THE FRANCO REGIME
1936–1975

Stanley Payne is Hilldale-Jaime Vicens Vives Professor of History at the University of Wisconsin-Madison. He is the author of a number of books on modern Spanish history, all of which have been translated into Spanish.

Also by Stanley Payne

Spanish Catholicism
Fascism: Comparison and Definition
A History of Spain and Portugal
Basque Nationalism
The Spanish Revolution
Politics and the Military in Modern Spain
Falange: A History of Spanish Fascism

THE
FRANCO REGIME
1936–1975

Stanley G. Payne

PHOENIX
PRESS

5 UPPER SAINT MARTIN'S LANE
LONDON
WC2H 9EA

A PHOENIX PRESS PAPERBACK

First published in Great Britain
in 2000 by Phoenix Press,
a division of The Orion Publishing Group Ltd,
Orion House, 5 Upper St Martin's Lane,
London WC2H 9EA

A CIP catalogue record for this book is
available from the British Library.

Printed and bound in Great Britain by
Clays Ltd, St Ives plc

ISBN 1 84212 046 8

To Julia

Contents

Contents

Part IV: Developmentalism and Decay, 1959–1975

Illustrations

Maps

Preface

The Franco regime was one of the longest-lived of right-authoritarian systems and during its later years one of the most extensively studied. Biographies of Franco himself are relatively numerous, and there have been several efforts to deal more broadly with the history of the regime, though some of those published within Spain have taken the character of histories of the opposition or diatribes against the dictatorship rather than serious efforts to deal with its history. More than a decade after the death of Franco the time seemed propitious to attempt a general account of the regime with the benefit of some historical distance and perspective.

The present work consists of a political history of the regime in the fundamental sense and is in no way intended to serve as a general history of Spain in this period. It is neither a history of the Civil War, nor of the Spanish economy under Franco, nor of society and social change, nor of intellectual, cultural, and religious affairs. It is not a history of Spain's international relations, either, and not a history of the opposition during these long decades. Though all these aspects are touched upon, they are treated only to the extent required by a political history of the regime itself. Two separate chapters dealing with social and economic policy are included not to attempt a full treatment of this dimension but simply to provide indispensable information for such areas and to permit some perspective on basic conditions and fundamental changes in Spanish life, without which alterations in the political climate and in the system itself would not be comprehensible. Moreover, this is not primarily a structural analysis and certainly not a sociological study of politics. For readers especially interested in such approaches, some work has already been done elsewhere, and references are provided in the notes.

It has become commonplace to observe that the Franco regime in certain respects was not one but several. The advantage of a historical approach is that it can delineate the primary changes as well as continuities within the system over its long life. The resulting book is long, as is required by the extent and complexity of the subject matter, and it is limited primarily by the unavoidable constraints of containing within one sizable volume what can be grasped by the reader and bound by the publisher. Even so, some major themes have had to be treated rather briefly and most details left out.

My hope is to have achieved a greater perspective and impartiality than have previous works, though readers and specialists will have to judge that for themselves. I am indebted to my reviewers, Richard Gunther of Ohio State University and Juan J. Linz of Yale University, who have improved the study a good deal with their comments and criticism and have saved it from at least some of its shortcomings. My thanks also go to Sandra Heitzkey of the Wisconsin History Department, who typed most of the manuscript, and once more to Mary Maraniss of the University of Wisconsin Press, who has guided yet another of my books to publication with skill and precision. Elizabeth Steinberg, the Executive Editor of the Press, has as usual supervised and coordinated the process with shrewd judgment and professional efficiency.

Madison, Wisconsin   January 1987

Chronology

1892	December 4	Birth of Francisco Franco Bahamonde at El Ferrol (Galicia)
1898		Defeat of Spain in Spanish-American War and loss of remaining colonial empire
1923	September 13	Beginning of Primo de Rivera dictatorship
1931	April 14	Proclamation of Second Republic
1933	November 19	Center-Right wins general election
1934	October	Leftist insurrection in Asturias
1936	February 16	Popular Front wins general election
	July 17–18	Beginning of military insurrection and civil war
	October 1	Franco takes power as Generalissimo and Chief of State in Nationalist zone
1937	April 19	Unification of Falange Espanola Tradicionalista as official state party
1938	January 30	Formation of first regular cabinet
1939	April 1	End of the Civil War
	August 8	Second government formed
	September 4	Spain declares neutrality in European war
1940	January 26	Law of Syndical Unity
	March 1	Law for the Repression of Masonry and Communism
	June 13	Spain moves from neutrality to "nonbelligerance"
	June 14	Spanish troops enter Tangier
	October 16	Serrano Súñer appointed foreign minister
	October 23	Hitler and Franco meet at Hendaye
1941	February 12	Franco and Mussolini meet at Bordighera
	May 20	Partial cabinet reorganization; Carrero Blanco appointed subsecretary of the presidency
	June 28	Recruitment of Blue Division begins
1942	August 16	Begoña incident
	September 3	Third government formed; Gómez Jordana replaces Serrano Súñer as foreign minister

1943	March 17	Cortes opens
	October 1	Spain returns to official neutrality
	November 12	Blue Division withdrawn
1945	March 19	Don Juan's Lausanne Manifesto against Franco
	July 17	Fuero de los Españoles promulgated
	July 18	Fourth government formed; Martín Artajo appointed foreign minister
1946	March 1	France closes border with Spain
	December 12	United Nations votes diplomatic boycott
1947	July 6	Referendum on Law of Succession
1948	February 10	French border reopened
	August 25	Franco and Don Juan meet on yacht *Azor*
1950	November 4	United Nations revokes boycott
1951	March 1	General strike in Barcelona
	July 19	Fifth government formed
1952	April 1	End of rationing
	November 18	Spain admitted to UNESCO
1953	August 27	Concordat with Vatican
	September 26	Pact of Madrid bases agreement with United States
1955	December 14	Spain admitted to United Nations
1956	February 8–11	Student incidents in Madrid
	April 7	Spain recognizes independence of Morocco
1957	February 25	Sixth government formed, including "technocrats" of Opus Dei; Falangist proposals definitively rejected
	November 22	Moroccan attack on Ifni
1958	May 17	Law of Principles of the Movement
1959	April 1	Franco inaugurates Valley of the Fallen
	July 22	Stabilization Plan announced
	December 23	Eisenhower visits Madrid
1961	December 24	Franco injured in shotgun accident
1962	February 9	Spain requests negotiations with EEC
	April–June	Outburst of strikes and oppositionist activity
	June 5–8	Munich meeting of democratic opposition
	July 10	Seventh government formed; Muñoz Grandes named vice-president
1963	April 20	Execution of Grimau
	December 28	First Development Plan announced
1964	April 1	"Twenty-five Years of Peace" campaign begins
1965	February 11	Eighth government formed
1966	March 18	Press Law of Fraga Iribarne
	December 14	Referendum on Organic Law of the State
1967	September 21	Carrero Blanco appointed vice-president
1968	October 12	Guinea becomes independent
1969	January–March	State of exception
	July 22	Juan Carlos recognized as successor
	August 8	MATESA affair made public
	October 30	Ninth ("monocolor") government formed

1970	December 3–28	Burgos trial of ETA activists
1973	June 8	Carrero Blanco named prime minister
	December 20	Carrero Blanco assassinated
	December 29	Arias Navarro named prime minister
1974	February 12	Arias Navarro promises reforms
	July 9	Franco seriously ill
	July 19– September 3	Authority provisionally transferred to Juan Carlos
	October 29	Pío Cabanillas dismissed as information minister
1975	April	State of exception in the Basque provinces
	June	Democratic opposition forms Platform of Democratic Convergence
	September 27	Execution of five terrorists followed by protests all over western Europe
	October	Crisis with Morocco over Spanish Sahara
	November 20	Death of Franco
	November 22	Juan Carlos crowned King of Spain

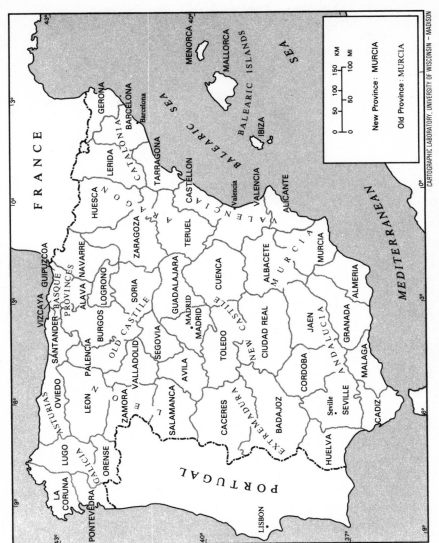

Provincial divisions of modern Spain

New Province: MURCIA

Old Province: MURCIA

PART I

Origins

1

The Politics
of Modern Spain

Commentary on modern Spain has largely revolved around concepts of difference, and in fact it was the idea of difference that was eventually converted into a positive slogan by the Spanish tourist industry of the 1960s. For historians and political observers, the difference has been that the perceived prototype of western modernization and the Spanish pattern vary considerably. This has led to considerable exaggeration and distortion on the one hand and defensive ethnocentric hyperbole on the other.

It is obvious enough that the formative period of Spanish and of all western history, the Middle Ages, was unique in Spain because of the Muslim conquest and intimate confrontation with Islamic civilization. Yet Spanish culture stems from the Christian north, not Al-Andalus, and reveals a fidelity to major aspects of medieval western Christian culture unequaled elsewhere. A dividing line between western and Levantine or Muslim civilization has always remained firmly set at the southern frontier of Hispanic Christendom. The only notable difference between Spain and certain of the most advanced areas of western Europe lay in a disparity of economic and technical-educational development. Spain's lag was partially overcome in the late fifteenth and sixteenth centuries, but the primary short-circuiting (to use Sánchez Albornoz's term) of Spanish development occurred in the seventeenth century, the period in which the advanced societies of northwestern Europe surged ahead of the rest of the continent.

During the seventeenth century Spain fell into a typically southern and eastern European pattern of ruralism, archaism, and slow economic development. Even in the seventeenth century, however, Spain's institutional and juridical structure remained typically western and distinct from the serf societies east of the Elbe. The eighteenth century, by comparison, was a period of recovery, though not of truly accelerated development.

The Old Regime in Spain was a victim of Napoleonic imperialism and of the first era of colonial liberation. Early introduction of modern parliamentary and constitutional liberalism (1810) gave Spain one of the longest modern political histories of any country in the world, exceeded among larger states only by Great Britain, the United States, and France. Early nineteenth century Spain was clearly not, by any normal set of criteria, properly prepared for modern liberalism, yet its precocious development seemed possible to the small minority of early Spanish liberals. One reason for this was the very long, if uneven, history of parliamentary institutions in Spain, for the initial late twelfth-century Cortes of León may have been the earliest of all medieval parliaments, antedating the Magna Carta. Another was the long and deep tradition of *fueros* (group rights and privileges), individual law and inheritance, and recognized autonomies within the peninsula. Yet another was the strong legalist-constitutionalist tradition of Spanish scholars and intellectuals, first fully developed by the theologians and philosophers of the sixteenth and seventeenth centuries and further elaborated by the late eighteenth-century Catholic enlightenment in Spain. The primary limitation of tolerance and freedom among formal institutions had come from the Inquisition, whose authority was seriously undermined by the modern rationalist culture that by the early nineteenth century dominated most educated opinion in Spain.

These factors help to account for the early emergence of minority, upper-class liberalism in Spain, but were far from sufficient to guarantee success for the nineteenth-century liberal polity. Popular illiteracy, extreme factional division, profound regional differences, and lagging, highly uneven economic development were only some of the major handicaps it faced. Thus the record of Spanish liberalism from 1810 to 1936 was complex, halting, and to the casual student confusing in the extreme, sometimes seemingly more Latin American than European. Focusing on a myriad of discordant details can, however, easily obscure the overall pattern as well as the primary factors at work.

If one looks at modern politics in broad historical perspective, Spain's experience in many respects turns out to be more typical than has often been assumed. Only a small minority of modern representative polities have undergone a long-term peaceful evolutionary development without a phase of breakdown. They are almost without exception either English-speaking or small states in northern Europe (including Switzerland). Most European and all non-European states have experienced convulsion and breakdown at least once, and the majority more than once. The truth is that the Spanish pattern is typical and the Anglo-American atypical.

The great majority of modern polities with a political history of a century or more have passed through a series of five major phases or sequences between 1800 and 1950: (1) convulsive, unstable early liberalism; (2) stable, elitist, minoritarian (censitary) liberalism; (3) democratization involving new political and social conflict, normally leading to breakdown; (4) an authoritarian phase or interlude (sometimes occurring in two distinct phases); followed in most west European continental countries by (5) a period of stable, institutionalized liberal democracy leading to systems of social democracy.

The stage of convulsive liberalism in Spain was long, from 1810 to 1874, compounded by riots, military revolt, civil war, and severe regional discord. Only the fraternal Hispanic countries of Latin America went through such a lengthy period of convulsion. Part of the reason for this—and indeed the principal distinction of Spanish liberalism—lay in the extreme precocity of Hispanic liberalism compared with its social and economic bases. The nineteenth-century Spanish political intelligentsia and elites persistently pushed through sweeping constitutional reforms, for brief periods giving Spain the most democratic suffrages and the most liberal political structures in continental Europe (in four distinct cycles: 1820–23, 1836–43, 1854–56, 1868–74). No other polity attempted such advanced political structures on the basis of such limited education, so little civic training, such an unproductive economy, such poor communications, such extreme regional dissociation, and so much institutionalized opposition in sectors of the Church and Carlism. Stability was eventually achieved by a more modest, restricted form of liberalism in the oligarchic system of the restored monarchy of 1874.

In most modern states the initial period of convulsion similarly issued into a phase of relative stability based on elitist, oligarchic suffrage and leadership. In the case of Spain, universal male suffrage was reintroduced in 1890, but its effects were at first spurious if for no other reasons than the illiteracy, lack of civic interest, and poor communications among the lower classes. The existing patronage and party-boss system, commonly known as *caciquismo*, largely contained or deflected popular voting for about thirty years.

The late nineteenth-century structure of censitary liberalism did represent the major established interests and achieved sufficient coherence to maintain stable government over two generations. In southern Europe, the elitist liberal systems were strong enough to endure major national crises and catastrophes such as Spain's humiliation in 1898 and the Tragic Week of 1909, Italy's defeat in Ethiopia and the subsequent crisis of 1898–99, and the great peasant revolt of 1907 in Romania.

By the beginning of the twentieth century, elitist liberalism was giving way to a process of democratization that opened a new series of deeper

Table 1.1. Historical Sequences of Political Change

	Early Convulsive Liberalism		
England 1640–68	France 1789–1830	Bulgaria 1879–87	Russia 1904–17
USA 1774–87	Spain 1810–74		
	Latin America ca. 1810–80		
	Portugal 1820–51		
	Greece 1829–64		
	Serbia 1829–1903		
	Hungary 1848–67		
	Romania 1859–79		
	Japan 1868–77		
	Stable Elitist Liberalism		
England 1688–1867	Portugal 1851–1910	Spain 1875–1909	
	Italy 1860–99	Germany 1871–1918	
	Argentina 1861–1919	Romania 1879–1916	
	Greece 1864–1909	Bulgaria 1887–1919	
	Austria 1867–1918	Brazil 1889–1930	
	Hungary 1867–1918	Serbia 1903–15	
		Japan 1877–1919	
	Democratization		
France 1848–49	Italy 1899–1922	Germany 1918–33	Japan 1920–31
USA 1828–76	Austria 1918–33	Romania 1917–30/38	
England 1867–1918	Spain 1909–36	Hungary 1918–20	
	Greece 1909–36	Serbia-Yugoslavia 1919–29	
	Portugal 1910–26	Bulgaria 1919–23/34	
	Argentina 1916–30	Brazil 1930–32/64	
	Russia 1917		
	Authoritarianism		
France 1852–70	Italy 1922–43	Japan 1931–45	
	Spain 1923–30		
Russia 1917–	1936–76	Germany 1933–45	
	Portugal 1926–74		
	Poland 1926–	Greece 1936–40	
	Yugoslavia 1929–	1967–74	
	Argentina 1930–32		
	1943–55	Romania 1938–	

conflicts. This marked the start of mass politics and broad voter participation, and expanded the political arena to include new issues of popular welfare and social legislation. The new problems of participation, government services, and social and economic redistribution, together with the rise of the revolutionary ideologies and the threat of leftist regimes, generated severe stresses and cleavages that overloaded the systems of most other countries.

Three unique factors conditioned such turmoils in Spain: the high cost of civil and colonial wars in the nineteenth and early twentieth centuries and their retarding effect; the centrifugal pressures of regionalism in the early twentieth century; and the general absence of nationalism. After being freed from French occupation by 1814, Spain escaped involvement in the major alliances and rivalries of the nineteenth century and the world wars that followed, and therefore it has been easy to overlook the cost of warfare to Spain in recent history. The nineteenth century was a time of repeated civil war (1821–23, 1833–40, 1869–76) as well as of frequent military revolt and political insurrection. In addition, there were major costly colonial wars in 1810–25, 1868–78, 1895–98, and 1919–26, and many lesser campaigns in between. Spain, the great neutral, probably spent more years during the entire period engaged in warfare of one serious kind or another than did any other European state. The effect of these in exhausting the public treasury and restricting economic growth was considerable—one of the major negative influences of the nineteenth century—yet since the conflicts were basically between Spaniards, they failed even to produce a sense of national unity, much less Spanish nationalism.

The relative absence or weakness of nationalism in Spain, otherwise quite remarkable in comparison with other European countries, is less mysterious in the light of Spanish history. Spain is an old state even though it has never been a fully unified and centralized country. The first and for a long time the largest of the great European empires, it was more secure in its international role than most other lands. After the empire declined, Spain remained uninvolved in great power rivalries and suffered no foreign threat. The country had scant external economic ambitions or interests and coveted no one else's territory. Compared with Italy, for example, there was no irredentist problem, and the issue of Gibraltar could not serve as a substitute. Up until World War I the pace of social and structural change was slow, retarding any general political mobilization and also, with the sole exception of Catalonia, discouraging any significant internal threat or challenge to established Spanish identity. Cultural transformation was equally measured; radical new ideas of the nineteenth century had little resonance until after the beginning of the twentieth.

Common Spanish identity has indeed had a specific basis and even a sort of historic ideology. It stemmed, first of all, from geographic propinquity and interassociation, but even more from common values in the several sectors of the Christian resistance society descended from the early medieval Romano-Visigothic population of northern Spain. The first expression of what may intelligibly be termed the Spanish ideology was formed during the reign of Alfonso II of Asturias (791–842), if not earlier, identifying the native Spanish with Latin Catholicism and embracing an historic mission to regain the lost patrimony of the Visigoths while ex-

tending the borders of the faith. During the eleventh century the ideology of reconquest was generalized, and subsequently the concept of
crusading and the "divine war" was adopted and normalized. By the sixteenth century this concept had become inflated, at least among some
Spaniards, into the notion of Spaniards as the new chosen people of God,
charged with a broad world-historical mission.

The first major disillusionment with the Spanish ideology set in before
the middle of the seventeenth century, and by the eighteenth century
much of the earlier mind-set had faded away. It was revived by neotraditionalist thinkers in the nineteenth century, and in fact neotraditionalist
Carlism became the only vigorous form of Spanish nationalism in that period. The fact that Spanish identity and the earlier Spanish sense of mission had been so completely identified with Catholicism proved a considerable hindrance in an era of modernization and incipient secularization.
In the late nineteenth and early twentieth centuries any pronounced
sense of Spanish nationalism tended to be confounded with reactionary
Carlism and with clericalism, thus divorcing it from the mainstream of
public affairs.

The possibility of a Spanish nationalism was further retarded by Spain's
peculiar structure of reverse regional roles in the nineteenth and early
twentieth centuries, for the regions that dominated governmentally were
not those that led the way in economic and cultural modernization. The
latter normally provided new foci of leadership and identity in other
countries. In Spain the industrial and commercial leader was Barcelona,
which also happened to be the center of a somewhat distinct culture that
eventually became the focus of a centrifugal regionalist nationalism, with
a crippling effect on the Spanish polity. The same was subsequently true
of Bilbao and the Basque industrial zone. Rural Castile and Andalucía, by
contrast, lacked the social structure, economic base, or new culture to foster a dynamic modern Spanish nationalism. Resistance to Catalanism, in
turn, took the form not of positive Spanish nationalism but of a sterile and
negative anti-Catalanism that further undermined the polity.[1]

In the Spanish case, the standard vertical problems of social and economic conflict arising from modern commercialism and industrialization
were thus profoundly exacerbated by horizontal problems of regional and
national integration. It is true that only a few small, relatively united
kingdoms such as England and Portugal had overcome regionalism under
the Old Regime, but in most of western Europe regional identities were
either eroded or effectively repressed during the course of the nineteenth

1. The best brief treatment of the development of the regionalist problem is Juan Linz,
"Early State-Building and Late Peripheral Nationalisms against the State: The Case of
Spain," in *Building States and Nations,* ed. S. Eisenstadt and S. Rokkan (London and Bev-
erly Hills, 1973), 32–116.

century. In Spain, nineteenth-century liberalism was too weak to accomplish the one or the other. Pre-modern Spain had been a monarchical confederation of distinct constitutional kingdoms and had never formed a fully centralized system. It remained the home of four distinct languages (Castilian or Spanish, Catalan, Galician, and Basque or Euskera) whose cultures were in fact revived and expanded by nineteenth century romanticism. Modern economic and cultural change did not unify Spain but threatened more and more to break it apart.[2]

To recapitulate, the chief reasons for the absence of Spanish nationalism may be summarized as follows:

1. Spain's situation of absolute independence since the eleventh century, in which it became the first truly world empire in history and for long ranked among the established powers
2. The nature of the traditional Spanish state, a sort of dynastic confederation of strongly pluralist character despite so-called Habsburg "absolutism"
3. The peculiar and exclusive mutual identity of traditional Spanish culture and religion, which created a climate of national Catholicism that endured for centuries and ended only with the full secularization that occurred late in the twentieth century
4. Absence of foreign threat after the Napoleonic wars
5. The long domination of classic liberalism, lasting nearly a century, conditioning formal culture and discouraging new military ambitions or the development of a modern radical right
6. The unique reverse role of regional nationalism, which absorbed much new energy
7. Neutrality in World War I
8. All this influenced and conditioned by, and to some extent even predicated upon, a slow pace of modernization, further accompanied by the absence of new political, economic, or cultural ambitions that might have stimulated nationalism

The political expression of regional nationalism received its first major stimulus from the Spanish disaster of 1898, which destroyed the remnants of the old empire and seemed to symbolize the failure of modern Spain as a state and system as well. The disaster also sparked a diffuse reform

2. In this connection, one of the most interesting recent efforts to explain the pathology of modern Latin American institutions is Claudio Véliz's *The Centralist Tradition of Latin America* (Princeton, 1980). The Spanish antecedent of the centralist tradition which Véliz finds in Latin America was not that of the Spanish system as a whole but of the strong monarchy of Castile, which organized its colonial empire under a tight central bureaucracy that had scant counterpart within the Hispanic peninsula. Even after nineteenth century liberalism centralized Spanish government, Spanish centralism remained considerably less rigorous and thorough than that of the corresponding liberal systems of France and Italy.

movement known as Regenerationism. In ideas, this produced a genre sometimes known as "disaster literature" (some of which had appeared before 1898) that suggested a variety of prescriptions and reforms for Spain's ills in a manner reminiscent of seventeenth-century *arbitristas*.

One strain of Regenerationism marked a new departure, introducing for the first time the notion of some sort of nonreactionary (non-Carlist or traditionalist) modernizing alternative to liberal and left revolutionary norms. Since the defeat of Bravo Murillo's restrictive constitutional elitism in 1852, Spanish politics had been totally preoccupied with clashing doctrines of liberal parliamentarianism and leftist democracy, opposed by the counterplay of reactionary Carlist monarchism, increasingly feeble after 1876. Some contributions to the disaster literature took a different approach, rejecting traditional monarchism but leveling their main blasts against corrupt parliamentarianism, which was accused of distorting Spanish life and making almost impossible the education, reform, and development of the country. A transition period of some sort of authoritarianism was occasionally suggested as a vague alternative.

Most prominent among Regenerationists was the autodidact and polymath Joaquín Costa. With roots deep in rural Aragon, Costa formulated the need for a development policy based on education, irrigation, and agrarian improvement, together with an emphasis on technology. He was also apparently the first to coin the phrase "revolution from above," and occasionally argued the need for an "iron surgeon" to remove impediments to progress. Costa never developed a coherent, clearly articulated political doctrine or program. At one point he identified the iron surgeon with Jesus Christ (not uncommon among Spanish progressives before secularization) and never espoused any clear-cut authoritarian alternative to liberalism.[3]

Second only to Costa among Regenerationist theorists was Ricardo Macías Picavea of Valladolid. His *El problema nacional* (Madrid, 1899) insisted that civic representation could be made more authentic only by doing away with the liberal oligarchy in parliament and replacing it with corporate representation of economic and professional groups, whose political arm would be a corporative "national council." Macías Picavea saw no way to break through to a new system other than by means of a providential temporary dictator, whom he termed "an historic man." Several

3. The authoritarian strain in Costa was apparently first emphasized by Dionisio Pérez, *El enigma de Costa: ¿revolucionario, oligarca?* (Madrid, 1930), in a treatment at least in part provoked by Primo de Rivera's invocations of Costa. More recently, this aspect has been singled out by Enrique Tierno Galván, *Costa y el regeneracionismo* (Barcelona, 1961). See also Cirilo Martín Retortillo, *Joaquín Costa* (Barcelona, 1961); Alberto Gil Novales, *Derecho y revolución en el pensamiento de Joaquín Costa* (Madrid, 1965); Rafael Pérez de la Dehesa, *El pensamiento de Costa y su influencia en el 98* (Madrid, 1966); and Jacques Maurice and Carlos Serrano, *Joaquín Costa: Crisis de la Restauración y populismo (1875–1911)* (Madrid, 1977).

other Regenerationist texts echoed these sentiments, though usually in more or less euphemistic terminology. The last of the notable Regenerationist writers, Julio Senador, preached a new ruralism and a return to the soil in his *Castilla en escombros* (Madrid, 1915). He denounced the futility, in his view, of an elitist parliament, and favored boycotting the university system, which reinforced oligarchy and the exploitation of the countryside. True justice could be introduced not through constitutionalism as it functioned in Spain but only through abrupt, presumably authoritarian change.

In contrast, the literary figures composing the belletristic Generation of Ninety-Eight were not primarily interested in politics and practical affairs. A number of them, however, reacted defensively on behalf of Spanish culture and in reevaluation of certain aspects of modernization. While Regenerationists denounced the barrenness of the Castilian landscape, Azorín and Antonio Machado emphasized its esthetic charms and seemed to suggest that it nourished a certain spiritual force. Miguel de Unamuno opposed the "Japanization" of Spain. "Let others invent," he proclaimed, insisting that the reform of Spain must not lead to betrayal of its spiritual heritage. Though some aspects of *noventayochista* thought have been judged "decidedly reactionary,"[4] Regenerationists and *noventayochistas* were nearly all predominantly liberal; none directly embraced the traditional Spanish ideology, at least until after World War I. At that point one of the most talented essayists of the period, Ramiro de Maeztu, renounced his earlier liberalism in favor of corporatism and a new hierarchy. He later developed the fullest and most extreme twentieth-century statement of the traditional Spanish ideology in his *Defensa de la Hispanidad* (1934).

Regenerationism influenced both of the established political parties after 1900 and helped to introduce numerous partial reforms, yet no radical transformation occurred. Its banner was soon grasped by the new Conservative chieftain, Antonio Maura, who adopted Costa's slogan "Revolution from above" and dominated politics during much of the first decade of the century. Proud, austere, and gravely impressive in manner and appearance, Maura was the outstanding parliamentary orator of his generation. He became perhaps the most admired and the most hated public figure in Spain, and one of the few with genuine charisma. Maura believed in a sort of *Rechtsstaat*, a rigorously orderly and constitutional system permitting a narrow formal democracy while encouraging economic development. His leitmotiv was the rallying of the *fuerzas vivas* (loosely, "silent majority"), the Catholic, law-abiding, but frequently apolitical middle classes. Maura did carry out a number of important reforms (for example, legalizing strikes) but at the same time drew sharp limits to

4. Donald L. Shaw, *The Generation of 1898 in Spain* (London, 1975), 208.

change. His plan for limited local self-government was blocked by parliamentary opposition, while his special legislation to repress anarchist terrorism was frustrated by an ad hoc alliance of establishment Liberals and leftist Republicans. He was finally forced from the prime ministership (never to return as independent leader) by these same elements in 1909 after the call-up of reserves for military service in Morocco resulted in the rioting and repression of Barcelona's "Tragic Week."[5]

Reaction to the subsequent semiostracism of Maura (a sanction in large measure self-inflicted by the haughty leader) produced a minor movement of rightist protonationalism, the Maurist Youth, organized in 1914. After Maura refused to collaborate regularly with a political system that, in his view, compromised with subversion, this small band of enthusiastic supporters championed his ideas outside the mainstream of parliamentary politics. They stood for Spanish patriotism, Catholic values, and stern opposition to the left, combined with new political and economic reforms. Yet though ever more critical of the established system, neither they nor their leader could arrive at any clear-cut systematic alternative to parliamentary government. The Maurist Youth were groping after a modern, radical, and also right-wing nationalism that was never fully defined.[6]

Reformism increasingly gave way to paralysis in the Spanish parliamentary system, yet the established middle-class Liberal and Conservative parties remained in place, however fragmented and ineffective. Unable to adjust to an age of democratization and mass mobilization, they nonetheless retained firm control of the electoral mechanism and levers of power, and after 1918 the Spanish electorate responded with growing abstentionism.

The breakdown of the parliamentary system that finally came five years later had no single cause. As in Italy in 1922, economic conditions were not a direct factor, since by that time the postwar slump had been largely overcome. The immediate causes were all in one way or another political. A mass working class left finally emerged after 1917 in Catalonia and a few industrial centers, employing tactics of violence and even terrorism. Yet the principal revolutionary force was anarchosyndicalism (the CNT), which could never be a major threat to the system because of the very anarchism of its organization and tactics. Regional nationalism grew

5. There is no adequate study of Maura. See Diego Sevilla Andrés, *Antonio Maura* (Barcelona, 1954); Rafael Pérez Delgado, *Antonio Maura* (Madrid, 1974); and the interpretation offered by his great-grandson, Joaquín Romero Maura, in the latter's translation of Raymond Carr, *España, 1808–1939* (Barcelona, 1966). Maura's ideas may be found in his *Ideario político*, ed. J. B. Catalá y Gavila (Madrid, 1953); and in J. Paulis and F. de Sorel, *Maura ante el pueblo* (Madrid, 1915).

6. Javier Tusell and Juan Avilés, *La derecha española contemporánea. Sus orígenes: El maurismo* (Madrid, 1986), offers an excellent study of the eclecticism and ambiguities of *maurismo* after 1913.

stronger at the end of World War I, but the main Catalanist middle-class party (the Lliga) was soon forced to trim its sails drastically in the face of the internal class struggle in Catalonia. To an even greater extent, Basque nationalism lost its main voter support to a conservative reaction in the Basque provinces.[7]

The breakdown was caused by the general loss of confidence in parliamentary liberalism, combined with the nasty stalemate of colonial war in Morocco. The failure of the dominant parties to function with unity and efficiency, to provide access and participation, and to solve problems eroded at least temporarily their support even among the middle classes, from whom their only broad support had ever come. The most immediate dilemma was military, however. Though Spain was the least and most reluctant of all twentieth-century European imperial powers, it had been drawn into the vortex of French imperialism on the eve of World War I in Morocco, the only area where Spain was conceived to have real interests. Madrid had obtained only the northern 5 percent of Morocco in the settlement of 1912, and made little effort to occupy that until the World War had ended. Its forward policy between 1919 and 1923 brought virtual disaster. Northern Morocco was the scene of the most skillful and determined native military resistance anywhere in the Afro-Asian world at that time. Spanish positions throughout the eastern zone of the Protectorate collapsed in the face of the assault of Abdul Karim's Riffi kabyles in 1921.[8] Though part of the territory had been shakily reoccupied by 1923, there was growing demand for "responsibilities," a special inquiry and prosecution of military and civilian figures deemed responsible for the disaster, not excluding the king himself. This brought one sector of the Army command to plot overthrow of the government and possibly of the system itself.[9]

The Pretorian Tradition

Since the inception of modern politics, the most common means of institutional or normative breakthrough in Spanish affairs had been military intervention. Given the political and economic (though not social or demographic) weakness of the middle classes, together with the profound

7. See Ignacio de Loyola Arana Pérez, *El monarquismo en Vizcaya durante la crisis del reinado de Alfonso XIII (1917–1931)* (Pamplona, 1982).

8. An overview of the Spanish experience in Morocco is provided by Víctor Morales Lezcano, *El colonialismo hispanofrancés en Marruecos (1898–1927)* (Madrid, 1976), and *España y el Norte de Africa: El Protectorado en Marruecos, 1912–1956* (Madrid, 1984).

9. The principal study of the final phase of Spanish liberalism is Thomas G. Trice's "Spanish Liberalism in Crisis: A Study of the Liberal Party during Spain's Parliamentary Collapse, 1913–1923" (Ph.D. diss., University of Wisconsin, 1974). The role of the crown is analyzed and ably defended by Carlos Seco Serrano's *Alfonso XIII y la crisis de la Restauración* (Madrid, 1979). See also Vicente R. Pilapil, *Alfonso XIII* (New York, 1969). In many ways the ablest defense of the pre-1923 parliamentary regime is still the Conde de Romanones, *Las responsabilidades del antiguo régimen de 1875 a 1923* (Madrid, n.d.).

internal division of the nation's leadership and elite, groups of the military were called upon time and again to supplement or replace civilian initiative. This created what without exaggeration may be called the pretorian tradition of modern Spanish politics. Pretorianism should not be confused with militarism, for Spain in modern times has been the least militarist of all the larger European countries. Pretorianism refers to the political rather than military hypertrophy of the military.

In the nineteenth century Spain exhibited the prototype of modern political pretorianism, at least among European countries. Its nearest competitors in this model were Portugal and Greece, who equaled the Spanish level of pretorianism for only comparatively brief periods. It is important to grasp that the pretorian phenomenon was reactive, not initiatory: it was a response to grave civic problems and disunity sometimes approaching political vacuum and breakdown. So long as regular civilian government was reasonably stable and effective and was supported by a near-majority of the politically active society, there was scant tendency toward pretorian activity, even in Spain. Pretorianism was more a response than spontaneous subversion. It was eagerly sought by key political activists, so that officers who preferred to restrict themselves to professional roles very often had to resist strong pressures and tempting inducements from civilian conspirators. Nineteenth-century liberals frequently confessed their reliance on the military. During that period, no change of regime (as distinct from government) in either a more radical or more conservative direction was made without either strong pressure or outright revolt by important elements of the Army. This variously took the form of intrigue or manipulation, the *cuartelazo* (a kind of barracks revolt or sit-down strike), a direct attempt at coup d'etat, or the more typically Spanish *pronunciamiento* (a term originating in 1820). The latter, as the word indicates, was a "pronouncement" that might take the initial form of pressure, manipulation, or outright insurrection. It was not necessarily aimed at immediate military occupation or overthrow of the government per se, but simply at rallying broader military or political support to effect changes in personnel, policies, or in extreme cases, the regime itself.[10]

10. For a broad treatment of modern Spanish pretorianism, see my *Politics and the Military in Modern Spain* (Stanford, 1967) (hereafter cited as *Politics and the Military*); as well as the revised Spanish edition of this work, *Ejército y sociedad en la España liberal (1808–1936)* (Madrid, 1977). The most comprehensive of the recent Spanish accounts is Carlos Seco Serrano, *Militarismo y civilismo en la España contemporánea* (Madrid, 1984). Miguel Alonso Baquer, *El Ejército en la sociedad española* (Madrid 1971), provides a brief general treatment; while his *El modelo español de pronunciamiento* (Madrid, 1983) offers an analytical taxonomy of types of intervention. Julio Busquets Bragulat, *Pronunciamientos y golpes de Estado en España* (Barcelona, 1982), presents a list and description of all the main attempted coups and pronunciamientos; and a patriotic-conservative viewpoint may be found in José Ramón Alonso, *Historia política del Ejército español* (Madrid, 1974). The police and juridical functions of the military are well defined in Manuel Ballbé, *Orden público y militarismo en la España constitucional (1812–1983)* (Madrid, 1983).

In the process, the Spanish military developed a special role and identity that gave it partial institutional autonomy, yet most of the time the officer corps was itself almost as divided as political society in general. It is thus probably incorrect to conceive of the nineteenth-century Spanish pretorian military as a "corporate army" in the strict sense.[11] The officer corps was not only extremely heterogeneous in social origin but sometimes also closely and divisively linked with mutually conflicting political and cultural subsectors of the broader society. Though senior generals normally took the lead, middle-rank officers were often the most energetic pretorians. Their status was sufficient to give them influence, yet they had less to lose than their seniors and were less identified with whoever happened to be in power. Most officers never participated in overt pretorian activity but simply followed orders, from whatever source. Moreover, during the nineteenth century, political insubordination normally did not extend far down the military hierarchy. It was rare for NCOs to exercise political initiative, and mutiny in the ranks was rarer still.

Before 1923, military dictatorship was never at issue. Pretorian rebels worked within the institutional framework of the liberal system and never sought to replace the regular structure of government with a military directory. Politicized officers identified with standard civilian parties and doctrines, serving as the military wing of a broader political formation. Whenever a general ruled, it was at least nominally as constitutional prime minister and as the leader of a primarily civilian political party. The only military chiefs to serve as heads of state before Franco were General Baldomero Espartero, for two years (1841–43) regent during the minority of Isabel II before he in turn was overthrown by a broadly based civilian-military revolt, and General Francisco Serrano, head of two brief interim regimes between 1868 and 1874.

The prevailing political sympathies of the military can be divided into several general phases. During phase 1 (1820–74), the primary tendency of military intervention was liberal, even though almost every liberal initiative was contested (and sometimes nullified) by a conservative one. Phase 2 (1874–1936) can be most easily described as centrist, though with an increasing tendency toward conservative and even right-authoritarian positions. The predominant political tone of the military became fully rightist and authoritarian only in phase 3, beginning with the inception of the Civil War and the Franco regime in 1936.

It could be argued that the basic political values of the officer corps changed rather less than it might seem at first glance. The liberalism of the classic age of nineteenth-century pronunciamientos was rarely demo-

11. The best comparative typologies are S. E. Finer, *The Man on Horseback* (New York, 1962); and Amos Perlmutter, *The Military and Politics in Modern Times* (Cambridge, 1977).

cratic and was normally middle-class elitist. As the political framework
began to shift first in a democratic-radical and then in a left-collectivist
direction, the original liberal posture tilted toward the right even though
its basic values and attitudes altered very little. The officer corps had
been predominantly of middle-class origin since the late eighteenth century, with an increasing tendency toward self-recruitment from the sons of
both officers and NCOs. Its ideals of patriotism, progress, and order were
served by middle-class nineteenth-century liberalism but not by radical
democracy, collectivism, regional nationalism, or other subversions of the
nineteenth century order.

The stabilization of liberalism under the restored constitutional monarchy after 1874 has often been given credit for restoring order and discipline and maintaining civilian dominance for half a century, but such a
conclusion is partially misleading. The two-party system as consolidated
in the late nineteenth century maintained the pattern of fusion of military
and political elites. A major revolt or pronunciamiento was avoided for
nearly fifty years, but the military did retain a relative institutional autonomy and the senior hierarchy enjoyed a good deal of political influence,
providing a number of transitional prime ministers.[12]

The military began to play a more overt, and corporate, political role
during the new systemic stresses of the early twentieth century. The first
major initiative was the *Cu-cut* incident of 1905, an officers' riot that
sacked a Catalanist journal which had satirized the military. This resulted
in the Law of Responsibilities (1906), which placed cases of libel and
slander against military institutions under the jurisdiction of military
courts. Much more important were the effects of the political radicalization and economic distortions of World War I. In Spain's protorevolutionary year of 1917, the officer corps itself began to fragment for the first time
since 1873. Middle- and junior-rank officers began to form "Juntas militares" in peninsular garrisons, creating a sort of officers' trade-union
movement to protest low pay, favoritism, and political manipulation by
the senior command. They also acted as an influential pressure group
against the Madrid government, demanding reform and forcing the resignation of two different cabinets in 1917–18.

The other two main sources of political pressure against the regime, the
reformist liberals from the periphery and the revolutionary working-class
movements, both hoped for some degree of military support, or at least
benevolence, during 1917. Yet this almost completely failed to materi-
alize, and the Spanish breakthrough of 1917 fragmented and splintered
before it began to mobilize significant support. The officers' Juntas made
it clear that they were seriously interested in little more than corporate

12. Daniel R. Headrick, *Ejéricito y política en España (1866–1898)* (Madrid, 1981), provides an excellent account of the politics of the Spanish Army in the late nineteenth century.

and professional privileges, and opposed the political radicalism of both the liberal and the revolutionary left. During the last years of the constitutional regime, the Juntas were largely neutralized through a series of carrot-and-stick manipulations, leaving the military even more divided than before.[13]

Thus there was no clear or simple military alternative to the liberal regime in 1923. Just as the aversion to parliament and the oligarchic system had produced no civilian consensus or alternative, so no outside faction or conspiracy was ready to step in. One group of four senior generals, known as the Quadrilateral, conspired during the summer of 1923 to promote a temporary military government that would press the struggle in Morocco to a victorious conclusion and silence critics at home, but it lacked sufficient support or leadership to carry off a coup. Speculation concerning several senior generals scarcely transcended gossip.

Only the decisive initiative of Miguel Primo de Rivera, captain general of Barcelona, created the pronunciamiento of September 13, 1923, that overthrew constitutional government altogether. Descended from an illustrious military family and himself the product of a military career that spanned more than three decades, Primo de Rivera was slow to develop political ambitions. He had served in Morocco, Cuba, and the Philippines, and in fact harbored few illusions about Spanish colonialism.[14] Impressed by Regenerationism and the tradition of liberal pretorianism, Primo was convinced that only temporary military government could create unity, solve Spain's problems, and institute necessary reforms.

Timing of the pronunciamiento was triggered by several key events: resignation of three ministers of the latest Liberal government on September 3 to protest renewal of Spanish military initiative in Morocco, the parade of left Catalanists in Barcelona on September 11 which dragged the Spanish flag on the ground without remonstrance from the authorities, and the scheduled report of a joint parliamentary committee on September 16 concerning political culpability in the 1921 disaster. The threat of force by Mussolini in taking over the Italian government in the preceding year and France's invasion of the Ruhr a few months earlier may have encouraged the use of force in Spain, but there is little direct evidence of this. The decision to act was evidently made on September 8–9 when Primo visited the Quadrilateral in Madrid.[15]

13. Carolyn P. Boyd, *Pretorian Politics in Liberal Spain* (Chapel Hill, 1979), is equally perceptive and useful for the first quarter of the twentieth century. Gabriel Cardona, *El poder militar en la España contemporánea hasta la Guerra Civil* (Madrid, 1983), provides a lucid general narrative and analysis covering the period from 1874 to 1936.

14. Maj. Gen. Miguel Primo de Rivera y Orbaneja, *Cuestión del día: Gibraltar y Africa* (Cadiz, 1917), is an early pamphlet that helps to explain Primo's reputation as an *abandonista*.

15. According to Primo de Rivera's own account in his *La obra de la Dictadura* (Madrid, 1930), 12–13.

The revolt began in Barcelona as a classic pronunciamiento, with a limited local takeover in the Catalan capital by its captain general, who called upon the rest of the Army and other patriotic Spaniards to rally round. In fact—also in the traditional style—all but one of the other captains general sat on the fence. The pronunciamiento succeeded above all because the Liberal government did almost nothing to defend itself. The issue was finally decided two days later by the Crown, as Alfonso XIII, without invoking constitutional limits or procedures, transferred power to what would become the first direct military dictatorship in modern Spanish history.[16]

16. For further details on the pronunciamiento, see ibid., 241–73; and *Politics and the Military,* 187–207.

2

An Authoritarian Alternative: The Primo de Rivera Dictatorship

Few heads of government have come to power in twentieth-century Europe with a less explicit political theory than Miguel Primo de Rivera. His assumption of power was predicated on a ninety-day emergency military directory to deal with such pressing problems as attempted subversion, the stalemate in Morocco, administrative corruption, and national political reform. Primo's only professed ideology was that of constitutional liberalism. He continued to insist that the parliamentary constitution of 1876 was the law of the land and at first even denied that he was a dictator in any genuine sense, insisting in his first public statement, "No one can with justice apply that term to me."[1]

It is generally agreed that the establishment of the Dictatorship was greeted with relief and broad, if shallow, support from the public. José Ortega y Gasset hailed the new government in Madrid's leading daily, *El Sol*, as a splendid opportunity to cut the Gordian knot restraining true modernization and regeneration. Much enlightened opinion seemed more or less to agree.

As it turned out, the ninety-day Military Directory, composed of eight brigadiers and one admiral, governed for twenty-seven months until December 1925. There was little domestic reform though much authoritarian centralization of administration. The only positive achievement of this period was to reorganize the forces in Morocco and take advantage of French cooperation in an expanded war that brought victory by the end of

1. M. C. García-Nieto, J. M. Donézar, and L. López Puerta, eds., *La Dictadura, 1923–1930* (Madrid, 1973), presents a collection of basic documents.

1925 and complete pacification of the Protectorate within three more years.[2]

The government took advantage of the economic prosperity of the 1920s (*los felices años veinte*) to concentrate on internal development. Public works expanded rapidly, and construction of a modern highway system was begun. The young finance minister, José Calvo Sotelo, instituted a tax reform that was proportionately the most significant to occur until after the end of the Franco regime half a century later.[3] The marketing of petroleum was nationalized under a state consortium (CAMPSA), and plans were initiated for major irrigation and hydroelectric projects.[4]

Politics and government remained unsolved problems. The only theoretical alternative within Spain was right-wing Carlism, whose theorists had formulated doctrines of state corporatism under a neotraditional monarchy, grounded spiritually in a rigorous return to a Counter-Reformation style of Catholicism.[5]

Fascism in the strict generic sense was not at issue,[6] if for no other rea-

2. The basic studies are Shannon E. Fleming, "Primo de Rivera and Abd el-Krim: The Struggle in Spanish Morocco, 1923–1927" (Ph.D. diss., University of Wisconsin, 1974); and S. E. Fleming and A. K. Fleming, "Primo de Rivera and Spain's Moroccan Problem, 1923–1927," *Journal of Contemporary History* (hereafter cited as *JCH*) 12:1 (Jan. 1977), 85–100. For the origins of the conflict, see Germain Ayache, *Les origines de la guerre du Rif* (Paris, 1981).

3. Calvo Sotelo's *Mis servicios al Estado* (Madrid, 1931) is the only memoir of any importance to have come out of the Dictatorship. For a critique of his financial management by an opponent, see Q. Saldaña, *Al servicio de la justicia* (Madrid, 1930), 91–115. Marqués de Santa Cara, *En honor de la verdad: La Dictadura española* (Madrid, 1930), 119–33, offers a defense.

4. The best treatment is Juan Velarde Fuertes, *Política económica de la Dictadura*, rev. ed. (Madrid, 1973). It should be noted that since the years of World War I, Spanish industrial and financial leaders had looked toward a more integrated national economic policy. See Santiago Roldán and J. L. García Delgado, *La formación de la sociedad capitalista en España, 1914–1920* (Madrid, 1973), 1:325–93. The full range of the Dictatorship's reformist policies is examined in James H. Rial, "The Reforms of the Dictatorship of Miguel Primo de Rivera" (Ph.D. diss., Northwestern University, 1978).

5. The outstanding Carlist theorist of the early twentieth century was Juan Vázquez de Mella y Fanjul, who tried to update traditionalism in terms of a more practical and modernized semi-authoritarianism. See Martin Blinkhorn, *Carlism and Crisis in Spain, 1931–1939* (Cambridge, 1975), 1–40.

6. In this work the word *fascism* used generically will not be capitalized; when the word is capitalized, it will refer to the Italian party or regime. The typological definition of fascism employed here is that which I first discussed in my *Fascism: Comparison and Definition* (Madison, 1980), 7, consisting of three sets of characteristics:
A. The fascist negations:
   Antiliberalism
   Anticommunism
   Anticonservatism (though willingness to undertake temporary alliances with groups from any other sector, most commonly the nationalist right)
B. Ideology and goals:
   Creation of a new nationalist authoritarian state based not merely on traditional principles or models

son than that no fascist party, movement, or even individual ideologue existed in Spain. Though imitative fascist-style grouplets had begun to appear in such diverse countries as France, Portugal,[7] and Romania as early as 1923–24, the nearest Spanish equivalent was a tiny circle in Barcelona called El Cruzado Español (The Spanish Crusader), whose overt symbolic connotations were in fact more specifically traditionalist and Carlist than fascist.[8] Primo de Rivera himself had explicitly disavowed Italian inspiration.[9]

    Organization of some new kind of regulated, multiclass, integrated national economic structure, whether called national corporatist, national socialist, or national syndicalist

    The goal of empire or a radical change in the nation's relation to the international system

    Specific espousal of an idealist, voluntarist creed, normally involving the attempt to realize a new form of modern, self-determined, secular culture

C. Style and organization:

    Emphasis on esthetic structure of meetings, symbols, and political choreography, stressing romantic and mystical aspects

    Attempted mass mobilization with militarization of political relationships and style and with the goal of a mass party militia

    Positive evaluation and use of, or willingness to use, violence

    Extreme stress on the masculine principle and male dominance, while espousing the organic view of society

    Exaltation of youth over other phases of life, emphasizing the conflict of generations, at least in effecting the initial political transformation

    Specific tendency toward an authoritarian, charismatic, personal style of command, whether or not the command is to some degree initially elective

This typology does not propose to establish a rigidly reified category that would describe every conceivable characteristic of every fascist-type party or exactly fit each one. Nor should it be taken to imply that the individual goals and characteristics identified were necessarily in every item unique to fascist movements, for most would be found in one or more other species of political movement. The contention would be rather that *taken as a whole* the definition would describe what all fascist movements had in common without trying to describe the unique characteristics of each. Such a broad definition can identify a variety of allegedly fascist movements while setting them apart from other kinds of revolutionary or authoritarian nationalist movements.

    7. A modest expression of a Portuguese fascism emerged in 1923 amid the remarkable turmoil of the Portuguese First Republic. It apparently revolved around Raul de Carvalho's journal *A Ditadura*, subtitled *Periódico do Fascismo Português*. By early 1924, the subtitle had been changed to *Jornal de Accão Nacionalista*, joining forces with a right-authoritarian nationalist group after it failed to win support under the fascist rubric. This effort, like some of the first attempts at a Spanish fascism nearly ten years later, was primarily financed by elements of big business. See António José Telo, *Decadência e queda da Iª República portuguesa* (Lisbon, 1980), 252–53.

    8. The first abortive steps toward a fascist or a new radical-right style of agitation during the early 1920s were concentrated in Barcelona, probably because of the more dynamic and modernizing atmosphere there than in Madrid and because of the much stronger mobilization of the left-revolutionary threat there (just as Italian Fascism was born in Milan, not in Rome). A publication called *La Camisa Negra* appeared in Barcelona in December 1922 but did not survive its first issue. Javier Jiménez Campos, *El fascismo en la crisis da Iª Segunda República* (Madrid, 1979), 97–98.

    9. To the excited query of a Barcelona journalist on the day of his pronunciamiento,

I. Origins

General Miguel Primo de Rivera while dictator in 1928

On the other hand, he and Alfonso XIII visited Rome within two months of Primo's takeover, marking the first triumphal foreign visit by any Spanish chief of state in the twentieth century (and, aside from

Primo responded: "It has not been necessary to imitate the Fascists or the great figure of Mussolini, though their deeds have been a useful example for everyone. But in Spain we have the Somatén [a civilian militia in Catalonia] and we have had Prim [principal military founder of the democratic constitutional monarchy of 1869], an admirable military and political figure." *Dos años de Directorio Militar,* ed. Marqués de Cáceres (Madrid, 1926), 2–5.

Franco's meetings with Salazar and Mussolini, the last until the reign of Juan Carlos). Mussolini hailed Primo de Rivera as the "head of Spanish fascism," while Primo called Mussolini his inspirer and teacher.[10] Both the Spanish dictator and the king viewed Mussolini's regime as the most friendly foreign power, if for no other reason than that it was the only other authoritarian west European state. Alfonso XIII confessed to the Italian ambassador his foreknowledge of plans for the pronunciamiento,[11] while Primo is said to have admired Mussolini more than any other contemporary statesman, extolling him in Rome as a "figure of worldwide dimensions," "apostle of the campaign against revolution and anarchy," who had achieved "order, work, and justice."[12]

Nonetheless, the extremely cordial relations between the two Latin dictators did not yield results. Trade between their countries more than doubled within the next three years, but that stemmed from the general economic expansion of the period. Though a Treaty of Friendship and Conciliation between Rome and Madrid was signed in 1926, Spain refused to yield to Italy a most-favored-nation status in exemption from its high tariff and had to turn toward collaboration with France to put down the revolt in Morocco. Even Spanish admirers knew little about Fascism, and at that point Spain held no priority in Mussolini's thinking. In 1927 the Duce would announce that Fascism was "not for export," and though Primo de Rivera sought some more direct point of political convergence with the Italian government, he never found the means or formula.[13]

A feasible alternative to parliamentary liberalism was not to be found as readily in Italian fascism as in some other variant of the corporatist ideas that had been advanced with increasing frequency since the late nineteenth century. For that matter, the Mussolini system itself did not fully take shape until 1926, while the Spanish cultural environment, influenced little by the intellectual revolution of the 1890s,[14] was unprepared for specific radical fascist ideas. On the other hand, modern corporatist economic representation was advocated in Spain as early as 1872 by Eduardo Pérez Pujol, professor of law at the University of Valencia, to remedy the social tensions that came to the fore under the democratic monarchy of Don Amadeo (1870–73). The Valencian chapter of the Sociedad Económica de Amigos del Pais, which in the late eighteenth century had along

10. Gabriel Maura Gamazo, *Bosquejo histórico de la Dictadura* (Madrid, 1930), 51–52.
11. *Documenti Diplomatici Italiani*, 7th ser., 1922–1935 (Rome, 1955), 2:251.
12. Jacinto Campella, *La verdad de Primo de Rivera* (Madrid, 1933), 19.
13. Relations between Primo de Rivera and Mussolini are studied in Javier Tusell and Ismael Saz, "Mussolini y Primo de Rivera: Las relaciones políticas y diplomáticas de dos dictaduras mediterráneas," *Boletín de la Real Academia de la Historia* 179:3 (Sept.–Dec. 1982), 413–83; and in John F. Coverdale, *Italian Intervention in the Spanish Civil War* (Princeton, 1975), 1–35.
14. On the prefascist ideas of the era of the 1890s, see Zeev Sternhell, in *Fascism: A Reader's Guide*, ed. W. Laqueur (Berkeley, 1976), 320–37; and my *Fascism*, 39–41.

with its counterparts pressed for elimination of the traditional guild system, in 1879 recommended a reorganized guild system to rectify the excesses of rampant individualism. From the time of Leo XIII, recommendations for some form of corporatism had come from the ranks of Spanish Catholicism, and the most prominent traditionalist politician of the early twentieth century, Vázquez de Mella, corresponded with the internationally known theorist Albert de Mun and preached corporative representation. Corporatism had also figured increasingly in electoral and parliamentary proposals, particularly on municipal and provincial levels, introduced by some of the more conservative elements of the main political parties. For example, Primo de Rivera's labor minister, Eduardo Aunós, had been a Maurist in his political youth and had subsequently figured in the Catalanist Lliga. Both of those groups had favored partial corporatist representation. Spain's most prestigious intellectual, José Ortega y Gasset, had at least temporarily come out for corporatism in 1918,[15] and at approximately the same time the Spanish Socialist Party had urged the government to form state labor regulation boards and mixed juries of worker and employer representatives.

The most likely organizational basis for any drastic new alternative on the right lay in Catholicism. Under the parliamentary regime, there had been no separate organized political form of Catholicism (save for the remnant of Carlism) because the Church had become increasingly identified with the established system during the second half of the nineteenth century. Catholic opinion had thus been represented primarily by the old Conservative Party, but elimination of the party system opened new possibilities. Though the Conservative Party elite generally rejected the new government, many conservative Catholics and Carlists greeted it warmly. In the last months of 1923 members of the Asociación Católica Nacional de Propagandistas (ACNP; National Association of Catholic Propagandists), led by Angel Herrera, began to organize a new civic group that would support the new government while representing Catholic and patriotic opinion. What began in the conservative and Catholic rural and small-town society of Castile and León as the Unión Patriótica Castellana was expanded into a national organization, the Unión Patriótica, in a meeting at Valladolid in April 1924, and was quickly adopted as the new political front of the regime.[16]

The Unión Patriótica was not so much a political party as the civic organization of a government opposed to parties. It was based on patriotism, religion, and the established institutions (except parliament), and its pro-

15. See Gonzalo Redondo, *Las empresas políticas de José Ortega y Gasset* (Madrid, 1970), vol. 2.
16. Cf. Nicolás González Ruiz and Isidoro Martín Martínez, *Seglares en la historia del catolicismo español* (Madrid, 1968), 111–33.

gram was never concrete. "Law" in Spain still ultimately meant the liberal constitution, and thus Primo's declaration to the press on April 15, 1924, "There is room in the party for all those who respect the constitution of 1876," a qualification repeated once more five months later.[17]

The Unión adopted as its slogan "Monarchy, Fatherland, and Religion," which sounded like nothing so much as a rewording of the traditional Carlist emblem "God, Fatherland, and King." In a set of programmatic norms issued on May 1, 1925, Herrera declared that the purpose of the Unión must eventually be to serve as the transition "civil dictatorship" after the military dictatorship came to an end.[18] During the next five years the Union functioned, officially at least, in every province of Spain, and claimed at one point more than a million members.

Its doctrines were based on a revival of the historic Spanish ideology and attempted to create a sense of positive nationalism in Spain. They emphasized hierarchical and authoritarian leadership, with Primo de Rivera as Jefe Nacional, and the ultimate goal of some kind of corporative system. Though the UP's doctrines remained vague in detail, they clearly pointed toward a permanent right-authoritarian alternative for Spanish government.[19] The UP became the first significant force of Spanish nationalism, and inaugurated a new style of mass rally that would later reappear among both left and right during the Second Republic.

After gaining control of the situation in Morocco, Primo de Rivera replaced the Military Directory in December 1925 with a "civilian" government, civilian at least to the extent that it was composed of government ministers, five of the nine portfolios being held by conservative civilian appointees, the rest by military men. The dictator himself was of little help in political definition. He favored the phrase "First live, then philosophize,"[20] bearing heavily on the regime's "simplicity." His supporters used the terms *intuicismo* and *intuicionismo* to describe this approach.[21] Though his ablest associate, the thirty-three-year-old finance minister Calvo Sotelo, warned that a government-created party was "doomed to sterility,"[22] Primo de Rivera was determined to build one by expanding the UP. Conceiving of the civilian government as based on the UP, Primo stressed that it was to be neither of the left nor the right and would even

17. *El pensamiento de Primo de Rivera* (Madrid, 1929), 109.
18. González Ruiz and Martín Martínez, *Seglares,* 133.
19. On the Unión Patriótica, see the key political study by Shlomo Ben-Ami, *Fascism from Above: The Dictatorship of Primo de Rivera in Spain, 1923–1930* (Oxford, 1983), 126–68; and Julio Gil Pecharromán, "La Unión Patriótica," *Historia 16* 9:96 (April 1984), 28–37. The most extensive exposition of the UP's ideas is José Ma. Pemán's *El hecho y la idea de la Unión Patriótica* (Madrid, 1929).
20. Pemán, *El hecho,* 113.
21. Cf. José Pemartín, *Los valores históricos en la Dictadura* (Madrid, 1929), 637.
22. Calvo Sotelo, *Mis servicios,* 331.

welcome nonmonarchists. In August 1927 he defined the UP as *una con-ducta organizada* ("an organized way of life").[23] It was not "doctrinaire, personalist," but was somehow "apolitical" and purely patriotic. Primo de Rivera did not altogether deny similarities between the UP and Italian Fascism, but he distinguished between the latter as an "armed force" and the UP as a Christian movement, "virtually a sanitizing civil crusade."[24]

The major expansion of the UP as a bureaucratic political organization occurred in 1926–27. Though some support was obtained from most of the main political and social sectors, *upetistas* were, as Calvo Sotelo noted, "mostly rightists,"[25] and there was a particular influx of Carlists.[26]

The most notable government innovation was a limited system of state-supervised labor arbitration, the first step toward corporatism. The new labor minister, Eduardo Aunós, became especially interested in the Italian system of national syndicalism just being developed at that time. He later wrote:

> The Dictator had the kindness to support my wish to observe achievements being made in Italy and invited me to go there to gain a deeper understanding. Needless to say, I was received with the utmost cordiality by Italian Fascists, who generously assisted my investigations. I went to Italy in April 1926 and was the recipient of high distinctions and immense satisfactions. Among these was being received by the Duce, who repeatedly expressed his warm sympathy for the regime and the men who were governing Spain. Bottai, whom I had the honor to visit, extended himself to assist my search. . . . I brought back a wealth of studies and observations that would serve to complete the ideal corporative project that I had already partially drawn up.[27]

The result was the Spanish decree law on economic corporations promulgated on November 26, 1926, which theoretically divided the entire Spanish economy into twenty-seven economic corporations. Each was to be represented by freely elected *comités paritarios* (parity committees) for both workers and employers on the local level, *comisiones mixtas* on the provincial level, and corporation councils on the national level.[28] Aunós liked to point out that this was a theoretically more complete and hierarchical structure than that of Italy and was also more democratic.[29] It was in a sense even more democratic than the recent Belgian arbitration and negotiation tribunal law of May 1926, under which delegates had ultimately to be ratified by the state.

23. *La Nación* (Madrid), Aug. 6, 1927.
24. Ibid.
25. Calvo Sotelo, *Mis servicios*, 332.
26. Maura Gamazo, *Bosquejo histórico*, 247.
27. Eduardo Aunós, *La política social de la Dictadura* (Madrid, 1944), 58–59.
28. The text of the decree and Aunós's own explanation is given in his booklet *Organisation corporative nationale* (Madrid, 1927).
29. Aunós, *Política social*, 64. He elaborated his concepts further in his *La organización corporativa del trabajo* (Madrid, 1928); *Las corporaciones del trabajo en el Estado moderno* (Madrid, 1928); and *El Estado corporativo* (Madrid, 1929).

In fact, the Spanish corporative system remained largely undeveloped. The largest labor organization in Spain, the anarchosyndicalist CNT, had been formally dissolved and driven underground by the Dictatorship. Its rival, the much smaller, more moderate and disciplined Socialist UGT, was willing to participate in the new system. In the process, it was able to elect numerous local delegates to the comités paritarios and expand its own membership by more than a third.[30] The other sectors most represented were Catholic labor groups. Altogether, by May 1929, a total of 450 comités paritarios had been formed, representing more than 320,000 workers and nearly 100,000 employers.[31] This represented only about 15 percent of the total national labor force and not even half the industrial workers, the ones primarily represented.

The condition of Spanish labor under the Dictatorship varied widely. General wage levels did not rise, despite relatively high production and employment levels in industry. Overall real wages declined 3 percent between 1925 and 1930. Skilled workers in Vizcayan industry, strongly represented by Socialist and Basque unions, gained a nominal increase of 8 percent in wages over five years. The addition of not inconsiderable fringe benefits meant an even greater increase in real income. Yet the destitute farm laborers of the south probably saw their meager incomes decline even further. Most noteworthy perhaps was the more careful regulation of female labor, and the wages of women in some fields increased 12 percent over five years.[32]

After three years in power, Primo de Rivera showed not the slightest inclination to return to military command, and so finally had to consider state reorganization and constitutional reform. According to Calvo Sotelo, there was strong encouragement from Rome.

> When Aunós returned from Italy [in April, 1926], . . . the Duce, who is not an eminently political man in vain, transmitted through the former his resolute advice that Primo de Rivera convene a parliament. The system or procedure was not the important thing; in his judgment, what was essential was that it be begun and continue. "That is the costume that must be worn in international society," Mussolini said. This recommendation deeply impressed Primo de Rivera, not because he felt such extraordinary sympathy for the Italian statesman but because the two regimes had a very similar origin and it was logical that they develop according to analogous norms. At first, Primo de Rivera decided to speed up [new parliamentary] elections. However, advisers from the UP and perhaps one or two officious friends—some friends can be fatal—led him away from that path.[33]

30. José Andrés-Gallego, *El socialismo durante la Dictadura (1923–1930)* (Madrid, 1976), treats this development.

31. According to figures given by Aunós in a speech of May 3, 1929, published in his *La organización corporativa y su posible desenvolvimiento* (Madrid, 1929).

32. Aunós, *Política social*, 86–89. For more-detailed treatment of the regime's economic policy and of conditions in Spain during these years, see Ben-Ami, *Fascism from Above*, 240–318.

33. Calvo Sotelo, *Mis servicios*, 336.

Primo de Rivera delayed action until October 1927, when he finally convened a consultative National Assembly in Madrid. Of its four hundred members, some—such as the top officials of the Unión Patriótica—were ex officio members by reason of function or office, some were directly appointed by the government, and some were chosen by approved social, economic, and cultural organizations. Before the National Assembly's final session in June 1928, a constituent committee was named to prepare the draft of a new Spanish constitution. This body was dominated by ultraconservative monarchists under the secretaryship of the right-wing Andalusian writer and politician José María Pemán. Its proposal, eventually presented in July 1929, provided for a drastic increase in royal executive power. The crown was to have responsibility for appointing the government, its approval would be necessary for all legislation, and parliamentary votes of confidence would be proscribed. Membership in future parliaments would be divided equally between deputies chosen through corporative representation and those chosen by direct elections, though the latter for the first time would be based on full universal suffrage, with women granted the right to vote and hold office. The Spanish senate would be replaced by a small consultative Consejo del Reino (Council of the Realm), half of whose members would be appointed by the government and half selected by corporate elections.

During the summer of 1929 the proposed draft was subjected to extensive criticism in the only lightly censored Spanish press.[34] It found little favor. Primo de Rivera had never thought the matter through, and along with some in his cabinet was quite skeptical of such an increase in royal power. Even the king doubted that he could accept greater authority in this manner.[35]

Meanwhile opposition to the Dictatorship mounted on the center-right more effectively than on the left. University students had come out in opposition, and middle-class liberals were turning to new semiclandestine republican parties. By late 1929 the officer corps of the Army, parts of which had always been restive, were beginning to turn against Primo de Rivera. The Dictator's health declined seriously as a result of diabetes. Unable to see his way clear to remaining in power or preparing for a new system that would continue the dictatorship, he resigned at the end of January 1930.

Primo de Rivera had initiated a movement away from the parliamentary liberalism that had governed Spain for a century and toward right-authoritarianism. Yet he never clearly conceptualized the process and al-

34. See Mariano Gómez, *La reforma constitucional en la España de la Dictadura* (Valencia, 1930).

35. On the failure of Primo de Rivera's efforts at new political institutionalization, see Ben-Ami, *Fascism from Above*, 206–39.

ways drew back from any sharp conclusions. The Dictator himself could not altogether move beyond the framework of liberalism. Nearly two decades later, his labor minister Aunós gave a lecture in Madrid entitled "The ideology of Primo de Rivera as chief obstacle to his work," emphasizing that "to no one is it a mystery that the Marqués de Estella [Primo's family title] was fundamentally a liberal. He passed his life amid principles, theories, and facts of liberal significance."[36]

The regime has been judged variously by political and historical opinion. The Socialist leader Indalecio Prieto termed Primo "a dictator without corpses," which was true enough, and added, "If only all dictatorships—though I do not desire any more—were like his."[37] The Dictatorship was the object of much execration in 1931, but the years under Primo were regarded with nostalgia by more than a few Spaniards, after the horrors of the Civil War, as the last "good times" before the onset of the depression and increasing political violence. Primo himself certainly drew less personal hostility than most dictators because of his personal good humor and unpretentiousness and because of the relative mildness of his regime.

At the same time there is no denying that his government offered most of the ingredients for an institutionalized right-nationalist dictatorship in Spain. These included the first modern outline of an organic authoritarian state, organized along corporative lines and strongly identified with right-wing Catholicism. Though the Dictator himself and his leading followers could not fully conceive a completely rounded ideology and a finished new state system, they provided some of the fundamental concepts and principles which the Franco regime would later elaborate more fully.[38]

In political framework, sequence, and type of regime, Primo de Rivera's

36. Eduardo Aunós, *Semblanza política del general Primo de Rivera* (Madrid, n.d.), 28–29.

37. Quoted in Carlos Fernández, *El general Franco* (Barcelona, 1983), 43.

38. This is the main thesis of Ben-Ami's *Fascism from Above* and of his earlier article "The Dictatorship of Primo de Rivera: A Political Reassessment," *JCH* 12:1 (Jan. 1977), 65–84. However, despite the title of his book, which is by far the best study of the regime, he agrees that the dictatorship was not really fascist. Seco Serrano, *Militarismo y civilismo*, 303–64, emphasizes the Regenerationist roots of the dictatorship.

Earlier works include Gamazo, *Bosquejo histórico de la Dictadura;* Dillwyn F. Ratcliff, *Prelude to Franco* (New York, 1957); Jordi Cassasas Imbert, *La dictadura de Primo de Rivera* (Barcelona, 1983); and the Marxist treatment by José García, *Diktatura Primo de Rivera* (Moscow, 1963). The anthology *La Dictadura de Primo de Rivera juzgada en el extranjero* (Madrid, 1931) indicates that foreign opinion was often benevolent.

There is no reliable biography of Primo de Rivera. The best account of his personality is Jacinto Capella, *La verdad de Primo de Rivera* (Madrid, 1933). Other sketches are admiring apologia: Emilio R. Tarduchy, *Psicología del Dictador* (Madrid, 1930); Eduardo Aunós, *Primo de Rivera, soldado y gobernante* (Madrid, 1944); Francisco Cimadevilla, *El general Primo de Rivera* (Madrid, 1944); Miguel Herrero García, *El general D. Miguel Primo de Rivera* (Madrid, 1947); Cesar González Ruano, *El general Primo de Rivera* (Madrid, 1954); and Ana de Sagrera, *Miguel Primo de Rivera: El hombre, el soldado y el político* (Jerez, 1973), which concentrates on the earlier years.

dictatorship was less like that of Mussolini than like the south and east European military takeovers and dictatorships of the period: the Pimenta de Castro (1915), Sidonio Pais (1917–18), and corporate military dictatorships (1926) in Portugal that eventually led to Salazar's Estado Novo by the early 1930s; the authoritarian governments of 1926 in Poland and Lithuania; the short-lived Pangalos regime in Greece (1926) and that of Uriburu in Argentina (1930–32); and more marginally, the Averescu government in Romania in the early 1920s and the overthrow of Stambuliski in Bulgaria (1923). These military coups in primarily agrarian countries in no case rested on a fascist movement nor did they directly create an institutionalized new authoritarian regime, though the 1926 takeovers in Portugal and Poland did eventually lead to institutionalized regimes some years later. As far as Italy is concerned, the Primo de Rivera government should not be compared to Fascism, which it resembled little, for want of institutionalized mobilization or categorical Fascist doctrine.[39] Rather, it should be compared to the similar phase in the initial breakdown of the liberal system, which occurred during World War I. That in turn led to institutional destabilization, further democratization, political mass mobilization, and prerevolutionary conditions, just as were produced by the

39. These distinctions were clearly seen by the only near-contemporary study that I have found, Wolfgang Scholz's *Die Lage des spanischen Staates vor der Revolution (unter Beruck-sichtigung ihres Verhältnisses zum italienischen Fascismus* [*sic*]), Dresden, 1932. Scholz correctly noted that though both countries were underdeveloped, Spain was distinctly more so and had a specific tradition of military pretorianism to which Primo could be related. He further observed that the equivalent "idea world" of Fascism was lacking in Spain. There existed in Italy a broader Fascist culture that enjoyed considerable support from the intelligentsia. In Spain, practically the entire intelligentsia had turned against the dictatorship by the late 1920s.

Probably the only sophisticated commentary on Italian Fascism written in Spain under the dictatorship is in two works by Francesc Cambó, leader of the moderate wing of political Catalanism: *Entorn del feixisme italiá* (Barcelona, 1925), originally a series of newspaper articles published in *La Veu de Catalunya* in mid-1924; followed by a broader and more comparative book-length essay, *Las Dictaduras* (Barcelona, 1929). In his 1924 articles, Cambó shrewdly observed that what was beginning to develop as the ideology of Italian Fascism was produced at least partially ex post facto, organized in a more conservative context and often in sharp contrast to some of Mussolini's own pre-1922 ideas. Writing at the time of the Matteotti crisis and soon after a personal interview with Mussolini, Cambó expressed his doubt that Fascism would be more than a temporary counterrevolutionary force. In his subsequent book, Cambó put forward a theory of dictatorship as a consequence of relative backwardness and as a strictly transitory response to current problems. Finally, he emphasized that one of the worst problems caused by temporary dictatorships established to deal only with specific crises was to find simple and inexpensive means of bringing them to an end and completing the transition back to representative government. There is further commentary by Philip V. Cannistraro and James W. Cortada, "Francisco Cambó and the Modernization of Spain: The Technocratic Possibilities of Fascism," *The Review of Politics* 37:1 (Jan. 1975), 66–82. "El Capitán Centellas," in *Las dictaduras y el señor Cambó* (Madrid, 1929), presented a reply from the regime's viewpoint.

The two principal Spanish Marxist critiques of the regime were by Andrés Nin, *Las dictaduras de nuestro tiempo* (Madrid, 1930); and Joaquín Maurín, *Los hombres de la dictadura* (Madrid, 1930).

aftermath of the Primo de Rivera regime, the depression, and the Second Republic in Spain. In the early twentieth century Spanish political development lagged a decade or more behind that of Italy, and its economic expansion even more.

Nearly all the early efforts at overriding parliament and establishing military regimes in southern and eastern Europe failed. They succeeded, in most cases, only during the second, more radicalized phase of the 1930s, the primary early exception being, of course, Italy, which led the way in introducing a noncommunist authoritarian regime and thereby also gave rise to the confusing terminology that labelled all such regimes fascist.

Emergence of the Radical Right:
The Unión Monárquica Nacional

The collapse of the Dictatorship brought the downfall of the Spanish monarchy within fifteen months, for recognition of the Dictatorship by the Crown in 1923 had seriously compromised the legitimacy of Alfonso XIII. Had the state moved vigorously to restore the political system through full and free elections soon after the departure of the dictator, it is at least theoretically possible that constitutional monarchy might have survived. Yet seven years of dictatorship had undone the old parliamentary parties, and they were being replaced by more radical new semiclandestine republican organizations. Don Alfonso feared to proceed directly to new elections and passed more than a year under an epigonic *dictablanda* (a mildly authoritarian government) that eroded the Monarchy's remaining credibility. When municipal elections were eventually held in April 1931, the victory of republican candidates in the larger cities was accepted by much of Spanish opinion as a valid plebiscite. Without formally abdicating, Alfonso XIII quickly departed Spain and the Second Republic was inaugurated. Though elsewhere in southern and eastern Europe during the depression year of 1931 forces of authoritarian nationalism were either in power or rapidly growing in strength, Spain seemed to be registering the final triumph of liberalism.

Indeed, the majority of Spanish monarchists in 1930–31 did not contest this in itself but simply the form of the liberalism—democratic republican rather than constitutional monarchist—that would predominate. Only one small group of diehard supporters of Primo de Rivera stood against the liberal tide. In April 1930 they organized a new Unión Monárquica Nacional (UMN) whose monarchism was strictly sui generis, for it vehemently opposed the current political line of the Monarchy. Led by the Conde de Guadalhorce, public works minister of the Dictatorship, the UMN stood for a new regime of strong nationalism based on outright

authoritarian rule and the willingness to employ violence. It glorified the
historic Spanish ideology and sought the full restoration of traditional
Spanish values. Though Fascism was hailed, a particular interpretation of
religion formed much of its ideological basis. The economic program of
Primo de Rivera was invoked to demonstrate the path to further development, a path that would guarantee the interests of workers and peasants.
Government should rest on popular support but not on parties and elections. The UMN proposed to repress all regionalism in the interest of
"Spain, One, Great, and Indivisible," reviving a slogan of the Dictatorship. Its position was categorical: if an atomistic, democratic republic
were inaugurated even by means of free elections, the new regime should
be crushed through armed force.[40] The leading theorists and propagandists of the UMN were drawn from the front echelon of ideologues of the
Primo de Rivera regime: José Ma. Pemán, Víctor Pradera, and Ramiro de
Maeztu.

The UMN was flanked by various other tiny rightist-monarchist groups
such as Reacción Ciudadana and Acción Nobiliaria, some of which carried
over into the early Republican years. Its most notable counterpart, however, was the Partido Nacionalista Español, founded in the same month
by José María Albiñana, a physician and sometime medical school professor. The PNE shared the general right-radical ideology of the *ume-
nistas,* its two principal features being an extreme emphasis on Spanish
neoimperialism (the predilection of Dr. Albiñana) and the formation of a
political militia called Legionarios, the first of various "shirt" formations,
left and right, of Spain in the 1930s.[41]

What distinguished the UMN and PNE from fascists in Italy and elsewhere was first, their rigorously right-wing defense of vested interests
and opposition not only to socialism but also to any form of economic radicalism or reorganization, and second, their extreme ideological reliance
on conventional forms of traditional culture, especially religion. They
were obviously opposed to any recirculation of elites. Thus they formed
the Spanish variant of the radical right movements then flourishing in
continental Europe, sometimes in conjunction with, sometimes in competition with, fascism.

José Antonio Primo de Rivera, eldest son of the late dictator, served as
vice secretary-general of the UMN. His primary political passion was and

40. The only study of the UMN is Shlomo Ben-Ami, "The Forerunners of Spanish Fascism: Unión Patriótica and Unión Monárquica," *JCH* 9:1 (Jan. 1979), 49–79, which employs
a broad typology of fascism.
41. See Manuel Pastor, *Los orígenes del fascismo en España* (Madrid, 1975), 38–61; Javier Jiménez Campo, *El fascismo en la crisis de la Segunda República española* (Madrid,
1979), 78–83; Julio Gil Pecharromán, "Albiñana, el rey de los ultras," *Historia 16* 45 (Jan.
1980), 29–36; and Luis Palacios Buñuelos, *Elecciones en Burgos, 1921–1936: El Partido Nacionalista Español* (Madrid, 1981).

long remained the vindication of the work of his father, which he now crystallized in a radical, authoritarian nationalist form. Later, after 1933, he would emerge as the principal leader of Spanish fascism, but only with considerable equivocation and only after adopting more radical positions on economics and other issues.

The UMN admired the fascist example and together with Albiñana's group tried to copy aspects of fascist style. Mass meetings, heroic and violent rhetoric, and efforts at paramilitary organization were of course characteristic of many forms of radical movements. The UMN's efforts at proselytizing, beginning in the summer of 1930, were quite unsuccessful and failed to convert the main sectors of monarchists and moderate conservatives. When the Republic began, there was once again little alternative to neoliberalism and the left in Spain.

3

The Second Republic

The political history of the Second Spanish Republic is one of the most controversial and mythified in twentieth-century Europe. The Republic began peacefully with relatively broad acceptance, though attitudes naturally differed considerably among various elements of Spanish society. Within two years it produced a series of reforms—some of debatable wisdom or effectiveness—and the most fully mobilized politics that Spain had ever known. Within three more years it had produced the most remarkable case of political decay and polarization in twentieth-century Europe, breaking down into a massive revolutionary/counterrevolutionary civil war.

Even professional historians do not agree how this came about. The propaganda that found wide acceptance abroad during the Civil War and World War II, attributing all this to a rightist plot against democracy, is no longer accepted, but no clear and simple alternative consensus exists. The Republican experience can be viewed as conflict and breakdown among parliamentary forces,[1] as the failure of a reform effort,[2] or as a revolutionary process,[3] as well as the breeding ground of a rightist conspiracy.[4] In fact it was all these[5] and more.

1. An excellent brief political analysis of the breakdown will be found in Juan J. Linz's study in *The Breakdown of Democratic Regimes: Europe* (Baltimore, 1978), ed. J. J. Linz and A. Stepan, 142–216.
2. The best defense of the Republic as a left-liberal reform process is still Gabriel Jackson, *The Spanish Republic and the Civil War, 1931–1939* (Princeton, 1965).
3. See my *The Spanish Revolution* (New York, 1980).
4. Cf. Paul Preston, "Alfonsist Monarchism and the Coming of the Spanish Civil War," *JCH* 7: (July–Oct. 1972), 89–114.
5. There are two multivolume right-wing political histories that narrate the events of the Republic in great detail, the first published by Josep Pla in 1940 and the second by Joaquín

Spain was obviously in a weak position to make a democratic republic work. Though its modern political experience was one of the longest in the world, mobilized democracy was a novelty. The country had just gone through eight years of authoritarian rule and in 1931 had to start over again with mostly new parties and organizations and new leaders. For the first time the revolutionary left became a fully organized mass force, and to the vertical split which this created was added the horizontal cleavage of accelerated regionalism and regional nationalism. Moreover, all other parliamentary systems in southern and eastern Europe had either broken down or would be breaking down about the same time.

In 1931 Spain had a total population of about 23,500,000, of whom 35.51 percent were active, a figure that held fairly constant throughout the first half of the century. Agriculture employed approximately 49.5 percent of the labor force, service occupations 25 percent, and industry only 25.5 percent. Significant industrialization was centered in Catalonia and the two northern Basque provinces. Barcelona had just over, Madrid just under, a million inhabitants. The next largest city was Valencia, with only 320,000. Spain remained an agricultural, predominantly rural and small-town, society, though with significant urban nuclei. Nearly one-third of the population was illiterate, though the great majority of adult males could read and write.

Yet despite widespread illiteracy and a primarily agrarian and backward economy, it would be a mistake to view the Spain of the 1930s as over-whelmingly rural and stagnant. The preceding decade had been some-thing of a boom period of rapid industrial growth and urbanization. The industrial labor force had grown by nearly a quarter in only ten years, pro-portionately the most precipitous rise in such a short time in all Spanish history,[6] and the larger cities had rather suddenly assumed a greater im-portance than before. Madrid, long a primarily political and administra-tive center, acquired greater economic weight and for the first time shel-tered a sizable working class, whose discontent would become a major factor in the next few years.[7]

The depression had a destructive impact upon politics almost every-where. Though it was long thought, from a superficial reading of some statistics, that its impact in Spain was comparatively slight, the Spanish economy by 1930 had become increasingly integrated with the world

Arrarás in 1956–64. Ricardo de la Cierva, *Historia de la Guerra civil española. I: Perspec-tivas y antecedentes 1898–1936* (Madrid 1969), presented a detailed political history of the Republic. Most recently, important new perspectives have been provided by P. Preston, ed., *Revolution and War in Spain 1931–1939* (London, 1984).

6. This has been pointed out by Shlomo Ben-Ami, "The Republican 'Take-over': Prelude to Inevitable Catastrophe?" in Preston, *Revolution and War*, 14–34.

7. Santos Juliá Díaz, *Madrid, 1931–1934: De la fiesta popular a la lucha de clases* (Ma-drid, 1984).

economy, even though it did not depend on industrial exports. Agricultural depression, in Spain as in many other countries, commenced well before the end of the twenties, and in overall terms Spain suffered approximately as much unemployment as Italy and more than France. Industrial production declined about 6 percent in 1931–32 before largely recovering in 1935. General unemployment, however, rose steadily, fueled by agricultural depression. Inadequate statistics make it impossible to distinguish between full mandatory unemployment (*paro forzoso*) and rigorous under- or limited term employment, but the strict unemployment figures rose from 200,000 in 1931 to at least half a million—by some reckonings higher—in 1936. These translate into rates of only 5 to 12 percent, but this is misleading because of the very high degree of seasonal or underemployment in agriculture, which actually made economic conditions much worse. While urban labor was not generally faced with massive unemployment on the scale of the major industrialized countries, landlessness and profound poverty among so much of the rural population in the southern half of the country created socioeconomic stress virtually unknown elsewhere in western Europe.[8]

At least as important, however, was the impact of the radical new trends in general European politics during the thirties. The depression decade produced crisis in many parts of Europe, featuring the rise of powerful new currents and the reactivation of temporarily dormant forces. It gave major impetus to fascist-like movements in central and east-central Europe, while invigorating Communist and Socialist parties in highly diverse lands. The resulting new polarization first took shape elsewhere, but the steady expansion of competing radicalisms in Europe soon influenced affairs in Spain as well. Within less than two years, both left and right would draw new and much more radical inspiration from events abroad, while their fears would be intensified by the violent and authoritarian victories of opposing tendencies elsewhere. The influence of pan-European trends toward extremism and polarization thus grew apace.

Yet unlike similar experiences in other lands, Spain's ultimate breakdown into fully polarized revolutionary/counterrevolutionary civil war occurred without involvement in foreign war, occupation, or defeat and without any very extensive or direct foreign intervention in its affairs. Thus the Republic's traumatic history must be approached first of all in terms of domestic forces, beginning with the three key national political divisions: the Left Republicans, the Socialists, and the Catholic conservatives. Of all parties, the Left Republicans were nearest the fulcrum of power under the Republic. Led by the eloquent and acerbic writer Manuel

8. Juan Hernández Andreu, *Depresión económica en España, 1925–1934* (Madrid, 1980), is the principal study of the depression in Spain.

Manuel Azaña Díaz, prime minister and president of the Second Republic

Azaña[9]—a sometimes vigorous leader of high ideals and vehement antipathies—they were a product of the new middle-class radicalism that developed in the late 1920s in reaction to the dictatorship.[10] They tended to reject the "historical" Republicans, above all the Radical Republican Party of Alejandro Lerroux, as excessively moderate, compromising, and corrupt. Their favorite allies, on whom their general strategy was based, were the Socialists, whom they simply assumed would continue to support a lower-middle-class, primarily liberal-democratic strategy. The great weakness of Azaña's leftist Republicans was their intolerance and arrogance, grounded in fanatical anticlericalism. They admitted little compromise with Catholics and conservatives, insisting that the Republic function on their principles or not at all. In this they gained their end, though the result was the latter, not the former. The constitution forced through by the Left Republicans and the Socialists deprived Catholics of civic and cultural rights, in that it not only separated church and state but was designed to make Catholic education and certain aspects of normal religious functioning illegal and impossible. The Republic thus began on the basis of exclusivism rather than equal rights and participation.

The Socialists, who became one of the two largest political forces in Spain, were a standard quasi-Marxist party stemming from the Second International. Their history had been one of failure and moderation. The Republic provided their first opportunity to participate in a coalition government, which they accepted with enthusiasm as the first step toward a social democratic and ultimately socialist system. When the initial coalition came apart because of internal feuding between Republican groups and rising middle-class discontent, it was not the Socialists who took the initiative in breaking it up.[11]

The Republican-Socialist coalition of 1931–33 faced serious obstacles and suffered from profound disagreement over both the principles and

9. There is no adequate study of the paradoxical Azaña, whose leadership proved so fateful. An apologium is presented by Juan Marichal in his prologue to Azaña's *Obras completas,* 4 vols. (Mexico City, 1966–68); and in *La vocación política de Manuel Azaña* (Madrid, 1968). Frank Sedwick, *The Tragedy of Manuel Azaña and the Fate of the Spanish Republic* (Columbus, Ohio, 1963), is superficial; as is Emiliano Aguado, *Don Manuel Azaña Díaz* (Barcelona, 1972). The anthology *Azaña* (Madrid, 1980), and Josefina Carabias, *Los que le llamábamos Don Manuel* (Madrid, 1980), are two later publications by Azaña's admirers. On his party and its politics, see Eduardo Espín, *Azaña en el poder: El partido de Acción Republicana* (Madrid, 1980); and, more broadly, Juan Avilés Farré, *La izquierda burguesa en la II República* (Madrid, 1985).

10. Shlomo Ben-Ami, *The Origins of the Second Republic in Spain* (Oxford, 1978), provides an extensive account of the political origins of the Republic and some of its principal forces.

11. Though not fully satisfactory, the only survey done in any detail is Manuel Contreras, *El PSOE in la IIa República* (Madrid, 1981). Brief general discussions will be found in Manuel Cantarero del Castillo, *La tragedia del socialismo español* (Madrid, 1971); and Ricardo de la Cierva, *La historia perdida del socialismo español* (Madrid, 1972).

pace of socioeconomic reform. Though one of Spain's main problems was that of the rural poor, who were either proletarianized or underemployed, the Left Republicans, concerned primarily with the nineteenth-century political and cultural revolution, shrank from the expense of radical agrarian reform.[12] Their models were the anticlerical regimes of France, Portugal, and Mexico and not the recent changes in agrarian eastern Europe, whether populist or Communist. While the Socialists controlled the Ministry of Labor and were able to stimulate wages, they became increasingly dissatisfied with the resistance to structural change.

The Republic was vehemently rejected by the extreme left, which consisted of the world's only mass anarcho-syndicalist trade union confederation, the CNT, a minuscule Spanish Communist Party (PCE), and a small independent Leninist movement in Catalonia (BOC-POUM). The CNT fell under control of revolutionaries of the Federación Anarquista Ibérica (FAI),[13] who insisted on immediate overthrow of any form of capitalism in the name of "libertarian communism," a decentralized anarchist form of revolutionary communalism. Manipulating a mass trade union movement of nearly a million, they engaged in three different amateurish efforts at revolutionary insurrection in 1932–33, contributing to the destabilization of the Republican-Socialist coalition.[14]

In the 1920s Spanish Communism had become a mere branch of the Soviet-controlled Third International. During the first four years of the Republic, the Soviet line called for immediate revolution. Though the PCE at first had only a few thousand members, it engaged in incendiary activities aimed at the overthrow of the Republic.[15] Since the nominal Spanish Communist Party was little more than a tool of Moscow, the true candidate for that role was in fact the small independent Leninist party, the Bloque Obrero-Campesino (BOC; Worker-Peasant Bloc), organized in Catalonia by Andrés Nin and Joaquín Maurín. Former adherents of the Third International, Nin and Maurín had lost all illusions about the Soviet Union. Their independent Leninist party, small though it was, would re-

12. The prime study of the Republican agrarian reform is Edward E. Malefakis, *Agrarian Reform and Peasant Revolution in Spain* (New Haven, 1970); to which Federico Bravo Morata, *La reforma agraria de la República* (Madrid, 1978), adds little. See also Leandro Benavides, *La política económica de la Segunda República* (Madrid, 1972); and, on the Republican reforms in general, Manuel Ramírez Jiménez, *Las reformas de la IIa República* (Madrid, 1977).
13. See Juan Gómez Casas, *Historia de la FAI* (Bilbao, 1977).
14. The principal account of the CNT in these years is John Brademas, *Anarcosindicalismo y revolución en España (1930–37)* (Barcelona, 1974). For a general history of Spanish anarchism, see Robert W. Kern, *Red Years, Black Years: A Political History of Spanish Anarchism* (Philadelphia, 1978); and Juan Gómez Casas, *Historia del anarco-sindicalismo español* (Madrid, 1969).
15. The most informative treatment of the PCE during the Republic is still Eduardo Comín Colomer, *Historia del Partido Comunista de España*, 3 vols. (Madrid, 1965–67).

main a thorn in the flesh of the Communists as an alternate form of Spanish Marxist revolution.[16]

The Republican-Socialist coalition broke down in 1933, not because of opposition on the right or extreme left but because of internal division. The largest Republican group, the Radical Republican Party, reflected the nomenclature as well as the characteristic of its French counterpart, being radical in name only. It represented the most common denominator of middle-class republicanism, for which socialism was anathema, and was, like its French counterpart, a political radish: "red" on the outside but thoroughly "white" on the inside. The Radicals finally withdrew from the coalition altogether, leaving the more genuinely radical Left Republicans a small minority with the Socialists.

Disillusion with the sectarian consequences of Republican government and resentment stemming from social and economic conditions were compounded by the somewhat heavy-handed tactics of Republican police administration. The new leadership was determined not to fail through timidity or weakness, and full civil rights rarely obtained under the Republican regime, which regularly placed varying limits on free speech and the right of assembly. Though the abuse of military powers by the monarchy had been much criticized, the new regime imposed conditions of martial law on May 12, 1931, less than a month after it had assumed power. Not only was the paramilitary rural police force of the Civil Guard not abolished, but it was flanked by a special new paramilitary Republican urban police, the Assault Guards, and under Republican government a variety of special military jurisdictions over aspects of civilian activity were perpetuated. A strong Law for the Defense of the Republic was enacted in October 1931, followed by a relatively restrictive new Law of Public Order in June 1933. The latter provided for three different levels of suspension of constitutional rights: a state of exception, a state of alarm, and a state of war (providing for prosecution by court-martial). During the last three years of the Republic, one or the other of these three constitutional states of exception was in effect either on a national or regional basis almost continuously.[17] At varying times both conservatives and would-be revolutionaries protested in almost equivalent terms the rigor of Republican police measures.[18]

The coming of the Republic had taken conservative and Catholic opin-

16. The best treatment of the BOC-POUM is Víctor Alba's *El marxisme a Catalunya 1919–1939*, 4 vols. (Barcelona, 1974–75). See also Francesc Bonamusa Gaspar, *El Bloc Obrer i Camperol* (Barcelona, 1974), and *Andreu Nin y el movimiento comunista en España (1930–1937)* (Barcelona, 1977).

17. These measures are summarized in detail by Ballbé, *Orden público*, 317–96.

18. The major "police scandal" of the early years of the Republic, the Casas Viejas affair, is elucidated in detail by Jerome Mintz's fascinating historico-anthropological reconstruction *The Anarchists of Casas Viejas* (Chicago, 1982).

ion by surprise. Conservative forces failed to organize adequately to contest the first parliamentary elections and thus had been meagerly represented in the drafting of the new constitution. Outrage over its sectarian and anticlerical nature, combined with fear of the revolutionary left, led to a major comeback by the right in 1932–33. This chiefly took the form of a mass Catholic political party, something that had never before existed in Spain.

The new Confederación Española de Derechas Autónomas (CEDA; Spanish Confederation of Autonomous Rightist Groups), soon became the largest single political force in Spain. The CEDA was Catholic and rightist but not extremist. It held to strictly legal means of opposition as a parliamentary electoral party but did aim at drastic constitutional reform and seemed, albeit vaguely, to espouse some form of new Catholic corporate state.[19] It was quickly labeled "Spanish fascism" by the left.

Local elections in 1933 revealed the extent to which the Republican-Socialist coalition had lost favor with Spanish voters. By that time, the left-liberal entente was in a state of collapse. In the ensuing national elections of November 1933, the Left Republicans and Socialists ran separate tickets and each suffered a smashing defeat. In contrast, the CEDA and the Radicals formed several provincial alliances and ran one-two in the national returns.

The parliamentary logic of such an outcome would normally have dictated a governing coalition led by the CEDA, which had gained a small plurality of the vote. The Republican president, however, was the moderate Catholic liberal Niceto Alcalá Zamora, who was determined to preserve the basic institutions of the Republic and feared that the CEDA and its leader, the eloquent young parliamentary spellbinder José María Gil Robles,[20] would push the Republic into a Catholic corporative system. For the next year, he therefore appointed a series of short-lived minoritarian Radical party governments under Lerroux.

The Radicals were primarily interested in avoiding trouble and making the most of their personal opportunities and were quick to achieve an unenviable reputation for financial corruption. The advantage which they offered was a program of live-and-let-live, middle-of-the-road republi-

19. The most extensive scholarly study of the CEDA is José Ramón Montero, *La C.E.D.A.*, 2 vols. (Madrid, 1977). A different perspective is presented in volume 1 of Javier Tusell Gómez, *Historia de la democracia cristiana en España* (Madrid, 1974); and in R. A. H. Robinson, *The Origins of Franco's Spain* (Pittsburgh, 1970). On the policies of the main conservative agrarian and industrialist interest groups, see Alejandro López López, *El boicot de las derechas a las reformas de la Segunda República: La minoría agraria* (Madrid, 1984); and Mercedes Cabrera, *La patronal ante la II República* (Madrid, 1983).

20. Biographies of major figures are generally wanting in modern Spanish historiography. Gil Robles himself has published one of the ablest memoirs of the period, *No fue posible la paz* (Barcelona, 1968). José Gutiérrez Ravé, *Gil Robles, caudillo frustrado* (Madrid, 1967), presents a rightist critique of his leadership and policies.

canism, but one doomed to failure because of their own minority status and ineffectiveness.[21] Given the temporary disarray of the left, they could govern only on the sufferance of the *cedistas,* who held a plurality of seats. The latter finally insisted on at least a limited coalition as the price of further support. On October 1, 1934, three of the most moderate CEDA leaders—not including the feared Gil Robles—entered the cabinet in a new reorganization of the Radical government.

This was made the excuse for a full-scale insurrection by the revolutionary left. During the preceding year much of the Socialist Party had undergone a process of "Bolshevization"—a term used by its own proponents. "Bolshevized" Socialists sought, somewhat confusedly, direct revolutionary confrontation. Meanwhile, during 1933, the Leninist BOC had taken the lead in attempting to form a new Alianza Obrera (Worker Alliance) with all other revolutionary worker groups. The Socialists tried to patch over their own internal differences between moderates and revolutionaries and took the lead in the Alianza Obrera, joining forces with the POUM and the minuscule Spanish Communist Party. Leaders of the Alianza Obrera agreed that the entrance of *cedistas* into the cabinet marked the beginning of a "fascist takeover" like those of Italy, Germany, and Austria.[22]

The horizontal cleavage of regional radicalism further intensified Republican political conflict. Catalanism presented the main challenge, fueled by the persistent strength of the Catalan language and its culture, the rise of modern Catalan industry as the largest single focus of economic development in Spain, and finally the emergence of a radical lower-middle-class "left Catalanism."[23] In 1932 Catalonia gained a generous though not absolute system of regional autonomy under the Republican reforms, yet extreme Catalanists chafed under the limitations that still existed. After a series of disappointments in relations with Madrid, their leaders agreed to engage in revolt parallel to the revolutionary left.

Basque nationalists, by comparison, tended to be more conservative, though no less sweeping in their goals. Relatively unified behind Catholic principles, they did not find it easy to work with the anticlerical Republic,

21. For the Radicals, see Octavio Ruiz Manjón, *El Partido Republicano Radical 1908–1936* (Madrid, 1976).

22. Paul Preston has analyzed the polarization between the two mass parties, the CEDA and the PSOE, in *The Coming of the Spanish Civil War, 1931–1936* (London, 1978). Andrés Blas Guerrero, *El socialismo radical en la IIa República* (Madrid, 1978), treats the rise of revolutionary socialism in 1933–34; and Marta Bizcarrondo, *Araquistain y la crisis de la Segunda República en España: "Leviatán" (1934–1936)* (Madrid, 1975), studies the party's outstanding radical intellectual.

23. On the radical Catalanists, see Joan B. Culla i Clara, *El catalanisme d'esquerra* (Barcelona, 1977).

and adopted an independent centrist position almost equidistant from left and right.[24]

The revolutionary insurrection of October 1934 was a dismal fiasco in Madrid and Barcelona but achieved striking success in the northwestern mining and industrial region of Asturias. This was the only area where the Alianza Obrera was effectively organized. Revolutionary miners seized control of the district and held it for ten days until the revolt was finally suppressed by large-scale military intervention. A wave of repression followed, with as many as 20,000 leftists imprisoned. There were numerous killings in Asturias, first by the revolutionaries in power and then by the military during the repression, and the stories of this were considerably magnified by both sides. The Asturian insurrection constituted the first direct revolutionary insurrection in western Europe since the Paris Commune (equaled only by outbursts in Italy and Germany before and after World World I), and initiated a drastic polarization of Spanish opinion.[25]

The October insurrection was formally directed against "fascism" at a time when fascism scarcely existed in Spain. This was later admitted by some leftist commentators, who then sometimes tried to justify the insurrection on more general grounds. In fact—just as the military revolt of 1936 sparked the leftist revolution that it was designed to avoid—the revolutionary insurrection of 1934 provoked more of the rightist polarization and movement toward a sort of fascism that it was designed to prevent.

El Sol, Madrid's leading moderate newspaper, warned specifically against such an outcome. In an editorial on Septmeber 9, 1934, criticizing ever more frequent outbursts of radical strike activity less than a month before the insurrection, it pointed out that

> an arm which is too often employed in inappropriate situations ends up injuring itself to the point where it can no longer be used when the propitious moment arrives not only because it tires and the edge is dulled, but also because the appropriate reaction grows, perfecting contrary arms, to counteract it.
>   . . . By using all revolutionary means with ill-measured frequency to fight against a fascism which does not exist, except as a pallid imitation, what definitely might happen is the production of the necessary conditions, the soil, the climate, for the growth of fascism. Not the gentleman's fascism which we have

24. Basque nationalism under the Republic is treated in my *Basque Nationalism* (Reno, 1975), 117–56.
25. Adrian Shubert, *Hacia la revolución (Orígenes sociales del movimiento obrero en Asturias, 1860–1934)* (Barcelona, 1984), presents a lucid account of the background of the revolt. The insurrection itself is treated in Francisco Aguado Sánchez, *La revolución de octubre de 1934* (Madrid, 1972); Bernardo Díaz-Nosty, *La comuna asturiana* (Madrid, 1974); J. A. Sánchez G. Sauco, *La revolución de 1934 en Asturias* (Madrid, 1974); N. Molins i Fabrega, *UHP: La insurrección proletaria de Asturias* (Madrid, 1977); Amaro del Rosal, *1934: movimiento revolucionario de octubre* (Madrid, 1984); P. Ignacio Taibo, *Asturias 1934*, 2 vols. (Madrid, 1984); and the collective work *Octubre, 1934: Cincuenta años para la reflexión* (Madrid, 1984).

[in Spain] by reason of style, but the true and fearful one, against which the arms raised by the liberal state are no good. In a not dissimilar manner fascism was engendered in other countries.

The following year, 1935, was a time of reaction and relative immobility. The CEDA's influence increased, and several of the Republic's earlier reforms were temporarily shelved, but the prime minister's position remained in the hands of the Radicals or moderate independents.[26] At length, Gil Robles and the CEDA rebelled against being denied access to the government leadership to which their plurality might presumably have entitled them, refusing to support another ministry led by a smaller party. President Alcalá Zamora thereupon placed the government in the hands of a personal crony and nonparty independent at the close of 1935 and subsequently scheduled new elections for February 1936. His goal was to reorganize some sort of moderate centrist Republican coalition that could overcome the deepening polarization between left and right, a project that failed completely.[27]

The moderate left had already begun to reorganize, Left Republicans and moderate Socialists proposing a new coalition as early as the spring of 1935. This was the remote origin of what became the Spanish Popular Front, whose development owed nothing to the Communists, the latter being included only upon the insistence of the Bolshevized sector of the Socialists.[28] For the elections of 1936, therefore, the left was united, with even an undetermined degree of voting support from the anarchists. Rightist parties, led by the CEDA, formed an electoral bloc of their own. Center forces, in contrast, found themselves isolated between left and right, while the Radical party, discredited by failure and the exposure of financial scandals, began to disintegrate. In the 1936 elections, 73 percent of the eligible Spanish electorate cast ballots. According to the most thorough study, the Popular Front drew 34.3 percent, the rightist coalition 33.2 percent, and the shrunken center only 5.4 percent.[29] Though the plurality in the popular vote was rather narrow, the Spanish electoral list system, derived in part from that of Italy in 1924, disproportionately rewarded coalitions with pluralities. After the new parliament met in March

26. The most able of these, Joaquín Chapaprieta, has presented a defense of a viable Republican policy during these months in his memoir, *La paz fue posible* (Barcelona, 1971).
27. Alcalá Zamora has presented his own defense in his *Memorias* (Barcelona, 1977). An earlier memoir and exordium, *Régimen político de convicencia en España* (Buenos Aires, 1945), offered an incisive and only partially exaggerated list of the mistakes and shortcomings of the rightist parties during 1933–35 (pp. 33–35).
28. There are two studies of revolutionary Socialist policies by Santos Juliá, *La izquierda del PSOE (1935–1936)* (Madrid, 1977), and *Orígenes del Frente Popular en España 1934–1936)* (Madrid, 1979).
29. Javier Tusell Gómez et al., *Las elecciones del Frente Popular en España*, 2 vols. (Madrid, 1971).

and disqualified a few of the rightist deputies earlier elected, the leftist parties held about two-thirds of the seats.

Had the Popular Front produced a stable governing coalition, this would have provided the basis for firm and effective rule. Though the Popular Front remained, it had no governmental dimension, for the Socialists refused to participate in a "bourgeois" regime. Thus a minority Left Republican government under Azaña took power, only to see that power disintegrate, along with law and order, in many parts of Spain. By the early spring of 1936 the country moved into what most historians agree was a prerevolutionary situation. The two mass movements of Socialists and anarchists competed with each other (and sometimes clashed violently) in radical activism, promoting mass strikes and revolutionary land seizures that were sometimes legitimized ex post facto by the increasingly impotent Republican government. The moderate president, Alcalá Zamora, was impeached on a technicality by the left so as to eliminate the last nonleftist leadership in the state. He was succeeded by Azaña, who as Republican president lapsed into paralysis. For five months some of Spain's principal cities and a portion of the southern countryside were the scene of intermittent violence between the revolutionaries and their foes, while social strife and economic disorder mounted.[30]

30. On conditions in the spring of 1936, see Luis Romero, *Por qué y cómo mataron a Calvo Sotelo* (Barcelona, 1982); my *The Spanish Revolution*, 185–214; and Ricardo de la Cierva, ed., *Los documentos de la primavera trágica* (Madrid, 1967).

4

The Nationalist Opposition

The principal opposition to Republican reformism and the possibility of revolution took the form of conservative political Catholicism, the CEDA. Though the CEDA was not merely a conservative party or a loyal opposition to the revolutionaries and the Left Republicans, neither did it represent fascism or the radical right. Its leaders insisted on constitutionalism and legal, parliamentary tactics, eschewing violence, street action, and paramilitary militias. The CEDA represented above all the Catholic middle classes and smallholders of northern Spain. As indicated earlier, it became the largest mass party in the country, and its leaders were fairly confident of winning power by electoral means. Indeed, they increased their vote in 1936 over that of 1933 and remained the most popular single party in Spain only five months before the Civil War.

After Catholicism, the most pronounced characteristic of the CEDA was ambiguity, and its ultimate goals remained vague. It espoused Catholic corporatism and a reform of the Republican constitution, which opponents charged would simply convert Spain into an authoritarian corporate state. Before long, many of the ordinary members and followers of the party were looking back with nostalgia on the monarchy, while its youth branch, the Juventudes de Acción Popular (JAP; Popular Action Youth), adopted some of the outward trappings of fascism, talking of the need for strong leadership and a powerful state. Yet the ambiguity of the JAP was demonstrated by their party salute: the right arm raised only halfway, then drawn back across the chest. They abhorred the fascist-like squadrism of anarchists, Socialists, and Communists and refused to compete in such endeavors. Moreover, they officially denied that their stress on authority and leadership was to be interpreted as support for a fascist type of authoritarianism.

46

The Radical Right

It was only natural that a moderate right-wing movement like the CEDA would win the backing of the great bulk of middle-class Catholic and conservative opinion in Spain. By definition, the conservative middle classes wanted to avoid trouble, and a moderate legalistic alternative reflected their habits and values fully. Small groups of the Spanish right, however, disagreed with the moderate reaction and propounded a more radical alternative. While most monarchists followed the CEDA, a select group of doctrinaires and activists organized for a new system.

The new radical right formed around a journal called *Acción Española* that began publication at the close of 1931. The activists of *Acción Española* were drawn from three areas: *maurista* conservatism, social Catholicism, and Carlism. Each of these Spanish sources was quickly superseded in the thinking of the group, for classical *maurismo* had been too legalistic and parliamentarian, the nascent Spanish social Catholicism of the early 1920s too heterogeneous,[1] squeamish, and even democratic, and Carlism too reactionary and backward-looking.[2] The group's principal backing came from wealthy conservatives, above all the well-organized Bilbao industrial-financial elite.[3]

The very title of *Acción Española* made the inspiration of the French Maurrasian radical right obvious; Italian Fascism was a more distant secondary source. Chief foreign collaborators were members of Action Française, followed by Portuguese Integralists and National Syndicalists and a few Italian Fascists. *Acción Española* generally approved of Hitlerism but criticized the German movement for its secularism and demagogy, holding that the *Fuehrerprinzip* was no substitute for a monarchy.

Acción Española pledged to revive the traditional Spanish ideology, grounded in religion and in strong monarchist institutions. It derived much inspiration from the Primo de Rivera regime, with which nearly all its members had been associated; the critique of the regime's failure[4] was a prime goal of the journal. Blame was placed on the lack of elite support and the absence of a vision of a modern new authoritarian structure.

The editor of *Acción Española* was Ramiro de Maeztu, formerly a leading *noventayochista* writer who had converted to the principles of authority and religion at the time of World War I. Maeztu was to give the

1. On the heterogeneity of early Spanish social Catholicism, see Oscar Alzaga, *La primera democracia cristiana en España* (Barcelona, 1973).
2. Raul Morodo, *Acción Española: Orígenes ideológicos del franquismo* (Madrid, 1980), is a thorough ideological study, superseding Luis Ma. Ansón, *Acción Española* (Zaragoza, 1960), briefer and more general. See also Santiago Galindo Herrero, *Los partidos monárquicos bajo la Segunda República* (Madrid, 1956).
3. An inventory of backers is presented in Morodo, *Acción Española*, 65–73.
4. As first articulated by Victor Pradera, *Al servicio de la Patria: Las ocasiones perdidas por la dictadura* (Madrid, 1930).

José Calvo Sotelo, head of the rightist Bloque Nacional under the Republic

final major historical definition to the traditional Spanish ideology three
years later when he published his *Defensa de la Hispanidad* (1934), a polemic in defense of traditional Hispanic culture and religion, both European and American, as opposed to Soviet socialism and Anglo-American
materialistic liberalism.[5]

5. *Obra de Ramiro de Maeztu* (Madrid, 1974). The principal studies are Vicente Ma-
rrero, *Maeztu* (Madrid, 1955), 367–750; and, more briefly, Ricardo Landeira, *Ramiro de
Maeztu* (Boston, 1978), 68–96, 114–31. A lucid overview and interpretation is presented in
Douglas Foard's "Ramiro de Maeztu y el fascismo," *Historia 16* 4:37 (May 1979), 106–15.

The group's key political leader was José Calvo Sotelo, former Young Maurist and finance minister of Primo de Rivera. Forced to flee abroad in 1931, he was converted to right radicalism under the influence of Action Française and French and Italian ideas while in exile in France. Calvo Sotelo's return to Spain was made possible first by his election to the Tribunal de Garantías Constitucionales and finally by election to the Cortes on the monarchist Renovación Española list in 1933. The latter, *Acción Española*'s political branch, had been organized earlier in the year after the CEDA rejected the group's principles. The CEDA in turn was denounced by Calvo for being too moderate, compromising, and ambiguous—insufficiently nationalist and authoritarian—whereas Renovación Española itself proved to be too small and narrow a sect. He was ready at one point in 1934 to enter Falange Española, the new fascist party to be discussed below, but was rejected by its leaders as too dangerous a rival and as too "rightist."

Calvo consequently tried to form a broader new movement of the radical right, which took shape as the Bloque Nacional, organized in December 1934 in the wake of the October insurrection in Asturias. Calvo and the *Acción Española* writers proposed not the restoration but the "installation" (*instauración*) of an authoritarian new monarchy, which would have to be preceded by an indeterminate period of dictatorship. In its founding manifesto, the Bloque called for creation of a "totalitarian state" in Spain to concentrate and direct national energies. The directly elected Cortes was to be replaced by an "organically" organized corporate chamber, analogous to that of Italy or Portugal, and social and economic problems resolved through state regulation, economic intervention, and reflationary policies. Calvo Sotelo clearly understood that this was not likely to come about through political mobilization but would probably require forcible intervention by the military. The new state would adopt a militantly nationalist policy and foster the development of the armed forces in particular. It would reject laicism and restore the Catholic identity of Spanish government.

The radical right of *Acción Española* and Calvo Sotelo differed from generic fascism not in any squeamishness about violence and dictatorship, or even in any differences over the goal of empire, but in their distinct socioeconomic strategies and cultural formulae. *Acción Española* invoked traditional rightist elites and feared the development of new competitors, even if nationalist in orientation. Both the neomonarchists and Spanish fascists strove for a corporate state, but for the latter this meant the mobilization of labor and a drastic new articulation of national interests behind national syndicalism. In religious and cultural matters, the neomonarchists were clerical and neotraditionalist, the incipient Spanish fascists Catholic but nonclerical and zealous to combine traditionalism with modernization.

Unlike many other rightists and even the Falangist leaders themselves, however, Calvo Sotelo was not unwilling to be labeled a fascist. His own definition of fascism seems to have been loose, referring rather vaguely to authoritarian nationalism and corporatism. On the other hand, though he sometimes referred to his own goals of corporative state economic regulation and interventionism as "economic leftism," he found the national syndicalism of the Falangists too radical and subversive of capitalism.

In practice, the Bloque Nacional proved a political failure, drawing little popular support and winning few seats in the final Republican elections of 1936. During the final political crisis of the Republic, however, with Gil Robles's moderate conservatism discredited and the Falangist leaders imprisoned, Calvo Sotelo emerged as the primary leader of the rightist opposition. His murder by Republican police in July 1936 was calculated to decapitate that opposition but instead became the final spark that set off the Civil War. It was an unprecedented crime, the only instance in the history of west European parliamentary government in which the leader of the parliamentary opposition had been murdered by the government police, and it dramatized the severe limitations to constitutional government and civil rights that had developed by then in Spain.

Analysis of the formal structure of the Franco regime in its plenitude—especially the "high phase" of Franquism from 1937 to 1959—soon reveals that the Franquist system was built on the ideas and doctrines of Calvo Sotelo and the *Acción Española* group more than on those of José Antonio Primo de Rivera and the Falangists. The reliance on the military, a corporative Cortes, and the *instauración* of monarchy all corresponded to this doctrine. The only notable Falangist component, the syndical system, never came close to achieving the Falangist goal of a national syndical state, but simply functioned as an agency of state regulation more or less along lines conceived by Calvo Sotelo. Moreover, the intensely Catholic character of the eventual Franquist system in its heyday corresponded much more to the concepts of *Acción Española* than to those of the Falangists.[6]

6. The best general treatments are those of Morodo, *Acción Española;* of Robinson, *Origins of Franco's Spain;* and, more briefly, Robinson's "The Monarchist Myth of the Franco Regime," *Iberian Studies* 2:1 (Spring 1973), 18–26.

In addition to the memoir on his work under the dictatorship, cited earlier, Calvo Sotelo published two collections of his writings in the early 1930s, *En defensa propia* (Madrid, 1933), and *La voz de un perseguido;* 2 vols. (Madrid, 1933), and he outlined some of his economic concepts in *El capitalismo contemporáneo y su evolución* (Madrid, 1935).

Two preliminary studies of the early part of his career are Manuel Pi y Navarro, *Los primeros veinticinco años de Calvo Sotelo* (Zaragoza, 1961); and Julián Soriano Flores de Lemus, *Clavo Sotelo ante la Segunda República* (Madrid, 1975). All biographical accounts have been written by admirers. The principal are Aurelio Joaniquet, *Calvo Sotelo* (Madrid, 1939); Eduardo Aunós, *Calvo Sotelo y la política de su tiempo* (Madrid, 1941); and General Felipe Acedo Colunga, *José Calvo Sotelo* (Barcelona, 1957). Eugenio Vegas Latapié, one of the leading theorists of *Acción Española*, published *El pensamiento político de Calvo Sotelo* (Madrid, 1941); as well as his own *Escritos políticos* (Madrid, n.d.); and subsequently, his own *Memorias políticas* (Barcelona, 1983).

More clearly than either the moderate Gil Robles or the radical Primo de Rivera, Calvo Sotelo grasped that the most feasible alternative to the Republican system was neither conservative parliamentarianism nor a popular national syndicalism but an integrated mobilization of all the resources of the counterrevolutionary right. The difference, of course, was not a matter of tactics but of values. To the CEDA leader such an extreme of dictatorship was repugnant, while to the Falangist it was inadequate and reactionary. Calvo Sotelo's politics became those of catastrophism. The rightist reaction of the military on which he came to rely could only be achieved in a situation of intense polarization and impending cataclysm. Hence the irony that Calvo Sotelo's own assassination formed an integral part of that very process on which he depended to realize his ideas and achieve his goals.

The Revival of Carlism

Spain's classic radical right, indeed the original nineteenth century prototype of such a force, and practically the only mass movement of the preceding century in the peninsula, was Carlism. Defeats in two civil wars, combined with extensive social and cultural change, had decreased Carlism's following considerably by the early twentieth century, but just as the emergence of the anticlerical First Republic had reawakened Carlism in 1873, so the anticlericalism and radical mass leftist politics of the Second Republic revived Carlism in the early 1930s. A more contemporary and integrated doctrinal base had been provided during the early years of the century by the theorist Juan Vázquez de Mella y Fanjul, who cast Carlist principles fully in the mold of right-wing Catholic corporatism under the leadership of traditionalist but theoretically decentralized monarchy.

During the first phase of the Republic the main branches of Carlism were reunited and given vigorous leadership by a new secretary general in Seville, Manuel Fal Conde. The Carlists joined with the Alfonsine monarchists of Renovación Española behind Calvo Sotelo's Bloque Nacional, though the association remained an uneasy one. The Carlists in fact enjoyed rather more popular support than Calvo Sotelo's monarchists, though their following was disproportionately concentrated in the northeastern historically autonomous province (formerly kingdom) of Navarre and adjacent territories.

The principal new statement of Carlist doctrine was Víctor Pradera's *El Estado nuevo* (1935). In it he defined Catholic identity and a form of so-

---

It may be noted that beginning in 1933 quite a number of books on corporatist doctrine appeared in Spain, some of them by independent right-wing doctrinaires. Perhaps the best were Eduardo Aunós, *La reforma corporativa del Estado* (Madrid, 1935); and Joaquín Azpiazu, *El Estado Corporativo* (Madrid, 1936).

cietal corporatism, under monarchy, that would be autonomous from the state though partially regulated by it and that would also be compatible with partial regional decentralization. Though the Carlist youth association, like the CEDA's JAP, suffered from aspects of the vertigo of fascism and sometimes used fascist-like slogans, the Carlists differentiated their traditionalist, ultra-Catholic, monarchist, and partially decentralized corporatism from the radical centralized contemporary authoritarianism of Italy and Germany.[7]

Falange Española

In discussing the origins and development of generic fascism in Spain, it is first of all important as a matter of historical perspective to understand that antifascism as a serious force preceded it and always exceeded it in strength down to the Civil War. The revolutionary left in Spain, first in the form of the CNT and then subsequently in the Marxist parties, was actively organized to combat fascism even before it clearly existed in Spain. Antifascism became a major category of activity for the Communist International soon after Mussolini's March on Rome in 1922, at a time when a threat of genuine fascism existed in few countries. It is probably correct to say that antifascism, not only in Spain but as a general force throughout Europe, was always more broadly diffused than fascism, and much greater in strength.

The obvious source of inspiration for a Spanish fascism was the Italian prototype, but the latter had, as indicated, attracted surprisingly little attention during its early years. The publication *La Camisa Negra* died at the beginning of 1923 as soon as it was born, and the abortive attempts to form various isolated little nationalist militia groups in 1931 such as Hueste Española or Cruzados de Cristo had no significance.

The first figure to directly adopt the doctrines of Italian Fascism in Spain was the avant-garde litterateur Ernesto Giménez Caballero, editor of *La Gaceta Literaria* (Spain's leading avant-garde literary review in the late 1920s)[8] and organizer of the first movie club in the country. In 1929 Giménez Caballero suddenly espoused fascism, which he interpreted as the modern form of Latin Catholicity, the national cultural and spiritual salvation of southern Europe against the Protestant North. "GC"'s fascism was more esthetic than political and somewhat bizarre in doctrine, but the prevailing attitudes of the Spanish intelligentsia were so overwhelm-

7. The basic study is Martin Blinkhorn, *Carlism and Crisis in Spain, 1931–1939* (London, 1975), 1–206. A Carlist narrative will be found in Luis Redondo and Juan Zavala, *El Requeté* (Barcelona, 1957), 225–310.

8. See Miguel Angel Hernando, *La Gaceta Literaria (1927–1932): Biografía y valoración* (Valladolid, 1974).

ingly liberal that this leader of the Madrid literary new wave and one of the country's fashionable cultural figures found himself almost immediately ostracized, condemned to being a "literary Robinson Crusoe."[9]

The first fascist political group in Spain was formed not by the esthete Giménez Caballero but by Ramiro Ledesma Ramos, an underemployed university graduate who had earlier specialized in mathematics and philosophy. Here again the inspiration was primarily Italian, for the title of the group's weekly, *La Conquista del Estado,* was copied from a sometime Italian publication of the same name by the radical Fascist writer Curzio Malaparte. Ledesma was followed by a mere handful of ten young students or ex-students in their twenties, and began publication in March 1931, one month before proclamation of the Republic. In August a radical nationalist organization appeared in Valladolid called Juntas Castellanas de Actuación Hispánica, organized by a radical right-wing Catholic lawyer and former teacher Onésimo Redondo Ortega. The two joined forces in October 1931 to form the first categoric Spanish fascist political organization, the Juntas de Ofensiva Nacional Sindicalista, a typically verbose Spanish formulation that resulted in the acronym JONS and the term *jonsistas* for the members.

Ledesma was the most trenchant intellectual in the entire history of Spanish fascism. With a well-trained and incisive mind, writing with a mordant pen, he dealt more directly with some of the problems of a fascism in Spain than any of his followers or the later epigoni of the movement. The JONS adopted a generically fascist program (consistent with the definition established at the end of chapter 2), affirming extreme nationalism, dictatorship, violence, and the expansion of empire. For Ledesma, true fascism was a revolutionary doctrine that engaged in competition with the revolutionary left. The JONS's economic program of national syndicalism was derived in large measure from that of the revolutionary national syndicalists who created the first doctrinal basis for Italian fascism,[10] though it was readily assumed to parallel that of the German National Socialists. In fact, neither Ledesma nor any of his colleagues ever elaborated any precise, detailed socioeconomic theory, nor was Ledesma able to develop any plans for direct action, because the group had no more than about two thousand followers in central and north central Spain. It lacked resources for propaganda, and its only sig-

9. Giménez Caballero has been studied by Douglas Foard, "Ernesto Giménez Caballero and the Revolt of the Esthetes" (Ph.D. diss., Washington University, 1972), of which a version was translated by the elderly Giménez Caballero for publication in Madrid in 1975; and more briefly in Foard's article, "The Forgotten Falangist: Giménez Caballero," *JCH* 10:1 (Jan. 1975). Giménez Caballero's two principal fascist works were *Genio de España* (Madrid, 1932) and *La nueva catolicidad* (Madrid, 1933).

10. David D. Roberts, *The Syndicalist Tradition and Italian Fascism* (Chapel Hill, 1979).

Ramiro Ledesma Ramos, co-founder of the JONS

nificant financial support was a limited subsidy from big business circles in Bilbao, interested in subsidizing some sort of radical nationalism, fascist or otherwise, to combat the left. Hence the little band functioned like many small radical groups—primarily by rhetoric.[11]

A more vigorous, better-financed attempt at a Spanish fascism was essayed by elements of the extreme right in 1933. The triumph of Hitler stimulated interest in Spain also, not so much among potential fascists—of whom there seemed to be so few—but among right radicals or potential right radicals, who were distinctly more numerous. The principal organized pressure group of the extreme right in Spain was composed of the representatives of leading financiers and industrialists in Bilbao, who had successfully promoted conservative and then right-radical politics since the turn of the century. During the summer of 1933 they conducted a search for the possible leader of a counterrevolutionary, demagogic Spanish fascism.

The leader who came to the fore was José Antonio Primo de Rivera, eldest son of the late dictator, who was in the course of evolution from conservative and authoritarian monarchism to a more radical brand of nationalist authoritarianism that at first was not unlike that of Calvo Sotelo. By 1933 the younger Primo de Rivera—soon to become generally known as José Antonio—had become interested in something rather like fascism (Italian-style) as the vehicle for giving form and ideological content to the national authoritarian regime attempted so uncertainly and unsuccessfully by his father. Unlike Ledesma, who initially had greater insight, José Antonio was not at first averse to using the label "fascist," though it was decided to call the new movement that he founded with a group of col-

---

11. "Ramiro . . . could never find the frontiers which separate the fluidity of real life from imagined existence, which only possesses us in fleeting moments of enchantment. . . . One cannot well ascertain if Ramiro dreamed in order to act or longed for action in order to dream." "It is difficult to find in the work of Ramiro, so tied to the concrete, a concrete norm about anything in ordinary life. When he talks of social affairs he loses himself in vague rhetoric which would never satisfy anyone who is in open struggle with life, and when he speaks to us on his own account of the economic order of the State the same thing happens. The worst occurs when, perhaps taking note of this vagueness, he endeavors to tell us something concrete about things he has not studied, for then one sees only too clearly that he has wanted to convince us with an artificial argument." "The work of Ramiro . . . did not propound anything concrete; it was rather the expression of a human lack we shall continue to feel so long as the present spiritual state of Europe endures." Emiliano Aguado, *Ramiro Ledesma en la crisis de España* (Madrid, 1941), 114–15.

Ledesma has been the subject of two full-length biographies, both entitled *Ramiro Ledesma Ramos*. The first, by Tomás Borrás (Madrid, 1972), is superficial and totally admiring, while the second, by José Ma. Sánchez Diana (Madrid, 1975), has somewhat greater depth. There is a brief treatment in my "Ledesma Ramos and the Origins of Spanish Fascism," *Mid-America* 43:4 (Oct. 1961), 226–41. His earlier technical writings on philosophy were later collected as *Los escritos filosóficos de Ramiro Ledesma* (Madrid, 1941).

The political writing of the jonsista co-leader Redondo was brought together in the *Obras completas de Onésimo Redondo* (Madrid, 1940), and the early struggles of the JONS in Valladolid are chronicled in Víctor Fragoso del Toro, *La España de ayer* (Madrid, 1965), vol. 1.

leagues in October 1933 by the more original title Falange Española
(Spanish Phalanx).[12]

The Falange began with much more financial support from those in big
business close to the radical right than did the JONS, promping the latter
to merge with it in early 1934, the resulting organization being called
Falange Española de las JONS. During the next two years, and indeed all
the way down to the beginning of the Civil War, the Falange was distinguished primarily by its insignificance. Like the Romanian Iron Guard
and several other European fascist movements, it relied primarily on its
student clientele, but unlike the Romanian movement, it completely
failed to generate any broad lower- or middle-class support.

The only advantage of this period in the wilderness was that it gave the
movement's leaders some time to reflect on what they were about. After a
year or so, José Antonio Primo Rivera began to move "left," as the national syndicalism of the Falangists took on more radical overtones. There
was a somewhat belated reaction to the danger of mimesis, as Ledesma
complained of the "mimicry" shown by Falangists, and before the close of
1934 Falangist leaders were denying that they were fascists.

José Antonio had had a personal interview with Mussolini early in October 1933, a few weeks before the founding of the party, but became increasingly aware of the Duce's opportunism. Criticism of the conservatism of the Italian regime was not uncommon among Falangists, though
it was muted. In May 1935 José Antonio visited the offices of the CAUR,
the so-called Fascist International, in Rome, but did not see Mussolini
again, and in September of that year attended the international meeting
of the CAUR in Montreux as an observer. He also visited Nazi Germany
very briefly in the spring of 1934 but did not find the experience particularly attractive and did not have a personal meeting with Hitler.

Part of this effort to distinguish the movement from Italian Fascism was
a genuine expression of difference and part was simply a concern to avoid
the charge of imitation.[13] José Antonio and the other Falangists admitted
that they had much in common with the Fascists but also insisted on the
Spanishness and singularity of Falangism.[14]

12. It may be noted that at that time the radical-right Jeunesses Patriotes in France maintained a student auxiliary called Phalanges Universitaires, though there is no direct evidence that this influenced the Spanish choice of name.

13. According to a document released many years later by his biographer, Felipe Ximénez
de Sandoval, José Antonio, in his brief remarks as an observer at Montreux on September 1,
1935, assured other European fascists of his moral support and sense of common identity,
but explained that the sensitivities of Spanish nationalism and the subversive nature of other
international forces in Spain made it politically infeasible for Falangists to participate in any
international association at that time, though he said that he hoped to be associated with
them in the future.

14. Redondo insisted that Italian Fascist doctrine was too mutable and pragmatic to be
easily defined, much less be considered equivalent to Falangism: "Nor does it suit us to ac-

It was all rather bewildering to Italian Fascists. During the "universal Fascism" phase of the mid-1930s, would-be Italian taxonomists somewhat inconclusively decided that Falangists were indeed fascists because of their belief in "authority, hierarchy, order" and their antimaterialist Falangist "mysticism,"[15] and the Falange later became one of a number of foreign movements to draw modest subsidies from the Italians.

Unlike some other fascist movements, the Falangists did develop an official program, the Twenty-Seven Points, before the close of 1934. These exhibited all the main points of fascistic doctrine, and in the economic sphere called for development of a national syndicalist state. No detailed blueprint of the national syndicalist state was developed, however, and the economic goals remained imprecise. The official Falangist program declared, "We repudiate the capitalist system," but like many other fascist movements, made a strong point of protecting "private property" from "grand capital." The only direct anticapitalist feature was point 14, stating, "We defend the tendency toward the nationalization of bank services and, through corporations, that of the major public services." José Antonio would later declare that "property, as we now conceive it, is coming to an end,"[16] but his aim was to guarantee that property fulfilled social responsibilities and not to seek its elimination. Falangist rhetoric followed the productionist line of early Italian Fascism, and José Antonio spoke of converting Spain into a "gigantic syndicate of producers," but the precise articulation of this remained unclear. In speeches during 1935 José Antonio did emphasize the expropriation of large landed estates to create in certain areas a drastic smallholders' reform combined with large cultivation units not held as latifundia. The solution to perpetual underemployment was clearly seen to lie in industrialization that would absorb excess labor.[17]

The most lengthy early attempt to elaborate this program was José Luis

---

cept the dialectic—which ought to be called dialectic rather than doctrine—of Mussolini, on relations between the state and individuals: what in this is called *fascist doctrine* is, in our judgment, a transitory tactic, incongruous as a fixed entity, which the combative and constructive talent of Mussolini has been adapting to fit his particular and very personal inspiration in order to govern Italy during recent years. . . . What there is not, rightly speaking, is a doctrine of public law, however much there may appear to be; *fascism* changes its course, as the calendar changes, in the passage of a year; we cannot even be sure that the 'doctrine' which appears most characteristic and fundamental, that of the semipantheistic supremacy of the state over everything else, will be maintained by Mussolini until his death." *El Estado Nacional* (Valladolid), May 15, 1933.

15. Michael Ledeen, *Universal Fascism* (New York, 1972), 100, 110–11.

16. *Obras completas de José Antonio Primo de Rivera* (Madrid, 1952), 427.

17. Years later Manuel Fuentes Irurozqui published a small book, *El pensamiento económico de José Antonio Primo de Rivera* (Madrid, 1957), which, contrary to its intention, pointed up the fact that José Antonio generated little economic thought. The nominal number-three figure in the movement, Julio Ruiz de Alda, generated even less, as evidenced by his *Obra completa* (Barcelona, 1939).

de Arrese's *La revolución social del nacional sindicalismo*, written in 1936 but not published until 1940 following the end of the Civil War. For Arrese, the "social revolution" of national syndicalism consisted of an assortment of limited proposals, such as profit sharing, vague workers councils in factories, a family wage, restoration of municipal patrimonies for communal support, and the aforementioned nationalization of banking and credit. In general these did not go as far toward "semisocialism" as the original proposals of German national socialists and Italian national syndicalists.

A mystical sense of nationalism was the outstanding feature of Falangism. José Antonio stressed the "eternal metaphysic of Spain" in contrast to its present miseries, and national unity—requiring the suppression of partyism and dissident regionalism—held the highest priority. Together with most of the radical right, Falangists insisted that Spain had declined ever since it ceased to be an empire, and that unity could be achieved only by offering common participation in a transcendent cause. Borrowing a concept of Ortega y Gasset, José Antonio declared Spain to be "una unidad de destino en lo universal" (a unity of destiny in universal affairs). Spanish people could enjoy unity, freedom, justice, and prosperity only as part of a successful nation, which in turn could flourish only by fulfilling a broader destiny. The Falangist program proclaimed "We have a will to empire," and yet the Falangist leaders made it categorically clear that they harbored no dreams of foreign conquest. "Empire" meant above all the projection of Hispanic culture and values.[18] Though José Antonio sometimes spoke of drastic changes in the offing in foreign affairs, he also declared the era of colonial conquest at an end,[19] and showed clear interest only in some kind of federation with Portugal and the development of a sort of cultural leadership or hegemony over Spanish America.

In religious affairs Falangism officially proclaimed its Catholicism but distinguished itself from the clericalism of the right and insisted on the separation of church and state. Spanish nationalism must ineluctably be Catholic or it would not be Spanish, and moreover most Falangist members were personal believers. Yet many millions of Spaniards had themselves ceased to be Catholic, and Falangists did not propose to subject them to a religion-dominated state.

18. This was stressed in detail by Redondo during the first months of the JONS, in *Libertad* (Valladolid), no. 2, Aug. 31, 1931. Ledesma similarly declared, "There are many feeble and sickly spirits who think this matter of empire means the launching of armies across the frontier. It is scarcely worth the effort to deny such foolishness." Quoted in Manuel Cantarero del Castillo, *Falange y socialismo* (Barcelona, 1973), 167.

19. In a speech of March 17, 1935, José Antonio stated: "Today every piece of land on earth has an owner and every conquest would be an act of depredation and robbery. But the domain of the spirit has no limits and there indeed conquests may be carried to the fullest extent. . . ." Quoted ibid., 168.

That Falangism exhibited certain distinct characteristics of its own is undeniable, but these did not prevent it from sharing the general qualities and characteristics that would compose an inventory of generic fascism.[20] As hypernationalists, all fascist groups by definition revealed certain distinct national traits. Falangism was, for example, more Catholic than Italian Fascism (for whom religion was marginal, even if stressed during the Fascist/National Socialist polemics of 1933–34). The Falangists' concept of the "new man" incorporated nearly all the qualities of the traditional Catholic hero, while fusing it with certain twentieth-century components, yet this was by no means uncommon among certain fascist movements. The Romanian Iron Guard, for example, was considerably more thoroughgoing and fanatical in its religious identity, and Boleslaw Piasecki's Polish "Falanga," whose name was derivative, was also more extreme and pronounced in its Catholicism.[21]

Though Ledesma was originally the more salient theorist, his rival José Antonio soon achieved undisputed leadership in the movement, and this was so despite the ambivalence of his personality. He was perhaps the most ambiguous of all the European national fascist leaders. Major personal characteristics may have disqualified him for successful leadership: a fastidious estheticism combined with a genuine if sometimes contradictory sense of moral scruple, a cultivated intellectual tone of distance and irony, and, for a Spanish politician, a remarkably limited spirit of sectarianism and group rivalry.[22]

20. Javier Jiménez Campo, *El fascismo en la crisis de la Segunda República espanola* (Madrid, 1979), is perhaps the best study of original Falangist doctrine. Bernd Nellessen, *Die verbotene Revolution (Aufstieg und niedergang der Falange)* (Hamburg, 1963), also devotes considerable attention to ideas; as does Patricia Root Fouquet, "The Falange in Pre-Civil War Spain: Leadership, Ideology and Origins" (Ph.D. diss., University of California, San Diego, 1972). For an exposition of the intellectual background of Falangist ideas from a neo-Falangist viewpoint, see Salvador Broca, *Falange y filosofía* (Salou, 1976).

21. For further examples of the fascist identity of early Falangism, see Raul Martín, *La contrarrevolución falangista* (Paris, 1971), 66–85; and, for an idealized comparison with the Romanian movement, Horia Sima, *Dos movimientos nacionales: José Antonio Primo de Rivera y Corneliu Zelea Codreanu* (Madrid, 1960).

22. In 1935, Ledesma's mordant pen etched an essentially accurate sketch: "It is characteristic of Primo de Rivera that he operates on a series of insolvable contradictions traceable to his intellectual formation and the politico-social background from which he emerged. His goals are firmly held, and he is moved by a sincere desire to realize them. The drama or difficulties are born when he perceives that these are not the aims in life which truly fit him, that he is the victim of his own contradictions, and that by virtue of them he is capable of devouring his own work and—what is worse—that of his collaborators. Behold him organizing a fascist movement, that is, a task born of faith in the virtues of impetus, of an enthusiasm sometimes blind, of the most fanatical and aggressive national patriotic sense, of profound anguish for the social totality of the people. Behold him, I repeat, with his cult of the rational, . . . with his flair for soft, skeptical modes, with his tendency to adopt the most timid forms of patriotism, with a proclivity to renounce whatever supposes the call of emotion or the exclusive impulse of voluntarism. All this, with his courteous temperament and his juristic education, would logically lead him to political forms of a liberal, parliamentary

José Antonio Primo de Rivera, first Jefe Nacional of the Falange

Perhaps the best brief portrait of José Antonio was written by one of his most sensitive and able young supporters, Dionisio Ridruejo:

> In 1935, outside of Falangist circles, I personally became acquainted with José Antonio Primo de Rivera, an appealing and intelligent man of great gallantry and dialectical elegance, possessed of sure personal honor, who added to

type. Nonetheless, circumstances hindered such a development. To be the son of a dictator and live tied to the social world of the highest bourgeoisie are things of sufficient force to influence one's destiny. They swayed José Antonio in that they forced him to twist his own sentiments and search for a politico-social attitude that might resolve his contradictions. He searched for such an attitude by intellectual means, and found it in fascism. Since the day of this discovery he has been in sharp conflict within himself, forcing himself to believe that this attitude of his is true and profound. At bottom he suspects that it is something that has come to him in an artificial, transient way, without roots. That explains his vacillation and mode of action. It was these vacillations which made him at times prefer the system of a triumvirate, curbing his aspiration to the *jefatura única*. Only when, because of the internal crisis, he saw his preeminence in danger did he determine to take it over. It is strange and even dramatic to watch a man not lacking in talent struggle valiantly against his own limitations. In reality, only after overcoming these limitations can he hope one day to achieve victory." Ramiro Ledesma Ramos, *¿Fascismo en España?* (Madrid, 1935), 186–88.

these qualities a note of delicacy and timidity that was enormously attractive. He impressed me as has no other man since and I seemed to see in him the model that every young man instinctively seeks to follow and to imitate: something like the older friend who guides the rebellious energies of adolescents when they feel the need to break with their immediate surroundings. . . .

I never have, and never shall, cease to feel for the figure of José Antonio the great respect and vivid affection that he inspired in me then, though many of his ideas now seem to me immature and others contradictory and mistaken. I still believe in his good faith, firmly demonstrated by the extraordinarily human behavior that preceded his death. In truth José Antonio did not possess that histrionic facility of fascist—and nonfascist—leaders and always seemed to be taking a critical attitude toward himself, seeking something which he never succeeded in finding. In personal conversation—even with a very young person like myself, who showed him unconditional admiration—he did not hide his doubts about the quality of the small band that followed him. He tried to distinguish his movement from the fascist model, and did not renounce the hope of gaining an audience among the men of the left who might make his own political party superfluous by taking the [nationalist] direction that he sought. He believed in the threat of communist revolution, but he feared no less that the country might fall into the hands of the traditional right, which he considered the surest means of guaranteeing that the revolution would be ultimately unavoidable and irremediable.[23]

Like most fascist movements, the Falangists placed great emphasis on style. Literature and poetry, specifically, were major interests of José Antonio, and the poetic style of a crusader—"half-monk" and "half-soldier"—was preached to the followers of what he sought to define as a "poetic movement." Though modern cultural romanticism was rejected as a source of confusion and degeneration, Falangist rhetoric was romantic in the extreme: "Life is not worth living if it is not to be consumed in the service of a great enterprise, and we know none greater than that of building the new Spain."[24]

This did not at first involve the employment of violence, which was well

23. Dionisio Ridruejo, *Escrito en España* (Buenos Aires, 1962), 13. For many years the semiofficial biography of José Antonio was Felipe Ximénez de Sandoval, *José Antonio (Biografía apasionada)*, rev. ed. (Madrid, 1980). One of the best biographical sketches is Ian Gibson, *En busca de José Antonio* (Barcelona, 1980). Antonio Gibello, *José Antonio: Apuntes para una biografía polemica* (Madrid, 1974), is one of the better accounts by his admirers; to which J. M. Nin Cardona, *José Antonio: La posibilidad política truncada* (Madrid, 1973), mainly a collection of quotations, adds little. The latest additions to this literature are Arnaud Imatz, *José Antonio et la Phalange Espagnole* (Paris, 1983); Carlos de Arce, *José Antonio: Biografía* (Barcelona, 1983); and Gibello, *José Antonio, ese desconocido* (Madrid, 1985). His speeches and writings have been published as *Obras completas* (Madrid, 1952); *Textos inéditos y epistolario de José Antonio Primo de Rivera* (Madrid, 1956); and *Ultimos hallazgos de escritos y cartas de José Antonio Primo de Rivera* (Madrid, 1962), the last edited by A. del Río Cisneros and E. Pavón Pereyra.

24. "Paradise is not rest. Paradise is against rest. In Paradise one cannot lie down; one must hold oneself upright, like the angels. Very well: we, who have already borne on the road to Paradise the lives of the best among us, want a difficult, erect, implacable Paradise; a Paradise where one can never rest and which has, beside the thresholds of the gates, angels with swords." *Obras completas*, 566. On its style and the Falange as a "poetic movement," see my *Falange: A History of Spanish Fascism* (Stanford, 1961), 38–51.

taken care of by leftist antifascists. During the Falange's first several
months of existence, nine of its members were murdered by the left without a single fatal counterattack by Falangists.[25] Spokesmen of the right said
that José Antonio's party smelled more of Franciscanism than of fascism
and actively incited it to take up arms against the left, something which
began only in June 1934.

Of all national fascist leaders, he was probably the most repelled by the
brutality and violence associated with the fascist enterprise. In the post-
fascist era much has been made by his admirers of José Antonio's "humanism," his opposition to total dictatorship, his stress on the individual personality and "man the bearer of eternal values," and his Catholicism.[26] Yet
in the Joseantonian formulation these did not necessarily contradict fascism; fairly similar usages might be found among some nominally leading
figures of Italian Fascism. José Antonio stopped using the term *fascist* before the end of 1934 and the term *totalitarian* before the end of 1935, and
he occasionally referred to rightist conspirators as "fascist windbags" (*fascistas llenos de viento*); yet however diffident and differential may have
been his approach, he never renounced the basic fascist goals in politics.

Up until the spring of 1936, the Falange probably never had more than
ten thousand regular members. The two or three thousand rightists who
had joined it during its first months soon dropped out, leaving it primarily
a student movement of very young men. Its most effective branch was in
fact the student organization, the SEU (Sindicato Español Universitario),
which became increasingly active and pugnacious and was later able to
dominate the streets around several Spanish universities, at least part of
the time.[27] Though the membership showed a good deal of enthusiasm,
there was little leadership, organizational ability, or clarity of thought.
With few exceptions, the second-rank leaders were mediocre, and much
depended on personal connections and favoritism within the party structure. Though he himself indulged these tendencies, they also worried and
discouraged José Antonio, who declared to his close friend Ramón Serrano
Súñer late in 1934: "If blood had not already been shed, I would dissolve
the Falange today. What would be the fate of these lads if they should
triumph? How would they be employed in formal circumstances? Many of
them would have to be shipped off to the Congo."[28] These were particularly fateful problems for a party with the ambition and later the opportunity to become a *partido único*.

25. Documentation may be found ibid., 51–58.

26. The most systematic exposition along these lines is Adolfo Muñoz Alonso, *Un pen-
sador para un pueblo* (Madrid, 1969); but see also Cecilio de Miguel Medina, *La personali-
dad religiosa de José Antonio* (Madrid, 1975).

27. David Jato, *La rebelión de los estudiantes* (Madrid, 1967), is a narrative of the early
SEU by one of its former members.

28. Serrano Súñer to Carlos Rojas, June 16, 1972, in Rojas, *Prieto y José Antonio: Socialismo y Falange ante la tragedia civil* (Barcelona, 1977), 145.

The strongest nuclei of the Falange were to be found in Madrid[29] and in the Valladolid district of León–Old Castile. The myth of Castile and the history of Castilian leadership in Spanish culture and history was important in Falangist doctrine as a counterweight to regional nationalism in the peninsula's periphery.[30] When all is said and done, the major Falangist appeal had to be made to the rural and small-town society of north-central Spain, which was Catholic and also conservative. Yet these regions were primarily mobilized by the conservative and Catholic CEDA, and showed no interest in a radical fascist alternative until the political breakdown of the system began in the spring of 1936.

An effort was also made to develop a nationalist, anti-Marxist trade union movement in several large cities, the CONS (Confederación Obrera Nacional-Sindicalista). Only one significant antileftist syndical group had heretofore emerged, the Barcelona-based Sindicatos Libres, but they were tarred with the label "scab union" and for the most part collapsed at the beginning of the Republic.[31] Though the CONS claimed a nominal membership of 25,000 by early 1935, this figure seems doubtful, for they failed altogether to make any impression on the urban working classes.[32]

While suffering the implacable hostility and violence of the left, the Falangists also encountered increasing difficulty in their relations with the right, their primary source of financial support. In August 1934 a pact was signed with Renovación Española in which the Falange pledged to do

29. In Madrid, the largest local *Jons* (as local groups were called) membership was drawn, according to a surviving document from the beginning of 1936, from the following social groups:

Laborers and service employees	431	Women	63
White-collar employees	315	Adult Students	38
Skilled workers	114	Small businessmen	19
Professional men	106	Officers and aviators	17

The laws of the Republic, however, prohibited minors from being officially affiliated with political parties. More than half of the Falangist activists were probably underage members of the SEU whose names could not appear on the regular party membership lists. In Cantarero del Castillo, *Falange y socialismo*, 31, there is a pertinent list of reasons why at least a small number of affiliates were attracted to the movement before 1936.

30. With regard to Catalonia, it may be noted in this connection that one current of radical Catalanism aimed at a sort of fascistic regional nationalism in opposition to the Spanish state, fomenting a violent and authoritarian form of micronationalism that would suppress the revolutionary left and create a state corporatism in imitation of Fascist Italy. The leader of this current was Josep Dencás, councillor of the interior in the Catalan regional government of 1933–34. During the Civil War several of his associates tried to negotiate Italian protection for an antileftist Catalonia. The only account is J. M. Morreres-Boix, "El Enigma de Josep Dencás," *Historia Nueva* 21 (Oct. 1978), 94–104; though Dencás published a self-serving apologium, *El 6 d'octubre des del Palau de Governació* (Barcelona, 1935). Other examples of a potential regional or micronational fascism in conflict with a central-state fascism might have been found in Yugoslavia.

31. The fundamental study is Colin M. Winston, *Workers and the Right in Spain, 1900–1936* (Princeton, 1984); see also his "The Proletarian Carlist Road to Fascism: Sindicalismo Libre," *JCH* 17:4 (Oct. 1982), 55–85.

32. Emilio Gutiérrez Palma, *Sindicatos y agitadores nacional-sindicalistas 1931–1936* (Valladolid, 1938), is the only extended account of the early CONS.

nothing to hinder the activities of the monarchists, in return for a monthly subsidy,[33] but this was soon discontinued. The hemorrhage of right-wing members continued, for they found the Falange insufficiently monarchist and clerical.[34] Ramiro Ledesma turned against José Antonio early in 1935, charging that he lacked toughness and aggressiveness in leadership, and ended being expelled from the party himself.[35]

The year 1935 was a time of penury for the Falange. On June 3 the Italian Foreign Ministry directed the Italian press attaché in Paris to subsidize the Spanish movement in the amount of 50,000 lire (about $4,000 US) per month, but after six months this was cut in half.[36] Such modest assistance—evidently much less than that provided by the Soviet Union to the Spanish Communist Party at the time—came nowhere near meeting the financial needs of the party. It was during this desperate period of isolation and lack of resources that Falangist spokesmen, led by José Antonio, redoubled emphasis on some of the more radical aspects of their program ranging from drastic socioeconomic change to the need for new and younger elites, and also made futile efforts to generate some sort of armed revolt against the Republican system.

Antifascism more than ever seemed more powerful than fascism in Spain, for in the aftermath of the 1934 insurrection and the repression that followed, antifascism became a central rallying point for the left. Ramiro Ledesma shrewdly observed at that time that if fascism meant radical politics, mass organization, violent tactics, and arbitrary government, in Spain, the rightists were "*apparently fascist but, in many instances, essentially antifascist*,"[37] either because of their legalism, squeamishness about violence, or reluctance to engage in drastic demagogy or mass organization. Conversely, the leftists were "*apparently antifascist, but in*

33. A copy of the text of this agreement was originally given to me by Pedro Sainz Rodríguez in Lisbon in May 1959. It has since been published by Gil Robles in *No fue posible la paz*, 442–43.

34. Cf. the Marqués de la Eliseda, *Fascismo, catolicismo, monarquía* (Madrid, 1935).

35. Ledesma subsequently received subsidies from monarchists and then from the German consulate in Barcelona to publish two short-lived independent fascist periodicals. During 1935 he published two books, a doctrinal statement called *Discurso a las juventudes de España* and a pseudonymous memoir of his brief political career, *¿Fascismo en España?* (Madrid, 1935), one of the most interesting sources on the early Falange.

36. John F. Coverdale, *Italian Intervention in the Spanish Civil War* (Princeton, 1975), 57–58. For more treatment of the financial problem, see my "La Financiación del Falangismo, 1931–1936," *Historia 16* 2:9 (March 1978). It is interesting to note that in dealings with the Italians—and specifically in an analysis of the Spanish situation prepared for them in August 1935—José Antonio was not reluctant to assert the fascist identity of the Falange. The latter has been published by Angel Viñas, who also presented the pertinent data on the Italian subsidy in his *La Alemania nazi y el 18 de julio* (Madrid, 1974). The fullest account of both Republican government and Spanish party relations with Fascist Italy will be found, however, in Ismael Saz's *Mussolini contra la II República* (Valencia, 1986).

37. *¿Fascismo en España?*, 38. (Italics in the original.)

many characteristics and aims, essentially fascist"[38] because they exhibited those basic qualities of fascism just referred to. The Spanish right harbored a not inconsiderable number of "fascistized"[39] elements who exhibited some of the external trappings and rhetoric of fascism but little in the way of full fascist doctrine, organization, and practice.

Indeed, Mussolini had originally been impressed by the Republican army minister and prime minister Manuel Azaña as the nearest thing to a fascist type of leader in Spain—a very considerable rhetorical exaggeration—because he seemed to be the only strong leader in the country. Though Giménez Caballero had been the first to translate the Italian Fascist Malaparte's *Technique of the Coup d'Etat*, it was read as eagerly among some of the anarchist elite of the FAI as among Falangists.[40] The principal "shirt movements" in terms of size, street dominance, and violence were those of the left, and only the left had risen violently and in significant numbers to try to overthrow the Republican system.

Abandoned by both the self-styled "left fascists" of Ledesma and the radical right, the Falangists redoubled their fascistic radicalism without drawing any response whatever. The very qualities displayed in their propaganda—demagogy, secularism, and socioeconomic extremism—made them anathema to the middle classes and the right. The question mark that Ledesma placed in the title of his memoirs that year—*¿Fascismo en España?*—seemed fully appropriate. In the final Republican elections of February 1936, the Falangist ticket gained only 44,000 votes in all Spain—about 0.7 percent of the total. Only in five areas did it gain more than 1 percent: in Zamora (1 percent), a conservative and largely agrarian area; in Santander (1.99 percent), a northern district of somewhat similar characteristics with a strong local Falangist nucleus; in Madrid (1.2 percent), where most of the vote was drawn from middle-class districts; in Valladolid, (4.16 percent), probably the most significant regional nucleus of Falangist strength, where a particular effort had been made among the lower-middle-class and agrarian population; and in Cádiz (4.6 percent), where the Primo de Rivera family connections were strongest.[41]

This was probably the weakest showing of fascism in electoral competition in any European country where a national fascist party contested elections. Even in social democratic Scandinavia, domestic Nazi parties managed to win at least 1 or 2 percent of the national vote. Fascism was extremely weak in Spain for somewhat the same reasons enumerated for the weakness of nationalism in general in chapter 1. A neutral in the First

---

38. Ibid.
39. On p. 47, Ledesma provides a list of those whom he considered merely *fascistizados*.
40. Cf. Fidel Miró, *Cataluña, los trabajadores y el problema de las nacionalidades* (Mexico City, 1967), 54–55.
41. These computations were made by Jiménez Campo, *El fascismo*, 236, 307–8.

World War, Spain lacked the many frustrated army veterans who played such key roles in the early phases of Fascism and Nazism in Italy and Germany. In Spain, mobilized nationalism was inverted—expressed through the intense regional nationalism of Catalans and Basques directed against the Spanish nation-state. Another key factor was the limited secularization of rural and provincial society in much of the country, particularly in the north. There, as in Austria and Slovakia, the most obvious and attractive cross-class alternative to liberal politics was political Catholicism. Moreover, the nominal electoral success of the CEDA from 1933 down to election day in 1936 gave this tactic the appearance of victory. Fascism enjoyed much less cultural reinforcement in Spain than in central Europe, for the cultural and intellectual ferment of the 1890s had achieved less resonance in the peninsula. There was a rightist/Catholic culture of considerable force, but not a secular/vitalist/Darwinist cultural environment of any vigor. Finally, as far as political revolutionism was concerned, the left seemed able to enforce a monopoly of its several brands, since during the 1930s the left had greater success and support in Spain than anywhere else in the world. Thus Spain offered distinctly less opportunity for fascism as the consummation of a sort of frustrated, deviant revolution than did central Europe.[42]

The fascist movement in Spain could not even profit from the incipient breakdown of the Spanish polity after the elections, because one of the last effective measures taken by the Republican government in the spring of 1936 was the official suppression of the Falange. Though disillusioned young rightists began to flock to the clandestine, partially disarticulated movement after the Popular Front's triumph, the eventual collapse of political order erased the very possibility of a political victory in the Italian or German sense, something which Falangists had never seen as a real opportunity at any time. The hope of the nationalist opposition no longer lay in political mobilization but in military action.

42. The reasons for the weakness and early failure of fascism in Spain are discussed more broadly in comparative terms in my "Spanish Fascism in Comparative Perspective," in *Reappraisals of Fascism,* ed. H. A. Turner, Jr. (New York, 1975), 142–69; and "La derecha en Italia y España (1910–1943)," in *Política y sociedad en la España del siglo XX,* ed. S. G. Payne (Madrid, 1978), 185–204.

5

Franco and the Military

The decisive victory of the left in the parliamentary elections of 1936, followed by the decline in public order and the incipient collapse of parliamentary and constitutional government, provoked widespread apprehension and fear among the middle and upper classes and in the conservative north. Some in the extreme right began to plot rebellion within no more than a fortnight of the political change, yet most conservative sectors seemed paralyzed, and months of conflict and disorder passed before a coherent revolt began to take shape. Only during its final phase did the leader who eventually emerged from the process as its dominant figure commit himself to it completely.

Francisco Franco Bahamonde, at one point the youngest general in Europe and later the most prestigious figure in the Spanish Army, was born on December 4, 1892, in El Ferrol, the Galician seaport that is Spain's chief naval base on the northern coast.[1] He was the second son of an old naval family, originally from Andalucía on the father's side, that had furnished naval officers in the direct male line uninterruptedly for six generations in El Ferrol, spanning nearly two centuries. Franco's parents were unusually ill matched. His father, Nicolás, a naval paymaster and supplies

---

1. The many biographies of Franco are briefly evaluated in the selected bibliography. Here it may simply be noted that by far the best informed of the official and semiofficial biographies is Ricardo de la Cierva, *Francisco Franco: Un siglo de España*, 2 vols. (Madrid, 1973), a revised edition appearing in 1986. The best critical biographies are J. W. D. Trythall, *El Caudillo: The Political Biography of Franco* (New York, 1970); Carlos Fernández, *El general Franco* (Barcelona, 1983); and Juan Pablo Fusi, *Franco: Autoritarismo y poder personal* (Madrid, 1985). The most-detailed treatment of Franco's subsequent political career and regime is Luis Suárez Fernández, *Francisco Franco y su tiempo* (Madrid, 1984), 8 vols. (hereafter cited as *FF*).

officer, was a capable professional who eventually retired at the close of his career at the level of Vice-Admiral. Though the stories of his drinking and gambling may be exaggerated, Nicolás Franco was highly unusual among senior naval officers as an agnostic and freethinker who scoffed at much of conventional morality. He was a strong-willed, vehement man who disciplined his sons rather harshly, and he found the piety and Catholic moralism of his somewhat dull and unimaginative wife increasingly distasteful as the years passed. Franco's mother, Pilar Bahamonde, was ten years younger than the husband from whom she differed so greatly in temperament and outlook. The Bahamonde family stemmed in part from the minor Galician aristocracy and was distantly related to the novelist Emilia Pardo Bazán, and there is also some indication that the Francos of Andalucía had a degree of aristocratic ancestry.[2] Doña Pilar seems to have been a gentle, high-minded, and self-sacrificing middle-class wife and mother, typical of the period, who found her husband's personal and philosophical extravagances incomprehensible. Don Nicolás had earlier fathered an illegitimate son while a naval officer in the Philippines,[3] though this was not revealed to the rest of the family until 1950. And in 1912, when he was reassigned to Madrid, he abandoned the family altogether, setting up housekeeping with a servant girl with whom he lived for the rest of his life (evidently going through the simulacrum of a non-Catholic "popular wedding") and by whom he may or may not have had a daughter.[4]

There were four Franco children, in order of birth Nicolás, Francisco (known as Paco or Paquito), Pilar, and Ramón (a second daughter died in early childhood). Of the boys, Paco was clearly the most affected by his family's drama, identifying with his mother and learning from her a quiet manner, stoicism, restraint, self-control, Catholic religiosity, family solidarity, and respect for traditional principles. At the same time, he failed to absorb her gentleness and capacity for self-effacement. Many years later, after Franco's death as chief of state, the playwright Jaime Salom wrote a play entitled *El Corto Vuelo del Gallo (The Short Flight of the Cock)*, advertised as "The Story of Franco through the Erotic Life of His Father." Of all his children, the elder Franco seems to have had the least sympathy

2. Persistent rumors about Franco's alleged Jewish ancestry have no clear foundation, and Harry S. May, *Francisco Franco: The Jewish Connection* (Washington, D.C., 1978), is somewhat fanciful. Proportionately more Jewish people, however, were absorbed into the societies of Spain and Portugal in the fifteenth and sixteenth centuries than into those of any other countries in European history. A significant portion of the Spanish and Portuguese populations have some remote Jewish ancestry; if this were true of Franco he would simply be in the position of millions of other Spaniards.

3. Carlos Fernández, *Franco*, 21.

4. The best portrait of Nicolás Franco is that penned by his eldest granddaughter, Pilar Jaraiz Franco, *Historia de una disidencia* (Barcelona, 1981), 53–55.

for the compulsive and withdrawn Paco, whose personality was most like that of the mother. In spite of this, Franco appears to have had an otherwise normal and not especially unhappy childhood, but he fully reciprocated his father's antipathy. Though the other children later visited their father in Madrid from time to time as adults, there is no indication that Franco did so. It is not even clear that he saw his father after 1912, and when their mother died in 1934, the children ignored their father as much as possible in the funeral arrangements.

The three brothers were each distinct in personality, sharing only an unusual zeal to advance themselves or gain recognition, a compulsion possibly related to their family background. Nicolás, the oldest and the only one of normal height, was the most conventional. He followed family tradition, gained entrance to a naval career at a time of severe cutbacks and sharp competition, and won a commission as a naval engineers' officer. He then transferred to the Naval Construction Corps, which was understaffed and offered faster promotion, and in 1921 reached a rank equivalent to that of an army lieutenant colonel, this at a slightly younger age than was later the case with his more famous brother. At the age of thirty-five he resigned to become the director of a successful commercial shipyard in Valencia. A sybarite and something of a dandy, Nicolás devoted his time variously to business and an extravagant night life (keeping extraordinarily late hours), without manifesting the same thirst for heroic deeds that motivated his younger brothers. He was fun-loving and full of jokes and by far the most conventionally human of the brothers.[5]

The drastic reduction in admissions to the naval officers corps during the first part of the century made it impossible for Paco and Ramón to follow in the path of their predecessors. Paco gained entrance instead to the Infantry Academy at Toledo and became a cadet at the age of fourteen, the youngest and also one of the smallest of the new officer candidates. At Toledo Franco would grow to his adult height of slightly more than five feet four inches and prove himself as a determined, hard-working cadet, though his performance was not at all distinguished (he graduated 251st in a class of 312).[6] He may not have been the object of as much hazing and ridicule as has sometimes been alleged, but he would continue to be known by a diminutive of one form or another for many years, and he was commonly referred to as Franquito or even Lieutenant Franquito. This was not only because of his short stature (for there were many small officers in the Spanish Army, some even shorter than Franco) but also be-

5. Ramón Garriga, *Nicolás Franco, el hermano brujo* (Barcelona, 1980), is the only biography and rather short on new facts.

6. For more-detailed treatment of Franco's early years, see George Hills, *Franco: The Man and His Nation* (London, 1967), 15–80. Louis Moreno Nieto, *Franco y Toledo* (Toledo, 1971), provides an admiring sketch of Franco at the Infantry Academy.

cause of his weak and lispy, decidedly high-pitched voice, which may have been affected by life-long sinus or bronchial abnormalities.[7]

The youngest brother Ramón, whom Doña Pilar had wished to dedicate to the priesthood, did much better, becoming a cadet junior officer (*galonista*) and eventually graduating 37th in a class of 413, though he had the advantage of being a year older than Paco when he entered the Academy. Ramón soon volunteered for the glamorous new military aviation, and eventually in 1926 at the age of thirty became the Spanish Charles Lindbergh, senior pilot of the *Plus Ultra,* the plane that made the first transatlantic crossing to Buenos Aires. At that point he was more famous and certainly more popular than his Army brother Paco. A daredevil and publicity-seeker, the diminutive Ramón (at scarcely more than five feet three the smallest of the brothers) emulated his father's personal life but sought even greater recognition by trying to organize the first Spanish round-the-world flight, a project doomed to frustration. He later turned as an alternative to radical left-wing politics, and was one of the military conspirators who promoted the coming of the Second Republic in 1931.[8]

Franco was commissioned a second lieutenant in 1910 at the age of seventeen. His original request for assignment to combat service in the Spanish zone of Morocco was denied, presumably because of his age and lack of a particularly distinguished record, but eighteen months later he was sent there; it was the only path to rapid promotion within the Spanish Army. Franco's first tour of duty in Morocco lasted more than four years, from 1912 to 1916. He displayed courage, discipline, and determination in his first skirmishes with hostile native kabyles and went through a number of encounters without a scratch. The style of the Spanish *africanistas* (officers in Morocco) was often a rather careless one that relied on guts and toughness much more than on planning and technique. Franco's calm self-control, practical and impersonal attitude, courageous example, and insistence on order and discipline enabled him to become an effective platoon and then company commander despite his youth. He was more resourceful as a combat leader than his record might have indicated, and he became one of the minority of officers who tried to deal seriously with maps, fortifications, and the technical preparation of armed columns. Instead of carousing with cards, wine, and whores, as many of his comrades did, Franco devoted himself to work.[9] He was finally seriously wounded in

---

7. In his memoir *Cuarenta años junto a Franco* (Barcelona, 1981), Dr. Vicente Gil, Franco's longtime personal physician, cites an interview with Franco's odontologist, Dr. José Iveas, in *Sabado Gráfico,* which reported that he suffered from a deviated septum and normally breathed through his mouth, affecting his quality of speech (p. 42). Gil adds that Franco had great difficulty with such fundamental throat-clearing techniques as coughing and gargling.

8. Ramón Garriga, *Ramón Franco, el hermano maldito* (Barcelona, 1978).

9. Three years after Franco's death there appeared a little book with the hyperbolic title *Las cartas de amor de Franco* (Barcelona, 1978), ed. Vicente Gracia, consisting of reproduc-

the abdomen on June 29, 1916, while leading troops in action near Ceuta.

It was already becoming well known that Franco's courage was equaled only by his ambition. Officers in the Spanish Army who suffered major wounds in combat were routinely granted promotion; when this was at first denied Franco because of his youth, he did not rest until his petition was carried all the way to the king. He was finally promoted to the rank of major before his twenty-fourth birthday, a breathtaking rise in the bloated, seniority-dominated Spanish officer corps of the period, making him its youngest *jefe* (senior officer). In 1917 the *comandantín* or "little major," as he was called, began a tour of domestic duty as commander of the infantry battalion at the Oviedo garrison in Asturias. He applied for admission to the Escuela Superior de Guerra (Superior War College) to supplement his limited technical training, but was rejected on the grounds that his rank was already too high to permit him to register for the studies undertaken by other outstanding young officers his age. Franco returned to Morocco to help organize the new Tercio, Spain's Foreign Legion. Destined to serve as elite shock units, the Tercio volunteers gained the grim sobriquet *Los novios de la muerte*—The Bridegrooms of Death.[10] Franco was twice recommended for promotion during the intense fighting of 1921–22, but this was impossible until after his thirtieth birthday. In 1923 he was made commander of the Legion[11] after his predecessor, like so very many Legionnaire officers, had been killed in combat.

---

tions of several postcards he had mailed in 1912–13 to Sofía Subirán, a colonel's daughter in one of the garrisons, whom he admired. These missives are friendly and polite, not true love letters.

After Franco's death, Sofía Subirán, by that time an elderly widow, was quoted as describing the youthful Franco as "a bit dull [*soso*] and very timid. A good person, but indecisive. Very quiet and reserved. . . . As a man he was courteous and attentive, quite a gentleman. He did have a bit of spirit, but in a delicate way. He treated me with exquisite delicacy, as though I were a supernatural being. He was very serious, too serious. He was Galician, very much his own kind of person." Franco did roller skate, but was not much of a dancer. "He was too clumsy for that. He used to sit beside me and talk." *Interviu*, no. 79 (1977), quoted in Enrique Salgado, *Radiografía de Franco* (Barcelona, 1985), 69. Other early romantic interests of Franco are recounted in Carlos Fernández, *Franco*, 174–76.

10. On the Legion, there is John H. Galey, "Bridegrooms of Death: A Profile Study of the Spanish Foreign Legion," *JCH* 4:2 (April 1969), 47–63; Sgt. Federico Ramas Izquierdo, *La Legión: Historial de guerra (10 septiembre 1920 al 12 octubre 1927)* (Ceuta, 1933); *La Legión Española*, 2 vols. (Madrid, 1973); and Carlos de Arce, *Historia de la Legión Española* (Barcelona, 1984).

Of 20,883 officers and men who eventually served in eight battalions during the balance of the Moroccan campaigns, approximately 2,000 were killed and 6,096 wounded.

11. The writer Arturo Barea, a recruit in Morocco during those years, paraphrased the remarks of a veteran Legionnaire as follows:

"You see, Franco. . . . No, look. The Tercio's rather like being in a penitentiary. The most courageous brute is master of the jail. And something of this sort has happened to that man. He's hated, just as the convicts hate the bravest killer in their jail, and he's obeyed and respected—he imposes himself on all the others—just as the big killer imposes himself on the whole jail. You know how many officers of the Legion have been killed by a shot in the back during an attack. Now, there are many who would wish to shoot Franco in the back, but not

   The only complete book that Franco ever wrote, his *Diario de una Bandera* (*Diary of a Legionnaire Battalion*), was published in 1922 while he was a major in the Tercio. (Gossip had it that the manuscript was ghost-written by a Catalan journalist, Juan Ferragut.) He later wrote a number of articles for the professional *Revista de Tropas Coloniales*. His book contained a certain amount of romantic rhetoric suitable to its topic, but also revealed growing awareness of and concern for its author's public image. As a child he had lived through the disaster of 1898 at Spain's leading naval base, and as a mature officer had witnessed another national humiliation in Morocco in 1921. Hence Franco showed a special concern for patriotic spirit and pride and for devotion to national honor. Like most serious officers, he also wanted to see the Army supplied with the best and most modern weapons, and as a strong advocate of mobility approved enthusiastically of the formation of the first squad of armored cars and mini-tanks in 1922. Franco was not a major innovator, but placed great importance on the value of proper equipment and of *saber manera* (know-how).
   Franco was married in October 1923 to Carmen Polo y Martínez Valdés, daughter of a wealthy upper-class Asturian family. He had met her as a fifteen-year-old at a society picnic in Oviedo six years earlier, and after being rejected by the father of another upper-class Galician girl whom he tried to woo, Franco pursued the young Asturian girl with the tenacity and determination that he demonstrated in his profession. As her only serious biographer describes her, Carmen Polo "without being a great

---

one of them has the courage to do it. They're afraid that he might turn his head and see them just when they have taken aim at him.
   ". . . It wouldn't be difficult to fire at Franco. He takes the lead in an advance, and—well, if somebody's got guts, you just have to admit it. I've seen him walk upright in front of all the others, while they hardly dared to lift their heads from the ground, the bullets fell so thick.
   ". . . Believe me, it's sticky going with Franco. You'll get whatever's due to you, and he knows where he's taking you, but as to the treatment you get. . . . He simply looks blankly at a fellow, with very big and very serious eyes, and says, 'Execute him,' and walks away, just like that. I've seen murderers go white in the face because Franco had looked at them out of the corner of his eye. And he's fussy! God save you if anything's missing from your equipment, or if your rifle isn't clean, or you've been lazy. You know, that man's not quite human and he hasn't got any nerves. And then, he's quite isolated, I believe all the officers detest him because he treats them just like he treats us and isn't friends with any of them. They go on the loose and get drunk—I ask you, what else should they do after two months in the firing line?—and he stays alone in the tent or in barracks, just like one of those old clerks who simply must go to the office, even on Sundays. It's difficult to make him out—it's funny, because he's still so young." Auturo Barea, *The Forging of a Rebel* (New York, 1946), 365–66.
   All aspects of this portrait need not be accepted as fully accurate, but it helps to show the kind of impression Franco made on his military contemporaries. Years later, Franco remarked to his cousin Salgado Araujo that he had once had an insubordinate legionnaire shot simply by personal command without proper recourse to court-martial. He then ordered the remainder of the battalion to march past the cadaver, and later credited the whole procedure with the rapid and complete restoration of discipline. Francisco Franco Salgado Araujo, *Mis conversaciones privadas con Franco* (hereafter cited as *Conversaciones privadas*) (Barcelona, 1979), 184–85.

beauty had an aristocratic profile, elegant movements, and a genuine vivacity."[12] She soon reciprocated her suitor's interest and affection, finding
in him a glamorous national hero who, despite his fundamental introver-
sion, could be talkative and lively on social occasions. The fact that he had
a weak, high-pitched voice and was a trifle shorter than she proved no
obstacle to love. The obstacle was Carmen's snobbish father, who had little
respect for young officers of modest means and was heard to say on one
occasion that "letting her marry that fellow would be like having her
marry a bullfighter," or words to that effect. The courtship was interrupted for two and a half years by Franco's Moroccan service of 1920–23,
but Carmen was as faithful and determined as her betrothed. Franco's personal reputation was further enhanced among his troops by the legend
that he had twice postponed his marriage to serve combat duty; combat
was something that most Spanish officers of the period avoided at all
costs. When the wedding finally took place during a brief leave of absence
from the Legion, Franco's prestige had risen so high that he had been made
a *gentilhombre de cámara* (gentleman of the bedchamber) of Alfonso
XIII, whose personal representative acted as *padrino* (godfather) at the
ceremony.

This love match, for it was indeed that, proved a highly successful marriage by any standard. The Francos established a conventional, upper-
middle-class Catholic household, finally blessed after three years with the
birth of their only child, a daughter also named Carmen (more commonly
known as Carmencita).[13] His felicitous and secure family life further reinforced Franco's conservative and religious values, and helped to sustain
the Catholic identity that some claimed had become attenuated during his
first years as an officer.[14]

Franco played a major role in the decisive Moroccan campaigns of
1924–25 that broke the back of the native insurgency. He led the first
assault wave in the landing on the northern coast of the stronghold of the
Riffi leader Abdul Karim that was possibly the largest successful amphibi-
ous operation under fire in military history to that date. The legend of
Franco's *baraka* (good luck) became more strongly established than ever;
legionnaires and other veterans claimed they were never defeated when
Franco was in command. At barely thirty-three years of age he was promoted to brigadier, reportedly the youngest general on active duty in any

12. Ramón Garriga, *La Señora de El Pardo* (Barcelona, 1979), 18.
13. The Franco brothers were decidedly not prolific. Each had only one child, Nicolás an
only son from two marriages, Ramón an only daughter from two marriages. By contrast Pilar,
the only sister, made a conventional upper-middle-class marriage to a wealthy civil engineer
and gave birth to ten children, whom she had to raise herself after being early widowed. For
her version of family history, see Pilar Franco, *Nosotros, los Franco* (Barcelona, 1980).
14. With regard to Franco's religious devotion, it may be noted that as an eighteen-year-
old second lieutenant he had entered the lay association of the Adoración Nocturna in 1911.
FF, 1:99.

Franco and his daughter Carmencita during the Civil War

European army. The fourteen-year "African period" of his life then came
to an end, but it had laid the basis for his fame and for his personal ascendancy in the Spanish Army. In the later years of his life the African days
were the days he looked back on with nostalgia. For him they were a
youthful time of heroics and uncomplicated patriotism and a time of personal happiness climaxed by his marriage. Henceforth his life would become increasingly complicated, and increasingly involved in politics.

For the next two years Franco was assigned command of the first brigade of the garrison in Madrid, giving him an opportunity to gain some
knowledge of the capital's politics and culture, meet a new branch of elite
society, read more widely, and improve his professional contacts and education. The Primo de Rivera dictatorship then in power was in fact never
especially popular with the military, whose priorities and structure it attempted to manipulate, and elements of the officer corps schemed and
plotted against it from beginning to end. In 1924 Franco had dramatically
confronted the dictator at a meeting in Morocco over the latter's plan for
temporary strategic withdrawal. Despite that incident, Primo de Rivera
appreciated Franco's professionalism, discipline, and abstention from political intrigue. He planned to overcome the limited training and intra-
corps sectarianism of different branches of the Army by reestablishing an
Academia General Militar in Zaragoza to provide common professional
training for all new career officers. When the Academia opened early in
1928, Franco was named its first director.

Franco at that time was not experienced in large-scale military command and organization nor did he have advanced technical training. He
had a great deal of small and medium-unit combat experience, of course,
and organized a new officer training school that stressed military funda-
mentals, logistics, and basic organization, with a strong emphasis on professional and patriotic mystique. Franco considered morale and attitude
of the utmost importance and strove to build a firm and spirited professional psychology while providing training by some of the best technical
instructors the Spanish Army had to offer. Personally, he attempted to
supplement his own limited formal education with a range of reading and
also found time for contemporary literature, his favorite author being his
fellow-Galician Valle Inclán.

The approximately three and a half years that Franco spent in Zaragoza
were happy and rewarding. They included his first and only foreign travel,
a brief professional visit to Germany, where he was especially interested
in the Infantry Academy at Dresden. In Zaragoza the Francos scored
their first major social success, establishing themselves with the provincial elite. In 1929 a street was named after the general in the Aragonese
capital. His attractive sister-in-law, Zita, who lived with them for a period, became engaged to a suave, astute young lawyer, Ramón Serrano

Súñer, member of one of the elite corps of the Spanish state administration, the Abogacia del Estado (equivalent in some ways to the French Inspection des Finances). A dapper, handsome, blue-eyed man, Serrano Súñer was well connected with conservative political circles and would later play a major role in the development of his brother-in-law's political career.

By the end of the 1920s Franco the military hero had also become part of the political establishment. Having been named a gentilhombre de cámara of the crown, Franco was strongly identified both with the monarchy, and through his appointment to the Academia, with the dictatorship. He evidently observed the latter's weakening and collapse in 1929–30 with some dismay; he would later incorporate major aspects of Primo de Rivera's politics, especially the eclectic and syncretistic policies that tried to combine government by experts or technocrats with an appeal to populism and the middle classes in a corporativistic framework. Yet Franco was far from an uncritical admirer of Primo de Rivera, and took note of his clumsiness, his tendency toward hasty improvisation, and his gratuitous provocation of political hostility. Much worse for Franco than the collapse of the dictatorship was the subsequent downfall of the monarchy, which placed in jeopardy the basic principles of authority, right-wing patriotism, and traditional continuity that Franco had learned to hold dear since childhood. The process of concession and liberalization had gotten entirely out of control, and it may well have been from this experience that Franco learned, as some of his biographers suggest, that authority once assumed should never be set aside or reduced, lest its entire structure erode. He himself instinctively sprang to the defense of the monarchy; at the time of the first minuscule Republican military revolt at Jaca in December 1930, Franco immediately mobilized his cadets and sent them out to bar the road south to the rebels.

Within three months the new Republican regime closed the Academia General Militar as militarist and elitist and tending to form the wrong esprit de corps. In a notable farewell speech to his cadets, the outgoing director made clear his loyalty to the monarchy while urging officers to strict discipline under the new regime. Franco was left without active assignment for six months, and for the next three years would be on the political defensive. The conflict with the Republic even altered his external personality. The Franco of the 1920s had been jolly, vivacious, and talkative, as demonstrated by newsreel shots of the period. Always fascinated by motion pictures, Franco had even performed briefly as an actor in one movie production. But after 1931 "the jovial, extroverted, party-going Franco will be changed forever into the withdrawn, monosyllabic, indecisive [and ever-calculating] Franco."[15]

15. Ricardo de la Cierva, *Historia del franquismo* (Barcelona, 1976), 1:99.

The Republican experience was at first much easier for his brothers. Nicolás got along well enough with moderate liberal politicians, whereas Ramón immediately became a hero of the new regime. He had been one of the leaders of an abortive military revolt against the monarchy at the end of 1930 and was made director of aviation by the Republic for a short period, then was elected to parliament on the Radical Socialist ticket— developments which Franco found mortifying in the extreme.

The Spanish Army was a major target of Republican reformism. Manuel Azaña, the new minister of war, was determined to shake up Army organization and above all to create a new set of institutional and political relationships, to put the Army in its proper place. On one occasion, with his usual rhetorical excess, he called it *trituración* (pulverizing). A main concern was the hypertrophy of the officer corps, whom a very generous policy of voluntary retirement at virtually full pay reduced by 37 percent in little more than a year, from about 22,000 to less than 12,400.[16] Promotions carried out by the dictatorship were revised but not drastically revoked, and Franco kept his brigadiership, though not the same place on the seniority list. An attempt was made at democratization and a special new structure created for NCOs, but the basic framework of the officer corps did not change. There was no genuine structural reorganization but rather a new combination of basic units into a broader system of "organic divisions." For 1932 basic military expenses were reduced by more than 15 percent, though that was more than balanced by the costs of the new retirement system. The supply of military equipment, always poor, deteriorated further.

The Army had not moved a finger to preserve the monarchy and in general was not hostile to the Republic at its inception. Within less than a year, however, that attitude began to change as a result of the sectarian character of Republican administration, growing political and social disorder, and the adversary attitude gratuitously adopted toward the military. The reforms probably had little effect on the military capacity of the armed forces, and in fact the voluntary retirement system may have worked against the Republic's political interests, for there is impressionistic evidence that the more liberal officers tended disproportionately to resign their commissions.[17]

A handful of officers began to plot against the new regime as early as the autumn of 1931. Franco, who avoided direct association with politics and acted as if he paid no attention to such affairs, was definitely not one of them. Though a monarchist at heart, he was respectful of the established

16. The basic study of the structure and scope of the Azaña reforms is Michael Alpert, *La reforma militar de Azaña (1931–1933)* (Madrid, 1982). Julio Merino, *La tragedia de los generales españoles 1936* (Barcelona, 1985), 97–219, presents a negative critique.

17. For an overview of relations between the Army and the Republic, see my *Politics and the Military in Modern Spain* (Stanford, 1967), 256–313. Francisco Bravo Morata, *La República y el Ejército* (Madrid, 1978), adds little.

order, and during these years not unwilling to achieve a modus vivendi with a responsible Republican liberalism. He was returned to active duty early in 1932 as commander of the infantry garrison at La Coruña in his native Galicia.

An abortive military revolt did occur in Seville on August 10, 1932, led by General José Sanjurjo, Franco's former immediate commander in Africa, recently deposed by Azaña as head of the rural constabulary, the Guardia Civil. The *sanjurjada* was a feeble revolt that drew the active participation of only a handful of officers, none of them with commands of any significance. Its political base was heterogeneous and confused. Monarchists and other rightist enemies of the Republic played a significant role, but it was not formally a monarchist pronunciamiento per se, for chastened liberals and conservative Republicans had also intrigued with Sanjurjo, who at first pretended no more than the overthrow of the present Republican-Socialist administration. The pronunciamiento collapsed immediately, leading to the capture and imprisonment of its leader, followed by a further swing to the left in Republican politics.[18]

Franco steadfastly refused involvement in such machinations, despite his hostility to the new regime, for he fully grasped their superficiality and futility. He was in turn rewarded by being named military commander of the Balearic Islands district—a more important post in a better climate—in February 1933. He threw himself into the development of a new defense plan for the islands that occupied much of his time for the next year and a half. As usual he was accompanied as personal aide by his first cousin and lifelong friend Francisco Franco Salgado Araujo, called "Pacón" by the family and intimates (to distinguish him from Franco, who was Paco). Salgado Araujo had been the general's assistant for several years and followed him in each change of assignment. Amid the changing fortunes of Spanish affairs it was obviously important to have a close relative and friend as principal aide and confidant. In the Balearics, moreover, he renewed professional contact with an able young naval lieutenant, the beetle-browed Luis Carrero Blanco, then studying at the French Naval War College, whom he had first met during the Moroccan campaigns.

The electoral victory of the center-right near the end of 1933 drastically altered the political situation and was personally quite advantageous to Franco. With his brother-in-law Ramón Serrano Súñer a CEDA deputy and a key leader in its youth movement (JAP), Franco's relations with the triumphant CEDA were excellent. The moderate Republicans (misleadingly named Radicals) who then took over the government had always stressed positive contacts with the military, and Franco found himself on good terms with several Radical politicians, one of whom, Diego Hidalgo,

18. See the section "La Sanjurjada" in *Historia 16* 7 (Aug. 1982), 43–67, and F. Olaya Morales, *La conspiración contra la República* (Barcelona, 1979), 175–238.

the new war minister, promoted him to major general (general of division, in the Spanish nomenclature) in March 1934.[19]

From the end of 1933 Franco was able to spend more and more time on leave in Madrid, where he had retained the home originally occupied in 1926. It was there that his mother died rather suddenly of a lung infection in February 1934 at not quite seventy years of age. As the months passed, Franco's contacts with center-right politicians increased; for the first time in his career, he was on the verge of becoming an overtly political general, identified with national conservative policies.[20] An urgent personal letter from the Falangist leader José Antonio on September 24, 1934, warning Franco to be on the alert against an imminent revolutionary insurrection, told him nothing of which he was not already aware.

The revolt broke out on the morning of October 5, and within less than twenty-four hours the government had installed Franco in the Ministry of War as special technical advisor in charge of coordinating its suppression. This was accomplished effectively but with no little bloodshed, accompanied, as indicated in chapter 3, by excesses and atrocities on both sides. Franco remained in the ministry until February 1935, when he was named commander-in-chief of Spanish forces in Morocco. The new center-right administration under Lerroux and the CEDA wanted to restabilize Spain's military institutions and guarantee the support of the antileftist sectors of the officer corps. During the next three months in Morocco, Franco did all he could to tune up the forces in the Protectorate, itself perfectly peaceful and quiet since 1928, and to maintain their status as the most militarily reliable units of the Spanish Army.

Franco had thus been catapulted by events and political connections into the role of key figure of the Spanish Army. Under the center-right administration, he had ironically become the "number-one general of the Republic," in La Cierva's phrase, though hardly the leading Republican general in a political sense. The leader of Spanish conservatism at the time, Gil Robles, later offered the following description of Franco's status and reputation at this juncture:

> The officers of his generation were impressed by a series of qualities that invested him with undeniable prestige. There was his courage, less theatrical

19. Hidalgo praises Franco highly in his memoir, *¿Por qué fui lanzado del Ministerio de la Guerra?* (Madrid, 1934).

20. To Franco's relief, his brother Ramón had finally begun to settle down. Ramón had made something of a fool of himself in the national parliament after being elected on the Radical Socialist ticket in 1931. By 1933 his political ambitions had disappeared, as had the wild behavior of early years when he had gone "fag-bashing" with Air Force buddies in Madrid's homosexual bars. His first marriage to a cabaret dancer was dissolved, and he had settled down to middle-class respectability with a new wife. In 1934 the new government assigned him to Washington, D.C., as Air Force attaché, a position that Ramón seems to have enjoyed. His first wife, Carmen Díaz, has left a memoir, *Mi vida con Ramón Franco* (Barcelona, 1981).

than that of other companions in the Moroccan campaigns, but which, after being subjected to the decisive test of fire on numerous occasions, became legendary; foresight and sure instinct that enabled him to measure the strength of the enemy in order to attack coldly when the latter was weakened; the cult of discipline, which he did not hesitate to sustain with means as harsh as might be necessary, though without failing to watch over the well-being of his troops with extreme care and striving to avoid wasting lives in combat; careful preparation of operations, indispensable in a colonial campaign, where it is more important to avoid dangerous improvisations than to develop grand strategic concepts; exact knowledge of the enemy's weak points in the material and in the moral order; avoidance of any kind of dissipation that might distract him from achieving his goals, maturely conceived and implacably pursued. . . . All this contributed to surrounding Franco with a special aura that was recognized by friends and enemies, and to create a zone of isolation and reserve about him that enhanced his reputation.[21]

Franco's physical image was not that of a glamorous hero. His short and somewhat muscular frame had added considerable weight in recent years, thickening his figure in a manner accentuated by the rather clumsily tailored uniforms of the period. His soft and high-pitched voice was equally disadvantageous, much better attuned to quiet commands and private conversation than public oratory. Yet these physical limitations merely pointed up the fact that there was nothing cosmetic or superficial in Franco's professional prestige and personal charisma among the military, for it was based on solid achievement and the personal experience of command.

In May 1935 the power of the CEDA increased as Gil Robles moved into the government as minister of war. For the *cedista* leader, this was the most important cabinet post except prime minister, for it provided opportunity to strengthen the armed forces and guarantee their bulwark against the revolutionary left. He understood clearly the nature of the political role of the Spanish Army in the past, for, as he later wrote,

> the intervention of the Spanish Army in politics during the past 150 years has obeyed the inexorable law of the material world and the moral order: the horror of a vacuum. When it acted in this area it did so in order to substitute for nonexistent or fictitious political forces. Had the national panorama presented social groups and political parties of sufficient solidity, the Army would have remained subordinate to civil authority and would not have exceeded the functions that strictly pertain to it.[22]

Gil Robles was convinced that the military were no danger to solid conservative interests but that they in turn required proper leadership to protect Spanish institutions from subversion. Within a matter of days he named Franco chief of the Army's General Staff to supervise the strengthening and reorganization of Spain's forces. The CEDA leader considered

21. Gil Robles, *No fue posible la paz*, 777.
22. Ibid., 232.

him the most appropriate choice both because the military looked more to Franco than to any other single figure and because he fit absolutely the political requirements of the CEDA: he was disciplined and legalistic, firmly Catholic and conservative.

There was much to do to rebuild the Army as a military institution, for equipment and combat training were both lacking. This had not been for want of expenditure, since Azaña's generous retirement policy had ended by increasing the overall military budget, even though expenditures for material had been somewhat reduced. The technical inadequacies of the Spanish military long antedated the Republic. Under Gil Robles and Franco a series of new appointments placed the Army once more under the direction of conservative professionals earlier relieved of command or shunted aside. Somewhat more was spent on combat equipment and preparation for direct action. General Emilio Mola, former commander-in-chief in Morocco and the Monarchy's last director general of security (in charge of police and constabulary), expelled from the officer corps by the Republic, had been restored to rank and was now placed in charge of preparing a new plan for combat mobilization. By July a new three-year Spanish rearmament program had been approved by the government. Moreover, Franco began to keep records on political attitudes among officers and on the percentage of rank-and-file recruits affiliated with leftist organizations (around 25 percent, as it turned out).

These policies were suddenly threatened by the collapse of the governing *cedorradical* coalition early in December. The Republican president, Alcalá Zamora, then refused to authorize a new coalition representing parliament, but appointed an extraparliamentary caretaker cabinet that would proceed to the new elections which would give the recently defeated left a chance to return to power. The prospect of civil war loomed on the horizon, and several generals in the Ministry of War urged a coup d'etat. This contradicted Gil Robles's whole policy, and he could not bring himself to that, referring the matter to his chief of staff. Approximately a year earlier Franco, as special advisor, had rejected proposals for a coup after several leading leftists had been amnestied. In the more dramatic circumstances of December 11, 1935, he restated his position, saying that the Army was too divided to be employed in a political coup, an appreciation which was entirely correct. The caretaker cabinet that governed Spain for the next two months reassigned many of the top commanders recently appointed but left the scrupulous Franco in his post as chief of staff. The dilemma of December 11 repeated itself on February 17, 1936, the morrow of the rather narrow but absolutely decisive victory of the Popular Front in the latest Republican elections. Several key generals as well as rightist politicians urged Franco and the caretaker prime minister, Portela Valladares, to annul the electoral results and declare a state of emergency. Though one general tried to rouse the Madrid garrison to direct revolt, Franco refused once more to act except on authorization from his constitutional superiors. His only initiative was to request them to declare a temporary state of martial law to maintain public order until the electoral process had been fully completed and certified,[23] which they refused to do. A new Left Republican government under Azaña took over within two more days.

Though various small groups of officers began to plot against the new government almost immediately, Franco was neither an extremist nor a catastrophist. Agreeing to some extent with José Antonio, he pointed out that technically only the most moderate sector of the Popular Front was represented in the government, that the left was divided, and that the worst might be avoided. Thirty years later he reminisced: "I always said to my companions, 'While there remains any hope that the Republican regime can still prevent anarchy or will not surrender itself to Moscow, we must support the Republic, which was accepted by the king first, by the monarchist government afterward, and then by the Army.'"[24]

The military policy of the new administration was to cut back the rearmament program and switch many of the top commands, removing the more conservative officers and placing reliable Republicans or liberals in most of the top posts. Franco was demoted to military commander of the Canary Islands, with headquarters in Tenerife. Though this was a major comedown, he responded with his usual caution. Early in March he met in Madrid with a number of his closest military associates who were also being reassigned. They agreed to keep in touch and to prepare for any deterioration of the political situation but to attempt a direct military revolt only if the revolutionary left should seize the government. In the interim, coordination would be provided by a junta of nine generals who were remaining in Madrid, some of them without active assignment.

Conspiracy had first been actively begun by monarchists, both in the planning of the sanjurjada and afterwards. Small detachments of Carlist militia (Requetés) had trained off and on for several years in Navarre. Agents of the Alfonsine monarchists had been in contact with the Italian government from early 1932, and in March 1934 representatives of Renovación Española and the Carlists signed an agreement with Italian authorities that promised Italian arms and a subsidy of one and a half million pesetas (around $150,000) to assist an anti-Republican revolt. About one-third of the money was paid, but few arms ever arrived, after the Italian government lost interest in the maneuver.[25]

23. *Conversaciones privadas*, 522–23.
24. Ibid., 452.
25. On the Italian dimension of anti-Republican conspiracy, see Coverdale, *Italian Intervention*, 41–58.

A secret, primarily rightist association, the Unión Militar Española, had existed among the officer corps of the Army since the winter of 1933–34. It was neither uniform nor tightly organized but consisted of a decentralized network of cells and groups that often had little mutual association. For some, the UME was simply a patriotic officers' association to protect the integrity of the military and defend the Fatherland, while for others it was a rightist political organization designed to combat and defeat the left in any way possible. The Junta Central of the UME in Madrid endeavored to supervise the association and by 1935 was looking into the possibility of an eventual military revolt, but with little success. The Popular Front's victory stimulated UME affiliation, and a circular distributed toward the end of March claimed that the UME had enrolled 3,436 officers on active duty, 2,131 NCO's and troops, and 1,843 officers either in the Reserve or retired.[26] If these figures were correct—and they may not be far off—they indicated that more than a third of the officers on active duty were associated with the UME. Yet the UME remained amorphous, without tight organization or general agreement, and many of its members seem to have considered it more a professional than a political organization.[27]

The very small leftist sector of the armed forces had organized its own Unión Militar Republicana Antifascista (UMRA) to counter the UME and the right in general. Its membership was exiguous by comparison, but some of its key activists were members of or sympathizers with the revolutionary Socialists and Communists, and a few held key positions within the police as well.

The Falange had begun to conspire seriously against the Republican system during the preceding year, though its only plan for armed insurrection (in the late spring of 1935) had to be abandoned as hopeless. Like Franco, José Antonio Primo de Rivera responded to the leftist victory with caution. Though his movement preached catastrophism, he was not entirely convinced that all was lost politically, and he was more determined than ever that his followers not fall into the clutches of the extreme right, who had always sought to use them as shock troops for political violence. The national Falangist leadership in Madrid was, however, arrested by the government in mid-March on the grounds of inciting to sedition and violence, and most of its top members never regained freedom. Though the charges brought against them were at least in part substanti-

26. For the development of the UME, see my *Politics and the Military*, 293–317; and on the rightist conspiracies in 1934–35, Olaya Morales, *La conspiración*, 265–308.

27. In a memo written decades later, Franco declared that he had made contact with UME conspirators in 1935 but urged them to reject "narrow conspiracies and nineteenth-century military pronunciamientos," for any future movement would have to be "supported by the people." According to Franco, he advised them that they all ought "to hope that the Republic would surmount its difficulties." Quoted in *FF*, 1:291.

ated, leaders of all the revolutionary left groups could have been similarly prosecuted with equal justification. This was but one aspect of the partisanship of Popular Front rule, and left the Falangists with little choice but to join forces with the right in revolt. That was made the easier because party membership began to grow very rapidly after the leftist victory, as disillusioned Catholic youth abandoned the CEDA in droves to join the militant fascists.

By April 1936 conspiracy against the government abounded on the right. UME groups were plotting all óver Spain with little in the way of coordination, the right-wing Junta of Generals sat in Madrid trying ineffectually to coordinate whatever efforts it could, leaders of Renovación Española were inciting the military to action, the Carlists had formed their own Supreme Carlist Military Junta across the border in St. Jean de Luz, and the Falangists were also beginning separately to prepare for action. Some of the most moderate sectors of the JAP, such as those connected with the Christian Democratic Valencian branch (DRV), had begun to plot independently if ineffectively within days of the Popular Front victory. More than a little of this was known to the government, but not surprisingly they were skeptical that this kaleidoscope of potential insurgency could ever be pulled together successfully.

PART II

The Civil War,
1936–1939

6

The Rebellion of the Eighteenth of July

The Spanish crisis of the spring and summer of 1936 was in key respects the Spanish variant of the revolutionary or protorevolutionary crises that afflicted various eastern and central European countries between 1917 and 1923. The Spanish case was unique in that it occurred half a generation later and was not triggered by world war or the breakdown of defeat. In Spain, mass mobilization and polarization were triggered instead by the intersection of the growth of major new political and social forces in a time of generalized depression, innovative but weak domestic institutionalization, and increasingly unstable international conditions whose vicarious influence became rapidly more pronounced.

The emergence of the only major violent twentieth-century revolution in a west European country was due first of all to the convergence of a remarkable and unique complex of conflictive factors. By the early 1930s Spain had become a free, open, and democratic country—something which up to that date had never existed in eastern or parts of central Europe—permitting maximal expression and mobilization in a society that at the same time remained backward and undeveloped economically compared with northwestern Europe. The contradictions between a sophisticated and progressive northwest-European type of culture and politico-civic framework on the one hand with an underdeveloped southern European social and economic structure on the other resulted in proportionately the broadest and most varied mobilization of competing mass revolutionary movements seen in any land before or since. Yet this revolutionary upsurge had also to face a sizable moderate and conservative middle-class society and a large Catholic rural sector in the north, parts of which were increasingly influenced by new nationalist and authoritarian doctrines. Serious horizontal regional splits then further complicated and reinforced these major vertical sociopolitical divisions.

Though all major revolutions have responded opportunistically to uniquely favorable opportunities, the Spanish revolution was also unusual in that it finally exploded directly only in response to the counterrevolution attempted by the preemptive strike of the military. One of its most important characteristics was that the Spanish revolution was the only pluralistic, genuinely multiparty and multiideological violent revolution among the significant conflicts of the century, for the revolutionary left reflected the extreme diversity of Spanish society itself. The protagonists of revolution thus sputtered and agitated through the spring of 1936 without producing revolutionary unity or a dominant, hegemonic force, and for the moment lacked either the plan, means, or will to carry the process of protorevolutionary subversion to a direct climax. Strikes and disorders hit a high point during the first three weeks of June and then declined somewhat by the beginning of July. The middle-class Left Republican government of Azaña and Casares Quiroga gambled on the revolutionaries burning themselves out and then returning to Republican reformism or being abandoned by their supporters. Indeed, there existed no clear indication that the protorevolutionary process was about to come to any immediate climax or that it was yet capable of directly overturning the government. What was clear by the late spring of 1936, however, was that the Spanish system was ceasing to govern effectively and that the country's institutional and economic structures were being directly undermined by a peculiar process of protorevolutionary stalemate, a process that no society can long withstand. This fact was publicly recognized by the Socialist leader Prieto as early as May 2.

So pluralistic and indeterminate a process, however, also retarded the multiple military conspiracies against the left. Plotting against the government was simultaneously being carried on by (a) the Junta Central and local groups of the UME; (b) the nominal Generals' Junta in Madrid; (c) various individual commanders and officers in the provinces; (d) the almost acephalous Falangists; (e) the Carlists; and (f) various other provincial rightist groups. Coordination developed only slowly, incompletely, and with considerable difficulty. The chief organizer was General Emilio Mola, known for his leading role in Morocco and service as the last national police chief under the monarchy. Relegated to the provincial garrison of Pamplona by the Azaña government, he found Carlist Navarre a congenial environment for conspiracy. Mola's own views were in some respects moderate, and he had never joined the UME. Though in contact with the Madrid Junta, he had written an official letter to government leaders in mid-April to protest the abuse to which the Army was subjected by revolutionaries. This drew no response other than an inspection visit to check his own command, and at that point (on April 20) UME leaders in north-central Spain recognized Mola as head of planning for an anti-government move by forces in that region.[1]

A national network of conspiracy began to take shape a month later, for the response of the military was cumulative. Only as incidents and tensions spread and became more intense was a broad reaction mounted. Moreover, the question of authority and legitimacy proved difficult to resolve. Since none of the senior active generals wanted to lead, the only central figure was General José Sanjurjo, Lion of the Riff, another hero of the Moroccan campaigns and former director of the Civil Guard, who had led the very small, abortive attempt of 1932. He had first been approached in his Lisbon exile by the Carlists, who wanted to use his name to provoke an armed rebellion of their own. Sanjurjo was willing to transmit his personal authority as coordinator of a revolt to Mola, since Mola indicated in correspondence that he was planning a broad national reaction and wished to install Sanjurjo as head of an interim junta once the coup was effected. These arrangements were not worked out until the end of May. By that time Mola had begun to draw up detailed sketches and timetables for the convergence of rebel forces to seize power in Madrid.

Relations with civilian groups remained vague or nonexistent. Mola was disgusted with Republican politics of both the conservative and leftist variety. He sketched a plan for an interim military directory that would completely replace the existing authorities, derogate the 1931 Constitution, suppress all revolutionary groups, and strengthen the armed forces as basis of the new state. The social reforms of the Republic, as well as separation of church and state, were to be maintained. The question of restoring the monarchy was scarcely considered, for monarchism had little support in Spain. There was some suggestion that power would eventually be handed over to a reformed parliamentary regime, probably organized along corporative lines with a more restricted or indirect suffrage.[2] No commitments of that sort were actually made, however, for

1. Of the several biographies of Mola, see, particularly concerning his role in the conspiracy, General Jorge Vigón, *Mola (El conspirador)* (Barcelona, 1957); and B. Félix Maíz, *Mola, aquel hombre* (Barcelona, 1976). In English there is Hugh R. Wilson, *The Man Who Created Franco: General Emilio Mola* (Elms Court, Devon, 1972), brief but not unperceptive. Mola was recognized as a commander of both organizational and literary ability. The memoirs of his early career and other writings were later published in his *Obras completas* (Valladolid, 1940).

2. In a draft sketch dated June 5, Mola proposed the following measures for the new government (quoted in Joaquín Arrarás, ed., *Historia de la Cruzada española* [Madrid, 1941], 3:449):

> "Separation of church and state, freedom of cults and respect for all religions.
> "Creation of a *carnet electoral* [electoral card], excluding illiterates and those guilty of social crimes. . . .
> "Special regional arrangements, handling agrarian reform through financing small family farms and collectivities where feasible.
> "Restoration of the death penalty for crimes that cause death or disability.
> "The new government will pledge itself not to change the Republican regime, main-

Mola was determined that the revolt be an Army movement, not obligated to any special interests. The only precise plan was for an all-military directory, even if temporary, that would seize full power over the state apparatus. Mola was authoritarian but not fascist. Like most officers, he was basically uninterested in political parties and doctrines. His sketch for the new junta was based on simple predicates of unity, authority, and order.

The civilian rightists were impotent and had no alternative to leaving matters in the hands of the military. Parliamentary government in the normal sense had largely ceased, even though the constitution still formally existed and parliament continued to meet. In the words of a leading Socialist historian,

> the parliament, as soon as it began to function, asphyxiated the government. It acted as a sounding board for civil war, reflecting and aggravating the nation's own turbulence. The deputies insulted and attacked each other by design; each session was in continuous tumult; and since all the representatives—true representatives of the nation—went armed, a catastrophe could have been expected any afternoon. In view of the frequency with which firearms were exhibited or referred to, it was necessary to resort to the humiliating precaution of frisking the legislators as they entered.[3]

Gil Robles and the main CEDA leaders finally changed their policy. Faced with the failure of their gradualist, constitutionalist approach, they eventually released their followers from responsibility to the party, advising them to act according to their consciences but not to compromise the party itself in illegal activities.

In this situation it was the leader of the radical right, Calvo Sotelo, who became head of the parliamentary opposition, rather than the moderate Gil Robles. He eventually received vague information about Mola's plans and offered full support. Financiers associated with both the monarchists and the CEDA provided financial backing. On June 16, in a parliamentary session of extraordinary drama and tension, Calvo Sotelo was threatened with death by Communist deputies and made an eloquent speech declaring his acceptance of his role as political leader of Spanish nationalism and rightism, together with the open threat of assassination this entailed.[4]

---

taining all social reforms legally obtained, reenforcing the principle of authority and the organs of state defense, developing the Army and Navy to a level of efficiency, creating a national militia, organizing premilitary instruction in schools, and adopting whatever means may be necessary to create a strong and disciplined state."

It is important to make clear, however, that this was little more than a personal draft of Mola's, since the leaders of the conspiracy never came to any clear and full agreement concerning the structure and policies of the new government which they proposed to establish.

3. Antonio Ramos Oliveira, *Historia de España* (Mexico City, 1952), 3:244.

4. Extracts of this speech have been widely quoted. The text may be found in R. de la Cierva, ed., *Los documentos de la primavera trágica* (Madrid, 1967), 495–567.

The only political organization actively involved in plans for revolt was the Falange, which had vainly attempted to win military backing for an antigovernment coup during the preceding year. This effort had not, however, diminished the concern of José Antonio and some other Falangists about the danger of becoming political prisoners of a merely right-wing military movement. José Antonio, from prison, continued to warn his followers about the danger of being coopted but was left with no alternative but to join forces with military conspirators. The Falange was too weak and fragmented to act on its own, and by May 29 José Antonio was able to establish direct contact with Mola, whose seriousness and organizational ability he respected.

The chief problem in organizing the conspiracy was the Army itself. The officer corps was also a bureaucratic class, and the great majority of its members were not eager to involve themselves in a desperate undertaking that might easily lead to their ruin. They had to be concerned about their families and pensions. The Republican government still existed, and the Constitution was still nominally the law of the land, even though less and less enforced. The revolutionaries had not yet tried to take over the government directly; after a few more months they might begin to settle down, and then the crisis would ease. Military activism had been a disaster in Spanish politics between 1917 and 1931; most officers were aware of this and all the less eager to throw themselves into the fray. Furthermore, the ferocious propaganda of the left made it clear that in any radical confrontation, defeated military dissidents would not be treated as leniently as in an earlier generation.

Given these doubts and hesitations, some of the leading would-be rebels apparently committed themselves fully to the conspiracy only after reaching the negative conclusion that it would be more dangerous for them if they did not. The best example is that of Franco himself. As earlier indicated, Franco had been involved in one form or another of plotting against the Popular Front government from the beginning, yet he was most reluctant to pledge himself to any specific proposal for armed revolt. The spring of 1936 was a time of supreme tension for Franco. On his arrival in Tenerife he had been greeted by chalked signs on walls from leftists pledging his death, and faithful military subordinates eventually mounted a twenty-four-hour guard around both the commander and his family to avert personal attack. His own attitude grew increasingly grim, and his thoughts turned more often to religion than at any previous time in his life. Franco's practice of almost daily devotions dated from these months. This intensified religious life in turn contributed to what eventually became a sense of mission, of a special providentiality manifested in his national role.

Conservative politicians recommended that Franco allow his name to appear on the rightist list for a special parliamentary by-election in May. The Popular Front regime had quickly proceeded to amnesty all the revolutionaries and criminals involved in the 1934 insurrection, while beginning the arrest and prosecution of those who had acted to uphold the Constitution. It was feared that Franco would be next on the government's list; a seat in parliament would presumably grant immunity from such prosecution. But this move was nullified by José Antonio Primo de Rivera, whose name had also been placed on the rightist list in Cuenca in the hope that a parliamentary seat would free him from prison. José Antonio insisted that Franco's name be withdrawn, since its extreme rightist and military connotations would be certain to elicit even stronger leftist and government opposition to the conservative list in Cuenca than there would otherwise be. Moreover, José Antonio, who had always looked to Franco as one of the key leaders of the Spanish Army, had been disillusioned by his only meeting with the general in which Franco had avoided discussion of fundamental issues, deflecting the conversation into small talk and polite discourse[5]—a deeply ingrained habit of the cautious general. He furthermore pointed out that Franco was unprepared for parliamentary life, lacking regular political experience and oratorical skill, and thus might easily be made a fool of in the intensely hostile debate that characterized Spain's representative forum. The latter point probably influenced Franco as much as José Antonio's political argument, for he was well aware that his brother Ramón had failed disastrously as a parliamentary deputy and had declined sharply in prestige. With this danger in mind and faced with severe pressure from the left, Franco agreed to withdraw his name from the Cuenca elections.[6] In a subsequently famous speech on May 2, the moderate Socialist leader Indalecio Prieto hailed Franco's withdrawal with prophetic words, warning of the danger of military revolt: "General Franco, because of his youth, his skills, his circle of friendships in the Army, is the man who at a given moment could lead a military movement of this type with the maximum probability of success, because of his professional prestige."[7]

Yet Franco himself was not convinced of either the necessity or the success of any military movement. His own subsequent version was that he had always been in favor of the revolt but had insisted that it must be a "joint action" by the Army that would achieve "surprise." At any rate, his reluctance was such that one of the senior conspirators, General Luis Orgaz, exiled by the government to the Canaries, tried to convince him that playing a leading role in the rebellion would be like eating a *perita en*

5. Ramón Serrano Súñer, *Entre el silencio y la propaganda, la Historia como fue: Memorias* (Barcelona, 1977), 56. (Hereafter cited as *Memorias*.)

6. Ibid., 56–58.

7. José Pla, *Historia de la Segunda República española* (Barcelona, 1940), 4:437–38.

dulce (candied pear), and that if he did not, some one else would simply seize the opportunity to take his place. Franco was not fooled by such talk, for he knew that at the very best a military revolt would be risky and extremely difficult.[8] On the one hand he bargained with Mola for a key command, that of the elite combat units in Morocco, but hesitated to fully commit himself.[9] As late as June 23 he wrote a personal letter to the prime minister, Casares Quiroga, in the latter's dual capacity as minister of war, to protest not so much the current "grave problems of the Fatherland" as the government's present treatment of the Army and of senior conservative commanders. He protested that "those who present the Army as disloyal to the Republic misrepresent the truth" and urged instead "measures of consideration, equanimity, and justice."[10]

José Antonio Primo de Rivera had different but equally grave doubts. A circular of June 24 sent to local Falangist leaders throughout Spain warned:

> The political projects of the military . . . are not usually distinguished for their relevance. Those projects are almost all based on an initial error: that of thinking that the ills of Spain are due to simple disarrangements of internal order and will disappear when power is handed over to those [reactionary politicians] previously referred to, who are charlatans lacking any historical understanding, any authentic education, and any desire that the Patria break forth once more on the great paths of its destiny.
>
> The participation of the Falange in one of those premature and ingenuous projects would constitute a grave responsibility and would entail *its total disappearance, even in case of triumph*. For this reason: because all those who count on the Falange for such undertakings consider it . . . only as an auxiliary shock force, as a species of juvenile assault militia, destined the day after tomorrow to parade before these conceited oligarchs reestablished in power.[11]

Nonetheless, the best terms that José Antonio could gain from Mola provided only for a limited autonomy, promising freedom of propaganda and proselytizing under the new military regime but no place in its government. Thus by June 29, José Antonio sent from his prison cell instructions to Falangists to collaborate in the military revolt, but stipulated that these would be valid for only eleven days. According to Franco's brother-in-law, Serrano Súñer (a close friend of José Antonio), the Falangist leader by this time would have preferred a new government of national con-

---

8. According to a conversation of April 27, 1968, in *Conversaciones privadas*, 526.

9. The most direct testimony will be found in Serrano Súñer's *Memorias*, 52–60. Serrano declares that at the beginning of March, before going to the Canaries, Franco had suggested that a sizable sum of money be placed at his disposal to enable him to organize a revolt from a secure place of exile in southern France where his family would be fully safe. It is doubtful that Franco harbored such an unrealistic idea for very long.

10. This famous letter, which apparently never drew a reply, has been extensively quoted, as in La Cierva, *Franco*, 1:430–31.

11. Primo de Rivera, *Obras completas*, 935–36.

centration representing all the patriotic sectors of politics willing to cooperate—from moderate left to the right—rather than an armed revolt that would divide Spain down the middle.[12]

Such a choice was not that of the government, which proved totally unable to come to grips with the situation. One of the leading leftist chroniclers of the period has reported that between February 17 and July 17 in Spain there were 213 attempted assassinations, 113 local general strikes, and 228 partial shutdowns, with total casualties of 269 killed and 1,287 wounded.[13] The government headed by Azaña's crony Casares Quiroga took the position that all difficulties stemmed from rightist provocation and that there was no need for measures to require the left to obey the law. In the speech of May 2 previously cited, the Socialist Prieto warned his fellow leftists nonetheless that "a country can survive a revolution, which is ended one way or another. What a country cannot survive is the constant attrition of public disorder . . . in a constant state of uneasiness, anxiety and worry."[14]

A leading Spanish scholar of a subsequent generation has observed:

> What strikes the reader of the political literature of the time—the newspapers and the speeches, even in Parliament—is the constant reference to the willingness to announce or encourage the use of force to achieve goals, the assertion of readiness to die for a cause, the frequent description as one of latent civil war. This atmosphere became intolerable and led participants to believe that the solution lay only in defeating and outlawing their opponents and establishing their own order.[15]

On May 25 the small Partido Republicano Nacional, the most moderate and constitutionalist of the liberal Republican groups, after earlier refusing to be associated with the Popular Front, urged a total revision of government policy. It recommended abolition of all shirt movements and political militias, immediate prosecution of all incitements to violence, and the direct imposition of constitutional authority. Several moderate spokesmen urged formation of a multiparty government endowed with decree powers. The most widely publicized proposal was made by Miguel Maura, the Republic's first minister of the interior, in six articles in Madrid's leading daily, *El Sol*, between June 18 and 27. Maura declared that his fear was not so much that Spain might fall under a Communist-style

12. Serrano Súñer, *Memorias*, 60.
13. José Peirats, *La C.N.T. en la revolución española* (Toulouse, 1951), 1:121. Though rightist spokesmen gave somewhat higher figures, the statistics cited may be fairly accurate. Juan Linz arrived at the same number of 269 fatalities in political incidents and assassinations for the period February 3 to July 17 inclusive. Of this total, 150 took place in cities and 119 in small towns and rural areas. Madrid led the way with 45 killings, the next most violent cities being Seville, Málaga, and Granada. Barcelona, the onetime "Chicago of the Mediterranean" (as it had sometimes been called in earlier years), was relatively quiet, with only 3. Linz, *The Breakdown of Democratic Regimes: Europe*, 188.
14. Pla, *Historia*, 4:437–38.
15. Linz, *Breakdown*, 189.

dictatorship as that the country would soon disintegrate in unprecedented anarchy:

> Peaceful citizens, whatever their political sympathies, now believe that the laws are a dead letter and that public insults, assaults, arson, property destruction, homicide, and attacks on the armed forces have ceased to count in the penal code when committed by those in red and blue shirts [the newly unified Socialist-Communist youth] or under the starred emblem of the hammer and sickle. The clenched fist has become safe conduct for the worst excesses.
>
> A reaction against this was inevitable and gives cause for concern in taking a form that is called "fascism," . . . though of authentic Italian Fascism it has only the name and a few doctrinal postulates of which the majority of its affiliates are ignorant.
>
> Today the Republic is no more—though I would like to believe unconsciously—than the tool of the violent, revolutionary sector of the working classes, which, shielded by the liberal democratic system and the blindness of certain leaders of the Republican parties, is preparing in minute detail an assault on the government and the extermination of capitalist and middle-class society. . . . They tell us this themselves in their newspapers and public meetings.
>
> . . . If the Republic is to be this, it is inexorably condemned to swift extinction at the hands of those who claim to be its defenders, or, which is more probable, at the hands of a reaction from the opposite direction.

Maura called for a multiparty "national Republican dictatorship" to save the country, but added, "I do not harbor the slightest hope that my reasoning could convince those who currently bear responsibility for government."

Up to that point the government nonetheless seemed justified in treating any danger from the right with contempt, for Mola continued to encounter so much difficulty in gaining full commitment to an armed revolt that by the first of July he was on the verge of abandoning the whole enterprise and retiring from the Army. Encouraging reports came in during the next few days, and the first concrete date considered for the revolt was July 10, but this had to be given up when one of the leading Falangists involved was arrested.[16]

Mola grew increasingly concerned about mustering the necessary strength, and began to doubt that military conspirators alone would suffice. He had little faith in the amount, quality, or reliability of the support that would be received from Falangists. The only alternative worth

16. The fullest account of the development of the military conspiracy is in Ricardo de la Cierva, *Historia de la guerra civil española* (Madrid, 1969), 735–816. See also Olaya Morales, *La conspiración*, 309–81; and, for a briefer account in English, my *Politics and the Military*, 314–40.

Officers involved in the conspiracy represented political opinions ranging from moderate liberalism to the extreme right. The dominant note was that of corporate action by the military, presumably within some sort of Republican but antileftist framework. Guillermo Cabanellas, *Cuatro generales, I: Preludio a la Guerra Civil* (Barcelona, 1977), 425–43, particularly emphasizes the moderate and corporate aspect of much of the conspiracy.

considering was the Carlist militia in Navarre, but the Carlist leaders were even stickier to deal with than the Falangists. The secretary-general of the Carlist Communion, Manuel Fal Conde, insisted upon political guarantees and at least two out of three seats in the new junta for the Carlists. Mola refused such terms; he knew that both orthodox monarchism and Carlism were weak in the country and that the pronunciamiento would succeed only if it could be presented as a patriotic national reaction led by the Army alone without being tied to special parties. The local Carlist militia were, as it turned out, eager to strike against the leftist regime. Navarrese leaders undercut the Carlist hierarchy by making an arrangement on July 12 to provide full assistance in return for being allowed to use the old monarchist bicolor flag and exercise local control of affairs in Navarre. This, however, was rejected by the supreme Carlist leadership on the following day, promoting the Navarrese to make a desperate effort at a final compromise. Seeing that the Navarrese militia, and presumably other Carlists elsewhere, were determined to join any military move against the current government, the national Carlist representatives in St. Jean de Luz across the French frontier finally accepted a vague compromise with Mola on July 15. Six days earlier Sanjurjo had sent dual letters to Mola and Fal Conde simultaneously, trying to suggest terms of a strictly military cabinet to be led by himself with the goal of putting a complete end to the liberal and parliamentary system. That amounted to much less than Carlism, and Mola's pledge simply promised "agreement with the orientations of General Sanjurjo's letter of the ninth, and those which he may determine in the future as head of government."[17] No clear and firm agreement had been reached as to political goals, but Carlist support for the revolt had been fully pledged.

Elsewhere the situation remained confused and problematic; as late as July 12 Franco is said to have sent an urgent message to Mola expressing further reluctance to go through with the armed revolt.[18] Most officers would act only on regular orders from above, which were not likely to be forthcoming. The conspiracy was further weakened by the fact that it

17. Even after July 15 Fal Conde tried to negotiate with Sanjurjo precise terms to guarantee a Carlist restoration, but this last effort was overtaken by events. The most complete study of the role of Carlists in the conspiracy is an unpublished work by Julio Arostegui, which will form part of a broader history of Carlism in the Civil War. See Antonio Lizarza Iribarren, *Memorias de la conspiración* (Pamplona, 1969); Tomás Echeverría, *Cómo se preparó el alzamiento: El General Mola y los carlistas* (Madrid, 1985); and the less complete accounts by Blinkhorn, *Carlism and Crisis*, 228–50, and Jaime del Burgo, *Conspiración y guerra civil* (Madrid, 1970).

18. According to Ramon Garriga, on July 13 when Mola received Franco's message of the preceding day expressing continued reluctance, despite the plans already underway to fly him to Morocco to take command of the forces in the Protectorate, Mola temporarily changed the arrangement to have General Sanjurjo, overall commander of the rebels, flown from Lisbon to Spanish Morocco to lead the revolt there. *Los validos de Franco* (Barcelona, 1981), 25.

was primarily based on preemptive considerations. A successful counter-revolution could be mobilized, it seemed, only in the face of a matured revolutionary threat, yet the forces of the left kept hanging fire. The extent of economic disorder was great, there was considerable violence in certain areas, and the government made it clear that it was a partisan of the left and would make no effort toward impartial administration vis-a-vis the center and right. But the left was altogether disunited, and there was as yet no revolutionary action directly aimed at the immediate overthrow of the Republican state.

The final blow in the storm of strikes, riots, arson, property confiscations, street disorders, and murders was struck in Madrid on the night of July 12–13. Leftist police officers, some of them recently reappointed by the Left Republican minister of the interior, in collaboration with a group of Socialist gunmen murdered one of the two leaders of the parliamentary opposition, Calvo Sotelo, after arresting him in the middle of the night.[19] This was a crime unprecedented in the annals of west European parliamentary government, for never before had a government's own security forces, in collaboration with revolutionary gunmen, sequestered and murdered in cold blood the leader of the opposition.[20] To many it indicated that revolutionary radicalism was out of control and the constitutional system at an end. For the next thirty years the supporters of the military revolt would refer to fake documents alleging that the murder of Calvo Sotelo was but the prelude to a Communist plot to seize power by the end of July. In fact no concrete leftist plan to take over the government by a specific date has ever been revealed, and though the Communists paid much more attention to military preparation than did the other larger leftist movements,[21] they were in no position to seize power at that

19. There are two recent accounts of this magnicide: Ian Gibson, *La noche en que mataron a Calvo Sotelo* (Barcelona, 1982); and Luis Romero, *Por qué y cómo mataron a Calvo Sotelo* (Barcelona, 1982).

20. The immediate provocation for this assassination was the killing on the preceding evening of Lt. José Castillo of the Republican Assault Guards, a weekend instructor of the socialist militia. Castillo in turn had been killed because of his strong leftist identity and because he was blamed for the death of one Falangist and the serious wounding of a Carlist in police incidents. Violence had spiraled in this manner since the first outbursts attending the leftist victory in February. Literally hundreds of Falangists had been arrested for their part in these affrays, but leftist gunmen scarcely ever appeared in court, because, as Romero succinctly put it, "the police never arrested leftists."

From the first hours the Republican authorities, and subsequently their supporters for many years, tried to establish an equivalence between the killing of a police officer by parties unknown (presumably Falangists or Carlists) and the calculated assassination of the co-leader of the parliamentary opposition by Republican police. They seemed oblivious of the fact that such a rationale equated the institutions of the Republic—in this case, its police and security system—with political reprisal or terrorist groups. But that, of course, is the whole point.

21. Most of the leftist political violence in the Madrid region, the most heated in all Spain, seems to have been carried out by Socialists rather than Communists. Only the Communists, however, had organized a serious paramilitary formation, the Milicias Anti-fascistas

time. All the leftist groups, on the other hand, indicated that they considered the days of the nominal parliamentary government to be numbered and expected some sort of revolutionary regime to follow in the near future. This was clearly stated in manifold public pronouncements during the spring and summer of 1936.

Gil Robles had warned earlier in a speech to the Cortes that "half a nation will not resign itself to die"[22] at the hands of the left, and the dramatic killing of Calvo Sotelo finally decided thousands of waverers. It apparently was also the final element in Franco's own decision. Elaborate plans were already being implemented to fly him to Morocco in a chartered British plane, and his last hesitations were overcome by this stark demonstration that no one would be safe from the Popular Front. Events also strengthened the sometimes uncertain resolve of José Antonio Primo de Rivera, who from his prison cell in Alicante sent word to Mola that unless a final date for revolt was set within seventy-two hours, the Falangists would begin by themselves.

The military rebellion was finally scheduled by Mola to start on July 18, 19, and 20 in a series of zones, spreading from Morocco to the southern part of the peninsula and then to the northern garrisons. It was precipitated in Morocco on July 17 because of an informer, but the rebels quickly gained control of the entire Protectorate, despite the fact that a majority of its Spanish population had voted for the Popular Front. Nonetheless, because of the many loose ends and Mola's staggered timetable, no generalized revolt in the peninsula garrisons took place for thirty-six hours.

There was subsequently much speculation as to why the left Republican government did not take more stringent measures both before and during the crisis to avert a major revolt. The conspiracy was not exactly a secret, for though the details were not known to the government, rumors had flown for months, certain civilian contacts had been arrested, and most of the active plotters were known to be hostile to the government. The government had, in fact, taken more than a few measures to keep the Army under control. Nearly all the top command assignments had been changed, and most of the new senior commanders were, as events proved, loyal to the existing regime. Many civilian activists, mainly Falangist, had been arrested, and some of the top conspirators had been placed under surveillance.

From the viewpoint of Azaña and Casares Quiroga's government of the Republican Left, its military policy seemed sensible and coherent. Both

---

Obreras y Campesinas (MAOC), begun on a very small scale in 1933 and later partly staffed with leaders trained in the Soviet Union. In addition, the Communist Party operated a special Anti-Military Bureau to collect information and form subversive cells among privates and NCOs.

22. La Cierva, *Los documentos de la primavera trágica*, 607–9.

Azaña, since May the impotent president of the Republic, and his prime minister, Casares Quiroga, doubted the ability of military conspirators to generate an effective pronunciamiento. There had scarcely been a well-organized revolt in the history of the Spanish Army. Successful pronunciamientos had won their goals in the past not so much because of their strength as because of the weakness or unpopularity of the governments whom they overthrew. The 1932 affair had been grotesquely arranged. Government authorities calculated that they could count on the support of more than half the population, including most of the best-organized and most active political groups. In such circumstances, a confused and weakly organized revolt could be easily isolated and stamped out.

This calculation was reinforced by a negative concern of the Left Republican leaders. Having unbalanced the political system to gain power, they had tied themselves to the revolutionary left and found it impossible to enforce many of the norms of the Constitution. But they were not themselves revolutionaries and did not want to establish a new revolutionary government. Their ideal was the status quo of March or April 1936, and they hesitated to play the Kerensky role assigned to them by the revolutionaries. Premature efforts to crack down on the Army might remove the last counterbalance to the extreme left and make the Republican government a prisoner of the revolutionaries (as indeed occurred after July 18 once the revolt removed the military from the political equation of the Republican zone).

The most serious miscalculation by government leaders resulted from their relative ignorance of the exact capacity and temper of the armed forces. They did not appreciate the dedication and determination of the hard-core rebels, who were totally committed to the proposition that the last opportunity had come to save their country from revolutionary destruction and bolshevization. Moreover, they overestimated the loyalty of the police forces to the leftist regime and they did not fully appreciate the importance of the units in Morocco. The government relied too much on the senior progovernment generals but did not gauge the weakness of these aging, sometimes inept bureaucrats in the military structure. In Morocco and a number of other key garrisons the elderly commanders were simply swept aside. The Eighteenth of July was not a generals' revolt in the strict sense; it was joined by only 7 of the 27 major generals (including 3 of 12 divisional commanders and 4 of 21 major generals with active commands) and 20 of the 35 brigade commanders.[23] Most generals were either loyal to the government or sat on their hands and did nothing.

23. The computation of Vicente Palacio Atard in *Aproximación histórica a la guerra española (1936–1939)* (Madrid, 1970), 41–42, is partially corrected by Gabriel Cardona and Joan Villarroya, "La represión contra los militares republicanos," *Historia 16* 8:92 (Dec. 1983), 33–36.

Though some sort of rebellion occurred in 44 of the 51 Spanish army garrisons, the initiative was taken by only a limited portion of the officer corps. When all is said and done, the Spanish military revolt of 1936 stands as an audacious coup by a comparatively small number of determined military conspirators. Probably no more than 1,000 officers—not all of them on active duty—served as the nucleus, and they came mostly from the activist middle and junior strata of the officer corps. Their resolution served to stiffen reluctant colleagues, overthrow senior commanders, and in a minority of cases bring whole garrisons out in revolt. In some cases it was managed by sheer bravado, courage, and personal example.

Among the few regions in which the revolt was simple and secure were Morocco and Navarre, at the antipodes of Spanish territory. In Morocco the military forces were powerful and fairly well united, with only a minority of officers reluctant to join the movement. In Navarre, Mola encountered no difficulty because of the strong civilian support among right-wing Carlists.

But in most regions the garrison forces were neither strong nor united. Civilian support was often uncertain at best, and at worst the rebels were likely to meet concerted resistance either from loyal armed police or the organized worker groups, or both. Because of low budgeting and summer leaves, the available manpower of the Army was only slightly more than 50 percent of its strength on paper. Materiel was scanty and obsolescent and supplies low. Save among a rightist minority, there was little enthusiasm in Spanish society for a military dictatorship. Moderate and conservative elements of the middle classes, while full of hate for and fear of the left and grave concern over the Azaña regime, were not necessarily eager for a military coup and in the first two or three days of the revolt showed considerable disorientation.

The rebellion was a success in only about one-third of the peninsular garrisons, and these were located mainly in the more conservative provinces of the north and northwest, where there was a good deal of civilian support for an organized antileftist move and the revolutionary forces were comparatively weak.[24] Conversely, the only province that voted for the conservative list in February but was dominated by the left after July 18 was the northern coastal district of Santander. There the leftist parties

24. The most detailed account of the revolt from the Nationalist perspective will be found in Arrarás, ed., *Historia de la Cruzada española,* vols. 3 and 4. The extensive early memoir and journalistic literature relating to it is listed in F. Amador Carrandi, *Ensayo bibliográfico de las obras y folletos publicados con motivo del Movimiento Nacional* (Granada, 1940). A less detailed, somewhat more balanced general treatment has been provided by Guillermo Cabanellas (son of one of the top rebel commanders) in his *Cuatro generales: La lucha por el poder,* 13–195.

There were several early descriptions of the revolt in the northwest, but the only serious study is Carlos Fernández, *El alzamiento de 1936 en Galicia* (La Coruña, 1982).

were more unified and seized the initiative themselves in a direct takover of authority under a Popular Front coalition on July 19.

The keys to a quick coup were the large cities, for there lay the centers of authority, communication, and resources and also of organized leftist strength. The rising failed in four of the six major cities—Madrid, Barcelona, Valencia, and Bilbao. It enjoyed spectacular and improbable triumph in Seville and Zaragoza. In Seville this was largely due to an extraordinary bravura performance by a grizzled sixty-year old veteran, Queipo de Llano. Initially he had only a handful of officers to rely on, and virtually no troops, but by clever bluff and manipulation he rallied nearly the entire garrison and most of the police as well.[25] The divisions within the revolutionary movements and their uncertain tactics accomplished the rest. Zaragoza was the headquarters of the anarchosyndicalist CNT and supposedly a stronghold of the left, but there the garrison and police acted swiftly and in full cooperation, dominating the city before the anarchosyndicalists could react.

In the three largest cities, Madrid,[26] Barcelona,[27] and Valencia,[28] the revolt never had much chance of success. The organized revolutionary groups were so large compared to the military, and the support of the police so uncertain, that only in Valencia might a positive result have been expected. In Madrid and Valencia the revolt was uncoordinated in the extreme. Though UME elements and various cliques of retired officers had been conspiring in both garrisons for several years, recent reassignments had broken up whatever unity existed earlier. Confusion among the military was almost total. There was never any rebellion at all in Valencia, where the main troops were confined to barracks for nearly two weeks and finally overwhelmed by the left.

The two main demands by reluctant officers were that the order to rebel must come through proper channels from senior commanders and that the armed police must support the Army. This last point was indeed

25. The only biography of Queipo is Gen. José Cuesta Monereo and Antonio Olmedo Delgado, *General Queipo de Llano* (Madrid, 1957); but see Ian Gibson, *Queipo de Llano: Sevilla, verano de 1936* (Barcelona, 1986). Manuel Barrios, *El último virrey* (Barcelona, 1978), is merely a badly written diatribe.

26. There are two accounts of the revolt in Madrid by Maximiano García Venero, *Madrid julio 1936* (Madrid, 1973), 283–410, and *El general Fanjul* (Madrid, 1967).

27. The best account of the revolt in Barcelona is Manuel Cruells, *La revolta del 1936 a Barcelona* (Barcelona, 1976). Military preparations and actions of the Catalan regional government are narrated in Federico Escofet, *De una derrota a una victoria: 6 de octubre de 1934–19 de julio de 1936* (Barcelona, 1984). The chief Nationalist descriptions are Francisco Lacruz, *El alzamiento, la revolución y el terror en Barcelona* (Barcelona, 1943); and José del Castillo and Santiago Alvarez, *Barcelona: Objetivo cubierto* (Barcelona, 1958). The failure there was doubly portentous since it led to the capture and execution of Manuel Goded, probably Franco's chief personal and political rival among the rebel commanders.

28. Arrarás, *Cruzada española*, 5:463–522; Gabriel Araceli, *Valencia 1936* (Zaragoza, 1939), 11–31.

important, for the forces of the Civil Guard and Assault Guard were nearly as numerous as the Army in the peninsula. They were more carefully trained and selected, in most cases more professionalized, and almost as well equipped. Though many of the police were antileftist, they tended to follow the general trend of each province. In most large cities they accepted the bent of the population and fought valiantly for the leftist authorities. In many rural provinces, however, they went over to the rebels, and the support of the police was sometimes a decisive factor.

A revolt that failed in more than half the national territory can scarcely be called a success. What it achieved was not a successful coup but the establishment of several nuclei of armed power in the north, west, and far south that could be coordinated into a major movement against the leftist regime, creating the conditions for full-scale civil war. This situation was grasped by government leaders on the night of July 18–19, bringing the resignation of Casares Quiroga's Left Republican cabinet and the appointment of an ephemeral compromise ministry under the moderate José Martínez Barrio that tried vainly to make a deal with the insurgents. The only version of Martínez Barrio's proposition that is at all likely to be accurate is that given by one of his cabinet members, Ramón Feced, to the writer García Venero.[29] Martínez Barrio apparently offered an across-the-board compromise, bringing one of the rebels into the cabinet, promising an abrupt about-face on internal policy, a national coalition government, and the disarming of the leftist militia. At an earlier date, such a compromise might well have succeeded and preserved constitutional government in Spain, but it came too late. Lines were too sharply drawn, and the chief conspirators had made solemn pledges which Mola refused to break. Moreover, it is not clear that the compromise could have been enforced on the left, for virulent opposition from the Socialists removed the Martínez Barrio government before it had actually been fully invested with powers.

In less than ten hours, the Left Republican government veered sharply from an across-the-board compromise in favor of the insurgent right to an almost complete capitulation to the revolutionary left. This wild careening in itself reveals the confusion and irresolution of Azaña and his colleagues of the middle-class left. The result was not so much a compromise with the revolutionary left as the transfer of effective power to them. The key decision here—the "arming of the people" (meaning not of course "the people" but the organized revolutionary groups)—was not made officially in Madrid until the afternoon of July 19, though some arms had already been distributed to the Socialists the night before. Within a few more days the vestiges of the Republican system were replaced by the Spanish revolutionary confederation of 1936–37, eventually to be super-

29. García Venero, *El general Fanjul*, 287–90.

seded by Juan Negrín's new People's Republic in 1937. The irony of this situation was that the military revolt thus created in the part of Spain that it failed to occupy exactly the situation that it was designed to avoid. A preemptive counterrevolutionary coup set off the revolution. The latter could only begin by superseding the remaining power of the Republican government, a circumstance that the military revolt first made possible.

The question has been asked many times whether the outbreak of the Civil War could have been avoided. Of course it could have, but not by mid-July 1936. By that point the degree of political hatred and polarization was so great that some sort of blow-up became inevitable. The main responsibility was borne by those on whose shoulders government authority rested—the middle-class Republican Left of Azaña, which was in control of executive power from February 19, 1936, to the outbreak of the Civil War. The standard apology for the Azaña administration has been that it did nothing to contribute to the prevailing polarization but was merely the victim of it, attacked by extremes of right and left. This contention will not withstand examination. Save for a few hours on the morning of July 19 when a belated effort was made to draw back from the precipice, the Azaña administration was more the accomplice than the victim of the revolutionary left. Such a policy was an inevitable consequence of the anticonstitutional distinction made by the middle-class left from 1931 onwards between "true Republicans"—those of the left—and reactionaries or cryptofascists—those of the right. Representative national government was not possible on such terms, and even though the terms ultimately proved suicidal for the middle-class left, Azaña was not willing to alter them until it was too late. The replacement of Left Republican government by pluralistic revolutionary dictatorship in late July 1936 was a not-illogical consequence of its theory and tactics.

The revolt was primarily an Army affair. In general, naval officers tended to be more conservative, and air force officers more liberal or radical, than those in the Army. Though the Navy would be crucial in guaranteeing transportation for the vital Moroccan forces, Mola and his associates were not able to organize coordinated action. The proportion of naval officers committed to the revolt was at least as high as in the Army, yet naval forces were dominated by the left all along the eastern and southern coasts of Spain. A key factor here was the initiative of a junior leftist radiotelegraph officer who at a crucial moment almost single-handedly seized control of the main radio naval transmitter on the southern coast, blocking rebel communications and rallying naval units to the left.[30] Moreover, despite the strong antileftist attitude of naval officers, an effective revolt

30. The initiative of this officer, Benjamín Balboa, is described in Daniel Sueiro, *La flota es roja* (Barcelona, 1983).

was especially difficult to arrange in the Navy because of the poor relations between officers and men. Though Communist and Socialist influence was weak, anarchosyndicalism flourished in most of the port towns. When naval commanders tried to swing their vessels behind the revolt on July 19, mutineers seized control of most ships, precipitating mass slaughter of officers. In contrast, there was little mutiny from the ranks in Army units that attempted rebellion. Army life was more open, with better relations between officers and men and less intense class consciousness among the lower ranks. Practically the only units of the Navy won by the rebels were those in the northwest where control of facilities was achieved not so much by the naval command as by successful Army forces.[31]

The Air Force was of course the newest branch of the armed forces. Its lack of tradition, its consciousness of innovation and the requirements of technological modernization had made it the most "futurist" arm of the military, and its most radical sector had acquired a pseudorevolutionary aura following the political acrobatics of Ramón Franco in 1930–31. The Air Force had the largest minority of proleftist officers of any part of the military, and the majority opposed the revolt. Only about 25 percent of its units and planes lined up on the insurgent side, placing the latter under a distinct handicap until this was removed by German and Italian aid.

The original revolt of July 17–20 was carried out as a nominally Republican rising, not a monarchist, fascist, or even completely militarist rebellion. Save for the compulsory "Viva España!" the most common slogan in the first military proclamations was "Viva la República!" Some pronouncements went even further. Franco's first official statement on July 19 ended with the invocation of "Fraternity, Liberty, and Equality" [sic]. Nearly all insurgent forces fought under the Republican flag during the first weeks of the Civil War. Mola and other leaders had been careful throughout to hold monarchists at some distance (save in Navarre), realizing that to tie the movement to monarchism would isolate it even within the Army, and much more within the country as a whole. Thus in some ways the revolt began, or seemed to begin, in the tradition of the nineteenth-century liberal pronunciamientos. It does not appear that there was any clear understanding or agreement concerning exact goals in the minds of most officers supporting the revolt other than the overthrow of Azaña's administration, throttling of the revolutionaries, and establishment of more moderate and nationalistic government.

Mola and most of the key leaders, however, planned from the start to replace the whole Republican regime, as it was constituted, with a military directory, at least for the moment. That was why Martínez Barrio's compromise on the morning of July 19 had been rejected. The appearance of moderation or liberalism in many of the first local Army pro-

31. José Cervera Pery, *Alzamiento y revolución de la Marina* (Madrid, 1978).

nouncements was the result of confusion or differences among regional commanders, and also of the fact that Mola and other leaders preferred to let the movement appear comparatively liberal in its opening days so as to minimize opposition. On the other hand, if the revolt had achieved rapid success, the military directory of 1936 would probably have retained more moderate or liberal features compared with the rigorous Franco regime that was later hammered out under conditions of revolutionary civil war.

Just as rebel propagandists often harped on the alleged imminent target date for the outbreak of a Communist takeover—for which no concrete evidence has ever been presented—so leftist propagandists similarly relied for years on the equally fictitious theme of "international fascist conspiracy," endeavoring to explain the Civil War in terms of planned aggression by Hitler and Mussolini. This has been thoroughly disproved by historical study, which has found no evidence of direct contacts between the leading military conspirators and the German and Italian governments before the end of the first week of the Civil War. Carlist leaders and Alfonsine monarchist plotters had negotiated with Italian authorities since 1932 and had even signed an agreement with them in March 1934 that pledged Italian supplies and money for an armed attempt at monarchist restoration. This plan never developed, because there was no interest in or support for monarchism in Spain. Army leaders were not a party to it, and the agreement was not directly applicable to the situation that developed after July 17, 1936. There were various contacts between German officials and local Nazi leaders in Spain or Morocco on the one hand and Army conspirators on the other, but none of these ever reached the level of official government understanding. Some minor arms agreements were negotiated with German firms, but this was done mainly by civilian conspirators and on the private level of German business, just as individual Republican arms purchases were negotiated with German firms during the early weeks of the Civil War.[32]

Considerable stress has been laid on the political and military miscalculations involved in the revolt. It is probably correct that many of the plotters did not appreciate fully the leftist groups' capacity for immediate paramilitary response, since the speed of reaction and the initial unity of the left in key areas did sometimes come as a surprise. Yet the very reason for the rebellion was fear of the strength of revolutionary groups, a power that was growing week by week. In a sense, the revolt was a gamble to take over the government before the counterrevolutionary forces grew weaker by comparison.

It was never seriously supposed by Mola that the regime would fall in a

32. The definitive study of Spanish-German relations for these months is Angel Viñas, *La Alemania Nazi y el 18 de julio*, rev. ed. (Madrid, 1979).

seventy-two-hour coup d'etat. The most sober calculations were based on
the likelihood that the revolt in Madrid would fail, and that it would be
necessary to concentrate forces from both the secure garrisons in the
north and the units from Morocco in the south against the capital. Mola
apparently thought that this might take up to two weeks. Hence a "little
civil war" was envisioned, though not a major one. The geographic scope
and sequences of the initial struggle—through the beginning phases
down to about the first of November—were at least partially foreseen.
What was not envisioned was the military extent of the struggle or its duration, or the initial success of the leftist forces in blockading the straits
and preventing a rapid build-up in the south. This, along with the slowdown in the north, nearly wrecked the whole plan. But then Mola and the
most perspicacious rebel leaders knew that it was a dubious, touch-and-go
affair with a fifty-fifty chance of failure. That was one of the main reasons
why otherwise-sympathetic officers were reluctant to be involved. As early
as May 31 Mola had sketched an emergency plan for retreat to a northern
redoubt based in Navarre if efforts to take Madrid should fail.[33]

Rapid escalation of the conflict into total civil war greatly expanded the
struggle, made it a major international issue, threatened the national sovereignty of Spain, and enormously radicalized the issues on both sides of
the barricades. This virtually ended the prospect of representative government in Spain for the next generation, regardless of who won, and
turned the military revolt in the direction of a more radical and authoritarian military regime whose contours had been but dimly perceived by
most of those engaged in the military conspiracy of 1936.

33. La Cierva, *Historia*, 775–76.

7

Establishment of the Franco Dictatorship

Mola and the other leading conspirators had always been eager for Franco to play a major role in the revolt against the Popular Front, but there had never been discussion of anyone other than José Sanjurjo as primary leader. Though he was also senior to the main rebel chiefs, Sanjurjo's primacy was based on his leadership of the abortive 1932 revolt and was recognized by all the other conspirators. A plane was sent to fly him from his Lisbon exile to rebel territory on July 20. Its fiery crash on takeoff left Sanjurjo dead and the rebel movement without a leader.[1]

Franco, as usual, had much better luck. The private British plane chartered to fly him to Spanish Morocco made the trip successfully, landing him in the Protectorate's capital of Tetuan on July 19.[2] During the next few

1. There is an account by Sanjurjo's pilot, Juan Antonio Ansaldo, who survived, in the latter's memoir *¿Para qué . . .?* (Buenos Aires, 1953), 140–43. Cf. Federico Bravo Morata, *Franco y los muertos providenciales* (Madrid, 1979), 49–96.

2. Perhaps the most direct and graphic account of Franco's flight is by his cousin and aide, Lt. Gen. Francisco Franco Salgado-Araujo, *Mi vida junto a Franco* (Barcelona, 1977), 152–64. The background is related by Luis Bolín, who helped to make arrangements, in his *Spain: The Vital Years* (London, 1967), 159–66; and in Douglas Jerrold, *Georgian Adventure* (London, 1939), 370ff.

Other arrangements were made to place Franco's wife and daughter aboard a German freighter bound for France, where they spent three months with Doña Carmen's former French governess. Her account of this is presented in Carmen Polo de Franco, "¿Que hacía Ud. mientras su marido se alzaba en armas?" *Y (Revista para la mujer nacional-sindicalista)* (June, 1938).

According to Ramón Garriga, leftist crewmen of the *Uad Arcila*, the Spanish gunboat which transferred them to the German vessel, tried to rebel while Franco's family was on board but were put down. In most of the Spanish Navy, the revolt and takeover by leftist sailors was successful, so that the General's wife and daughter just missed falling into leftist hands. Cf. Garriga, *La Señora de El Pardo*, 91–93; and *Los validos de Franco* (Barcelona, 1981), 28–30.

weeks he worked feverishly to prepare forces for the march on Madrid, but was left temporarily isolated by the Republican command of the sea. This desperate situation led to his early and independent contacts with Rome and Berlin, seeking some form of support to transfer his forces logistically and to muster more for an assault from the south. It also left him out of the first political steps taken by Mola in the core of the rebel zone.

On July 19, after declaring martial law in Pamplona, Mola hastily re-edited his earlier political sketch for the new military directory. The new draft proposed a corporative economic administration, a system of cooperatives, and the continuation of a moderate program of agrarian reform. Freedom of education was to be generally permitted, but encouragement of "anarchy" and pornography were rigorously prohibited. Concerning religion, Mola's memorandum stated: "We are Catholic, but respect the religious beliefs of those who are not. We believe that the Church ought to be separate from the State, for this benefits both institutions."[3] In general, this sketch was a faithful reflection of the peculiar combination of authoritarianism and liberalism that informed Mola's political attitudes. In at least two cities, Zaragoza and Mahón (on Menorca), the first municipal governments set up by the Army rebels were not staffed by conservatives but by the Radicals and other center elements.[4]

Four days later, on July 23, Mola officially set up a seven-member Junta de Defensa Nacional in Burgos to serve as the executive leadership of the military movement.[5] Membership was based in part on seniority but was also calculated to reflect the several sectors of the officer corps that had participated in the revolt. Nominal president was General Miguel Cabanellas, highest in seniority among the rebel generals and one of the least enthusiastic. His district headquarters at Zaragoza was one of those responsible for appointing local luminaries of the Radical Party to major posts—Cabanellas had earlier been a Radical Cortes deputy. He had quickly made concessions there to avoid antimilitary sentiment, and was considered by other rebel leaders to be wavering and indecisive.[6] Within little more than forty-eight hours, Mola had decided that Cabanellas must be replaced at Zaragoza with a more determined and ruthless commander, but because of his rank he could only be kicked upstairs. A week earlier Cabanellas had feared that he might have to shave off his white beard and flee across the Pyrenees disguised as a priest.[7] Instead he found himself

3. Félix Maíz, *Alzamiento en España* (Pamplona, 1956), 307–10.
4. Cf. Arrarás, *Cruzada española*, 4:315.
5. The official decrees were published in most north Spanish newspapers and are presented in *La historia de España en sus documentos. El Siglo XX: La Guerra (1936–1939)*, ed. Fernando Díaz-Plaja (Madrid, 1963), 173–76.
6. Joaquín Pérez Madrigal, "Veinticinco anos después," *¡Qué pasa!* (July, 1965); Arrarás, *Cruzada española*, 4:218.
7. José María Iribarren, *Con el general Mola* (Zaragoza, 1937), 169.

the puppet leader of the rebellion, for there was some hope that the image of this elderly Mason and well-known liberal as nominal Junta president would help rally the moderates and undecided. (It might be noted also that the naming of a moderate, very senior figure as the initial leader subsequently became rather common in new military regimes elsewhere.)

In addition to Cabanellas, the Junta was initially composed of Mola, the retired generals Miguel Ponte, Fidel Dávila, and Andrés Saliquet (who had played key roles in the revolt in Old Castile and earlier formed part of the shadow "Generals' Junta" in Madrid), and two lieutenant-colonels from the General Staff, Federico Montaner and Fernando Moreno Calderón,[8] who represented the UME. It was rumored in Burgos that the generals hoped to include distinguished civilians as subordinate members,[9] but the factionalism of Spanish politics made this seem inadvisable.[10] In accordance with Mola's plans, some kind of patriotic junta—usually with civilian members or advisers in subordinate roles—was being set up in almost every province dominated by the rebels, but the real government in the insurgent zone was obviously the new self-appointed military hierarchy. Theirs was the main responsibility, and when the Junta members signed their first decree in Burgos, Moreno Calderón is said to have murmured, "If Spain does not respond, this is our death sentence."[11] Despite the lack of seniority or official authority of some of the new rebel commanders, very nearly one hundred percent of the officers in the rebel-controlled areas rallied to the insurgent cause. This demonstrated considerable unity among the military in revolt. The major exceptions were a number of the highest-ranking commanders, who were simply swept aside and arrested, and eventually in some cases executed.

The Junta de Defensa Nacional was not dominated by Mola but worked as a team. While Mola served by general consent as overall military commander in the north, the administrative work was supervised by the Junta's two staff officers, and Cabanellas signed the decrees. On July 30 a representative of the Navy, Captain Francisco Moreno Hernández, who earlier had been placed in charge of that portion of the fleet under rebel command, was added to the Junta. On August 3, as his African units were beginning their drive north against Madrid, Franco was invited to become the ninth member, followed by Queipo de Llano and Orgaz.

By August the insurgents had baptized their movement "Nationalist." Though the rebels tried to reassure the lower classes about their eco-

8. Most of these figures were unknown to the Spanish public. During the following winter a series of cheap booklets were published in Avila to popularize leading military commanders.

9. Antonio Ruiz Vilaplana, *Doy fe: Un año de actuación en la España de Franco* (Paris, 1938), 224–26.

10. Iribarren, *Mola*, 106–7.

11. Ibid., 122.

nomic aims, the bulk of their support came from the lower-middle and middle classes and the conservative north generally, so that the term Nationalist was soon understood to denote an affirmation of religion, tradition, and Spanish patriotism, with little of the radical connotation found in some other countries.

It was above all the outbreak of violent mass revolution in the Republican zone, with its church burnings, economic appropriations, and many thousands of murders, that quickly rallied the more conservative half of the Spanish population to the Nationalist cause. Almost equally important was the identification of the revolt with religion, which soon began to convert the revolt into an official crusade and provided its primary cultural, emotional, and spiritual support.

Representatives of the monarchy were kept at a distance. When Don Juan, third son of Alfonso XIII, slipped across the French border to volunteer for the Nationalist army, he was sent back again by Mola without being permitted to see any of the Junta members.[12] Mola also declined to receive other members of the royal family, including Air Force general Don Alfonso de Orleans-Bourbon, a cousin of the former king.[13] After a few weeks, the old monarchist flag was adopted throughout the Nationalist zone in place of the Republican banner, but this was the only symbol of identification with the monarchy.

The Burgos Junta's only firm plan seems to have been to maintain an all-military government, at least until the war was won. Administration was loose, and the Junta made no effort to govern the southern zone directly. The core of it was under the personal rule of Queipo de Llano, who administered all western Andalusia (and subsequently much of the southern part of Nationalist Spain) from his headquarters in Seville. The main field units advancing to the north were directed by Franco, commander of the Army of Africa and of the South, who was largely absorbed in military affairs. There is no evidence that the Burgos Junta was especially concerned during August and early September with putting the Nationalist government on a more orderly foundation, even though the scope and complexities of the conflict were spreading beyond its control.

The first general to raise the question of the nature of the future Nationalist regime was the monarchist Alfredo Kindelán, one of the creators of the Spanish Air Force under Alfonso XIII, a personal friend and devoted follower of the ex-king, and commander of the air force of Franco's Army of the South. When he first assumed command of the African forces, Franco had requested that Kindelán send a formal message to Don Alfonso (residing in Rome), as well as to Hitler and Mussolini. Franco

12. Francisco Bonmatí de Codecido, *El Príncipe Don Juan de España* (Valladolid, 1938), 229–36.
13. According to Don Alfonso, in Peter Kemp, *Mine Were of Trouble* (London, 1957), 25.

pointedly addressed the missive to "His Royal Highness Don Alfonso de Borbón," not "His Majesty Alfonso XIII," as the monarchists would have preferred.[14]

In an interview with a Portuguese journalist on August 10, Franco declared categorically: "Spain is Republican and will continue to be so. Neither the regime nor the flag have changed. The only change will be that crime is replaced by order and acts of banditry by honest and progressive work." Then he added more ominously, "Spain will be governed by a corporative system similar to those installed in Portugal, Italy, and Germany."[15] This distinction undercut much of the reassurance in Franco's first remarks. Moreover, only five days later, at a major ceremony on the Feast of the Assumption (August 15) in Seville, Franco replaced the Republican flag with the traditional red and yellow banner of the monarchy, hailing it as the authentic flag of Spain for which patriots had given their lives in a hundred battles.

When asked privately by Kindelán if he really intended to work for a restoration, Franco replied that the return of the monarchy must be the eventual goal but could not be considered for the moment, for there were too many Republicans—or at least nonmonarchists—in the ranks of the Nationalist movement. Somewhat reassured, Kindelán insisted that a single unified command be created as soon as possible. Trusting Franco's discretion and knowing his qualities of leadership, he suggested that Franco be made commander in chief and also be named regent until it was possible to bring back the king. Franco, however, rejected the notion of a regency, saying that it would weaken the unity of the movement. Nor is there evidence that he was at first eager to have personal supporters work to install him as commander in chief of the Nationalist Army. Perhaps, calling to mind the fate of Primo de Rivera, he felt that the position of an interim leader or dictator was not a strong one. On the other hand, Franco's current status as commander of the Armies of Africa and of the South of Spain gave him control of the most important of the Nationalist forces and carried with it none of the compromising responsibility of political leadership.

Franco was undoubtedly in the strongest individual position of any Nationalist general, and within his own command he had exercised forthright leadership from the start. His messages and proclamations during the first days and weeks made no reference to Sanjurjo, Mola, or even the Junta de Defensa Nacional. From the beginning, foreign journalists as well as the German consul in Tetuán referred to Franco as the key leader of the rebel movement. In addition to the unqualified obedience of his own key forces, Franco also had the most capable military staff to admin-

14. According to Jean Créac'h, *Le Coeur et l'épée* (Paris, 1959), 175–76.
15. *The Times*, Aug. 11, 1936; Cabanellas, *Cuatro generales*, 2:354.

ister his sector. He relied on veteran officers from the Protectorate and also on a nucleus of reliable officers who had recently served him in Tenerife, headed by the astute and lively Major Lorenzo Martínez Fuset of the military Juridical Corps. He also maintained a small political and propaganda group, eventually headed by his brother Nicolás. Franco had further enhanced his position by being more active than Mola in effecting contact with the German and Italian governments. Thus the first material supplied by Mussolini and Hitler was directed to Franco's forces, and German and Italian contacts made it clear that they regarded Franco as the dominant Spanish commander.

The month of August was occupied almost entirely with military problems, as Franco wrested control of all southwestern Spain from the Popular Front forces. During September his troops entered the Tajo river valley and began to drive northeast directly toward Madrid. As the war entered a decisive phase, the question of command became increasingly urgent.

Despite his growing preeminence, Franco at first showed little inclination to assert political leadership. According to Cabanellas, "Franco was not prone to commit himself or to reveal his sentiments. [He was] apparently sincere in his outward behavior, informal in manner, readier to listen than to advance opinions, never given to argument, rigidly disciplined in his dealings with superiors, and agreeable in his dealings with subordinates, . . ."[16] It is doubtful that he would ever have advanced his name for head of the Nationalist movement without the assistance and vehement encouragement of a small group of devoted associates. Chief among these were his brother Nicolás, who had helped win aid from the Portuguese regime and was now acting as his political secretary in Cáceres (Franco's headquarters during September); General Alfredo Kindelán; several other monarchists such as the veteran general Luis Orgaz, his close associate, and José Sangróniz, Franco's diplomatic adviser; the often-mutilated former Legionnaire commander Millán Astray, acting as a kind of propaganda chief; and Col. Juan Yagüe, one of the few Falangist officers and head of the shock units advancing on Madrid.

Mola was only a brigadier in rank and had already disclaimed any ambition to become commander in chief. Though Franco was far from the most senior, Cabanellas was a liberal Mason, Queipo a former Republican of dubious background and scant political prestige, and the elderly Saliquet a nonentity.

The issue began to come to a head in mid-September as the final drive on Madrid approached. This would be the decisive battle and required a maximum of coordination. The need for a military commander-in-chief

16. Cabanellas, *Cuatro generales*, 2:327.

Franco and Yagüe in Seville, August 1936

was logical and evident, for Franco had already encountered considerable friction with Queipo in the south, and there were sharp altercations between Mola and Yagüe on the central front. Thus Franco's request for a meeting of a now-expanded Junta de Defensa to discuss the problem of a unified military command was readily accepted and scheduled for September 21, the main session taking place at a private estate beside the Salamanca airfield.

The only version we have is that of Kindelán:

> During the morning session, which lasted three hours and a half, we discussed various topics of importance, but none as important as that of the *mando único*. I pointed this out three times without managing to bring the

issue to discussion, despite having been actively supported by General Orgaz. I seemed to observe, with disillusion, that my aims were not shared by the majority of those assembled.

When the afternoon session began at four, I firmly introduced the question, without the slightest reticence, encountering a hostile reception from various members. General Cabanellas was clearly opposed, declaring that the question was premature and that it was possible to have a unified command without it being led by a single person, since there were two ways to direct a war: by a Generalissimo or by a Directory or Junta. I agreed, adding: "There are indeed two methods of directing a war: with the first you win, with the second you lose." My proposal was finally put to a vote and was approved with only General Cabanellas dissenting. Then came the vote on the name of the person who should be named Generalissimo. Since it began with the most junior officers and the two colonels excused themselves because of their rank, I decided to reduce tension and break the ice by asking to vote first, and did so in favor of Franco. My vote was immediately joined by those of Mola, Orgaz, Dávila, Queipo de Llano, and all the rest, with the exception of Cabanellas, who said that, as an opponent of such a system, it was not up to him to vote for someone in a post which he deemed unnecessary.[17]

The *Anuario Militar* for 1936 listed Franco only twenty-third in seniority among major generals, and he was outranked in years of service by Cabanellas, Queipo, and Saliquet, yet no one else had as much combat experience and military prestige or as much political tact and influence abroad. Franco already had made a compromise of sorts with Moroccan authorities in the Protectorate that secured the Nationalists' rear guard, providing Spain with a valuable staging area and thousands of combative mercenaries.[18] Not only was Franco's name the best known among the insurgent generals, but it was less directly associated with political activity odious to moderate Spanish opinion. Mola was still remembered as the police chief of the *dictablanda* of 1930–31 and was now becoming known as "the Carlist general" because of the tens of thousands of Requetés flocking to the Army of the North. His name had acquired a negative, even reactionary connotation, and the tall, bespectacled, homely general was not unaware of this. There is no indication that Mola particularly coveted the *mando único* for himself, and no evidence of any opposition on his part to Franco. The meeting adjourned with the understanding that

17. Alfredo Kindelán, *La verdad de mis relaciones con Franco* (Barcelona, 1981), 29, which supplements his earlier chronologically confused *Mis cuadernos de guerra* (Madrid, 1945). See also La Cierva, *Franco*, 1:506–9, who also had access to the unpublished diary of Mola's aide, Maj. Emiliano Fernández Cordón.

18. See Shannon E. Fleming, "Spanish Morocco and the *Alzamiento Nacional*, 1936–1939: The Military, Economic and Political Mobilization of a Protectorate," *JCH* 18:1 (Jan. 1983), 27–42. A subsequent proposal by Moroccan nationalists to organize a large-scale native revolt in the Protectorate in return for autonomy was rejected by the Republican government as too drastic and likely to jeopardize Republican relations with France, as well as the stability of the Popular Front government. Abdelmajid Benjelloun, "La retaguardia de Franco, en peligro," *Historia 16* 9:102 (Oct. 1984), 12–18.

Franco's election as commander in chief was to remain secret until formally announced by the Burgos Junta.

What had been agreed to, however, was only the naming of Franco as military commander in chief, not dictator or chief of state. The Junta de Defensa remained intact, nor was there a precise deadline for the assumption of powers. Several days passed without a word from Burgos, with no indication of any official announcement. Moreover, the post of military generalissimo alone was considerably less than Franco's backers wanted. Together Nicolás Franco, Kindelán, Millán Astray, and Yagüe met with the general and convinced him to call forthwith another meeting of the Nationalist hierarchy, this time to clarify the powers of generalissimo and define his position as that of chief of state for as long as the war lasted. An important role was apparently played by Yagüe, who had relinquished command of the field units southwest of Madrid on the twenty-first and devoted the following crucial week to political intrigue. At a public celebration before Franco's headquarters in Cáceres on the twenty-seventh—following announcement of the breakthrough of the first Nationalist forces to the relief of the defenders of the Alcázar of Toledo—Yagüe publicly hailed Franco as *jefe único*.[19]

The decisive meeting of the Junta de Defensa was held in Salamanca on the following day, September 28. Nicolás Franco arrived there on the eve to secure local political support, and several companies of Carlist and Falangist militia were stationed at the airport to protect and cheer Franco,[20] and possibly also to intimidate any opposition. Kindelán presented a new draft decree, article 3 of which stated: "The office of Generalissimo will also carry the function of Chief of State so long as the war may last. For this reason it has authority over all national activities: political, economic, social, cultural, etc."[21] This proposal came as something of a shock, even though several had been informed beforehand, and it aroused considerable opposition. Yagüe joined the main group at lunch and pressed the case for Franco, possibly hinting at insubordination among the elite combat units. What happened during the afternoon session is unclear. Mola and Queipo de Llano departed after lunch, and the extent of agreement that ensued is not certain.

According to the version provided by his son,[22] Cabanellas returned to

19. On the role of Yagüe, see Juan José Calleja, *Yagüe, un corazón al rojo* (Barcelona, 1963), 116; and José Ignacio Escobar, *Así empezó . . .* (Madrid, 1974), 149–50. Some commentators also allege strong pressure from German contacts, such as the Abwehr chief Admiral Canaris and Johannes Bernhardt, Nazi party chief for Spanish Morocco. Cf. Ramón Garriga, *Nicolás Franco*, 100–104, which fails to cite any evidence.

20. Gonzalo Redondo, *El Requeté* (Barcelona, 1957), 338–39; Kindelán, *Mis cuadernos*, 54.

21. Kindelán, *La verdad*, 31.

22. Cabanellas, *Cuatro generales*, 2:336–38.

Burgos that night unsure how to proceed. He opposed the elevation of Franco but could count on little support from the other generals, and was aware that his personal aide was in collusion with Franco's backers. He placed telephone calls to both Queipo and Mola. The former recommended that he hold out, but Mola counseled acquiescence in handing over the reins of government to Franco, which Cabanellas finally decided to do.

Before the decree was issued the next day, its text was further revised. In return for substituting the phrase "Chief of Government" for "Chief of State," the temporal limitation on Franco's powers was dropped.[23] As officially published under Cabanellas's signature on September 29, it read: "In accordance with the resolution adopted by the Junta de Defensa Nacional, General Francisco Franco Bahamonde is named Chief of the Government of the Spanish State, and will assume all the powers of the new State."[24]

This terminology may have been in part a stratagem to placate Cabanellas, Mola, and Queipo, who according to one source favored a Portuguese-style arrangement whereby the powers of chief of government, or prime minister, were separated from those of head of state (president or king).[25] More crucial, however, was elimination of the time limit—duration of the war—without general discussion or agreement. Whatever the original intention or agreement, the distinction between chief of government and chief of state was immediately ignored. Within twenty-four hours of Franco's official investiture at Burgos on October 1, newspaper and radio announcements, doubtless upon instruction, referred to Franco as "Chief of State," the title employed in his first government order of that day.[26]

As usual, the forty-three-year-old general did not cut a dashing figure in the official ceremonies by which he took power. A hostile writer has described him thus:

> On the low stand in the throne room, placing him higher than the audience, appears the figure of Francisco Franco, with the prominence of his stomach marked and his thrown-back shoulders accentuating his natural thickness. In such a posture, his figure seems even more diminutive, reduced to a shapeless

23. Different versions of this maneuver are given by Créac'h, *Coeur et l'épée*, 181–82; and by Charles Foltz, Jr., *The Masquerade in Spain* (Boston, 1948), 178. Cf. Jorge Vigón, *Mola* (Barcelona, 1957), 252–54; and La Cierva, *Franco*, 1:512. Franco's chief juridical aide, Lt. Col. Martínez Fuset, at that time one of his most influential counsellors, has often been given credit for arranging the change. Serrano Súñer, however, declares categorically in his *Memorias*, 163–64, that the change was inspired by Alfonsine monarchist politicians, and particularly by José Yanguas Messía, a former minister of the Primo de Rivera regime. These versions need not be considered mutually exclusive.

24. The text appeared in this form in the *Boletín Oficial de la Junta de Defensa Nacional*, Sept. 30, 1956. (Hereafter cited as *BOJDN*.)

25. According to Cabanellas, *Cuatro generales*, 2:338–40.

26. So it appeared in the *Boletín Oficial del Estado*, Oct. 2, 1936.

ball. His face is round, with an incipient double-chin, his hair black, with strong and pronounced brows, his nose straight, the small moustache closely trimmed, the advancing baldness of his head pronounced. His glance, however, is keen and intelligent. On the right hand he wears a gold ring which seems to cut into the finger now grown thicker. His clothing is poorly cut, for his short sleeves are hidden from sight and the whole uniform looks too small.[27]

The investiture speech was brief and simple, though delivered with the vehemence and emotion typical of Spanish public orators of that era. Its most striking passage declared, "You are placing Spain in my hands. My hand will be firm, my pulse will not tremble, and I shall try to raise Spain to the place that corresponds to her history and her rank in earlier times."[28] That night he delivered a longer radio speech, written by his legal aide, Martínez Fuset, which declared that "Spain would be organized under a broadly totalitarian concept of unity and continuity." It promised "a regime of authority and hierarchy" that would be based on organic, corporative representation and, "without being confessional," would "respect the religion of the majority."[29] It reiterated the nationalist and populist themes of the Primo de Rivera dictatorship—to that date Franco's closest model—without specifically invoking the particular doctrines of either the monarchists, Catholics, Carlists, or Falangists, the principal civilian groups in the Nationalist zone. For the next thirty-nine years, Franco would claim that he had not sought power, but answering the call to "save Spain," had found authority thrust upon him by his colleagues. As witness to the purity of his mandate he could cite his earlier hesitation in seeking supreme power.

In this fashion a determined handful took advantage of the great need for unity among the Nationalist commanders to promote the most prestigious of the rebel generals to the position of generalissimo and chief of state as well. After the second meeting on the twenty-eighth of September, Franco had seen the green light and no longer showed the slightest reluctance about assuming supreme power, though he was very careful to spare the feelings of his colleagues. Mola doubtless had ironic thoughts about the course of events, in view of his considerable difficulty in getting Franco to rebel in the first place. Nevertheless, he gave way to Franco's

27. Cabanellas, *Cuatro generales*, 2:351. This may be compared with another hostile impression written about that time by the American journalist John Whitaker, who interviewed Franco: "Personally I found Franco shrewd but disconcertingly unimpressive. I talked with him first when he was still slender, and later after he had gone to fat. A small man, he is muscular; but his hand is soft as a woman's, and in both instances I found it damp with perspiration. Excessively shy as he fences to understand a caller, his voice is shrill and pitched on a high note, which is slightly disturbing since he speaks quietly, almost in a whisper. Although effusively flattering, he gave no frank answer to any question I put to him; I could see that he understood the implication of even the most subtle query. A less straightforward man I never met." John Whitaker, *We Cannot Escape History* (New York, 1943), 105.

28. Cabanellas, 351.

29. *FF*, 2:111–13.

elevation with good grace, readily conceding the many advantages that Franco's backers enumerated.[30] The monarchist politicians had labored to promote Franco's accession, the Falangists were without a leader, and the Carlist chief Fal Conde had been called away to Vienna by the death of the Pretender that same September 28. Both the Catholic conservative Gil Robles and the veteran Republican centrist Lerroux were supporting the Nationalists from exile,[31] but the only civilians to have had a hand in the entire maneuver were, first and foremost, Franco's brother Nicolás, and, much more secondarily, a few monarchist politicians like Sangróniz and Yanguas Messía, in or near Franco's personal entourage. It had been primarily, though not quite exclusively, a military affair.

The preferred title soon became Caudillo, a classic Castilian term for leader that dated from the Middle Ages. In the 1930s it had a fascist flavor as the Spanish equivalent of Duce or Fuehrer. Yet it possessed a freshness altogether preferable to the frank appellation Dictator sometimes employed during the Primo de Rivera regime, and even very briefly by part of the press in the Nationalist zone. The latter usage was quickly suppressed, even though the word, with its evocations of Primo de Rivera, no longer had particularly negative connotations for much of the Spanish middle classes. Franco immediately became the subject of a public litany of adulation, orchestrated by the increasingly organized and disciplined press of the Nationalist zone, that far exceeded anything ever accorded any other living figure in Spanish history. It would continue to mark public discourse for the next quarter-century, declining somewhat only in the later years of the regime.

Franco immediately replaced the Junta de Defensa with a new "Junta Técnica" composed of seven commissions to supervise state administration. Each commission had a president, who served as chief administrator, and three of these posts went to members of the Acción Española group, giving them the greatest visibility in this first phase of administration. General Fidel Dávila, one of Franco's backers and a bureaucratic-administrative officer par excellence, was made president of the Junta Técnica and also chief of the Army General Staff. He was the only member of the Junta de Defensa to have a position in the new government. Setting the first example of what became a standard practice of kicking upstairs unwanted notables, Franco made Cabanellas the inspector general of the Army, an honorific post that deprived him of both political power and active military command. He also created a General Secretariat of the Chief of State under his brother Nicolás (who served as his chief political ad-

30. According to Mola's secretary Iribarren, in an interview in Pamplona, Dec. 15, 1958.
31. In a letter to Vicente Serra of Sept. 11, 1936, Lerroux declared that Spain now needed a Roman-style legal dictatorship to save it from the Popular Front. Quoted in Armando Boaventura, *Madrid-Moscovo: Da Ditadura a Republica e a Guerra Civil de España* (Lisbon, 1937), 245–47.

visor), a Secretariat for Foreign Relations, and a General Goverment Ministry or Ministry of the Interior, which was assigned to another trusted general.[32] All this amounted to little more than an ad hoc administration for fighting a civil war, but it would serve for sixteen months until the first regular government was formed.

Franco's rule could never have succeeded had it not been immediately accepted by at least a sizable minority of the Spanish population, and indeed a majority within the original rebel zone. All Spaniards who felt threatened by the Popular Front—from upper-class monarchists to ordinary middle-class people to the smallholder peasants of the northern provinces—rallied to Franco as their leader in a desperate revolutionary struggle.

Though Franco and other rebel commanders had been careful to avoid attacking the basic principles of constitutional republicanism in the first days of the revolt, the outbreak of full revolution in the Republican zone stimulated an increasingly right-wing polarization under the Nationalist banners. By the autumn of 1936 the Nationalist zone not only had a new government but was undergoing a cultural counterrevolution of unprecedented proportions for any western country in the twentieth century. Religious revivalism was in full swing, at least on the public level, and nationalism was held to require the restoration of traditional values and attitudes on a remarkable scale. Schools and libraries were purged not only of radical but of nearly all liberal influences, and Spanish tradition was upheld as the indispensable guide to a nation that had lost its path by following the principles of the French Revolution and liberalism.

The Nationalist writer Federico de Urrutia summarized the new spirit: "This is our ultimate guideline. To be what we were before rather than the shame of what we have been recently. To kill the dead soul of the nineteenth century, liberal, decadent, Masonic, materialist, and Frenchified, and to fill ourselves once more with the spirit of the sixteenth century, imperial, heroic, sober, Castilian, spiritual, legendary, and chivalrous."[33]

The Nationalist cultural counterrevolution bred a spirit of discipline, unity, and self-sacrifice that proved highly effective militarily. It was this cultural counterrevolution, whose religious aspects will be surveyed in chapter 10, that provided the emotional and ideological underpinning of the Nationalist cause during the next two and a half years of bitter civil war.

32. Official decrees were published in the new *Boletín Oficial del Estado*, beginning on October 2, 1936. Those discussed in this work can be found in the *Boletín* (hereafter cited as BOE). The early legislation of both the Junta de Defensa and the Junta Técnica was collected in José P. San Román Colino, ed., *Legislación del Gobierno Nacional* (Avila, 1937).

33. Quoted in Refael Abella, *La vida cotidiana durante la Guerra Civil: La España nacional* (Barcelona, 1973), 109.

8

The Nationalist War
Effort

The initial odds in the Civil War scarcely favored the Nationalists. Not only had Mola's plan for a quick seizure of the capital been foiled, but the Popular Front dominated most of the larger cities, all the industrial areas, most of Spain's financial resources, most of the existing stock of military materiel, and the bulk of the Navy and Air Force. Moreover, the political militias formed by the revolutionary organizations at first considerably outnumbered the military auxiliaries of the Nationalists.

Greater parity existed in the division of regular Army forces, though exact estimates have differed considerably.[1] It will never be possible to arrive at precise totals, first of all because there are not complete records, and secondly because of the inaccuracy or misleading character of records that do exist. The Army was not at full strength when the conflict began, because of incomplete recruitment and even more because at least one-third of the nominal 180,000 troops under arms were on summer leave. As far as can be determined, existing Army forces divided about equally

1. The most careful estimates will be found in Ramon Salas Larrazábal, *Historia del Ejército Popular de la República* (Madrid, 1973), 1:181–210, and *Los datos exactos de la Guerra Civil* (Madrid, 1980), 55–94; Michael Alpert, *El Ejército Republicano en la Guerra Civil* (Barcelona, 1977), 23–37; and Ricardo de la Cierva, "The Nationalist Army in the Spanish Civil War," in R. Carr, ed., *The Spanish Republic and Civil War* (London, 1971), 188–212.

For an overview of the war, the best general account is Hugh Thomas, *The Spanish Civil War*, 2nd ed., rev. and exp. (New York, 1977). The best Spanish accounts are Ricardo de la Cierva, *Historia ilustrada de la Guerra Civil española*, 2 vols. (Barcelona, 1970), favorable to the right; and M. Tuñón de Lara et al., *La Guerra Civil española 50 anos después* (Barcelona, 1985), favorable to the left. See also Guillermo Cabanellas, *La guerra de los mil días*, 2 vols. (Buenos Aires, 1973); and Estado Mayor Central del Ejército, *Síntesis histórica de la Guerra de Liberación 1936–1939* (Madrid, 1968), a one-volume Nationalist military account.

There are a variety of memoirs by Nationalist veterans. Among the more notable are Jorge Vigón Suerodíaz, *Cuadernos de guerra y notas de paz* (Oviedo, 1970); and José Ma. Gárate Córdoba, *Mil días de fuego* (Barcelona, 1972).

Republican troops during the first months of the Civil War

between Republicans and Nationalists—around 55,000 for each side, though the actual available manpower may well have been less than that in both cases. Moreover, the Republicans retained the services of at least 60 percent of the 5,300 Air Force personnel, nearly two-thirds of the 20,000 Navy personnel (though minus many of their officers, slaughtered by crewmen in the first days), and slightly more than half of the armed police. Thus the Republican forces began with a slight numerical advantage in organized personnel, in addition to general air and naval control.

This nominal advantage was, however, soon eroded by the effects of the revolution, which was determined to destroy the remains of the regular armed forces and replace them with political militia. Thus during the first weeks of the Civil War those military units remaining in the Republican zone were progressively dissolved by the revolution until few remained. Of the slightly more than 15,000 officers in the Spanish Army in 1936, at least half found themselves in the Republican zone. Only a small minority of these rebelled during the weekend of July 18, but approximately 3,000 were purged during the next few weeks. Some 1,500 were sooner or later executed and the remainder imprisoned. Another thousand or so managed either to flee the Republican zone or find hiding within it, while approximately 3,500 served the Republican forces during the Civil War.

The result was the replacement of the regular Army in the Republican zone during late July and August with a series of revolutionary militia units and columns that relied mainly on political volunteers although integrating some loyal regular troops and police. Even those Army officers clearly loyal to the Republic were rarely trusted, and consequently the new revolutionary militia lacked training and discipline. Its military value was extremely low.[2]

Thus the first major advantage enjoyed by the Nationalists lay in superior military leadership, organization, and quality. The second lay in their complete control of the elite sector of the Spanish Army, the well-trained and equipped units, mostly of volunteers, stationed in Morocco. They numbered 47,000 on paper (33,000 Spanish, 14,000 Moroccans), but their actual effectives were probably 20 percent fewer. Though better led than the Republicans, the Nationlist forces in the peninsula were increasingly outnumbered, generally poorly armed and supplied, and at first not altogether reliable politically in some cases.

Therefore Franco's Army of Africa was the main hope for victory, but as a result of the general failure in the Navy it found itself bottled up in Morocco, unable to cross the straits. With the large cities and industrial zones largely in Republican hands, Mola lacked the strength in the north to move effectively against them. After ten days of intermittent fighting on several improvised fronts, the most important of which was the effort to advance through the mountains north of Madrid with several small columns, he was in danger of running out of ammunition. The Popular Front forces dominated the main sources of supply, and the new wartime government of José Giral, organized on July 19, immediately asked for material from the new Popular Front government of France. Aid was pledged a day later, and the pledge became public knowledge very soon afterward. By that time most foreign observers judged that the rebellion was a failure, and therefore, as J. W. D. Trythall writes, "Franco's slogan, 'Blind faith in victory,' was an apt one. Everybody with his eyes open was giving long odds against his victory."[3]

The search for foreign assistance thus assumed vital importance during the first weeks. Rightist conspirators had looked for arms and support abroad, primarily from Fascist Italy, ever since 1932, yet the old agreement between monarchists and Italian authorities signed in early 1934 subsequently became a dead letter.[4] A visit had been made by General Sanjurjo to Berlin in March 1936, apparently to seek assistance for the revolt, but at that time no effective conspiracy existed and there is no evidence that any promises or support whatever were provided by German

2. See the works by Salas Larrazábal and Alpert cited in note 1; and also Cristóbal Zaragoza, *Ejército Popular y militares de la República (1936–1939)* (Barcelona, 1983).
3. *El Caudillo* (New York, 1970), 94.
4. Coverdale, *Italian Intervention*, 43–65.

authorities. Various contacts were developed during the spring and early summer of 1936 by rightist conspirators, including agents of Mola, but these had to do with individual second-level diplomatic representatives, minor officials of the Nazi Party abroad and private German arms dealers, not with responsible authorities in Berlin.[5]

Outbreak of the Civil War surprised officials in Rome and Berlin about as much as elsewhere, but Franco dispatched his first representatives to Rome on July 19,[6] the same day that he landed in Spanish Morocco, and four days later another little delegation was sent off by air to Berlin.[7] Mola also dispatched small missions to Rome and Berlin,[8] though each arrived three days after those of Franco, which appeared in the two capitals on the twenty-second and twenty-fifth, respectively. The ambassadors of Mola, composed of monarchists associated with the earlier agreement of 1934, were influential in carrying the day in Rome, while Franco's emissaries, led by the two top Nazi leaders among the tiny German colony in Spanish Morocco, were effective in Berlin. On July 27 Mussolini decided to send 12 bombing planes and a small amount of other equipment to the rebels. On the preceding day, Hitler came independently to the same decision, agreeing to send 26 transport planes and other equipment, designed above all to move Franco's elite troops to the peninsula. Two special holding companies were created to handle shipments between the two countries.[9] On July 26 the Portuguese government of Salazar promised full cooperation with the Nationalists, covering their western border.

Even before the first foreign planes arrived, Franco initiated the first airlift in military history with several Spanish aircraft on July 20, flying small numbers of troops across the straits to Nationalist Andalusia. One small convoy managed to make the crossing on August 5, and the Republican blockade was broken altogether by the end of September. Over sev-

5. For years the standard Republican line was to inflate this into the charge that the Nationalist movement was little more than a Nazi-Fascist plot. The last nominally scholarly work to take such notions seriously was Dante A. Puzzo, *Spain and the Great Powers 1936–1941* (New York, 1962), though the significance of the early contacts was also exaggerated in Robert A. Friedlander, "The July 1936 Military Rebellion in Spain: Background and Beginnings" (Ph.D. diss. Northwestern University, 1963), 66–132. All this is placed in proper perspective in the definitive study by Angel Viñas, *La Alemania Nazi y el 18 de julio* (Madrid, 1974; rev. ed., 1977), 117–299.
6. Coverdale, *Italian Intervention*, 66–72.
7. Viñas, *Alemania Nazi*, 312–27.
8. The personal account of Mola's emissary to Berlin is given in José I. Escobar, *Así empezó* (Madrid, 1974), 57–90.
9. The principal studies of German policy in the Spanish war are Manfred Merkes, *Die deutsche Politik im spanischen Bürgerkrieg 1936–1939*, rev. and exp. ed. (Bonn, 1969), which concentrates on 1936–37; and Hans-Henning Abendroth, *Hitler in der spanischen Arena* (Paderborn, 1973). Economic policy is treated by Glenn T. Harper, *German Economic Policy in Spain During the Spanish Civil War 1936–1939* (The Hague, 1967). There are also Albert C. Horton, "Germany and the Spanish Civil War" (Ph.D. diss., Columbia University, 1964); and a major unpublished book-length study by Prof. Robert H. Whealey.

Heavily loaded troop ship carrying Franco's units across the straits from Morocco in September 1936

eral months, 24,000 of the best troops in the Spanish Army were transferred to the peninsula, where Franco began his drive to the north at the beginning of August.

Assisted by soldiers from the peninsular garrisons and thousands of Falangist and rightist volunteers, the troops moved steadily north, then northeast, toward Madrid. Time and again the Army of Africa outmaneuvered, outfought, and destroyed more-numerous Republican columns. Relying primarily on small cadres of veteran personnel, its strength was obviously quite limited and its progress less rapid than planned. One of its more resourceful commanders, Col. (later Lt. Gen.) Carlos Asensio, who took over some of the advance units on September 21, ruefully observed twenty-five years afterward: "For lack of effectives, our advance turned out to be terribly slow."[10] Armored vehicles were virtually nonexistent, and the Army of Africa often traveled on foot, though it sometimes employed trucks and buses.

It cannot be said that either Franco or Mola showed much strategic imagination. At the time that effective conjunction was made between

10. Quoted in my *Politics and the Military*, 383.

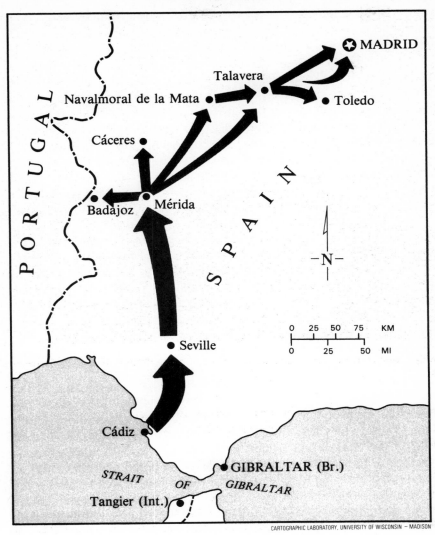

Route of the Army of Africa

the northern and southern Nationalist zones in mid-August, Mola already held a position that was only about 40 kilometers north of Madrid, yet no effort was made to transfer any of Franco's elite units northward where they might have quickly broken through to the capital. Instead, Franco continued to plod directly ahead, first occupying all of southwestern and west-central Spain, which took six weeks.

During September the Nationalist advance slowed. Republican forces were more concentrated as Franco's troops neared Madrid, while their control of the air became more effective as the fighting drew nearer their bases in central Spain, impeding daylight maneuvers by the Nationalists. Even when he got nearer Madrid in late September, Franco made no effort at a grand strike that might have quickly overcome a partially undefended city. Instead he delayed, to divert a major portion of his limited resources to relieve the Alcázar de Toledo, where 2,000 defenders had withstood an epic siege of more than two months.[11] This was typical of Franco's priorities throughout the war, determined first of all to consolidate his general position before advancing further, attuned to political and psychological symbols, and responding to major commitments of the enemy more than to a rapid and imaginative independent strategy that might have brought the conflict to an early conclusion.

It has been argued that the failure to move on Madrid as rapidly as possible at the close of September may have been Franco's major error of the war.[12] Discouragement and demoralization among the capital's Republicans was at its height at the end of summer, though whether the degree of disorientation was great enough to have allowed a very small Nationalist strike force to seize a large city in a *coup de main* can never be known. Franco had on the other hand major strategic reasons for closing his right flank before undertaking the decisive operation of the war, for even after the relief of Toledo his right flank was weakly held and for some months in danger of being turned.

At any rate, when the direct advance on Madrid was resumed in October, resistance stiffened. The first all–Popular Front government, organized the preceding month under the Socialist Largo Caballero, had begun to build a new Republican People's Army whose manpower exceeded that of the Nationalists. Major Soviet supplies arrived during October, creating a Republican armored regiment composed of Soviet tanks and crews, guaranteeing Republican air control through Soviet planes and pilots, and once more assuring overall superiority in equipment and supplies.

By that point the Spanish conflict had become an international issue of major dimensions, even though the official policy of all the powers was nonintervention. An international agreement to this effect, promoted by Britain and France, was signed by all the principal European states, though it was consistently ignored by the Soviet Union, Italy, and Germany (and occasionally later also by France). An International Non-Intervention Committee began regular meetings in London in September to supervise the agreement, and has been scored by historians ever since as a model of diplomatic insincerity and hypocrisy.[13]

11. The best description is by Cecil Eby, *The Siege of the Alcazar* (New York, 1965).
12. Cf. the remarks by Serrano Súñer in his *Memorias*, 132.
13. On international diplomacy and the Spanish war, see Norman J. Padelford, *International Law and Diplomacy in the Spanish Civil Strife* (New York, 1939); Patricia A. M. Van

The Spanish left was consistently supported militarily by the Soviet Union and only intermittently obtained assistance from France.[14] The Nationalists enjoyed solid backing from beginning to end from the right-authoritarian regime of Salazar in Portugal, which believed that its own vital interests were at stake in Spain,[15] but the major military support of the Nationalists came from Italy and Germany.

Mussolini at the very least hoped to avoid a leftist regime in the west Mediterranean and probably, more ambitiously, hoped to expand Italian power and influence.[16] Hitler's goals were more limited. He wished to defeat a leftist regime, bring a friendly movement to power, tip slightly the balance of power in the southwest, and probably most important in the later phases, distract international attention from his own actions in central Europe.[17] This did not preclude the private sale by several German firms of modest arms consignments to the Republic during the early months of the conflict. After making their decisions to intervene separately and independently, Hitler and Mussolini took the first step toward cooperation on August 4, and in fact this mutual concern initiated the relationship that became the Rome-Berlin Axis in October. There was no mention of Spain in *Mein Kampf*, and Hitler had no very clear ambitions in the Mediterranean area, which he left primarily as an area of Italian initiative. Hitler did hold a certain limited respect for Spaniards in his racial hierarchy, though he believed that their superior Germanic elements had been seriously diluted and corrupted by Moorish influence, which, together with religion, explained to Hitler the decline of Spain after the sixteenth century.[18]

Thus the first small shipments of German and Italian planes were followed during August and September by modest consignments of conventional arms, and two squadrons of light tanks were organized in conjunction with the Army of Africa. When the first large shipments of Soviet

---

der Esch, *Prelude to War* (The Hague, 1951); and William E. Watters, *An International Affair: Non-Intervention in the Spanish Civil War* (New York, 1971). The chief Spanish accounts are Pedro Schwartz, *La internacionalización de la Guerra Civil española* (Barcelona, 1971); F. V. Sevillano Carbajal, *La diplomacia mundial ante la guerra española* (Madrid, 1969); and Luis García Arias, *La política internacional en torno a la guerra de España* (Zaragoza, 1961). On the British role, see William L. Kleine-Ahlbrandt, *The Policy of Simmering: A Study of British Policy during the Spanish Civil War* (The Hague, 1962).

14. For the French connection, see David W. Pike, *Les français et la guerre d'Espagne* (Paris, 1975); and J. M. Borrás Llop, *Francia ante la Guerra Civil española* (Madrid, 1981).

15. Iva Delgado, *Portugal e a guerra civil de Espanha* (Lisbon, 1980), provides a brief account of Portuguese policy.

16. Coverdale, *Italian Intervention*, 72–84.

17. Viñas, 330–401; Merkes, *Deutsche Politik*, 20–50; Abendroth, *Hitler*, 15–73; Horton, "Germany" 24–35; and Denis Smyth, "Reflex Reaction, Germany and the Onset of the Spanish Civil War," in Preston, *Revolution and War*, 243–65.

18. To place Hitler's attitude toward Spain in the perspective of his general policy and world view, see the references to Spain in Norman Rich, *Hitler's War Aims*, 2 vols. (New York, 1973).

weapons and personnel tipped the balance by early November, Hitler decided on a counterescalation of his own, shipping a whole small German air corps, the Condor Legion of approximately 100 combat planes. It was assembled during November.[19]

By this time the shock units of the Nationalist forces were so depleted that the first direct assault on the defenses of Madrid on November 8 was made by scarcely 12,000 troops divided into several columns.[20] Fully armed militia defending the capital numbered approximately 18,000,[21] but at least as many more were rapidly being organized, and the arrival of the first Communist-organized International Brigades helped tighten the defense. These forces were now in the process of being reorganized as regular "mixed brigades" under regular army discipline. For a week, small Nationalist columns tried to ram their way across the Manzanares River into western Madrid. A major effort by Asensio on November 15 with 18 light Italian tanks (little more than armored cars) managed to place 1,500 troops on the other side of the river near the University, where they were pinned down. After November 21, the Nationalists went over to the defensive in this sector. The rebel command was momentarily shaken and Major Castejón, a badly wounded column leader, remarked despairingly to the American journalist John Whitaker, "We who made the revolt are now beaten."[22]

Three efforts to outflank the Madrid defense line to the north, made in late November, mid-December, and early January, ended in failure,[23] for the terrain northwest of Madrid—uneven, occasionally wooded, dotted with low hills and scattered villages—is not well suited to mobile warfare. The last of the attacks employed 12,000 troops, the largest single concerted Nationalist force yet committed, and was supported by German planes and artillery and Italian tankettes, but it had to be suspended on January 9. Improved equipment and organization, revitalized morale, and the advantage of numbers and interior lines enabled the new People's Army to build a successful defense. Indeed, the Nationalist line was stretched so thin by the new year that a determined counterattack by several Republican brigades might have disrupted the entire front.

19. The principal study is Raymond L. Proctor, *Hitler's Luftwaffe in the Spanish Civil War* (Westport, Conn., 1983). See also Col. Hugo Sperrle, "Die Legion Condor," in *Die Wehrmacht,* May 30, 1939; and Karl Ries and Hans Ring, *Legion Condor 1936–1939* (Mainz, 1980); Ramón Garriga, *La Legión Condor* (Madrid, 1975); Ramon Hidalgo Salazar, *La ayuda alemana a España 1936–1939* (Madrid, 1975); and, for an apologium, Wilfred von Oven, *Hitler und der spanische Burgerkrieg: Mission und Schicksal der Legion Condor* (Tübingen, 1978).

20. José Manuel Martínez Bande, *La Marcha sobre Madrid* (Madrid, 1968), 114–16.

21. Martínez Bande, "La lucha en torno a Madrid en el invierno de 1936–1937," *Revista de Historia Militar,* no. 11 (1962), 171–202.

22. Whitaker, *We Cannot Escape History,* 103.

23. Martínez Bande, *La lucha en torno a Madrid* (Madrid, 1968), 11–69.

Members of the International Brigades

Though Hitler decided on December 22 not to expand Germany's commitment any further, the Italian government was being drawn deeper into the conflict. Germany and Italy, having become allies for the first time in their Spanish intervention, had officially recognized the Nationalist regime on November 18, and Mussolini committed Fascist prestige to Franco's victory, whatever the cost. Italian air support had helped the Nationalists hold the key Balearic island of Mallorca against Catalan assault,[24] and before the close of 1936 Mussolini had decided to send Franco not only much more materiel but also a whole Italian artillery corps and several divisions of Italian troops and Fascist Party militia. These forces arrived during January and February 1937. Though Franco stubbornly defended the autonomy of his command, on January 26 he was forced to accept in principle the concept of a joint German-Italian staff of ten military advisers to help plan future operations. The system was never actu-

24. Concerning Mallorca, see Josep Massot i Muntaner, *La Guerra Civil a Mallorca* (Montserrat, 1976).

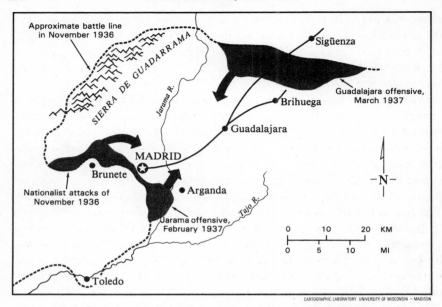

Approximate battle line
in November 1936

SIERRA DE GUADARRAMA

Jarama R.

Sigüenza

Guadalajara offensive,
March 1937

Brihuega

Guadalajara

MADRID

Brunete

Nationalist attacks of
November 1936

Arganda

Tajo R.

Jarama offensive,
February 1937

−N−

0   10   20   KM

0   5   10   MI

Toledo

CARTOGRAPHIC LABORATORY. UNIVERSITY OF WISCONSIN – MADISON

Nationalist advances in the Madrid area, November 1936–March 1937

ally implemented, yet the Italians insisted that a large part of the nearly
49,000 troops being sent to Spain would be used first in a new offensive in
the south.[25]

By early 1937 Franco had occupied nearly 60 percent of Spanish soil,
but the Popular Front forces still held slightly over half the south behind a
line running from Madrid to the east of Cordoba, curving farther east beyond Granada and then turning west of Málaga to the southern coast.
Concentrating his attention on the Madrid front and secondarily on political issues, Franco allowed regional commanders considerable autonomy,
and Queipo de Llano held the south with a motley force of second-class
troops, Civil Guard units, and Falangist militia. A convergent Spanish-
Italian operation to seal off Málaga ended with the capture of the city on
February 8.[26]

Simultaneously a new Nationalist offensive was launched on the Madrid front, this time trying to outflank the city from the south across the
Jarama river. The main assault was begun on February 6 by five reinforced brigades totaling 18,500 men, but lack of reserves made it impossible to sustain momentum. After nine days, initiative passed to the more

25. For the Italian escalation, see Coverdale, *Italian Intervention*, 153–86. About 43
percent of the Italian troops sent to Spain were regular army personnel.
26. Martínez Bande, *La campaña de Andalucía* (Madrid, 1969); and Ismael Saz and Javier Tusell, *Fascistas en España* (Madrid, 1981), 42–47.

numerous Republican forces, who also began to win temporary control of the air with further Soviet assistance. By the time that it was finally broken off near the close of February, the Jarama engagement had become the bloodiest battle thus far,[27] yet had resulted in no more than minimal success for the Nationalists.

With Franco's best forces momentarily exhausted, the Italian Corpo di Truppe Volontarie (CTV) took the main initiative early in March in the boldest move yet attempted on the Madrid front, endeavoring to strike southward from Guadalajara, northeast of the capital, to cut it off from the east. The resultant Battle of Guadalajara, perhaps the most famous single encounter of the Spanish war, began on March 8. Roads were few and poor and the weather soon turned very bad, handicapping movement. The attempted advance of a Nationalist division farther west was stopped by Russian tanks. Though the Italians gained ground, they failed to achieve a breakthrough and were met with stiff counterattacks. The struggle was broken off on March 14 far short of its major objective. Thanks to the bitter weather and the inadequacy of training, maps, equipment, air support, and leadership among the Italians, and thanks to the aggressiveness of the main new Popular Front brigades, the Republicans had won a major psychological victory.[28] This was not totally disheartening to the Nationalists, however.[29] Franco had never asked for the entry of large numbers of Italian troops and resented the independence of the Italian command.

The failure to seize Madrid during the winter of 1936–37 made it clear that a mass, twentieth-century army would have to be developed for a long war, a project on which the Largo Caballero government in the Republican zone had been embarked since the preceding October. Soon after Franco became generalissimo, his German advisers began to urge him to declare mass conscription. Because of the political unreliability of much of the population, Franco was not eager to do this. Broad conscription measures, however, had been taken by local commanders in certain areas such as Mallorca and western Andalusia, where in one of his first

27. Martínez Bande, *La lucha en torno a Madrid*, 71–111.

28. Coverdale, *Italian Intervention*, 199–260; and Coverdale's article "The Battle of Guadalajara, 8–22 March 1937," *JCH* 9:1 (1974), 53–57. See Ramón Garriga, *Guadalajara y sus consecuencias* (Madrid, 1974). Italian military activity has been treated in some detail by José Luis Alcofar Nassaes, *CTV: Los legionarios italianos en la Guerra Civil española, 1936–1939* (Barcelona, 1972); *La aviación legionaria en la guerra española* (Barcelona, 1975); and *La marina italiana en la guerra de España* (Barcelona, 1975).

29. Indeed, many Nationalists felt that the pushy, somewhat supercilious Fascists had gotten their comeuppance. Some of Franco's troops threw back the original Italian sneers about primitive Spanish transportation with the following ditty, set to the tune of a popular Italian song:

Guadalajara no es Abisinia.	Guadalajara is not Abyssinia.
Los españoles, aunque rojos,	Spaniards, even if Red,
son valientes:	are brave:
Menos camiones y más cojones.	Fewer trucks and more guts.

decrees Queipo had called up the draft quotas for the years 1931–35 inclusive.[30] The Burgos Junta had mobilized the draftees of 1935 by August, but this had brought in little more than 20,000 recruits in the northern part of the insurgent zone, which in turn led the Junta on August 26 to call up the contingents for 1931–34. When this mobilization was completed early in 1937, some 270,000 recruits had been assembled.[31] On February 22, 1937, the first quarter of the 1937 draft was summoned as well.

Though a significant minority in the Nationalist zone opposed the regime, most of the middle classes and Catholic peasantry responded effectively to the nationalist appeal. By and large, morale was good and there was widespread determination to defend religion and the national way of life against the revolution and against what was perceived to be a threat of foreign domination. In this even the aristocracy, a privileged and sometimes corrupt class, set an example, and the proportion of volunteers from the aristocracy was at least as high as from other strata of society.[32]

The social response on behalf of the counterrevolutionary cause was thus much greater in Spain than was subsequently the case in similar conflicts in less developed countries in later years. Perhaps only in Finland and the Baltic area during the civil wars of 1917–18 was there a similarly enthusiastic outpouring on the part of the more conservative population in opposition to the left. In other conflicts in the Third World or the Balkans in following decades mobilization by conservatives tended to be considerably weaker, probably because of the more limited civic development in those societies.

The military effort had depended on independent volunteering from the outset. Not only the Carlists and Falangists but most of the individual rightist groups as well organized political militia in various provinces.[33] The major exception was the pacific and legalist CEDA, which had simply fallen apart under the pressure of events. The front lines were discontinuous, and in some sectors local groups filled in the gaps under the general military command. This was especially the case in the conservative north,[34] where less than half the Nationalist manpower had consisted of regular soldiers during the first months. In Aragón, for example, the local Nationalist militia around Zaragoza and Teruel held a defensive front,

30. Queipo's decrees are collected in Julio Ramón-Laca, *Bajo la férula de Queipo* (Seville, 1939).

31. Vigón, *Mola*, 304.

32. Rafael Abella, *La vida cotidiana durante la Guerra Civil: La España nacional* (Barcelona, 1973), provides a good description of the character of the rear guard in the Nationalist zone.

33. Local groups formed during the first weeks in the Nationalist provinces bore such names as Guardias Cívicos, Caballeros de Santiago, Caballeros Patriotas, Voluntarios de España, and Caballeros de La Coruña.

34. Martínez Bande, *La guerra en el norte (hasta el 31 de marzo de 1937)* (Madrid, 1969).

stiffened by some Army troops and Civil Guard units, against as many as four times their number of Catalan revolutionary militia.[35]

For numbers of volunteers and spirit of self-sacrifice, the heroic province par excellence was Carlist Navarre. During the first week of fighting, eleven different columns (mainly of civilian volunteers) were organized in Pamplona, ranging from 200 to 2,000 men each. During the course of the Civil War, Navarre provided 11,443 volunteers for the Carlist militia, 7,068 for Falangist units, and 21,950 volunteers and recruits for the regular Army.[36] This amounted to a total of 40,461 volunteers and recruits from a provincial population of 345,883—nearly 12 percent of the population, the highest proportion in Spain. Of these, 4,552 died in combat or of wounds (the Navarrese normally forming part of the shock units), a percentage of 13.2, more than double the rate of 5.69 for all Nationalist forces.[37] On November 8, 1937, in official recognition of Navarre's remarkable contribution, Franco officially awarded the Gran Cruz Laureada de San Fernando, Spain's highest military decoration, to the province as a whole.

It is not possible to give as precise figures for the Nationalist zone as a whole as for Navarre. Certainly the largest contingent of militia were Falangists, but the statistics of more than 200,000 that have been given for Falangist volunteers probably include duplications. Falangist militiamen were often of heterogeneous background, for Falangist recruiters told former leftists and trade unionists that the best proof of their loyalty to the Nationalist cause would be to volunteer for Falangist shock battalions. The most careful study concludes that the number of Nationalist militia certainly exceeded 170,000,[38] the majority Falangists but with a wide variety of other elements also, including thousands of Carlist volunteers from provinces other than Navarre. Altogether, more than 17,000 militia were killed or died of wounds and more than 85,000 were wounded (though both these statistics may include duplications). It seems clear that more than 20 percent of the 820,000 men who served in the Nationalist Army alone (exclusive of other service arms) were provided by the political militia, who suffered a similar, possibly even greater, proportion of the casualties.[39]

Another source of manpower was Morocco, which provided nearly

35. See Martínez Bande, *La invasión de Aragón y el desembarco en Mallorca* (Madrid, 1970).

36. According to statistics compiled by Julio Aróstegui, published in Ramón Salas Larrazábal, *Cómo ganó Navarra la Gran Cruz Laureada de San Fernando* (Madrid, 1980), 26.

37. Ibid., 33.

38. The most thorough study is that of Rafael Casa de la Vega, *Las milicias nacionales*, 2 vols. (Madrid, 1977). Cf. his totals in 2:1005–8.

39. Ibid.

60,000 volunteers, mainly in 1936–37. Moreover, contrary to the indications of some Nationalist historians, Moroccan units were frequently used as shock troops and may have suffered nearly 50 percent casualties.[40]

The largest group of foreigners were the more than 70,000 Italian military personnel who served in Spain, primarily during 1937. As many as 10,000 German military personnel may have been in Spain at one time or another (two or three times the number of Soviets), but unlike the Italians, they served in advisory roles as often as in combat. European volunteers were few compared with the Communist-organized International Brigades in the Republican Army. The largest contingent came from neighboring Portugal, whose total has been estimated as high as 20,000, though the only serious study reduces the figure to less than half that.[41] The second largest group were the French, though the most loquacious were the Irish,[42] who saw very little combat.

Preparation of a large cadre of reliable officers was crucial. The first step was taken by the Burgos Junta on September 4, 1936, when it decreed organization of a series of courses in Seville and Burgos for the training of *alféreces provisionales* (provisional second lieutenants). Young men between twenty and thirty years of age, of sound political background, and possessing a professional license or the equivalent of a bachelor's degree were eligible. This meant primarily university students or graduates from the middle classes. The training of alféreces provisionales was greatly expanded in October and November, when three new schools were set up. Between the autumn of 1936 and the spring of 1937 hundreds of German military specialists and instructors were sent to the Nationalist zone to provide training.[43]

On the morrow of the stalemate at Guadalajara, the training program was brought under one chief, General Luis Orgaz. A devoted monarchist, he was also a committed *franquista* who had helped elect Franco to the *mando único*. After serving as high commissioner of the Protectorate during the autumn of 1936, he had replaced Mola as commander of the central front following the failure of the first assault on Madrid. A decree of March 25, 1937, named him "general in charge of mobilization services

40. Raymond L. Proctor, who has made the most precise study, presents a total of 62,271 Moroccan volunteers, with possibly as many as 5,000 or more killed. "The Spanish Army and the Nationalists' Moroccan Allies," *Bulletin of the Society for Spanish and Portuguese Historical Studies* 9 (Oct. 1984), 18–19.

41. Cesar Oliveira, *A consolidação do salazarismo e a guerra civil de Espanha* (Lisbon, 1987).

42. The short-lived Irish "Blueshirt" battalion produced two memoirs: Eoin O'Duffy, *Crusade in Spain* (Clonskeagh, 1938?); and Seumas MacKee, *I was a Franco Soldier* (London, 1938).

43. Oberst Freiherrn von Funck, "'Funker' and 'Drohne' hilfen Franco," *Die Wehrmacht*, May 30, 1939, is a brief contemporary German account.

and the recuperation of personnel, materiel, cattle, and automobiles, and of the preparation and instruction of officers in rearguard academies."[44] During the next two years his bureau, the MIR (Mobilization, Instruction, and Recovery), expanded the number of training schools to 22, with at least a few German advisors in almost every one. In January 1937, the age requirement for officer candidates was lowered to eighteen years, and by the end of the war the program had commissioned 29,023, while approximately 19,700 NCOs were trained in other sections. With the addition of naval and air force officers, the total came to 30,311.[45]

When the MIR began operating, the Nationalists had already drafted 350,000 recruits. In March 1937 the regime called up *reemplazos* from 1927 onward and mobilized combatworthy males in the Nationalist zone between the ages twenty-one and thirty-one. The age limit was steadily lowered until by August 9, 1938, the first trimester of 1941, made up of eighteen-year-olds, was drafted. This provided another 450,000 recruits by the beginning of 1939.[46] From start to finish, the Nationalist forces mobilized well over one million men—the greatest concentration of military manpower in Spanish history.

Only during the final year of the war did this swelling mass of manpower take full organizational form. The leaders of the Nationalist Army, from Franco, Mola, and Cabanellas on down, had gained their combat and command training in Morocco in campaigns of small engagements organized around small combat groups and mobile columns. The informal and heterogeneous character of the first months of the conflict, combined with the long distances to be covered and the noncontinuous character of the front, encouraged the continuation of ad hoc and composite combat groups and columns. From battalions and columns in 1936, the organizational structure moved into more composite brigades and larger groups in 1937, but the general conversion of the Nationalist Army to divisional structure took place only at the end of that year.

Selected elite units continued to do a disproportionate share of the fighting and suffered high losses. Among the best were the First, Fourth, and Fifth Navarrese Divisions (based originally on Carlist militia battalions), commanded by García Valiño, Alonso Vega, and J. B. Sánchez; the Twelfth, Thirteenth, and One-hundred-and-fifth Moroccan Divisions, composite groups mostly of Spanish troops led by Asensio, Barrón, and López Bravo; and the Eighty-second, Eighty-third, and Eighty-fourth

44. Quoted in Lt. Col. Fernando Gil Ossorio, "Oficiales provisionales," *Revista de Historia Militar*, no. 9 (1961), 121–45.

45. José Ma. Gárate, *Alféreces provisionales* (Madrid, 1976), 331–32.

46. "Ejército Nacional: Organización," in *Enciclopedia Universal Ilustrada, Suplemento 1936–1939*.

Galician Divisions, commanded by Delgado Serrano, Martín Alonso, and Galera.[47] Some of these suffered casualties greater than their original numbers, but replacements were fed in from the best new manpower so that their special quality as elite units would not be lost.

Probably the most important element of the new conscript army was the alféreces provisionales. Though their military training was deficient, they were enthusiasts of the Nationalist movement and of relatively advanced educational background. What they lacked in technical preparation they made up in courage and personal example. Their losses were high—approximately 3,000 were killed—which led to the phrase "alférez provisional, cadáver efectivo" ("provisional lieutenant, permanent corpse").

For ordinary recruits, basic training was brief, lasting only thirty days. By 1937 medical services were fairly well organized but living conditions remained crude. There were standard problems with lice and petty thievery. Relations between officers and men were formal and highly disciplined, and in general the recruits responded reasonably well. They appreciated the fact that their own commanders provided better preparation, organization, and leadership than existed on the Republican side.

Tactics and performance followed a fairly rigid pattern. Despite an occasional experiment in mobile warfare attempted by German advisors, the larger Nationalist units advanced in a straight line. Superior organization and leadership gave them greater cohesion than the Republicans, particularly on the offensive, though this advantage was only relative. Even in the Fourth Navarrese Division, according to one of its alféreces, some of the old-line regular officers could not read complex field maps. The Nationalist Army never became a first-rate twentieth-century military machine; it won because it held certain advantages over the less effective contingents of the Popular Front.

The Republican forces generally had the advantage of numbers and materiel throughout the first year of the Civil War, as well as that of usually acting on the defensive. Their greatest liability was failure to overcome their lack of military leadership and effective organization. In forming a new revolutionary People's Army during 1937 that used the Communist red star and clenched fist as its insignia and salute, the Popular Front passed from disorganized to organized militia but never altogether to a regular army, even though it had the look and structure of one. Units retained political identities and loyalties that were not overcome. Though the Soviet system of political commissars was introduced, this had only limited effect. Soviet advisors exercised much more influence than did

47. For sketches of Franco's leading generals during and after the Civil War, see Teresa Suero Roca, *Los generales de Franco* (Barcelona, 1975); and Carlos de Arce, *Los generales de Franco* (Barcelona, 1984).

Nationalist artillery on the Somosierra front north of Madrid, 1937

the German and Italian staffs in the Nationalist zone, and largely controlled the Republican Air Force and Navy.

By 1937 a network of espionage and guerrilla groups had been organized behind Nationalist lines by the Soviet NKVD chief Alexander Orlov, who supervised Republican intelligence and counterintelligence activities. Orlov, who had organized Red partisans during the Russian Civil War, wrote:

> The Russians regarded Spain as a testing ground for perfecting the Soviet guerrilla science accumulated since the October Revolution and for acquiring new experience. We started from scratch and within ten months [that is, by July 1937] we had 1,600 regular guerrillas trained in the six schools which I organized in and around Madrid, Valencia and Barcelona, and about 14,000 regular guerrillas, who were trained, supplied and led by our instructors on the territory of Franco, mostly in the hills from which they could descend to harass moving enemy columns, attack supply convoys and disrupt communications.[48]

Orlov's account can be misleading, however, insofar as leftist guerrilla units were rarely a major problem behind Nationalist lines, Ernest Hemingway notwithstanding. Much of the Nationalist zone was based on po-

48. Manuscript prepared by Alexander Orlov, dated April 1, 1968, in response to my questionnaire.

litically conservative territory in which leftist guerrillas did not have enough civilian support to attain maximum effectiveness. Their high point of efficiency probably came in Asturias during the fall and winter of 1937–38, when several Army divisions had to be deployed to hold them in check. Conversely, a small group of antileftist guerrillas operated among the conservative peasants of northwestern Catalonia in 1938.

Military intelligence was more effectively organized by the NKVD:

> In Spain the Soviets tested the system and methods of their military intelligence, which proved effective beyond all expectations. With the help of the Soviet long-standing network of spies in Berlin and Rome and with my own network on the territory of Franco, I was able to provide Prime Minister Negrín and his Chief of Staff Vicente Rojo with the strategic plans of the Nationalist High Command and with the *Order of battle* [italics Orlov's], before and during each important engagement with the enemy.[49]

This may or may not be an exaggeration, but in general both sides collected considerable military intelligence concerning the other's plans and development.[50] The Nationalists had many sympathizers in the Republican zone, and a number of the professional officers who remained in Republican service turned out to be disloyal. In general, however, Nationalist intelligence was apparently the less thorough of the two, for the major Republican offensives of 1937–38 all came as at least partial surprises to the Nationalist command.

Following the Republic's successful defense of Madrid in the fall and winter of 1936–37, the Spanish conflict had become a fully mobilized modern war of partially international dimensions. After Guadalajara, Franco made his most astute strategic decision of the war when he accepted the vigorous argument of his capable chief of staff, the monarchist general Juan Vigón, who urged him to give up attempting to seize Madrid directly and instead launch a major offensive to eliminate the northern zone of Republican territory—Vizcaya, Santander, and Asturias. For nine months, weak Nationalist forces had manned the irregular lines holding this northern sector in isolation.[51] Containing most of Spain's heavy industry, it was a valuable prize in a longer war of attrition. It was also an easier target than the central Republican zone, while its conquest could decisively swing the balance of power.

By that point, Franco had also come to the conviction that a rapid victory might no longer be desirable, because of the enormous problems of

49. Ibid.
50. On the Nationalist intelligence services, there are Armando Paz, *Los servicios de espionaje en la Guerra Civil española (1936–1939)* (Madrid, 1976); D. Pastor Petit, *Espionaje (España 1936–1939)* (Barcelona, 1977) and *Los dossiers secretos de la Guerra Civil* (Barcelona, 1978); and José Bertrán y Musitu, *Experiencias de los Servicios de Información del Nordeste de España (S.I.F.N.E.) durante la guerra* (Madrid, 1940).
51. Martínez Bande, *La guerra en el norte (hasta el 31 de marzo de 1937)* (Madrid, 1969).

purging and consolidating politically each conquered province. As he explained at some length to the Italian ambassador, Roberto Cantalupo, he planned to proceed methodically step by step, adding victory to victory, consolidating each position before moving on[52]—a policy typical of his *hábil prudencia*.

Mola, commander of the Army of the North, was given direction of the campaign. His removal as head of the assault on Madrid in late autumn had led to hard feelings, but he devoted himself to military affairs, stayed out of politics, and in the spring of 1937 returned to the center of action. For the first time the Nationalists were able to muster a slight superiority in manpower, as they attacked each of the three northern Republican districts separately and in isolation, moving from east to west. A force of 50,000 of the best Nationalist troops (organized around the four reinforced Navarrese brigades) was supported by 50 batteries of artillery, most of which was Italian, and by the bulk of the German and Italian aircraft. This gave the Nationalists a decisive advantage in technology and firepower. Amid bad weather in April and May, they advanced slowly but steadily against the outgunned Basque defenders of Vizcaya.[53]

During this campaign there occurred the most famous single incident of the Spanish Civil War, the bombing of the small Basque city and foral center of Guernica on April 26. In the wake of the attack, the greater part of the city (some 70 percent of the buildings) burned and several hundred people died. In 1937 Guernica was a small industrial center of slightly more than 4,000, famous for having been at one time the seat of the province's provincial assembly. An enormous propaganda campaign developed, partly originated by the British correspondent Geoffrey Speer[54] and soon expanded worldwide by the propaganda facilities of the Republic, the Third International, and their sympathizers. According to the ensuing legend, Guernica was a peaceful civilian center without any value as a military target, and bombed on a market day when its population was swollen by country people. Moreover, the attack was presented as a deliberate experiment in massive terror-bombing by the leaders of the German Condor Legion. The subsequent painting by Picasso may have contributed more than any other single factor in making the incident world famous.

All details of the Guernica operation will never be fully clarified, but the fundamental facts have been established by consulting surviving German and Italian records and by direct inquiry into the military situation of Guernica and the Basque front at that time. By April 26, the main Basque defense line to the east had been turned, and Guernica marked one of the

52. Roberto Cantalupo, *Embajada en España* (Barcelona, 1951), 190–95.
53. Martínez Bande, *Vizcaya* (Madrid, 1971), 11–148.
54. Geoffrey Speer, *The Tree of Gernika* (London, 1938).

The town of Guernica after the bombing, 1937

two principal routes of retreat toward Bilbao. The city was a district communications center, and contained three military barracks and four small arms factories. The bombing of cities had been made routine practice during the first week of the Civil War by the Republicans, who on several occasions early in the conflict boasted of the damage done to Nationalist-held cities. There is no evidence of any special experiment or massive terror-bombing. Guernica was a routine target of particular importance because of the circumstances of April 26, but it received no special treatment. Though the chief objectives were the nearby bridge and other transportation and communication facilities, many incendiary bombs were also dropped on the town itself, with the aim of destroying much of the city to block retreat of Basque troops through it. The assault was carried out by 3 Italian medium bombers that dropped almost 2 tons of bombs and by 21 German medium bombers (18 of which were obsolescent Ju-52s) that discharged a maximum of 30 tons. This amounted to no more than a third of the effectives of the Condor Legion, and only one bombing run was made. The bridge remained intact, but many bombs fell within the city, where flames spread rapidly because of the extent of wooden construction, the narrowness of the streets, the loss of water pressure, and the lack of fire-fighting equipment.[55]

The destruction of Guernica was an immediate embarrassment to Franco and his new government. Rather than admitting the facts and placing them in the full perspective of the war, Nationalist authorities denied any responsibility whatever and charged that the burning of the city was a deliberate act of leftist arson. This fabrication, once adopted as an official position, was persistently maintained almost to the end of the regime, and is an excellent example of the way in which fundamental facts of the Civil War were obscured by the propaganda inventions of both sides.[56]

Moreover, Mola failed to exploit adequately the breakthrough in the Vizcayan front during the last days of April. The Basques managed to restore a shorter defensive line during May, and the Nationalist offensive slowed. On June 3, Mola left Burgos by plane for a routine report to Franco's headquarters in Salamanca. Shortly after taking off, his plane crashed against a mountain, killing all aboard. Rumors immediately began to circulate that certain agents, working for either the Germans or Franco, had sabotaged the plane to get rid of Mola. The German ambassador wrote that Franco was "undoubtedly relieved by the death of Mola."[57] Certainly the sudden demise of the principal architect of the Nationalist conspiracy, an influential general both anti-Falangist and anti-monarchist, eased the Generalissimo's political problems, yet neither Mola's widow nor his personal secretary ever found any evidence of sabotage,[58] and as far as can be determined the crash was the result of mechanical or operational accident. The manuscript that Mola had been preparing about the conspiracy and the beginning of the Civil War was quickly confiscated, however,[59] and Franco, who had made a number of hazardous trips by plane during the preceding year, stopped flying altogether. The fate of

55. The most accurate and informative study is Jesús Salas Larrazábal, *Guernica: El bombardeo* (Madrid, 1981). See also Klaus A. Maier, *Guernica, 26. 4. 1937: Die deutsche Intervention in Spanien und der "Fall Guernica"* (Freiburg, 1975); and Angel Viñas, "Guernica: Las Responsabilidades," *Historia 16*, no. 25 (May 1978), 127–43, reprinted in Viñas's *Guerra, dinero, dictadura* (Madrid, 1984), 98–140.

The Guernica raid may be compared with the most extensive series of bombardments conducted by Franco's forces, aimed at Barcelona. See J. Villarroya i Font, *Els bombardeigs de Barcelona durant la guerra civil (1936–1939)* (Barcelona, 1981).

56. The propaganda surrounding this incident is documented in detail in Herbert R. Southworth, *Guernica! Guernica!* (Berkeley, 1977).

57. *Documents on German Foreign Policy, 1918–1945* ser. D (Washington, D.C., 1950), vol. 3, no. 361, p. 410.

58. According to Mola's secretary, José María Iribarren, in conversation with the author in Pamplona, December 1958. The text of the "Extracto de las Diligencias Instruidas" for the investigation of Mola's death reveals nothing special.

59. Again according to Iribarren. Cf. Bravo Morata, *Franco y los muertos providenciales*, 149–81.

Sanjurjo and Mola was sufficient to ground him for the remaining thirty-eight years of his long life. Mola was succeeded by Fidel Dávila, a loyal *franquista* from the first moment and a man more used to the desk than the battlefield, unlikely to create friction in the high command.

After the weather cleared in June, a week of hard fighting sufficed for the occupation of Bilbao, precipitating the collapse of the remainder of the Republican resistance in Vizcaya.[60] All the while, however, the main part of the People's Army was building up a preponderance of force. Organizational deficiencies prevented it from launching the first major Republican offensive of the war in time to relieve the pressure against Vizcaya, but on July 6 more than 60,000 of the best-trained and equipped troops in the People's Army, supported by nearly 100 Soviet tanks and sizable air units, began an assault fifteen miles northwest of Madrid, near the town of Brunete. It achieved complete tactical surprise, punching a hole through the thinly held Nationalist line almost immediately. Failure to exploit this initial success decisively revealed the limitations of the central sector of the new People's Army. There were few roads, communications became snarled, and the attacking units failed to keep moving. Field officers let their forces be tied down in frontal attacks or sieges of a handful of fixed positions where the Nationalists had dug themselves in. After the first day, a cautious and uncertain Republican command halted the advance. Nationalists hurried reinforcements in from the north and other areas and their week-long counteroffensive then regained most of the ground lost,[61] leaving some of the best People's Army units dispirited and exhausted. The People's Army chief of staff, Vicente Rojo, has suggested that a major Nationalist assault against Madrid at that time might have brought the war to a speedy conclusion.[62]

Such a risky (and imaginative) undertaking would have been contrary to Franco's cautious, methodical nature. A new setback around Madrid might have had serious psychological and political consequences. After a five-week delay, the offensive in the north was resumed. Santander fell in August, and the Republican sector of Asturias was occupied in September and October.[63] Though hundreds of leftist guerrilleros remained in the hills, delaying redeployment of the Nationalist forces for a month or more, the northern zone had been completely conquered, and the balance of power in Spain now swung decisively in favor of Franco. This crucial campaign would later be remembered with nostalgia by senior of-

60. Martínez Bande, *Vizcaya*, 149–220.
61. Martínez Bande, *La ofensiva sobre Segovia y la batalla de Brunete* (Madrid, 1972); and Rafael Casas de la Vega, *Brunete* (Madrid, 1969).
62. Vicente Rojo, *España heroica* (Buenos Aires, 1942), 111. Col. Segismundo Casado, the last Republican commander of Madrid, concurred (in conversation with the author in Madrid, February 1963).
63. Martínez Bande, *El final del Frente Norte* (Madrid, 1972).

ficers of the Nationalist Army because of the respect felt for the Basques and the comparatively smooth relations maintained within the Nationalist forces. The Army held key advantages and once more demonstrated its offensive superiority. Though casualties were rather heavy,[64] in this campaign the Republican forces lost 100,000 in prisoners alone. The northern provinces had provided the highest rate of volunteers and some of the best soldiers for the People's Army, and their loss would never be made good.

Meanwhile, the People's Army command tried another strategic diversion, this time in the northeast on the Aragón front. Commentators have criticized the Republican command for commencing a major operation in a mountainous area so near the main axis of Franco's strength in the north central region of Spain. For political and logistical reasons, however, Republican strategy was based on concentration near the major population centers, and in the Zaragoza sector "many soldiers" had deserted the Nationalists during the first months, leading the Republican staff to consider this a weak point. On August 24, eight columns totaling at least 80,000 troops struck the irregular Nationalist line north and south of Zaragoza and on both sides of the Ebro River. Initial gains were made in the Belchite sector to the south, but in many ways the battle of Belchite was a repetition of Brunete and was even less effective as a strategic diversion. It constituted the Nationalists' most remarkable defensive action in the face of a major Republican offensive, for the disproportion of attackers to attacked was even greater than at Brunete. Half the Nationalist battalion bearing the brunt of the assault was wiped out and all its officers and sergeants killed, but no breakthrough occurred. Only one major Nationalist unit was detached from the northern campaign, and by the end of September part of the small strip of territory lost to the People's Army had been recaptured.[65]

Even more important, the war of logistics and supply shifted decisively in favor of the Nationalists during the last months of 1937, as a result of the almost complete success of Nationalist naval warfare, strongly supported by Italy. Nothing better illustrated the greater aggressiveness and superior military leadership of the Nationalist forces than did the war at sea. Despite the naval superiority originally held by the Republicans, Franco had decided immediately after his assumption of the *mando único* in October 1936 to attack Republican shipping whenever possible. Though at first he lacked the means to do so effectively, the naval offensive that began in August 1937 with the active participation of Italy's Mediterranean fleet (mainly submarines) proved devastatingly effective. In the face of this ruthless campaign waged in defiance of international law, the So-

64. The *Enciclopedia Universal Ilustrada* states that approximately 7,000 died of wounds.
65. Martínez Bande, *La gran ofensiva sobre Zaragoza* (Madrid, 1973).

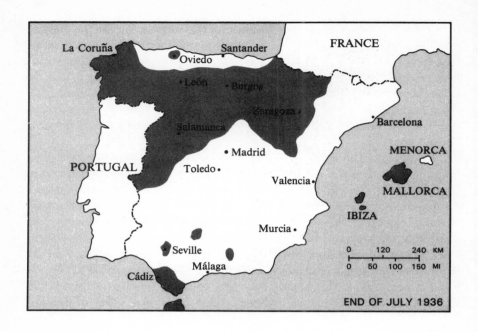

END OF JULY 1936

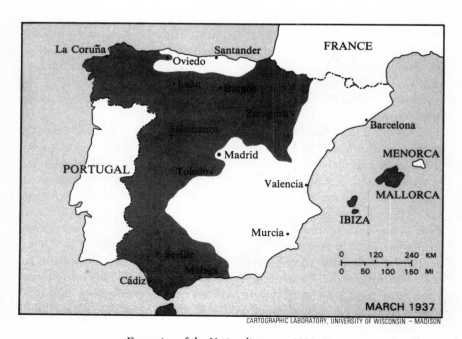

MARCH 1937

Expansion of the Nationalist zone, 1936–39

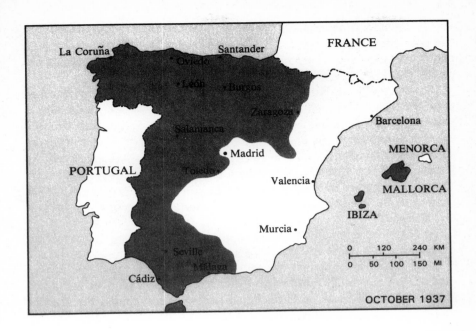

OCTOBER 1937

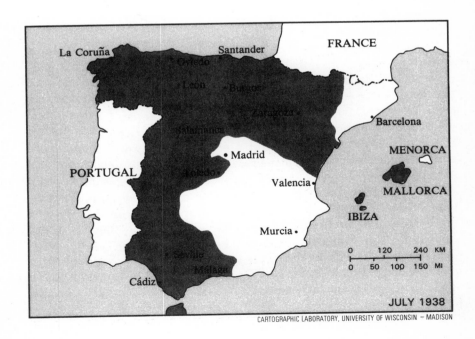

JULY 1938

CARTOGRAPHIC LABORATORY, UNIVERSITY OF WISCONSIN – MADISON

viet Union largely abandoned the direct Mediterranean route to Republican ports after September 1937. The replacement route to French ports, requiring transhipment across France, was much more uncertain and impeded the flow of Republican supplies.

By late 1937 both Hitler and Stalin became somewhat more detached from the Spanish struggle. The Soviet regime began to reduce the flow of materiel to the Republic, doubting the prospect of victory and the utility of maintaining its previously high commitment, while Hitler observed to his military advisors on November 5 that "a 100 percent victory for Franco" was not desirable "from the German point of view." Germany's "interest lay rather in a continuance of the war and the keeping up of the tension in the Mediterranean" to distract international concern from central Europe.[66]

Yet the existing level of German support was maintained, and after the conquest of the north and the restriction of Republican supplies the war became distinctly easier for the Nationalist command, now able to concentrate on one single continuous front. Franco had well over half a million troops under arms, and this figure was swelling rapidly. For the first time he was near overall parity of numbers and, thanks to continued Italian and German aid, had the benefit of an increasing superiority in materiel. Republican casualties during the past year, by comparison, had been heavy. According to one source, the People's Army counted 49,000 dead and some 200,000 wounded during 1937,[67] in addition to losing more than 100,000 men as prisoners.

Nevertheless, the Republican command believed that it could not afford to relinquish the initiative. Learning that Franco planned a major new offensive in the Guadalajara region for early winter, the leaders of the People's Army chose to forestall it with a preemptive move of their own. Nearly 100,000 troops were assembled for the largest Republican effort of the war, though only 40,000 were committed to the first phase of a new offensive east of Guadalajara. Here the front turned sharply north at right angles near the provincial mountain capital of Teruel, in Nationalist hands since the beginning of the war. Once more the first assault achieved surprise, breaking through to a depth of 10 kilometers in twelve hours before losing steam. German and Italian advisers urged Franco not to be dissuaded, but to withdraw to a more easily defended line in Aragon so that the main Nationalist forces could proceed with their new Guadalajara offensive. The Generalissimo, however, remained acutely sensitive to political and psychological factors of prestige. He felt it dangerous to concede the Republicans the smallest territorial gain and therefore canceled

66. *Documents on German Foreign Policy*, 4:37.
67. According to the Republican military psychiatrist Emilio Mira, in his *Psychiatry in War* (New York, 1943), 73.

his own plans, ordering preparations for an all-out counteroffensive. Bitter sub-zero weather, by far the coldest encountered in major operations during the Civil War, impeded realignment, and the Teruel garrison finally surrendered on January 7 after suffering more than 75 percent casualties. This was the first and only time that a Republican offensive managed to conquer a provincial capital. Franco, meanwhile, was roundly criticized by the Italians for "indecisiveness."[68] His counteroffensive could not begin until the weather improved on January 17, but when it did it made steady progress, exhausting the last Republican reserves. With complete air control and superiority in artillery, the Nationalists finally retook Teruel on February 22 in what was proportionately the bloodiest campaign of the war.[69] Coming after the heavy losses of 1937, it seemed to weaken the People's Army almost beyond repair.[70]

The corner of the Nationalist line southeast of Zaragoza lay less than 100 kilometers from the Mediterranean. With his main forces concentrated in this area, Franco decided to undertake a two-pronged advance east and southeast to cut the Republican zone in two. Weak and exhausted People's Army units collapsed before the offensive that began on March 7, and major breakthroughs were made at every point of advance. German and Italian armor, supplemented by captured Soviet vehicles, totaled nearly 200 tanks, yet this was not blitzkrieg, for small armored units were used mostly in conjunction with the infantry and hardly at all as independent offensive force. At some points the Republicans were scarcely fighting back; a few of the best Nationalist divisions were semimotorized and in one area advanced nearly 100 kilometers in eight days. When they stopped to regroup after twelve days, the main assault forces had suffered only one percent casualties.[71] Lérida, the first Catalan provincial capital to fall, was taken early in April, while an even more powerful attack was launched in the southern part of the Aragón front. Its objective was the sea, and despite having to traverse rugged terrain, the troops made steady progress. On Good Friday, April 15, the Fourth Navarrese Division occupied the seaside town of Viñaroz, slicing the Republican zone in two.

68. Count Ciano, the Italian foreign minister, noted in his diary on December 20, 1937: "Our commanders are restless, quite rightly. Franco has no idea of synthesis in war. His operations are those of a magnificent battalion commander. His objective is always ground, never the enemy. And he doesn't realize that it is by destruction of the enemy that you win a war." *Ciano's Diary, 1937–1938* (London, 1952), 46.

69. The best general studies of this major battle are Martínez Bande, *La batalla de Teruel* (Madrid, 1974); and Rafael Casas de la Vega, *Teruel* (Barcelona, 1973) and *Alfambra: La reconquista de Teruel* (Barcelona, 1976).

70. The Nationalists took 17,000 more prisoners during January and February and claim to have buried 14,000 enemy corpses during this period, according to Manuel Aznar, *Historia militar de la guerra de España* (Madrid, 1958), 2:422.

71. According to Gen. Antonio Aranda, "La guerra en Asturias," in *La guerra de liberación española* (Zaragoza, 1961).

Nationalist infantry from one of the elite Tercio units on the assault in Aragon, 1938

Within four days Franco's forces had opened a wedge to the sea that was 70 kilometers long.[72]

While excitement over a possible sudden end to the war mounted among the Nationalists, Franco made another questionable decision. Though his leadership was firm and obviously successful—his forces were never clearly defeated in a major engagement—some of his major strategic choices during the war have been questioned, with his conduct in 1938 probably the most criticized. In April 1938 the collapse of Republican strength in the northeast opened the way for a rapid occupation of Catalonia and the seizure of Barcelona, the current Republican capital, bringing total control of the border with France. It has sometimes been said in Franco's defense that he feared the reaction of France if Nationalist forces, drawing on German and Italian assistance, took over the entire French border area during the tense pre-Munich spring of 1938, while years later Franco alleged that the Nationalist zone at that point would have benefited more from the incorporation of Valencia than Barcelona (although he failed to accomplish this).[73] Moreover, there is indirect in-

72. Martínez Bande, *La llegada al mar* (Madrid, 1975).
73. On March 2, 1957, he told his cousin Salgado Araujo that he preferred to conquer Valencia because its citrus production would provide badly needed foreign exchange, whereas in the case of Barcelona he lacked the means at that point to import the cotton necessary to maintain its textile industry. *Conversaciones privadas*, 202.

dication in German sources that Hitler himself may have discouraged Franco from the immediate occupation of Catalonia, preferring to drag out the war in Spain to distract Mussolini and others, maintain French anxiety and continue Franco's dependence on Germany, though available evidence is inconclusive. At any rate, Franco renounced the major triumph that lay within his grasp, and concentrated strength for an advance southward toward Valencia, whose capture would begin to seal off the largest remaining Republican zone. Here, however, the two prongs of advance had to move along a narrow coastal road and through rugged hilly terrain southeast of Teruel. Progress was slow and the advance had to be temporarily halted in June, but the Nationalist confidence was so great that the government's newly organized tourist bureau announced a series of motor tours to former battlefields beginning on July 1. The renewed offensive against Valencia made slow but steady progress until July 25,[74] when it was broken off to repel a sudden Republican counteroffensive in Catalonia.

The reconstitution of the People's Army in Catalonia during the late spring and early summer of 1938 ranks as one of the major achievements of the Republican war effort. It was facilitated by major new military shipments from the Soviet Union and France. The new Republican Army of the Ebro, composed of three reorganized corps, attacked across the bend of the Ebro river about 20 kilometers north of Tortosa in the early hours of July 25. The main assault by pontoon crossing came as a partial surprise, and within little more than 24 hours the Republicans occupied a bulge southwest of the river about 20 kilometers long and 15 kilometers deep. As in earlier offensives, the People's Army proved incapable of exploiting its advantage fully, and the Nationalists soon stabilized their line about 15 kilometers west of the bend in the Ebro.[75]

Tension already existed at Franco's headquarters, caused by the resentment of a number of his top generals at the unimaginative and plodding frontal assault against the defenses of Valencia. The Republicans' Ebro offensive did relieve the pressure in the south, for Franco once more decided to abandon his own objectives and switch to a battlefield chosen by the enemy. Popular Front propagandists loudly proclaimed that the Ebro effort was an all-out offensive designed to break the enemy, and Franco apparently felt that for political and psychological reasons he could not afford to let the Republicans retain the ground they had won. Though a counteroffensive would have been easier in the north Catalan zone, Franco transferred the bulk of his artillery and aircraft to the Ebro, gradually building up decisive superiority in firepower. The Republican units had

74. Martínez Bande, *La ofensiva sobre Valencia* (Madrid, 1977); Aznar, *Historia militar*, 3:120–69; Lojendio, *Operaciones militares*, 491–526.

75. The best Nationalist accounts are Luis Ma. Mezquida y Gené, *La batalla del Ebro*, 3 vols. (Madrid, 1963–70); and Martínez Bande, *La batalla del Ebro* (Madrid, 1978).

little opportunity to fortify their new line, but in the words of a leading Nationalist general, tried to hold on from "newly improvised positions, which they defended primarily with hand grenades and antiquated machine guns."[76]

Though local Nationalist counterattacks began in August, it took at least six weeks to complete the full buildup, and even after that the advance was slow. Kindelán has written that this sluggishness was due to the "depressive effect that the Red offensive had on our troops and some of their commanders, producing temperamental aberrations . . . , logistical errors, and exaggerated meticulousness in preparing the operations."[77] Moreover, the losses of two years of fighting and the problems of staffing a mass army had lowered the quality of Nationalist field officers. In the early phases of the Ebro struggle, "the deficient quality of officers at battalion and company level was evident. . . . Exaggerating a bit, it could be said that every intermediate-level [professional] infantry officer with field experience had died by the end of the second year of the war."[78] The artillery was similarly affected, for despite comparatively light losses, batteries that could once have been moved in four hours now required twelve hours to change positions.[79] The slowing down of Nationalist operations especially infuriated Mussolini, who on August 24 "used violent language" in blaming Franco for "letting the victory slip" when it was "already in his grasp."[80] Some of Franco's own commanders apparently felt the same way and the Nationalist leadership probably suffered more from internal tension during the late summer of 1938 than at any other point in the war.

The main phase of the Nationalist counteroffensive began on September 3. It was supported by more than 300 cannon on a 10-kilometer front that mounted the most sustained artillery barrage of either side during the conflict.[81] Yet even Franco became uneasy at the slow pace of advance at a time when international tension in Europe was mounting. The tension was temporarily relieved after the British and French capitulation at Munich late in the month, but in the final week of October Franco moved his headquarters uncommonly close to the front and evidently demanded more action from his corps commanders.[82] By November 16 his objective had been achieved and all the ground west of the Ebro reconquered. The

76. Lt. Gen. Carlos Martínez de Campos, *Dos batallas de la Guerra de Liberación de España* (Madrid, n.d.), 32.

77. Kindelán, *Mis cuadernos*, 148.

78. Ibid., 163.

79. Ibid.

80. Ciano, *Diary*, 146.

81. Maj. Ignacio Moyano, "De la batalla del Ebro: La acción de la Artillería," *Ejército*, no. 23 (December 1941), 18–27.

82. Martínez de Campos, *Dos batallas*, 33.

duration of the Ebro campaign did encourage a new scheme for arbitration of the conflict that attempted to make use of the good offices of the Vatican and of the monarchy,[83] but in the end the complete victory won by Franco strengthened his hand against any political concessions.

Nationalist casualties may have exceeded those of the enemy,[84] although the Republicans lost another 20,000 troops as prisoners. But the Nationalist forces suffered only moderate structural damage save among the Navarrese divisions, while the Republicans would be unable to make good their losses. A comparison of the sources of manpower of the opposing armies was made by checking the ages of 11,831 prisoners taken by Yagüe's corps. Only 47 percent of these came from the age groups being drafted for the Nationalist forces: 10 percent were younger and 43 percent were older men.[85] When the Nationalist offensive was resumed in Catalonia in December, there was no stopping it. By February 1939 all northeastern Spain was occupied,[86] while a Republican diversion on the Andalusian front was effectively contained. Final victory was in sight.

The final month of the war was anticlimactic militarily. On March 4 the Republican military command in Madrid, strongly supported by Anarchists and some Socialists, openly rebelled against the government of Republican prime minister Juan Negrín, which it denounced as a mask for Communist domination. Ironically, the Spanish Civil War thus ended as it had begun, with one portion of the Republican Army rebelling against the current Republican government on the grounds that it was being dominated by foreign Communist influence, an allegation much more nearly correct in 1939 than in 1936. A mini–civil war in the Madrid area between Communists and anti-Communists was then won by the latter, and on March 17 the revolutionary red star was officially eliminated as the insignia of the Republican People's Army. The new leadership in Madrid hoped that it would be possible for a new anti-Communist government led by professional military officers to make a reasonable peace with Franco. Such was not the case. The Nationalist Caudillo had always insisted on unconditional surrender, and on March 26 launched the final "Ofensiva de la Victoria," which encountered almost no resistance. The last Republican units surrendered in Alicante on April 1, bringing an offi-

83. On these murky maneuvers, see Antonio Marquina Barrio, "Primero la victoria, luego el rey," *Historia 16* 4:35 (March 1979), 23–36.

84. Though earlier Nationalist sources listed lower figures, Salas Larrazábal states that the Nationalists lost nearly 6,500 dead at the Ebro. *Ejército Popular*, 2:2021–22.

85. Aznar, *Historia militar*, 3:264. By the beginning of 1939 the People's Army had mobilized a total of 916,677 men from a steadily shrinking population base, according to copies of People's Army reports in Moscow, cited in the Soviet Army General Staff's *Katalonskaya operatsiya* (Moscow, 1940), 19. Salas Larrazábal, *Ejército Popular*, insists on an even larger figure.

86. Martínez Bande, *La conquista de Cataluña* (Madrid, 1979).

cial announcement from Franco (ill at the moment with high fever from a flu) that the war had ended.[87]

Franco's decisive contributions to winning complete victory lay not in any remarkable aspect of his strategy but in his shrewd administration of each major area of government: military, political, and diplomatic. In Paul Johnson's words, he maintained "a cold heart and a cool head,"[88] prudently developing and concentrating military resources for total victory. Equally important was his maintenance of political unity—in contrast to the disunity and conflict among Republicans—while his deft management of relations with Germany and Italy guaranteed adequate materiel for his troops without seriously compromising his government's independence. Taken as a whole, this was a remarkable performance and not one performed by a rear-guard general, for Franco frequently inspected his battlefronts near the firing line.

Militarily, the Nationalist Caudillo was "no genius but very thorough and calm; he never reinforced failure and he learnt from mistakes."[89] He devoted considerable attention to practical matters such as training, logistics, supply, communications, and the use of topography. Thanks to its professional leadership and organization, the Nationalist Army maintained superior operational efficiency throughout. Franco was able to move major units and respond to enemy attacks much more rapidly than the Republicans. Quiet fronts were defended with minimal contingents, while the main striking power was concentrated for offensive action. In contrast, Republican political and regional division tied down large reserves on inactive fronts even when they were vitally needed elsewhere. Moreover, though the war was ultimately won because of superior offensive strength and cohesion, it should not be forgotten that the stoutest defensive battles were also those waged by the Nationalists. The defense of the Alcázar de Toledo and the less heralded but longer siege of a small group of Civil Guards and volunteers at the sanctuary of Santa María de la Cabeza in Jaén[90] were epics of determination. Though the Popular Front forces also achieved high morale and firm discipline at times, their tone inevitably sagged under constant defeat. The Republican chief of staff, Vicente Rojo, refused to return to the main Republican zone after the conquest of Catalonia. Several months later, writing in disgust at the disunity in Popular Front ranks, he stated categorically, "In the social and

87. There are numerous accounts of the last phase of the war. The most recent synthesis, written from a moderate Nationalist viewpoint, is Servicio Histórico Militar, *El final de la Guerra Civil* (Madrid, 1985). Ironically, this final month of victory also produced perhaps the greatest individual Nationalist disaster of the conflict, the sinking of the troopship *Castillo de Olite* off Cartagena, resulting in 1,200 deaths.

88. Paul Johnson, *Modern Times* (New York, 1983), 331.

89. Ibid.

90. There is a description in Julio de Urrutia Echaniz, *El cerro de los héroes* (Madrid, 1965).

human order, Franco has triumphed . . . for he has achieved moral superiority at home and abroad."[91]

Whereas the Popular Front forces began with superiority on land only in numbers and materiel but not in leadership and combat quality, they had categorical superiority in the air[92] and at sea.[93] This advantage was wasted by timidity and ineptitude. The initial blockade of Morocco, partially broken by Franco on August 5, 1936, was voluntarily withdrawn by Republican authorities near the end of the following month. Because of defection or murder of most of the officers, the majority of Republican warships lacked combat effectiveness. Similarly, the Republican air force pursued unproductive tactics, squandering its initial superiority. From late 1936 to late 1938 the fleet and the main part of the air force were under the direct control of Soviet advisors who imposed the cautious defensive strategy then in vogue in the Soviet naval and air forces. Thus the Nationalists soon came to dominate both the air and the ocean, thanks in part to the more aggressive tactics of German and Italian units assisting them and the open intervention of the Italian navy in the Mediterranean in 1937–38. Though the British Navy eventually acted to protect neutral shipping part of the time, the major role played by Franco's foreign allies, combined with the sinking of a large number of non-Spanish vessels, underscored the extent to which the Nationalists and their Axis associates were willing to violate international law at sea.

The war at sea thus ultimately became as great a disaster for the Popular Front as the war on the land. Both Republicans and Nationalists began with one battleship each, though the former had three cruisers compared with one for the latter. At the end of the war both had three. The Republicans began with a 10 to 1 advantage in destroyers and 12 to 0 advantage in submarines. At the conclusion the ratios were 9 to 5 and 6 to 3, respec-

91. Vicente Rojo, *¡Alerta los pueblos!* (Buenos Aires, 1939), 274–75.

92. The chief studies of the air war in Spain are Salvador Rello, *La aviación en la guerra de España*, 4 vols. (Madrid, 1969–72); and Jesús Salas Larrazábal, *La guerra de España desde el aire* (Madrid, 1969). See also the works on the German Condor Legion and the Italian aviation cited earlier.

93. The best study of the maritime aspects of the war will be found in an article by Willard C. Frank, Jr., "Naval Operations in the Spanish Civil War, 1936–1939," *Naval War College Review* 37:1 (Jan.–Feb. 1984), 24–55, which provides an excellent synthesis combined with judicious global statistics. See also Adm. Juan Cervera Valderrama, the Nationalist naval chief of staff, *Memorias de guerra* (Madrid, 1968); Francisco Moreno, *La guerra en el mar* (Barcelona, 1959); Rafael González Echegaray, *La marina mercante y el tráfico marítimo* (Madrid, 1977); and Ricardo Cerezo Martínez, *Armada española siglo XX* (Madrid, 1983), vol. 3. In "La estrategia naval en la Guerra Civil Española," *Revista de Historia Naval* 2:6 (1984), 5–24, Cerezo divides Nationalist naval strategy into three main phases: the first defensive phase of July 19 to September 29, 1936, in which the Nationalists dominated only the Bay of Biscay; a second phase of equilibrium from September 1936 to October 1937, in which the Nationalists controlled both the north and the Straits of Gibraltar, with the Republican fleet controlling the Mediterranean coast; and the final phase from October 1937 on, in which the Nationalists and their allies maintained the offensive, partially blockading the Republican Mediterranean coast as well.

tively. The most thorough and objective study concludes that the Republicans lost 554 ships of all types, 144 of them to Italian and German (primarily Italian) action, and that 106 foreign ships bearing Republican supplies were also sunk, 75 of them by Italian and German action. By contrast the Nationalists lost only 31 ships of all types, 9 of which were apparently sunk by Soviet action.[94]

Thus in the long run Franco was more fully supplied by his German and Italian supporters but until 1938 did not have the vast disproportion of means often alleged by the Republicans. Moreover, he was able to avoid the kind of foreign domination exercised by Soviet military and Comintern advisors over major aspects of the Republican effort. His government was officially recognized by Rome and Berlin on November 18, 1936,[95] at a time when the fall of Madrid was still thought to be imminent. Ten days later, on November 28, he signed a secret treaty of mutual friendship and assistance with Italy which provided for benevolent neutrality in the event of armed conflict with a third power, mutual respect for territorial integrity, and closer economic relations. The Italian commitment had become massive by early 1937, yet despite the presence of German and Italian advisors, Franco was as successful as the Republicans were unsuccessful in maintaining his independence of command. There were only very occasional direct interventions limited to specific instances, such as the order given by Mussolini in mid-March 1938 for Italian planes based on Mallorca to carry out several terror raids of intimidation against Barcelona (raids that, according to the German ambassador, left Franco "pale with anger"). Otherwise, Mussolini merely fumed in Rome about the slowness and alleged ineptitude with which Franco conducted his war.[96]

Relations with Nazi Germany were much more difficult in every way. On the one hand, the German Führer was more detached than Mussolini and less willing to make major commitments of materiel, while on the other, German representatives were pushy and meddlesome, did much more to interfere with domestic politics, and steadily increased their pressure for major economic concessions in return for war supplies. Hitler obviously attached less importance to the war in Spain than Mussolini, but this did not prevent German representatives from bombarding Franco with all manner of gratuitous advice, occasionally intriguing with sectors of the Falange, or criticizing the "reactionary" and "clerical" qualities of his new government. Franco in turn often simply told both German and Italian representatives what they wanted to hear: that he would expand the popular base of the Spanish state, curb the harshness of the repres-

94. These statistics are drawn from Frank's study.

95. The first country to officially recognize the Franco regime was El Salvador, which did so on November 10, 1936.

96. This is treated in depth by Coverdale, *Italian Intervention*.

sion, institute social reforms, prosecute the war vigorously, and alter the institutions of Spain to make them more fascist in character.[97] The arrogance and pretentiousness of their German and Italian allies often provoked resentment among the Nationalists, yet this resulted only in scattered minor incidents and did not materially interfere with the war effort.

Unlike the Republican government, which paid for almost every bit of materiel that it received from the Soviet Union and elsewhere with gold (virtually liquidating the gold reserves of the Bank of Spain),[98] Franco obtained the great bulk of his arms and other supplies on credit. The most thorough study indicates that Italy, the main supplier, provided $355 million worth of military goods and Germany a total of $215 million, while $76 million came from other countries. Thus the Nationalists obtained approximately $645 million of materiel in toto, compared with aggregate Republican expenditures of approximately $775 million. The Italian materiel was provided almost entirely on credit, which was in turn paid off by the Nationalist government over a long period of nearly thirty years until the last lira had been returned. The Germans were more demanding, insisting on hard currency as much as possible and major raw material concessions. During the final year of the conflict the Nationalist government was able to pay about $300,000 to each of its Axis suppliers in hard currency.[99]

The German government was particularly interested in making a major penetration of the Spanish mining industry, whose raw materials could be of prime importance for German military production. Franco and his ministers held them off as long as they could, stressing the complexity of the industry and its problems and the need to secure more data, while insisting that Spanish law did not permit changes in favor of new foreign ownership by a "provisional" government such as the wartime Nationalist regime. On March 20, 1937, Franco found it expedient to sign a secret protocol with the German government pledging the two regimes to friendly relations and mutual cooperation, more or less along the lines of the earlier secret treaty with Italy.[100] Nonetheless, after the conquest of Vizcaya in mid-1937 Franco was in a stronger position economically, and the bulk of Vizcayan iron ore was regularly shipped to Britain to obtain foreign ex-

97. For brief summaries of Franco's wartime relations, see the chapter by Charles R. Halstead in *Spain in the Twentieth-Century World*, ed. J. W. Cortada (Westport, Conn., 1980), 41–94; and that by Robert H. Whealey in *The Republic and the Civil War in Spain* (London, 1971), 213–38.

98. The definitive study is Angel Viñas, *El oro de Moscú* (Barcelona, 1979).

99. See Robert Whealey, "How Franco Financed His War—Reconsidered," *JCH* 12:1 (Jan., 1977), 133–52.

100. Horton, "Germany and the Spanish Civil War," 123–24. The Marxist account of German economic policy by Marion Einhorn, *Die oekonomischen Hintergruende der deutschen faschistischen Intervention in Spanien 1936–1939* (Berlin, 1962), is somewhat distorted.

change for purchases of other items in the western markets, such as American trucks and oil, that could not be obtained from Germany. Before the end of that year Burgos and London established regular relations through formal agents, though Britain had not yet officially recognized the Franco regime.

The Nationalist success in splitting the Republican zone in two in April 1938 brought the government official recognition from the Vatican and a number of Latin American countries. Yet the slow progress of the Valencian offensive that followed made Franco more reliant than ever on Axis support as war clouds gathered in Europe. The first real German breakthrough came in June 1938, when Franco felt compelled to allow establishment of a new German mining company that would hold more shares in mining ventures than was normally permitted foreign groups by Spanish law. This concession was extended further in November, when to insure German support for the last phase of the war, the German share in five Spanish mining groups was permitted to increase to between 60 and 75 percent.[101]

The Munich crisis raised the direct possibility of a general European war that might have disastrous consequences for Nationalist Spain. Franco immediately made it clear that he had no intention of being dragged into a German war, assuring both Britain and France of his absolute neutrality in the event of a general conflict. This galled both Rome and Berlin, and yet the logic of such a step could not be totally denied. In turn, Franco encountered no difficulties with France early in 1939 as his forces occupied all northeastern Spain.

On March 31, 1939, the next-to-last day of the war, Franco signed a new German-Spanish treaty of friendship with Hitler, but this did little more than confirm the provisions of the secret agreement of March 20, 1937. It provided for mutual consultation on all common interests and benevolent neutrality in the event of war. Four days earlier the Spanish regime had become a signatory to the Anti-Comintern Pact, indicating its general ideological sympathy with the other anticommunist authoritarian regimes.[102]

Though the Nationalist movement was exclusively Spanish in origin, there is no doubt that Italo-German aid to Franco greatly exceeded in quality and effect, and also somewhat exceeded in sheer quantity, the assistance from the Soviet Union and elsewhere received by the Popular Front regime. The number of German military personnel in Spain was evidently at least twice as great as that of Soviet personnel, and the 70,000 Italian troops in Spain at the high point of CTV participation in the late

101. Glen T. Harper, *German Economic Policy in Spain during the Spanish Civil War 1936–1939* (The Hague, 1967), 116–20.

102. The best treatment of German-Spanish relations during the final phase of the Civil War will be found in Robert H. Whealey, "German-Spanish Relations January–August 1939" (Ph.D. diss., University of Michigan, 1963), 51–148.

A detachment of the Condor Legion on parade during the Civil War

winter and spring of 1937 exceeded the total number of foreign volunteers in the International Brigades.[103]

In most instances such matters can be dealt with only in terms of approximations, for there are no central record respositories for quantities of foreign assistance received by either side that have yet been discovered, and scholars are in broad disagreement as to the various totals, as indicated in the accompanying table 8.1.

It can be concluded that both sides received very approximately the

103. Nationalist historians such as Martínez Bande and Salas Larrazábal continue to insist on totals of 100,000 or more for International Brigade membership. It is not impossible that they are correct, but their logic and evidence are nonetheless not convincing. The only account with direct access to pertinent records is that of the Soviet scholar K. L. Maidanik, who cites the figure of 31,237 as drawn from Soviet Army records (which normally got extra copies of major Republican People's Army documents) in his *Ispanskii proletariat v natsionalno-revoliutsionnoi voine* (Moscow, 1960), 206. Other Soviet sources give only slightly higher figures. Verle B. Johnston, *Legions of Babel* (University Park, Pa., 1967), 88, suggests a total of 35,000; but the principal Spanish study, Andreu Castells, *Las Brigadas Internacionales en la guerra de España* (Barcelona, 1973), raises this to 59,000. See also R. Dan Richardson, *Comintern Army* (Lexington, Ky., 1982).

Table 8.1. Estimates of Foreign Assistance during the Spanish Civil War

	The brothers Salas Larra-zábal	Sov. Acad. of Sciences	Frank	García Deleyto	Laureau	Llera	Petrucci	Sanchís
To Republicans								
Soviet tanks		362	362	575				
planes	1111	806	806		922	806	1244	1409
cannon		1555	1555					
Other tanks			16+	45				
planes	364		383					
cannon			243					

	The brothers Salas Larrazábal	Coverdale	Frank	García Deleyto	Tusell/ G.Q. Llano
To Nationalists					
Italian tanks	150	157[a]	157	157	over 150
planes	656–700	759	763		over 600
cannon	ca. 1,000	1801	1801		over 1800
German tanks	111		150	170	
planes	593		708		
cannon	737		409		

Sources: Willard C. Frank, "Naval Operations in the Spanish Civil War, 1936–1939," *Naval War College Review* 37 (Jan.–Feb. 1984), 24–55; Pablo García Deleyto, "Los tanques en la guerra civil," *Historia 16* 5: 52 (Aug. 1980), 29–43; Armando Llera, "Armas rusas en la guerra civil," *Historia 16* 7: 75 (July 1982), 11–21; Jesús Salas Larrazábal, *Intervención extranjera en la guerra de España* (Madrid, 1974); Académie des Sciences de l'URSS, *La solidarité des peuples avec la République Espagnole* (Moscow, 1974), 511–63: J. Tusell and G. G. Queipo de Llano, *Franco y Mussolini* (Madrid, 1985), 19.

[a]Coverdale's figure also includes armored cars. For that matter, the Italian tanks sent to Spain were only light "tankettes," in no way comparable to the more formidable Soviet models.

same number of planes from abroad. If the figures for the Republic by the Salas Larrazábal brothers are somewhat exaggerated, it should be remembered that the Popular Front forces began with a greater proportion of the original Spanish Air Force. The Nationalists were probably given the most artillery. The Republicans not only received more tanks than did Franco's army—by one scholarly calculation nearly twice as many—but the quality of the Red Army armor that they received was superior, in some cases by a wide margin, and the first shipments were accompanied by Soviet crews who took the tanks directly into action. The complaint registered by some People's Army veterans that the Soviet materiel was worn out or inferior does not seem to be justified in most cases. The Soviet planes serving on the Madrid front clearly outperformed German and Italian fighters until the first Messerschmitts arrived, Soviet artillery was rather better than the Italian pieces that provided most of Franco's equipment, and Soviet tanks were more heavily armored and possessed greater firepower than any of the German and Italian models.

Performance and effectiveness were quite a different matter. It is true that the International Brigades (which by 1938 were predominantly Spanish, not international) played an important role in the People's Army, but the Italian infantry had a better record with the Nationalists than they are usually given credit for. By the fall of 1937 they had been pared down by more than 35 percent and were further reduced in number by 1938, but the remaining Italians performed creditably[104] once the poorer troops were sent home. The German and Italian air force personnel serving with the Nationalists consistently outperformed their Soviet and Republican counterparts, while the Italian artillery also contributed effectively. The timid defensive tactics imposed by Soviet advisors on the Republican air force and navy were little short of disastrous, while Soviet units rarely intervened directly in the Mediterranean against the enemy's shipping as the Italians did with such frequency and telling effect.

A prime characteristic of the Spanish Civil War, both politically and militarily, was that what was actually taking place was often misrepresented as something that it was not. False political representations had their counterpart in false, misleading, or incomplete military conclusions. Thus there has been considerable exaggeration about the military experimentation supposedly carried on during the Spanish war and the lessons derived from it. Tactics and materiel were a unique blend of World Wars I and II. Both sides obviously had the opportunity to employ a number of minor military innovations, such as more rapid-firing new weapons, but none of these were revolutionary. For the purposes of World War II, the conclusions drawn by European armies were perhaps more inaccurate and misleading than they were pertinent and helpful.[105]

The Germans profited most, but even then only partially. The most significant new factor demonstrated in Spain was the effectiveness of German tactical air support, which played a major role in several key Nationalist victories. And it was in Spain that German fighter pilots first developed the standard western "Finger Four" formation, later also used by the RAF and USAF. Many of the German aces of the early phase of World War II got their first combat experience in Spain, and the Luftwaffe developed

104. Coverdale, *Italian Intervention*, 396, points out that of the total of approximately 78,000 Italian military personnel of all arms who at one time or another served in Spain, about 5 percent were killed, close to the percentage for Nationalist forces in general.

105. Maurice Duval, *Les leçons de la guerre d'Espagne* (Paris, 1938), a book published in the final year of the conflict, proved less than sagacious in the drawing of "lessons."

new night flying expertise. The general conclusion drawn by the Luftwaffe was that strategic bombing of cities and industry deserved much
less emphasis than did tactical bombing in support of land operations, an
emphasis that would cost the German war effort dear from the autumn of
1940 on. Contrary to other assertions, the German blitzkrieg was never
tested in Spain. Tanks of adequate quality were not mass-produced by the
Germans until the Spanish war was nearly over, and almost none were
available to send to Spain. Air power was much more important than armor in assisting Nationalist breakthroughs.

Italy, the power most committed to the Spanish struggle, failed to
profit from it militarily. This was not because, as has sometimes been alleged, Italian military supplies were seriously depleted by shipments to
Spain. Most of the Italian materiel sent to Spain, while adequate in the
somewhat antiquated technological context of the Spanish struggle, was
old and of little value in combat of the level of World War II, and the volume in which it was provided was not great enough to seriously challenge
the output of Italian industry. Rather the opposite was true: the partially
anachronistic character of the Spanish war, together with the relatively
superior performance of the Nationalist troops using Italian weapons,
lulled the Italian leadership, which never seriously planned or prepared
for involvement in a massive world war, into a false sense of complacency.
Even the frustration of their lightly armed infantry in the face of Soviet
tanks at Guadalajara made scant impression.

Nor did Soviet military leadership prove demonstrably more sagacious
in learning from the Spanish conflict. Though they did grasp the importance of increasing the strength of their tank armor, they were already
headed in that direction anyway, whereas the limited utility of armor in
Spain further convinced them that a tactic of dispersal among infantry
units—the very opposite of the German massed armored blitzkrieg—was
the appropriate tactic for European war. Similarly, the disastrous failure
of Soviet aerial tactics in Spain—which emphasized group combat and
the defensive over individual tactics and the offensive—produced scant
change in their approach until after 1941.

After 1939 it became fashionable to refer to the Spanish conflict as the
opening round of World War II in Europe or to employ some equivalent
concept, but such an interpretation is exaggerated. It makes almost equal
sense to turn the proposition directly around and conclude that the Spanish struggle was in fact the last and most radical round of World War I. The
revolutionary breakdown of institutions in Spain had no counterpart anywhere else in Europe during the late 1930s but was in key respects analogous to the revolutionary breakdown of institutions in many areas of
central and eastern Europe between 1917 and 1920. Radicalization and
breakdown came later in Spain because of its noninvolvement in World

War I; lacking the stimulus of wartime stress and radicalization, these processes took longer to work themselves out in a strictly peacetime and domestic context. As a revolutionary/counterrevolutionary civil war—which was the essence of the Spanish conflict—it was directly analogous to the struggles immediately after World War I in Russia, Hungary, the Baltic area, and to some extent Germany. This had no counterpart at all during the early round of World War II, similar patterns beginning to emerge in Yugoslavia and Greece only after 1941. Similarly, the creation of a new revolutionary Red or People's Army, accompanied by the exacerbation of nationalism or in opposition to it, was a product of World War I but was not typical of the early phases of World War II in Europe. Even in the employment of military tactics and materiel, the Spanish conflict reflected World War I as much as its successor, with the prime exception that the use of air power was much more sophisticated.

As a focus of international attention and intervention, the Spanish war certainly contributed to the dynamics of international affairs, but it was not of truly crucial concern to any of the great powers, except perhaps insofar as Italy could have been considered a great power. The Spanish war did provide the original opportunity for creation of the Rome-Berlin Axis in October 1936, yet the Axis did not participate jointly in the beginning of the general European war. On the side of the left the Spanish war featured an attempt to form a sort of international Popular Front, led in part by the Soviet Union, but that proved a complete failure. World War II was begun by Hitler only after Stalin reversed the policy in which Soviet intervention in Spain had been based, and had instead come directly to terms with Hitler for the division of power that would make possible a broader European war. That is, World War II could only begin after the nominal alliances of the Spanish Civil War had been reversed. The first, purely European phase of World War II was made possible by alliance of the two rival revolutionary imperialisms, Nazi and Soviet, against the western democracies and the smaller states. Not only had the two revolutionary imperialisms backed opposing sides in Spain, but democracy in the western sense was never the primary issue. It was rejected by the Nationalists from the start, while the pluralistic Popular Front regime that governed the Republican zone largely smothered democracy beneath the revolution.

As Raymond Aron correctly observed in his *Mémoires*, the only part of World War II that was to any degree foreshadowed or anticipated by the Spanish conflict was the war that began in June 1941 when Hitler attacked the Soviet Union. That was why Nationalist Spain, though itself never more than semifascist, sent volunteers to fight on the Russian front while remaining neutral in other phases of the war that involved powers with whom the Franco regime had no direct quarrel. Conversely, the worldwide struggle that was finally joined in December 1941 when Japanese and American participation produced a truly global conflict showed no very recognizable political reflection of the Spanish war, for the conservative support that was Franco's chief domestic mainstay was to be found as often as not on the side of the anti-German coalition.

9

Franco's Wartime

Government

Radicalization of the Civil War into an intense revolutionary-counter-revolutionary struggle demanded a firm political structure and definition for the nascent Nationalist regime. How to accomplish this was not altogether clear to Franco, who inevitably had to devote most of his time during the first months of his *caudillaje* to pressing military affairs. He also had to find time for personal contacts with foreign representatives and to not infrequent pronouncements designed for public relations within the Nationalist zone. Thus more than six months passed before he began the construction of a new political system.

All leftist and liberal parties were outlawed soon after the beginning of the war. All conservative and rightist groups contributed to the organization of militia forces and to the economic support of the new regime, although Gil Robles had fled the rebel zone early in the war after threats of lynching from Falangists. The latter held him responsible for José Antonio's failure to win a seat in the 1936 elections, a failure that cost José Antonio parliamentary immunity and indirectly his life. Full support from what had recently been the largest of Spanish political parties was nonetheless pledged by Gil Robles from his new residence in Lisbon, in a letter of October 7, 1936, declaring to the leader of the JAP militia the group's complete subordination to the new military command.[1]

With moderate conservatism discredited by the terms of Civil War, the key political movement in the Nationalist zone was the burgeoning Falange. It mobilized the great majority of militia volunteers, and the political membership of the party, which had already multiplied during the

1. José Ma. Gil Robles to Luciano de la Calzada, quoted in La Cierva, *Franco*, 1:534–35. This letter was published in the press of the Nationalist zone on October 28.

Manuel Hedilla Larrey, leader of the Falange early in the Civil War

spring of 1936, doubled twice over during the first months of the Civil War. Its radical nationalism, fascistic authoritarianism, and violent, military tone enabled it to win members away from more moderate groups and among the apolitical middle classes, while its loudly publicized national syndicalist social and economic program was heralded as the only norm that would enable Spanish Nationalists to win the political and social war against the revolutionary left. Falangists proclaimed that only a national revolution could defeat the Marxist revolution.

The Falangists had the numbers and the propaganda but suffered from two profound weaknesses. The party had developed into a mass movement only under conditions of civil war that were totally dominated by Franco's new military government through martial law. Secondly, its leadership was very weak. All the top figures in the party had been in Republican jails since March 1936. The only one to be liberated, Onésimo Redondo, was killed while leading a militia column in the first days of fighting northwest of Madrid. With the fate of José Antonio Primo de Rivera still undecided in the Republican zone, the remaining second-level leaders of the party, on September 4, 1936, ratified the governance of a seven-member Junta de Mando (Command or Governance Committee) under Manuel Hedilla.

Hedilla was the former Falangist provincial chief of Santander, and had played a key role in the party during the conspiracy as a clandestine *inspector nacional* trying to reorganize various of its sections. A former ship's mechanic and small businessman, he had little formal education but considerable practical sense and a reputation for honesty. During the fall and winter of 1936–37, Hedilla struggled to give a new structure to what was suddenly a mass organization. He tried with very limited success to coordinate far-flung militia activities and began to form a new party treasury to pay volunteers three pesetas a day (compared with ten pesetas daily paid Republican *milicianos*, a good example of the disparity in demagogy and discipline in the two zones). The skeleton of a new administrative system of party services was intended to serve as the beginning of a parallel state structure, while the Sección Femenina quickly blossomed into the largest and by far the most effective women's auxiliary service organization in either zone. The Falange's Auxilio Social soon became the leading secular welfare organization in Nationalist territory, helping to care for victims of the war and the orphans created by the Nationalists' own bloody repression.

Aside from the militia recruitment, however, the main Falangist achievement during Hedilla's brief period of leadership lay in the development of its press and propaganda. Daily or weekly newspapers were established in almost every province of the Nationalist zone, and in some, the most important local organ more or less voluntarily agreed to become the district

Falangist mouthpiece. Falangist propagandists drew considerable hostility and criticism because of their rhetorical excesses and their habit of wearing pompous uniforms far from the heat of battle, yet they created the major publicity force in Franco's territory. Moreover, they had the leadership or collaboration of a considerable roster of intellectuals and writers, mostly of the younger generation—essayists such as Eugenio d'Ors and Pedro Laín Entralgo, scholars such as Antonio Tovar and Martín Almagro, young poets such as Dionisio Ridruejo and Luis Rosales, the psychologist José Lopez Ibor, the Catalan novelist Ignacio Agustí, and many others.[2]

José Antonio Primo de Rivera was meanwhile executed in the Republican provincial prison of Alicante on November 20, after conviction by a "People's Court" of the kind recently instituted in the Popular Front zone, for his participation in organizing the conspiracy and revolt. He had been considerably chastened by the development of the Civil War, and among his papers was left a proposal drafted after the conflict was about a month old. It was the strongest statement in his entire career of the essential ambiguity—unusual among Spanish politicians—that surrounded his political attitudes. During the year preceding the Civil War he had blown alternately hot and cold, occasionally seeking an alternative leader for the Falange so that he might abandon politics, at other times actively conspiring against the Republic and contemplating collaboration with the authoritarian right in order to do so effectively. José Antonio nonetheless distrusted the latter profoundly and had always been painfully aware that his young Falangist militants lacked the maturity and political ability to assume power. He considered the Civil War the national disaster that it was, and proposed an armistice on the basis of a compromise "national pacification" government of moderate liberals and middle-class centrists.[3] It was similar in concept to the Martínez Barrio compromise attempted by Republican authorities on July 19—Martínez Barrio and Sánchez Ro-

2. On the Falange early in the Civil War, see Ricardo de la Cierva, "La trayectoria de la Falange hasta la unificación de 1937," in *Aproximación histórica a la guerra española (1936–1939)* (Madrid, 1970), 205–40; my *Falange,* 116–31; Maximiano García Venero's pro-Hedilla account, *Falange en la guerra de España: La unificación y Hedilla* (Paris, 1967), 161–306, and his anti-Hedilla reversal, *Historia de la unificación* (Madrid, 1970), 71–114; and the anti-Falangist critique by Herbert R. Southworth, *Antifalange* (Paris, 1967), 109–39. On the growth of its propaganda facilities, see María Antonia Estévez, "El nacimiento de la propaganda azul," *Historia 16* 1:9 (Jan. 1977), 21–28.

3. The text is given in *Falange,* 133–35. The Socialist leader Indalecio Prieto collected José Antonio's private papers written in jail and was impressed by what he found. Prieto later wrote: "The philosophical affirmation that there is some truth in all ideas has a long history. This comes to my mind on account of the manuscripts which José Antonio Primo de Rivera left in the Alicante jail. Perhaps in Spain we have not examined with serenity our respective ideologies in order to discover the coincidences, which were probably fundamental, and measure the divergences, probably secondary, in order to determine if the latter were worth being aired on the battlefield." Prologue to *Palabras de ayer y hoy* (Santiago de Chile, 1938), 17.

mán were his proposed leaders—but of course that was an option even less acceptable to the opposing sides a month later. Meanwhile, two efforts were made to rescue José Antonio, one by local Alicante Falangists and a second by a group of Falangists sent from the Nationalist zone with the limited assistance of Franco and of German naval forces and diplomatic personnel, who attempted to bribe local Popular Front officials. Both efforts were complete failures,[4] and the execution of the Jefe[5] left the rapidly expanding Falange of the Nationalist zone without an authentic and recognized leader.

The movement's most important function during the first months of the Civil War was the organization of many tens of thousands of military volunteers. Cooperating fully with the military command, Falangists were also allowed to organize two small military training schools for their own cadres, at Seville and Salamanca.[6] Yet a Carlist announcement on December 8 of a plan to form a separate Carlist military school quickly led to Franco's first political crackdown among the Nationalists. The Generalissimo viewed the publicity and air of independence that attended the project as a clear violation of the prerogative of military command. The project was canceled and the Carlist leader Manuel Fal Conde exiled from Nationalist territory a few days later.[7]

Franco increasingly recognized the need to create some distinctly new form of political organization in order to avoid Primo de Rivera's mistake of failing to proceed to the direct institutionalization of a new system. He was impressed by the potential of Catholic corporatism, as he indicated in his first public statements, and had paid particular attention to the chief theoretical definition of the Carlist program articulated in 1935 by Víctor Pradera.[8] Franco evidently felt restricted by the lack of fully trusted political collaborators, however, and relied above all on his brother Nicolás and a handful of trusted military subordinates.

In these circumstances the arrival in the Nationalist zone on February 20, 1937, of Franco's brother-in-law, Ramón Serrano Súñer—just es-

4. Angel Viñas, "Berlin, Salvad a José Antonio," *Historia 16* 1:1 (May 1976), 41–56, reprinted in Viñas's *Guerra, dinero, dictadura* (Madrid, 1984), 60–97; *Falange*, 135–38. These accounts are corroborated by several unpublished statements by Falangist survivors involved in the same activities. See, further, the remarks of Federico Menéndez Gundín in *Historia 16* 1:3 (July 1976). A different perspective will be found in Bravo Morata, *Franco y los muertos providenciales*, 97–146.

5. The text of José Antonio's trial circulated in typescript among Falangists for many years. One version, with various errors, was eventually published by José Ma. Mancisidor, *Frente a frente: José Antonio Primo de Rivera frente al Tribunal Popular* (Madrid, 1963). Some details are clarified in Luis Covarrubias Arriazu, "¿Quién ordenó el fusilamiento de José Antonio?," *Nueva Historia*, no. 22 (Nov. 1978), 67–69.

6. *Falange*, 142–47.

7. Blinkhorn, *Carlism*, 271–279.

8. Cf. Franco's prologue to the 1945 Madrid edition of Pradera's *El Estado nuevo*.

caped from prison in Republican territory—assumed major importance. Unlike Franco, the slender, blue-eyed, prematurely white-haired Serrano was a man of culture and sophistication, an elite *abogado del Estado* with an outstanding university and professional record. Serrano had been a parliamentary deputy and youth leader of the CEDA, and his political orientation was toward what the left called clerical fascism. A former student at the University of Bologna, Serrano admired the Fascist system, though his personal inclinations were more Catholic, conservative, and legalistic. He had been radicalized by the trauma of the Civil War, both his brothers having been killed by the Red terror in Madrid, and in later years he declared that he had felt totally "benumbed" by the time that he arrived in Salamanca.[9] Serrano had also been a close friend of José Antonio Primo de Rivera since student days, and he harbored a strong ambition to realize as many of the original Falangist goals as possible within the structure of a new juridically defined and institutionalized system. He soon replaced Nicolás Franco as the Generalissimo's primary political counselor and assistant[10] and helped resolve the chief domestic problem of the Nationalist zone, giving political structure and organization to a new authoritarian system.

Nicolás Franco's efforts to form an Acción Ciudadana, primarily of middle-class conservatives and moderates (it was sometimes referred to imprecisely as the Partido Franquista) were thus dropped, for the Acción Ciudadana was too much like the amorphous "Unión Patriótica" of Primo de Rivera. The goal almost inevitably would have to be a more radical and sophisticated state party of at least semifascist contours, organized on the basis of the Falange but integrating other Nationalist elements as well. The first measure of multigroup unification, logically, had been military. On December 22, 1936, in the wake of the Fal Conde incident, Franco unified all the diverse civilian political militias of the Nationalist zone under military command, to which of course they had been subject since the beginning of the conflict. By early 1937 some of Franco's publicists were starting to employ the slogan "Una Patria, Un Estado, Un Caudi-

9. The Serrano Súñer of 1937 has been described thus: "He was very slender and always dressed in a black business suit. His hair, which had been blond, was already white though abundant. His features were delicate and his hands unusually fine and well-manicured. His gestures were free though measured. He was very thin and when relaxed slightly bent as though oppressed by a great weight. His gestures were melancholy . . . and he exhibited unusual courtesy." Dionisio Ridruejo, *Casi unas memorias* (Barcelona, 1976), 96. Serrano has given his own presentation of his background in his *Entre Hendaya y Gibraltar* (Mexico City, 1947), 19–64, and in his subsequent post-Franco *Memorias* (Barcelona, 1977), 157–73. There is a sort of authorized biography by Fernando García Lahiguera, *Ramon Serrano Súñer: Un documento para la historia* (Barcelona, 1983).

10. During the wartime housing shortage, the Serrano Súñer family shared the official residence of the Francos.

llo,"[11] obviously inspired by the Nazi "Ein Volk, Ein Reich, Ein Fuehrer." Albiñana's tiny Partido Nacionalista Español, the smallest of the right-wing groups, announced on January 8 that it would merge with the Carlists. One group of Falangist leaders met with the top Carlist authorities at Lisbon in the middle of the following month to discuss a much broader unification of the two largest and most active Nationalist political forces.[12] Throughout the winter months, the German ambassador Faupel urged Franco to create a dynamic new state party on the German model,[13] while lesser NSDAP representatives urged Falangist leaders to copy German ways. Italian pressure was less overt, though in March 1937 the Fascist *gerarca* Robert Farinacci was sent to Spain on a fact-finding mission, and also in the vain hope of persuading the Falangists to support a monarchist restoration in the person of a prince from the House of Savoy. He found the Falangists much too radical and antimonarchist for this, and his report describing them as a sort of "leftist" group caused "great scandal" in Rome.[14] Later Serrano would recall that "the Italians particularly urged a political unification, though they did so with tact and discretion."[15]

Franco had begun to work on vague plans for unification by the beginning of 1937. According to Serrano, "he was already developing the idea of reducing the various parties and ideologies of the [Nationalist] movement to a common denominator. He showed me the statutes of the Falange on which he had made copious marginal annotations. He had also made comparisons between the speeches of José Antonio and those of Pradera."[16] Carlism, as Serrano put it, "suffered from a certain lack of political modernity. On the other hand, a good part of its doctrine was included in the thought of the Falange, which furthermore had the popular social revolutionary content that could permit Nationalist Spain to absorb Red Spain ideologically, which was our great ambition and our great duty."[17] Yet the Falange was filled "even with masses coming from the Republic and from syndicalism. . . . Its leaders were old provincial chiefs, usually little known, and extremely young squad leaders, in many cases merely improvised."[18] Carlist and other rightists sometimes made jokes

---

11. Within the Falange itself this was particularly encouraged by the new Falangist paper *Arriba España* of Pamplona, directed by the extravagant Navarrese priest Fermín Yzurdiaga, whose pompous rhetoric led the Falangist wit Agustín de Foxá to exclaim, paraphrasing the leftist slogan, "Yzurdiaga will be the tomb of fascism."

12. On the Carlist relation to the Nationalist unification process, see Blinkhorn, *Carlism*, 279–89.

13. *Documents on German Foreign Policy*, vol. 3, no. 229, pp. 267–70.

14. According to Cantalupo, *Spagna*, 148–57.

15. Serrano, *Memorias*, 255.

16. Serrano, *Entre Hendaya y Gibraltar*, 33.

17. Ibid., 32.

18. Ibid., 25–26.

about the Falangists as the "FAIlange" (referring to the acronym of the Iberian Anarchist Federation) or as being "our Reds." Such a party would need firm control, subordination, and combination with contrasting conservative elements.

The prospect of some form of political unification excited considerable rivalry and infighting among Falangist leaders. The party's former Madrid circle, grouped around José Antonio's cousin Sancho Dávila, maintained the cult of "El Ausente" ("The Absent One") and did all they could to avoid recognition of Hedilla's authority in the party. Whereas the Falangist leaders in the principal northern provinces and the writers of the party apparatus supported Hedilla, the "legitimists," led by Dávila and the militia chief Agustín Aznar, based themselves on southern sections of the party and on Madrid refugees. In March they began a direct intraparty conspiracy aimed at ousting Hedilla.

By early April Hedilla was consulting with certain of the Carlist leadership and monarchist politicians with the aim of creating a broader political fusion that would cooperate with the politically unorganized Franco regime. The CEDA youth movement, JAP, had held an assembly of its own on March 19 which affirmed its willingness to cooperate in the political development of the new state. What Franco did not want, however, was a broad new political movement created independently of his government. On April 11 he asked Serrano Súñer to draft terms of a broad fusion of political groups under the new state, and on the following day he informed some of his strongest supporters among the Carlist leadership that he would soon proceed toward a political unification.

After Hedilla somewhat languidly called a meeting of the Falange's National Council for April 25 to deal with the issues of leadership and unification, the "legitimist" conspirators seized the initiative on April 16, meeting in Falangist national headquarters with part of the Junta de Mando to declare Hedilla deposed. He was replaced with a triumvirate—the original Falangist executive structure—composed of Dávila, Aznar, and José Moreno (a provincial boss), with Rafael Garcerán, a former legal aide to José Antonio who had not even been a member of the party before the war, as secretary. The self-appointed triumvirs then scheduled a separate meeting of their own for the National Council, confronted Hedilla with a series of faits accomplis—reading off a list of his real and imagined deficiencies as head of the Junta de Mando—and ended by calling on Franco at his headquarters to inform him of developments.

Hedilla apparently also made direct contact with the Generalissimo, who in all this was taken by surprise. After dark a group of *hedillistas* then descended on the residences of Dávila and Garcerán. The former was taken prisoner at the cost of one Falangist killed on each side, while the latter held off assailants with pistol fire, after which all concerned were arrested by forces of the Civil Guard. Dávila and Garcerán—at that point the only triumvirs in Salamanca—were charged with armed rebellion for trying to undercut Hedilla at the very moment he was clumsily attempting to promote some sort of political unification.[19]

On the evening of the eighteenth Hedilla convened a hastily called meeting of the Falangist National Council. The need for election of a new Jefe Nacional to replace José Antonio was then agreed upon, with Hedilla receiving ten of twenty-two votes cast, eight abstaining and one going to each of four other candidates.[20] Hedilla then sped to Franco's headquarters, where the Generalissimo even introduced him from the balcony to a crowd of Franco's admirers.

On the following day, April 19, while the National Council was holding its concluding session, Franco and Serrano Súñer added the finishing touches to their own arrangements, announcing the fusion of Falangists and Carlists into a new organization called the Falange Española Tradicionalista y de las J.O.N.S. Franco's unification decree emphasized the need for an organized political basis for the new state and declared that "as in other countries of totalitarian regime," traditional and newer forces must be combined. The Falange's Twenty-six Points (minus the last article that rejected fusions) were announced as the "programmatic norm" of the new state, though making it clear that since "the movement that we lead is precisely this—a movement—more than a program, it will not be rigid or static, but subject, in each case, to the work of revision and improvement that reality may counsel,"[21] a point that Franco made even more forcefully in his radio address that night. Monarchist restoration was not rejected by the new political structure, for Franco specified that "when we have put an end to the great task of spiritual and material reconstruction, should patriotic need and the wishes of the country support it, we do not close the horizon to the possibility of installing in the nation the secular regime that forged its unity and historical greatness,"[22] carefully employing the Acción Española term for the *instauración* of a more authoritarian monarchy rather than the *restauración* of the old parliamentary regime. All other parties were dissolved, but the FET was theoretically open to all followers of the Nationalist movement, though regular membership would subsequently be made subject to certain restrictions.

19. The most reliable accounts of the events of April 16 will be found in La Cierva, "Trayectoria de la Falange,"; and Ridruejo, *Casi unas memorias*, 87–96. See also Angel Alcázar de Velasco, *Los siete días de Salamanca* (Madrid, 1976). Sancho Dávila's own *José Antonio, Salamanca . . . y otras cosas* (Madrid, 1967), is much less than frank.

20. See Vicente de Cadenas y Vicent, *Actas del último Consejo Nacional de Falange Española de las J.O.N.S. (Salamanca, 18-19-IV-37)* (Madrid, 1975), though this contains a few obvious inaccuracies.

21. *Palabras del Caudillo* (Madrid, 1943), 9–17.

22. The text appeared in the *BOE*, April 21, 1937, and may be found in F. Díaz-Plaja, ed., *La historia de España en sus documentos* (Madrid, 1972), 3:297–99.

Franco saluting a crowd from the balcony of the Salamanca city hall, 1937

Franco made himself *jefe nacional* of the new FET, with a secretary, Junta
Política and National Council to be named subsequently by himself. Five
days later (April 24) the raised-arm Fascist salute of the Falangé was made
the official salute of the Nationalist regime. This was accompanied by
adoption of the other Falangist slogans and insignia for the FET and in
some measure for the regime: the blue shirt, the official appellation *com-
rade*, the red and black flag, the yoked arrows symbol, the anthem "Cara
al Sol" ("Face to the Sun"), and the slogan "Arriba España" ("Upward
Spain").

Creation of the official FET represented the triumph of the "fascistized" rightists, originally denounced by Ramiro Ledesma in 1935,
over the core fascists of the old Falange, and was an absolutely logical and
necessary measure for Franco in an all-out revolutionary civil war. Three
days later, he appointed a new Junta de Mando, with Hedilla the first
member designated. Though most Falangists had been willing to accept

some form of unification, Franco's seizure of power was too much for a number of them, including Hedilla, who at first refused to cooperate.

The resulting "Hedilla affair" climaxed on April 25, when Hedilla was arrested. On the preceding day, the Secretariat of War in Franco's Junta Técnica had ordered the incorporation of the Falangist militia by the regular Army, bringing immediate dissolution of the separate Falangist officer-training school near Salamanca. When its members were moved to other facilities in Avila, some resisted. Government authorities subsequently produced a telegram from Hedilla, dated April 22, urging Falangists not to collaborate in the new FET, and a number of Falangist public demonstrations against the unification took place in several cities in the interim.[23]

Though Hedilla had refused his new position in the FET Junta de Mando, he denied all charges of rebellion, but to authorities his actions were profoundly subversive of the new political structure. Hedilla and a number of other recalcitrant Falangists were tried for rebellion by court-martial early in June and sentenced to death. The sentence was reduced first to life imprisonment and then to a twenty-year prison term in the Canary Islands, where Hedilla was kept for four years, part of the time in rigorous solitary confinement, before being paroled to the Balearics and allowed to reconstruct his life working in private industry.[24] A score or more of other Falangist diehards (none of them of the top rank) were also prosecuted and sentenced to shorter terms.

The Carlists accepted the unification with skepticism but better grace than did many of the Falangists, and the other political forces in the Nationalist zone made haste to cooperate. From Lisbon, Gil Robles wrote on April 25 with directions for the dissolution of Acción Popular, the largest nucleus of the old CEDA.[25] There was no serious challenge to Franco's leadership from any source.

The aim was a semi-fascist *partido único*, though one not slavishly based on foreign imitation. In an interview published in a pamphlet called *Ideario del Generalísimo*, released just before the unification, Franco declared, "Our system will be based on a Portuguese or Italian model, though we shall conserve our historic institutions." Later in an *ABC* (Seville) interview on July 19, Franco would reiterate that the goal was a "totalitarian state," yet the context in which he always placed this term, invoking the institutional structure of the Catholic Monarchs of the

23. See *FF*, 2:200–209.
24. Hedilla's first apologia appeared in a series of letters published in a clandestine pamphlet entitled *Cartas entrecruzadas entre el Sr. D. Manuel Hedilla Larrey y el Sr. D. Ramón Serrano Súñer* (Madrid, 1948). It was presented in more detail in García Venero's *Falange en la guerra de España*, 287–427, a book subsequently reprinted as *Testimonio de Manuel Hedilla* (Madrid, 1970). There is a critique in Southworth's *Antifalange*, 176–240.
25. The text may be found in José Gutiérrez Ravé, *Gil Robles, caudillo frustrado* (Madrid, 1967), 198–99.

fifteenth century, indicated that what Franco had in mind was not any system of total institutional control such as that of the Soviet Union or of radical fascists—a true functional totalitarianism—but simply a unitary and authoritarian state that permitted varying degrees of traditional pluralism. As he put it, ambiguously, in an interview for the *New York Times Magazine* in December 1937, "Spain has its own tradition, and the majority of the modern formulas that are to be discovered in the totalitarian countries may be found already incorporated within our national past."[26] In February, before the unification, Franco had declared that it was not a matter of the Falange being a fascist movement. "The Falange has not called itself fascist; its founder declared so himself." The habit at first common in the press of the Nationalist zone of calling the Falangists, and sometimes other Nationalist military groups, fascists was not generally used by 1937. All that Franco had been willing to concede before the unification was that the supposed nonfascist character of the Falange in general "did not mean that there are not individual fascists [within it]." Its function after the unification was to incorporate, in Franco's words, the "great unaffiliated neutral mass" of Spaniards,[27] and doctrinal rigidity was clearly not to stand in the way.

Serrano Súñer was delegated by Franco to carry out the transformation and organization of the new FET, and the Caudillo in fact preferred that his brother-in-law become its first secretary-general.[28] Serrano was shrewd enough to perceive that this would be keenly resented by the *camisas viejas* (party veterans; lit. "old shirts"). Instead, during the following few weeks he carried on a series of negotiations with some of the old Falangist leadership, especially the central core of camisas viejas associated with José Antonio's younger sister Pilar, head of the party's Sección Femenina.[29] This included such figures as Aznar, the militia leader José Antonio Girón of Valladolid, Fernando González Vélez, the serious and intelligent *jefe provincial* from León, and Dionisio Ridruejo, the intense young poet and incumbent provincial leader of Valladolid. A vague but effective understanding was soon reached. The Falangists would fully accept Franco's new hierarchy, an organized national political system and state would be developed, and after the war a sincere attempt would be made to carry out the national syndicalist program.

The great majority of those Falangists who had earlier been arrested, some of them mere rank-and-file militants, were soon released. More than a few Falangists continued to harbor private reservations, while

26. *Palabras del Caudillo*, 406.
27. Ibid., 167.
28. According to Serrano Súñer in Heleno Saña, *El franquismo sin mitos: Conversaciones con Serrano Súñer* (Barcelona, 1982), 69.
29. *Entre Hendaya y Gibraltar*, 42.

others, such as the national councillor and jefe provincial of Seville, Martín Ruiz Arenado, were willing to be convinced of Franco's sincerity. At any rate, they had no choice. Almost all accepted Serrano's argument that it would be better for them to participate and have the new FET set up and administered primarily by Falangists rather than by a motley assortment of Carlists, monarchists, and various right-wing opportunists, and some resolved to build as strong a core of camisas viejas within the organization as they could. González Vélez was a strong advocate of this tactic of boring from within, and he was given Hedilla's vacant seat on the new Junta Política, becoming its first chairman.

Work on the new organization proceeded through the summer, and the first party statutes, released on August 4, 1937, preserved much of the original structure but made the system even more hierarchical and authoritarian. The role of Franco was defined in the following terms in articles 47 and 48:

> The Jefe Nacional of F.E.T. y de las J.O.N.S., supreme Caudillo of the Movement, personifies all its values and honors. As author of the historical era in which Spain acquires the means to carry out its destiny and with that the goals of the Movement, the Jefe, in the plenitude of his powers, assumes the most absolute authority. The Jefe is responsible [only] before God and history.
> . . . It is up to the Caudillo to designate his successor, who will receive from him the same authority and obligations.

An early article also provided that the Caudillo would secretly designate his successor, to be proclaimed by the National Council in the event of his death or incapacity. The jefe nacional held direct authority to appoint provincial chiefs and members of the National Council, though henceforth in theory the advisory Junta Política would be chosen half by the jefe nacional, half by the National Council. The *jefe locales* and *secretarios locales* of the party would be selected by the jefes provinciales.

Two categories of members were established for the FET: *militantes* and *adheridos* (adherents). The status of militantes was reserved for those affiliated with the Falangists and Carlists before unification, for military personnel, and for those recognized for their special service. Ordinary new affiliates were relegated to the category of adheridos and were expected to "serve the F.E.T. without any of the rights of members," full membership being granted only after a lengthy period of service. Twelve special "National Services" were created paralleling the state system: External Affairs, National Education, Press and Propaganda, Sección Femenina, Social Works, Syndicates, Youth Organization, Justice and Law, Initiatives and Orientations of the Work of the State, Communications and Transportation, Treasury and Administration, and Information and Investigation. So elaborate a structure of service cadres were designed to compensate for the lack of preparation in the new Falangist leadership by training elite cadres that could later help administer the one-party state.[30] A subsequent law of October 30, 1937, required the approval of local Falangist and Civil Guard chiefs for anyone recommended for a position in local or provincial government; such double authorization was declared necessary until construction of the new "totalitarian state" was completed.[31]

The FET effectively fulfilled its function as an official political and doctrinal organization for the remainder of the war. Its membership eventually soared to more than 900,000 by 1942—by far the largest political group in Spanish history—and yet membership soon came to have a relatively limited significance. All Army officers became ipso facto affiliates of the FET, and a law of October 1, 1938, gave anyone jailed in Republican territory for nominally political reasons automatic membership. Anyone who proposed to get ahead, hide a liberal or leftist past, or merely cooperate with the regime for the duration was likely to join. Serrano later admitted that "a large number of party members never became more than nominal affiliates. In reality they preserved their own personal identities as representatives of more or less surreptitious currents of free opinion,"[32] little influenced by the official Twenty-Six Points. The FET's new National Service of Information and Investigation was soon charged with a purge of undesirables in party membership, but the expulsion of 1,500 affiliates for disciplinary reasons during 1937–38[33] had little effect on the size or zeal of the new state party's following. Much more extensive was the work of special commissions set up throughout the Nationalist zone to purge libraries of literature that was *disolvente* (licentious) and *inmoral*.

Serrano knew that he was already being referred to as the *cuñadísimo* (brother-in-law-in-chief), and rather than become secretary of the party he sought to avoid further exposure to the ire of camisas viejas. They pressed for the exchange of Raimundo Fernández Cuesta, last regular secretary of the original party, a loyal friend and follower of José Antonio who

30. The limited functions of the various National Services are treated in Ricardo Chueca, *El fascismo en los comienzos del régimen de Franco: Un estudio sobre FET-JONS* (Madrid, 1983), 233–64.

31. Clyde L. Clark, *The Evolution of the Franco Regime* (Washington, D.C. [?], n.d.), 2:639.

32. *Entre Hendaya y Gibraltar*, 60.

33. The principal purge of some of those guilty of disciplinary infractions and of common crimes was carried out during the second half of 1938. *Boletín del Movimiento de Falange Española Tradicionalista* (hereafter cited as *BMFET*), nos. 22 and 23 (June 15 and Oct. 10, 1938). According to Chueca, *El fascismo*, 192–93, the number of expulsions from the FET for disciplinary reasons during its first fourteen years varied as follows:

1937	204	1942	777	1947	145
1938	1,303	1943	437	1948	85
1939	556	1944	519	1949	143
1940	685	1945	270	1950	178
1941	825	1946	198		

continued to languish in a Republican jail. An exchange was also favored by the Republican defense minister Indalecio Prieto, impressed with the papers which José Antonio left behind before execution. Prieto had already sent copies of José Antonio's final statements into the Nationalist zone, hoping to provoke dissension, and he calculated that the return of Fernández Cuesta might rouse the camisas viejas to action.[34]

That was hardly to be the case. The former secretary general arrived in Nationalist territory in October 1937. In one of his first public addresses Fernández Cuesta insisted that the Falangists were "revolutionary, profoundly revolutionary,"[35] but he immediately grasped the power alignment in the new regime. After giving every indication of accepting Franco's leadership, he was reappointed to his old post on December 2, 1937. Fernández Cuesta understood that he could not provide independent direction, and is supposed to have lamented privately that he was "being named secretary in order to fail."[36] He carried out the primarily bureaucratic and propagandistic role that Franco intended, and in a New Year's Day interview said to fellow Falangists: "Sincerity and affection oblige me to say to the Old Guard that it must have an understanding spirit, and not lock itself up in exclusiveness or adopt repulsive airs of superiority, but receive with love and comradeship all who come with good faith to Falange Española Tradicionalista."[37] Fernández Cuesta was later blamed by many camisas viejas, perhaps not altogether fairly, for the bureaucratic stagnation into which the movement was sinking. His prestige declined steadily during the later months of the Civil War.

Only Serrano Súñer enjoyed the full confidence of the Generalissimo. He was dapper, alert, and sensitive, always dressed in a well-tailored dark business suit, the only important person in Salamanca or Burgos who felt no compulsion to sport a uniform. Serrano would later declare that his goals were "to help establish *effectively* the political *jefatura* of Franco, to save and realize the political thought of José Antonio, and to contribute to establishing the National Movement in a *régimen jurídico,* that is, to in-

34. During the latter part of 1937 there appeared a series of leaflets attacking the capture of the Falange, signed "Falange Española Auténtica." The sheets were printed in foreign territory, probably in France, and made little impression on the old Falangists, most of whom were being placed in positions within the new FET.

There was even more to it than that, according to a speech delivered by Franco on April 19, 1938: "To this effect propaganda was sent into our zone, and in return for treason, certain prisoners in Republican jails were allowed to escape into our territory under the obligation to agitate among our rear guard. Attempts to infiltrate the cadres of our organizations multiplied, and efforts were made to sow rivalry and division within our ranks." *Palabras del Caudillo,* 46. For further discussion and references, see Sheelagh Ellwood, *Prietas las filas: Historia de Falange Española, 1933–1983* (Barcelona, 1984), 203–6.

35. Raimundo Fernández Cuesta, *Discursos* (Madrid, 1942), 76.

36. According to Serrano Súñer, *Memorias,* 255.

37. Quoted from *La Voz de Galicia* in *FE* (Seville), Jan. 4, 1938.

stitute a state of law."[38] By the beginning of 1938 he had helped establish a central state administration, prepared new legislation defining the powers of Franco and the state, and played a key role in the organization of ministerial departments to form Franco's first formal cabinet. He then became the regime's first minister of the interior, as well as national chief of press and propaganda for the FET.[39] A Falangist pedigree was built up for Serrano, and his relationship with José Antonio was widely publicized.[40]

While one of Serrano's primary tasks was to deal with the regular Falangists, development of the FET had to be conducted in balance with the various other factions behind the National Movement—the several "ideological families" of the new regime, as they would later be termed by commentators. Both brothers-in-law revealed undeniable skill in this enterprise, which was ultimately the responsibility of Franco himself. The German ambassador noted:

> [Franco] has very cleverly succeeded, with the advice of his brother-in-law, . . . in not making enemies of any of the parties represented in the Unity Party that were previously independent and hostile to one another, . . . but, on the other hand, also in not favoring any one of them that might thus grow too strong. . . . It is therefore comprehensible that, depending on the party allegiance of the person concerned, one is just as apt to hear the opinion . . . that "Franco is entirely a creature of the Falange," as that "Franco has sold himself completely to the reaction," or "Franco is a proven monarchist," or "he is completely under the influence of the Church."[41]

The roster of the first National Council of the FET was not complete until October 19, 1937. Of its fifty members, a maximum of twenty could be considered genuine Falangists (whether camisas viejas or serious neo-Falangists), while thirteen were Carlists, four were monarchists, and seven (later eight) were military commanders.[42] According to Serrano Súñer, at the first assembly of the National Council its leading military member, Queipo de Llano—who encountered increasing difficulty adjusting to the full authoritarianism that he had helped bring about—complained that all appointments were being made by one man. Franco observed wryly that this was "not a parliament" and soon ended the council meeting.[43] The first National Council convened only a few times, and its insignificance was extreme.[44] Little more could be said for the Junta Polí-

38. *Entre Hendaya y Gibraltar,* 31.

39. His major speeches during 1938 were published as *Siete discursos* (Bilbao, 1938).

40. The fullest expression of this came in the later book by the Falangist journalist Angel Alcázar de Velasco, *Serrano Súñer en la Falange* (Madrid, 1941).

41. Report from Eberhard von Stohrer, May 19, 1938. *Documents on German Foreign Policy,* vol. 3, no. 586, pp. 657–63.

42. Cf. Ridruejo, *Memorias,* 121.

43. Saña, *Conversaciones,* 148.

44. Serrano observed wryly, "Its life was not precisely intense." *Entre Hendaya y Gibraltar,* 65.

tica. According to Serrano, "Its labors were rather insignificant, serving only to prevent the party and the state from losing official contact with each other. In some cases the meetings (it should not be forgotten that the official party, like the National Movement itself, was a conglomerate of forces) were strained and even agitated. The political life of the regime resided in the ministries."[45]

It was Serrano more than Franco who bore the brunt of the enmity aroused by the new political alignment. His bitterest foes were monarchists, who realized that with the unification he was trying to lay the basis for a corporative, authoritarian, and presumably nonmonarchical state. This would create a major obstacle to restoration, and monarchists launched an extensive whispering campaign against Franco's "evil genius," the *cuñadísimo*. To counter this and other maneuvers by monarchist activists, Serrano, before the end of 1937, wrote directly to Don Juan, the young heir to the throne, in Estoril. In Franco's name, he asked for the monarchy's support of the Nationalist government for the duration of the conflict, pledging that afterwards the question of the monarchy would be taken up. According to Serrano, Don Juan promised full support in reply.[46]

In his *ABC* interview of the preceding July, Franco had enunciated his standard line for monarchists: "If the time for a restoration should arrive, the new monarchy would of course have to be very different from the one which fell on April 14, 1931: different in its content and—though it may grieve many, we must obey reality—even in the person who incarnates it. . . . [That person] ought to have the character of a pacifier and ought not to be numbered among the conquerers."[47] This last qualification defined exactly the role of King Juan Carlos after Franco's death nearly forty years later, though the eventual course of events was not precisely what the Generalissimo intended. In an article published in *La Revue Belge* on August 15, 1937, he added the seemingly democratic stipulation that "with regard to the future regime in Spain, the people itself will decide. I have already said that if the Spanish express the desire to return to the system of government that gave Spain its past greatness and lasted more than a thousand years, the decision belongs to them."[48] But his practical conclusion was that all concrete measures would be postponed for the duration, without any specific promises about what would then take place.

45. Ibid., 66.
46. Serrano, *Memorias*, 164.
47. *Palabras del Caudillo*, 168–69.
48. Ibid., 161.

Franco's First Regular Government

Had it been possible, Franco would also have preferred to postpone the organization of a regular government system and council of ministers until after the end of the conflict, but its duration made that impossible. In what was evidently intended as a symbolic gesture, Franco chose January 30, 1938, eighth anniversary of the downfall of the Primo de Rivera dictatorship, to announce a new administrative law establishing the structure of his government, with the names of his first regular cabinet ministers appearing on the following day. Article 16 of the new decree on government and administrative structure officially stated the powers of dictatorship, stipulating, "The Chief of State possesses the supreme power to dictate juridical norms of a general character."[49] This law also stated that the office of President of Government (prime minister) was "attached to that of Chief of State," permanently reserving the position for Franco. However, Serrano Súñer, who drafted the decree, also arranged to have the preamble declare, "The organization being carried out will remain subject to the constant influence of the National Movement, with whose influence . . . the administration of the new state is to be impregnated [sic]." Moreover, the law established certain procedural requirements for Franco's exercise of power when it declared that "the dispositions and resolutions of the Chief of State" much first be "proposed by the minister of the branch involved" and subjected to the "prior deliberation of the council of government" before becoming law.[50] This procedure was followed during 1938, though sometimes ignored during the years of World War II.

The new cabinet, appointed on January 31, replaced the Junta Técnica with regular government ministries and provided the first clear example of what would become Franco's typical balancing act, giving representation to all the main political currents. The senior position went to the able and respected Lt. Gen. Francisco Gómez Jordana, who became vice-president of the cabinet and foreign minister. Eight months earlier, at the beginning of June 1937, Jordana had replaced Dávila as president of the now-superseded Junta Técnica del Estado, and had managed to bring greater order into domestic administration. A member of Primo de Rivera's Directorio Militar and former high commissioner of Morocco, he was a monarchist moderate and Anglophile of the old school whose appointment greatly angered Falangists. The Ministry of Justice went to the Conde de Rodezno, the most sophisticated and urbane of the top Carlists, who proceeded to dismantle much of the liberal and laicizing legislation

49. A subsequent decree of April 22, 1938, repeated that the chief of state would assume "all the absolute powers of the state" in order to carry out "totalitarian aspirations." Clark, *Evolution*, 2:90.

50. These aspects are emphasized by Serrano's biographer, García Lahiguera, 124.

of the Republic. The minister of defense was Gen. Fidel Dávila, also moderate and astute and a former *primorriverista* who had recently commanded the victorious Nationalist campaign in the north. Finance went to Andrés Amado, a former collaborator of Calvo Sotelo who had the equivalent position in the Junta Técnica. A naval engineer officer and old childhood friend of Franco, Juan Antonio Suanzes, became the first minister of industry. The Catholic monarchist Pedro Sainz Rodríguez was appointed minister of education, the civil engineer Alfonso Peña Boeuf minister of public works, and the elderly but notorious primorriverista Gen. Severiano Martínez Anido became minister of public order. The only posts given Falangists were the Ministry of Agriculture, for Fernández Cuesta (who had no qualifications whatever in that area—an indication of the low priority given agriculture in the new regime), and the inevitably Falangist Ministry of Syndical Action and Organization, which went to the neo-Falangist Pedro González Bueno. Of eleven positions, three thus went to veteran generals who had collaborated with Primo de Rivera, two to right-wing monarchists, one to a Carlist, two to relatively apolitical technicians, and three to Falangists (including Serrano Súñer), only one of whom was a camisa vieja.

Though the new government promised to begin construction of the "national syndicalist state," it represented primarily the military and the old right, not the erstwhile national syndicalists of the new partido único. Subsecretaryships and other top administrative positions were filled in about the same political proportions as the ministries, with a high proportion of *abogados del Estado*, civil engineers, and technicians, especially from Aragon, the prewar home of Serrano Súñer. Technical personnel were of course more effective than Falangists in technical administration, and it was the state apparatus, not the party, which dominated affairs in the Nationalist zone.

That administrative apparatus was widely scattered, for the Nationalist government never acquired a full-fledged capital during the war. None of the provincial capitals of northern Spain possessed adequate facilities and housing for a national government. The nearest thing to a civil administrative center was Burgos, which was the site of several ministries, but two were located in Vitoria, two in Santander and one each in Bilbao and Valladolid. The Ministry of Defense was to be found in Salamanca, Franco's military headquarters.

The principal function of the FET was social and propagandistic. Strict control of the press was juridically defined by a tough new press and censorship law introduced on April 22, 1938, by Serrano Súñer in his role as national delegate of press and propaganda of the FET. This established a rigid system of control and prior censorship, with state propaganda and censorship at this juncture the only significant official preserve of the

FET. Serrano found a trio of ardent young camisas viejas for major appointments, making José Antonio Giménez Arnau the FET's national press chief,[51] Dionisio Ridruejo national propaganda chief and Antonio Tovar head of National Radio. Censorship was at first placed under the Falangist National Direction of Propaganda, headed by Ridruejo, while a network of forty-five daily newspapers, numerous radio stations,[52] and many specialized publications was built up between 1936 and 1943.[53] At this point Ridruejo and Tovar, who became close friends of Serrano, represented the most ardent element of Falangism and burned to create a genuinely revolutionary and totalitarian system.

Social Policy

Demogogy was a feature of more than Falangist rhetoric, for tough talk about "capitalism" had also been characteristic of the military leadership, particularly during the early phase of the Civil War. Nationalist commanders had threatened stiff sanctions against employers who failed to honor the existing social legislation of the Republic,[54] and Franco had promised "all possible reforms within the capacity of the nation's economy. We balk at nothing that the country's economy can stand. No use in giving poor land to poor peasants. It is not land alone that counts, but money to work it. Another twenty-five years will see the break-up of the big estates into small properties and the creation of a bourgeois peasantry."[55] In a subsequent interview he emphasized that the goal of the Nationalist movement was not to "defend capitalism" but to save the national interest of Spain. "We came," he said, "for the middle class and the humble class," not the wealthy. Franco promised state regulation of large concentrations of wealth and an agricultural development program featuring easier credit, the cultivation of unused land, reforestation, stimulation of the cattle industry, and special encouragement for such

51. Giménez Arnau prepared the first draft of the new press and censorship law. There are a few remarks about his work as national press chief during 1938–39 in his superficial autobiography, *Memorias de memoria* (Barcelona, 1978), 95–106.

52. On Nationalist radio during the Civil War, see Jesús García Jiménez, *Radiotelevisión y política cultural en el franquismo* (Madrid, 1980), 1–77.

53. A full list of FET publications will be found in Chueca, *El fascismo*, 461–70. On the party's general role in press and propaganda during the early years of the regime, see 276–94. A general outline of press policy during the early years of the regime is given in Manuel Fernández Areal, *La libertad de prensa en España (1938–1971)* (Madrid, 1971), 15–55; and Javier Terrón Montero, *La prensa en España durante el régimen de Franco* (Madrid, 1981), 54–64.

54. An early announcement by Franco and a proclamation by Cabanellas's replacement at Zaragoza to this effect are reprinted in G. Orizana and José Manuel Liébana, *El Movimiento Nacional* (Valladolid, 1937), 55–57.

55. *Chicago Daily Tribune*, July 27, 1936.

cash crops as tobacco, cotton, and flax.[56] Queipo de Llano, for his part, had declared, "We realize that the problem of class hatred can only be solved by the removal of extreme class distinctions. We realize, also, that the wealthy, by means of taxation, have to contribute toward a more equitable distribution of money."[57] Mola had early plumped for a "representative" kind of corporatism.[58] During the first months of the Civil War especially, the Nationalist press carried dire warnings addressed to "capitalists" demanding their conformity and financial contribution before it was too late.

This reflected the consistently populist line of Nationalist propaganda and policy, which was not at all structurally anticapitalist, however. Little in the way of absolute systemic change was promised, but much was proposed along the lines of populist and nationalist reform to regulate large property and industry and to provide greater opportunity for small business and greater social justice for the lower classes.

After the organization of the first regular government in 1938 it became necessary to give social policy a sharper focus. The new Council of Ministers approved a proposal that a *fuero del trabajo*—a "labor charter"—be prepared to fulfill the same function as the Carta del Lavoro in Fascist Italy. Two draft projects were commissioned, one by González Bueno, the minister of syndical organization, and his associates; the second by two of the more radical neo-Falangists with academic backgrounds, Joaquín Garrigues and Francisco Javier Conde, with the collaboration of Dionisio Ridruejo. The latter draft was originally entitled "Carta del Trabajo," reflecting Italian inspiration, but turned out to be quite radical, placing the national economy under the control of the proposed state syndical system, with its entire program based on an explicitly anticapitalist concept of property. The Garrigues–Javier Conde project was championed in the council of ministers by Fernández Cuesta but immediately rejected. The González Bueno project, conversely, was of a much more conservative, paternalist-capitalist nature and was referred to the National Council of the FET for further polishing.

This provoked a general free-for-all in the National Council. Carlists and other rightists offered amendments to make the proposed *fuero* more conservative, while Falangists countered with amendments to make it more radical. Serrano tried to salvage the situation by recommending that the most acceptable outcome would be a general statement of aims and

56. This was reflected in the first official agricultural program distributed by the FET, *El futuro de la agricultura nacional-sindicalista* (Valladolid, n.d., 1938?), which took much the same line.
57. *The Times* (London), April 18, 1937.
58. Ibid., March 8, 1937.

ideals, and Franco directed that a third draft be prepared by a bipartite commission headed by Ridruejo and Eduardo Aunós, Primo de Rivera's minister of labor.[59]

The resulting Fuero del Trabajo, approved on March 9, 1938, differed from the Fascist Carta del Lavoro primarily in its reflection of some of the principles of social Catholicism.[60] It proclaimed an economic middle way equidistant from "liberal capitalism" and "Marxist materialism," leading its defenders later to claim that the Fuero was not merely a statement of labor relations but of a new structure of economy. It declared labor both a duty and a right and defined capital as "an instrument of production." State protection was promised in limiting the work day and in guaranteeing Sunday rest, holidays, annual vacations, and the development of recreational facilities. The principle of a minimum wage was endorsed, together with family assistance and the goal of a "gradual but inflexible" increase in the standard of living. Point 10 promised basic social securities such as sickness, unemployment, and retirement insurance, while strikes and lockouts were both proscribed as "crimes against the supreme interest of the nation." Special labor courts were planned to adjudicate between capital and labor. Social justice within large industrial enterprises was made the special responsibility of an ambiguously defined *jefe de empresa*. The most radical provision was that which obligated the state to "endeavor to endow each peasant family with a small parcel of land," while protecting long-term rent leases and working toward the ultimate goal that the land "eventually belongs to those who work on it."

At the same time, it was made clear that the economy would continue to rest on the basis of private property, whose protection was guaranteed. The state was envisioned as undertaking direct economic initiatives only when private enterprise failed or "the interests of the nation required it." The Fuero promised protection to artisans, as well as guaranteeing enough income to entrepreneurs to make it possible for them to increase wages. Point 9 promised regulation of credit to make it available for large and small loans.

Construction of national syndicalism nominally began with the creation of the Ministry of Syndical Action and Organization on January 30, 1938, to be comprised of five National Services: Syndicates, Jurisdiction and Housing of Labor, Social Security, Emigration, and Statistics. A subsequent decree of April 30 elaborated the upper echelon of the syndical bu-

59. This account is based on interviews with Dionisio Ridruejo in Madrid, Jan. 10 and 19, 1959, and his description in *Casi unas memorias*, 195; and on *FF*, 2:288–89. Garrigues gave a formalistic explanation in his *Tres conferencias en Italia sobre el Fuero del Trabajo* (Madrid, 1939).

60. Cf. J. J. Azpiazu y Zulaica, *Orientaciones cristianas del Fuero del Trabajo* (Burgos, 1939).

reaucracy. A Central Syndical Council of Coordination was provided for and national syndicalist centers were to be established in each province.[61] On May 13 provisions were made for the establishment of labor magistrates to adjudicate between capital and labor.

Three months later, Fernández Cuesta made the following distinction between the nascent Spanish national syndicalism and Italian Fascist corporatism:

> Neither is the vertical syndicate a copy of the corporation. In those countries in which the governors have encountered, on coming to power, as in Italy, a class syndicalism that they could not dismantle, they have seen themselves forced, as a lesser evil, to convert it into state syndicalism and afterwards to create supersyndical organs of interconnection and self-discipline in defense of the totalitarian interest in production. Those organs are the corporations. The corporation, then, had a forced basis in class syndicalism. The vertical syndicate, on the other hand, is both the point of departure and of arrival. It does not suppose the previous existence of other syndicates. Broad horizontal structures do not interfere with it. It is not an organ of the state, but an instrument at the service of its utilitarian economic policy.[62]

The Falangist state, he said, would not be a syndicalist state per se:

> When we say "the national syndicalist state" we are referring to only one aspect of the state, the economic aspect. We mean that the state, to discipline the economy, employs the instrument of the syndicates, but we do not mean that the state is mounted solely and exclusively on the syndicates or that the sovereignty of the state lies in the syndicates.[63]

González Bueno enjoyed little success as minister of syndical organization. Wartime conditions were disturbed and the authority of his ministry was limited. A professional engineer, he lacked full capacity for the job. Three small syndical organizations already existed in the Nationalist zone: the CESO (Spanish Confederation of Worker Syndicates), the Catholic confederation that counted probably no more than 300,000 affiliates; the Carlist Obra Nacional Corporativa, organized after the start of the war with modest membership;[64] and the original Falangist syndicates. The latter consisted of the CONS (National Syndicalist Worker Confederation) and the CENS (National Syndicalist Entrepreneurial Confederation), the two exiguous economic groups launched in 1935 that maintained small nuclei in various provinces of the Nationalist zone. The Carlist Obra Na-

61. See the discussion in Miguel A. Aparicio, *El sindicalismo vertical y la formación del Estado franquista* (Barcelona, 1980), 53–80.

62. Raimundo Fernández Cuesta, *Intemperie, victoria y servicio: Discursos y escritos* (Madrid, 1951), 91.

63. Ibid., 101–2. See also Luis Mayor Martínez, *Ideologías dominantes en el Sindicato vertical* (Valencia, 1971), a *tesis de licenciatura* that briefly synthesizes Nationalist syndical theory, in its several variants, during the Civil War.

64. J. M. Arauz de Robles, *Obra Nacional Corporativa* (Burgos, 1937).

cional Corporativa had even published its own *Plan* of corporative theory in May 1937, though a series of steps had been taken between April and June of that year to bring together the Falangist and Carlist syndical groups, even if only on paper.

Confusion abounded with regard to the development of a national syndicalist system, and before the ministry was created, Fernández Cuesta had had to order all local press and syndical chiefs to "ABSTAIN COM-PLETELY FROM PUBLISHING ANY STATEMENT THAT MAY PRETEND TO IN-TERPRET THE POINT IN QUESTION [on syndicates]."[65] Some provincial leaders referred to González Bueno as the "minister of syndical disorganization," and a few even resigned.

The first step began late in April with the beginning of the formation of a Central Nacional-Sindicalista for each province, to be headed by a provincial delegate of syndicates who was both a provincial FET leader and a state official. The Centrals did not so much organize syndicates as begin to create "syndical services" that dealt with particular economic problems such as agricultural credit, fertilizers, rural cooperatives, and fishing and construction materials—branches of economic administration and assistance more than syndical organization. This was followed in July by creation of "commissions to regulate production" for major economic sectors. Their function was to arrange allocation of imports and organization of exports and to otherwise serve mainly an informational role.[66] Little was done to actually organize syndicates while the war lasted, and the first formal plan of syndical organization, drawn up late in 1938, was officially canceled in January 1939.[67]

In agriculture even less was accomplished. Though Fernández Cuesta might repeat in some detail variations of José Antonio's proposals for agrarian reform,[68] there was no intention of introducing even minor reform as long as the war lasted. The Nationalist zone benefitted from the fact that it included the greater share of Spain's farmland and concentrated on obtaining steady, normal production from the existing structure of agricultural exploitation. It never faced the severe food shortages, sometimes bordering on starvation, that afflicted the larger Republican cities in 1938–39.

65. *BMFET*, no. 11 (Jan. 1, 1938).
66. Cf. Aparicio, *Sindicalismo vertical*, 39–51.
67. Chueca, *El fascismo*, 348–49, 473–77.
68. "Syndical exploration of large unirrigated units; division of irrigated land into family units; the immediate start of irrigation in those areas where such facilities have already been prepared; determination of the kind of cultivation in each zone according to the conditions of exploitation; the movement of masses of peasants off those lands where it is impossible to live, because of sterility . . . to others more fit for production." Fernández Cuesta, *Discursos*, 104. There was of course no explanation of where the necessary new land and capital were to be found other than the vague implication that it would be from state assistance and requiring large owners to play a more socially constructive role.

The most effective social activity of the FET during the Civil War was not that of the syndicates but was the work of the Sección Femenina, whose membership expanded to approximately 580,000 by the end of the conflict.[69] The Sección Femenina created a conservative social and moral framework for female activism that took hundreds of thousands of women out of their accustomed routine to a greater extent than anything existing on the Republican side. It provided practical assistance on a large scale in the form of nursing and support for the Nationalist army.[70]

Significant political divergence also developed within the female auxiliary leadership, however. After the political unification, Carlist women's auxiliaries led by María Rosa Urraca Pastor were given direction of the Service of Fronts and Hospitals and did not cooperate fully with the national leadersip headed by Pilar Primo de Rivera. More serious was the autonomous development of Auxilio en Invierno (Winter Aid), created in Valladolid by the local Falangist leader Javier Martínez de Bedoya and Mercedes Sanz Bachiller, widow of the top early Falangist chief Redondo (and who later married Bedoya). Their organization was patterned on the Nazi Winterhilfe and received some limited technical assistance from Germany. In late 1937, after a long visit of Sanz Bachiller to the Third Reich, the organization was renamed Auxilio Social and officially made the national social assistance agency of the regime. Womanpower was provided by a decree of October 7, 1937, which established the obligation of six months "social service" for all unmarried women between seventeen and thirty-five. Though not absolutely compulsory, this was an almost indispensable requirement of all young women who sought any form of employment or professional qualification.[71] A severe personality conflict and power struggle developed between Pilar Primo de Rivera and Mercedes Sanz, and it was not fully resolved by a subsequent decree of December 28, 1939, that subordinated the social welfare agency to the Sección Femenina.[72] Though the FET's women's auxiliary never achieved its goal of the political education and indoctrination of Spanish women as a whole, its far-flung programs had a significant impact on the well-being of the less fortunate in the Nationalist zone, produced much more tangible results than did the work of its male counterparts, and contributed more than a little to the good morale and relative social cohesion of the zone.

Just as all political factions effectively supported the Nationalist war effort, all helped to promote aggressive gestures of nationalist culture. This involved such trivial matters as the common word *restaurant*, here-

69. *La Sección Femenina: Historia y organización* (Madrid, 1952), 20.
70. See María Teresa Gallego Méndez, *Mujer, Falange y franquismo* (Madrid, 1983), 47–59; and Mercedes García Basauri, "La Sección Femenina en la Guerra Civil Española," *Historia 16* 5:50 (June 1980), 45–56.
71. Fundamentos del Nuevo Estado (Madrid, 1943), 126–29.
72. The struggle over Auxilio Social is treated by Gallego Méndez, *Mujer*, 59–66.

tofore usually rendered in Spanish just as in French and English, but which now received an obligatory *e* at the end in all commercial eating establishments to make the word sound more Spanish. The new minister of justice, the Conde de Rodezno, promoted legislation on May 18, 1938, requiring that all newly christened Spanish children receive appropriate Spanish names not identified with foreign cultures or religions.

Internal Politics in 1938

Amid such paroxysms of patriotism Franco experienced few political problems in the first phases of construction of his regime. Though political figures from various backgrounds might occasionally be disciplined for stepping out of line, the only ones to draw Franco's special ire were a handful of Falangist zealots. For example, when three young leaders— Ridruejo, Pedro Gamero del Castillo, and Juan José Pradera—were authorized by the party's National Council to draw up a new organizational scheme for the FET, they quickly presented one that would have greatly increased the party's direct influence over the state and guaranteed the autonomy of its militia. Franco angrily quashed it,[73] for at no time had he the slightest intention of presiding over a party-dominated state.

This incident served only to increase Franco's suspicion of old-guard Falangists. The two most troublesome were González Vélez, from Leon, and Agustín Aznar, the militia leader. González Vélez was highly critical of the failure to develop mass national syndicalism during the war and proposed to lead a vague "Frente de Trabajo," whose name was derived from the Nazi Arbeitsfront. But, as Serrano put it much later,

> from an anti-Franco point of view in not accepting the results of unification, the most dangerous Falangist was not Vélez, but Agustín Aznar, since he was a man of limited ideas, but firm, a fighter, quite valiant and intolerant. He was the real leader of the Falangist resistance. And with him there were many more. . . . This group of irreduceable Falangists maintained constant communication with the Falangists fighting at the front, with whom they wanted to meddle.[74]

As Franco received more and more information on these activities and about political contacts made with several key commanders, Franco had both González Vélez and Aznar arrested and court-martialed in mid-1938. As usual, it was up to Serrano to mediate between Franco's wrath and the resentment of other Falangist leaders. Aznar, who was married to a cousin of José Antonio Primo de Rivera, soon had his sentence commuted to a term of internal exile and was set free after the war ended, but González Vélez was held in prison longer.[75]

73. There is an interesting account of this incident, narrated by Ridruejo, in Julián Lago, *Las contramemorias de Franco* (Barcelona, 1976), 119.

74. Saña, *Conversaciones*, 153.

75. Ibid., 152–54; Ridruejo, *Casi unas memorias*, 122–27; Serrano Súñer, *Memorias*, 262–64.

Despite their aversion to radical Falangism, the Carlists presented few problems, concentrating above all on military responsibilities. They held only twelve or thirteen (depending on individual categorization) of the fifty seats in the party's National Council, and only eight of the jefaturas provinciales. Of the National Delegations of the FET, only two of the politically least important—Health and Hospitals and Front-line Aid (Frente y Hospitales)—were directed by Carlists. Don Javier, the Carlist pretender, had determined soon after the unification that the Traditionalists would create no political problems for Franco as long as the war lasted, but in a brief visit to Spain at the close of 1937 he did condemn all those Carlist national councillors of the FET who had sworn a personal oath to the Movement and Franco without receiving personal permission.[76] He was ordered out of Spain, and Fal Conde was not permitted to return until after the war was over. At the lower levels of common FET membership, ordinary Carlists withdrew more and more, and in some districts never really participated directly in the new state party. In general, the closest collaboration came from the Navarrese Carlists who had so zealously supported the Nationalist movement from the beginning.[77]

The only conflict with monarchist politicians during the latter part of the war came in April 1938, when the Acción Española writer Eugenio Vegas Latapié was relieved of his seat on the National Council. At that point some within the *Acción Española* group began to end their direct collaboration with the regime, though in the beginning a number of the monarchist politicians had played a more prominent role in Franco's system than any Falangists. The only direct representative of Alfonsine monarchism in the first regular cabinet was the minister of education, the obese scholar Sainz Rodríguez, who carried out a general reorganization of the secondary education curriculum during 1938, introducing greater authority and an emphasis on religion, patriotism, and the traditional humanities. Yet his suspicion of Franco continued to mount, and his steady stream of jokes abut the Caudillo sometimes got back to Franco himself. Tension grew, and Sainz Rodríguez asked to be relieved of his post as soon as the war ended.[78]

Only two of the Nationalist generals created any political difficulties during the second half of the war: Queipo de Llano, and, what may seem surprising at first, Juan Yagüe, who had played a key role in Franco's rise to leadership. Queipo ruled most of Andalusia as a sort of personal vice-

76. Both these pronouncements are in the unpublished Carlist "Libro Blanco," 28–37.

77. Blinkhorn, *Carlism*, 293–94.

78. Sainz Rodríguez has given his own version of his fifteen months as a cabinet minister in his *Testimonio y recuerdos* (Barcelona, 1978), 253–74. His educational reform generally followed the pattern of the earlier Gentile reform in Fascist Italy, differing in its greater emphasis on religion. A study of Nationalist cultural and educational policy will be found in Alicia Alted Vigil, *Política del nuevo Estado sobre el patrimonio cultural y la educación durante la Guerra Civil Española* (Madrid, 1984).

Franco on an inspection tour during the Civil War

royalty as long as the war lasted.[79] Though he never challenged Franco directly, he felt increasingly restricted by the growth of an organized bureaucracy and state party in 1938. Queipo was extremely touchy about his own domain and complained angrily of the young Falangist civil governor of Seville, Pedro Gamero del Castillo, with whom he did not get along. In February 1938 he flew to Salamanca to demand that Serrano depose Gamero, which Serrano refused to do. Serrano did propose to Franco that it would be better to coopt Queipo further by bringing him into the cabinet as minister of agriculture (to replace the somewhat inept Fernández Cuesta), but Queipo had the wit to avoid such an assignment.[80] It was at this point that Queipo de Llano's nightly radio broadcasts from Seville, which he had carried on in a coarse but witty and often quite effective fashion since the start of the Civil War, were brought to a close.

The only more or less genuine Falangist among the Army commanders was Yagüe, who by 1938 commanded an entire corps on the main active front in the northeast. He evidently became disillusioned with Franco only a few months after he had helped push him through as Caudillo, turning to grumbling and dissident conversations from early 1937 on. He was infuriated by Franco's decision to halt the spring offensive of 1938 on the border of Catalonia and drive south against Valencia instead. On the first anniversary of the political unification in April 1938, he gave a speech in Zaragoza (the principal city to the rear of his corps) in which he acknowledged the courage of the Republicans, spoke on behalf of the political prisoners on both sides who were defending their ideals, and attacked the administration of justice in the Nationalist zone for its partiality.[81] For this Franco relieved him of command of his corps for several months, a comparatively mild measure, and then reinstated him.

Nor did Franco's Axis suppliers make any notable effort to meddle in domestic politics. The Italians never really had such ambitions, and Faupel's replacement as German ambassador, Dr. Eberhard von Stohrer, who arrived in Salamanca in October 1937, was much more discreet than his predecessor. He emphasized to Berlin that Germany should "avoid any interference in Spanish domestic affairs."[82]

We have thus far confined ourselves to indicating our particular sympathies for the movement in the Falange which is called the "original Falange," the "revolutionary Falange," or the "camisas viejas," which is closest to us ideologically and whose aims, in our opinion, also offer Spain the best guaranty for the establishment of a new and strong national state which could be useful to us. We

79. Many of his decrees and official dispositions have been collected in Julio Ramón-Laca, *Bajo la férula de Queipo* (Seville, 1939).

80. Serrano has given his account of this in his *Memorias*, 214–219; and in Saña, *Conversaciones*, 97.

81. Cf. the remarks of the German ambassador von Stohrer, *Documents on German Foreign Policy*, vol. 3, no. 586, pp. 657–63.

82. In a report of February 1938, ibid., no. 529, pp. 590–99.

have, therefore, readily placed our experience at the disposal of the Falange, have shown our party organizations, social institutions, etc., in Germany to picked representatives of the Falange, and have advised them upon request. We have thereby considerably lightened their task here, but we have naturally not been able to strengthen them to the extent that the victory of this element is assured.[83]

The Falangists in turn generally felt strong sympathy for the German and Italian parties. There was considerable propaganda interchange and the Falange organized pro-German "galas" and sent leaders of the Auxilio Social to Germany to observe Nazi social programs, but that was the limit. "On request, the Falange receives from the German press office a wealth of material on German conditions and the organization, etc., of the NSDAP. There is no importunate propaganda or 'intervention in the internal affairs' of Spain. Any objection of this type formerly made can at most refer to the beginnings of the Falange (the Hedilla affair)."[84] Statements like that of Franco in July 1937 that his regime would "follow the structure of totalitarian regimes such as Italy and Germany"[85] were pleasing to the Axis states and reassured them about the future direction of Spanish affairs.

Despite the Falange's total subordination to a state founded by military men, Franco's victory in the Civil War gave it considerable prestige as partido único among authoritarian nationalists elsewhere, especially in Catholic countries. At least two parties were named after it—Boleslaw Piasecki's Falanga in Poland and the Falange Social Boliviana in Bolivia. During the early years of World War II it had more than a little influence on the more radical youth among the Chilean Christian Democrats, and later still, the *Obras* of José Antonio were read by Fidel Castro in the Sierra Maestra.[86] That all these elements evolved in different directions is not in itself surprising in view of the eclecticism and contradictions of European fascist doctrine.

The dominant political factor in Nationalist Spain remained the ever-victorious military and political leadership of Franco, which towered over the new civic landscape. Though in general he lacked the esthetic qualities of charisma, there is little doubt that on its own terms the leadership of Franco acquired fully charismatic dimensions during the Civil War. The status of Caudillo, though never well worked out in theory,[87] was im-

83. Ibid.
84. Ibid., vol. 3, no. 455, pp. 480–84.
85. *Palabras del Caudillo*, 119.
86. Hugh Thomas, *Cuba or the Pursuit of Freedom* (London, 1967), 807, 822, cites several sources.
87. The only serious attempt to define the charismatic terms of Franco's caudillaje in Weberian theory were several articles and essays by Francisco Javier Conde, beginning with his "Espejo del caudillaje" (1941), reprinted in his *Escritos y fragmentos politicos* (Madrid, 1974), vol. 1. These were followed nearly twenty years later by Pascual Marín Pérez, whose

plicitly based upon a charismatic, supranormal legitimacy. The aspects of Franco's career and leadership that contributed to this were various: (1) his remarkable personal history and reputation stemming from combat days in Africa, where he seemed always to triumph, while other officers fell dead, wounded, or in defeat; (2) the dramatic circumstances of Spain and the military movement in 1936, which created a broad popular movement out of nothing, and recognized the personal eminence of Franco over all the other Nationalist leaders—a veritable raising of the leader on the shields of the military elite, as in ancient Visigothic times; (3) the undeniable effect of what had become the Nationalist propaganda machine; (4) the development of a personal style in Franco, not flashy, or glamorous, or even eloquent, but one that was self-assured, comfortable, convincing in command, and able to communicate basic principles and concerns to his followers; (5) the affirmation of the new Nationalist culture, which recognized authority and continuity based on a kind of historical-cultural legitimacy that Franco incarnated; (6) on that basis, the appeal to traditionalism and the combination of the higher Spanish tradition with effective new apsects of modernization; above all else (7) Franco's sure and steady victorious leadership in the Civil War, ever confident and seemingly well-organized, which never took a step back and scarcely lost a battle; climaxed by (8) the development of a new state system which represented the synthesis of these achievements, of the historic national culture and tradition and the requirements of twentieth-century government, and supposedly marking the beginning of a new historical era.

By the close of the Civil War the regime was not only militarily victorious but economically successful as well. Throughout the conflict it had maintained a stable paper currency and exchange rate without any gold reserve or central banking system, while the Republican peseta had collapsed well before the end of the war. This was a notable achievement, and seemed to indicate a capacity for economic as well as military leadership (and provided little warning of the dark days that would ensue soon after the fighting was concluded.)

Propagandistic exaltation of Franco began to hit its stride in 1937, though it did not reach a peak until 1939–40. The state Delegation of Press and Propaganda dated from February 1937, preceding formation of the official party and the full government administration. Shortly before the first anniversary of his rise to power, October 1 was officially declared that Fiesta Nacional del Caudillo. Franco's name was increasingly invoked on every possible occasion; "Franco, Franco, Franco" became a slogan and

---

El caudillaje español (Madrid, 1960) was the last major attempt to define theoretically a Franquist doctrine of caudillaje. See the discussion in Juan Ferrando Badía, *El régimen de Franco: Un estudio político-jurídico* (Madrid, 1984), 47–65.

Nationalist troops entering the Valencia region at war's end, 1939

chant equivalent to "Duce, Duce, Duce." The style was overtly fascistic, totally different from the impersonal, quiet, and largely constitutional authoritarianism of neighboring Portugal. At the same time, much more was made of Franco's military leadership than could have been done at that point in either Italy or Germany. "The Caesars were victorious generals" was a common slogan, and at times the caesar image was invoked almost as much as in Italy. In the terms of comparative politics, the symbolic legitimization was thus more pretorian or Bonapartist than directly fascist.

The physical appearance continued to betray the military and political image. Despite the emphasis traditionally placed by Spanish society on sartorial elegance, several years would pass before the Generalissimo finally acquired a competent tailor. As it was, his squat, roundish figure, ill-fitting uniforms, moist hands, timid manner, high-pitched voice, and tendency to waddle a bit as he walked were an enemy cartoonist's delight and the target of sarcasm even among a few of his senior generals and cabinet members. The monarchist education minister, Sainz Rodríguez, bitingly observed, referring to the Caudillo's daughter: "This Carmencita resembles her father more every day in her voice."[88] The garrulous and vulgarly macho Queipo de Llano, who detested Franco's style and manner, preferred to call him in private "Paca la culona" (perhaps best rendered as "Fat-fanny Francie"). Nearly two decades would pass before Franco would go on a rigid high-protein diet and become more svelte and distinguished in appearance as an aging dictator than as the victorious middle-aged Caudillo of the Civil War years.

Formation of Franco's first regular government in 1938 marked the end of the eighteen-month political career of his brother Nicolás, who was increasingly relegated to a secondary role after the arrival of Serrano Súñer. Nicolás headed a major Nationalist delegation to Rome in the late summer of 1937 to obtain increased support from Italy, and Franco originally planned to appoint him minister of industry in the new cabinet on the basis of his brother's experience in running a shipyard. Serrano Súñer manged to convince Franco that that would be "too much family" and would inevitably antagonize the public. Nicolás was subsequently made ambassador to Lisbon (where he had already represented the new regime as special agent), a post that he held for more than two decades.[89]

Late in 1938 Franco lost his younger brother Ramón, from whom he had long been alienated and who had decided to leave his diplomatic post in Washington, D.C., and join the Nationalists only after the Civil War was some three months old. Ramón subsequently received command of the naval air unit on Mallorca, where he found less than universal acceptance and admiration,[90] given his leftist antecendents, even though he had abjured his radical past. Whatever the perception of his colleagues, the middle-aged Ramón Franco was considerably changed from his youth. He had become more serious and even withdrawn, devoting himself exclusively to his profession and his family. He took part in a number of combat missions over the Mediterranean but on October 28, 1938, disappeared on a flight in very bad weather; his corpse was later found floating in the water.[91] Franco showed little desire to remember his younger brother, virtually severing relations with Ramón's widow (even though she was not a

88. According to Cabanellas, *Cuatro generales*, 2:513.

89. Some information of Nicolás Franco's career in Lisbon is provided in Garriga's *El hermano brujo*.

90. Kindelán, the Nationalist Air Force commander so active in elevating Franco to the jefatura única, felt obliged to write a letter to his commander-in-chief on Nov. 26, 1936, informing him that the appointment of Ramón had "been received very badly by the aviators, who show unanimous desire that your brother not serve in aviation, at least not in a position of active command." A facsimile is in Salgado Araujo, *Conversaciones privadas*, 441.

91. Various rumors were spread concerning what seems to have been a straightforward accident. See Pilar Jaráiz Franco, *Historia*, 138–42; and the report of the officer who discovered the body in Pilar Franco, *Nosotros*, 200–213.

demimondaine like the first wife) and daughter for the remainder of their lives.[92]

In August 1937 the official residence was moved to Burgos, the nearest thing to a Nationalist capital, where a large heterogeneous household (of which Serrano Súñer's own sizable family formed a part for many months) was established in the Palacio de la Isla, an old aristocratic residence. There the Franco family followed a generally austere regimen, with little evidence of the pomp and ostentation that would come later. The Generalissimo devoted himself to work with little respite. He avoided personal confrontation with subordinates; whenever anyone was discharged, the message would come in the form of an impersonal written order. In personal interviews and conversations he remained, as always, cautious and reserved. Ridruejo has written that when he was first ushered into Franco's headquarters he was "surprised to find a person more timid than arrogant."[93] As usual, save in formal meetings of his military staff or political cabinet, he preferred the chatter of small talk to the serious discussion of fundamental issues. He did not even fully share his counsel with Serrano; Doña Carmen was his only true intimate. His personal comportment could range to extremes, for he might exhibit genuine tears of grief and outrage over fresh reports of bloody atrocities in the Republican zone while maintaining an icy coldness in moments of danger or tension in military command or when ratifying the executions of convicted leftists.[94] What never altered was his imperturbable self-confidence—amounting to an overwhelming sense of self-righteousness—in the justice of his mission and the adequacy of his leadership.

92. Garriga, *El hermano maldito*, 278–306.
93. *Casi unas memorias*, 96.
94. One of the best personal sketches of the Franco of these years is that of Sainz Rodríguez, *Testimonio y recuerdos*, 323–43.

10

Civil War as Crusade

Religious concern played no overt role in the rebellion of the eighteenth of July that began the Civil War. Mola's original sketch for the new Nationalist system planned to retain not merely a republican form of government but also the Republic's separation of church and state. The first appeals of the Nationalist leaders made no special call for Catholic support. Some, in fact, had little concern for the defense of Catholicism—especially such Masons as Cabanellas and Queipo de Llano—while others were reluctant to complicate the situation further by giving a religious coloring to their movement. The insurgents hoped for extensive middle-class support and had no interest in antagonizing moderate anticlericals. Only four of the original ten members of Mola's Junta de Defensa Nacional could have been identified as overt political supporters of Catholicism in preceding years. Moreover, in his first address as chief of state, Franco promised merely that his state, "without being confessional, will respect of the majority of the Spanish people, without tolerating interference of another power within the state."[1]

The counterrevolutionary goals of the revolt nonetheless made conservative Catholics its natural allies from the very start. Some Catholic rightists participated marginally in the preparation of the rebellion, and in Navarre a part of the clergy aided military preparations of the Carlist militia. More important, in most cases the revolt was initially successful in

1. *FF*, 2:113. Indeed, the first religious leader to invoke publicly the righteousness of the Nationalist cause was no Catholic but the semipuppet caliph of the Protectorate, Muley Hassan, who proclaimed in July 1936 that Moorish volunteers for Franco's forces were participating in a jihad against atheists. Hilari Raguer, *La espada y la cruz* (Barcelona, 1977), 64.

those provinces where public opinion supported the right. In the Popular
Front zone, the revolutionary forces unleashed the most extensive persecution ever experienced by Roman Catholicism at any point in its modern history (with the sole exception of that inflicted on the small Catholic
minority in Russia during the Communist revolution). A total of 6,832
clergy were slaughtered in the leftist zone, the great majority even without the simulacrum of condemnation by revolutionary tribunals.[2]

As news of the explosive revolution and mass atrocities in the Popular
Front zone crossed the lines, the volume of Catholic support became
overwhelming. This in itself was hardly surprising; only a diametrically
opposite result would have been remarkable. As it was, Catholic backing
in terms of political support, military volunteers, financial assistance, and
perhaps above all, spiritual motivation and cultural legitimization became
the most important single domestic pillar of the Nationalist movement.

As the initial revolt stalled militarily, then broadened into full-scale
civil war, the military leadership moved to take advantage of Catholic
backing. By the end of July General Mola, the organizer of the rebellion,
used the phrase "the true Catholic Spain." In a radio address of August 15
he hailed "the cross that was and remains the symbol of our religion and
our faith,"[3] pledging to raise it over the new state. Such pronouncements
thenceforth became increasingly frequent. The first formal disposition in
recognition of the new regime's Catholicism came on September 4, when
it was ordered that school textbooks in the Nationalist zone be revised in
accordance with Catholic doctrine and that educational activities be segregated by sex.

Within thirty days of the outbreak of the conflict Church leaders began
to speak in favor of the military movement. Bishop Mateo Múgica of
Vitoria, issuing a pastoral instruction written by the primate, Gomá, denounced Catholic Basque nationalists for establishing a political entente
with leftist revolutionaries in two of the Basque provinces. Bishop Olaechea of Pamplona, center of the fervently Catholic province of Navarre
whose volunteers poured into the insurgent cause from the beginning,
declared on August 23, 1936, "This is not merely a war that is being waged
but a Crusade."[4] When General Franco, soon to be named Nationalist
commander-in-chief, moved his headquarters to Salamanca in the following month, Archbishop Pla y Deniel handed over the archdiocesan residence for Franco's official use. In a pastoral, "Las Dos Ciudades," issued
on September 30, Pla recited the long record of Republican persecution

2. The most authoritative study is Antonio Montero Moreno, *Historia de la persecución
religiosa en Espala 1936–1939* (Madrid, 1961). See also José Sanabre Sanromá, *Martirologio*
(Barcelona, 1943).

3. Felipe Bertrán Güell, *Preparación y desarrollo del Alzamiento nacional* (Valladolid,
1939), 243; Manuel Tuñón de Lara, *El hecho religioso en España* (Paris, 1968), 134–35.

4. Quoted in José Chao Rego, *La Iglesia en el franquismo* (Madrid, 1976), 26.

and stressed that the Church could not be criticized because it had "openly and officially spoken in favor of order against anarchy, in favor of establishing a hierarchical government against dissolvent communism, in favor of the defense of Christian civilization and its bases, religion, fatherland and family, against those without God and against God, and without fatherland. . . ."[5]

Despite the cautious tone of Franco's address on assuming the powers of head of state on October 1, this tendency toward absolute identification of the Nationalist cause with the church soon became even more accentuated. Franco had been raised as a devout Catholic. Though such a domestic background had no discernable effect on his brothers, Franco's attitude had always been much more respectful. He had given little outward indication of religious faith as a young officer in Morocco, but marriage reenforced his Catholic identity. By 1936, if not before, he had come to believe that Catholic faith and Spanish nationalism were inseparable, fully subscribing to the traditional Spanish ideology that stressed a special national relationship to Catholicism and a unique religious mission for Spain. His eldest niece declared that "his faith was genuine and by no means a mask of accommodation, even though his way of understanding the Gospel might leave a good deal to be desired."[6] Indeed, religious faith was for Franco an important aspect of the personal sense of destiny that he had developed.

During his first weeks as chief of state he nonetheless felt his way carefully, for the Spanish hierarchy as a whole did not endorse his new regime nor did the Vatican seem eager to grant official diplomatic recognition. Thus the regime first appears to have officially labeled itself a Catholic state in a minor decree of October 30 establishing the *plato único* (a day of the week in which restaurants served single-course meals as a symbol of austerity). The role of military chaplains was officially instituted in the Nationalist Army on December 6, though they had served with some volunteer units (mainly Navarrese Carlists) from the beginning. Subsequent negotiations with the Church concerning the regulation of their activities nonetheless proved surprisingly tense and difficult.[7]

The primate and archbishop of Toledo, Cardinal Isidro Gomá, supported the Nationalists from the beginning. He reported to the Vatican on October 24,

> It can be said that the situation created in Spain by the war has been much more effective than a system of missions in reviving Christian faith and piety.

5. Ibid., 25.

6. Jaraiz Franco, *Historia*, 37.

7. Antonio Marquina Barrio, *La diplomacia vaticana y la España de Franco (1936–1945)* (Madrid, 1983), 54–59. There are several memoirs by military chaplains of the Civil War. Fernando Pérez Escribano, *La Cruzada del escándalo* (Madrid, 1969), is one of the better ones.

The destruction of our churches, the profanation of objects of great devotion, and the slaughter of priests have struck a responsive note in the simple soul of the people, which expresses itself in splendid acts of piety. There is no public meeting related to the war not characterized by religious solemnity. Towns that in recent years had fallen into indifference have given proof of great fervor, not only in public acts but especially in the frequency of sacraments. . . .[8]

Gomá soon acceded to demands of the Nationalist government that the leading Church officials in Vitoria, ecclesiastical center for the Basque provinces, be removed because of their equivocal attitude toward Basque nationalism. The primate also showed understanding with regard to the Spanish Nationalists' own atrocious treatment of certain Basque priests involved in Basque nationalist political activities, some sixteen of whom had been executed. All sixteen had been tried by summary court-martial for secular political deeds,[9] but after Gomá's protest to Franco and to Dávila, the head of the Junta Técnica, on October 26, Franco ordered an immediate end to such condign punishments for Basque nationalist priests involved in politics,[10] and none were executed during the remainder of the war.[11]

According to Marquina Barrio, "Gomá always drew favorable conclusions from his interviews with Franco,"[12] whose evident piety and apparent good faith impressed the Cardinal. He was slow to grasp that Franco understood Catholic policy sui generis and, despite his intention to gain maximum support from religion, had no intention of becoming a "clerical politician," for he wanted "little interference from the Church and less from the Holy See"[13] in political matters. Thus in the late autumn of 1936 Gomá accelerated his efforts on behalf of the new regime. On November 24 he published a pastoral, "El Caso de España," specifying his position: "This most cruel war is at bottom a war of principles, of doctrines, of one concept of life and social reality against another, of one civilization against another. It is a war waged by the Christian and Spanish spirit against another spirit. . . ."[14]

8. Marquina Barrio, *Diplomacia vaticana*, 46. The most extensive study of Gomá is Ma. Luisa Rodríguez Aisa, *El cardenal Gomá y la guerra de España* (Madrid, 1981).

9. According to La Cierva, *Franco.*, 1:537-38. Basque nationalist priests routinely played political roles. Among the Spanish Nationalists, priests sometimes carried out very limited functions in local militia during the first months of the Civil War, much to the disgust of anticlericals such as Cabanellas in the insurgent command. Cf. Cabanellas, *Cuatro generales*, 2:361.

10. Marquina Barrio, *Diplomacia vaticana*, 48-49.

11. Though other sources state that two of the sixteen were killed even after Gomá's protest. Cf. Hilari Raguer, "El Vaticano y la Guerra Civil Española," *Cristianesimo nella Storia* (April 1982), 162. The fullest account of the prosecution of Basque nationalist priests during the Civil War is "El clero vasco ante los tribunales," in E. Apaiz Talde et al., *Historia de la Guerra Civil en Euskadi*, vols. 7-8 (San Sebastian, 1982).

12. Marquina Barrio, *Diplomacia vaticana*, 60.

13. Ibid.

14. *Iglesia, Estado y Movimiento acional* (Madrid, 1963), 21-23.

Several weeks later Gomá traveled to Rome to argue in favor of Vatican support for the Franco regime. Though the Vatican, like most Catholic opinion around the world, naturally favored those who defended Catholicism against one of the most severe persecutions in its history, Pius XI found it impolitic to have to take sides formally. A small number of devout Catholics had remained with the Popular Front regime, the Catholic Basque nationalists had recently won autonomy and concluded a deal with the Republic, and the Spanish Nationalists, accused of many murders and excesses of their own, could only inspire caution. The first ambassador of the insurgents to the Vatican was the seventy-six-year-old Marqués de Magaz, former senior member of Primo de Rivera's Military Directory and onetime representative of the earlier Spanish dictatorship to the Holy See. His stiff-necked and arrogant behavior, verging on discourtesy, achieved very little in Rome, where he was received simply as the agent of the Nationalists. His recall by Franco, coinciding with Gomá's visit to Rome, improved relations, and when Gomá returned to Spain on December 19, he was named "confidential and semiofficial [oficioso] representative" of the Holy See to Franco's government, and Franco's new representative to the Vatican was subsequently accorded the status of chargé d'affaires.[15]

On December 29 Franco and Gomá signed an informal six-point agreement, much more a gentleman's agreement than a formal treaty, whereby Franco promised full freedom to the Catholic Church for its activities. He pledged to abstain from unilateral control of spheres of overlapping competence between church and state and to bring Spanish legislation into conformity with church doctrine.[16] A feeble Vatican effort to propose mediation in the Spanish conflict was brushed aside several months later,[17] and during 1937, relations between the Church and the new state began to be regularized. Wartime conditions precluded resumption of the old ecclesiastical budget, and in some respects required ecclesiastical assistance to the state, but a long series of measures were adopted to establish Catholic norms in most aspects of culture and education and to foster religious observance. The Marian cult and all traditional symbols were restored in public schools, Corpus Christi was declared a national holiday once more, and Santiago was restored as patron saint of Spain. More and more regulations followed, not to be fully completed for nearly a decade.

Though the Vatican remained reluctant to commit itself, Franco urged the Spanish Church hierarchy to issue an official statement in order to dispel false impressions abroad. Gomá was himself eager to have the leadership of the Church in Spain take an official stand through a collective pas-

15. Concerning these discussions with the Vatican, see Rodríguez Aisa; Marquina Barrio, 50–52; and the article by Raguer.
16. Anastasio Granados, *El Cardenal Gomá, Primado de Espana* (Madrid, 1969), 99–100.
17. Marquina Barrio, *Diplomacia vaticana*, 62–63.

toral. On March 10, 1937, Cardinal Pacelli, Vatican secretary of state, wrote to Gomá, "The Holy Father leaves it fully up to your prudent judgment."[18] This opened the way for the negotiation and writing of the famous Collective Letter of the Spanish hierarchy that was published on July 1, 1937, soon after the final collapse of Catholic Basque resistance in Vizcaya.

This major document, forty-two pages long, provided a long and detailed statement of the Spanish Church's position on the war along with a carefully argued justification. It catalogued the deficiencies of the prewar Republic and the latter's failure to observe democratic procedure or maintain civil rights, then discussed in detail the onslaught of the Spanish anarcho-Marxist revolution, which it termed simply Communist. The hierarchy rejected the frequently advanced interpretation that the Civil War was essentially a class war, terming it primarily an ideological conflict, a war of ideas. They pointed out that all the wealthier provinces of Spain—those with the highest per capita income—were dominated by the left, while the Nationalist movement was based primarily on the poorer and agrarian regions, whose predominant philosophy was Catholic, not collectivist/materialist.

The hierarchy disclaimed any desire for conflict with the left. They observed that the Church did believe in the doctrine of just war and in the past had helped to organize armed crusades, but emphasized that this was not their position: "The Church has neither desired nor sought this war and we do not think it necessary to vindicate it against the charges of belligerence with which the Spanish Church has been censured in some foreign newspapers."[19]

In these circumstances the Church leaders believed that Catholics had no alternative but to support the "civic-military movement," as they termed it, of Franco. The adjective *national* as applied to Franco's forces was deemed fully justified. The Spanish prelates held that the values of the insurgents corresponded to the Spanish national spirit and were shared throughout Spain. They also insisted that the cause of the insurgents was national in its aim of restoring the culture and ethos of Spanish society in consonance with its own history.

Thus with the exception of two dissident prelates who refused to sign,[20] the Spanish hierarchy endorsed the struggle of Franco's regime in the

18. Quoted in Raguer, *La espada*, 103.

19. Cardenal Isidro Gomá y Tomás, *Pastorales de la guerra de España* (Madrid, 1955), 147–89.

20. Five bishops failed to sign the Collective Letter, but in the case of three this was because of geographical obstacles and problems of communication. The principal dissident was the Catalan prelate Vidal i Barraquer, archbishop of Tarragona, who maintained a liberal stance in exile. See Ramon Muntanyola, *Vidal i Barraquer, cardenal de la pau* (Barcelona, 1970), 502–689.

Civil War. What it did not do, however, was endorse the Franco regime as a specific form of government or as an end in itself.

> With respect to the future, we cannot predict what will take place at the end of the struggle. We do affirm that the war has not been undertaken to raise an autocratic state over a humiliated nation but in order that the national spirit re-regenerate itself with the vigor and Christian freedom of olden times. We trust in the prudence of the men of government, who will not wish to accept foreign models for the configuration of the future Spanish state but will keep in mind the intimate requirements of national life and the path marked by past centuries.[21]

The Collective Letter made it clear that the Church leadership had no intention of endorsing any specific form of authoritarianism. Apparently with Fascism and Nazism in mind, it warned against the influence of "foreign ideology on the state that would tend to divert it from Christian doctrines and influence."[22] The new Spanish government, still not fully defined in mid-1937, was seen by the Church hierarchy, not necessarily incorrectly, as primarily a right-wing traditionalist/nationalist regime.

The new state was nonetheless slowly proceeding to absorb the political and social activities of prewar Catholic organizations. The Catholic trade union federation, CESO, was absorbed into the nascent national syndical system during the following year, and the Catholic university student group, Confederación de Estudiantes Católicos, survived only a little longer until it was similarly subsumed into the SEU, the Falangist student organization. Of all Catholic political and social groups, only the agrarian organization, CONCA, endured into the post–Civil War period with its identity and independence at least partially intact, though reduced in support and range of action.

The Falange had always affirmed Catholicism as religion but before the Civil War had evinced considerable ambiguity about its political and institutional relation to the Church. One of its original financial backers, the wealthy and ultra-Catholic Marqués de la Eliseda, had left the party in 1935 because of that ambiguity.[23] The party program spoke merely of the "concord of interests" between church and state, while even Onésimo Redondo, the most overtly Catholic of the founders of the party, had declared that in order to be "totalitarian" and truly nationalist the new state could not merely "defend religion" or be "confessional."[24] Some of the most radical Falangists, who insisted on the predominance of party and state, provided the only undercurrent of anticlericalism to be found in the Nationalist zone.

21. Gomá, *Pastorales.*
22. Ibid.
23. Eliseda presented his own position in his *Fascismo, catolicismo, monarquía* (San Sebastián, 1935).
24. Onésimo Redondo, *El Estado nacional* (Madrid, 1943), 46.

   This was made much less disturbing by the frequent and open declarations of Catholic orthodoxy from the official Falangist organization, both old and new. Manuel Hedilla, for example, had always been careful to distinguish Falangism from secular foreign fascisms, declaring in a newspaper interview early in the conflict: "The pagan sense of the cult of Fatherland and subordination to race, force, and so forth that one finds among some foreign movements of a similar type is substituted in ours by a strong dose of religious spirituality, which is very much in accord with our traditions." [25] The official statutes of the new FET declared the goal of the movement to be restoration of Spain's "resolute faith in her Catholic and imperial mission." The first article recognized "the Christian freedom of the person," while article 23 stipulated the naming of a national director of religious education and attendance. This was but part of a trend that the German ambassador found quite alarming in its "reactionary" and "clerical" quality. Indeed, when Franco emphasized that Spanish "totalitarianism" would be derived from the monarchism and cultural policy of the Catholic Kings, he was not merely coining a symbolic phrase. The Franquist regime was embarked on the most traditionalist, indeed reactionary, cultural policy of any twentieth-century Western state, bar none. It was an enterprise virtually without parallel.

   Though this was not fully defined in explicit political philosophy, it was enough for nearly all Church leaders and the great majority of Catholic laymen. Perhaps the nearest thing to a discussion took place in the influential Jesuit journal *Razón y Fe* in October 1937. José Azpiazu, discussing the concepts of the traditional state and the totalitarian state in an article so entitled, inquired:

> What is the concept of the totalitarian state and what does it represent? Above all—in Spain more than anywhere else—it represents a strong and complete type of state, shorn of the weaknesses and hesitations of the liberal and socialist state, a power representing all the vital forces of the nation. . . . For many—though mistakenly, in our judgment—the totalitarian state means a state that takes into its hands the direction and control of all the affairs of the nation. Such a concept is totally false and one must expunge it. If that were true, the totalitarian state would be equivalent to the socialist state or, at least, very similar to it.
>
>   . . . . The state must assist the Church in achieving her most holy goal of the salvation of man to the greatest degree possible. This is not different from the goal of the state but simply superior to it. So that if we should try to define the essence of the totalitarian state in a single phrase, we would say that the Spanish totalitarian state should not be totalitarian in the objective sense—that would be equivalent to a socialist one—but in the subjective sense of a total and sovereign power, strong and not limited, directive and not frustrated. . . .
> If it were thus, let us have the totalitarian state, for that would be equivalent to

25. Reprinted by *Arriba España* (Pamplona), Jan. 6, 1937.

the total resurrection of the pure and authentically traditional Spain, without shadows of foreign systems nor the mixture of non-Catholic doctrines.[26]

Azpiazu correctly introduced the distinction between a structurally totalitarian socialist system of the Leninist-Stalinist pattern and the essentially Mussolinian type of political dictatorship of limited scope that employed the rhetoric and coined the phrase of totalitarianism. What he failed to do altogether was to define the structural, philosophical, or functional nature of a Spanish totalitarianism as distinct from that of Fascist Italy beyond the general insistence that Spanish nationalism could only be exclusively Catholic. Totalitarianism therefore merely stood for some form of an authoritarian system—though not at all structurally totalitarian in the comparative empirical sense—and for cultural and religious unity. Unity was, in fact, the common theme of both religious and secular commentators.

In the same number of *Razón y Fe,* a well-known Jesuit writer, Constantino Bayle, engaged in similarly fuzzy qualifications. He argued that the National Movement, as Franco's state party was now called, was not necessarily fascist, since it was also pluralist. For Bayle, there was no clear content to the term fascist. If fascism were to mean law and order and the resurrection of the national spirit, he was for fascism. "If that is meant by fascism, then we are in agreement. . . . And, carefully examined, the party or organization for whom the term is least ill-suited [the Falange] stands for nothing else [no otra cosa es]."[27]

There were a number of ideologues in the Nationalist zone who specifically espoused the term fascism, though this was never official policy, but also insisted that its definition in Spain must be consubstantial with Catholicism. Probably the most widely read new book of political doctrine published in the Nationalist zone during the Civil War was José Permartín's *¿Qué es lo nuevo?* (1938), which declared that "fascism is, in brief, the Hegelian fusion of state and nation. Consequently, if Spain is to be national, and is to be fascist, the Spanish state much necessarily be Catholic." The 1940 edition elaborated further:

26. J. Azpiazu, S. J., "Estado tradicional y Estado totalitario," *Razón y Fe* 37:477 (Oct. 1937), 186–87, in J. J. Ruiz Rico, *El papel político de la Iglesia católica en la España de Franco* (Madrid, 1977), 67. It might be noted that Padre Azpiazu was perhaps the leading authority in the Spanish clergy on the theory of corporatism. He had earlier published *El Estado Corporativo* (Madrid, 1936) and later brought out *El Estado Católico* (Madrid-Burgos, 1939), as well as the booklet *¿Corporativismo o nacional-sindicalismo?* (Pamplona, 1938). In the latter work Azpiazu correctly warned of the danger of exaggerated state power in a state national-syndicalist system, and pointed out that the mere organization of state-sponsored vertical syndicates would not, by mere mechanical means, eliminate class antagonisms. In general, however, he agreed with the primary Church position that accepted the legitimacy of the Nationalist state system.

27. Quoted in Ruiz Rico, *Papel político,* 68.

The New State must be founded on all the principles of traditionalism in order to be genuinely national and Spanish. Thus in Spain the Falange must become the technique of traditionalism. Our fascism, our Hegelian juridical absolutism, must necessarily be grounded in its form on a historical-Catholic-traditional basis. Spanish fascism thus becomes the religion of religion. The Italian and German fascisms have invented nothing new for us. Spain was already fascist four full centuries before them. When it was united, great and free, Spain was truly so; in the sixteenth century, when state and nation were identified with the eternal Catholic ideal, Spain was the model nation, the *alma mater* of western Christian civilization.

This simple identification of "Spanish fascism" with the traditional Spanish ideology—ignoring many of the radical innovations and totally distinct philosophies of Italian Fascism and German Nazism—was echoed by other Nationalist writers.[28] A Falangist priest from Navarre, Fermín de Yzurdiaga, even served as the national chief of press and propaganda of the FET in 1937, endeavoring to popularize the nationalist-Catholic slogan "Por el imperio hacia Dios" ("For the empire toward God").

Yet most Catholic opinion had little desire to be identified with or use the nomenclature of fascism, preferring instead to invoke the Nationalist cause as a crusade pure and simple.[29] A sizable literature developed in this vein during 1937–38, devoted to justifying the initial rebellion, the concept of the just war, and the crusading quality of the Nationalist movement.[30] Conversely, there was no trace of self-criticism or any public sign

28. Such as the formerly dissident Marqués de la Eliseda, who found in the new regime and its FET his ideal form of fascism, as he defined it in *El sentido fascista del Movimiento Nacional* (Santander, 1939). Cf. Federico de Urrutia, *Por qué la Falange es católica* (Madrid, 1939); and Pedro Laín Entralgo, *Los valores espirituales del nacionalsindicalismo* (Madrid, 1941).

29. To cite six examples collected by one historian: the archbishop of Valladolid: "The most holy war witnessed by the centuries" (Mar. 30, 1937) and "[Nationalist troops are] crusaders for Christ and for Spain" (Mar. 28, 1937); the archbishop of Granada: "We find ourselves once more at Lepanto" (Oct. 1937); the archbishop of Cordoba: "The most heroic crusade registered by history" (Dec. 30, 1937); the bishop of Tuy: "This is not a civil war but a patriotic and religious crusade"; the bishop of Tenerife: "Of all the just and holy wars known to history, none is more sacred and just." Chao Rego, *La Iglesia*, 26, 377–79.

30. Fray Ignacio González Menéndez-Reigada, *La guerra española ante la moral y el Derecho* (Salamanca, 1937); Julio Meinville, *¿Que saldrá de la España que sangra?* (Buenos Aires, 1937); Juan de la Cruz Martínez, *¿Cruzada o rebelión? Estudio histórico-jurídico de la actual guerra de España* (Zaragoza, 1938); Constantino Bayle, *Sin Dios y contra Dios* (Burgos, 1938); A. de Castro Albarrán, *Guerra santa: El sentido católico de la guerra española* (Burgos, 1938); José Joaquín Azpiazu y Zulaica, *¡Por Dios y por la patria! El patriotismo como virtud cristiana* (Burgos, 1938). For a critique, see Herbert R. Southworth, *Le mythe de la croisade de Franco* (Paris, 1963).

One of the most extreme and categorical political endorsements of the regime by a cleric was Menéndez Reigada's *Catecismo político español* (Salamanca, 1937), subsequently declared an official school text by order of the Ministry of Education on March 1, 1939. It declared the Iberian peninsula to be "providentially placed by God in the center of the world," and solemnly informed its readers that there were three types of "totalitarian states": the materialist, the pantheist, and the Christian. "The Spanish state has adopted the form of the Christian totalitarian state, because that is what is most appropriate to the struc-

of concern over the harshness of Nationalist policy, which involved extensive political executions, ultimately reaching into the tens of thousands. There were occasional instances of private intercession by an individual priest or prelate, but it never went beyond that.

Cardinal Gomá remained adamant throughout the war in his faith in the righteousness of the Nationalist cause, a faith equally certain that the Crusade would lead to a profound spiritual awakening in Spain. At the May 1938 International Eucharistic Congress in Budapest, he declared that the Civil War could not end in compromise but that the left must surrender completely. Near the conclusion of the fighting, his pastoral "Catolicismo y Patria" intoned: "Let us give thanks to God that he has willed to make of Spain a Christian people from the heights of [state] power. This is declared, moreover, by the new legislation of the state, informed by Catholic spirit in its broad trajectory. And our hope is confirmed, dear diocesans, by the undeniable religious resurgence that we have observed in the liberated portion of our beloved archdiocese."[31]

Formal derogation of some of the main Republican anti-Catholic legislation was nonetheless delayed by the Franco regime until the spring of 1938, when both its military dominance in the war and the recognition and support of the Vatican seemed assured. In March of that year obligatory religious instruction was restored in public schools, crucifixes mandatorily reinstalled in all classrooms, the validity of religious marriage emphasized, and plans announced for a new religiously inspired secondary school curriculum. The only lingering expression of anticlericalism might be found among the radical elements of the Falange. In rare moments of belligerence, a Falangist newspaper might declare that papal politics were not infallible and denounce the Franciscan aspects of Catholicism.[32] A brawl in Seville during the autumn of 1938 between a Falangist youth demonstration and a religious procession created a major scandal, which the government tried to cover up.[33]

That the last expressions of Falangist anticlericalism were not eliminated altogether was due to the fact that they played a role in Franco's political balancing act. He administered a primarily but not totally clerical regime, and he wanted to reserve other, nonclerical cards to play, though his public posture of total piety could never admit it.

---

ture and tradition of the Spanish nation." Such a state would "regulate, harmonize and channel all, . . . private and collective rights," because it was "superior to all individual interest [bienes particulares]."

31. *Iglesia, Estado y Movimiento Nacional*, 35–37.

32. *Unidad* (Santander), May 23, 1937; *Sur* (Málaga), Dec. 12, 1937; *FE* (Seville), Jan. 1, 1938; *Hierro* (Bilbao), Mar. 7, 1938.

33. Report of the German ambassador von Stohrer. *Germany and the Spanish Civil War*, vol. 3, no. 699, pp. 796–801.

During the Festival of Victory held in Madrid's Church of Santa Barbara on May 20, 1939, Franco offered the public prayer: "Lord God, in whose hands is right and all power, lend me thy assistance to lead this people to the full glory of empire, for thy glory and that of the Church. Lord: may all men know Jesus, who is Christ the son of the Living God."[34] It was an unusual invocation of empire during the era of World War II, though one fully consistent with the traditional Spanish ideology.

34. *Iglesia, Estado y Movimiento Nacional*, 45–46.

11

The Repression

Revolutionary civil wars of the twentieth century have generally been marked by a high degree of political violence against civilians. It has been observed that civil wars tend to be much more conflicts of principle than are most international struggles, while those of this century have been stimulated by intense ideological and moralistic passion. In the past, civil wars might take a heavy toll of life on the regular battlefield—as in the case of the English conflict of the 1640s and the American Civil War of the 1860s—yet be generally free of atrocities against civilians. This was presumably due to the fact that despite the intense differences in political principle that divided the participants in these earlier conflicts, they continued to share a certain common world outlook, religion, or sociomoral framework. Mass atrocities against civilians at the time of the great English civil war were directed almost exclusively against Irish Catholics—beyond the general pale of English civilization. By contrast, nearly all the twentieth-century conflicts have reflected intense civilizational and ideological conflicts that demonize the enemy and serve psychologically and emotionally to legitimate the most extreme and atrocious measures.

These were initiated by Lenin's imposition of the Red terror in 1918, to which the counterrevolutionaries responded, though in somewhat lesser degree. The Hungarian revolution was characterized by considerable atrocity, albeit not of the Russian scale, and widespread violence against civilians was also a feature of the subsequent civil wars in Greece and in east Asia. Even in restrained and legalistic Finland, the civil war of 1917–18 took a proportionately heavy toll of life during or in the aftermath of a four-month conflict—about one percent of the total Finnish population,[1] roughly equivalent, for its duration and the population involved, to the loss of life in Spain during a three-year conflict.

From the very beginning, the political violence that attended the struggle in Spain attracted widespread publicity and revulsion, not because it was more severe than in other revolutionary civil wars but simply because it was the first to be widely publicized, and took place in a western country at that. On any reasonable comparative scale, political violence against civilians in Spain would have to be rated somewhere in the middle range among conflicts of this type. It was more severe than that of Hungary, rather less than that of Russia, and as indicated, about the same as that of the only example to be found in Protestant Scandinavia.

Political violence had already become a major factor in mutual polarization before the war began. All the left revolutionary groups made repeated appeals to the legitimate use of revolutionary violence, as did the Falangists, and the rightist radicals differed only in the greater decorum of their outward expression of such urges. When the Civil War began, violence came naturally to the left, who had long been primed for it and incited to it by their propaganda media and had actively practiced it in Asturias, Barcelona, Madrid and elsewhere. The same might be said of the Falangists, who had lost about sixty of their number as fatalities to leftist violence before the war began and had slain an approximately equal number of their enemies.

From the start, both sides blamed the other for having initiated political executions and reprisals, and each claimed that the repression was much more widespread and vicious in the opposing zone. Vague references in the planning of the conspirators that were later published might be taken as tenuous indication that a very harsh policy was planned from the beginning.[2] In fact, the first general slaughter—and one that imme-

1. The principal study of the fatalities in the Finnish Civil War is Jaakko Paavolainen, *Poliittiset väkivaltaisundet Suomessa 1918*, 2 vols. (Helsinki, 1967). It arrives at a total of 31,000 or about 1 percent of the Finnish population of 3,200,000. The bulk were direct or indirect victims of the White terror, which killed about 8,400 outright. Another 11,800 (included in the total) died afterwards in camps.

By comparison, the numbers executed by left and right in the Hungarian revolution and counterrevolution of 1919 were relatively minuscule. Cf. Andrew C. Janos, *The Politics of Backwardness in Hungary 1825–1945* (Princeton, 1982), 197–202. The most lethal of all the revolutionary civil wars was that which took place in Yugoslavia during World War II. There the triangular conflict between Croatians, Serbs, and Communist Partisans was inextricably mixed with the consequences of foreign occupation and vicious Nazi repression. The official Yugoslav statistics for total nonnatural deaths above the prewar norm is 1.7 million, about 12 percent of the population, and much of this stemmed from the civil war itself. The Russian civil war of 1918–21 was proportionately almost as destructive, if the millions of deaths resulting from the subsequent famine are added to those slain in combat and in the accompanying repressions.

2. For example, Mola's "Instrucción Reservada Número Uno," prepared at the close of April 1936, stated: "It should be understood that the action must be violent in the extreme, in order to subdue the enemy—who is strong and well-organized—as soon as possible. All

diately received widespread photographic publicity if only because of its location—was the killing of rebels captured by leftist militia at the Montaña barracks in Madrid on July 20,[3] the third day of the conflict. By that time, executions had already taken place in Nationalist-dominated territory, and atrocity then followed atrocity.

A common distinction between the Red and White terrors in Spain that has sometimes been made by partisans of the left is that the former was disorganized and spontaneous, and largely suppressed after about six months, while the latter was centralized and systematic, continuing throughout the war and long afterward. This distinction is at best only partially accurate. In the early months the Nationalist repression was not at all centrally organized, whereas that in the Popular Front zone had more planning and organization than it is given credit for. This is indicated by the many executions in areas where social conflict was not particularly intense, and by the fact that many of the killings were done by revolutionary militia coming in from other districts. Nor did the political executions in the Republican zone end after the close of 1936, though they did diminish in volume.[4]

On July 28, 1936, the Burgos Junta declared total martial law throughout Nationalist Spain.[5] In Valladolid a *consejo de guerra* was set up within twenty-four hours of the rebel takeover. Further Junta rulings on August 31 and September 8 directed all Army and Navy courts to conduct proceedings as swiftly as possible and to suspend jury trials even for civil cases.[6] It was considered necessary to take strong measures from the start to establish control of a chaotic situation, but Mola himself was surprised by the rebels' ferocity. The memoir of his secretary reflects the attitude of the rebel command. For example, early in the conflict Mola had occasion to order that a truckload of captured militiamen be executed at the side of the road. When he changed his mind and rescinded the order, a staff colo-

---

the leaders of political parties, organizations, or trade unions not in favor of the movement will be arrested and exemplary punishments applied, so as to stifle strikes or rebellions." Quoted in Felipe Beltrán Güell, *Preparación y desarrollo del Movimiento Nacional* (Valladilid, 1938), 123. Mola even drew up a subsequent plan calling for summary execution of all who opposed the revolt. Quoted in Garriga, *Los validos de Franco*, 34.

3. An American correspondent reported, "The memory of that shooting of the Madrid officers is one of the strongest motives in the hearts of the White Army. I have seen officers carrying pictures of the shootings, clipped from foreign publications. There were some remarkable pictures." H. R. Knickerbocker, *The Siege of Alcazar* (Philadelphia, 1936), 22.

4. This issue has been most accurately addressed by Ramón Salas Larrazábal, *Los fusilados en Navarra en la guerra de 1936* (Madrid, 1983), 71–75. The largest single slaughter in the Republican zone, the killing of several thousand prisoners from the city's political prisons at Paracuellos del Jarama in the late autumn of 1936, has been analyzed by Carlos Fernández, *Paracuellos del Jarama: ¿Carrillo culpable?* (Barcelona, 1983); and Ian Gibson, *Paracuellos: cómo fue* (Barcelona, 1983).

5. *BOJDN*, July 29, 1936.

6. Ibid., Sept. 1 and 9, 1936.

nel complained, "General, let us not have to repent afterwards for mildness!"[7] Mola was said to have remarked, "A year ago I would have trembled
to sign a death sentence. Now I sign more than ten a day with an easy conscience."[8] At Seville, Queipo de Llano was even more outspoken. In his
nightly radio broadcasts he made direct references to the brutal reprisals
being carried out, apparently in order to terrify leftist listeners into
submission.[9]

Juridical and police power was not centralized in the Nationalist zone
until more than eight months had passed. Local and regional military authorities thus held direct responsibility for police action and proved implacable in execution. Franco himself set an important precedent during
the first days of the revolt in Morocco when, shortly after arriving to assume command, he approved the execution of his own first cousin, Major
Ricardo de la Puente Bahamonde, who had resisted the rebellion as commander of the Tetuan airfield.[10] Almost all the high-ranking officers in the
Nationalist zone who had refused to join the rising were shot during the
first year of the Civil War.[11] Even Franco proved unable to save the life of
one of his most valued subordinates at the old Zaragoza General Military
Academy, General Miguel Campins. As commander of the Granada garrison Campins had been reluctant to support the revolt, and the Nationalist commander-in-chief of Andalusia, Queipo de Llano, quickly relieved
him of command, subjected him to court-martial, and flatly rejected
Franco's personal request that the death penalty be reconsidered.[12]

The objects of the repression were leftist leaders and activists in general and anyone suspected of opposing the Nationalist movement in particular. There was randomness in the repression on both sides, but active
figures of the political opposition were marked men (and women), and
thousands of ordinary affiliates, members, and militiamen were shot as

7. Jose María Iribarren, *Con el general Mola* (Zaragoza, 1937), 94. After its publication
following the death of Mola, this book was immediately suppressed by the Nationalist government, though Mola had personally approved the manuscript before publication and
thanked the author for rendering a faithful account.

8. Ibid., 245 (and according to a handwritten correction made in Iribarren's personal
copy).

9. *ABC* (Seville), July 22–27, 1936, and elsewhere in Gibson, *Queipo de Llano*.

10. Many were of course shot for less. Cf. the remarks of Franco Salgado-Araujo in his
memoir *Mi vida junto a Franco*, 167–69. This grim incident did not, by the way, poison
family relations, for one of La Puente Bahamonde's brothers later served as assistant head of
Franco's personal military staff (segundo jefe de la Casa Militar). Jaraiz Franco, *Historia*,
83–85.

11. Altogether, 25 of Spain's 85 generals on the active list in 1936 were executed during
the Civil War, 17 in the Republican and 8 in the Nationalist zone. Two admirals were also
executed. There are some general remarks in Gabriel Cardona and Joan Villaroya, "La represión contra los militares republicanos," *Historia 16* 8:92 (Dec. 1983), 33–36.

12. Franco Salgado-Araujo, *Mi vida*, 185–88, and Garriga, *Los validos de Franco*, 37–38.
The execution of Campins occurred in mid-August 1936, some six weeks before Franco's elevation to the jefatura única.

well.[13] Of the two terrors, the White terror of the Nationalists was probably the more effective, not because it killed more people but because it was more concerted.

Though the military authorities were responsible for the great majority of the death sentences, executions were usually carried out either by the Civil Guard or by Falangists and other civilian militia. The first official circular of the Falangist Junta de Mando under Hedilla on September 9, 1936, tried to eliminate spontaneous acts of repression on the part of Falangist militia, ordering them to strictly obey local military command, which in many localities directed Falangists whom to arrest or shoot. Hedilla soon protested to Mola over the killing of *gente de alpargatas* (ordinary workers) and such incidents as the strewing of the Irún highway (near the French border) with corpses. A subsequent circular in November attempted to reduce Falangist participation in the repression. In his Christmas Eve radio address, Hedilla limited the Falangists' role to the purge of the leaders of the left and of "murderers," saying that in many areas there were "rightists who are worse than the Reds" and charging Falangists to protect ordinary rank-and-file leftists who had committed no crime.[14] Eventually, in January 1937, he endeavored unsuccessfully to withdraw Falangists from participation in the repression altogether.[15] The climate of passion and hatred was such that, given the ruthless ferocity of the repression, there were very few protests among the more conscientious or squeamish Nationalists, even on the part of the clergy. During the first weeks, executions even became public spectacles in some areas, and on September 25, 1936, the Valladolid newspaper *El Norte de Castilla* protested the attendance of children and girls at such scenes. Finally on November 15 the ardently pro-Nationalist bishop of Pamplona, Olaechea, preached a sermon "No More Bloodshed," which asked only that no more irregular killings occur outside the formal juridical process (though in Nationalist Spain the latter simply meant summary court-martial). Even Nazi and Fascist visitors were sometimes appalled, and occasionally suggested that the high level of violence might be counterproductive.

After Franco took over the jefatura única in October 1936, some effort began to be made to centralize the repression and assert the new government's control over courts-martial and the entire juridical process in the

13. Many of the published sources that have been frequently cited in the general literature are not reliable as objective accounts. The two principal eyewitness denunciations of the Nationalist repression published during the Civil War were Antonio Bahamonde y Sánchez de Castro, *Un año con Queipo de Llano* (Barcelona, 1938); and Antonio Ruiz Vilaplana, *Doy fe: Un ano de actuación en la España de Franco* (Paris, 1938). For an overall sketch, see Hugh Thomas, *The Spanish Civil War* (New York, 1977), 258–68, 514–16; and Guillermo Cabanellas, *La guerra de los mil días* (Buenos Aires, 1973), 2:838–68.

14. Quoted in Abella, *Vida cotidiana*, 158.

15. According to the testimony of Hedilla himself in García Venero's *Falange en la guerra de España*, 227–50.

Nationalist zone. Franco's chief administrator in this area was Major (soon Lt. Col.) Lorenzo Martínez Fuset, a professional officer of the Military Juridical Corps from the Canaries and head of the military juridical section at his headquarters in Salamanca.[16] When the capture of Madrid and the fall of the Republic appeared imminent at the beginning of November, it was Martínez Fuset who organized a new Auditoria de Guerra del Ejército de Ocupación, (Military Court of the Army of Occupation), endowed with eight separate military tribunals to begin the purge of Madrid and other main Republican centers. It soon developed that this plan was premature, however, and the process of establishing central authority over courts-martial and repression proved no simple task. During the first months only the main northern Nationalist zone was brought under any semblance of coordination. The gravest problem presented to Franco in this regard during his first weeks as chief of state was the complaint of the Church's primate, Cardinal Gomá, concerning the summary court-martial and execution of Basque nationalist priests, a process that Franco quickly brought to an end. The extension of central authority also brought with it some lessening of the extreme rigor of the repression, for Franco had begun to recognize that the number of shootings carried out by local authorities was excessive and might even be counterproductive for the Nationalist cause.

The final incentive for national integration of the Nationalist system of courts-martial was provided by the aftermath of the Nationalist/Italian conquest of the Málaga district in February 1937. There the victorious Spanish Nationalists under Queipo de Llano extended the practices common to the Seville district during preceding months, featuring summary executions in newly occupied areas often without even the simulacrum of a court-martial. This appalled their Italian allies, who were sometimes reluctant to hand over Republican prisoners directly to the Nationalist forces for fear of what might be done to them. The defeat of Italian troops in the Guadalajara offensive only a month later further increased the concern of the Italian commanders, eager to avoid reprisals by Republicans against Italian soldiers held prisoner.[17]

The atrocities in Málaga and Italian protests apparently moved Franco to further action. A regularized Nationalist court-martial system was established in the southern sectors for the first time, with five military

16. On the career of Martínez Fuset, see Garriga, Los validos de Franco, 15–125.

17. Italian representatives were given to more than a little hyperbole and self-righteousness about conditions in Spain. Mussolini's special envoy Farinacci thus reported after his visit in March 1937, "To tell the truth, Red and Nationalist atrocities are equivalent here. It is sort of a contest to see who can massacre more people, almost a sport. It seems impossible that a day can go by without a certain number of people being sent to the other world. . . . The population is used to it by now and pays no attention; it is only we sentimentalists who create a tragedy over people who don't deserve it." Quoted in Coverdale, *Italian Intervention*, 191.

courts set up in Málaga to channel the repression. On March 4 Franco informed the Italian ambassador that he had given firm orders against shooting Republican POWs in order to encourage more to desert, and said that death sentences by court-martial would be limited to leftist leaders and those personally guilty of crimes, and that even in those cases only slightly more than 50 percent of those condemned would actually be executed. At the end of the month Franco informed the Italian ambassador that he had commuted the death sentences of nineteen convicted Freemasons in Málaga and removed two military judges there whose verdicts had been unjustifiable.[18]

The end of March 1937 thus seems to have been the date at which Franco imposed the requirement that all death sentences passed by military courts must be sent directly to the Asesoría Jurídica of Martínez Fuset at his headquarters for review before sentence was carried out. Fuset organized these verdicts for Franco sometimes on a daily basis, and from that point the Generalissimo is said to have personally reviewed capital sentences of all courts-martial for political crimes. According to one version,[19] Franco initialed all the names on such lists either with an *E* for *Enterado* (standing for "Informed and approved") or a *C* for *Conmutado* ("Commuted"). When the condemned was indicated to have been guilty of heinous personal crimes such as rape or murder, Franco is said to have sometimes added the words *garrote y prensa,* indicating that he should be executed by *vile garrotte* (strangulation with a metal collar) and the action should be announced in the press, something that was not ordinarily done. It has been claimed that Franco was more inclined to leniency in the cases of anarchists than of Marxists or Freemasons, believing the former more honest and redeemable and not under the influence of international forces emanating from Moscow or foreign Masonic headquarters. Conversely, Franco was not above occasionally intervening personally to direct more rigorous prosecution and sentencing (at least in a few cases), as he himself reminisced in later years.[20] The Generalissimo would also entertain rare personal representations from visitors urging greater clemency, but such visitors were few and received scant attention.[21]

The regular government apparatus of the Nationalist state seems to

18. Cf. Garriga, *Los validos,* 68–69.

19. Ibid., 70–72.

20. Franco would later observe that he had twice intervened to see to it that the son of the Republican general Miaja was tried and condemned. Cf. Ramón Soriano, *La mano izquierda de Franco* (Barcelona, 1981), 146–47.

21. For example, the Catholic Action leader Francisco Herrera Oria made several protests to Franco in 1937, and Franco soon stopped receiving him altogether. Later, after Herrera Oria criticized continuation of the dictatorship, he was sent into internal exile for six months in 1939. See the account by Herrera Oria's son in *Los confinados* (Barcelona, 1976), ed. J. A. Pérez Mateos, 81–90.

have played little role in the repression, even during the latter stages of the Civil War. The elderly General Severiano Martínez Anido, notorious persecutor of anarchists during the early 1920s and a minister of the Primo de Rivera regime, was made chief of internal security on October 31, 1937, and then became minister of public order in the first regular government of 1938, but his sphere was to uphold public morality and decency, censor movies and plays, and discourage cheating in the marketplace. After Anido's death in December 1938 his ministry was incorporated into Serrano Súñer's Ministry of the Interior, which at no time exercised juridical responsibility over the repression.

It will never be possible to measure the exact scope of the repression, for few records were kept in the early months, and later more formalized data for the period after March 1937 were apparently destroyed during the 1940s for reasons of political prudence. The technique of investigating formal records of deaths and burials cannot produce fully complete data either, for every single death was not formally recorded, though the vast majority were. Vague devices of statistical projection have been used by various writers in forming "guesstimates," but these have usually been subject to more than a little bias and have almost always returned inflated figures, sometimes in the range of 200,000 or more deaths at the hand of the Nationalists during and after the Civil War. Conversely, by the time the conflict ended, Nationalist propagandists routinely spoke of half a million deaths at the hand of the Red terror. During the later years of the regime this was officially reduced to a total of 61,000 (including the nearly 7,000 slain clergy).

The only systematic study is that of Ramón Salas Larrazábal, *Pérdidas de la guerra* (Barcelona, 1977), based on an analysis of all recorded deaths and his finding that almost all deaths were recorded, although sometimes tardily. Salas's conclusions challenge the conventional wisdom, which has either postulated a level of Nationalist executions far higher than that of the left[22] or has judged both repressions to have been of approximately the same magnitude.[23] Salas calculated that Nationalist executions during the Civil War amounted to 35,021, followed by 22,641 during the four years that followed (after which large-scale executions ceased), whereas those carried out in the Republican zone during the war amounted to 72,344. The largest number of executions by the Nationalists were carried

22. Perhaps the classic in this regard is Gabriel Jackson, *The Spanish Republic and the Civil War, 1931–1939*, 535; followed by Ramón Tamames, *La República: La era de Franco* (Madrid, 1973), 349–50, which accepts Jackson's figures; and for the postwar period, by Elena de la Souchère, *Explication de l'Espagne* (Paris, 1962).

23. For example, Thomas, *The Spanish Civil War*, 265–66; La Cierva, in Carr, ed., *The Republic and Civil War*, 202; and also in general terms my *Politics and the Military*, 415, and *The Spanish Revolution*, 225, which awarded the contest to the Nationalists, though in the latter case because of the additional number of postwar executions.

out in the provinces of Córdoba and Málaga (which top the list at 3,864 each), followed in descending order by Zaragoza, Badajoz, Seville, Granada, and Oviedo. Madrid, Barcelona, Valencia, and Ciudad Real are also among the eleven provinces with the largest number of executions, though in these cases because of the number carried out after the war ended.

Though Salas's work is by far the most systematic and probably comes near the truth in its global conclusions, it is nevertheless far from definitive. It is first of all not entirely clear that all executions were registered, even in subsequent years, though certainly the vast majority were. Beyond this lies the problem of complete and systematic investigation for every registry throughout Spain, beyond the task of a one-man investigation, and thus Salas has relied on certain totals and projections which are in some cases evidently incomplete. The figure for the number of Republican executions is perhaps too high by 10 percent or so, while that for Nationalist executions is probably an underestimation by an equal or greater order of magnitude. Such a conclusion is further indicated by the only detailed provincial study by Salas, dealing with Navarre. After examining 43 municipalities covering most of the province, he has raised the total of Nationalist executions there from 948 to approximately 1,160[24]— an increase of more than 20 percent. Projecting the same proportionate adjustment nationally, this would produce an estimate of at least 42,000 executions by the Nationalists during the Civil War. Moreover, Salas subsequently raised his calculation of the number of postwar executions to approximately 28,000 to 30,000 for the entire period down to 1950. This would result in total Nationalist executions of 70,000 to 72,000 from beginning to end, almost exactly equal to the total in his computation of Republican executions during the Civil War.

The only region that has been thoroughly and definitively studied is Catalonia, with results that generally substantiate Salas's original conclusion.[25] More thorough investigation has raised his figure of 3,527 for

24. Salas Larrazábal, *Los fusilados en Navarra en la guerra de 1936*, cited above. Salas's statistics for Navarre have been challenged by the documentation of the Colectivo Afán, which collects many statements from relatives and friends of those executed in Navarre in its *NO, General! Fueron más de tres mil los asesinados* (Pamplona, 1983).

25. Josep M. Solé i Sabaté, *La repressió franquista a Catalunya, 1938–1953* (Barcelona, 1985), tabulated 3,385 executions in Catalonia, and in addition some 30 to 40 ad hoc shootings without trial or sentencing. Of these, 62.1 percent had taken place by the end of 1939 and another 22.4 percent in 1940. There were proportionately more executions in rural than in urban areas. Those killed were predominantly from thirty-three to forty-one years old (with an average age of thirty-eight), and in Catalonia those executed in urban areas came especially from the CNT and in rural districts from the Esquerra. Though these totals are very close to Salas's figures, Solé is quite critical of Salas's methodology (pp. 265–66). He also observes that both sides exaggerated the extent of the repression in the opposing zone during the war on the false assumption that the high rate of executions of the first six months was continuing.

Zaragoza province—third highest in the Nationalist zone—to 3,890 through 1943 (the end of Salas's original research) and to 4,075 through 1945,[26] though this remains within the 20 percent margin of error suggested above. A study of Galicia suggests that his statistics for that region were too low by approximately 30 percent,[27] while other scholars offer much higher totals for Nationalist executions in the provinces of Córdoba[28] and Granada.[29]

Concerning the total loss of life inflicted by the Civil War, for some time it has been appreciated by scholars that the *millón de muertos* (one million dead) cherished by both sides for years was a mythic and emotional concept that did not correspond to the facts. This had been shown as early as 1942 in the work of Jesús Villar Salinas, *Repercusiones demográficas de la guerra civil española*, which demonstrated that the number of deaths directly attributable to the war could not have exceeded 350,000, and that the category of a million could be reached only by invoking reduction in demographic potential in addition to deaths. According to the latter calculation, a deficit of approximately a half million births resulted, to which might be added the number of permanent emigrés, thus reaching a total figure of a million or more. Salas effectively supports these general conclusions. His overall totals are shown in table 11.1.

The youngest of the Salas Larrazábal brothers, Jesús, has employed a simpler methodology to arrive at slightly different conclusions.[30] He has noted that soon after the end of the Civil War the Servicio Histórico Militar calculated Republican war dead at 83,000, and he uses lower, probably more nearly correct figures for foreign deaths. Altogether he calculates Nationalist military fatalities at 75,000 or less and the total number of executions at no more than 100,000 (60,000 in the Republican zone, 40,000

26. Fernando Baeta in *Sábado Gráfico*, Nov. 21, 1979, 18–19; and *Cambio 16*, Dec. 30, 1979, 82–85. Considerable attention was drawn by discovery in late 1979 of the remains of several hundred bodies in a common grave at Zaragoza, which may correspond to the numerous members of the Bandera "General Sanjurjo" (a battalion of the Legion in the Nationalist Army, recruited by Falangists among peasants in the leftist Ribera district of Navarre and Zaragoza), who were shot in the face of a threatened mutiny in 1937.

27. Carlos Fernández, *El alzamiento de 1936 en Galicia* (La Coruña, 1982).

28. Francisco Moreno Gómez, *La Guerra Civil en Córdoba 1936–1939* (Madrid, 1985), 513, suggests 7,700 deaths attributable to the Nationalist repression in Cordoba province during the three years of the Civil War, more than three times the number executed by Republicans in the leftist-controlled sector of the province. This is not entirely convincing.

29. Ian Gibson continues to increase his estimates of the extent of the Nationalist repression in Granada, raising the total to 5,000 or more in *Granada en 1936 y el asesinato de Federico García Lorca* (Granada, 1979), 126. Alberto Reig Tapia, *Ideología e historia: Sobre la represión franquista y la Guerra Civil* (Madrid, 1984), presents an extensive discussion of the literature on the repression and a severe critique of Salas Larrazábal. On the other hand, the leftist historian Manuel Tuñón de Lara has tended to reduce some of his own earlier estimates in the direction of those of Salas. Cf. Tuñón de Lara, *La Guerra Civil Española*, 423.

30. J. Salas Larrazábal, "Los muertos de la Guerra Civil," *ABC* (Madrid), July 21, 1977.

Table 11.1. Deaths Caused by the Spanish Civil War

	Nationalist	Republican	Total	% N	% R
	During the War				
Combat deaths	59,500	60,500	120,000	49.6	50.54
Foreign combat deaths	12,000	13,500	25,500	47.06	52.94
Civilian deaths from military action	4,000	11,000	15,000	26.66	73.33
Executions and murders	72,500	35,500	108,000	67.13	32.87
Total	148,000	120,500	268,500	55.12	44.88
	During the Postwar period (to Dec. 31, 1961)				
Executions	—	23,000	23,000	—	100.00
Killed in World War II	4,500	1,500	6,000	75.00	25.00
Killed in guerrilla activity	500	2,500	3,000	13.21	83.33
Murdered by guerrillas	1,000	—	1,000	100.00	—
Total	6,000	27,000	33,000	18.18	81.82
	Deaths above the Norm Caused by Illness				
During the Civil War (and to end of 1939)	16,000	149,000	165,000	9.70	90.30
During 1940–43 inclusive	75,000	84,000	159,000	47.17	52.83
Total	91,000	233,000	324,000	28.10	71.9
Grand total	245,000	380,500	625,500	39.17	60.83

Source: Ramón Salas Larrazábal, *Pérdidas de la guerra* (Barcelona, 1977), 428–29.

in the Nationalist). No provision is made for civilian deaths from military actions, but if these are subtracted from total combat fatalities, the distribution suggested by Jesús Salas may in fact be more accurate than that of his brother. The totals in his statistics are based on an accurate global calculation of adult masculine mortality over the norm in the active age groups during this period, but the distribution by categories is derived from uncertain sources or in some cases intuitively estimated.

The general conclusion that there were less than 300,000 violent deaths from all causes during the Civil War years is almost undoubtedly correct, as is the one that the numbers of fatalities in the contending armies were approximately equal. Though the Nationalists were militarily more efficient, they were normally on the offensive, which ordinarily brings higher casualties, and thus these two factors tended to balance each other. On the other hand, the calculation by Ramón Salas of a distinctly higher number of excess deaths for the Republican zone also seems logical, for mortality from disease and malnutrition was considerably less in the better-fed, less-disrupted Nationalist territory. The rather low figures for civilian deaths caused by military action are also plausible. Though the Republicans initiated military attacks on civilian targets, their

air raids of this sort were very few and quite weak. Franco and his allies
limited themsleves for the most part to a certain number of raids on Madrid and Barcelona (as well as that on Guernica). Franco generally preferred to avoid destruction of civilian areas, and the noted "terror raids"
on Barcelona in 1938 were carried out by comparatively small Italian
units on direct orders from Mussolini and soon came to an end. Other civilian casualties sometimes resulted from artillery fire, but such victims
were relatively limited in number.

The total mortality from violence during the Spanish conflict thus
amounted to only slightly more than 1 per cent of the Spanish population
of 25 million. To this, however, must be added the death from disease and
malnutrition of about 165,000 more, together with the loss through permanent exile of approximately 162,000 Republicans.[31]

Even though the casualties of the Civil War have usually been exaggerated, the effect of the accompanying trauma on Spanish society is
scarcely susceptible to exaggeration. The complete destruction of the
regular polity, the impact of revolution on half of Spain, the ubiquity of
internecine violence, and enormous privation and suffering for half the
country, climaxed by the shock and discouragement of defeat, left much
of the population shell-shocked and psychologically adrift. A great many
of the people living in the former Republican zone felt at least temporarily submissive and willing to accept any reasonable program of reconciliation and reconstruction.

The triumphant Nationalist regime had no such plan of reconciliation in
mind. The Civil War had been persistently defined as conflict between
the "true Spain" and the "anti-Spain," the forces of light and the forces of
darkness. Tens of thousands of Catholics and conservatives had been murdered in cold blood by the Popular Front, and many of Franco's adherents
had no intention of forgiving anyone even remotely connected with leftist
politics. Thus the regime would continue to divide Spanish life into categories of victors and vanquished for many years after the close of the war,
and this had the political advantage of binding most of Franco's followers
into firm support of his postwar system. A decree of April 9, 1938, required all persons of legal age, for the first time in Spanish history, to hold
a personal identification card.[32]

31. At one point (the end of February 1939) nearly half a million Republicans had gone
into exile, primarily into France after the fall of Catalonia. The majority of these returned
before the end of the year. The best studies are by Javier Rubio García-Mina, *La emigración
española a Francia* (Barcelona, 1974), and *La emigración de la Guerra Civil de 1936–1939*,
3 vols. (Madrid, 1977). His final conclusions are summed up in Rubio's article "Las cifras del
exilio," *Historia 16* 3:30 (Oct. 1978), 19–32. For descriptive data, see José Luis Abellán,
ed., *El exilio español de 1936*, 6 vols. (Madrid, 1978).
32. This legislation establishing the Documento Nacional de Identidad does not appear
to have been fully implemented until a later period. More important in the early years of the
regime was the official *salvoconducto* required for domestic travel.

Thus the close of the Civil War did not bring an end to the repression but instead facilitated its more efficient systematization. The wartime purges and courts-martial had rested on a most tortured juridical basis, applying the category "military rebellion" to those who technically had refused to support military rebellion, and refusing to apply the technical provisions of the Code of Military Justice that gave the rank-and-file of military units declared to be in revolt the right to submit without further penalty or prosecution.[33] Eventually a new juridical basis would be worked out for the repression, and as one major step in the new process of juridical legitimization, a special commission was appointed on December 21, 1938, to prepare an indictment of the legality of the Republican Popular Front regime of July 1936. This was composed of noted scholars and jurists, including several former cabinet members of the monarchy and the early Republican period. Its lengthy report, impugning Republican legitimacy, was published by the new Editora Nacional in mid-1939.[34] This provided a theoretical justification for the conclusion of a postwar study of the crime of military rebellion which declared, "Defense of the old [Republican] political order constitutes the true rebellion."[35]

The end of the war did not bring to an end the militarization of the system of justice in Nationalist Spain. The state of martial law that had been declared by the Junta de Defensa Nacional on July 28, 1936, remained in effect and would not be repealed by Franco until April 7, 1948. Nominal political crimes would continue to be prosecuted by military courts, and both the Civil Guard and armed police would be commanded by Army officers and would be subject to military discipline. This situation, it should be pointed out, was not as unprecedented in Spain as in some other Western countries, for between 1934 and 1936 more than 2,000 civilians had been prosecuted by court-martial for their participation in the 1934 insurrection.

To establish standards for political prosecution, a special Law of Political Responsibilities promulgated on February 9, 1939, established penalties for political and politically related activities retroactive to October 1, 1934. The law had been drafted by the somewhat befuddled González Bueno, minister of syndical organization, with the aid of a small team of jurists. Its jurisdiction covered all forms of subversion and aid to the Republican war effort and even examples of "grave passivity" during the war.

33. Serrano Súñer, *Memorias*, 243–52, presents a critique of the nominal juridical basis of the repression during the Civil War.

34. Ministerio de Gobernación, *Dictamen de la Comisión sobre la ilegitimidad de poderes actuantes en 18 de julio de 1936* (Madrid, 1939). One year later the state prosecutor's office initiated an official investigation into the Red terror, the results being published in 1943 as *La dominación roja en España: Causa General instruida por el Ministerio Fiscal*, 3rd ed. (Madrid, 1953).

35. Fernández Asiain, *El delito de rebelión militar* (Madrid, 1943), quoted in Ballbé, *Orden público*, 402.

Categories of persons automatically indicted by the law included all members of revolutionary and left-liberal political parties, though not automatically rank-and-file members of leftist trade unions, and anyone who had participated in a revolutionary People's Court in the Republican zone. Membership in a Masonic lodge was also automatic grounds for prosecution, despite the fact that the first head of the Nationalist Junta (Cabanellas) had been a Mason. Regional courts were established for each region of the country, with one central National Tribunal in Madrid. Three different categories of culpability were defined, with penalties ranging from fifteen years to six months.[36] For those convicted, the tendency was to impose heavy sentences at first and then reduce them later.

In addition to formal imprisonment, the law also provided for a variety of other penalties. These included partial or complete restrictions of personal and professional activities, and various categories of limitations of residence, ranging from expulsion from the country to internal exile, banishment to one of the African colonies, or house arrest. Wide-ranging economic sanctions were also included, which might extend from specific fines or levies to the confiscation of certain categories of goods or even total confiscation of personal estates.

At the time of the final surrender, the prison population in Nationalist Spain was listed at 100,292,[37] though this figure does not include the huge camps set up to process the 400,000 or more Republican troops who surrendered in the last days of the war, as well as some 70,000 who voluntarily returned from France during the final month. During 1937–38 ordinary Republican troops taken prisoner had been freed almost immediately if no evidence of political initiative or affiliation was found, and a good many were rapidly redrafted into the Nationalist forces, which led to more than a few desertions. Most of the great mass of Republicans taken in 1939 were soon released, but nonetheless the incorporation by the Nationalist state of approximately one-third of Spain during the first three months of that year led to the greatest single wave of political arrests in the country's history.[38] At the close of 1939 the prison population stood at 270,719, though within a year or so that level began to drop rapidly.

36. Máximo Cajal, ed., *La Ley de Responsabilidades Políticas, comentada y seguida de un apéndice de disposiciones legales y formularios más en uso* (Madrid, 1939); Manuel Mínguez de Rico, ed., *Ley de Responsabilidades Políticas y de depuración de funcionarios políticos* (Madrid, 1939); Luis Benítez de Lugo y Reymundo, *Responsabilidades civiles y políticas* (Barcelona, 1940).

37. *Anuario Estadístico de España 1944–1945.*

38. There are several memoirs by leftists arrested in the end-of-the-war roundup, such as José Ma. Aroca, *Los republicanos que no se exilaron* (Barcelona, 1969); Eduardo de Guzmán, *El año de la victoria* (Madrid, 1974); and Angel Ma. de Lera, *Los que perdimos* (Barcelona, 1974). Cf. Juan Llarch, *Campos de concentración en la España de Franco* (Barcelona, 1978); and Angel Suárez-Colectivo 36, *Libro blanco sobre las cárceles franquistas, 1939–1976* (Paris, 1976), 63–85.

Table 11.2. Prison Population of Spain
(as of December 31 of each year)

1939	270,719	1945	43,812
1940	233,373	1946	36,379
1941	159,392	1947	38,139
1942	124,423	1948	37,451
1943	74,095	1949	36,127
1944	54,072	1950	30,610

Source: *Anuario Estadístico de España, 1944–1950.*

The best that can be said for the Nationalist repression is that it was not a Stalinist-Hitlerian type of liquidation and was not categorically applied by such automatic and involuntary criteria as race or class. It did tend, however, to be applied by general category to certain levels of responsibility in leftist and Republican political parties and trade union movements. Under such terms, cases were then dealt with on an individual basis according to the newly imposed legal criteria under military judicial process. As the most thorough scholarly investigator of this purge has put it, "The repression was constant, regular, and methodical. It was not arbitrary in character, even though it often seemed so. The repression was frightful, but it was also selective and rational."[39]

There was no death penalty for political crimes as such, but numerous death sentences were pronounced on those convicted of political crimes of violence (a fairly elastic category in the immediate aftermath of the war).[40] Executions were carried on, at a decreasing rate, well into 1944, though their total for the years following the Civil War was undoubtedly much smaller than the vast figures of 200,000 or more imagined by foes of the regime. Once more, the most detailed study has been carried out by Ramón Salas Larrazábal; it concludes that the approximate number of political executions by the regime during the first six postwar years of 1939 to 1945 was 28,000.[41] After that point, direct execution became a rarity.

39. Solé Sabaté, *La repressió franquista,* 268.
40. The most notorious single case of injustice was arguably that of the respected Socialist leader Julián Besteiro, who had always opposed the revolution and Civil War, and played a courageous role in helping to bring it to a close. Nonetheless, though old and quite ill, he was condemned to a thirty-year term, basically for having been a major figure in the Socialist Party, and he died in prison in 1940. See Ignacio Arenillas de Chaves, *El proceso de Besteiro* (Madrid, 1976). Several key leftist leaders, such as the former president of the Catalan Generalitat Lluis Companys and the CNT moderate Joan Peiró, were later extradited from France by German occupation authorities to be tried and executed in Spain.
41. Salas has found that during the first three postwar years of 1939 to 1941 there was an excess mortality (compared with prewar averages) of approximately 200,000 due to illness, primarily the result of malnutrition and other shortages during the war and immediately afterward. A total of 115,000 violent deaths were recorded for the years 1939 to 1945 over

Franco did recognize some theoretical responsibility to heal the wounds of fratricide and bring the country together, but his method would be entirely his own and very slow to produce any such results. In a speech of December 31, 1939, he declared, "It is necessary to liquidate the hatred and passions left by our past war. But this liquidation must not be accomplished in the liberal manner, with enormous and disastrous amnesties, which are a deception rather than a gesture of forgiveness. It must be Christian, achieved by means of redemption through work accompanied by repentance and penitence."[42] Franco and his associates are said to have been particularly influenced by the prewar penal studies of a Jesuit, Julián Pereda, which emphasized that the goal of penal correction was rehabilitation and that the opportunity to work rather than merely be confined was an important aspect of this. Work would enable criminals in some sense to make restitution for their crimes, but should also be recognized and rewarded with modest wages.[43]

A decree of June 9, 1939, therefore established provisions for reducing sentences by up to one-third in return for volunteering for labor projects, and on September 8 arrangements began to create several "militarized penitentiary colonies" to assist in reconstruction.[44] The antecedents for this program lay in the Batallones Disciplinarios de Soldados Trabajadores (Punishment Battalions of Soldier Laborers) organized during the latter part of the Civil War for certain categories of ex-Republican POWs who were judged in some fashion "politically responsible" or not rehabilitated whether or not charged with individual crimes. A small number of Nationalist troops convicted of infractions were also in the battalions.[45] Par-

---

and above the prewar averages, but most of these correspond to "war wounds" that were actually inflicted during the war, to "civil executions" (referring to executions in the Nationalist zone during the conflict), and to "homicides" (referring mainly to executions in the Republican zone). Because of wartime conditions such deaths had not been registered earlier. Political executions in the postwar years were, according to Salas, registered mainly under the category "judicial executions" and totaled some 23,000, to which figure he is inclined to add an additional 5,000 deaths listed in other categories. Salas Larrazábal, "Tiempo de silencio, cárcel y muerte," in Diario 16, *Historia del franquismo* (Madrid, 1985), 18–19.

Finally, it should be added that Republican exiles who escaped to France were not free from imprisonment or death. Many were held in camps by French authorities for months under harsh conditions little or no better than those of some of the imprisoned in Spain, and German occupation forces later deported thousands to imprisonment or slave labor in Germany. One of the most extensive studies of Spanish Republicans in wartime France, Antonio Vilanova's *Los olvidados* (Paris, 1969), concluded that at least 5,000 Spaniards (and perhaps more) died in German camps, while another thousand or more perished as laborers or in other jails (pp. 199–201).

42. Quoted in Max Gallo, *Histoire de l'Espagne franquiste* (Paris, 1969), 1:102.

43. George Hills, *Franco* (London, 1967), 338–39.

44. Clark, *Evolution*, 1:160–61.

45. Conditions in these units varied considerably. There is a glowing testimonial to the humane treatment by the commander of one disciplinary battalion by a former member in *Cambio 16*, Jan. 14, 1985.

ticipants in the postwar penitentiary colonies were primarily Republican POWs charged with comparatively minor offenses or those with only a limited amount of time left on their sentences. Penal labor was involved in many projects during the immediate postwar period, especially in Morocco and Andalusia. The most important, however, was the special war memorial called the Valley of the Fallen, later to house Franco's own tomb. Plans for this were announced April 1, 1940, the first anniversary of the end of the war.[46]

The sort of rehabilitation that was attempted with political prisoners was not so much political as spiritual. During the first years after the Civil War the Catholic clergy played a prominent role in the penal system, holding obligatory religious services and attempting to catechize and convert many of those in jail. Nuns were particularly important in helping to administer prisons for women. For several years prison chaplains published a journal called *Redención* (*Redemption*), which published the confessions and stories of the conversion of convicted prisoners.

An active political opposition, along with very limited guerrilla activity, continued to exist. When a leading military police inspector was ambushed and killed on the Madrid-Lisbon highway on July 27, 1939, the response was swift and brutal: sixty-seven members of the underground United Socialist Youth (a joint Communist-Socialist organization) were rounded up and immediately tried, bringing rapid execution for at least sixty-three, including eleven young women, some of them under twenty-one years of age.[47] The vindictive policies of the regime and the political encouragement provided the left by outbreak of general war in Europe combined to spark a further recrudescence of opposition activity by early 1940.

The Law of Political Responsibilities was thus supplemented on March 1, 1940, by a new Law for the Suppression of Masonry and Communism. This new blanket legislation was so titled because Masonry was held to be the chief source of spiritual and cultural subversion in contemporary society (this had become the number-one individual mania of Franco and some of his chief collaborators), while communism—a term referring vaguely to much of the radical and revolutionary left in general—was considered the primary political foe. Terms of the new law made it "a crime to belong to Masonry and to Communism" because in all the ills of Spain since 1800 "there is always discovered the joint action of Masonry and of the anarchizing forces, served in their turn by hidden international forces."[48] Its provisions thus included "Trotskyists, anarchists, or similar

46. See Daniel Sueiro, *La verdadera historia del Valle de los Caídos* (Madrid, 1976).

47. Hartmut Heine, *La oposición política al franquismo* (Madrid, 1983), 65–66; J. García Blanco-Cicerón, "Las 'trece rosas,'" *Historia 16* 10:106 (Feb. 1985), 11–29.

48. La Cierva, *Franco*, 1:167; Clark, 1:224. On the regime's anti-Masonic mania, see Daniel Sueiro and Bernardo Díaz Nosty, *Historia del franquismo* (Madrid, 1977), 1:121–40.

elements," as well as Masons and Communists. Under the continuing terms of martial law, the new decree would be enforced by military tribunals. Three years later, on March 2, 1943, Franco's council of ministers approved yet another measure making any form of infringement of the laws on public order a matter of military rebellion. By that time, with domestic and international tensions mounting and the European war nearing Spain, the mere passing of so-called seditious rumors could place an accused person before a court-martial.

Thus the close of the Civil War brought neither reconciliation nor political disarmament. The new Nationalist state was a rigorous and punitive dictatorship determined to carry out a political and cultural counter-revolution, to suppress all signs of opposition and firmly establish the dominance of the victors.

Yet neither Franco nor most other top officials had any desire to run a system of concentration camps in Spain, and after a year had passed there was increasing concern to reduce the numbers of political prisoners. Franco took the first step on October 1, 1939, the third anniversary of his accession to power, when he pardoned all former members of the Republican armed forces who had been sentenced to terms of less than six years. This affected only a comparatively small number, however, and on January 24, 1940, a number of special military juridical commissions were created to review all sentences to date, with the power either to confirm or reduce but never to extend them. By the spring of 1940 there were still more than a quarter-million prisoners in Spanish jails. On May 8 the director general of prisons sent a special report to Franco pointing out that only 103,000 of them were serving confirmed sentences. The military court system proceeded rather slowly and in the year after the fighting had ended produced only 40,000 confirmed convictions. In addition to the latter group, another 9,000 had received death sentences, but most of these were still subject to appeal or reconfirmation. The fact that so many prisoners were potentially on death row was leading to riots and other acts of indiscipline, and consequently the Generalissimo was asked to do all that he could to speed up the juridical process before conditions in the overcrowded jails became unmanageable. Franco responded by increasing the number of tribunals and juridical personnel, incorporating more junior officials from the Military Juridical Corps.[49]

On June 4, 1940, the limited amnesty of the preceding fall was extended by granting provisional liberty to all political prisoners serving sentences of less than six years. From that time on, the prison population began to drop. Forty thousand political prisoners were freed on April 1, 1941, second anniversary of the end of the war, when the same terms were

49. *FF*, 2:383–84.

granted to all serving sentences of up to twelve years. This was extended to fourteen-year terms on October 16, freeing at least 20,000 more. During the winter of 1941–42 more than 50,000 more were released. An equally large group was amnestied on December 17, 1943, when provisional liberty was granted those with sentences of up to twenty years. During this same period, down to December 1943, approximately half of the 50,000 death sentences passed had been commuted to lesser terms.[50]

Harsh though it was, the situation in Spain thus does not compare unfavorably with the aftermath of other revolutionary-counterrevolutionary civil wars, whether won by left or right. In view of the many thousands who were slaughtered in the leftist zone, there is no particular reason to think that conditions would have been significantly better had the Republic triumphed; indeed, had it won under the Communist hegemony created in 1937–38 they would undoubtedly have been much worse. The sole example of a more clement resolution of a revolutionary twentieth-century civil war would be that of Greece during the early 1950s, but the government coming out of that war was incorporated within the framework of postwar democratic Europe, while the Franco regime of the early 1940s struggled to survive amid world war and manifold dangers from within and without that were much more severe than those faced either by a relatively secure Greece or by the Soviet Union during the relatively peaceful 1920s. In March 1944 the minister of justice Eduardo Aunós is said to have informed a British journalist that about 400,000 had passed through the regime's prisons since 1936,[51] but the number still being held continued to drop sharply, sinking to less than 55,000 by the close of 1944 and to a nominal 43,812 a year later, of whom approximately 17,000 would be classified as political prisoners.[52] Compared with the numbers imprisoned by many Communist regimes or by Nazi Germany, this figure was quite small, amounting to less than one-tenth of one percent of the general population.

Though repression remained firm and rigorous, it had largely ceased to be murderous. Even the large round of postwar executions had not assumed the capricious and sometimes genocidal forms found in the worst dictatorships, so that no analogy for those years can be drawn with Stalinist Russia, Nazi Germany, the Khmer Rouge of Cambodia, or even the arbitrary, capricious, and massive "disappearances" in Latin American countries during the 1970s and 1980s. Moreover, regular political prisoners were for the most part cared for in prison, however meagerly, were not systematically starved to death, and were generally segregated from

50. *FF*, 2:386.
51. According to Garriga, *Los validos*, 171–72.
52. Cf. Fusi, *Franco*, 79.

common criminals, largely avoiding the victimization by the latter that has been common in so many other countries. Though it claimed tens of thousands of lives, the Nationalist repression recognized limits and normally respected its own rules. It also grew progressively milder with each passing year.

PART III

The Dictadura,
1939–1959

12

Semi-Fascism:
The New State
of 1939

Franco's complete victory in 1939 gave him greater power than any previous ruler of Spain. No king of medieval or early modern times held the overriding authority for central control and administrative penetration of an organized twentieth-century authoritarian regime. If scarcely half of the Spanish population at most had directly supported the Nationalist war effort, in 1939 most of the other half were disposed at least passively to accept Franco's rule, if for no other reasons than hunger, weariness, disillusionment, and the total disaster of their cause. In the abstract this gave Franco a remarkable opportunity to forge a new national consensus, but to him it meant the opportunity to impose absolute political control and a series of unilateral policies developed on an individual and ad hoc basis rather than according to any fully conceived grand design or plan.

The new regime was by far the most centralized in Spanish history. Only the provinces of Navarre and Alava, both of which had abjured Basque nationalism and made major contributions to the Nationalist victory, retained a degree of provincial self-administration. The regional autonomy statutes for Catalonia and the Basque provinces were completely annulled, and the two "special regions" were, again with the partial exception of Alava, brought directly under a uniform pattern of central administration. In the case of Catalonia, which was not occupied until near the very end of the war, a special occupation administration held sway from January 26 to August 1, 1939.[1] The use of Catalan and Basque in publications, the courts, and even in religious services was generally prohibited, and in Catalonia for the next year or two large public signs urged inhabitants to "speak the language of the empire" (that is, Spanish).

1. This is treated by the oppositionist *Catalunya sota el règim franquista* (Paris, 1973), 221–77.

The first months of peace involved a slow process of establishing the regime in the newly occupied capital of Madrid and of articulating an administrative network for Catalonia and the large zone of Republican territory occupied at the end of the war. Sudden expansion of the state system required rapid employment of thousands of relatively untrained personnel, resulting in a rather low level of competence and probably also encouraging the spread of corruption, which began to plague the regime during the first year of peace. A decree of August 25, 1939, reserved most state employment for active Nationalists, stipulating that 80 percent of all ordinary state jobs would be reserved for veterans of the Nationalist Army, civilians who had made special sacrifices for the cause, former prisoners of the Republicans, and relatives of victims of the Red terror.

Movement of the various ministries to Madrid was not entirely completed for months, and Franco himself only took up residence in the capital in October 1939, moving his family at first to the Castle of Viñuelas (a property of the Duque del Infantado) some 18 kilometers outside town. Five more months were required for the renovation of the new official residence of the chief of state, El Pardo, an eighteenth-century Bourbon palace on the northwest edge of Madrid, employed as a barracks for Communist troops during the war. Both its seclusion and the fact that a small hunting domain was attached made it ideal for Franco's purposes. Once the family had moved in early in 1940, it remained the official residence until the Caudillo's death.

A special summer home had already been provided Franco in 1938, when Julio Muñoz Aguilar, provincial governor of Franco's native La Coruña, carried out a subscription campaign (in fact, it was said, a virtual local tax assessment) to buy him an estate in his native district. These funds were used to purchase the Pazo de Meirás, an elegant rural estate that had once been the property of the noted Galician novelist (and distant Franco family relative) Emilia Pardo Bazán. The Pazo de Meirás would remain Franco's summer home until his death, and, unlike El Pardo, was his personal property. The devoted Muñoz Aguilar in turn became head of the Generalissimo's *casa civil* (household staff) for the first five years after the Civil War.

Franco dedicated much of the spring of 1939 to the first extended series of visits to diverse parts of Spain that he had been able to make. These trips—always made by high-speed limousine in a guarded motorcade, never by the aerial flights that had cost the lives of two of the highest Nationalist generals—were designed to make contact with the public all over the country and enhance the leadership of the Caudillo. Security was always extensive but neither as thorough nor as oppressive as in totalitarian societies. Each visit, normally to a large city or at least a provincial capital, featured one or more major public appearances and short speeches

Franco addressing a large political audience in Madrid soon after the Civil War

by Franco, and large cheering crowds were always guaranteed through the mobilization of the FET or the syndicates.

In 1939 the fascist style heavily predominated, with ritualistic invocations of "Franco, Franco, Franco." The Caudillo's name was being painted on the sides of public buildings throughout Spain, and his photograph placed in all public offices as well as on the faces of Spain's new stamps and five-peseta coins. Initial festivities were climaxed by a lavish victory march in Madrid on May 19, where ceremonies achieved a kind of apotheosis of personal acclaim of Franco.[2]

The leaders of the new Spanish state firmly believed that the European order was moving toward national "organic" authoritarian regimes, and for the first four years after the Civil War Franco ran the entire government as though it were an army, ruling by *leyes de prerrogativa*, personal decrees issued by the chief of state. A new Ley de la Jefatura del Estado (Law of the Head of State) was published on August 9, 1939, which further expanded Franco's powers as originally defined by the decree of January 29, 1938. The new measure declared that the powers of government were "permanently confided" to Franco, who was categorically relieved of the need to submit new legislation or decrees to his cabinet when "urgent problems" required it.[3] Revised statues of the FET, issued a few days earlier, further extended his direct control over the state party. Though postwar Spanish society and institutions were not at all totalitarian in terms of complete government control, the new government was in its own formal theory a more direct personal dictatorship than those of the Soviet Union, Italy, or Germany.

Political tensions within the Nationalist elite nonetheless tended to reintensify with the coming of victory. Principal protagonists were Serrano Súñer and the Falangists on the one hand and varying alignments or groups of high military officials, Catholics, conservatives, or monarchists on the other. The ambition of Serrano himself tended to grow rather than diminish, aiming at construction of a fully institutionalized and certainly partly fascist authoritarian system. During the final month of the war, he was embroiled in intense controversy with Gómez Jordana, the foreign minister, who keenly resented the steady encroachment of the *cuñadísimo's* influence. One minor counterweight, the monarchist education minister Sainz Rodríguez, had dropped out of the cabinet at the beginning of April. It was Serrano, not the foreign minister, who in the following month led the sizable state delegation to Italy, the new regime's closest ally, and he returned with a large collection of Fascist books for guidance in the further development of the Spanish system.

2. This is described in some detail in Sueiro and Díaz Nosty, *Historia del franquismo*, 6–20.

3. Cf. the remarks of García Lahiguera, *Serrano Súñer*, 142, and Ramón Tamames, *La República. La Era de Franco* (Madrid, 1973), 498.

Franco completely reorganized his cabinet on August 8, 1939, retaining only two of the incumbents, Serrano Súñer and Alfonso Peña Boeuf, the professional engineer in charge of public works. The principal changes had to do with the Falange and the military leadership. Five cabinet posts were given to Falangists and neo-Falangists, compared with two in the preceding government, reflecting an effort to approximate, at least symbolically, the new fascistic era that seemed to be dawning in European affairs. Yet three of the five new Falangist ministers were in fact Army men, beginning with Col. Juan Beigbeder, the new foreign minister, who had earned neo-Falangist credentials during the Civil War. To supervise the armed forces themselves, Franco had at first apparently planned a unified Ministry of Defense, perhaps headed by General Antonio Aranda, with subsecretaryships for three different branches. Yet this idea was soon given up because of the need to placate the various services and provide recognition for leading generals. Moreover, there was the danger of Aranda's own ambitions and the greater power that would have accrued to a single minister. Consequently three separate portfolios were created for the Army, Navy, and Air Force. Whereas the military had held four of twelve cabinet posts in Franco's first regular government, they held five of fourteen in the second. The Carlist Gen. José Enrique Varela became army minister, Adm. Salvador Moreno Fernández, Franco's best cruiser commander during the war, became navy minister, and Juan Yagüe, the nearest thing to a genuine Falangist general, was named Spain's first air force minister. Yagüe had no particular competence in this area, but he had shown signs of potential dissidence; such a post would deprive him of regular Army command, busy him with manifold new technical responsibilities, and placate Falangist sentiment. At the same time, a new Alto Estado Mayor (High General Staff) was created to coordinate certain aspects of planning for the military branches. The monarchist and anti-Falangist Gen. Juan Vigón, one of the most senior and sagacious of the Spanish generals, was appointed its first head, and he was also in charge of relations between Franco and the exiled Alfonso XIII, a touchy area for the Caudillo. The other civilian cabinet ministers were nominal monarchists of trusted loyalty, most notably the new Carlist minister of justice, Esteban Bilbao.[4] The post of vice-president of government, previously held by the outgoing foreign minister, Gen. Gómez Jordana, was replaced with a new subsecretaryship of the presidency of government (Franco's

4. For biographical sketches of all Franco's ministers down to 1970, see the Equipo Mundo's *Los noventa ministros de Franco* (Barcelona, 1970). Esteban Bilbao, who was quite loyal to Franco and also tended to purple rhetoric, was later given credit for coining the phrase "Francisco Franco, Caudillo de España por la gracia de Dios" ("Francisco Franco, Caudillo of Spain by the grace of God"), which began to appear on Spanish coins. Punsters quickly corrupted this to "Francisco Franco, Caudillo de España por una gracia de Dios" (Francisco Franco, Caudillo of Spain by a joke of God).

position), created to coordinate the work of the executive. This was assigned to the anti-Falangist and monarchist staff officer Col. Valentín Galarza, who had played a leading role in the 1936 conspiracy, and this virtually give the military a sixth cabinet position.

Though some at first dubbed this a Falangist government, it was obviously no such thing. The new cabinet represented Franco's regular balancing act between the various ideological "families" of the regime. The nearest thing to a true concentration of power was in the military, yet even they held little corporate power, the individual military ministers being carefully selected in terms of personality, loyalty, and political identity (or lack of it) to fulfill what were primarily individual roles. During the entire first phase of the regime down to 1945, military personnel would hold 45.9 percent of the ministerial appointments and 36.8 percent of all the top governmental positions,[5] concentrated primarily in the armed forces ministries and in Interior, which dealt with the police. Falangists, by comparison, would hold 37.9 percent of the ministerial appointments and only 30.3 percent of all the top administrative positions, concentrated above all in the party administration, Labor, and Agriculture.[6]

5. Miguel Jerez Mir, *Elites políticas y centros de extracción en España, 1938–1957* (Madrid, 1982), 230.
6. Ibid., 121. The new political personnel were genuinely new, "without political experience, and in their majority, men who, though they had previously belonged to various political parties or forces, had not held positions of leadership in them. Discontinuity is total with respect to the Republic and, . . . , even with respect to the Cedo-Radical biennium of 1933–35." C. Viver Pi-Sunyer, *El personal político de Franco (1936–1945)* (Barcelona, 1978), 191. The new political elite stemmed broadly from the middle and upper-middle classes, with generally urban and university-trained background. Thus the FET did not serve as a vehicle for working-class movement into politics but rather as a channel for alternating groups from the middle classes to move up. Few of the new political elite had significant prior connections with big business, finance, or large landholdings, though many developed such connections after moving into the government. See Viver Pi-Sunyer, 235–323.
According to Pi-Sunyer, 157, the political background of the regime's top personnel down to 1945 was as follows:

	No. of individuals	No. of positions
Military and UME	232	469
Falangists before July 18 with positions	82	226
Falangists before July 18 without positions	89	186
Falangists who joined before April 1937	41	116
JONS	26	63
Alfonsine monarchists	87	184
Renovación Española	13	30
Bloque Nacional	28	82
Union Monárquica Nacional (1930)	2	6
Acción Española	34	103

Just a few days before formation of the new government Franco had carried out his first postwar changes in the FET, which were completed with the new cabinet appointments. The new secretary general was General Agustín Muñoz Grandes, a professional officer and africanista who had played a major role in organizing the urban Assault Guards for the Republic in 1931–32. For most of his career he had been a professional soldier, and then police commander, who avoided involvement in politics. Thus he had refused to join the conspiracy and revolt of 1936. Though he was soon arrested by Republican authorities, in April 1937 a Republican court had completely absolved him of anti-Republican activities,[7] providing him with the freedom to leave Spain and to subsequently enter the Nationalist zone. Franco gave Muñoz Grandes a divisional command during the war, and he rose rapidly, thanks to his professional talents and a unique combination of austerity and ambition. Franco gave him the surprising post of head of the FET, as well as a cabinet seat, because of Muñoz Grandes's professed neo-Falangism (something in which he had not shown the slightest interest before mid-1937), but even more, to keep the organization under the authority of a military man. Muñoz Grandes was also named militia chief for the Falange, whose militia in fact would languish with low enrollment and in strict subordination to the military establishment.[8]

The other Falangist cabinet ministers were Serrano Súñer, who retained the Ministry of the Interior (now once more called Gobernación) and was named president of the FET's new Junta Política. A new vice-secretary general of the party was appointed in the person of Pedro Gamero del Castillo, a talented young right-wing neo-Falangist from Seville and something of a protégé of Serrano. Gamero was also made a minister

---

Carlist traditionalists	55	123
Catholics	39	83
ACNP (Catholic propagandists)	30	65
CEDA	72	122
Republican moderate liberals	7	13

7. *Gaceta de la República*, no. 112 (April 22, 1937). Though somewhat crude and lacking in advanced technical training, Muñoz Grandes was well regarded for his professional competence and enjoyed considerable esteem among his fellow officers. The initial Left Republican government of 1936 had reassigned him as a colonel of Moroccan troops. After he had refused to join the conspiracy, his old comrades asked him to resign that post so as not to create an obstacle to the revolt. Muñoz Grandes agreed to this, but after the war began was arrested and at first sentenced by the Republic to nine years imprisonment, leaving him embittered and eager to serve the Nationalist regime.

8. On the FET militia, see Chueca, *El fascismo*, 265–75. The law constituting the regular peacetime FET militia was not promulgated until July 2, 1940. The militia was charged with premilitary training and political education but never became obligatory and never mobilized any large number of Spanish youth. The officers in command were mostly strict professionals.

without portfolio, as was the camisa vieja writer and new vice-president of the Junta Política, Rafael Sánchez Mazas. Ramiro Ledesma had once sneeringly labeled Sánchez Mazas "the provider of rhetoric for the Falange." After spending the war in a Republican prison Sánchez Mazas seemed totally washed out and was hardly able to do even that, though he later registered a few strictly literary achievements.[9]

The new permanent statutes of the party maintained indefinitely the parallel system of Falangist Services and Delegations.[10] They created only the illusion of a parallel state structure, for most of the Falangist national delegates had no governmental authority whatever. An exception was the new syndical chief, Gerardo Salvador Merino, who was given explicit powers under the state to construct the new system of national syndicates. Falangist influence was diluted even within the new Junta Política, the party's advisory board, where the only camisa vieja among the nine members was Dionisio Ridruejo. The remaining eight were two neo-Falangists, two Franco-monarchists, two Carlists, one new *franquista* opportunist, and one Army officer. The membership of the third National Council of the FET was arranged in somewhat similar proportions. Of 100 members, only 24 were genuine camisas viejas, almost as many monarchists, nearly 20 Army officers, and only 7 Carlists.

By 1939 the FET organization claimed a nominal active male membership of approximately 650,000.[11] Most younger men of active age who hoped to get ahead in politics, obtain state employment, or flourish in various lines of professional or economic activity found it expedient to sign up, and FET membership would continue to increase for three more years, reaching an all-time high of 932,000 in 1942.[12] The FET bore responsibility for political indoctrination of the population and for providing the political infrastructure of the entire system.[13] Nearly all the new provincial governors and mayors were nominal members, but the bulk of the active male membership was relatively passive and only rarely mobilized. Hundreds of disillusioned camisas viejas, finding the new Spain not at all the dynamic and revolutionary national syndicalist system to which they aspired, had dropped out of active participation. Some effort would soon

9. There is an excellent sketch of Sánchez Mazas in Gregorio Morán, *Los españoles que dejaron de serlo: Euskadi, 1937–1981* (Barcelona, 1981), 134–48.

10. *Fundamentos del Nuevo Estado* (Madrid, 1943), 22–37; *Recopilación sistemática de la legislación del Movimiento Mayo 1937 a Diciembre 1943* (Madrid, 1944).

11. According to a report by the vice–secretary general to a meeting of the National Council in March 1963, cited in Joaquín Bardavío, *La estructura del poder en España* (Madrid, 1969), 117.

12. Ibid.

13. Perhaps its most widely diffused doctrinal pamphlet in the immediate postwar period, first published a few weeks after the war ended, was the FET's *Doctrina e historia de la revolución nacional española* (Barcelona, 1939).

be made in several of the larger cities to begin a network of Falangist *jefes de bloque* in imitation of the party "block chiefs" in Nazi Germany and the Soviet Union, but this stratagem soon languished and was never completed. In general, FET administration was content with a nominally large but little mobilized and basically passive membership.[14]

The regime placed considerable emphasis on youth, giving it frequent attention in state propaganda, and in theory this was another important focus of Falangist mobilization. During the first year of the Civil War, however, members of Acción Española had formed a Comisión de Cultura y Ensenañza (Commission on Instruction and Culture) in Burgos, and their associates were able to dominate policy in primary and secondary education under the new regime. The Falangist university student group SEU (Sindicato Español Universitario) had been officially revived in November 1937, however, and Falangist pressure managed to block a proposed new Law of University Reform sponsored by the right-wing Catholic Education Minister, Sainz Rodríguez, during the latter part of the Civil War. In September 1939 the SEU was given a monopoly in university student organizing,[15] to the consternation of Catholic groups. A circle of Young Turks formed around *Haz*, the official SEU journal, and was allowed considerable autonomy. Led by an ardent nineteen-year-old, Enrique Sotomayor, this group proposed to form a broad Frente de Juventudes (Youth Front) to diffuse Falangist ideology and mobilize the youth of Spain. The official SEU leadership, cautious and bureaucratic, opposed this, but Serrano Súñer brought the project to the attention of Franco, who approved it on August 16, 1939. Muñoz Grandes, the new Falangist secretary general, soon mounted a counterattack with the help of the SEU leaders, who feared a large radical youth organization beyond their control. Franco immediately had second thoughts, three days later balancing the appointment of Sotomayor as secretary general of the SEU with that of a "safe" camisa vieja, José Miguel Guitarte, to the higher post of jefe nacional of the proposed new front.[16]

Against the advice of other camisas viejas, Sotomayor accepted the leadership of the SEU. He and his handful of fanatical young associates planned a semiautonomous mass student organization to promote national revolution. They distinguished their Falangist syndicalism from Italian Fascism by its greater radicalism and authenticity, which was to be "morally

14. Serrano Súñer's speech to the opening meeting of the new Junta Política on October 31, 1939 did mention the need for a purge of the large opportunist membership in the FET. Serrano Súñer, *De la victoria y la postguerra (Discursos)* (Madrid, 1941), 78. Nothing seems to have come of this.

15. FET, *Falange ante la universidad* (Madrid, 1942).

16. *BMFET*, Aug. 20, 1939. Background material on Sotomayor was drawn from the personal files of his camisa vieja colleague, Carlos Juan Ruiz de la Fuente.

barbarous" and "Catholically barbarous," recapturing the dynamism and commitment of "primitive Christianity."[17] In fact, their initiatives were thoroughly squelched by bureaucratic superiors and Sotomayor resigned within three months. A long delay ensued before the official organization of the Frente de Juventudes to ensure its restriction and subordination. It was not officially formed until December 6, 1940,[18] and even then it never became a fully developed mass organization on the national level. The Frente de Juventudes's most extensive activities would have to do with camping and sports. Its main division, the Falanges Juveniles de Franco, according to its own statistics never mobilized more than 13 percent of the boys and 8 percent of the girls of Spain between seven and eighteen years of age—even at its height.[19] Membership was voluntary and members were primarily the children of ardent Nationalists, but even many of these received only limited political indoctrination.

To compensate for the feeble development of political theory thus far, an Instituto de Estudios Políticos was created under the FET on September 9, 1939. It was designed as a sort of brain trust for the new regime, combining features of an advanced training school for high-level party leaders with those of a study institute for policy and theory. The kind of

17. According to a published speech before the Falange of Madrid early in November 1939.

18. *La España franquista en sus documentos*, ed. F. Díaz-Plaja (Barcelona, 1976), 76–80. Sáncho Dávila, *De la O.J. al Frente de Juventudes* (Madrid, 1941), presents a brief bureaucratic statement on the transition from the wartime Organización Juvenil to the Frente de Juventudes.

19. The Frente de Juventudes was composed of five categories: Centros de Trabajo (Work Centers) for adolescent and teen-aged workers; Centros de Enseñanza (Instruction Centers) for secondary students in the cities; rural centers; the SEU; and the Falanges Juveniles de Franco. Only the last two were directly political, and even the Falanges Juveniles spent most of their funding on sports and outings. The Falanges Juveniles were divided into three age groups, and their membership was reported by *Arriba* on December 31, 1941, as follows:

Age	Males		Females	
7–10	(Pelayos)	162,738	(Margaritas)	94,484
10–14	(Flechas)	251,797	(Flechas)	126,590
14–18	(Cadetes)	150,464	(Flechas Azules)	57,878
		564,999		278,952

This amounted to only about 17.5 percent and 8.5 percent, respectively, of the male and female population of approximately six and a half million for these age groups in Spain. It may be compared with the figures for Fascist Italy, where approximately 65 percent of Italian juvenile males and 44 percent of females were nominal members of Fascist youth organizations in 1939. See Chueca, *El fascismo*, 311; and Juan J. Linz, "From Falange to Movimiento-Organización," in *Authoritarian Politics in Modern Society*, ed. S. P. Huntington and C. H. Moore (New York, 1970), 167.

Moreover, by 1943 membership was already in decline, though according to the statistics of the Falanges Juveniles the peak of their camping activity came in the years 1942 to 1945.

half-baked ideas sometimes served up during the Civil War, like those in one Falangist pamphlet which declared that "fascism is nothing else than the nationalization of the doctrines of Marx,"[20] obviously would not do, but it would take the Instituto several years to make any contribution.

The most active doctrinal publicist in the immediate aftermath of the Civil War was Juan Beneyto Pérez. In *El Partido* (1939), *El nuevo Estado español* (1939), and *Genio y figura del Movimiento* (1940), he proclaimed the "totalitarian" quality of the Franco state and its similarity to other one-party authoritarian regimes,[21] while limning out a theory of *caudillaje:*

> The concept of the Caudillo is a synthesis of reason and ideal necessity. It is not only force, but spirit; it constitutes a new technique and is the incarnation of the national soul and even of the national physiognomy. As a technique, it is the natural consequence and organic necessity of a unitary, hierarchical, and total regime. As an incarnation it is the exaltation of a mystique. It becomes a new concept by which a man arises as rector of the community and personifies its spirit, a concept which proceeds directly from the Revolution. It has a fully and typically revolutionary context, like the idea that nourishes it, . . .
>
> In the totalitarian regimes the Party appears exalted in this precise function of selecting the Jefe. . . . [In practice, it would seem to have worked exactly the other way around.]
>
> . . . As a minority, it is to integrate whatever is healthy and robust in national life. Therefore the unification itself has a task of selection, since it seeks homogeneity even in the solvency of its elements. . . . The Party thus becomes the depository of a force that is continually renewed and knows how to orient each generation in a revolutionary spirit. Thanks to the concept of the permanent revolution, and owing to the instrumentality of the Party, struggles disappear and all energy is concentrated on the task of national affirmation.[22]

The principal public event of the autumn of 1939 was a major drama of political liturgy—removal of the remains of José Antonio Primo de Rivera from his wartime grave in the Republican prison of Alicante to a posthumous apotheosis and final interment before the altar of the church at El Escorial, only a few feet from the traditional pantheon of the rulers of Spain. This was accomplished by successive relays of young Falangists who bore the vanished Jefe's bier on their shoulders during a ten-day trek across Spain between November 10 and 20, accompanied by organized baroque ceremony in each town through which they passed.[23] The cult of

20. Ricardo Gutiérrez, *Memorias de un azul* (Salamanca, 1937), 62.

21. Especially in *El nuevo Estado español* (Madrid, 1939), 39, 59–68. Cf. Luis del Valle, *El Estado nacionalista totalitario autoritario* (Zaragoza, 1940).

22. Juan Beneyto and J. M. Costa Serrano, *El Partido* (Zaragoza, 1939), 150, 156, 169. Four decades later, an elderly Beneyto would publish a very different book after the end of the regime, *La identidad del franquismo* (Madrid, 1979), which would interpret the regime and its institutions as a kind of absolute monarchy and neotraditionalist system, rather nearer the truth.

23. Samuel Ros and Antonio Bouthelier, *A hombros de la Falange: Historia del traslado de los restos de José Antonio* (Madrid and Barcelona, 1940).

El Ausente remained strong in the Falange,[24] serving as a kind of psychological transfer and compensation for the subordination of the FET in the new regime and the more remote charisma of the Caudillo. Political liturgy was then at its high point for the regime as a whole, as an extensive new politicized calendar of national observances was created during 1938–40.[25]

Yet of all the regime's political objectives, probably the most important during the autumn of 1939 was the negotiation of a new concordat with the Vatican, a proposal already broached before the end of the Civil War. Franco saw this as the logical culmination of his neotraditionalist religious policy, roofing the solid edifice of Catholic support that he had built for his new system. The government annulled the old Republican divorce law in September and on December 1 resumed the state ecclesiastical subsidy. Talk among Falangist anticlericals about a national church was quieted, and even *Arriba,* the central Falangist organ, underlined the mutual desirability of a treaty with the Vatican. A circular from Muñoz Grandes to all Falangist provincial chiefs on October 25 forbade imitation of such Nazi styles as "Nazi uniforms, goosestepping, raised arm ovations, etc."[26] in keeping with the spirit of the Spanish diplomatic offensive. If the Vatican had been willing to sign a concordat with Germany during Hitler's first year as chancellor, Franco felt that it ought to be all the more interested in such an accord with so ultra-Catholic a state as Spain during its first full year of government.

The Vatican did not see matters so simply, particularly since the Spanish government adamantly insisted on restoration of the right of presentation of bishops by the state. Outbreak of war in Europe further complicated the international outlook, while the somewhat arrogant demands of the regime placed a strain on relations with the Holy See. At one point the Spanish representative to the Vatican was withdrawn briefly, and no progress was made in negotiations during the fall and winter of 1939–40.[27]

The Armed Forces

Pride of place within the new state went to the armed forces, which had initiated the Nationalist movement and carried it to victory. During the first postwar phase of the regime the military played a much more important role in the government and the administrative system than did the

24. *Dolor y memoria de España en el segundo aniversario de la muerte de José Antonio* (Barcelona, 1939).

25. The major political holidays and special occasions are listed by Francisco Moret Messerli, *Conmemoraciones y fechas de la España nacionalsindicalista* (Madrid, 1942).

26. Quoted in La Cierva, *Franquismo,* 1:164.

27. These are chronicled in Marquina Barrio, *Diplomacia vaticana,* 155–242.

official *partido único*, holding more elite positions. The military not only provided the key martial underpinning of the state but also administered the repression and led the police forces, were responsible through ministerial appointments for much of national reconstruction and the new industrialization program, and even provided some of the key symbols and ideological components of the regime through the doctrine of military caudillaje.[28]

By 1939 the officer corps of the Spanish military and their leadership was in considerable measure a creation of Franco. Though senior officers antedated the Civil War Nationalist Army,[29] a new corporate group had been forged in one of the harshest of military experiences, bound to and identified with its Generalissimo. During the war Franco had astutely downplayed rewards and promotions, emphasizing common service and sacrifice, so that it had not been uncommon to find colonels commanding divisions and brigadiers entire corps. This had proven effective, focusing attention on performance, but a major round of promotions took place after the fighting was over that involved restoration of the ranks of lieutenant general and full admiral, abolished by the Republic. Though salaries remained low,[30] officers enjoyed special privileges, particularly their access to the well-stocked and low-priced commissaries that were a special contrast in a country beginning to suffer grave shortages. Former enlisted men were given preference in the newly announced government hiring quotas. On the whole the military were content and would remain the backbone of the regime, with little dissidence, until the time of Franco's death. They took pride in their overwhelming victory and in the place of honor they held in the new system.

It was this privileged status that made it possible for the only public signs of discontent in the immediate aftermath of the Civil War to be expressed by two of Franco's most restive generals, Yagüe and Queipo de Llano. Before his appointment as air minister, Yagüe was honored with a special military banquet in Madrid by old comrades, an act of veiled criticism of the regime. On July 18, a separate Carlist military banquet for senior Navarrese officers was held in Pamplona, leading to a new regulation that special military banquets obtain official approval. More overtly, an outburst by Queipo de Llano at public ceremonies in Seville on July 18, 1939, third anniversary of the rising, criticized new political oppor-

28. The principal study of the role of the military within the regime is José Antonio Olmeda Gómez, "La burocracia militar en España: Un análisis administrativo" (Ph.D. diss., University of Madrid, 1984).

29. Teresa Suero Roca, *Los generales de Franco* (Barcelona, 1975), provides brief biographical sketches of the principal figures.

30. A new salary scale in 1940 increased officers' salaries by from 17 to 40 percent, depending on rank. Eduardo San Martín Losada, *Sueldos, haberes y gratificaciones del personal del Ejército* (Madrid, 1943).

tunists and suggested that Seville merited the same national honor (the Gran Cruz Laureada) that Franco had recently awarded the city of Valladolid, a strong Falangist base. Queipo was immediately deprived of command and within a month shipped off to Italy, to serve first on a military mission and then as regular attaché for two and a half years before eventually being permitted to return to Spain in January 1942.[31]

The Army alone had come to number over 900,000 by the end of the war. On January 24, 1939, Franco decided to cut the postwar force to a nominal 24 divisions formed in 10 corps, one for each of Spain's eight regular territorial military districts plus two for the Moroccan Protectorate. At its lowest point Army manpower sank to about 230,000 early in 1940, in addition to 20,000 Moroccan troops. The spread of World War II soon encouraged as much expansion as the slender resources of the new state could afford, however. For much of the war, about 400,000 troops were maintained, the Army numbering about 365,000 in 1945. The numbers in the officer corps, nominally around 15,500 in 1940, rose to nearly 26,000 by 1945. Thus the old institutional scourge of a bloated officer corps, temporarily eliminated at least in part by the Republic and the Civil War, quickly reemerged under the new regime, because of the pressure of World War II and of domestic political considerations. Most of the added officers came from the ranks of the wartime alféreces provisionales, 8,937 of whom passed a series of further training courses and gained permanent commissions.[32] In addition, a new regulation of July 12, 1940 (the "ley Varela") empowered the armed forces ministers to carry out a thorough purge and reclassification of officers and NCOs, primarily with respect to political reliability. The military purge commissions created by this regulation expelled a small but undetermined number of Nationalist officers deemed to have been only "circumstantial" Nationalists during the war, insufficiently devoted to the cause, while a number of older officers who had retired under the Republic were recommissioned.

During the first months of peace the regime had great visions of restoring Spain's long-lost sea power. On September 8, 1939, it announced a ten-year naval armament program that proposed to build 4 battleships, 2 heavy and 2 light cruisers, 54 destroyers, 36 torpedo boats and 50 submarines within the next decade. Costs were estimated at approximately 5,500 million pesetas, to be paid at the rate of about 500 million per year. Of all the specific ambitions of the new state, this was the most grandiose

31. The best summary is in Carlos Fernández, *Tensiones militares durante el franquismo* (Barcelona, 1985), 13–21. See also Antonio Olmedo Delgado and José Cuesta Monereo, *El General Queipo de Llano* (Barcelona, 1957), 298–320. Franco later, in 1944, awarded the Gran Cruz Laureada to the city of Seville and to Queipo personally.

32. According to the reworking of Gil Ossorio's statistics by Julio Busquets, "Los Alféreces Provisionales hasta la creación de la Hermandad (1936–1958)," *Historia 16* 11:119 (March 1986), 43–55.

and disproportionate, and had to be abandoned soon after it was first announced. Between 1940 and 1945 the shrunken Spanish economy was able to construct only 3 submarines and 6 corvettes, while a fourth submarine was purchased from Germany. Two new destroyers were begun but only completed later. Naval personnel grew only slightly during World War II, increasing from about 1,600 officers and 20,000 men in 1940 to more than 2,600 officers and 23,000 men in 1945.[33]

Not to be outdone in ambitious planning, the new air force minister, Yagüe, presented a proposal to the government in October 1939 that would involve the acquisition of 3,740 combat planes during the coming decade. This proposal found less favor than the grandiose naval plan and was soon reduced by more than half, fixed at a rate of 150 planes per year that would involve little more than normal replacement of worn-out material. Thus the Air Force remained of modest dimensions, growing from 3,800 officers and 25,000 men in 1940 to nearly 4,000 officers and almost 31,000 men by 1945.[34]

Immediately after the Civil War the police underwent more extensive reorganization than the armed forces proper. At one point Franco considered abolishing the century-old national constabulary, the Guardia Civil, in favor of a new unified force for both towns and countryside, but was dissuaded. Instead, the Carabineros (border patrol) were merged with the Guardia Civil, the latter retaining its name and distinctive identity and uniforms. It numbered approximately 60,000 by 1941, or about 20 percent more than the two combined in 1936. The institution was placed under full military discipline and the command of career Army officers, who also held numerous intermediate posts. The Republic's special urban Guardias de Asalto were replaced by a new system of urban Policía Armada (Armed Police), which numbered 17,000 by 1942. All security forces together had an only slightly larger enrollment in the early 1940s than they had under the Republic, though they were employed much more vigorously.

The goals of streamlining and modernizing the armed forces were not, however, being met in any way, nor could they under the straitened circumstances of the Spanish economy. Most of the budget for the Army and Navy was still being spent on personnel, given the continued bloat in the officer corps. All that the regime managed to accomplish in fiscal terms—and this was not unimportant—was to reduce somewhat the armed forces' portion of the national budget, as indicated in table 12.1.

33. Ricardo de la Cierva, *Historia del franquismo* (Barcelona, 1976), 1:328–31.
34. A number of other expensive proposals by Yagüe, such as the creation of an independent antiaircraft arm, were also rejected. Moreover, the air force minister's practice of incorporating certain nonleftist Republican air force officers and giving them seniority credit for their wartime Republican service was quashed by Franco in a decree of Sept. 28, 1939, which denied all seniority derived from the wartime Republican forces. *FF*, 3:10.

Table 12.1. Percentages of the Spanish Budget Spent in
           Key Areas, 1940–45

	1940	1945
Armed forces	40.6	34
All police services	10.5	6.4
Education	6.4	5.4
FET	0.16	1.9

Source: Ricardo de la Cierva, *Historia del franquismo* (Madrid,
1976), 1: 340.

The Beginning of Autarchy

On the morrow of the Civil War it was much easier to do away with the
remnants of revolutionary style among the society of the former Republican zone than to deal with the economic problems resulting from the conflict. In the cities, the campaign to restore the wearing of hats and neckties was generally successful, but the effort to restore full production
encountered major obstacles. This was not because the Civil War itself
had been enormously destructive in strictly economic terms. Its results,
for example, could not in any way be compared with the massive destruction inflicted on areas of central and eastern Europe during the six years
that followed. The firepower available to both sides had been modest
compared to that routinely employed in World War II, and with the notorious exception of Guernica, Spanish cities had never been heavily
bombed. Even so, the losses had been costly and were proportionately
heaviest in shipping and transportation, with nearly 30 percent of the nation's maritime tonnage destroyed (primarily by the attacks of the Nationalists and their allies) and half the railway locomotives lost. Eight percent
of Spain's housing and more than a third of the livestock had been lost.
Though no more than 6 to 7 percent of the total national wealth had been
directly destroyed, the disruption of production was very great. By 1939
industrial output was 31 percent less than in the last prewar year, agricultural production had declined by 21 percent, the labor force had fallen by
half a million, and per capita income by approximately 28 percent.[35] Spain
thus faced a major task of reconstruction and development, compounded
by the long-term effects of the depression and the growing international
economic crisis that accompanied the outbreak of general war in Europe.

There is not the slightest evidence that Franco ever proposed to implement the national syndicalist revolution of which radical Falangists talked.

35. Most of these statistics are derived from Ramón Tamames, *La República, La era de
Franco* (Madrid, 1973), 357; but see also J. Ros Hombravella et al., *Capitalismo español: De
la autarquía a la estabilización (1939–1959)* (Madrid, 1973), 1: 166–70.

Just as his syncretist regime would never adopt full fascism, it would never consider a radically fascistic economic policy. In economics as in other areas the nascent regime combined ultraconservatism with ambitious renovationist schemes to develop the economy rapidly while transforming its social framework only by degrees and altering its basic financial structure very little, at least in the short run.

Nearly all confiscated or collectivized properties, urban and rural, were returned to previous owners or their heirs, usually restoring ownership and management on much the same terms as had existed in 1936. A small number of collectives not primarily based on revolutionary confiscation, however, were reconstituted as private property–based cooperatives. On the other hand, special patrimonies were created for key state agencies such as the FET by across-the-board confiscation of the holdings of leftist organizations and trade unions, a process not fully completed until 1945.[36]

More serious than wartime destruction for the economy as a whole was the fact that Spain possessed little domestic capital that could be mobilized for reconstruction. The state's gold reserves had been largely liquidated by the wartime Republican government,[37] it already held a considerable public debt, and the country lacked an efficient domestic capital market in which funds might be readily generated. A weak and inefficient fiscal system further limited public resources. Perhaps as much as 23 percent of Spanish industrial investment and bonds was held by foreigners.[38] The major single source of imports was the United States, but Spain's largest export market was Britain, followed by France and Germany. Much of the pattern of international trade had been disrupted by the Civil War, and the subsequent European war made it unlikely that it could be easily restored. All this depressed opportunities to earn foreign exchange or negotiate foreign loans. Yet as matters stood, Spain would need foreign loans or credits in the short run to import vitally needed materials ranging from basic food supplies to cotton and other goods used in textile production, the largest domestic industry. The United States did grant credits for the importation of cotton, but Britain and France were willing to provide credit only on stringent terms, while Spain's associates in Berlin and Rome had no extra capital to provide on any terms.

A nationalist program of economics was thus imposed by circumstances, at least to some degree, but it clearly corresponded to Franco's own predilections. His critics always derided his ignorance of the technicalities of

36. This phenomenon is discussed at some length by Sueiro and Díaz Nosty, *Historia*, 201–20.

37. The definitive study is Angel Viñas, *El oro de Moscú* (Barcelona, 1979).

38. Britain held about a third of foreign investment, followed by France, according to conclusions cited in Robert H. Whealey, "Economic Influence of the Great Powers in the Spanish Civil War," *The International History Review* 5:2 (May 1983), 229–54.

economics and the simplism of his ideas. In many ways this derision was deserved, though Franco did have a reasonably consistent general orientation. He had grown up in the Regenerationist era of the early twentieth century and always believed that the government should itself provide a concerted approach to economics. More recently, he had been impressed by the achievements of Hjalmar Schacht's policies in Germany and was convinced that orthodox liberal theories had become passé. Franco preferred a policy of nationalism and voluntarism that subordinated economic affairs to state policy in all those areas which the state might deem important. Its goal would be achieving national development and as high a degree of self-sufficiency as might be feasible. In this regard he assigned a high value to raw materials, with which he was convinced Spain was abundantly supplied, while downplaying the significance of capital and technology. In August 1938 he had gone so far as to declare to a French journalist, "Spain is a privileged country that can be self-sufficient. . . . We have no need to import anything."[39] Later, in December 1939, he spoke of Spain's opportunity to exploit untapped gold deposits,[40] which he apparently was convinced existed.

Franco therefore announced on June 5, 1939, that Spain must carry out reconstruction on the basis of economic self-sufficiency or autarchy, which, though foreign models were not invoked, implicitly paralleled the current policies of Italy and Germany. He declared, "Our victory constitutes the triumph of certain economic principles that reject the old liberal theories, under whose mythologies many foreign states were subjected to colonialism."[41] Thus, shaking off the constraints of the "liberal plutocracies" Franco inaugurated the era of autarchy in Spanish policy, which would continue with diminishing vigor for twenty years.

His basic ideas were outlined in an extensive document that he signed on October 8 entitled "Guidelines for a Plan of Reform for our Economy."[42] This laid out a vague ten-year plan to achieve economic modernization and self-sufficiency, proposing to simultaneously increase exports and reduce imports without relying on foreign investment. It revealed great faith in the economic potential of Spanish society and the adequacy of domestic raw materials. The effectiveness of statist direction and control was simply assumed. The goal was to meet the country's basic economic

39. *Francisco Franco: Pensamiento económico* (Madrid, 1958), 626. Critics might maintain that the title of this publication constituted an oxymoron. It is rather curious that twenty years after the Civil War a collection that included many of Franco's errors and extravagances would still be presented by state propaganda as "economic thought."

40. Carlos Velasco Murviedro, "Las pintorescas ideas económicas de Franco," *Historia 16* 8:85 (May 1983), 19–28.

41. *Palabras del Caudillo*, 135–45.

42. "Fundamentos y directrices de un Plan de saneamiento de nuestra economía armónico con nuestra reconstrucción nacional," published with commentary by Javier Tusell in *Historia 16* 10:115 (Nov. 1985), 41–49.

and defense needs primarily from domestic resources within only four years, another six being proposed as necessary to achieve full reconstruction and development.

Though this document called for each ministry to submit a detailed plan to the presidency of the government, no coordinated program emerged except for a loosely formulated "Plan of National Reconstruction" approved by the Council of Ministers that month. It proposed to eliminate the deficit in the external balance of payments within a decade, largely through a massive program of dam construction to boost electrical output and provide water for irrigation. The varied approaches to economics of the ideological "families" of the regime were as diverse and eclectic as the politics of the Nationalist elite in general. Falangists could present no clear, detailed program, nor did Franco wish to give any individual or group the power to develop or implement overarching policy.[43] It suited him to approach economic policy on an ad hoc basis, adding or dropping features or particular policies as circumstances warranted.

A Dirección General de Regiones Devastadas had already been set up during the Civil War, and 173 towns and villages were subsequently targeted for special attention in reconstruction. Most of these were very small but had had the misfortune to be on the front lines in major battles. Similarly, on July 6, 1939, an Instituto de Crédito para la Reconstrucción was created by the state to grant low-interest, long-term loans to individuals and enterprises trying to rebuild.[44]

The soundest economic administrator in the 1939 government was the new minister of finance, José Larraz, a portly business and financial expert who attempted to pursue a relatively vigorous and straightforward policy to unify the state budget and the national financial system, liquidate war debts, contain inflation, and put the burden of reconstruction on a sound financial footing. By the end of 1940 he had managed to unify the currency and deposits of the two former war zones. He also made an effort to integrate the various *cajas especiales* (special funds) that remained outside the central budget, some of which, like that of the FET, amounted to

43. The most prolific theorist of formalistic programs was the economic publicist Higinio París Eguilaz, whose book *El Estado y la economía: Política económica totalitaria* had appeared in 1938. This abstract work advocated long-range planning to span periods of from fifteen to twenty years, an inherently unrealistic notion. "Totalitarian policy" seemed to refer merely to some sort of state regulation and coordination that eschewed state socialism at least as much as it did purely laissez-faire liberal capitalism. París saw that at most only a relative autarchy could be attempted.

In his subsequent *Un nuevo orden económico* (Madrid, 1941), París proposed a "central directive organ" of the state over the economy, but this was to stimulate and regulate (not specifically plan) a mostly private economy. He did not suggest a systematically corporative structure but urged a "totalitarian policy of jobs creation" to coordinate new development. This was also another example of the vagueness and inflation with which the term *totalitarian* was used in the Spanish lexicon of the period.

44. *La reconstrucción de España: Resumen de dos años de labor* (Madrid, 1942).

as much as 400 million pesetas. At the close of 1940 he put through a Ley de Reforma Tributaria (Tax Reform Law) which contained certain improvements to make the system slightly less regressive and inefficient, but he was generally frustrated in his efforts to unify and reform the archaic Spanish financial system. Larraz finally resigned in disgust early in 1941, the first and for a long time the only minister of Franco to walk out on him.[45]

Much of the responsibility for implementing the policy of autarchy lay with the new minister of commerce and industry, the Army colonel Luis Alarcón de la Lastra, who survived in this exacting task for only a year before giving way to the Catalan businessman and neo-Falangist Demetrio Carceller. The latter had no faith in extreme autarchy, correctly gauging that Spain lacked the resources to implement it fully and that the governmental straitjacket which it required would hamper the economy.[46]

At no time did the regime pretend that Spain could become fully self-sufficient. The practical goal was the most efficient trade-off between domestic self-sufficiency and the international division of labor,[47] difficult to achieve in practice. Given the severe shortages afflicting the country, significant imports of food, petroleum, and raw materials were an absolute necessity. Autarchy therefore was directed toward improving the terms of foreign commerce and expanding domestic industry, where new projects were calculated above all in terms of foreign exchange costs.

The autarchist industrialization drive was initiated by a decree of October, 1939, creating the Law for the Protection and Development (Fomento) of National Industry, which provided a wide variety of incentives, tax benefits, and special licensing arrangements for creation of new factories. A subsequent Law for the Regulation (Ordenación) and Defense of National Industry of November 24 declared certain industries worthy of particular assistance, and remained in effect for twenty years. It also stipulated that every firm receiving any form of state financial or economic assistance must give preference to domestic products and services. This eventually culminated in the establishment in 1941 of the Instituto Na-

45. Larraz also rejected Franco's request to return ten years later. His role as finance minister is treated in passing in Juan Sardá's study, "El Banco de España (1931–1962)," in *El Banco de España: Una historia económica* (Madrid, 1970), 447–54. Cf. Jean Créac'h, *Le Coeur et l'épée* (Paris, 1959), 310.

46. As quoted in the *New York Times*, Feb. 29, 1940, cited in Trythall, *Caudillo*, 214.

47. "Autarchic policy should not be confused with the concept of a closed and isolated economy. There is no contradiction whatever between the concepts of relative autarchy and the need to export. Autarchic policy may undoubtedly produce a reduction in the volume of certain kinds of exports, but it can never be carried to the extreme of impeding the nation's provision of vital materials, for such a policy would provoke in turn a reduction in the purchase of vital products of this country by the nations affected. Everything depends on the balance established between the vital products necessary for the autarchic state and the vital products that this state supplies to other countries. . . ." R. Gay de Montellá, *Autarquía: Nuevas orientaciones de la economía* (Barcelona, 1940), 81, in Angel Viñas et al., *Política comercial exterior de España (1931–1975)* (Madrid, 1979), 1:206.

cional de Industria (INI), a state investment and holding company to stimulate industrialization, modeled on the Italian Istituto per la Ricostruzione Industriale. The decree of September 25, 1941, that founded the INI announced that its purpose was "to develop and finance, in the service of the nation, the creation and resurgence of our industries, especially those whose principal task is to resolve problems imposed by the country's defense needs or the development of our economic autarchy."[48] In particular, it would attempt to stimulate shipbuilding, steel and chemical production, and the domestic manufacture of cars, trucks, and airplanes. The INI's first head was the senior naval officer Juan Antonio Suanzes, childhood friend of Franco and son of one of his early school superintendents in El Ferrol. Suanzes would continue to direct the INI for more than twenty years.

Autarchist policy was full of inconsistencies and loopholes from the start and soon resulted in grave distortions. In addition to the emphases of the INI, it stressed war industries, railroad construction and repair, shipbuilding, roads, machine-tool production, domestic hydrocarbons, nitrogen, and cotton.[49] While rigid controls were set up for foreign exchange, imports, and certain domestic products, these barriers meant that rather artificial terms of cost allocation had to be projected for industrial development, based at first on the levels of 1935. Lack of market or other adjustments resulted in costs and prices that were set in an increasingly arbitrary and unrealistic manner, fueling inflation and impeding growth. As shortages arising from World War II intensified, this would also lead to costly and fruitless efforts to find replacements for imported petroleum by extracting oil from shale and bituminous coal (the chief fossil fuel deposits in the peninsula) and in official support for a dubious Austrian inventor who proposed development of an absolutely artificial form of synthetic gasoline.

Equally important, it discouraged the government from seeking a maximum of loans, credit, and investment from abroad because of regulations against foreign capital participation and the general disposition of state policy. Even in the straitened circumstances of 1939–40 it would have been possible to generate more foreign credits and capital investment, but the regime's approach was to beware of such opportunities and accept them only on the most favorable terms, depriving a struggling economy of the necessary support for expansion and new employment.[50]

Spanish policy also reflected the overconcentration on industry typical

48. Pedro Schwartz and Manuel Jesús González, *Una historia del Instituto Nacional de Industria* (Madrid, 1978), 1.

49. Viñas et al., *Política comercial*, 1:295–96. See the general discussion of immediate postwar policy and of autarchy on pp. 248–319, and also that in Ros Hombravella et al., *Capitalismo*, 1:78–98.

50. Cf. Manuel Jesús González, *La política económica del franquismo (1940–1970)* (Madrid, 1979), 46–47.

of twentieth-century agrarian countries eager to expand rapidly. Thus agriculture, the basis of the economy, was severely neglected. The main instrument of agrarian policy during the war had been the Servicio Nacional de Trigo (National Wheat Service) designed to channel marketing and stabilize prices. This was maintained in the postwar period at the cost of state subsidies, but investment stagnated. Spanish agriculture failed to recover its pre-1936 production at any point during the years of World War II, due to the effects of the Civil War, bad weather, and restrictive state regulations,[51] remaining in general terms nearly 25 percent below the admittedly unusually high levels of 1934–35.

Almost as soon as the agrarian former Nationalist zone and the more urban former Republican zone were integrated in the spring of 1939, massive food shortages began to develop in the country as a whole. On May 14, 1939, general rationing of certain staples was imposed and maintained at varying rates for more than a decade. Food supplies were allocated through the new General Commissary of Supplies (Abastecimientos) and Transports (CAT), which put into operation an increasingly complex and arbitrarily bureaucratic labyrinth of controls and procedures.

Austerity and self-sacrifice were announced as keynotes of the new economic policy. Raw materials were similarly rationed or allocated for industry, and government controls soon produced a widespread *straperlo* (the word came from a government financial scandal in 1935) or black market, which operated on nearly all levels of the economy, from simple consumer goods to major industrial supplies. State allocation became subject to extensive manipulation and bribery. Arrests and even a few executions were later carried out, but corruption developed into a system of its own. What the tensions and ideals of wartime had largely avoided were produced on a massive scale in peacetime as a result of the acute shortages and state controls.[52] For ordinary people in the former Nationalist zone, at least, the immediate postwar years were in some respects worse than the war itself.

During the five years that followed the Civil War there were at least 200,000 deaths from malnutrition and disease over and above the prewar death rate. Pulmonary tuberculosis carried off at least 25,000 a year, while in 1941 there were 53,307 registered deaths from diarrhea and enteritis, 4,168 from typhoid fever, and 1,644 from typhus.[53]

Nor did the new state generate the resources that could enable it to play a more dynamic social and economic role. The very conservative fiscal policies of the new regime reduced the percentage of national in-

51. This is emphasized in J. Clavera et al., *Capitalismo español: De la autarquía a la estabilización (1939–1959)* (Madrid, 1973), 1:92ff.

52. There is a general sketch of the straperlo in Sueiro and Díaz Nosty, *Historia del franquismo*, 221–40.

53. Sueiro and Díaz Nosty, *Historia del franquismo* (Barcelona, 1985 ed.), 1:135.

come collected in taxes from 17.83 under the Republic to 15.07 during the first five years after the Civil War. Increased military expenses and wartime shortages left little for new public works, for example, that might have palliated unemployment. The percentage of the national budget devoted to public works declined from 14.04 under the Republic to 7.74 during the first postwar years.[54] Official unemployment did descend from approximately 750,000 before the Civil War to 500,000 by the close of 1940 and eventually to 153,122 by the end of 1944, but such statistics hid the usual massive rural underemployment in parts of the country. In addition, wages remained extremely low and in real terms at first declined, as did the total labor force during the immediate postwar years (because of wartime losses, emigration, and a high rate of incarceration).

The new economic policies did not produce a system of national solidarity of the sort envisioned by the original Falangists or preached by the regime's own propaganda. Though they were undeniably aimed at increasing national economic production, their terms favored the established industrial and financial interests to the detriment of the defeated and of much of the rural population in general, part of which had fought for the Nationalists. The regime granted considerable autonomy to individual ministries and to major industrial and financial enterprises to conduct their own operations within their own spheres, which was not necessarily wrong, but their economic activity was not exposed to either general market forces or countervailing trade union or other interests. Those who could afford to pay could buy nearly anything they needed either at higher prices from legitimate enterprises or more frequently on the black market.

The years 1940–43 were the time of the most acute shortages and suffering for most of the population, though desperate conditions continued in the southern countryside for several more years. Depression and scarcity were to an extent dictated by the stringencies imposed at an international level by World War II, yet the regime's policies in key respects were scarcely well calculated to overcome them. To Franco, the suffering endured by Spanish people was in large measure a judgment elicited by the political and spiritual apostasy of half the nation. As he put it during a speech in Jaén on March 18, 1940, "The suffering of a nation at a certain point in its history is no chance: it is the spiritual judgment which God imposes for a corrupt life, for an unclean history."[55]

Foreign Policy: The Neutral Phase, 1939–1940

In 1939, Spanish policy was oriented toward Italy and Germany, the two powers who had made Franco's victory possible. They set the prime ex-

54. From a study by Jorge Esteban and Luis López Guerra, cited ibid., 137.
55. *Palabras del Caudillo* (1943), 157.

amples of the new national authoritarian state in Europe and constituted a new diplomatic and military alignment whose strength was steadily increasing. At the close of March 1939 Franco signed a treaty of friendship with Germany requiring mutual consultation in the event of an attack on either, and also joined the Anti-Comintern Pact, though the latter was a gesture without very concrete obligations. On May 8, the Spanish government officially withdrew from the League of Nations.

This did not mean that the Spanish regime was a satellite of either Axis power, for Franco's policy from beginning to end was based on pragmatism and his judgment of Spain's best interests.[56] Thus a ten-year treaty of mutual friendship had been signed with Portugal largely at Madrid's request just a few days before the German pacts, and this was harmonized with the traditional British alliance with Portugal.[57] Serrano Súñer's state visit to Rome immediately after the war ended[58] was designed to express in part the Spanish regime's sense of a closer identity with Italy than with Germany, and was partly a response to the fact that Italy had made a more extensive contribution to the Nationalist triumph. Ciano, Mussolini's son-in-law and foreign minister, returned the visit in July.

Franco held at bay a proposed visit from Goering in May 1939. To lead the Berlin counterpart of Serrano's visit to Rome he selected the semi-liberal and anti-Falangist General Antonio Aranda, one of his ablest and most intelligent commanders, who accompanied the returning Condor Legion to Germany. In Berlin Aranda stressed the importance of good relations with Britain and tended to downplay the role of the Falange.[59]

War debts to Italy and Germany were a heavy obligation. Italy was owed more than 7 billion lire, but the amount was generously reduced by Mussolini to only 5 billion (around $250 million), partly with the aim of facilitating Italian economic penetration of Spain. After long and hard bargaining, the twenty-five-year table of payments was established to begin in mid-1942. Payment was eventually completed exactly on schedule on June 30, 1967. Hitler's government was less generous than Mussolini's, having already formed seventeen German-dominated mining companies

56. This was stressed in Camilo Barcia Trelles's *Puntos cardinales de la política exterior española*, published in Madrid that summer. For a brief overview of the regime's foreign policy throughout its long life, see José Mario Armero, *La política exterior de Franco* (Barcelona, 1978).

57. See Charles R. Halstead's thorough study, "Peninsular Purpose: Portugal and Its 1939 Treaty of Friendship and Non-Aggression with Spain," *Il Politico* 45:2 (1980), 287–311.

58. Serrano's speeches in Italy are collected in his *De la victoria y la postguerra (Discursos)* (Madrid, 1941); and he has commented on this trip in Saña, *Conversaciones*, 135–39.

59. *Documents Secrets du Ministère des Affaires Etrangères d'Allemagne* (Brussels, 1946), vol. 3, no. 23, pp. 66–68; *The Daily Express* (London), June 19, 1939; *O Diario de Norte* (Porto), June 24, 1939. There is an extensive treatment in Robert H. Whealey, "German-Spanish Relations, January–August 1939" (Ph.D. diss., University of Michigan, 1963), 177–92. At that point Aranda seemed convinced that Franco held him in high esteem and that he was destined for greater influence.

in Spain pursuant to Franco's concessions in 1938 and demonstrating clear intentions of establishing a dominant economic position. One government report prepared for Franco complained that "the Germans consider Spain a colony of theirs."[60] The Spanish regime for the most part avoided any further commitments and blocked greater economic penetration. Debt negotiations were strung out for the duration of World War II, and only very limited payments were made before the obligation was unilaterally canceled by Spain in 1945.[61]

As tensions heightened during the summer of 1939, Franco used the phrase *hábil prudencia* (adroit prudence) to describe Spain's foreign policy at a July meeting of the FET's National Council. The regime was trying to build closer relations with Spanish American states, the Philippines, and even the Arab world in an effort to reestablish the historic dimensions of Spanish diplomacy and circumvent its restriction to a weak and passive role in Europe.

The new foreign minister in the 1939 government was Col. Juan Beigbeder y Atienza, who had served as high commissioner of Spanish Morocco during much of the Civil War and had earlier been attaché in Berlin. He was a somewhat odd choice, a tall, thin, and nervous eccentric who had in certain respects "gone native" in Morocco. According to Serrano, Franco at first thought the nomination was "crazy," but accepted it in part because Beigbeder's appointment would gratify the military. He had a record of solid accomplishment in maintaining the loyalty of the native Moroccan population during the Civil War[62] and he was, together with Yagüe and Muñoz Grandes, one of the major Falangist officers, having also been jefe territorial of the FET in Morocco, where he had strongly encouraged the partido único. Like many of Franco's senior officers, Beigbeder was relatively pro-German though not fanatically so.[63]

Hitler's signing of the Nazi-Soviet Pact only two weeks after the formation of the new Spanish government was a shock to Madrid, contradicting the basic orientation of Franco's policy. The Falangist organ *Arriba* could only headline it as a "Surprise, A Tremendous Surprise," but at first was at a loss to justify it. The imminent outbreak of war was received with dismay, for the Polish government was a Catholic national-authoritarian state that had much in common with Franco's, and the Generalissimo and other Spanish leaders feared another civil war throughout Europe that would

60. Quoted in *FF*, 3:53.
61. The war debts are treated in Jesús Salas Larrazábal, *La intervención extranjera en la guerra de España* (Madrid, 1974); and in the article "La financiación exterior de la guerra civil" in Angel Viñas, *Guerra, dinero, dictadura*, 168–204.
62. Charles R. Halstead, "A 'Somewhat Machiavellian' Face: Colonel Juan Beigbeder as High Commissioner in Spanish Morocco 1937–1939," *The Historian* 37:1 (Nov. 1974).
63. The only study of Beigbeder as foreign minister is Halstead's "Un 'Africain' Méconnu: Le Colonel Juan Beigbeder," *Revue d'Histoire de la Deuxième Guerre Mondiale*, no. 83 (July 1971), 31–60.

open the door to the Soviet Union, whose foothold in the Peninsula had been eliminated only six months earlier. Nonetheless, Franco apparently considered Poland at least partly responsible for the impasse with Germany, because it had refused any compromise over the Polish Corridor, and informed Mussolini (initiator of the Munich conference) that he was willing to attempt some sort of mediation if the Duce thought it useful. Mussolini replied that he would try to undertake the task himself, but when, on August 30 (less than forty-eight hours before the German attack), the French foreign minister suggested to the Spanish ambassador in Paris that Franco attempt mediation, Mussolini vetoed the enterprise as coming too late.[64] On September 3, when Britain and France declared war on Germany, Franco publicly called on all parties to reconsider their decisions and return to negotiation. His appeal for "voluntary limitation" of use of means of destruction was not categorically pro-Polish, however, even though Beigbeder informed Berlin that renewed negotiations for a Spanish-German cultural agreement could not take place. Spain's neutrality was announced the following day, and Franco followed this up by quietly denying opportunity for Germany to supply its submarines in Spanish ports. On September 6 he telegraphed the ambassador in Rome to urge Mussolini to work toward "Polish surrender" as soon as possible to avert Russian military advance into Europe. When Franco later publicly condemned the destruction of Catholic Poland, he did so more in terms of the Soviet advance than in rejection of the Nazi agression.[65] Only hardcore Falangists were pleased with the outbreak of the European war, which they were confident would vindicate the authoritarian new order.

Franco rejected a French proposal for a new nonaggression pact between France and Spain, partly because Paris had failed to ratify a recently negotiated commercial agreement, but continued to offer his good offices to Berlin for possible mediation. He made it clear that another German invasion of the Low Countries would be badly received in Madrid, while in Paris a conservative French cabinet minister asked Franco's ambassador there to sound out the possibility of further peace mediation by Mussolini. Strong sympathy was expressed for Finland when it was attacked by the Soviet Union in December. The Soviet attack had the effect of diminishing Germany's prestige in Spain, for Hitler was generally viewed as responsible for bringing the Soviet Union into eastern Europe, and a small amount of Spanish arms were subsequently made available to the Finns.

The new Spanish regime looked much more to Rome than to Berlin, seeing in Fascist Italy the nearest thing to a model. Mussolini and his subordinates were almost equally interested in cultivating a special relation-

64. Javier Tusell and Genoveva García Queipo de Llano, *Franco y Mussolini* (Barcelona, 1985), 46–49.
65. *Arriba*, Oct. 2, 1939.

ship with Spain, which they saw as an Italian associate and semisatellite.
Mussolini, bound to Hitler by a military pact, declared Italy only a nonbelligerent, but nonetheless toyed briefly with the notion of forming a
sort of neutral bloc of south European authoritarian regimes led by Italy.
Beigbeder recommended this idea to Franco, suggesting that the association of Spain, Italy, Portugal, and perhaps some of the Balkan states might
replace the Rome-Berlin axis with a new Rome-Madrid axis. Franco was
little impressed, doubting the significance of what he termed an "axis
without strength,"[66] but a few inquiries were made. As it turned out,
Mussolini soon dropped the notion.

In March 1940 the senior generals who made up the Consejo Superior
del Ejército (Senior Army Council) approved a statement prepared by
General Kindelán declaring it impossible for Spain to enter the conflict
because it lacked economic support and materiel. They also complained
of the extreme internal division within the FET and questioned its role as
partido único, declaring that the Army was "the only available instrument
for orienting Spanish politics."[67]

A new trade agreement was signed with Britain that month, granting
the hard-pressed Spanish economy modest credits,[68] and on April 26
Beigbeder asked for British and French recognition of the territorial integrity of a neutral Spain and its possessions in the event that war spread,
a recognition that was duly granted. Spain also signed commercial agreements with France and Portugal, and during 1940 had a greater volume of
trade with the Allies than with the Axis, managing to pay off a portion of
its wartime debt to Britain in pounds. However, Franco rejected the possibility of a 200-million-dollar loan from the United States for badly needed
railway equipment, fearing it would compromise Spain's freedom of action, and also spurned a French request in April 1940 for a pledge of continued Spanish neutrality in the event of Italy's entry into the war.

Tensions Within the FET and Syndical Organization

During the first phases of World War II, the Falangist organization was
involved in a series of fundamental political tensions and struggles that
were not resolved until the autumn of 1942. This was inevitable, given
the nominal bureaucratic monopoly of the FET, the wide disparity between the criteria of Franco and other political sectors and those of the
camisas viejas, and the encouragement that the more radical and ambitious elements in the Falange derived from the German victories during
those years.

66. Quoted in *FF*, 3:34.
67. Diario 16, *Historia del franquismo*, 164.
68. Michael Alpert, "Las relaciones hispano-británicas en el primer año de la posguerra:
Los acuerdos comerciales y financieros de marzo de 1940," *Revista de Política Internacional*,
Sept.–Oct. 1976, pp. 13–29.

The first change in the FET resulted from Muñoz Grandes's abrupt resignation as secretary general in March 1940. This had been one of Franco's least felicitous appointments. Though known to possess some skill in military organization and command, Muñoz Grandes had little political talent, and found it almost impossible to deal with the sprawling, amorphous, and internally disharmonious structure of the FET. He found his relationship with Franco equally unsatisfactory, complaining that whenever he raised serious issues of abuses and corruption or party reorganization with Franco, the Caudillo simply diverted it into his customary patter of small talk, evading all the major issues.[69] Franco left the FET under the nominal administrative control of its twenty-seven-year-old vice-secretary general, Gamero del Castillo, a young man of sense and discretion who would not cause trouble and lacked the prestige or independence to create a separate power base. Though nominal membership continued to increase, the FET organization itself would languish for the following year.

Its principal rivals were the military. Though most Army officers at least to some extent shared the Germanophile attitudes of Falangists vis-à-vis the European war, nearly all resented the bureaucratic monopoly of the FET, its ideological radicalism, and the elitist presumption of Falangist militants. Few officers took their membership in the FET very seriously, and almost all were gratified by the military decree of July 2, 1940, that reconstituted the Falangist militia strictly under military command.

Thoughout the World War II period, the most politically active figure in the military hierarchy was Aranda, who was overtly anti-Falangist. He had intervened several times as captain-general of Valencia during 1939 to moderate the repression after the city was occupied, and is even alleged to have executed several Falangists caught trying to drag Republican prisoners from military jails for summary execution.[70] Despite the Axis sympathies of most of the generals, during the months of "phony war" in 1939–40 they feared involvement in dangerous adventures, and Aranda's prestige increased. He hoped to replace Vigón as second head of the new Alto Estado Mayor, a post for which he was qualified, but by 1940 Franco had begun to question his loyalty, and thus taking advantage of Aranda's technical credentials, made him instead director of the Escuela Superior de Guerra (Senior War College), a less prestigious position that deprived him of command of troops.

While radical Falangists conspired for more overt fascistization, Serrano Súñer tried to work toward juridical institutionalization of the regime. In the summer of 1940, under Serrano's leadership, the Junta Polí-

69. See the remarks of his acquaintance, José Ma. Taboada Lago, *Por una España mejor* (Madrid, 1977), 182–92.

70. According to British diplomatic documents cited by Antonio Marquina Barrio, "Conspiración contra Franco: El Ejército y la injerencia extranjera en España: el papel de Aranda, 1939–1945," *Historia 16* 7:72 (April 1982), 21–30.

Ramón Serrano Súñer while Minister of the Interior, 1940

tica of the FET began to prepare the draft of a set of constitutive laws to regularize the regime's authoritarian structure without particularly reducing the powers of Franco. The text of this Ley de Organización del Estado was composed of five sections, dealing with the state, the powers of the chief of state, a proposed new corporative Cortes or parliament, the Junta Política of the FET, and the scope of a new national economic council. Article 1, echoing the text of the original Falangist program, declared the state to be "a totalitarian instrument at the service of the integrity of the Fatherland. All its power and institutions are devoted to this service and are subject to law and to the political and moral Principles of the National Movement." Twenty of the draft's thirty-seven articles were devoted to defining the scope and structure of the proposed new corporative parliament, which was to be rather like that of Fascist Italy. The most controversial aspect was article 28, which declared, "The Junta Política is the supreme political council of the regime and the collegial organ of coordination between the state and the Movement." Article 31 went on to stipulate, "The Junta Política must be heard in full session on matters that affect the constitutive power and the Fundamental Laws of the State, on international political treaties and concordats, on the declaration of war and the conclusion of peace. The competence of the Junta Política in those matters defined by the Statutes of the Movement remains unaltered."[71]

This alarmed non- and anti-Falangists because it threatened to give the upper echelon of the Movement a constitutive place within the structure of state power, and it elicited a formal letter of protest from Esteban Bilbao, one of the most influential representatives of Carlism within the regime, against the "systematic interjection of the Party" in the organs of the state.[72] Franco evidently agreed and ordered the project shelved.

Less easily short-circuited was the plot against Franco that had begun to gestate among a small core of camisas viejas. It has been estimated that as much as 60 percent of the original membership of the party had been killed during the war, but the vast majority of the surviving Falangists had remained in the FET, some in hope of being able to dominate the new structure and implement the original Falangist program. In the aftermath of the Civil War it had become clear that the new regime was essentially a rightist authoritarian system flavored with fascist rhetoric but little more, and a few decided to try to take action. Their attitude reflected that of a German diplomat who replied to the question "How do you find the new Spain?" by saying, "When I find it, I shall tell you."[73]

71. Quoted in Laureano López Rodó, *La larga marcha hacia la Monarquía* (Barcelona, 1978), 30–31.
72. Quoted by López Rodó, *Política y desarrollo* (Madrid, 1970), 18–19.
73. Report of von Stohrer, Feb. 19, 1939. *Documents on German Foreign Policy*, vol. 3, no. 740, pp. 843–51.

At the close of 1939 a small group met at the home of Col. Emilio Rodríguez Tarduchy, a veteran of Primo de Rivera's UP, the UME of 1933, and the original Falange. A clandestine junta política was formed, with Tarduchy as president and Patricio González de Canales, a militant young *camisa vieja* from Seville (who held posts in Falangist publications and state commercial administration) as secretary. Seven or eight other veterans, representing various small sectors of the Falange in diverse parts of the country, formed the rest of the junta's fluctuating membership.[74] Their most coveted ally would have been General Juan Yagüe, who was close to José Antonio de Girón and other key elements of the Falangist *ex-combatientes* but refused to move directly against Franco, insisting that the Falange must change the regime from within. Though the conspirators later claimed to have gained the support of several thousand Falangists in various parts of Spain, most of this was doubtless quite tenuous, and they completely lacked influence among key power holders.[75]

The clandestine junta then turned to outside support and especially to Hans Thomsen, Nazi Landesgruppenleiter for the NSDAP organization among German residents in Madrid. Thomsen, however, would or could offer German support only on terms that would have reduced Spain to the status of a satellite, while the conspirators were further discouraged by rumors that an opportunistic clique of rightist dissidents was also intriguing for German assistance. The German government is said to have refused its aid unless the Falangists would agree to place themselves under the direct orders of the Fuehrer.[76]

Franco meanwhile was aware of Yagüe's personal contracts with the German embassy and his sometimes public criticism of cabinet ministers and anti-Falangists in the regime. His insistence on a greatly increased air force budget was a source of conflict within the government, while political foes complained that he was an inveterate intriguer who sheltered Masons and former Republicans within the air force officer corps. The results of an earlier investigation of Yagüe's conduct had been delivered to the Generalissimo on February 8, 1940, but Franco apparently found them inconclusive. On March 15 the air force minister sent him a note complaining that the military judicial commissions had been much less lenient in reducing sentences of former Republican officers in his branch of service than in the Army and Navy, but this lament only renewed suspicion that Yagüe was politically soft on Reds. What finally brought matters to a head

74. Personal interviews with González de Canales and Luis de Caralt (a member of the clandestine junta from Barcelona) in Madrid and Barcelona during the first months of 1959. See Armando Romero Cuesta, *Objetivo: Matar a Franco* (Madrid, 1976), 65–78, which seems to consist primarily of the recollections of González de Canales.

75. Romero Cuesta, *Objetivo*, 78–98.

76. Ibid., 98–111.

was the new situation suddenly created by Hitler's triumph in the west in June 1940. This caused Franco to take much more seriously the rumors of German intrigue to provoke a change in the regime. When the military governor of San Sebastián invited the new German occupation authorities at the Spanish border to a reception at which he shouted "Viva Hitler," Franco quickly had him replaced. Yagüe was called in for a final dressing down by Franco in the presence of the army minister Varela on June 27, in the course of which he was summarily dismissed as minister.[77]

The Falangist plotters nonetheless continued their meandering course. After toying with and rejecting the notion of assassinating Serrano Súñer, they finally decided to face up to their only direct alternative—the assassination of Franco himself—at a final meeting in Madrid near the end of March 1941. They concluded that there was no one with whom to replace him and that Falangism lacked the support to do without him. In a meeting attended by five conspirators, the vote was four to nothing, with one abstention, against attempting assassination.[78] The conspirators attributed their failure to gain more support to the success of Gamero del Castillo in attracting Falangist veterans to positions in the bureaucratic structure of the regime.

The most important development within the Falangist sphere in the immediate postwar period was the elaboration of the national syndical system. In the 1939 government the functions of the Ministry of Labor were attached to those of the Ministry of Agriculture, held by the right-wing engineer Joaquín Benjumea Burín, while Gerardo Salvador Merino was named national delegate of syndicates of the FET, charged with construction of the new syndical system. Separation of the Ministry of Labor from the Syndical Organization itself would be maintained for many years.

Salvador Merino was a radical camisa vieja of Socialist Party origins[79] who had served as Falangist jefe provincial of La Coruña during a period of the Civil War, winning a reputation for worker organization and radical rhetoric. This, in fact, cost him his position as jefe, but he had proven

77. The memo prepared by Franco for this confrontation is quoted in *FF*, 3:146–47. It emphasized Yagüe's political dissidence much more than his German contacts. Such scenes were painful for Franco, who never overcame his relative timidity in personal contact, and he avoided them as much as possible.

78. Ibid., 111–18. For further references to clandestine Falangist activities during these years, see Ellwood, *Prietas las filas*, 206–10.

There is also some evidence of preparation by the CNT underground for an attempt on Franco during 1940. According to one version, an attempt was made to fire on his limousine on the Carretera de Extremadura in Madrid, but in a case of mistaken identity a government information officer riding in an offical limousine was killed instead. Cipriano Damiano González, *La resistencia libertaria (1939–1970)* (Barcelona, 1978), 81.

79. According to Serrano Súñer, he left the Socialist Party because one of its goon squads under the Republic tried to assassinate Merino's father, a CEDA activist, but only succeeded in murdering his mother instead. Saña, *Conversaciones*, 154. This is corroborated by Tomás Garicano Goñi in *Franco visto por sus ministros*, ed. Angel Bayod (Barcelona, 1981), 198.

willing to serve the FET and was known for intelligence and organizational ability of the sort needed to develop the new structure.

Salvador Merino was a rather cold, highly ambitious Falangist—and apparently an ardent Naziphile—who conceived the ambition of building a powerful and relatively autonomous syndical system as the decisive element in the new regime.[80] He quickly set up a structure of three sections and nine services under the Syndical Organization, and on January 26, 1940, the government issued the Law on Syndical Unity, subordinating all private economic associations to the new system, except for the liberal professions and for chambers of commerce. On Victory Day, March 31, 1940, the first anniversary of the end of the Civil War, Salvador Merino arranged for several hundred thousand workers to march in a gigantic Madrid parade,[81] drawing the ire of Army right-wingers. The Ley de Constitución de Sindicatos of December 6, 1940, rhetorically declared the syndicates "ordered in militia, under the command of FET de las JONS."[82] Membership was obligatory for owners and employers in the organs of economic control, but individual membership for workers theoretically was not.

Yet the strength of the Syndical Organization turned out to be considerably less than conservatives feared. The original concept of integrated "vertical" syndicates was abandoned, employers and workers being represented in separate sections, with the former relatively autonomous. Authority for national economic regulation lay mostly in the hands of central government agencies, not in those of the national syndicates. The structure of the Syndical Organization itself was totally hierarchical,[83] with all appointments made from the top down. Moreover, local worker sections were subdivided according to each branch of industry in every local district, fractionalizing the syndical network and thus avoiding strong central concentrations. It was even specifically stated that employers rather than workers would have the dominant voice in economic affairs.[84]

80. Interview with Gerardo Salvador Merino in Barcelona, April 2, 1959.
81. *Arriba,* April 1, 1940.
82. La Cierva, *Franquismo,* 1:186.
83. See the doctrinal sketch in Aparicio, *Sindicalismo,* 169–74.
84. The right-wing neo-Falangist José María de Areilza put the matter very clearly:
"The Spanish syndicate will thus be composed by integrating all employers in a specific branch or zone of production, grouped as employers, that is, bearing the representation of factories as a productive unit. No classist [workerist] entity as such is accepted in our structure, because it was not accepted in the original [Falangist] doctrine and also because the character of the War of Liberation, in which the immense majority of the proletarian organizations bore arms as organizations against the Nationalist Army, would have proscribed the resurrection of such organisms—even if they had Spanish labels and goals at the present time—as completely inopportune and contrary to national feeling. All the enterprises of Spain dedicated to the manufacture of a particular product or group of products are thus grouped together under the orientation, guidance and vigilance of the state. This great entity—whose deliberations will

The pace of organization remained slow. Full national syndicates were declared to have been organized in ten sectors of the economy—the most important being textiles and metallurgy—by the close of 1940, yet the number of workers organized totaled only about 110,000 in Madrid, possibly 300,000 in Barcelona, and approximately 107,000 in the mining and industrial province of Asturias.[85] A National Agrarian Council was set up for agriculture in June 1941, as the system slowly absorbed the functions of CONCA, the Catholic small farmer syndicate.[86]

Despite all these limitations, Salvador Merino himself aroused increasing apprehension among rivals in other branches of the state, as well as among those in the military who considered him a dangerous Falangist subversive, a sort of crypto-Red. Serrano suggested to him that he might be promoted to cabinet rank by being given the portfolio of the Ministry of Labor, but Salvador Merino refused to see the handwriting on the wall, and since the Ministry of Labor would have deprived him of his position as national syndical chief, rejected the offer. By that point Merino's principal inspiration seems to have been Nazism, and he evidently aspired to a leading role in the radical transformation of Spain. He happened to be in Berlin on May 7, 1941, at the time of the first post–Civil War political crisis in the Spanish regime (treated in the following chapter), and there he talked with Goebbels about the possibility of German support for a radical Falangist takeover.[87]

Salvador Merino had become a marked man for certain military and rightist elements in the regime. The initiative in hunting for his head was taken by the elderly Andrés Saliquet, captain general of Valladolid. Saliquet was an unconditional franquista, one of those who had originally elected Franco to the jefatura única, and thoroughly outraged by Merino's ambitions. Probably with the assistance of the military court system, he presented evidence that Merino had been a Freemason in the early years of the Republic. In July 1941 Salvador Merino was relieved of his post and sent into internal exile in the Balearics, and thus the most ardent pro-Nazi in Spanish government vanished from public life.[88]

His removal and the placing of the nascent Spanish syndical system under fully subordinated bureaucratic control can be compared in their

include a great variety of common problems, primarily economic, and which will serve as advisory organ to the economic ministries, directly bringing to them the voices and concerns of the producers—is what we term the Syndicates" (*Problemas técnicos de importancia económica en la nueva organización de España* [Barcelona, 1940], 496, quoted in Amando de Miguel, *Herencia del franquismo* [Madrid, 1976], 96–97).

85. According to Aparicio, *Sindicalismo*, 136.
86. The initial juridical theory and structure of the system is outlined ibid., 79–169. See also Chueca, *El fascismo*, 341–91.
87. Klaus-Jörg Ruhl, *Spanien im Zweiten Weltkrieg: Franco, die Falange und das "Dritte Reich"* (Hamburg, 1975), 70–71.
88. See Serrano's account in Saña, *Conversaciones*, 154–57.

effects to the *sbloccamento* (lit. "unblocking," but actually breaking up into weaker regional federations) of the original Italian Fascist national syndicalism under Edmundo Rossoni in 1928. Mussolini's earlier action is usually seen correctly as a further step of the Italian regime toward the right, and the same may be said of the elimination of Salvador Merino in Spain, even though it is doubtful that Falangist national syndicalism ever had the radical impetus of its Italian Fascist counterpart.

13

The "German Phase," 1940–1942

Hitler's startling conquest of France in the spring of 1940 drastically altered the foreign policy of the Spanish regime. Its orientation had always been pro-German, but the terms on which the war had begun, and the uncertain prospects in the early months, had inevitably dictated a policy of neutrality. Germany's sudden ascendancy changed that, opening a new period of temptation combined with danger for both Spain and its government. The pro-German alignment that Franco adopted was nonetheless characterized by his customary prudence and indirection and stopped short of outright belligerence. It also had implications for domestic politics, arguing for some the logic of a more strongly Falangist regime. In the end, Franco avoided both direct entry into the war and greater internal fascistization, but the policy of cautious opportunism and diplomatic zigzagging that ensued earned his government the enmity of both Nazi Germany and the western Allies. Though it managed to spare the people of Spain the horrors of involvement in World War II, it failed to make the most of Spain's status as a neutral power.

By June 1940 most political and military opinion in Spain had swung sharply in the direction of Germany. The goal of a new Spanish "empire" had always been part of the Falangist program, even though it had usually been expressed in cautious and nonaggressive, almost metaphysical, terms.[1] Franco's new state had proclaimed the mission of empire with vigor,

1. The FET's official statement, *El imperio de España* (Valladolid, 1938), had declared self-righteously that Spanish "imperialism is not going to be an imperialism of petroleum or rubber." Its task was to restore and lead pan-Hispanic unity and to achieve a "new Catholicity. . . . Spain aspires to the effective exercise of rights of defense and tutelage, . . . not the rights of protectorates but the rights of defense of Spanish civilization in the world."

albeit in rather abstract formulae, and its social pronouncements during the early years sometimes echoed the Italian Fascist emphasis on a high birth rate for future military manpower. This aimed not only at overcoming international dependency through autarchist economic development, but also at regaining Gibraltar from Britain and possibly expanding the modest Spanish possessions in northwest Africa at the expense of France. After the fall of France the attitude of most of the military hierarchy had changed in favor of getting in on the winning side, and Falangists were more ardent than ever in public expressions of Germanophilia.[2]

Franco was now firmly convinced of German victory and would remain so, though in diminishing degree, until mid-1944. Yet, though eager to adjust Spanish policy to the new situation, he did not abandon his habitual caution. On June 3, he prepared the text of a letter to Hitler (that would not be delivered for more than a week) congratulating him on the German victory and identifying Spain with the German cause, which he chose to define on this occasion as a continuation of the struggle against the same enemies whom the Spanish Nationalists had already fought. At the same time he detailed the economic and military deficiencies that made it difficult for Spain to enter the war at that time.[3] The next day Beigbeder handed the German ambassador a list of Spanish claims in northwest Africa. On June 9, the eve of Italy's attack on France, Mussolini urged Franco to join him, but the Caudillo, sensing the frustration that might attend Italian and Spanish participation as long as France and Britain were still resisting, politely declined in a cordial response.[4]

The Spanish regime nonetheless continued to feel especially close to Mussolini's government, which it considered its own representative within the Italo-German Axis. Ciano, who had established a close rapport with Serrano Súñer, requested him to convince Franco that even if Spain could not enter the war for the moment it should demonstrate solidarity with the Axis by altering its position of neutrality to a declaration of nonbelligerence.[5] Franco agreed immediately, and Madrid declared its new policy of nonbelligerence on June 12.

In a subsequent phase of weakened Axis power, Franco would insist that this merely expressed Spain's sympathy for Germany without chang-

2. It might be noted that a relative Germanophilia has been characteristic of modern Spanish attitudes. A postwar study, Alfonso Alvarez Villar's "Notas sobre la germanofilia en España," in the *Revista de Psicología General y Aplicada*, (1963), 1147–53, reported results of an opinion survey that showed highly positive attitudes toward Germans among the Spanish public. Qualities attributed disproportionately to Germans included great intelligence, extraordinary industriousness, a spirit of discipline, great patriotism and military efficiency, and the most outstanding capacity among all peoples for scientific investigation and philosophy, most of these being considered the opposite of salient Spanish characteristics.

3. Donald S. Detwiler, *Hitler, Franco und Gibraltar: Die Frage des spanischen Eintritts in den Zweiten Weltkrieg* (Wiesbaden, 1962), 22–23.

4. *Documenti Diplomatici Italiani*, ser. 9, vol. 4, pp. 620–30.

5. *Franco y Mussolini*, 74–78.

ing the actual terms of its neutrality.[6] It is nonetheless perfectly clear from the character of Spanish-German relations during the next eighteen months that the adoption of a position of nonbelligerence was the first step in an alignment with the Axis, though Franco hoped to set his own price for such alignment and to make it as high as possible.

Two days later, on June 14, Spanish troops occupied the international zone of Tangier, but this was cautiously announced as simply a temporary wartime administrative measure. Since France, Britain, and Italy—three of the zone's administering powers—were at war with each other, Spanish occupation would guarantee the neutrality of the zone and the adjacent Spanish Protectorate. The move was accepted by Britain (which officially reserved its full rights for the future),[7] while Franco prudently ignored the crowd of proexpansionist Falangists who gathered outside the presidency building to cheer the move. The aim of "Tánger español" had been on the agenda of Spanish nationalism for decades, and the vacuous Falangist writer Sánchez Mazas, minister without portfolio in the current government, was incited by young radicals to give an impromptu speech stressing that Tangier would always remain Spanish, an action that earned him a severe dressing-down from Serrano.[8]

Meanwhile, General Juan Vigón, the monarchist and pro-German head of the Alto Estado Mayor, was dispatched to Berlin with the text of Franco's earlier but still undelivered letter and the mission of discussing possible military terms of Spain's entry into the war. He met with Hitler and Ribbentrop on the sixteenth. The following day the Spanish government and its ambassador in Paris, José Félix de Lequerica, began the round of mediation between Hitler and the defeated French regime that eventually produced the armistice between the two powers some days afterward. On June 19 the Spanish ambassador in Berlin formally presented Spain's territorial claims: annexation of the entire Oran district of western Algeria, incorporation of all Morocco, the extension of the Spanish Sahara southward to the twentieth parallel, and the addition of the

6. This is the burden of the memoirs of the subsequent American ambassador, the Europeanist historian from Columbia University, Carlton J. H. Hayes, in his *Wartime Mission in Spain* (New York, 1946), 61–94. He declares that Franco once observed to him of Mussolini's last-minute attack on France, "No Spanish hidalgo would have done that." (P. 66.)

The recent memoir-history by Willard Beaulac, American counsellor of embassy and briefly chargé in Madrid from 1941 to 1944, *Franco: Silent Ally in World War II* (Carbondale/Edwardsville, 1986), inflates this thesis to an exaggerated degree, but contains much useful and accurate material on Spanish and Allied diplomacy.

7. See Charles R. Halstead and Carolyn J. Halstead, "Aborted Imperialism: Spain's Occupation of Tangier 1940–1945," *Iberian Studies* 7:2 (Autumn 1978), 53–71.

8. Serrano relates that he became so outraged at Sánchez Mazas's attempts to justify his speech that he attempted to punch him in the face. The Falangist writer managed to dodge the blow but fell to the floor in a state of collapse. Saña, *Conversaciones*, 169–70. On Spanish ambitions in Morocco, see Enrique Arqués, *El momento de España en Marruecos* (Madrid, 1942).

French Cameroons to Spanish Guinea. Moreover, Spain requested German heavy artillery and aviation to help conquer Gibraltar and German submarine support to assist in the defense of the Canary Islands, as well as large amounts of food, ammunition, fuel, and other materials. To the intense disappointment of officials in Madrid, Hitler refused to discuss the Spanish shopping list. In his hour of triumph he showed little interest in Spain one way or the other, though that attitude would soon change.[9] In response to such coolness, Franco temporarily suspended the resupplying of German submarines in Spanish ports that had been permitted on several occasions since the beginning of the year.[10]

Yet Franco had no real doubts as to who was becoming master of Europe. At the celebrations attending the anniversary of the Movement on July 18 he declared the Nationalist struggle in Spain to have been "the first battle of the New Order [in Europe]," adding that "we have made a pause in our struggle, but only a pause, for our task is not yet finished," and boasting that Spain "has two million warriors ready to fight [enfrentarse] in defense of our rights."[11] At this point Spanish diplomacy made an effort to detach Portugal from its traditional British alliance, bringing it into line with the Axis through a military pact with Madrid that would have virtually made Portugal a Spanish satellite. Salazar, unlike Franco, was genuinely neutral and firmly refused the offer, signing instead an additional Protocol to the existing Hispano-Portuguese treaty that merely provided for mutual consultation between Lisbon and Madrid in the event of foreign threat to the peninsula.[12]

From about the end of July, Hitler slowly developed more interest in Spain's entry into the conflict as a means of securing control of Gibraltar and thus strangling Britain's strategic position in the Mediterranean and Middle East.[13] In the last days of the month a small German military in-

---

9. The literature concerning Spain's non-role in World War II has become extensive. A bibliography to 1977 has been collected by Fredric M. Messick, "Spanish Neutrality in World War II: A Select Bibliography of Published Materials," *Iberian Studies* 6:1 (Spring 1977), 17–23. The chief Spanish diplomatic study is Victor Morales Lezcano, *Historia de la no-beligerancia española durante la Segunda Guerra Mundial (VI, 1940–X, 1943)* (Las Palmas, 1980), though the lengthiest Spanish narrative of politics and diplomacy during the war years is Ramón Garriga, *La España de Franco*, 2 vols. (Madrid, 1976). The regime's two principal memoir-apologia are Serrano Súñer's *Entre Hendaya y Gibraltar* (Mexico City, 1947); and José Ma. Doussinague, *España tenía razón (1939–1945)* (Madrid, 1950).

10. Charles B. Burdick, "'Moro': The Resupply of German Submarines in Spain, 1939–1942," *Central European History*, Sept. 1970, pp. 256–84.

11. Quoted in Garriga, *Yagüe*, 185. This imprudent speech was later excluded from the 1943 collection of *Palabras del Caudillo*.

12. Pedro Teotonio Pereira, *Memorias* (Lisbon, 1973), 2:213–32; and Charles R. Halstead, "Consistent and Total Peril from Every Side: Portugal and Its 1940 Protocol with Spain," *Iberian Studies* 3:1 (Spring 1974), 15–28.

13. Charles B. Burdick, *Germany's Military Strategy and Spain in World War II* (Syracuse, 1968), presents an inclusive account of German strategic planning with regard to Spain. The book by Detwiler previously cited deals primarily with the second half of 1940.

spection team traversed Spain in order to determine the planning, personnel, and equipment that would be required for a possible assault on Gibraltar, and on August 2 the elderly (almost octogenarian) and ultraconservative ambassador in Berlin, Magaz, who had at least some aversion to Nazism, was replaced by the fervently pro-Hitlerian General Eugenio Espinosa de los Monteros. Eighteen days later the Spanish government decreed compulsory two-year military service.

The Generalissimo and his most influential advisor, Serrano Súñer, were firmly convinced of eventual German victory and realized that Spain could profit from the coming New Order only if it entered the war in time. Yet they were apprehensive about involving their weak and unprepared country in the conflict as long as Britain retained significant powers of resistance. Whereas Germany for the time being had become almost self-sufficient, the Spanish economy could be totally devastated by a British naval blockade. To survive for even a brief period, it would require concrete guarantees of major assistance from Germany. Moreover, if a new Spanish empire were to be carved out of French Northwest Africa (concerning which contingency plans had been under way in the Spanish General Staff since June), new acquisitions would have to be firmly recognized and guaranteed by Germany from the beginning, when Spanish assistance still had value in Hitler's eyes. To wait until the final victory would be too late.

As German pressure increased, Serrano, even though not foreign minister, was deputed to head a special Spanish delegation to Berlin that departed on September 13. On arriving, he gave an interview to the Nazi party organ *Voelkische Beobachter* in which he stressed that the Spanish conflict had been a struggle against "the capitalism of the great democracies" similar to the *Kampf* of National Socialism,[14] employing the rhetoric of the radical sector of the Falange. Between September 15 and 25 Serrano engaged in several lengthy conversations with Ribbentrop and two shorter ones with Hitler. Franco hoped that Hitler would meet the Spanish terms, writing to his brother-in-law on the twenty-fourth, "We must guarantee the future with a pact [*protocolizar el futuro*], and though there is no doubt as to our decision, we have to be very careful about the details of an agreement and the obligations of each part."[15] In fact, Serrano was dismayed to find that Hitler wanted Spain to enter the war immediately while trusting in German good will to provide equipment and supplies, and refused to make any territorial commitments in northwest Africa, suggesting vaguely that Spain work out the details of a possible expansion with Italy. The foreign minister, Ribbentrop, was

14. Quoted in Sueiro and Díaz-Nosty (1985), *Historia*, 1:194.
15. From the full text in Serrano, *Memorias*, 342–48.

more aggressive and demanding, suggesting the cession to Germany of one of Spain's own Canary Islands as a naval base, together with at least one port in any southward extension of Spanish Morocco. On Franco's orders, this proposal was rejected with barely concealed indignation, and any agreement on entering the war for the moment was postponed behind a shield of Spanish territorial, economic, and military requests.[16]

Clearly the simultaneous and somewhat contradictory requirements of retaining Germany's good will, winning a place for Spain in the New Order, and avoiding premature entry into the war on hazardous terms created the most difficult and dangerous diplomatic challenge faced by the regime in its long history. To deal with it, Franco needed the most reliable assistance possible, and therefore on October 15, immediately after Serrano's return,[17] he appointed him foreign minister in place of Beigbeder. This was not to exchange an Anglophile for a Germanophile, as was often said then and afterwards, for Beigbeder was a very recent and tepid convert to anything approaching Anglophilia, while Serrano was no Germanophile in the strict sense but simply convinced, like nearly all the major figures in the regime at that time, that Spain must come to terms with Germany, albeit on terms that would safeguard her interests. Beigbeder was dismissed mainly because of his personal unreliability, his work as foreign minister having been haphazard. He often changed his position according to his audience, and had developed friendly relations with the new British ambassador, Sir Samuel Hoare. Moreover, Beigbeder was an inveterate womanizer with a taste for "exotic" ladies, who were said to include a Miss Fox in the employ of the British Secret Service.[18] Rumor had it that he had been bribed by the British ambassador,[19] and the Germans were increasingly reluctant to deal with him.[20] Equally important was Franco's concern to have his most trusted collaborator in charge of foreign affairs during this crucial phase. Because he was head of the Junta Política and in many ways the real leader of the FET, and because of his entrance into the Foreign Ministry at the time when Spain's ties to Ger-

16. Principal memoirs on the Spanish side are Serrano's *Entre Hendaya y Gibraltar*, 170; and Ridruejo's *Casi unas memorias*, 215–23; but a more objective account will be found in *Franco y Mussolini*, 103–07. See also Ramón Garriga, *Las relaciones secretas entre Franco y Hitler* (Buenos Aires, 1965), 141–66; and *La España de Franco*, 1:195–225.

17. Serrano made a stopover in Rome before returning to Madrid, venting his anger against the Germans with Ciano and Mussolini, whom he always held in high esteem. A decade after Mussolini's death, Serrano expressed his great respect for the Duce in several newspaper articles in 1954–55, later published in his collected essays, *Ensayos al viento* (Madrid, 1969), 123–33.

18. *FF*, 3:188.

19. Cf. David Jato Miranda, *Gibraltar decidió la guerra* (Barcelona, 1978).

20. Salgado Araujo, *Conversaciones privadas*, 12, claims that von Stohrer, the German ambassador, had requested that Beigbeder be allowed to see no major documents concerning Germany.

Franco and Hitler at Hendaye, October 23, 1940

many were closest, Serrano would often be called the "Axis minister," yet this was no more than a half-truth.

Three days after a quick visit by Heinrich Himmler to Madrid on October 20,[21] there occurred the only personal encounter between Franco

21. This has sometimes been presented as a professional visit to align Spanish police and intelligence services with those of Germany, but in fact it was extremely brief and primarily

and Hitler, the famous meeting at Hendaye on the French border. Franco presented what had now become the standard Spanish shopping list, territorial and economic, and was evidently prepared to enter the war at that point if Hitler would grant Spain control of most of northwest Africa.[22] This had been the dream of Spanish expansionists, such as they were, for forty years, and few ambitions were dearer to the heart of the Caudillo than domination of all Morocco and the Oran district. To the end of his days, Morocco would represent for Franco the golden illusions and fulfillment of his youth, and at one point he silenced the talkative Fuehrer with an hour-long monologue on the history of Spain's role in Morocco that reduced Hitler to yawns and probably also to the conclusion that Franco was no more than a provincial African colonialist. Unbeknown to the Spanish, Hitler had already decided to grant priority to a new alliance with what remained of Vichy France and had already said privately that there would be no point in alienating Vichy by giving away French colonial territory to a Spain that could not defend it. At Hendaye he told Franco that, given the need to conciliate France, he could offer Spain no guarantee at that time. After enduring some seven hours of the polite, fawning, and evasive but obdurate conversation of the "Latin charlatan," as he called Franco, Hitler later declared that he would prefer "having three or four teeth pulled" to enduring such an experience again.[23]

Up to this point Franco had apparently held the ingenuous conviction that Hitler was a great leader friendly to Spain, while all obstacles stemmed from various mediocre or ill-intentioned subordinates. Hitler's refusal to grant Spanish requests angered him, and yet he had to agree that given the need to conciliate Vichy France,[24] Hitler could not at that time recognize all Spanish territorial demands. Hitler and Ribbentrop insisted on the signing of a secret protocol that would guarantee Spanish war entry when Germany should see fit, but Franco and Serrano refused a unilateral German draft which they replaced with one of their own. This document

---

involved attending a bullfight, visiting a museum, and going on a quick hunting trip on the estate of the Conde de Mayalde, the monarchist aristocrat who then headed the Spanish police apparatus (Dirección General de Seguridad). Some details are given in Sueiro and Díaz-Nosty, *Historia del franquismo*, 1:182–86. It appears nonetheless true that the Spanish police did receive some technical assistance from the Gestapo during this period, though the extent is not known and direct documentation has not been found.

22. Serrano is categorical on this point in Saña, *Conversaciones*, 193. He candidly admitted to Charles Favrel of *Paris-Presse*, Oct. 26, 1945, that in 1940 he had little doubt of final German victory and that his "intention was to enter the war at the very end, at the moment of the final victory, exactly as Russia did against Japan."

23. There are extensive references to Hendaye in the literature. The fullest account is La Cierva's *Hendaya: Punto final* (Barcelona, 1981); and perhaps the best succinct treatment is in Detwiler, *Hitler*, 51–67. Serrano's reminiscences are in his *Memorias*, 283–324. See also Saña, *Conversaciones*, 190–98; and García Lahiguera, *Serrano Súñer*, 165–75.

24. Concerning Spanish relations with Vichy, there is a memoir by the Vichy ambassador, Francois Piétri, *Mes années d'Espagne* (Paris, 1954).

pledged Spain to adhere to the Tripartite Pact (the defensive alliance between Germany, Italy, and Japan) and to enter the war against Britain at
some unspecified date to be determined by the Spanish government after
further consultation with Germany and Italy. The secret protocol thus
lacked teeth and did not specifically bind Spain to any schedule of action.[25]

Pressure of a different sort was mounted by Britain. The British government had never been truly hostile to the Franco regime, and even
Jordana had admitted in 1938 that the British policy of nonintervention
during the Civil War had favored the Nationalists. London's concern was
to maintain Spain's neutrality and to keep Spanish territory free of German troops and bases. For the embattled British government, the strategic significance of Spain was threefold: (a) the fortress of Gibraltar controlled the mouth of the Mediterranean, vital to British interests; (b) the
northwest coast and the Canaries, together with Spanish Africa, offered
crucial access to the central region of the east Atlantic; (c) Spain was a
direct geographic link with Africa, and particularly French Northwest Africa, which might play a significant role in the future. The British ambassador, Hoare, and foreign minister, Halifax, formulated a policy during
the summer and fall of 1940 designed to promote political stability and
neutrality in Spain through the judicious use of British naval power to
provide adequate imports of food and raw materials to sustain the impov-
erished Spanish economy.[26] Moreover, in October the British government
was willing to go at least as far as Hitler in privately expressing that it was
"in principle sympathetic to the Spanish case"[27] for an expanded zone
in Morocco, declaring in a public statement of October 22 that Britain
looked "forward to seeing her [Spain] take her rightful place . . . as a great
Mediterranean Power. . . ."[28]

25. The existence of the secret protocol was finally demonstrated by Professor Carlos
Rojas of Emory University. La Cierva, *Hendaya,* 147–50; Serrano, *Memorias,* 311–312;
Saña, *Conversaciones,* 197–98; and García Lahiguera, *Serrano Suñer,* 172–74. A more
skeptical interpretation will be found in Tusell, *Franco y Mussolini,* 112–14.

26. Hoare's postwar memoir, *Complacent Dictator* (New York, 1947), was not entirely
frank regarding the degree of support for the regime that he encouraged. (Beaulac has observed that, given the author's distortions and his self-importance, the book might better
have been entitled *Complacent Ambassador.*) The definitive study is Denis Smyth, *Diplomacy and Strategy of Survival: British Policy and Franco's Spain, 1940–41* (Cambridge,
1986).

British Conservatives were not greatly troubled by "Spanish fascism." One of Churchill's
advisors described the FET in 1940 as not "totalitarianism but a muddle that defies description." (Smyth, 72.) On the other hand, Hoare developed a certain respect for Franco, who
he thought, however incorrectly, would never lead Spain into the war on his own volition.
Hoare wrote in May 1941: "General Franco is the Brer Rabbit of dictators. He lies very low,
often so low and so long that people think that he is dead or asleep. Then suddenly, when no
one is expecting it, he bobs up and gives evidence of unexpected agility. . . . It looks as if he
is only forced into active movement when he is in actual danger of being trodden underfoot."
(Quoted in Smyth, 77.)

27. Quoted in Smyth, *Diplomacy,* 97.

28. Ibid., 99. A minor crisis with Britain flared after the Spanish government, on November 3, 1940, abolished the main institutions of international administration in Tangier,

The British policy of discreet sympathy and economic cooperation was accompanied by more devious tactics, especially the systematic bribery on a massive scale of some ten high-ranking generals. Surviving documentation has not made it possible to identify the latter, though they evidently included Aranda. Using the good offices of the pro-Allied Juan March (perhaps Spain's wealthiest businessman and a key early financier of Franco), half the bribes were paid regularly in cash and the other half deposited in personal accounts in New York and Buenos Aires. Though it is doubtful that this bribery in itself greatly influenced the course of events, some idea of its scale may be gained from the fact that in the autumn of 1941 the British government was struggling to unblock some ten million dollars in personal accounts for Spaniards that had temporarily been frozen in New York banks.[29]

Meanwhile, Hitler peremptorily summoned Serrano Súñer to Berchtesgaden in mid-November to demand that a date be fixed for Spain's entry into the war. Before leaving Madrid, Serrano insisted on a formal meeting with Franco and the military ministers. England's recent success in the Battle of Britain had diminished ardor among the Spanish military hierarchy to enter the war on Hitler's side. Moreover, a six-page report prepared by the senior naval staff on November 11 emphasized the extreme military and economic hazards that would face Spain if it should enter the war while Britain still controlled the seas.[30] Anti-German opinion was discreetly led by the Carlist army minister, Varela, and by the semiliberal director of the Escuela Superior de Guerra, Aranda. Varela recommended that Serrano not even submit to the German insistence on an immediate visit. Such defiance was not possible, but Moreno, the naval minister, and the thoughtful Vigón, the new air minister, agreed that Spanish policy must remain as cautious as possible. At this time the only major interventionist sentiment was fostered by the two principal Falangist generals, Muñoz Grandes and Yagüe,[31] but neither any longer held a cabinet position.

At Berchtesgaden on November 18 Serrano complained to the Fuehrer about Germany's apparent lack of interest in implementing the article of the recent secret protocol that vaguely referred to Spain's colonial aims in

integrating that city (which had been militarily occupied in June) within the regular administrative structure of the Spanish Protectorate. After a series of relatively acrimonious exchanges, this matter was ironed out for the duration to the relative satisfaction of London. The written agreement of February 22, 1941, provided guarantees for British rights and interests, restated Britain's reservation of its original treaty rights, and included a Spanish pledge not to fortify the Tangier district. Ibid., 135–72.

29. Ibid., 35–36. Cf. Tusell, *Franco y Mussolini*, 82.

30. This has sometimes been referred to somewhat inaccurately as the Carrero Blanco report, though Capt. Luis Carrero Blanco was only one of a group of naval officers who prepared it. There has been considerable competition over who deserved the most credit. Cf. Fernández, *Franco*, 117–18.

31. According to Serrano Súñer in Saña, *Conversaciones*, 203, 208–9.

northwest Africa. Hitler candidly replied that under present circumstances Spain's acquisition of these territories could not be formally guaranteed, for if that led to disputes with other powers it would frankly be better for the time being to leave northwest Africa with Vichy and Gibraltar in the hands of Britain (!). He sought to avoid further diplomatic and military complications in the west Mediterranean area pending his final decision to proceed with the invasion of the Soviet Union. After Serrano explained with candor and in detail the disastrous state of Spain's military supplies and factories, compounded by severe shortages of basic raw materials and foodstuffs, Hitler finally slumped silently onto a sofa, realizing that Spain was probably in no condition to make a contribution to the war effort.[32]

When Serrano returned to Madrid on November 22, the National Council of the FET was in full session, a majority of its members favoring entry into the war. This, however, had little effect on Franco's policy, which further demonstrated the extent to which Franco's emasculation of the partido único served the purposes of his regime. Before the end of the month he assured the German government that Spanish preparations for war entry were about to begin, but still no date was set. As an inducement for Franco not to change his official stance, Britain renewed regular commercial relations under the old agreement, even though Franco restored supply facilities to German submarines on December 5.

More time was bought by requesting a new German military mission to discuss problems, which arrived on December 7 to urge that Spain be ready to enter the war by January 10. To Spain's good fortune, this mission was headed by Franco's old acquaintance Admiral Canaris, the head of German military intelligence, who evidently communicated to Franco that the military future would be most difficult and that immediate war entry was not really in Spain's interests. Canaris then reported to Berlin that Franco refused to alter his position. The German admiral apparently even recommended to Hitler that Spanish participation might be counterproductive in that it would open an enormous coastline to defend against the British.[33] Soon afterward the Fuehrer turned away from Operation Felix—the projected assault on Gibraltar—to concentrate on the first stages of planning for the Russian invasion, while observing in a letter of December 31 to Mussolini that Franco "had made the biggest mistake of his life" in not entering the war immediately.[34]

Nonetheless, after a brief respite, pressures were resumed during the first two months of 1941. After three ultimatums at diverse levels during

32. Ibid., 203–6.
33. Léon Papeleux, *L'Admiral Canaris entre Franco et Hitler: Le role de Canaris dans les relations germano-espagnoles, 1915–1944* (Tournai, 1977), 134–59.
34. Quoted in Tusell, *Franco y Mussolini*, 117.

Serrano Súñer, Franco, and Mussolini at Bordighera, February 12, 1941

late January produced no result, Hitler continued with a long, harsh letter to Franco on February 6, telling him in no uncertain terms that in "a war to the death" no "gifts" could be given Spain, and threatening him with the fact that should Germany ever lose, the Franco regime would have no chance of survival. By this point Franco's earlier enthusiastic appraisal of Hitler seems to have considerably moderated, and he resisted these pressures with his customary evasive tactics, accompanied by requests for large amounts of German supplies.

Hitler then turned the Spanish problem over to Mussolini, leading to the only meeting between the Spanish and Italian dictators at Bordighera on February 12. Franco and Serrano Súñer had tried earlier to use the cordial relationship between the two regimes to obtain Italian mediation in their suit with Germany, but Mussolini had shown ambivalence, fearing that Spanish ambitions might interfere with Italy's own prestige and goals in Africa. Late in 1940 the Spanish government had signed an agreement with Rome to obtain rubber and tin from Britain and the United States for transshipment to Italy, and Mussolini sustained these terms of friendship by making little effort to pressure or deceive Franco. He admitted that the initiative for the meeting came from Hitler and that the prospects were for a long war, while some in his retinue could scarcely hide their growing demoralization.[35]

Henceforth the German government desisted from overt pressure to force Spanish entry into the war, primarily because Hitler's priorities lay elsewhere and he did not judge Spanish participation to merit a very high price. The attitude toward Franco in the German regime was now universally negative (Franco in return had even denied to German officials that their aid was decisive in the Civil War), though ire was especially directed against the "clerical," "reactionary" and "Jesuitical" Serrano Súñer.[36] As usual, Franco ceded on several minor points, signing an agreement on German-Spanish cooperation in propaganda in Latin America and again renewing submarine supply facilities the first of March.

Sentiment to enter the war nonetheless dominated among Falangists (whether of the old or new varieties) and some of the military. This feeling increased with the next successes of the blitzkrieg in Yugoslavia and Greece during March and April 1941. The most notorious expression of Spanish expansionism was of course the publication with semiofficial approval of the book *Reivindicaciones de España* by the neo-Falangists José Ma. de Areilza and Fernando Ma. Castiella in April. Though not bellicose in tone, this volume declared that the Spanish conflict had been but the first phase of an extended world war, blamed Britain and France for originating the war, and defined what Spain wanted: Gibraltar, a protectorate over all Morocco, the Oran district of northwestern Algeria, expansion in equatorial Africa at the expense of British Nigeria and French possessions, and a slice of French northwest Africa to connect these ter-

35. Ibid., 120–21.
36. Various references in the Nazi literature have been collected by Saña, *Conversaciones*, 211–20, to which may be added the remarks of Ciano. Like many foreigners, Hitler was obsessed by the myth of the power of the Spanish Church, whose representative he made out Serrano to be.

ritories.[37] The book's clear and vigorous style, with its reasoned historical and geopolitical analysis and lack of shrillness, made it perhaps the most influential and successful piece of wartime propaganda among the more nationalistic elements of Spanish society.

Through the first months of 1941, Britain continued to follow its careful management of diplomatic and economic relations with Spain, on April 7 signing a new Supplementary Loan Agreement (against the opposition of the more pro-Axis members of the Spanish government) that extended further credits for imports to the peninsula. London was less successful in gaining full American cooperation for its policy of attraction toward Madrid. Opinion in Washington was more categorically anti-Franco, and some concern existed there about the extension of "Spanish fascist" influence to Latin America. As the new American counsellor of embassy in Madrid in 1941 was to write forty years later, American attitudes were "more emotional, more ideological, and more influenced by what they read in the press" than were those of the British.[38] Personal relations between Serrano Súñer and the American ambassador, Weddell, were virtually suspended for six months after an incident on April 19 in which Weddell used strong language to protest German influence in Spain. Though more normal relations were restored in the early fall,[39] Washington refused to give the degree of economic assistance to Spain that the British government deemed appropriate. The straitened British wartime economy could never provide all the consumer goods and fuel that Spain required, and indeed, by 1942 Spanish exports of iron ore and other vital raw materials to Britain reached such a volume that for the remainder of the war British authorities had difficulty balancing their accounts with Spain.[40]

By late April 1941 alarm in London about the possibility of German entrance into the Iberian peninsula or Franco's entry into the war—sparked by the dramatic German victories in Yugoslavia and Greece—rapidly increased. On April 23 Churchill ordered preparation of an expeditionary force ready to sail at forty-eight hours' notice to seize the Portuguese islands (the Azores and the Cape Verdes) if the peninsula fell under Axis control. On the following day his chiefs of staff requested per-

---

37. For more scholarly statement of some Spanish aspirations, see José Ma. Cordero Torres, *Misión africana de España* (Madrid, 1941), and *Aspectos de la misión universal de España* (Madrid, 1942).

38. Beaulac, *Franco*, 24.

39. See Charles R. Halstead, "Diligent Diplomat: Alexander W. Weddell as American Ambassador to Spain, 1939–1942," *The Virginia Magazine of History and Biography* 82:1 (Jan. 1974), 3–38; and the excellent portrait of Weddell in Beaulac, *Franco*, 95–120, who observes that "much of the fault was Weddell's" (p. 108).

40. Smyth, *Diplomacy*, 179–98. Cf. W. N. Medlicott, *The Economic Blockade* (London, 1952), 1:548.

U.S. Ambassador Weddell and German Ambassador Eberhard von Stohrer leaving the Palace of the National Council after announcement of the new Syndical law, December 6, 1940

mission to ready a force to seize the Canaries (Operation Puma), beginning construction of an expeditionary unit that at one point numbered 24,000.[41]

Such British concern at that juncture was exaggerated, but the Italian government made a new effort late in the spring of 1941 to draw the Spanish regime more publicly to the side of the Axis. On June 9 Serrano received a personal letter from the Italian foreign minister Ciano urging him to convince Franco that the time had come to announce Spain's adherence to the Tripartite Pact, as pledged in the secret protocol of the preceding autumn. Serrano seems to have agreed and had a very long talk with his brother-in-law, whom he declared not averse to this step, but he warned the Italian ambassador that it would be tantamount to a declara-

41. Smyth, *Diplomacy*, 223–28.

Falangists lead a mass demonstration in the center of Madrid on June 24, 1941, two days after the German invasion of the Soviet Union

tion of war by Spain. In such an event, the Spanish leaders expected Britain to seize at least one of the Canaries and blockade Spain, so that some sort of pledge of economic assistance would be needed. Yet a meeting between Ciano and Ribbentrop on the fifteenth indicated that Germany had no interest in offering even minor enticements to bring Spain into the war.[42]

That response, coupled with Germany's invasion of the Soviet Union on June 22, dampened Spanish interest in a more complete alignment with the Axis. Yet the attack on the Communist heartland elicited a strong emotional response, particularly from Falangists. Within forty-eight hours the government requested an opportunity for Spanish participation in some form short of official entry into the war. Before a huge crowd in front of Falangist headquarters on the twenty-fourth, Serrano Súñer delivered his famous "Russia is guilty" speech, invoking Soviet responsibility for the Spanish war and its loss of life and declaring that "the extermination of Russia is required by history and the future of Europe." The anti-Soviet

42. Tusell, *Franco y Mussolini*, 139–40.

struggle in the east was declared an extension of the Spanish Crusade in the Civil War, and Spain "a moral belligerent" in the new conflict.

Since Franco had no intention of declaring war on the Soviet Union at that point, Falangist leaders suggested the official formation of a "Blue Division" (dark blue was the Falangist color) of FET volunteers to fight beside the Germans on the Russian front. This found acceptance among Franco and other cabinet members, and registration of volunteers began on June 28, the seventh day of the German invasion. Falangist enthusiasm was intense; among the volunteers were six members of the National Council and seven civil governors, as well as some of the most militant younger leaders such as Enrique Sotomayor, soon to be killed in battle. Army commanders were themselves much less enthusiastic, and complained of Falangist domination of recruitment even among the regular military. As it turned out, however, nearly 70 percent of the volunteers came from the Army, as did nearly all officers, to ensure military leadership and coherence. Command was given to Muñoz Grandes, one of the best organizers among the few nominally Falangist generals. The first units of an initial force of 18,694 officers and men began to leave Spain on July 17 for further training in Germany, followed by a volunteer contingent of combat aviators who formed a "Blue Squadron." The Blue Division later formed as German Division 250 on the northern sector of the eastern front just below Leningrad. It entered into combat on October 4, under German command but always technically subordinate to the Spanish Ministry of the Army.[43]

The genuine enthusiasm among Spanish Nationalists was undeniable, and the summer of 1941 marked a peak in war feeling on behalf of Germany, the last major peak. This led Franco to present the most outspokenly pro-German speech that he ever delivered in his annual address to the National Council on July 17. He denounced the "age-old enemies" of Spain, with clear allusions to Britain, France, and the United States, who still engaged in "intrigues and treachery" against it. Franco insisted, "Not even the American continent can dream of intervening in Europe without exposing itself to catastrophe. . . . To say that the outcome can be reversed by the entry of a third party into the war is criminal madness. The issues of the war were wrongly presented, and the Allies have lost." His concluding sentence hailed Germany for leading "the battle for which

43. There are numerous accounts of the Blue Division. The best overall treatment is Gerald R. Kleinfeld and Lewis A. Tambs, *Hitler's Spanish Legion: The Blue Division in Russia* (Carbondale, Ill., 1979). Raymond Proctor, *Agonía de un neutral* (Madrid, 1972), provides a briefer account set in the context of Spanish-German relations. The early bibliography is listed in Werner Haupt, "Die 'Blaue Division' in der Literatur," *Wehrwissenschaftliche Rundschau*, vol. 4 (April 1959). For a Soviet presentation, see S. P. Pozharskaya, *Tainaya diplomatiya Madrida* (Moscow, 1971), 104–42.

Enlistment of volunteers for the Blue Division in Madrid, June 1941

Europe and Christianity have for so many years longed, and in which the blood of our youth is to mingle with that of our comrades of the Axis as an expression of firm solidarity."[44] Even the Axis ambassadors commented on the imprudence of these remarks.[45]

In the following month an agreement was signed with Germany to provide 100,000 workers for the increasingly strained German industrial force, though none left Spain for months. In the long run no more than 15,000 were sent, compared to approximately 10,000 Spanish workers who worked daily for the British in Gibraltar throughout the war. For that matter, Spanish consulates in France managed to recruit 40,000 unem-

44. *Arriba*, July 18, 1941.
45. The German ambassador, von Stohrer, reported that Serrano Súñer called the speech premature, because, in von Stohrer's words, "It suddenly opened the eyes of the English and the Americans about the position of Spain. Previously the English Government especially kept on believing that only he [Serrano] . . . was pushing for war, while the 'wise and thoughtful' Caudillo would preserve neutrality unconditionally. That illusion has now been taken from them. They had come to realize that Spain, in understanding with the German Government, would enter the war at a suitable moment." *Documents on German Foreign Policy*, ser. D, vol. 13, p. 223.

ployed Republican emigrés for German jobs,[46] whom Hitler later dreamed of converting into pro-German revolutionaries to overthrow Franco.[47]

If the invasion of the Soviet Union ended the main phase of direct German pressure on the Spanish government, it also had the opposite effect of heightening tension with Great Britain. The turning of Hitler's attention to the east left Britain much freer to undertake strategic initiatives in the Atlantic and west Mediterranean, while Spanish participation on the eastern front weakened Spain's status as a semineutral nonbelligerent. British planners once more toyed with the notion of seizing the Canary Islands as a strategic base but finally dropped it. In July Spanish authorities feared that Britain might intervene in the Iberian sphere by occupying the Portuguese Azores. On July 29 Serrano declared in a press interview that "Spain could not remain indifferent to an attack on the Portuguese possessions."[48]

Allied bases would eventually be established in the Azores two years later, with the reluctant support of Portugal. Yet after every consideration of direct action in the Iberian Peninsula, British planners always came to the conclusion, shared by their American counterparts in future calculations made in 1942–43, that a direct invasion would not bring the strategic or other advantages to justify the time and cost.[49]

Throughout 1941 the official British policy toward Spain remained that of attraction, though with a thinly veiled stick behind the carrot. At a private dinner in the Spanish Embassy in London on October 2, Churchill and other British government figures once more expressed their support for an expansion of the Spanish Protectorate in Morocco once the war was over, a position reiterated by Churchill at a British Defense Committee meeting two weeks later.[50] No more than Hitler, however, were the British willing to offer any concrete guarantees, and for exactly the same reason—fear of complicating their relations with the French. The Churchill government soon concluded that to encourage any further speculation was a mistake, directing Ambassador Hoare to offer no further verbal support, however vague, for Spanish ambitions.[51] More successful was the strong British protest, accompanied by direct evidence, about the provision of Spanish refueling facilities for German submarines (Operation Moro) that had been underway since March 1941, prompting Franco to terminate these arrangements in December.[52]

46. All these figures are from Trythall, *Caudillo*, 179.
47. *Hitler's Table Talk, 1941–1944*, ed. H. R. Trevor-Roper (London, 1953), 568.
48. Trythall, *Caudillo*, 180.
49. Antonio Marquina Barrio presented a brief comprehensive study, "España y los planes militares aliados," at the Primer Simposio "España y la Segunda Guerra Mundial," Madrid, Oct. 13, 1983.
50. Serrano Súñer, *Entre Hendaya*, 301–2; Smyth, *Diplomacy*, 202–3.
51. Smyth, *Diplomacy*, 203–5.
52. Ibid., 190.

The Political Crisis of May 1941

With Republican and leftist opposition still weak and vigorously repressed, Franco's principal domestic political problems concerned the management of the three main pillars of his power, the military, the Falangists, and the monarchists. Of these, the military would always be the most important, and senior commanders with few exceptions continued to support Franco's leadership. Though Spanish generals were mostly pro-German, there was little quarrel with his reluctance to enter the war, for military opinion generally agreed that the country was in no position to do so. Many senior officers disagreed sharply with other aspects of state policy, however. Criticism mounted over domestic policy, fueled by increasingly severe shortages (bread rationing had been introduced in January 1941), the rapid growth of corruption, and the frequent inefficiency of the new state system, with its often clumsy bureaucratic controls. Ever more intense hostility was focused on the pretensions of Falangists, and more concretely, on their primary spokesman, Serrano Súñer, whose political ascendancy was bitterly resented. Serrano was detested by the military and others not simply because of his power but also because of the manner in which he exercised it. Serrano Súñer did not wear his authority lightly; he was increasingly intemperate in speech and manner, arrogant and overweening, the object of constant attention in the official media. His pro-Axis statements, particularly those made to his favorite interlocutors of the Italian Fascist press, were more frequent and extreme than those of Franco. Army officers and anti-Falangists resented his pride, power, and leadership of Falangism, monarchists held him partly responsible for the regime's failure to recognize the monarchy, and malcontents and critics of diverse stripes detested him simply because he was the *cuñadísimo*, to the extent that the German intelligence chief could describe him in Berlin as "the most hated man in Spain."[53] Withal, he had more influence over Franco during the years of his ascendancy than did anyone else in the history of the regime; even Carrero Blanco in later years would not have the same personal authority with the Caudillo.

Yet the two scarcely saw eye to eye on all issues. Though they tended to agree on foreign policy, Serrano backed a more coherent and integrated, and to that extent a more fully fascist, political system than Franco was willing to permit. Franco's extreme personalism, suspicion, cautiousness, and refusal to commit himself to a systematic, juridically defined domestic

---

53. Quoted in Detwiler, *Hitler*, 71. Of the various jingles composed by Serrano's critics, the most telling was:

"Miradle por donde viene,   [Behold whence he comes,
el Señor del Gran Poder,   the Lord of Great Power,
antes se llamaba Cristo   who once was called Christ
y ahora Serrano Súñer."   and now Serrano Súñer.]

system all caused Serrano increasing frustration. He was also aware of the intense hostility, rumors, and gossip of which he was the object and found his position increasingly uncomfortable.

The administration of the FET under the vicesecretary general, Gamero, had turned into a pure holding action. On Serrano's advice, Franco himself assumed control of the Ministry of the Interior after Serrano had become foreign minister. There is no indication that he devoted much time to the task, and he certainly did not encourage any new domestic political initiatives during the winter of 1940–41. Gamero lamented in *Arriba* on January 19, 1941:

> Our finest colleagues and many others in Spain are daily asking a basic question. The question is about the present status of the Falange, about the proportion between the present problems of Spain and the actual possibilities of the party.
>
> For the truth is that the Falange neither rules a State of its own—which has not yet been built—nor combats an opposing state, which has been destroyed. . . .
>
> At the present time the Falange has been called upon to perform a dangerous duty of partial eclipse. It has to work in the most difficult circumstances, weakened by a deep substratum of political heterogeneity that at times reduces the visible result to zero.

Falangist assertiveness became more strident with the German military triumphs of 1940–41. While some radicals and Naziphiles conspired with German representatives,[54] FET leaders who had been collaborating with Serrano since 1937 urged him to take decisive action that would give the party greater power and coherence. The Falange's greatest influence lay in press and propaganda, dominated since 1938 by Antonio Tovar, press subsecretary under the Ministry of Interior, and by Dionisio Ridruejo, FET director general of propaganda. In March, Tovar had signed an agreement with Paul Schmidt, his approximate counterpart in the German Foreign Ministry, authorizing the German foreign news agency Transocean to make use of the Spanish press in news distribution. With the approval of Serrano, who continued to supervise aspects of the Interior Ministry and the FET, Tovar signed an order on May 1 freeing all press organs of the Movement from censorship,[55] thereby creating an independent fascist press in Spain. On the following day, Serrano delivered a vituperative speech in the town of Mota del Cuervo denouncing the domestic foes of Falangism, for which he claimed the right to dominate public policy,

---

54. Klaus-Jörg Ruhl, *Spanien im Zweiten Weltkrieg: Franco, die Falange und das "Dritte Reich"* (Hamburg, 1975), 25, 300. The south European authoritarian regime whose structure bore the greatest similarity to that of Spain at this moment was Romania. Its own fascistic movement, the Legion of the Archangel Michael—better known as the Iron Guard—had been in partnership with the military regime of Marshal Antonescu, but rose in revolt and was crushed in January 1941. A Falangist demonstration in Madrid in support of the Iron Guard was prohibited by Spanish authorities.

55. *FF*, 3:254–55.

stressing that "those who lead this task can be none other than the political minority moved by light and faith." It was not, Serrano insisted, a matter of "widening the base, but of tightening its coherence and of employing it in its full and rigorous meaning through those who understand and love the Falange . . . , and not through the eclectic centipede desired by those who are blind to our path." [56] To increase Falangist representation in the cabinet, Serrano suggested to his brother-in-law that the Ministry of Labor, languishing in the hands of the agriculture minister for a year and half, be given to the young camisa vieja activist from Valladolid, José Antonio Giron.

Franco agreed, but decided to balance this by appointing a close military associate as minister of the interior, on May 5 switching the staff officer and veteran Nationalist intriguer Col. Valentín Galarza, who had served as the subsecretary of his own presidency of the government since August 1939, to that post. A sometime monarchist, Galarza was above all a military bureaucrat devoted to the interests of the military elite. His appointment touched off a fire storm among hard-core Falangists, who considered domination of the Interior apparatus by what they termed the Casino Militar de Madrid a final insult to their own ambitions. Falangist loss of control of press censorship and Interior administration was followed two days later by other key appointments for enemies of the FET. A naval officer, Capt. Luis Carrero Blanco, replaced Galarza as subsecretary of the presidency, the Carlist Antonio Iturmendi was made subsecretary of the interior, and two leading monarchist generals, Orgaz and Kindelán, received the key posts of high commissioner of the Moroccan Protectorate and captain-general of Barcelona, respectively. Within twenty-four hours, *Arriba* carried a prominent article (May 8) entitled "Puntos sobre las íes: El Hombre y el Currinche" ("Dotting the i's: The Man and the Pipsqueak"), with a clear allusion to Galarza as the pipsqueak, and it was accompanied by the resignation of some ten jefes provinciales.

This created the most serious crisis Franco had faced since the unification of the FET, for Galarza and the military demanded revenge. The Generalissimo faced the need to somehow placate both sides. Tovar had already resigned, Ridruejo (probably the main author of the article) was fired, and Serrano even tendered his own resignation as foreign minister, which Franco refused. During the next fortnight Franco carried out a partial reorganization of his cabinet that retained all its military appointees but offered greater representation to carefully selected Falangists, a delicate balancing that worked quite well in the short run. Military interests were protected by the retention of the anti-Falangist and pro-neutralist Varela as minister of the army, while Galarza remained in Interior. At the

56. Quoted in *Franco y Mussolini*, 130.

same time, Falangists gained further recognition with three new cabinet posts. A reliable new secretary-general for the FET was appointed in the person of José Luis de Arrese, Girón became the regime's first real minister of labor, and Miguel Primo de Rivera, the superficial but ambitious playboy younger brother of José Antonio, became minister of agriculture. Primo de Rivera had been one of the jefes provinciales to resign in protest over the naming of Galarza, and had no real qualifications for his new ministry, but was delighted with the cabinet assignment.

The development of this crisis, following the first cabinet changes, had obviously taken Franco by surprise, and its two-week duration made it the longest cabinet crisis of the regime. The outcome by no means succeeded in relieving all the tension between the military and Falangists, but it did reveal Franco's growing skill in balancing them off against each other. Along with a number of other secondary appointments, this reorganization managed to meet the minimum demands of the military while conciliating their Falangist rivals.[57]

The appointment of Arrese turned out to be one of Franco's master strokes. Related by marriage to José Antonio's mother, he had literary ambitions and wrote the first attempt at a full exposition of a Falangist socioeconomic program.[58] Jailed as a camisa vieja rebel in April 1937, he had soon secured his release from prison and eagerly expressed his desire to collaborate with the regime. He was subsequently made jefe provincial of Malaga and became active in trying to promote social programs, though he still occasionally dabbled in "legitimist" camisa vieja maneuvers of the old Falangist Madrid leaders. Summoned by Franco to account personally for these velleities, Arrese's pleasant, fawning, and absolutely servile manner impressed the Caudillo, who correctly judged him to be fully serviceable.

Arrese would eventually complete the task of bureaucratizing and domesticating the Falange that Serrano had never been able to complete. Although there seems to have been some sort of initial understanding that Serrano Súñer would retain some control over the FET, once Franco found Arrese fully obedient and effective he was given more and more direct power over the organization. While maintaining a verbal radicalism that was pleasing to the old guard, Arrese did all that he could to expedite the buying off and domestication of the core Falangists. A few others were directly removed, beginning with the national delegate of syndicates,

57. The principal accounts of the 1941 crisis will be found in Tusell, *Franco y Mussolini*, 129–35; and La Cierva, *Franquismo*, 1 : 203–17. See also Serrano's version in Saña, *Conversaciones*, 158–62.

58. *La revolución social del Nacionalsindicalismo* (Madrid, 1940). These and Arrese's other Falangist writings and speeches were collected in his *Treinta años de política* (Madrid, 1966).

Franco, followed by Arrese, entering a meeting of the FET's National Council, December 8, 1942

Salvador Merino, who, as noted earlier, was discharged in July 1941 and expelled from the party. Meanwhile, Arrese found other docile appointees with camisa vieja credentials for major posts, men like José Luna Meléndez to replace Gamero as vicesecretary general and Fermín Sanz Orrio as the new national delegate of syndicates. The new Falangist leadership was further reinforced by the activity of Jose Antonio Girón, the minister of labor, who, like Arrese, was rhetorically demagogic but politically conservative and bureaucratic, thoroughly loyal to Franco.[59]

At this point the FET had reached its highest membership, with more than 900,000 registered in its several categories of affiliation, and in November 1941 Arrese announced the beginning of the second and last purge in the party's history. It was designed to eliminate crypto-leftists,

59. Girón's early speeches and writings as minister of labor were collected in his *Dos años de actuación al frente del Ministerio de Trabajo mayo 1941–1943* (Madrid, 1943).

former Masons, and those guilty of "immoral" activity or simply activity "incompatible" with the party.[60] For this purpose a new Inspección de Depuración (Purge Inspectorate) was created under a colonel from the Army's Juridical Corps, and during the next five years nearly 6,000 were expelled from the FET.[61] This was hardly an impressive number by the standard of twentieth-century purges, yet it was sufficient to help bring the organization more closely to heel. Cheerleading became an even more important function for the party under Arrese than before, and during 1942 a series of major marches and huge mass meetings were organized in various parts of Spain.[62] Restiveness and conspiracy among Falangists would not come to a complete end until 1944 with the irreversible decline of German military power, but the appointment of Arrese and his cronies nonetheless marked a major step toward the final domestication of the party.

Some elements of party structure were also realigned. On November 28, 1941, the echelon of twelve National Services parallel to the state that had been created in 1938 was abolished. It was replaced by four new vicesecretariats: that of the Movement (the party apparatus), Social Works (including syndicates and excombatientes, the Falangist war veterans' association), Popular Education (for press and propaganda), and Services (miscellaneous, including other aspects of communications, health, recreation groups, and so forth). For the first time, however, the post of jefe provincial of the FET was made synonymous with that of civil governor in the state structure. The pattern of syncretism that Franco had followed from the beginning continued to prevail in new appointments within the party, and at the next renewal of the National Council Franco awarded only about 40 of the 106 seats to genuine Falangists of any sort, while 20 went to Army officers and only half a dozen to Carlists.

Arrese's leadership particularly emphasized the Catholic identity of the FET—later termed by one sociologist *fascismo frailuno* (friar fascism)—and this helped to bring the party even more closely in line with the overtly religious character invoked by the regime's political syncretism. The Sección Femenina, at this stage still a sizable auxiliary, paralleled this orientation under the leadership of Pilar Primo de Rivera, promoting social doctrines of Catholicism, conservatism, and conformism.[63]

---

60. Ellwood, *Prietas*, 128–30.

61. Chueca, *El fascismo*, 198, gives the following figures for those expelled in all categories:

1942	631	1945	1,003
1943	1,962	1946	20
1944	2,087	Total	5,703

62. Ellwood, *Prietas*, 130–32.

63. On the Sección Femenina during the 1940s, see Gallego Méndez, *Mujer*, 76–201. The social service program for women was maintained for more than a decade after the war, though only about 25,000 women a year fulfilled the requirements for a certificate.

In the same vein was the appointment of Gabriel Arias Salgado to the newly created vicesecretariat of popular education within the FET, which replaced the old subsecretariat of press and propaganda in control of radio and press activities under the Ministry of the Interior. Arias Salgado, a relative of Franco's cousin Salgado Araujo, was not much of a Falangist at all but an ultra-right wing Catholic from the hard core of Catholic Action and the National Catholic Association of Propagandists (ACNP) who had once studied to become a Jesuit. His career had been patronized by Franco, and he was appointed to Popular Education by Arrese to help undermine Serrano Súñer's allies and reinforce a policy even more attuned to Catholic norms. Though Arias was strongly pro-Axis, the main thrust of his long-term censorship of Spanish publishing and radio would be more specifically the propagation of right-wing Catholicism.[64]

Franco made one other major appointment in conjunction with the 1941 political realignment. One of his most pressing needs was another military man to replace Galarza as subsecretary (or chief executive assistant) to Franco's presidency of the government, and for this he chose an aspiring naval officer, Capt. Luis Carrero Blanco, who would become his closest and most devoted subordinate and political associate for the next three decades until Carrero's spectacular assassination in 1973. Carrero was a career naval officer who up until the Civil War had been a professor in the Escuela de Guerra Naval in Madrid. He escaped the bloody purge that killed 40 percent of the naval officer corps in the Republican zone, thanks to his lack of political involvement and the fact that he had no active command. The slaughter of naval officers only hardened his extreme right-wing convictions. He gained asylum in the Mexican embassy and thence fled to the Nationalist zone, where during the last phases of the war he commanded first a destroyer and then a submarine. He was later made chief of operations for the Navy's General Staff.

Politically, Carrero Blanco was a discovery of Serrano Súñer and Gamero del Castillo, who had searched for reliable and interested military men to add to the FET's National Council, and it was there that Carrero came to the attention of Franco, who had had some marginal contact with him before the Civil War.[65] Carrero also played a role in the November 1940 naval report that underscored the negative prospects for entry into the war, which is said to have impressed the Generalissimo.[66] Carrero Blanco

64. Though it actually dated from 1936–37, the official Press of the Movement was constituted on June 13, 1940, and was the largest publisher in Spain, by 1944 operating 37 daily and 5 Monday newspapers, 8 weekly and 7 monthly magazines, as well as other publishing facilities. Aspects of Spanish press opinion during the war are presented in Conrado García Alix, *La prensa española ante la Segunda Guerra Mundial* (Madrid, 1974).
65. The principal biographical studies are Carlos Fernández, *El Almirante Carrero* (Barcelona, 1985); and the portrait in Garriga's *Los validos de Franco*, 214–368.
66. López Rodó, *Larga marcha*, 24, though López Rodó exaggerates the extent of Carrero's personal responsibility for the report.

Captain Luis Carrero Blanco, Subsecretary of the Presidency in 1941

had some skill as a writer, and his principal work, *España en el mar (Spain On the Seas)*, was published by the Editora Nacional at the beginning of 1941. It was devoted to the importance of sea power in Spain's past and future and expressed the author's personal convictions, which were ultra-Catholic as well as strongly anti-Semitic.[67]

In this beetle-browed, devoutly Catholic and conservative naval officer Franco would find an ideal, devoted and almost sycophantic executive assistant and adviser,[68] more suitable for his purposes than his brother-in-law and someone with whom he could he more comfortable. Carrero was genuinely self-effacing with Franco, and while aspiring to be the Caudillo's dominant *privado* in a personal sense, had no desire ever to hold the limelight directly. His own ideas ran more closely parallel to those of Franco than did Serrano's thinking, for Carrero was more conservative, more military-oriented and semimonarchist in his convictions. The notion that subsequently developed to the effect that Carrero had no ideas of his own was exaggerated, but Carrero was carefully attuned to Franco's wishes and extremely discreet in proffering his own advice. Differences of criteria between the two were surprisingly few, and Carrero became the nearest thing to a genuine alter ego that Franco would ever have. As this relationship began to develop during 1941–42, Serrano Súñer became more and more expendable. Carrero's own orientation was more genuinely neutralist, and the first significant influence that he had on Franco was evidently exerted in that direction. As his executive and administrative secretary he set much of Franco's agenda, filtering a large part of the information and advice that he received.

Thus the resolution of Franco's first major post–Civil War crisis, even though some of its aspects proved merely provisional, revealed once more his mastery of the major political forces behind the new regime. He retained the support of the military while rejecting their aim of a drastic downgrading of the Falange at a time when it seemed that the Axis was still winning the war. The manner in which he placated the Falangist opposition met his own terms far more than theirs, introducing the kind of Falangist leadership prepared to subordinate itself in return for a secondary place in the system. Moreover, Franco had brought to the top Falangist leaders who claimed authentic camisa vieja status, enabling him to work directly with the FET leadership rather than relying on the intermedia-

67. Spain's ideal would always be "the civilization that is based on the doctrine of Christ"; conversely, the Civil War was but one aspect of the continual "struggle between Christianity and Judaism." *España en el mar* (Madrid, 1949), 7, 9.

68. Carrero's extreme subservience eventually led to all manner of jokes, such as the one recounted by Garriga, according to which Carrero would respond to Franco's question "What time is it?" ("Qué hora es?") with "Whatever Your Excellency orders" ("La que mande Su Excelencia").

tion of Serrano Súñer. The outcome was therefore to widen Franco's political options on several fronts and make him less dependent on his brother-in-law than before.

Internal security was being tightened through renewed repression of the opposition, an attempt to organize local resources for defense in case of foreign invasion,[69] and new efforts to improve at least a few aspects of state administration, particularly with some measure of control over the burgeoning black market. Serious black market offenses had been nominally subject to the death penalty for more than a year, and in March 1941 a number of "crimes of treason" were given the same penalty under military court jurisdiction. In November, two black marketeers were executed in Alicante, one of them the camisa vieja José Pérez de Cabo, author of the first pre–Civil War attempt at a book on Falangist doctrine.[70] He had been involved in the anti-Franco conspiracy of the clandestine junta política, and friends later defended his name by claiming that the black market deals had been designed to finance the Falangist plot.[71]

Extreme shortages and privation for millions, accompanied by black-market operations of all kinds, reached a high point by 1941, the second severe "year of hunger" in a row for Spain. Crop yields for 1940 had been low, and the harvest was equally poor in 1941, its effects compounded by the war and the disruption of foreign trade, which depressed food imports far below need. Severe privation had become a major factor in foreign relations, restricting closer alignment with Germany and increasing somewhat the influence of Britain, whose control of the sea enabled it to regulate food imports into Spain.

Meanwhile there began to develop a "respectable" opposition among the most zealous of the monarchists who sought to replace Franco as soon as was feasible. This opposition, depending on the circumstances and personalities involved, ranged from loyal to Franco to semiloyal to directly subversive. On January 15, 1941, only two weeks before his death, the exiled Alfonso XIII abdicated on behalf of his third son and official heir, Don Juan (the Conde de Barcelona), on whom monarchist hopes would subsequently rest. Active conspiracy at that point, however, was limited to two veteran legitimists who lacked broad support or contacts: the Acción Española writer Eugenio Vegas Latapié (dropped from the National Council of the FET in 1938 because of his monarchist machinations)[72] and the aviator Juan Antonio Ansaldo, pilot of the plane in which

69. For example, on January 23, 1941, the Jefatura Nacional de Defensa Pasiva y del Territorio was created with the task of forming local committees of military officers in all districts of Spain to coordinate auxiliary local defense and mobilization of resources. Clark, Evolution, 1:331.

70. José Pérez de Cabo, ¡Arriba España! (Madrid, 1935).

71. Cf. Romero Cuesta, Objetivo, 72–74.

72. See his Escritos políticos (Madrid, 1942).

Sanjurjo was killed in 1936.[73] They could count on only a very few military figures, such as Kindelán, Franco's former air force commander and one of his key backers in 1936 (soon to be appointed to the important post of captain general of Barcelona), the former minister Beigbeder (who now lacked a major assignment), and the political gadfly Aranda (who favored the monarchy as the most constructive alternative rather than because of any innate monarchist convictions).[74]

Among other things, monarchists were apparently willing to discuss the alternative of an authoritarian German-backed restoration. Don Juan had earlier protested to the Carlist regent, D. Javier, that his own branch of the monarchy should not be thought of as necessarily committed to liberalism.[75] In April 1941, with Hitler's star in the ascendant, a representative in Berlin discussed German support for a restoration in Spain that would supposedly integrate the monarchy in the New Order.[76] Several months later, Maj. Gen. Juan Vigón, Franco's moderately pro-German air force minister who doubled as Don Juan's personal political representative in Madrid, was reported to be engaged in conversations about possible German assistance in the installation of an authoritarian monarchy in Spain,[77] though this cannot be corroborated directly. As late as May 1942 the Conde de Barcelona was rumored to be willing to consider an authoritarian restoration with German assistance and in conjunction with the Falange.[78]

Though Franco had managed to deflect the criticism of the military hierarchy, there was still restiveness over the dangerous international situation. There was even more dissatisfaction with the continuing institutional incoherence of the regime and the rivalry with Serrano Súñer and the FET, climaxed by the increasingly disastrous economic situation and the rampant corruption in which some military leaders were themselves involved. Conversations reflecting a common dissatisfaction continued among senior commanders in the summer of 1941, and during August Franco was visited by both the loyal Orgaz and the intriguer Aranda, who urged the dismissal of Serrano and greater caution and consultation in future foreign policy initiatives.[79]

73. On monarchist conspiracy in Spain during 1941, see Juan Antonio Ansaldo, *Mémoires d'un monarchiste espagnol* (Monaco, 1953), 146–60; and Rafael Calvo Serer, *Franco frente al rey* (Paris, 1972), 21–22.

74. The British, who had extensive dealings with Aranda and were apparently paying him a great deal of money, were less and less impressed with his successive confidences and conspiracies, considering him "unreliable and illogical," veering around "like a weathercock," according to diplomatic dispatches quoted in Smyth, *Diplomacy*, 215.

75. In a letter of March 8, 1940, partially quoted in La Cierva, *Franquismo*, 1:170.

76. Ruhl, *Spanien*, 69, 326.

77. According to the article on Aranda by Marquina Barrio previously cited.

78. Ruhl, *Spanien*, 98–99, 346–47.

79. Hartmut Heine, *La oposición política al franquismo* (Barcelona, 1983), 253–54.

General Antonio Aranda

Franco's first crisis of confidence in his brother-in-law seems to have developed during the following month. Part of the new cabinet was strongly anti-Serrano, and even the new Falangist ministers resented his influence. There is some evidence that Serrano made a direct offer to resign, all the while presenting himself as the victim of a right-wing monarchist conspiracy (though his enemies were much more numerous than that) and as Spain's indispensable representative for proper relations with the Axis. Serrano made some effort to mend his fences with his diverse antagonists, and managed to regain the Generalissimo's backing, weathering this new storm.[80] Franco, in turn, moved to protect himself against the mounting monarchist sentiment in the military command with a personal letter to Don Juan which stressed that the monarchy would eventually become the "coronation" of Franco's regime. The letter denounced the "blindness and incompetence" of those who tried to oppose the monarchy to his own "National Movement."[81]

In October 1941 Aranda took advantage of monarchist feelings to meet with some of the senior generals and seriously discuss the possibility of some sort of new military regency with or without Franco. There was evidently talk of such action, particularly in the event of German invasion, for some feared that Franco's government lacked the energy, efficiency, and popular support for effective resistance. Though Aranda mentioned a shadow "Generals' Junta" to British contacts,[82] it is rather doubtful that such a thing actually existed. However, at a meeting of the Consejo Superior del Ejército on December 15, 1941, Kindelán spoke candidly in Franco's presence about the opprobrium which the present situation was bringing on both Franco and the Army, stressing that generals should be removed from political positions, that the abuse of military justice for political and ordinary criminal prosecution should cease, and that rampant corruption and the influence of the Falange should be sharply curtailed.[83]

Franco was usually patient with critical generals as long as they did not speak out in public or engage in direct conspiracy, and he treated monarchists with considerable respect, subject to the same terms. His tactic had always been to assure them privately that restoration was the ultimate

---

(Heine, however, tends to accept at face value the considerably exaggerated claims made by Aranda et al. to British diplomats.)

80. Tusell, *Franco y Mussolini*, 144–46.

81. Pedro Sainz Rodríguez, *Un reinado en la sombra* (Barcelona, 1981), 349–50.

82. According to the article "Conspiracion contra Franco" by Marquina Barrio. Even the bizarre Beigbeder, however, cogently concluded that any alternative military regime "was bound in the end to fail, owing to mutual jealousies, inexperience, and competition for places among the generals concerned." (Quoted in Smyth, *Diplomacy*, 209.) Indeed, the British government discouraged any military revolt to replace Franco under the existing circumstances, judging that a new, weaker set of Army leaders would be more susceptible to German pressure.

83. Kindelán, *La verdad*, 46–49.

goal of the regime but that conditions of Civil War and World War were scarcely propitious, and he was not necessarily insincere in this. In a subsequent letter of May 12, 1942, he assured Don Juan that he planned eventually to make him king of Spain,[84] just as in November 1942, after the Allied landings in northwest Africa, he privately assured Kindelán that the special name designating his successor which he kept in a little box in his office was that of Don Juan.[85]

Foreign Policy in 1942

Expansion of the "last European war" into World War in December 1941 inspired further modification of Spanish policy. Franco could breathe a sigh of relief that he had resisted following up the agreement in the secret Hendaye protocol that Spain would join the Tripartite Pact (as Ciano had urged Serrano to do in 1941), for that would have set Spain at war with the United States after Pearl Harbor. To Franco this all meant that German victory, while still probable and desirable, would be slower and more difficult, and that a Spanish entry into the war in the near future would be even more costly and potentially disastrous. The new situation gave Spain slightly greater freedom to maneuver, but it also was capable of producing new dangers from either the Allies or Germany. Since American entry coincided with the stalemate of the German blitzkrieg before Moscow, it argued for Franco a lower profile for Spanish nonbelligerence in support of Germany. Therefore in February 1942 he dispatched the Army chief of staff, General Carlos Asensio, on an inspection tour of the Blue Division in Russia, and then requested provisional withdrawal of the Spanish unit, which Hitler did not grant. Soon afterward, supply facilities for German submarines were once more suspended just as the major phase of the Battle of the Atlantic began.

For Franco, all this was merely elemental discretion; it did not bring any modification of the generally pro-German stance of the Spanish press and public activities. There were still occasional demonstrations and stone-throwing incidents before the British embassy, while, partly because of a more aggressive American policy, relations with the United States embassy deteriorated.

In mid-February Franco had his first face-to-face meeting with Salazar at Badajoz (where, contrary to legend, he did not address the Portuguese leader in Galician but in Spanish). Though there could never be full collaboration between a genuinely neutral Portugal and a pro-Axis Spain, this encounter produced verbal reinforcement of the earlier 1939 Treaty of Friendship and Non-Aggression (the so-called Iberian Pact), and a gen-

84. Ibid., 42–46.
85. Ibid., 32–33.

eral understanding that the two Iberian regimes would consult on items of mutual concern and resist foreign intrusions into the peninsula. On a subsequent visit of the Spanish foreign minister to Lisbon the following December, this was officially announced somewhat pompously as the "Bloque Ibérico" (Iberian Bloc).[86]

Franco quickly made it clear that he was uninfluenced by Salazar's neutralism. On February 14, in a speech before the garrison of Seville, he declared: "The Allies are offering Europe as a possible prey to Communism. We have no fear that will actually happen; we are absolutely sure that things will not end thus; but if there should be a moment of danger, if the road to Berlin were left undefended, it would not be merely a division of Spanish volunteers who would go, but a million Spaniards who would offer themselves."[87]

Moreover, during 1941–42 Germany was trying to play a more direct role in Spanish domestic affairs. By that point the Madrid embassy had the distinction of being the largest German embassy in the world,[88] packed with press and propaganda personnel charged with influencing Spanish opinion and gaining a stepping stone to Latin America as well. Since 1940 German penetration of Spanish news media and of certain aspects of cultural life had been extensive. The German press attaché Hans Lazar was said to have no less than 432 Spanish names, including those of many journalists, on his payroll.[89] The Italians, whose efforts had exceeded those of the Germans during the Civil War, fell far behind; during 1941 approximately three times as many German as Italian films were shown in Spain. By the beginning of 1942 a German "Grosse Plan" was being implemented to diffuse German propaganda even more broadly and to move more actively into Latin America as well.[90]

German political and intelligence contacts operated on multiple levels. The ambassador and top attachés cultivated leading political figures from Serrano Súñer on down. Leaders of the Nazi party organization in Spain

86. The principal study is a paper by Ester Sacristán, "Las relaciones peninsulares durante la Segunda Guerra Mundial: La entente del Bloque Ibérico 1942," presented at the Symposium "España y la Segunda Guerra Mundial," Madrid, Oct. 13–15, 1983. It should also be noted that Salazar apparently raised one problem affecting intrapeninsular relations—the ambitions of radical Falangists who talked of taking over Portugal and even conspired with Nazis to that end. Franco completely disavowed any such ambitions and emphasized that such rhetoric stemmed from small radical groups with little influence in the FET.

87. *Palabras del Caudillo*, 204.

88. Ruhl, *Spanien*, 315.

89. According to La Cierva, *Franquismo*, 1:234. Hitler at one point gushed that "the Spanish press is the best in the world!" *Hitler's Table Talk*, ed. H. R. Trevor-Roper (London, 1973), 694.

90. In part, this developed from the first Schmidt-Tovar agreement of October 1940, signed by Antonio Tovar, then subsecretary of press and propaganda, whereby the official news agency, EFE, would relay to the Germans information from Latin America and in turn help to diffuse German propaganda there. German authorities later complained that they received little concrete benefit from this. Garriga, *La España de Franco*, 1:287–92.

Soldiers of the Spanish Blue Division on the Russian front

maintained their own relations, primarily with Falangists, while the main operation was probably based on the intelligence network first established by the SS Sicherheitsdienst Sturmbannführer Paul Winzer,[91] which had become quite active by 1940. In addition, there was at least one other

91. Ruhl, *Spanien*, 56–59.

smaller German network operated by the Abwehr (military intelligence). Closest German contacts were almost always with members of the Falange, and generally the more radical the Falangist the more pro-Nazi he proved to be. Yet the only active liberal conspirator in the military hierarchy, Aranda, also had contacts with the local Nazi leaders Bernhardt and Thomsen during 1941,[92] hoping to gain German acceptance of a non-Falangist military regime in Spain. The expulsion of several lower-level German diplomatic personnel for dabbling in domestic politics did little to discourage such machinations.

On the eastern front, German authorities tried to convince Muñoz Grandes and other Blue Division commanders of the need for a drastic change in Spanish policy, and seemed to be achieving some success. Muñoz Grandes was heard to say that things back in Spain were a mess and must be straightened out by a more effective government that would bring the country into the war. When word of these mutterings reached Franco, he relieved Muñoz Grandes of command in May 1942, innocently blaming it on the hostility of Varela and Serrano toward the Blue Division's commander. At Hitler's insistence, however, he nervously agreed to let Muñoz Grandes remain a little longer. Hitler apparently planned to give Muñoz Grandes a prominent place in the anticipated conquest of Leningrad during the summer of 1942, thus endowing him with the prestige to play a dominant role in Spanish affairs afterward. At a subsequent meeting with Hitler on July 12, Muñoz Grandes seems to have been thoroughly captivated by the Fuehrer's charm, readily agreeing that Spain needed a totally pro-German and anti-British regime. He declared that after the next victory on the eastern front his ambition was to return to Spain and become chief of government (a sort of prime minister) under a weakened Franco, eliminating Serrano Súñer altogether. Just how far Muñoz Grandes was prepared to go, and whether he merely told Hitler what the latter wanted to hear while directing his animus against Serrano and Varela rather than Franco, was not clear, but what he knew of the situation was enough to give Franco pause. There seemed the more reason for alarm in Madrid when only a few days later the German military attaché visited Muñoz Grandes's friend and sometime associate Yagüe at the latter's country home.[93]

Though the military situation of the Tripartite powers seemed even more favorable by July 1942 than at the beginning of the year, Franco was becoming increasingly cautious. His seventeenth of July speech, on the anniversary of the Nationalist rebellion, was worded with unusual care and pleased the American ambassador, who observed: "It announced that the form of government suitable to one country was not necessarily suit-

92. Ibid., 70.
93. Ibid., 111–14; Kleinfeld and Tambs, *Hitler's Spanish Legion*, 192–97.

able to others, and that the million Spanish soldiers would make their stand not before Berlin but at the Pyrenees."[94] Meanwhile, returning Blue Division veterans who might have been influenced by Muñoz Grandes were isolated as much as possible from positions of influence.

The Begoña Affair and the Political Crisis of August 1942

Tensions within the regime, already acute during 1941, increased sharply in the following year, to some extent following their own internal dynamic quite apart from the pressures of the international situation. Resentment among military commanders had first begun to come to a head during the winter and spring of 1941 and was only momentarily assuaged by Franco's cabinet reorganization. The main goals of the military—complete ouster of Serrano Súñer and the downgrading or even outright abolition of the FET—were far from realization. Franco had no intention of capitulating to the political demands of the military, which could only weaken his own authority. He deemed the FET a useful and necessary instrument, not least because he still expected the Axis to win the war. The FET enabled him to staff a continuing system and provided an alternative to monarchist and right-wing pressure.

In 1942, rivalry between the military and Falangists threatened to reach a new high. Strong pressure from senior commanders in January did lead top Falangists to become more circumspect and issue public statements emphasizing the need for unity between the party and armed forces. But this was the merest window-dressing, for the return of mild weather in March and April produced a long series of incidents between young Falangist militants and monarchists or Carlists, and between Falangists and Army officers.

Franco relied on Arrese and the more docile new Falangist leaders to keep party members in line, but the situation within the FET remained divided and unstable. Conversations between radical Falangists (and several main-line FET leaders as well) with German officials persisted on several levels, while the perpetual discontent of some of the camisas viejas continued to fester. Clandestine pamphlets appeared frequently, and by the spring of 1942 a new shadow "Falange Auténtica" announced its existence and was said to be carrying on contacts with high-ranking FET personnel, though Arrese monitored the situation to keep it from getting out of control.[95]

94. Hayes, *Wartime Mission*, 54.
95. Ruhl, *Spanien*, 115. An architect named Juan Muñoz Mateo was subsequently arrested in San Sebastián on November 2 and charged with having founded the Falange Auténtica to overthrow the government. *FF*, 3:359.

This sort of effervescence seems to have troubled Franco relatively little, for he evidently viewed it less as a threat than as a potential counterweight to his critics in the military. Early in March, to silence the latter, he even drafted the sketch of a new regulation to limit political activity by Army officers, but then thought better of it and dropped the proposal. Further incidents followed in succession. Just before the end of the month the new captain-general of Old Castile, the extremely pro-German Espinosa de los Monteros (recently ambassador in Berlin), made a veiled attack on Serrano Súñer in a public speech at Burgos. This virtually coincided with an incident in Madrid in which Felipe Ximénez de Sandoval, head of Serrano's diplomatic cabinet in the Foreign Ministry and supervisor of foreign news coverage by the Spanish press, provoked a Falangist assault on a young monarchist aristocrat, which backfired when the intended victim mastered his assailant and turned him over to the police. Franco responded to these incidents with his customary arbitrage. Both Espinosa and Ximénez de Sandoval were fired, though Ximénez was also publicly charged with homosexuality and expelled from the FET altogether. According to one version, the latter maneuver was inspired by Arrese to foster his more moderate anti-Serrano apparatus within the party. A few days later on April 2 a bomb went off in the car of Girón, the labor minister, injuring no one, and those responsible were never identified.[96]

Even within the Italian government increasing doubt developed as to the future stability of the Spanish regime, and for the first time Ciano showed interest in courting the monarchist pretender as an alternative, inviting Don Juan to a special hunting party in Albania during April.[97] As public insults from and incidents with Falangists increased, the commanders of the Madrid garrison even issued instructions in mid-April that officers carry sidearms when off duty. At that point, the minister of war, Varela, who was the chief representative of military opinion in the government, had a serious talk with Franco, insisting that the present political balance within the government and the FET could not continue. Either the party should become the genuine amalgam of Falangists and Carlists that had been announced in 1937, which would mean that half the positions in the party should be awarded Carlists or other elements, or it should be dissolved. Similarly, Varela outlined two different schemes of cabinet reorganization, each of which would drastically downgrade Falangist influence. Several weeks later, on May 4, a cabinet meeting exploded into violent recriminations between Falangist and Army ministers.[98]

96. Heine, *La oposición*, 257–58.
97. Tusell, *Franco y Mussolini*, 156–57.
98. Ibid., 158–59. The outrage of Army officers was reflected in a verse that circulated among the Madrid garrison:

Franco redefined his position in a speech before the Sección Femenina of the FET at the Castillo de la Mota on May 29, in which he invoked the "totalitarian monarchy" of the Catholic Monarchs as the inspiration of the regime. In this way he kept his peace with monarchists on the one hand and held to his own political formulae on the other. He denounced as the internal foes of the Catholic Monarchs the selfish and sectarian aristocracy, a scarcely veiled allusion to his own critics among the monarchist elite. Lauding the "totalitarian" character of the fifteenth-century monarchy, he also applauded its "racist" and anti-Jewish policies, in terminology unusual for Franco.[99]

While some generals grumbled about the need to replace what they called Franco's totalitarian rule with a collective military government that would prepare the return of the monarchy, a new series of public brawls erupted between Falangist activists and Carlist and monarchist youth in Madrid, Pamplona, Burgos, and Santiago de Compostela. Indirectly encouraged by Varela in the War Ministry, Carlists showed increasing signs of dissidence. By July their leaders in Navarre and the Basque provinces were said to be discussing the desirability of having their remaining representatives within the system retire one by one, and at a Carlist parade in Bilbao on July 18 cries of "Muera Franco!" ("Death to Franco!") were allegedly heard.[100] Street affrays between Falangists and their rivals were becoming more frequent in the larger cities,[101] and during the summer of 1942 tension remained high.

Though Franco stubbornly refused the military hierarchy the satisfaction of eliminating Serrano, the foreign minister's influence had declined since the cabinet crisis of the preceding year. If Arrese had not been able to bring the Falange totally under control, he was increasingly successful in making the FET apparatus more pliable than Serrano ever had, and his loyal collaboration gave Franco a reliable support he had not possessed before.[102] Serrano in turn grew increasingly exasperated. On a brief trip

---

La Falange a un militar
a traición apaleó
y . . . nada ocurrió.
Puede el baile continuar!
Ejército: has de aguantar
si es Falange quien te pisa
y poner cara de risa
si algún día esos cabrones
te bajan los pantalones
y te suben la camisa. . . .

[The Falange attacked
an officer from the back
but . . . nothing happened.
The dance can continue!
Army: you have to swallow it
if the Falange walks all over you,
and pretend to smile
if one day those cuckolds
pull down your trousers
and pull up your shirt. . . .]

99. *Palabras del Caudillo*, 211–16.
100. Ruhl, *Spanien*, 115.
101. Cf. Hayes, *Wartime Mission*, 56.
102. Arrese further ingratiated himself with such feats as turning out large crowds for Franco's visit to Catalonia in January 1942, after the Caudillo had been coolly received in Vizcaya. The applause in Barcelona was allegedly achieved by offering workers the day off at double wages to line the streets.

to Rome in June he complained of the constant maneuverings and petty conspiracies within the regime which Franco seemed to have little interest in eliminating.[103] While Muñoz Grandes and others intrigued with the Germans, Aranda held conversations with Allied representatives.[104] Meanwhile, one of Serrano's closest friends and collaborators within the FET, the poet and activist Dionisio Ridruejo, had become severely disillusioned, and renounced all his positions in the party in August.[105]

Serrano mounted a counteroffensive of his own, preparing new legislation to regain control of the foreign news censorship which he had lost to the FET's vicesecretariat of popular culture upon the expulsion of his aide Ximénez de Sandoval. Technically, this was presented as necessary for the proper conduct of foreign affairs, aligning the press with official policy, but it lacked the neutralist overtones that Serrano has alleged in his numerous memoirs.[106] This was demonstrated by the appearance in the Spanish press early in August of his article "España y la guerra mundial" ("Spain and the World War"), reprinted from its earlier publication in a

103. *Ciano's Diplomatic Papers,* 460–65.

104. In March 1942 Aranda had told the British that he could count on seven of the eight district captains-general to participate in a move against Franco, undoubtedly a bold exaggeration. Meanwhile, according to Marquina Barrio, the Allies made contact with native nationalists within the Moroccan Protectorate and even began to prepare a small contingent of Spanish Republican and American Lincoln Battalion veterans to initiate new resistance inside Spain.

105. In a letter to Franco of July 7, 1942, Ridruejo defined the "reality of the regime" as follows:

"1. Failure of the government's plan and its authority in economic affairs. Triumph of estraperlo. Disproportionate hunger among the people.

2. Weakness of the state on the one hand, which suffers the most intolerable interference in matters that affect its own political texture, while on the other, popular will is alienated by an exclusively conservative-style policy.

3. Abandonment of a military policy based on efficient foresight and, in exchange, permanence of the Army as the active watchdog of political life; something that is justified by the instability of the regime, in the interventionist tradition stemming from a century of civil wars that has still not been overcome.

4. Confusion and arbitrariness in the affairs of justice, with a sharpening of leftist resentment among extensive sectors of the people.

5. Incessant conspiracy among the reactionary elements, Anglophiles by opportunism, inviting intrigue by those who defend privilege and adopt positions opposing the regime and more concretely the Falange.

6. Complete forgetfulness of the original Falangist doctrine. A Movement inert and without program. Leaders of scant authenticity but great vulgarity. The crowd at the expense of demagogues." (*Casi unas memorias,* 236–40.)

These judgments are further elaborated in Ridruejo's letter of resignation to Serrano Súñer, Aug. 29, 1942, quoted in García Lahiguera, *Serrano Súñer,* 229–32.

After being fired by Franco from his position as director of propaganda in May 1941, Ridruejo had volunteered for the Blue Division, and his diary of the eastern front was posthumously published many years later as *Los cuadernos de Rusia* (Barcelona, 1978). Serrano wrote an account of Ridruejo's withdrawal from the regime in 1942 in Juan Benet et al., *Dionisio Ridruejo, de la Falange a la oposición* (Madrid, 1976). Ridruejo's first memoir, representing the perspective he formed during the 1940s and 1950s, was *Escrito en España* (Buenos Aires, 1964).

106. See also Garriga, *La España de Franco,* 1:234.

Nazi journal inside Germany. It reaffirmed the Spanish government's solidarity with the Axis and against "democracy and communism," the two foes in east and west. At that moment German and Japanese expansion was reaching its farthest points in the Soviet Union, North Africa, and East Asia, and Serrano seemed determined to justify his sobriquet Axis minister while attempting to recoup lost prestige in Berlin.[107]

Within the central state apparatus, Serrano's most influential foes, aside from the top military leaders, were Arrese and Carrero Blanco, Franco's new subsecretary of the presidency. Arrese schemed to eliminate Serrano's remaining influence in the FET, while Carrero saw Serrano as the ultimate rival in his personal relationship with the Caudillo. When Franco decided that summer to give the green light to the proposal first advanced two years earlier by Serrano and a subcommittee of the Junta Política, that a corporative Cortes or parliament be developed for the regime, he first charged Arrese with drafting the project, though it was later polished by Serrano.[108] Growing influence in the regime, meanwhile, in no way hindered Arrese from assiduous cultivation of the number-two political operative in the German diplomatic delegation (after the ambassador, von Stohrer), the embassy counsellor Erich Gardemann, encouraging him to believe that Arrese was working for pro-Nazi change in Spanish policy.

These rivalries finally came to a head after a bloody incident in the outskirts of Bilbao that turned into the most notorious cause celebre of the 1940s in Spain. As indicated, Carlist feeling in Navarre and the Basque provinces was strongly against the FET and the present structure of the regime. Feeling erupted once more at the annual memorial mass held August 16 in the sanctuary of the Virgen de Begoña in Bilbao, in memory of Requetés fallen in the Civil War. A small group of Falangist activists outside the church were identified at the ceremony, taunted (and allegedly faced with a few cries of "Muera Franco!"), and according to the Falangists, assaulted. The Falangists responded by tossing two hand grenades into the crowd of Carlists, which may or may not have caused fatalities (Carlist sources claim there were ultimately two deaths) but wounded between 30 and 117, depending on various accounts.[109]

107. Cf. Tusell, *Franco y Mussolini*, 165.
108. Saña, *Conversaciones*, 262–63.
109. Reconstructions of this incident vary considerably. The most detailed treatment is by Marquina Barrio, "El atentado de Begoña," *Historia 16* 4:46 (April 1980), 11–19, though some of his facts are probably wrong. See also Serrano Súñer, *Memorias*, 364–73; Saña, *Conversaciones*, 263–69; García Lahiguera, *Serrano Súñer*, 215–34; Garriga, *La España de Franco*, 1:428–30; and Ellwood, *Prietas*, 145–54. The Carlists launched their own version in a semiclandestine pamphlet, *El crimen de la Falange en Begoña: Un régimen al descubierto*.

As indicated in Marquina Barrio and Garriga, it was rumored that the whole incident was part of a Falangist plot intended to discredit either the Carlists or Serrano Súñer. The conspiracy theory hinges on the motives for the presence of Juan Domínguez and his five Falangist comrades at the Carlist rally. Another version, defended by Narciso Perales and

General José Enrique Varela during the Civil War

General Varela happened to be inside the sanctuary at the time of the incident. He immediately seized on it as evidence of a Falangist attack on the military (which he alleged might even have involved an assassination attempt), sending telegrams in this vein to all district captains generals and protesting vehemently to Franco. He was seconded by the interior minister, Galarza, who dispatched similar messages to civil governors throughout Spain. The six Falangists arrested in Begoña were then tried by court-martial.

Franco was greatly displeased by the initiatives of Varela and Galarza, which he considered excessive, imprudent, and even potentially insubordinate. Yet Varela succeeded in mobilizing the sympathies of much of the military hierarchy, and despite Falangist pressure, Franco hesitated to intervene in the court-martial (he scarcely ever intervened) even though he deeply resented the Carlist rally and the cries of "Long Live the King!" that had accompanied it. Several of the Falangists under indictment were Blue Division veterans who sought a regime under full control of the Falange, and entry into the war on the side of Germany. All six were convicted, two receiving the death penalty, and one of these, Juan Domínguez (a national inspector of the SEU and the person responsible for throwing the one grenade that exploded) was executed at the beginning of September.[110]

Meanwhile, Varela demanded of Franco direct political satisfaction against the Falange. According to one version,[111] the conversation became so hostile that Franco realized he would have no alternative but to dismiss Varela. He also decided to remove Galarza, whom he blamed for having run a slack ship and for having withheld information on the incident, as well as the FET vicesecretary Luna, who had been sent to Bilbao to collect information and was accused of involvement in the affair. No action, however, was taken against the principal Falangist leaders, who demon-

---

accepted by Serrano, has the Falangist group meeting a returning veteran from the Blue Division at the border and then stopping at the latter's home in Bilbao, where they learned of the Carlist ceremonial. The hand grenades thrown by Domínguez, according to this explanation, were souvenirs brought from the eastern front by the returning veteran. Yet details of this are in turn contradicted by the testimony of the military governor of Bilbao, presented by Javier Tusell in Diario 16, *Historia del franquismo*, 224.

110. The other death penalty was commuted, and all five surviving Falangists were finally pardoned and released in 1945. Domínguez was awarded a German medal for his service in Russia, and German authorities made an effort to intervene on his behalf. Apparently to counter this, the Falangist National Delegation of Information under Manuel Valdés presented a report accusing Domínguez of being paid by the British intelligence service. It is doubtful (though not impossible) that this charge was true; it may even have been concocted by the Arrese leadership in the FET to scapegoat Domínguez and wash their hands of him while maintaining positive relations with the military.

111. Marquina Barrio, "El atentado de Begoña." The transcript of a telephone conversation between Franco and Varela during the crisis is presented in López Rodó, *Larga marcha*, 503–7.

strated complete obsequiousness to Franco and dissociated themselves from the defense of the Falangists who were tried and convicted.

When Franco communicated these new personnel decisions to his subsecretary, Carrero Blanco, who had for some time been conniving with Arrese to eliminate Serrano, Carrero warned him that firing two Army ministers alone without firing their political counterparts would create serious complications. Serrano had done more than Arrese to try to save Domínguez, and Carrero warned that if Serrano were allowed to retain his ministry, the military and all other non- or anti-Falangists would say that Serrano and the FET had won a complete victory and that Franco was no longer in full control.[112] Franco seems to have required little convincing, for he had become increasingly restive with Serrano, who tended to contradict and criticize him more and more, and had already suggested resigning.[113]

Franco's cabinet reorganization, announced on September 3, sought to perfect the pragmatic equilibrium first attempted by the partial reorganization of the preceding year. The conservative and practical Jordana returned to the Foreign Ministry, and Varela was replaced by General Carlos Asensio, one of the most capable figures in the military hierarchy, a trusted and disciplined subordinate whom Franco had to press vigorously to accept the appointment.[114] Galarza was replaced by Blas Pérez González, a prewar University of Barcelona law professor who was also a major in the Army Juridical Corps. Pérez was an astute jurist and an administrator of unusual ability and self-control. He had made an outstanding career in the Nationalist juridical system[115] and was also a friend of Girón, the

112. According to the version that Carrero gave years later to López Rodó, in the latter's *Larga marcha*, 29–30.

113. Saña, *Conversaciones*, 271–74. There had been a further source of personal and family tension as a result of Serrano's extramarital affair with the wife of an aristocratic lieutenant colonel of Cavalry, which became the gossip of Madrid and was even mentioned in diplomatic reports. Cf. D. W. Pike, "Aspects nouveaux du role de l'Espagne dans la Seconde Guerre Mondiale," *Revue d'Histoire Moderne et Contemporaine* 19 (July–Sept. 1972), 516n, and "Franco and the Axis Stigma," *JCH* 17:3 (July 1982), 369–407; and Fernández, *Tensiones militares*, 41–43. This was about the nearest thing to a major sex scandal in the long and puritanical history of the regime.

114. Varela bitterly resented his ouster and lobbied among his fellow lieutenant generals to dissuade any of them from replacing him, probably alleging that the honor of the military hierarchy was at stake. Franco therefore went to Asensio, one of his best major generals, and chief of the General Staff under Varela. According to Serrano, the Generalissimo encountered further difficulty in convincing Asensio to accept the post, railing in exasperation, "What do you want? For me to be carried out of here some day feet first?" Saña, *Conversaciones*, 267.

115. Pérez González earlier had the courage to oppose the retroactive provisions of the regime's decrees establishing severe criminal penalties for membership in the Masonic order. This brought down upon him a libel campaign by the regime's ultras that he survived only after the bishop of Santa Cruz de Tenerife (his home diocese) testified personally to Franco on his behalf. The only study of Pérez González is in Garriga's *Los validos de Franco*, 126–213.

Blas Pérez González, Minister of the Interior, 1942–57

Falangist minister of labor. In addition, José Luna was replaced as vice-secretary of the FET, and during the next few weeks several of the more radical jefes provinciales were also removed.

These cabinet changes were quite effective. Pérez was in administrative and juridical terms the most careful and efficient interior minister that Franco ever had, holding this position through the entire post–World War II period of intensified opposition all the way down to 1957. Asensio became a reliable army minister, to whom Varela's type of independence was alien. His reputation for being strongly pro-German (which he was) pleased Berlin, which also found gratification in Serrano's ouster, while the British and American governments were equally pleased with the removal of the so-called Axis minister.

Of all the new appointees, the most important in broad historical terms was undoubtedly Gómez Jordana. He was genuinely neutralist in personal outlook and convictions, and soon brought a new tone, though not at first a new orientation, to foreign relations. A senior general of firm character, he was willing to stand up for policies in which he believed, while his diligent, workmanlike habits infused a new efficiency into the Foreign Ministry. Serrano, though not lacking in administrative ability, had often been distracted by his intermittently poor health and perhaps even more by his political interests and ambitions in other areas.

None of the major political contestants—the military, Falangists, mainline monarchists, or Carlists—were fully satisfied with the results. All things considered, the military gained rather more than the others, but this new balancing act by no means stilled Army criticism, which remained fairly vehement in some circles of the officer corps.[116] Yet the new combination of September 1942 was shrewdly chosen to balance all these forces off against each other, and proved the most manageable since the Civil War.

Franco thus survived two internal crises in less than eighteen months, demonstrating an increasing ability to manage the diverse elements of the Nationalist elite. For five and a half years, from February 1937 until September 1942, Serrano Súñer had played a vital role as *valido* (favorite) and a kind of second-in-command on whom Franco relied for both advice and key administrative leadership, in both domestic and foreign policy. Yet rather than becoming indispensable, Serrano eventually became a lia-

---

116. One anonymous military pamphlet soon afterward urged direct action to eliminate the FET altogether. To counter the concern of those who feared that Hitler would take this as anti-German, it alleged that "a military action by the Army would in Spain provide the same guarantees for Germany that the Army provided in Romania by combatting the pack of lunatics in the party." *Franco y Mussolini*, 170. This argument referred to the suppression of the Iron Guard by the Romanian Army in January 1941, after which the conservative, military-led nationalist dictatorship of Antonescu became an ally of Germany.

bility in both spheres. The terms of the new combination which followed made Franco, if anything, more dominant personally and more self-reliant politically than ever before. These same terms would serve him well for the equally uncertain and potentially even more dangerous climactic phase of the World War which followed.

14

From Nonbelligerence
to Neutrality,
1942–1945

As the war drew nearer to Spain in 1942–43, Franco's policy varied only slightly. He still expected and indeed hoped for an eventual German victory, while maintaining the nonbelligerent policy of *hábil prudencia* with its tilt toward the Axis.

The Allied landings in northwest Africa on November 8, 1942 (Operation Torch) brought the war closer than at any previous time. German forces acted swiftly to occupy the southern half of France previously controlled by the Vichy regime, sealing the entire Pyrenean border with Spain, now caught between two fires. A few hours after the Anglo-American landings began, a personal letter from Roosevelt was hand-delivered to Franco by the new American ambassador, Carlton J. H. Hayes.[1] A distinguished Columbia University history professor, Hayes had been in charge of the American embassy since the beginning of the year and had formed a rather positive impression of the Caudillo.[2] To the relief of the Spanish government, Roosevelt assured Franco that the Allied landings in northwest Africa involved no infringement of Spain's territorial sovereignty at any point, concluding with the categorical assurance "Spain has nothing to fear from the United Nations," as he titled the dis-

1. C. J. H. Hayes, *Wartime Mission in Spain* (New York, 1946), 89–91.
2. "The General, I soon perceived, differed notably from the caricatures of him current in the 'leftist' press of the United States. Physically he was not so short or so stout and he did not 'strut.' Mentally he impressed me as being not at all a stupid or 'me too' sort of person, but distinctly alert and possessing a good deal of both determination and caution and a rather lively and spontaneous sense of humor. He laughed easily and naturally, which, I imagine, a Hitler couldn't do and a Mussolini wouldn't do except in private." Ibid., 30.

parate anti-German coalition. The British government offered similar assurances, and Franco would later refer to this as his first guarantee that, if worst came to worst, his regime could survive the possible defeat of the Axis.

A new alarm was sounded at the cabinet meeting held on November 16, which was presented a report from the embassy in Berlin indicating that Hitler soon intended to request permission for the passage of troops across Spanish territory.[3] The Germanophile minority (Asensio, Arrese, Girón) apparently urged closer alignment with the Third Reich, but the majority supported the position of Franco and Jordana in favor of continued nonbelligerence.[4] The cabinet agreed that the entry of German troops had to be resisted, and on November 18 the Generalissimo ordered a partial mobilization[5] that for several months more than doubled the number of troops under arms. The gesture was not ineffective, reinforcing the impression in Hitler's mind that movement into the peninsula would not be worth the effort and would encounter stout resistance from the Spanish, who he had once said were the only Latins who would fight.[6] Before the end of the month Spanish ambassadors around the world were informed of the government's firm decision to resist any foreign occupation of the Balearics—a move reportedly under consideration by both the Allies and the Axis. At the same time that measures were taken to safeguard Spain's territorial integrity, every effort was made to avoid incidents with the Anglo-American forces in Morocco and to maintain German good will by expediting the shipment of strategic raw materials and doing nothing to curb Nazi influence in the Spanish press.

During the autumn of 1942 German schemes to engineer political change in Spain continued. The main contact was not the ambassador, von Stohrer, who was reserved for official diplomatic activities, but the Nazi party official and embassy counsellor Erich Gardemann. Since the beginning of the year the latter had held conversations with Arrese and Manuel

3. The German command developed two different contingency plans to counter a possible British (and later Anglo-American) landing in the Iberian peninsula. The first, Operation Isabella, prepared in May 1941, was the more ambitious, aimed not merely at driving any British forces out of the peninsula but at the capture of Gibraltar as well. One year later this was replaced by Operation Ilona, more modest in scope, aimed simply at countering an Anglo-American invasion and holding the north Spanish ports to protect the German position in France. (The code name changed from Ilona to Gisela in September 1942 following a security leak.) The fullest discussion of these plans will be found in Burdick, *Germany's Military Strategy*, 131–88.

4. Information reaching the Germans had it that the three leading Germanophiles were also supported by Blas Pérez and Primo de Rivera (Ruhl, *Spanien*, 189), while some Spanish commentators have recently suggested that they even recommended direct entry into the war, but reliable information is lacking.

5. *BOE*, Nov. 18, 1942.

6. Although Hitler's interest in moving troops into Spain peaked early in 1943 and did not die until April of that year.

Valdés, FET vicesecretary and Arrese's most trusted collaborator, who told him that what was needed for a fundamental change in Spain was German military assistance and another big German victory. Gardemann hoped to use Muñoz Grandes, Arrese, and Yagüe (in provincial exile since 1940) to convince Franco to change his policy and reorganize his cabinet, or failing that, to replace him with a pro-German general.[7] An effort to overthrow Franco directly was not likely to prosper, however, for the Army remained loyal, and no one else had major support in either the military or the public at large. Moreover, the Germans suspected that Arrese might be fundamentally faithful to Franco and merely playing a game with them. One hope was that upon his return from Russia, Muñoz Grandes could resume his old post as secretary of the FET, where he could mobilize the Falangists while the new pro-German army minister, Asensio, mobilized military opinion.

Yet by the time of the government change in September, Hitler himself had grown skeptical of any major change in Madrid. He was gratified by the ouster of Serrano Súñer but dismissed schemes of replacing Franco as "phantasy."[8] Yagüe had even told a German representative that the only appropriate change at this juncture would be in the direction of the monarchy.[9] He was therefore dropped by the Germans after Franco cleverly neutralized him by appointing him on November 12 commander of the Tenth Army Corps in Melilla, a region in which the high commissioner (Orgaz) and other top military staff were considered rather Anglophile and where the only adjacent military contacts were with the Allies.[10] This appointment in turn had the typically Francoist countereffect of checking any gesture of dissidence from the monarchist Orgaz, who protested the new assignment and at first attempted to resign.

During the final weeks of 1942 Franco made it clear that the Anglo-American offensive in the west Mediterranean had not changed his political orientation, engaging in what would be the last general round of publicly fascistic remarks. On the first anniversary of Pearl Harbor, he declared to the National Council of the FET: "We are witnessing the end of one era and the beginning of another. The liberal world is going under, victim of the cancer of its errors, and with it is collapsing commercial imperialism and finance capitalism with its millions of unemployed. . . ." After praising Fascist Italy and Nazi Germany, he insisted, "The historical destiny of our era will be realized either by the barbarous formula of Bolshevist totalitarianism or by the patriotic and spiritual one offered by Spain or by any other formula of the fascist peoples. . . . Therefore those

7. Ruhl, *Spanien*, 174–80.
8. Ibid., 119.
9. Ibid., 182.
10. See Garriga, *Yagüe*, 222–24.

who dream of the establishment of demoliberal systems in western Europe deceive themselves. . . ." [11]

Franco also agreed to let Arrese make the trip to Berlin that the Germans had been requesting for some time, but in return insisted that Muñoz Grandes—whose departure had been delayed for six months by Hitler—come back to Spain at once, nominally in order to serve as further liaison between Madrid and Berlin. Muñoz Grandes was only the second foreign officer to be decorated with the Eichenlaub zum Ritterkreuz of the Iron Cross, but when Hitler said goodbye to the hard-bitten Blue Division commander whom he admired, he realistically requested no more than that Muñoz Grandes try to see that Spain defend itself vigorously against any Allied invasion. [12] When Muñoz Grandes arrived in Madrid on December 17, he was met by the entire government and subsequently awarded the Palma de Plata, the Falange's highest decoration (the first such concession since the death of José Antonio), and promoted to lieutenant general, highest rank in the Spanish Army. But, according to Muñoz Grandes, Franco prudently left him without active assignment after he had turned down Franco's offer of a cabinet post or an ambassadorship. [13] His only other gratification was the purely verbal one of hearing Franco declare to the Escuela Superior de Guerra on the nineteenth that "the fate and . . . future of Spain are closely bound to German victory," [14] which Franco was still convinced would come.

In late December Raeder, the German naval chief of staff, insisted in Berlin that Germany must guarantee for itself the full security of the Iberian peninsula in order to achieve victory in the submarine war, and Muñoz Grandes and Asensio continued to speak encouraging words to German contacts, saying they were doing everything possible to convince Franco to alter his policy and enter the war. [15] It is doubtful that by the beginning of 1943 the Spanish military hierarchy harbored any eagerness for that prospect, however. The opinion of most commanders was quite the opposite, and as the full dimensions of Stalingrad started to unfold, the image of a German defeat began to form in the minds of some.

Gómez Jordana slowly but resolutely steered Spanish diplomacy toward a more detached and neutral course, showing considerable firmness and self-confidence in his administration of the Foreign Ministry, a deter-

11. *Palabras del Caudillo*, 523–27. Franco's official published version obviously aligned Spain clearly with the fascistic powers, but the phrase about the Spanish formula "or by any other formula of the fascist peoples" ("o por cualquiera otra de los pueblos fascistas") is often rendered in secondary works as "Spain and any other of the fascist peoples" ("España y cualquier otro de los pueblos fascistas").

12. Ibid., 190–97. Cf. Garriga, *La España de Franco*, 2:38–45.

13. Kleinfeld and Tambs, *Hitler's Spanish Legion*, 229–35.

14. *Informaciones*, Dec. 19, 1942, quoted ibid., 234.

15. Ibid., 236–37.

General Gómez Jordana, twice Foreign Minister, with Esteban Bilbao, the first president of the Cortes, in 1940

mination that he backed up on more than one occasion by offering to resign. Franco was increasingly willing to be convinced, however, and a
change of attitude was further encouraged by his subsecretary, Carrero
Blanco, a neutralist whose personal influence with Franco on this and
other issues was growing steadily. Carrero was apparently the author of an
interesting memo written shortly before the end of 1942 which declared
that Germany might eventually suffer "a defeat like that of 1918." Though
he characteristically blamed the war in part on "the fundamental Jewish
design of annihilating Europe," he observed that rather than face final
defeat Germany would probably "make an agreement with Russia, with
whom she has no fundamental religious or spiritual differences,"[16] a position that indicated that he had no illusions about the final tendencies of
Hitlerian philosophy.

One product of this altered perspective was a Spanish diplomatic campaign in January–February 1943 which attempted to form an understanding among the remaining neutrals (Sweden, Switzerland, and Ireland) to
help mediate a negotiated peace between the Allies and Germany that
would save Europe from Bolshevism. Spanish policy also envisioned
closer rapport among the remaining Catholic states in association with the
Vatican as a new alternate polarity of European diplomacy. Franco made a
public appeal for peace in speeches delivered in Andalusia early in May,
but Sweden and Switzerland refused to cooperate, while both Britain and
Germany completely rejected such a prospect. Only Italy, with the possible assistance of the Vatican, might have been interested.[17]

Henceforth Franco would expound his theory of the "three wars" underway and of Spain's distinct attitude toward each: neutral in the conflict
between the Allies and Germany, favoring Germany in its struggle with
the Soviet Union, and favoring the Allies in the Far Eastern struggle
against Japan. Franco was obviously veering towards genuine neutrality.
The neo-Falangist commerce minister, Demetrio Carceller, earlier pro-
German, had for some months been discreetly trying to realign Spanish
commercial and economic interests in accord with those of Britain and the
United States. In general, food supplies and economic conditions improved, and by the beginning of 1943 the period of the most intense suffering for much of the Spanish population was ending.

German pressure meanwhile increased once again, and on January 7,
the day after Franco launched his mediation proposal, a new Spanish ar-

16. Quoted in *Franco y Mussolini*, 181.
17. This was called Plan D after the director general of foreign policy in the Foreign Ministry, José Ma. Doussinague. See Doussinague, *España*, 139–70; Gallo, *Histoire*, 1:142–48;
and Marquina Barrio, 315–30. A broader analysis is offered in an unpublished paper by
Pablo Barroso, "España, Estados Unidos y las iniciativas de paz durante la II Guerra mundial," presented at the Primer Congreso Hispano-Luso-Norteamericano de Historia, Madrid, June 12, 1958.

maments commission left for Berlin with a shopping list of military items theoretically necessary for entrance into the war. Soon afterward, Arrese and a major Falangist retinue also departed for the German capital, where the Falangist secretary had an agreeable but nonetheless distant conversation with Hitler on the nineteenth. Arrese showed no interest in talking real policy as distinct from rhetorical anticommunism, while Hitler was annoyed that Franco's accompanying letter did not respond to his request for a clear commitment to resist the Allies militarily should they move into Spain.[18] The new ambassador in Madrid, von Moltke, insisted that at the very least the Spanish government sign a secret protocol pledging to resist forcibly any Allied incursion. Franco agreed to do so on February 12 provided that Germany guarantee new materiel, and Hitler indicated willingness to receive yet another Spanish commission, provided that it was top-level, to arrange such assistance. For this assignment Franco chose Carlos Martínez de Campos, one of his best-trained generals and a monarchist at odds with the pro-German elements. As it turned out, Hitler provided very little in the way of military assistance but managed to put on such a convincing display of German arms that the originally skeptical Martínez de Campos returned to tell Franco that Germany would yet win the war.[19]

This somewhat surprised Franco, who for the first time was beginning to conclude the opposite. Germany's declining fortunes apparently made it easier to keep potential dissidents in line within the regime. Franco finally came to a sort of understanding with Muñoz Grandes, whom he named head of his Casa Militar (personal military staff) on March 3. This kept him away from the command of troops and directly under Franco's thumb. Though the former Blue Division commander would continue to correspond with Berlin, his pro-German ardor had cooled and he had come to accept *hábil prudencia*. German maneuvering with members of the regime, always lacking in conherence, had come to a standstill.

Political Redefinitions

Changing political nuances progressively reflected the altered balance of the war. Franco never had difficulty restating his basic principles independent of an explicitly fascist context, and he had early mastered the art of altering his appeal to fit his audience. Personal visits to key regions continued at varying rhythms throughout the war years, and in a series of short speeches delivered in January 1942 during a brief tour of Catalonia—then the opposition region par excellence—he had refashioned

18. Ruhl, *Spanien*, 197–209; Garriga, *España de Franco*, 2:7–31.
19. According to an interview with Serrano Súñer in June, 1974, cited in Kleinfeld and Tambs, *Hitler's Spanish Legion*, 313, 398.

some of his main themes. Franco's chief appeal was never to fascist doctrine in general or Falangism in particular, but to a modernized version of the traditional Spanish ideology. In Catalonia he had invoked an idealized traditional society—not a fascist culture of "new men"—composed of "hidalgos" who lamentably had been turned into "proletarians" by "liberal democracy" and its accompanying liberal capitalism. All preceding regimes of the nineteenth and twentieth centuries, save that of Primo de Rivera, had contributed to this debacle. Only a modernized Catholic traditionalism as represented by the institutions and culture of his regime could redeem the situation, but this also required technical ability and should reflect an appropriate eclecticism. "We need competent ministers with administrative ability, and technical experts to lift the nation from the position to which it has sunk."[20] In this enterprise there was room for all, and especially for "Catalan producers and entrepreneurs who have an [economic] sensibility superior to that of the rest of the nation."[21]

For a leader without rhetorical ability, the thin-voiced Generalissimo was able to communicate some of his major points quite effectively. Though large portions of Spanish society remained unconvinced, his populist appeal was at one time or another aimed at every region and social group of the country.

During 1942 one notable effort was made to define the attributions of Franco when the (formerly Socialist) neo-Falangist law professor Francisco Javier Conde began to publish a series of articles in *Arriba*, later collected in the brochure *Contribución a la doctrina del Caudillaje*. Javier Conde, who had studied in Germany, applied the Weberian concept of charisma to establishing a theory of legitimacy. His lengthy explanation of the attributes of charismatic leadership in Franco's case emphasized that its source was not merely arbitrary power, that it was also based on a long record of achievement and popular support during the war, the meeting of manifold responsibilities and the upholding and incorporating of the legitimating qualities of traditional culture and institutions. This involved recognition by and affirmation of the national religion, the expression and acceptance of special qualities of leadership in time of crisis, and the development of a style and program to care for the needs of the people. In fact, during the 1940s when the Nationalists still retained a strong sense of unity and identity (despite their growing internal factional quarrels), this theorizing had some validity, especially in view of the absence of practical alternatives and the weakness of the state party mechanism itself, factors which Javier Conde, for obvious reasons, did not invoke.

The standard though ambiguous use of the term *totalitarian* in the regime[22] also began to undergo redefinition. This was initiated at the start of 1942, when Alfonso García Valdecasas, briefly cofounder of the Falange in 1933 and then the first director of the regime's Instituto de Estudios Políticos, published an article "Los Estados Totalitarios y el Estado español." He defined it in this way:

> In the original [Twenty-seven] Points of the Falange, the state is defined as a "*totalitarian instrument* at the service of the integrity of the Patria." It is, then, deliberately expressed that ours is an instrumental concept of the state. Every instrument is characterized as a medium for something, by a task which it serves.
> No instrument is justified in and of itself. It is worth while insofar as it fulfills the end for which it is destined. Therefore, the state is not for us an end in itself, nor can it find its justification in itself.
> . . . The state ought not to pursue ends nor undertake tasks that are not justified as a function of the integrity of the Patria. On the contrary, its forces are dispersed and wasted in improper enterprises, which, when attempted, aggravate the process of bureaucratization to which we have previously referred.
> . . . In order to justify itself in a positive sense, the state must act as an instrument for the achievement of ultimate moral values. . . .
> . . . Genuine Spanish thought refuses to recognize the state as the supreme value. This is the meaning of the polemical attitude of all classical Spanish thought against the *razón de Estado* enunciated by Machiavelli.[23]

At the Nazi-organized First Congress of European Youth, held at Vienna in 1942, parallel concepts were vigorously defended by the sizable Spanish delegation headed by the Falangists José Antonio de Elola and Pilar Primo de Rivera. It was careful to avoid identification with typically Nazi racist and paganizing statements, and insisted on amendments to the proceedings that recognized traditional Catholic morality, the importance of the family, and the secondary role of the state in education. Elola emphasized José Antonio's insistence that Spain had always exercised "the leadership of universal enterprises of the spirit."[24] Amid considerable tension, the Spanish delegation managed to gain establishment of a special congress commission on youth and the family, whose members were subsequently invited to Spain for the festival of the Immaculate Conception, converted by the Frente de Juventudes into the Día de la Madre, the new Spanish Mother's Day.[25]

This modification of its fascist character did not at all presage the eclipse of the FET, but it did further ideological evolution and redefinition. It

22. Confusion was sometimes expressed in the very title of hortatory publications such as Luis del Valle's *El Estado nacionalista totalitario autoritario* (Zaragoza, 1940).
23. *Revista de Estudios Políticos* 2:5 (Jan. 1942), 5–32.
24. Consejo Superior de Misiones, *Función espiritual de España en el Congreso de las Juventudes Europeas* (Madrid, 1943), 21.
25. According to Amando de Miguel, *Herencia del franquismo* (Madrid, 1976), 131–32. It is said that diplomatic intervention was necessary to enable the Falangists to remain at the Vienna Congress, which was publicly criticized by Elola after his return to Spain. Manuel Cantarero del Castillo, *Falange y socialismo* (Barcelona, 1973), 166.

was as if the Carlists rather than the Falangists were finally gaining the upper hand, ideologically if not in terms of personnel, for more clearly than ever before the Partido único was understood to function within a Catholic corporative context. The third National Council was appointed in November 1942 and its regular statutes issued the next month,[26] followed by a new Junta Política whose composition owed much to Arrese. The customary eclecticism prevailed, though care was taken to keep out the active monarchists.

In his National Council speech of December 7, 1942, which prophesied a future authoritarian Europe, Franco made it clear that he had no intention of modifying the authoritarian structure of the regime. He did, however, refer once more to the possible restoration of "the traditional system" (the monarchy), since, as he put it, "regimes and persons are to serve Spain, and not sacrifice the latter to the former."[27] This speech, totally inaccurate in forecasting the political future of postwar western Europe, was less inaccurate if viewed in the light of the general expansion of radical new authoritarian regimes throughout the world in the decades that followed. The tone and vocabulary would not be heard again after the winter of 1942–43.

As 1943 developed, Franco and the Falangist leadership under Arrese took steps to distinguish between Spanish Catholic authoritarianism and the central European regimes. In a major speech at Burgos on September 8, 1943, Arrese stressed that the Falange was an indigenous movement, not a foreign imitation or import. The ultimate goal of the FET and of the entire Franco movement was held to be not the construction of a totalitarian system but the integration of mankind into a universal community free of Bolshevism.[28] On September 23, instructions were issued forbidding anyone thenceforward to refer to the FET as a party; it was to be exclusively termed a movement, and on November 27, the FET's Delegación Nacional de Prensa dispatched categorical instructions to the party's press:

> The following must be kept in mind as a general norm: in no case and under no pretext shall foreign texts, doctrines, or examples be used to refer to the characteristics and political principles of our movement, whether in collaborative articles or editorial commentaries on other newspapers. The Spanish state is exclusively based on national political norms, principles, and philosophy. In no case will the comparison of our state with others that might appear similar be tolerated, and particularly the drawing of consequences from supposed foreign ideological adaptations for our Patria. The basis of our state must always be

26. *Fundamentos del Nuevo Estado* (Madrid, 1943), 37–46; *Recopilación sistemática de la legislación del Movimiento mayo 1937–diciembre 1943* (Madrid, 1944).
27. *Palabras del Caudillo*, 528–29.
28. Arrese, *Escritos y discursos* (Madrid, 1943), 219.

identified in the original text of its founders and in the doctrine established by the Caudillo.[29]

At a national meeting of Falangist *jefes provinciales* in mid-December, Arrese recommended some liberalization of the censorship and a reduction in certain government economic controls. He also urged a rapid end to prosecutions for political responsibilities dating from the Civil War, so as to achieve "national brotherhood" in "constructive tasks" of "deep community."[30]

While other declarations emphasized the function of "freedom" in Falangist doctrine,[31] Arrese made his primary theoretical effort in a brief work published in 1944 entitled *El Estado totalitario en el pensamiento de José Antonio,* which stressed the grounding of Falangist doctrine in Spanish history, tradition, and even theology (a partial but obviously not complete truth). The term totalitarian had been used persistently in the early epoch of the party and during the first six years of the regime, though primarily with respect to the goal of complete unity and the concentration of political power, not to advocate total control over all institutions.[32] Arrese did not dare a complete exegesis, since the term had sometimes been used loosely to compare Spain with Germany and Italy. Instead, he emphasized accurately that the term appeared infrequently in the political vocabulary of José Antonio and on those occasions had been used to mean not a state of total control but one of total involvement and service to all of society and all the national interest, and that it had been dropped altogether by 1935.

The chief institutional innovation accompanying this phase of redefinition was a new corporative parliament, called after Spanish custom the Cortes. Before 1943 the nominal structure of the Franco regime was the most purely arbitrary in the world. Stalin and Hitler went through the act of maintaining fictive and impotent parliaments, but not even that existed in Spain. On July 17, 1942, a government law first announced plans to

29. Díaz-Plaja, *España franquista,* 139–40.

30. Arrese, *Treinta años de política.* 470–72. Doussinague told the American embassy councillor that Franco, who had already spoken in a somewhat similar vein, had required Arrese to use such terms. Kleinfeld and Tambs, *Hitler's Spanish Legion,* 339.

31. E.g., Javier Martínez de Bedoya, "El sentido de la libertad en la doctrina falangista," *Revista de Estudios Políticos* 3:10 (July–Aug. 1943), 313–34.

32. The FET's *Notas sobre la Falange como partido único (Cuadernos de orientación política)* correctly distinguished between the Italian, German, and Soviet regimes respectively in terms of the subordination of the party to the state, identification of the party with the state, and subordination of the state to the party. It emphasized that the Spanish system was totalitarian with respect to the political power of the state, but by implication suggested that no broader structural totalitarianism was aimed at, which was obviously the case. It also declared that the Spanish system was based on "military unity" but had no "warlike objectives," which again distinguished it from other systems.

institute a corporative Cortes, a sort of reincarnation of Primo de Rivera's Asamblea Nacional on a permanent basis. In this, as in all other institutional changes, the regime made haste slowly. Arrese had drawn up the original project, which was further polished by Serrano Súñer. The function of the Cortes would be more technical than political. It would provide a covering of legitimization and support to the regime, but it would have the right to pass on legislation introduced by the government.

The convening of the Cortes was not announced until February 7, 1943, in the immediate aftermath of Stalingrad. Of the 424 seats in the first cortes, 126 were allocated to members of the National Council of the FET and other Falangist appointees, 141 to officials of the syndical system (also nominally Falangist), and 102 to mayors of the leading cities. Ex officio members included all cabinet ministers, the heads of leading state institutions such as the Supreme Court, and rectors of all Spanish universities (themselves government appointees under the Spanish system). Finally, 7 representatives were to be chosen by professional organizations, and 50 were designated personally by the Caudillo. In the first Cortes those chosen for the latter category were primarily conservative monarchists, to balance off the heavy FET and syndical representation.[33] Franco's undersecretary Carrero and a moderate Falangist were made vice-presidents of the new Cortes under the presidency of the Carlist Esteban Bilbao. Virtually all members were state appointees[34]; a more docile assembly could scarcely have been conceived.

Franco's speech at the initial session of March 17, 1943, hailed it as the beginning of an "institutional system of full juridical development." Comparing it with the old liberal parliaments, Franco declared, "We are installing an enlightened and paternal system of government [entirely free of] the foreignizing and Jeremiac labors of the liberals. . . . We seek liberty, but with order." He urged the *procuradores* (as members were called, restoring the terminology of the preliberal Antiguo Régimen) to "collaborate" with the government, which he said "does not presume to be infallible in its proposals," indicating that "disagreement" would also be welcomed,[35] a verbal show of objectivity that led astray none of the controlled membership. The first Cortes would show itself totally subservient to the government in every way.

33. *BOE,* July 19, 1942, in *Fundamentos del Nuevo Estado* (Madrid, 1943), 47–52.
34. See Rafael Bañón Martínez, *Poder de la burocracia y Cortes franquistas 1943–1971* (Madrid, 1978). Bañón Martínez found that over the life of the nine Cortes of Franco nearly one-third the seats, or 1,776 of approximately 5,400, were awarded to members of the state central administration, and nearly a fifth (933) under one guise or another to military officers. There was considerable continuity of membership, the same person commonly holding a seat through three or four different Cortes.
35. *Discursos y mensajes de S. E. el Jefe del Estado a las Cortes españolas 1943–1961* (Madrid, 1961), 9–17.

The Monarchist Offensive of 1943

The change in the balance of the war, together with the first sign of reform in the regime, provided direct encouragement to monarchists to
work toward an immediate restoration, arguably the logical replacement
for Franco in terms acceptable to Allied opinion. This tactic did not emerge
until 1942, for the royal family had strongly supported the Nationalist
cause both financially and politically during its early years.[36] The heir to
the throne, Don Juan, had twice presented himself as a military volunteer, first for the Nationalist Army in the rebel zone during the initial
weeks of the conflict and then, in writing several months later, for service
aboard the new Nationalist cruiser *Baleares* (which would have taken advantage of his early training with the British Navy). The Nationalist command had refused his services on both occasions, to avoid compromising
their own cause by such an association with the relatively unpopular monarchy and to avoid risking the life of the heir to the throne (the *Baleares*,
in fact, was sunk in 1938). During the first part of the European war Don
Juan had been friendly to the Axis (Alfonso XIII residing in Rome until his
death in 1941), and various intermediaries had sounded out German support for a monarchist restoration in Spain oriented toward the New
Order.[37]

The conversion of Don Juan to the cause of constitutional monarchy
and western democracy was thus a product of changing circumstances,
encouraged further by the geopolitical leanings of the queen mother, Victoria Eugenia, English in origin and a strong supporter of the Allied
cause. During 1942 his advisers and supporters swung heavily toward the
Allies, and one group even made plans with the British to establish a monarchist resistance government in the Canaries should Hitler invade the
peninsula. From his residence in Lausanne he began to mark a new line
immediately after the Allied landing in northwest Africa, declaring that
the future government of Spain "depended on the will of the Spanish
people."[38] On March 8, 1943, Don Juan wrote to Franco for the first time
in nearly a year, declaring that the continuation of Franco's "provisional
regime" was exposing Spain to grave risks and urging him to move quickly
toward restoration.[39] Monarchist supporters stepped up their activity,
creating excitement over a possibly imminent change of institutions.

36. The first biography of Don Juan to appear in Nationalist Spain, Francisco Bonmatí de
Codecido's *El Príncipe don Juan de España*, published in 1938, presented him as the logical
successor to the Nationalist movement, in values and goals.

37. Ruhl, *passim;* and Pedro Sainz Rodríguez, *Testimonio y recuerdos* (Barcelona, 1978),
279.

38. *Journal de Genève*, Nov. 11, 1942.

39. The text is given in López Rodó, *Larga marcha*, 34–35, 508–9.

Franco's own political orientation was ultimately monarchist, though quite circumstantially so, and he always held out the hope of an eventual restoration without directly committing himself to it. His subsecretary, Carrero Blanco, who had now replaced Serrano as his chief advisor, had prepared a memorandum for him soon after the last change of government, recommending categorically, "It is evident that the future of Spain . . . lies in a monarchy of the traditional [i.e., not constitutional] type. . . . If Spain is eventually to become a monarchy—which Your Excellency ought to constitute, since Spain remains in your hands as the fruit of victory—it must count on the king, and it is undeniable that, despite all the maneuvers of Carlists, there is no other [legitimate] king but Don Juan." [40] The key here, obviously, lay in the *instauración*, as the *Accion Española* theorists would have said, of a traditional monarchy as direct successor of the regime, exclusively dependent on the will and timing of Franco.

Franco thus waited two and a half months before replying to Don Juan on May 27 that his government was not simply transitory but represented an organized movement that was already in place and must obey its own rhythms, which only Franco was in a position to interpret. He revealed that he did consider the Pretender his potential successor, but only so long as the monarchy accepted the "standards of the Movement," which was not a political party but the basis of national unity "founded on eternal and incontrovertible principles." [41] Three days later the government announced the retirement from military service of one of the most active monarchists among the military, Galarza, who had returned to political conspiracy after his ouster as minister of the interior the preceding September. This followed by five months Franco's removal of Aranda, the most inveterate conspirator of all, from his post as head of the Escuela Superior de Guerra the preceding December. [42]

The Generalissimo sought to further solidify the armed forces behind him by accelerating the promotion of some of the younger generals who had won their spurs in the Civil War. The younger commanders were the

40. Ibid., 31–33.

41. Ibid., 511–15.

42. According to Marquina Barrio, Aranda told informants that his political stock rose considerably after the September 1942 cabinet change, but that he refused to accept any compromise with Franco other than the presidency of government and suppression of the FET. Whether or not that was so, Franco evidently decided there was no way to buy off or adequately compromise Aranda and so placed him on the *disponible* list without assignment, reducing his effectiveness as conspirator.

To stem further discontent among the monarchist military, Franco replaced Aranda with Kindelán (cf. the latter's *La verdad*, 55–57), despite a direct blast from Kindelán in the Consejo Superior del Ejército over a year earlier (Dec. 15, 1941), when he had demanded a drastic change in government personnel and policy. (Fernández, *Tensiones*, 66). This had the advantage of removing Kindelán from the potentially more influential post of captain general of Barcelona, which Franco filled with one of his most *incondicional* followers, Moscardó, even more tilting the balance in military command away from the monarchists.

most ardent supporters of the Nationalist cause and the regime *tout court* (though not of the FET, now relabeled the Movement) and were the least influenced by the monarchism of many of the senior generals. While Franco had removed Yagüe and several of the most pro-German commanders in 1940 to avoid their pressure and maintain political balance, by the same token, as the tide began to swing in favor of the Allies and monarchist militants, he relied more on pro-German and pro-Falangist generals such as Asensio, Yagüe, and Muñoz Grandes. This was symbolized by a major public ceremony at the Alcázar of Toledo on June 5 arranged by Franco's former classmates at the old military academy to honor the thirty-fifth anniversary of his entrance. The ceremony was accompanied by a strong speech by Yagüe pledging continued unwavering military support of the Caudillo.[43]

Nonetheless, soon afterwards Franco received the most direct challenge from inside the regime that he had yet faced, when twenty-seven monarchist procuradores of the new Cortes directly petitioned him to complete the "definition and ordering of the fundamental institutions of the state" by restoring the monarchy, which would be the best safeguard for the neutrality and integrity of Spain.[44] Among the signatories were sometime leading Falangists such as García Valdecasas and Gamero del Castillo, as well as one lieutenant general. Franco as usual failed to make any formal response, though on June 26 six of the signatories who also happened to be members of the National Council of the FET (such as Gamero and Valdecasas) lost their seats on the council. The only other formal reprisal was the exile to La Palma in the Canaries of a monarchist aristocrat whom Franco held most responsible for the petition, the Conde de los Andes. Meanwhile, to divide the monarchists and confuse the issue, the FET leadership subsidized a diversionary campaign on behalf of a secondary Carlist pretender descended through the female line from Don Carlos "VII."[45]

The overthrow of Mussolini in July, followed by Italy's withdrawal from the war less than two months later, had considerable impact in Spanish

43. Cf. Garriga, *Yagüe*, 229–30.
44. The full text is in López Rodó, *Larga marcha*, 37–38.
45. This was the nominally Austrian Archduke Carlos de Habsburgo-Lorena, son of the daughter of Carlos "VII" (the last Carlist candidate in the male line, Don Alfonso Carlos, killed in an accident in 1936). On the rival dynasty and conflicting legitimacies, see Jesús Pabón, *La otra legitimidad* (Madrid, 1945); Román Oyarzun, *Historia del carlismo* (Bilbao, 1939), 578–80; and Guy Coutant de Saisseval, *Les maisons imperiales et royales d'Europe* (Paris, 1966), 189–241, 387–411.

The original proponent of this gambit, a Carlist lawyer in Valencia, later wrote, "A hundred years of the government of Franco, with all the corruption of its administration, is preferable to one year of Don Juan, which would be the swift bridge to communism." Carmelo Paulo y Bondía to the author, March 2, 1959. See also Josep Carles Clemente, "El invento de 'Carlos VIII,'" in Diario 16, *Historia del franquismo*, 253.

political circles. This was compounded by the effect of a lengthy letter from the personal secretary of the current ambassador in Rome, Fernández Cuesta, to friends in Madrid, describing scenes of disorder in the Italian capital, attacks on Fascists and on party headquarters, and concluding with an analogy to potentially similar consequences in Madrid. This missive was widely copied and circulated throughout the capital among Falangist and government personnel. The Italian Fascist regime, since 1936 the chief foreign model for the new Spanish government, suddenly became the primary foreign model to avoid. Mussolini's successors hoped to use Spain's good offices and diplomatic channels to expedite negotiations with the Allies, but Franco and Jordana largely refused assistance, fearing to have Spain in any way involved in the Italian Fascist debacle. Mussolini's subsequent Salò Republic, organized as a German puppet in occupied northern Italy, was denied official recognition. Franco dispatched only a semiofficial personal representative, similar in status to the Spanish representative attached to De Gaulle's Free French government in London, and major Italian figures who sought Spanish passports and the opportunity to flee to Spain were almost always denied assistance.[46]

On August 2, Don Juan dispatched a virtual ultimatum to Franco by telegram, to which the Generalissimo replied several days later in terms of restraint yet absolute firmness, urging the Pretender to do nothing at that grave juncture to lessen Spanish unity or weaken the country abroad.[47] One week later the principal Carlist leader in Spain, Manuel Fal Conde, transmitted to Franco a letter signed by seventeen of the most influential Carlists reminding him that the monarchy for which monarchists in the Nationalist forces had fought during the Civil War was the traditional institution, not a liberal monarchy.[48] This welcome encouragement only strengthened what had become a posture of grim determination in the Generalissimo.

The only institution capable of forcing a change in government at this point was the one which had raised Franco to supreme power in the first place—the military. The political dissatisfaction of many senior commanders, so often near the surface the past three years, finally took concrete form in a letter signed by seven of the twelve lieutenant generals on September 8 and delivered to Franco three days later by the army minister, Asensio. It read:

> Excellency,
>   The high commanders of the Army are aware that it is the only organic reserve on which Spain can rely to subdue the grave crises that destiny may allot

46. The principal discussion will be found in *Franco y Mussolini*, 209–40. Fernández Cuesta presents his own anodyne account in his *Testimonio, recuerdos y reflexiones* (Madrid, 1985), 205–29.
47. López Rodó, *Larga marcha*, 41–42, 515–16.
48. *FF*, 3:427–28.

her in the near future. These authorities, wishing to give no excuse to enemies domestic or foreign by allowing them to think the Army's unity weakened or its discipline diminished, made certain that no subordinate ranks took part in the exchange of views to which patriotism obliged them. For that same reason, they employed the most discreet and respectful means to make known their concern to their only senior commander in the Army, doing so with affectionate sincerity, in their own names, and without claiming the representation of the entire armed forces, which was neither requested nor granted.

They are companions in arms who come to share their worry and concern with him who has achieved by his toil and his own merit the highest rank in the Armies of Land, Sea, and Air, won in a difficult and victorious war; the same who . . . placed in your hands seven years ago in the Salamanca airdrome the supreme powers of military command and of the state.

On that occasion, the correctness of our decision was crowned with glory by complete and magnificent victory, and the exclusive act of will of certain generals was transformed into national agreement by the unanimous assent, tacit or enthusiastic, of the people, to such a degree that prolongation of the mandate beyond the term foreseen was legitimate.

We hope that the discretion which then accompanied us has not abandoned us today as we ask our Generalissimo, with all loyalty, respect, and affection, if he does not think, as do we, that the moment has arrived to give Spain back a regime as fondly remembered by himself as by us; one that can uphold the state with the bulwarks of unity, tradition, and prestige inherent in the monarchical formula. The hour seems propitious to delay no longer the restoration of this authentically Spanish form of government, which created the grandeur of Spain and from which she departed to imitate foreign models. The Army will unanimously support Your Excellency's decision and stand ready to repress any attempt at internal disturbance and opposition, either open or covert, without the slightest fear of the Communist menace . . . or of foreign interference.

This, Your Excellency, is the request that your old comrades in arms and respectful subordinates address with the strictest discipline and most sincere loyalty to the Generalissimo of the Spanish armed forces and Chief of State.[49]

Though relatively obsequious in tone—a much harsher draft having been rejected by most of the signatories[50]—this was the only time in the thirty-nine years of the regime that a majority of Franco's senior generals asked him to resign. The five lieutenant generals who did not sign were Jordana, Vigón, Muñoz Grandes, Moscardó, and Serrador. The first two abstained because they were cabinet ministers but declared themselves in agreement with the letter. Queipo de Llano, who also supported it, had

---

49. The text was first made available to me by Eugenio Vegas Latapié in 1963.

50. The rejected version declared, "The political regime installed in Spain by the express decision of Your Excellency has officially defined itself as a totalitarian regime in the service of Falangist ideology. . . . This error is of such profound degree and proportions that its ultimate fate is tied to the adverse result of the war. . . . Therefore, to honor the truth we tell Your Excellency in this critical hour that the road you have undertaken is wrong and is not shared by the majority of Spaniards who initiated the National Rebellion of the Eighteenth of July, whose spirit has been totally deformed." It ended by demanding the "urgent and ABSOLUTE SUPPRESSION of the totalitarian regime and the NORMAL reestablishment of our traditional Catholic monarchy." Quoted in Tusell, *Franco y Mussolini*, 223.

been placed on the reserve list the preceding February, though only sixty-six years of age.

Though not explicitly stated, what the signatories seem to have had in mind was a Badoglio style of government initially, to carry out the preliminary moves away from fascism. It would perhaps have been led by Don Juan's second cousin and personal representative in Spain, Don Alfonso de Orleáns (an Air Force general), together with Kindelán and the archbishop of Valladolid, with the task of reforming the government drastically, disbanding the FET, and preparing for local elections to be followed by a legitimizing plebiscite on the monarchy.[51]

Franco demanded of Asensio absolute silence about the letter in his relations with the rest of the Army, to which the latter agreed. The Generalissimo promised simply that he would speak to the signatories himself in order to clarify the situation. They had made the mistake of not demanding a collective meeting, and Franco prepared to stand pat, while later speaking to some of them one or two at a time. Within the armed forces, he relied especially upon senior commanders who had not signed the letter, and upon stronger personal support among younger officers who were not Falangist in sympathies but retained great loyalty to the Caudillo as their victorious leader. Among the commanders on whom he could rely especially were Muñoz Grandes (who had been too committed to fascism to support the monarchists), García Valiño, the comparatively young head of the Supreme General Staff, Yagüe, the captain-general of Burgos, and Moscardó, captain-general of Barcelona.

At least two supporters of the letter changed their minds. Saliquet, the captain-general of Madrid, announced after talking later with Franco that he had made a mistake. As the weeks passed, Asensio also began to waver, particularly after an incident at the opening of the fall course at the Superior War College (Escuela Superior de Guerra) where Franco's appearance prompted prolonged ovations from a group of eighty junior officers and fifty sergeants.[52]

During late September and October the Generalissimo talked to a number of senior commanders, explaining patiently that though an appropriate restoration of the monarchy was the ultimate goal, the present situation was too dangerous both internationally and domestically to risk any immediate changes. Moreover, he told them that it was by no means certain that Germany would lose the war (for he had been informed of German "secret weapons"), and that in any event the Allies had assured him that they would not move against the Spanish government.[53] On October 1 he promoted Yagüe (who had proven fully faithful in the year since

51. According to Marquina Barrio.
52. Tusell, *Franco y Mussolini*, 224–26.
53. Créac'h, *Le Coeur*, 207–8.

he had been restored to command) and José Monasterio to the rank of lieutenant general. Monasterio was the only major general to have signed the collective letter, but he had almost immediately dissociated himself from it. This completely balanced the senior hierarchy, from Franco's point of view, for it broadened the top rank until there were at least as many opponents as proponents of monarchist pressure. The two most committed monarchists in the military at this juncture were Kindelán and Orgaz, but the former lacked an active command and top rank. Orgaz, the high commissioner of Spanish Morocco, talked somewhat loosely of trying to organize a coup from Morocco if all else failed, but such a plan never took concrete form.[54]

The final round in this opening phase of what would become a decades-long drama between Franco and the Pretender took place during the winter of 1944. Spanish intelligence intercepted a letter from Don Juan to his supporters indicating that he might be on the verge of a public announcement breaking all ties with the regime. Therefore, on January 6, 1944—the same day that Asensio, the army minister, organized a public ceremony of personal loyalty to Franco by the Army—Franco wrote once more to the Pretender reiterating his own position. Don Juan replied on the twenty-fifth insisting that Franco misunderstood the situation.[55] This produced a virtual breakdown in personal relations, though it did not take public form.

On February 29, the Infante Alfonso de Orleáns called on Asensio to inform him that the Pretender was on the verge of a public manifesto which the Franco regime would be unable to resist. In a moment of panic, Asensio wrote to Franco urging him to negotiate with Don Juan and offering his own resignation should the Caudillo find his own formerly fascistic sympathies an embarrassment. Franco seems to have ignored the matter altogether.[56] When a group of conservative university professors soon afterwards signed a manifesto in support of monarchism, four of them, including García Valdecasas, were exiled to remote spots in the provinces.

Franco's tactics relied on his perfect calm and air of absolute self-assurance, his refusal to react, become excited, or make the slightest real concession on the one hand while convincing nominal monarchists and their hangers-on of his indispensability on the other. The monarchists above all represented the social and economic elite; none more than they feared a leap in the dark. The danger that any serious attempt to remove Franco might open the door to subversion of the Nationalist state, inter-

54. Cf. Fernández, *Tensiones*, 101–4.
55. López Rodó, *Larga marcha*, 520–23.
56. Suárez Fernández has found a draft of a reply by Franco merely indicating his agreement with Asensio that Allied pressure on wolfram shipments ought to be more firmly resisted. *FF*, 3:489–90.

nal disorder, or further fratricide was sufficient to dissuade nearly all in time of test.

Politics and Diplomacy in
The Final Phase of World War II

Whatever Franco's personal opinion, the Supreme General Staff (AEM) completed a study of the European military situation on May 19, 1943, which concluded that German defeat would be the most likely outcome, leaving the Soviet Union dominant in Europe.[57] Despite the lack of response, the Generalissimo had not given up hope for his peace initiative, and on June 1 the ambassador in Berlin was instructed to urge the German government to modify its policy with regard to the Catholic Church, partly in the hope that the peace initiative could still be a useful tactic.[58] Throughout the spring of 1943 Hitler continued to show concern about a possible Anglo-American landing in the peninsula, but when he pressed Franco in June for further talks to prepare Spanish resistance, the Caudillo replied quite correctly that no such threat existed and refused to engage in further conversations.[59]

Allied pressure mounted in mid-1943 as the strategic situation shifted. Washington, particularly, began to take a stronger line against Madrid and planned to reduce drastically the oil exports vital to Spain's economy, though Ambassador Hayes managed to counter this by a strong stand in favor of maintaining the volume of oil shipment.[60] Jordana in turn responded to the course of events by insisting on June 1 that the government must take steps to control the pro-German propaganda which dominated the Spanish press.[61] Similarly he made a protest to the American ambassador over the release of the new American propaganda newsreel "Inside Fascist Spain," rejecting the application of this adjective to the Spanish regime. Having already established sound credentials regarding his own good faith and friendship toward Spain, Hayes replied in a long letter which listed in detail all the features of the government similar to those of Italy and Germany, as well as its special policies favoring the latter. Subsequently, following a frank discussion between Hayes and Franco on July 29, the tone of the Spanish press toward the Allies began to change.[62]

57. *FF*, 3:375–76.
58. Ibid., 379.
59. On June 14 Hitler finally canceled all plans for a countermove into the Peninsula, restricting German plans to defense of the Pyrenees. Burdick, *Germany's Military Strategy*, 187.
60. Cf. Hayes, *Wartime Mission*, 139–48; and Beaulac, *Franco*, 183–85.
61. *FF*, 3:375–76.
62. Ibid., 379. Cf. Beaulac, *Franco*, 175–77; and Hayes, *Wartime Mission*, 152–54, who apparently confuses the dates.

The collapse of Italy in September was directly reported in the Spanish press, possibly because of Jordana's insistence, and shortly afterward Franco, wearing an admiral's uniform rather than Falangist costume, announced on October 1 the end of Spanish nonbelligerence and the adoption of a policy of "vigilant neutrality." One week later British troops moved into the Azores in accordance with an agreement negotiated shortly before with the Portuguese government.[63]

In mid-October, however, the Spanish government was embarrassed by the so-called Laurel incident, occasioned by a friendly reply from the Foreign Ministry to the announcement of the assumption of power by Japan's new puppet regime in the Philippines. This was not tantamount to official Spanish recognition of the Laurel government (as was proclaimed indiscriminately by Tokyo, Berlin, and Washington), and in fact the Spanish government was currently protesting to Japan the treatment of the Catholic Church and Spanish nationals under the Japanese occupation system.[64] Nonetheless, the United States and Britain vigorously denounced the Spanish response to Laurel's official telegram, prompting a note of explanation by Madrid which denied any political significance or official recognition in the act, labeling it a mere act of courtesy toward the "Philippine people."[65]

With both western allies taking a strong line toward Madrid, in November the American government asked for a complete embargo on Spanish shipment of wolfram to Germany, which Franco refused. The Blue Division, however, was officially disbanded that month, ending Franco's major collaboration with Nazi Germany. Altogether, 47,000 Spanish officers and men had served on the eastern front, suffering about 22,000 casualties (47 percent), of whom approximately 4,500 died.[66] They had fought well, and may have helped Franco buy time from Hitler. Some volunteered to remain, but Franco limited these to three battalions (2,133 officers and men), so that this residual Blue Legion (as it was informally known) would be relatively inconspicuous. It in turn was dissolved on March 15, 1944, and the remaining troops incorporated into the Waffen SS (together with scores of new volunteers directly from Spain). Curiously, the remnants of the Spanish battalion of the Waffen SS helped to defend a part of Berlin

63. On Portuguese wartime diplomacy, see Hugh Kay, *Salazar and Modern Portugal* (New York, 1970), 121–70. The place of the Azores and the Canaries in the general strategy and diplomacy of the war is treated briefly in Víctor Morales Lezcano, "Canarias y Azores, los archipiélagos codiciados," *Historia 16* 3:26 (June 1978), 17–24.

64. According to a declassified United States government intercept, cited in Beaulac, *Franco*, 188–89.

65. James W. Cortada, "Spain and the Second World War: The Laurel Incident," *JCH* 5:4 (April 1970), 65–75.

66. Kleinfeld and Tambs, *Hitler's Spanish Legion*, 346. Proctor, *La agonía*, 265, gives slightly lower figures. The enlistment and casualty statistics include more than one enlistment and more than one casualty in the cases of certain soldiers, and possibly balance out proportionately.

(including the Fuehrerbunker perimeter) during Hitler's final days at the close of April 1945.[67]

Spain's policy had shifted so much that on December 15, 1943, the new German ambassador in Madrid reported that he had personally protested to Franco a long series of measures by the Spanish government that were harmful to the Axis, ranging from withdrawal of the Blue Division to free passage of refugees, the internment of German submarine crews, and various restrictions on German shipping. Franco merely responded that these measures were required to maintain Spain's security vis-à-vis the Allies and to that extent were actually in Germany's interest.[68]

Franco would subsequently claim that the most difficult time of all came in January 1944, when the regime feared that the Allies might open their second front against Germany in Spain before entering France,[69] while all danger from Germany still had not ended.[70] On February 7 he changed the priorities in Spain's defense plan, to guard against an Allied coastal invasion rather than a trans-Pyrenean German onslaught.[71]

Early in 1944 Allied economic policy toward Spain became much harsher, with an announced total suspension of oil shipments until the export of strategic raw materials to Germany was ended. Franco at first was prepared to withstand this pressure, despite the suffering which it would cause the Spanish economy, and was strongly backed by the chief Falangist ministers, Arrese and Primo de Rivera, together with General Asensio, who had swung back to a more pro-German line once more. Though Jordana protested to Hayes (correctly) that this violated the Allies' solemn promise that Spain had "nothing to fear" from them, he insisted to Franco that their country's economic survival depended on coming to terms with the Allies, and after further threats to resign finally carried his point.[72] Two years of diplomatic and commercial tension with the western democracies over wolfram exports and other shipments to Germany were finally ended by an agreement completed on May 1, 1944. It stipulated that Spain would reserve nearly all its wolfram for the Allies, close the German consulate in Spanish-occupied Tangier, and expel German information agents in return for adequate shipments of petroleum and other ne-

67. Miguel Ezquerra Sánchez, *Lutei até ao fim* (Lisbon, 1947). A Spanish edition of this memoir was published only after Franco's death.

68. *DGFP*, vol. 13, no. 314, Dec. 15, 1943.

69. Franco, *Textos de doctrina política* (Madrid, 1961), 167.

70. This was apparently due to misinterpretation of a German military document obtained by Spanish intelligence. *FF*, 3:477. In fact, German strategic planning after June 1943 never varied from the basic concept of Operation Nürnberg, which replaced all earlier plans and only envisaged defense of the Pyrenees from Allied attack from the south. Burdick, *Germany's Military Strategy*, 189–98.

71. Doussinague, *España*, 307.

72. According to Jordana's diary for this period, cited in Tusell, *Franco y Mussolini*, 245–48.

cessities.[73] A hopeful sign for the Spanish regime was the tribute which Churchill paid to the benefits of Spanish neutrality in an address to the House of Commons on May 24.[74]

Though Spanish diplomacy had ceased months ago to make any further overt efforts at general mediation, it did effectively follow up a request from the Vatican that the two neutral officially Catholic states (Spain and Ireland) mediate to spare Rome from military destruction in the face of the Allied advance. Here Spanish efforts were of some benefit in gaining for Rome the status of an open city that was respected by both sides. Moreover, during these weeks several Spanish diplomats made modest efforts to cooperate with right-wing German resisters who sought a separate peace for a non-Nazi German government to succeed Hitler.[75]

Probably the most truly neutral aspect of Spanish policy had been the regime's treatment of refugees, especially Jews. Altogether, during the first part of the war some 30,000 Jews had received safe passage through Spain, and there is no indication of any Jew who reached Spanish soil being turned back to German authorities. Approximately 7,500 more may have passed through between 1942 and 1944, and during the later phases of the SS roundup in Hungary and the Balkans Spanish consular officials managed to provide protection (through citizenship status) to more than 3,200 additional Jews, many of the latter Sephardic.[76]

Nonetheless, minor collaboration with Nazi Germany continued, at least through the last months of 1944, and the generally pro-German tone of the Spanish press did not change fully until the end of the war. The publishing event of mid-1944 was a book by the Falangist journalist Ismael Herraiz, *Italia fuera de combate*, which described the preceding two years in Italy with great sympathy for Fascism and Mussolini's new Salò

73. On the wolfram controversy and the course of relations with the United States, see James W. Cortada, *United States-Spanish Relations: Wolfram and World War II* (Barcelona, 1971).

74. Spanish-British relations during the Civil War and throughout World War II were expedited by the adroit hand of Franco's ambassador in London, the Duque de Alba, whose monarchist sympathies stood him in good stead with the British while in no way diminishing his service to the regime. See Rafael Rodríguez-Moñino Soriano, *La misión diplomática del XVII Duque de Alba en la Embajada de España en Londres (1937–1945)* (Valencia, 1971). Kim Philby, Iberian subsection chief for British intelligence, had clandestine access to Alba's correspondence and reported him exceptionally well informed on British politics. *My Secret War* (London, 1969), 60–61.

75. Cf. Doussinague, *España*, 294–300; and Ruhl, *Spanien*, 211–17.

76. The principal study is Haim Avni, *Spain, the Jews, and Franco* (Philadelphia, 1982). See also Federico Ysart, *España y los judíos en la Segunda Guerra Mundial* (Barcelona, 1973); and Chaim Lipschitz, *Franco, Spain, the Jews, and the Holocaust* (New York, 1984). Years later Franco would recognize that the "great crimes" of Nazi Germany, as he put it, elicited "worldwide condemnation" and "with every reason evoked the world's horror when it learned of the slaughter after the war was over." Salgado-Araujo, *Conversaciones privadas*, 307–8. It might also be observed in passing that during the Civil War, the Spanish Nationalists had received support from part of the Jewish community in northern Morocco, yet another reason why Franco was more open-minded toward Jews than toward Masons.

Republic, quickly going through several printings. Despite the May 1944 agreement with the Allies, Spain continued to provide certain kinds of intelligence facilities to the Germans, and made possible the first transfer of the new wonder drug penicillin from the west to Germany in October 1944.[77] This has led more than one commentator to conclude that Franco continued to try to hedge his bets as long as possible. That is probably correct, but the minor assistance that continued to be lent to Germany throughout 1944 and the favorable commentary in the Spanish press even into 1945 may as accurately be seen simply as the continuing expression of the undeniable pro-German sympathies felt by so much of Spanish government, military, and press personnel.

The success of the Allied invasion of France and the subsequent breakthrough finally convinced Franco that German defeat was indeed inevitable and not likely to be avoided by last-minute wonder weapons. The Allies were then granted overflight rights in Spanish air space for antisubmarine patrols and were also allowed to evacuate casualties from France through Barcelona. In one sense there is no doubt that the regime had become sincere in seeking closer cooperation with the Allies, for, as Franco explained to the American ambassador on July 6, he looked to them to defend Europe from Communism after the defeat of Germany.[78]

The foreign minister Gómez Jordana, who had labored diligently and consistently to move Spanish policy to constructive neutrality,[79] died suddenly at the beginning of August from the complication of a recent hunting injury. He was replaced by José Félix de Lequerica, who for the past five years had been ambassador to France and had helped to negotiate the armistice of 1940. A sophisticated sometime representative of the Vizcayan financial and industrial oligarchy, Lequerica had become known in occupied France as "more German than the Germans," and according to Serrano Súñer, lunched almost daily with the Paris Gestapo chief. Suave, witty, and opportunistic, he eventually gained the reputation of being the most cynical politician in the regime,[80] despite the considerable competition for that distinction. Though Carrero Blanco thought him crassly unprincipled, Lequerica suited Franco, at least at the moment, because of his sheer pragmatism and because he had burned all other bridges and was totally bound to the regime. He could be depended upon to stand fast for the regime come what might, while cleverly making use of every rhetorical argument to defend Franco's policies. The new foreign minister

77. Pike, "Franco," 386–87, lists various facets of these activities.

78. Hayes, *Wartime Mission*, 242–45.

79. Hoare described him to the British Foreign Office as "an authentic Anglophile" who had always expressed personal belief in an Allied victory. Tusell, *Franco y Mussolini*, 258.

80. There is a vivid sketch of Lequerica in Morán, *Los españoles que dejaron de serlo*, 110–20. He is supposed to have said of Franco, "That fellow—Galician, sly, taciturn, and slippery—reminds me of the old chief of the Conservative Party, the Conde de Bugallal."

emphasized such topics as Spain's traditional "democracy," the regime's Catholic identity, Spain's newly rediscovered "American vocation"—something that had largely ended in 1825—and the need for a "policy of Atlantic cooperation."

On August 21, 1944, direct instructions were finally given the Spanish press to observe genuine neutrality in commenting on international and military developments, with the express exception of those referring to the Soviet Union. The press was ordered to favor the United States in its treatment of the Pacific war and to be more positive in transmitting news of Allied advances in the west than in reporting Soviet advances in the east. Soviet actions on behalf of the Allied war effort were to be referred to as Russian rather than Soviet, while Communist political activities would still be condemned.[81] Barcelona was converted into a free port for transshipment of Allied materiel, and eventually in February 1945 American transport planes were given regular use of Spanish facilities.

Heartened by Churchill's speech the previous May, Franco wrote a personal and rather smug letter to the British prime minister on October 18, 1944, about the importance of closer friendship between Britain and Spain to save western Europe from Communism.[82] In this he considerably overreached himself; Churchill did not reply for three months, and then only to rebuke him in discouraging terms, while a subsequent personal letter from Roosevelt was even harsher in tone. To Franco, this further demonstrated the degree of domination by Masonry in both London and Washington. The British ambassador meanwhile stressed to Lequerica that the absence of democracy in Spain constituted an almost insuperable barrier to better relations, to which the latter replied with unassailable logic that this surely could not be the case in view of the Allies' good relations with Stalin.[83]

The Generalissimo tried once more in November through an interview with the United Press in which he insisted that his regime had observed "complete neutrality" during the war and "had nothing to do with fascism" because "Spain could never be joined to other governments that did not hold to Catholicism as first principle." He insisted that "institutions which produce excellent results in other countries lead to the opposite results here, due to certain peculiarities of the Spanish temperament." Inaugurating what would become a standard line for the remainder of the long history of the regime, he insisted that despite the absence of direct national elections, his regime in its own way constituted a "true democ-

81. Díaz Plaja, *España franquista*, 155–57.
82. La Cierva, *Franco*, II, 392–93. He also repeated briefly an earlier protest made by Jordana the preceding June concerning direct Allied support for subversive acts by enemies of the regime within Spain, including armed insurgency and terrorism.
83. Doussinague, *España*, 338.

racy," an "organic democracy" based on religion, local institutions, syndicates, and the family.[84] Simultaneously, government spokesmen drew attention to recent low-level syndical elections that had taken place on October 21–22,[85] and municipal elections were announced for some unspecified future date. Franco had been preparing for the need to present a new facade for the regime at least as early as December 1943, when he first instructed the minister of justice to prepare the draft of a human rights law.[86]

At approximately the same time, the question of future policy toward Spain was being extensively discussed in London. Churchill argued forcefully against any plan to intervene overtly in Spanish affairs, observing that the Spanish regime had "done us much more good than harm in the war." He went on to declare:

> I am no more in agreement with the internal government of Russia than I am with that of Spain, but I would certainly rather live in Spain than Russia.
>   . . . You need not, I think, suppose that Franco's position will be weakened by our warnings. He and all those with him will never consent to be butchered by the Republicans, which is what would happen. . . .
>   . . . Already we are accused in many responsible quarters of handing over the Balkans and Central Europe to the Russians, and if we now lay hands on Spain, I am of opinion that we shall be making needless trouble for ourselves. . . . Should the Communists become masters of Spain we must expect the infection to spread very fast through both Italy and France. . . .
>   . . . I should of course be very glad to see a Monarchical and Democratic restoration, but once we have identified ourselves with the Communist side in Spain which, whatever you say, would be the effect of your policy, all our influence will be gone for a middle course.[87]

Though neither Britain nor the United States decided to intervene directly in Spain, their policies toward Madrid nonetheless continued to harden. During the first months of 1945 the British and American embassies lodged repeated protests over what they termed the failure of Spanish authorities to implement fully the agreement of May 1, 1944, and its spirit. They listed the names of eighty-three German intelligence agents allegedly still operating in Spain and protested the continued liberty of movement of those agents who had been detained, the continuation of Lufthansa flights from Barcelona, and the persistent shipment of supplies in twelve Spanish vessels to several German-occupied ports on the French coast that had held out long after the Allied breakthrough.[88] The regime finally broke relations with Japan in April 1945 after Japanese forces had

---

84. Díaz Plaja, *La España política del siglo XX* (Barcelona, 1972), 4:149–52.
85. These were the first local elections within the syndical system for *enlaces sindicales* (partly analogous to shop stewards).
86. *FF*, 3:453.
87. Quoted in Smyth, *Diplomacy*, 247–48.
88. A more complete list may be found in Antonio Marquina Barrio, "La consolidación del franquismo," *Historia universal: Siglo XX* (Madrid, 1984–85), 20:120.

invaded Spanish diplomatic facilities in Manila and carried out a small massacre, but the new Truman administration in Washington seemed if anything more antagonistic than Roosevelt's, and the Allies' Potsdam Conference of July 1945 realized the regime's fears. Against the wishes of Churchill, it formally recommended to the new United Nations then being organized that relations with the Spanish government be broken and support be transferred to "democratic forces" in order that Spain might have a regime of its own choice.[89]

The founding meeting of the international organization at San Francisco that summer marked a complete victory for the diplomacy of the new Junta Española de Liberación formed by the Republican and leftist parties in exile. The government of Mexico, Latin America's most resolute foe of the Franco regime, presented a motion whose terms, effectively excluding the Spanish government from membership, were accepted by acclamation.[90] On June 30, in a frenzy of democratic fervor, the government of Panama broke relations with Madrid, which braced for similar actions from other countries. The new postwar tide of the left in western Europe, which swept the Labourites into the government of Britain and would soon place a leftist coalition in power in France, established new administrations whose leaders had already sworn hostility to the Spanish regime. The Soviet Union, ever Franco's most unremitting foe, went one step further, launching a diplomatic campaign against the five neutral governments it accused of favoring Germany during the war—Spain, Portugal, Sweden, Switzerland, and Argentina—urging active measures against them.[91]

Spanish Policy in World War II: Summary and Evaluation

Though forever afterward Franco would maintain that the Spanish government had always been essentially neutral and had "never" (a word he subsequently used in several formal interviews) contemplated entering the war on the side of the Axis, the historical record of the regime's heavy tilt in that direction is both clear and abundant. Spain was relatively neutral only during the first (1939–40) and last (1944–45) phases of the war, when German victory was originally in doubt and later virtually impossible.

Yet of all the achievements of the regime, none has received as much

89. *España y ONU (1945–1946): La "cuestión española." Documentación básica, sistematizada y anotada*, ed. A. J. Lleonart and F. J. Castiella y Maíz et al. (Madrid, 1978), 42–45.

90. Robert P. Huff, "The Spanish Question before the United Nations" (Ph.D. diss., Stanford University, 1966), 2–22; Lleonart and Castiella, *España y ONU*, 30–33; and Roger E. Sanders, *Spain and the United Nations 1945–1950* (New York, 1966), which presents a general summary.

91. For the Soviet interpretation of Spanish policy during the later phases of the war, see Pozharskaya, *Tainaya diplomatiya*, 189–241.

praise as that of keeping Spain out of direct military involvement in the war. The Caudillo would go to his grave with the nominal distinction of having been the only European statesman to decisively outmaneuver Hitler in personal negotiations, all others having been dragged to death or destruction (or to massive losses and near destruction, as in the case of Stalin).

In fact, between July and October 1940 and to some extent at several points afterwards, Franco was perfectly ready to enter the conflict on Hitler's side as soon as Hitler fully met his price. In this, as in certain other aspects of foreign policy, Franco was sometimes neither *hábil* nor *prudente*. The decision not to bring Spain in was initially made by Hitler rather than Franco, for Hitler never judged the value of Spanish participation worth the potential cost of alienating Vichy France through the loss of a large part of its African territory. Needless to say, neither Hitler nor Mussolini viewed Franco as an equal; they considered him an "accidental" military dictator of a weak country who lacked the status or credentials of a major statesman. Spain was relegated to the southern, "Italian" sphere, and the Mussolini government, though sometimes generous to Spain, looked upon the Franco regime alternately as a sort of younger brother and as a semisatellite. It was reluctant to recruit Spanish entry too seriously for fear of raising up another rival in North Africa.

Though the right terms might have brought Spain into the war as late as the spring of 1942, Franco became increasingly committed to a policy of *attentisme* after October 1940. He was indeed more prudent and calculating than Mussolini, in part because Spain was distinctly weaker than Italy. He grasped that a militarily insignificant Spain could gain maximal terms from Hitler only before, not after, its entry into the war, and therefore he stubbornly held out for his price, a policy usually encouraged by Serrano Súñer. Moreover, there was much internal disagreement about the war within the regime. Falangist enthusiasm for the Axis was tempered by the increasing opposition of much of the military, who together with much of Catholic and Carlist opinion tended more toward neutrality and sometimes even a pro-Allied posture. Monarchists, including the Pretender, to some extent played both sides, but made a definitive switch to a pro-Allied strategy late in 1942. The two ministers who did most to keep Spain out of the war were the army minister Varela, leader of anti-Falangist (and therefore to some extent antifascist) opinion between 1939 and 1942, and the steady, reliable, clear-minded Gómez Jordana, foreign minister from September 1942 to August 1944.

Though its geographic location gave it a certain importance, the Iberian peninsula was considered a secondary strategic theater by both sides. For most of the war, both had relatively similar minimum goals vis-à-vis Spain: to deny the peninsula and its resources to the other side, keeping

Franco out of the war and as favorably inclined toward them as possible. The main exception was the temporary shift in German policy during late 1940 and early 1941, when Hitler sought to encourage direct Spanish entry in order to cripple Britain's strategic position. Neither he nor the Allied leaders ever seriously planned to undertake the formidable problems of geography, logistics, and combat involved in trying to occupy the peninsula, though both sides toyed with such projects between 1941 and 1943. Though Hitler held the dominant leverage during 1940–42, at no time was Franco able to merely ignore Allied interests, and the balance began to swing in their favor during 1943. Through varying combinations of economic and diplomatic pressure, Britain and the United States "managed" the Spanish regime with increasing success and by 1944 were able to pressure Franco more overtly and effectively than had Germany and Italy.

A fuller perspective on the problems facing the Spanish regime can be gained through comparison with the policy of traditionally neutral Sweden, which in certain respects accommodated German pressure to a greater degree than did Spain. Stockholm permitted the passage of German troops across its territory, for long shipped large amounts of strategic raw materials to Germany, and at times denied sanctuary to escaping Baltic Jews in desperate search of asylum, a policy in direct contrast to that of Madrid. Similarly, neutral Turkey signed a nonaggression pact with Germany, beneficial to the latter, only four days before Hitler invaded the Soviet Union, and provided Germany with strategic chrome exports throughout the war.

The great failure of Franco's diplomacy was above all not to have returned to genuine neutrality in 1942 after American entry, when this might have been done without a particularly heavy cost and with even a positive short-term economic advantage to Spain and a longer-term political advantage to the regime. That this opportunity was not taken was attributable above all to the genuine pro-Axis sympathies of most of the top Spanish leaders, beginning with Franco himself, and to his personal conviction that Germany would still somehow find the means to avoid defeat. Thus the advantages of a policy of true neutrality in 1942–43, when it would really have counted, were lost. The cost for Spain was a continuing economic hardship that could have been partially alleviated by a more genuinely neutral policy, among whose benefits would have been a higher level of vital imports from the Allies and expanded export opportunities.

The ultimate shift in 1944 simply came too late. It convinced few among the Allies and was disdainfully exploited for whatever it was worth and then shown to be of little effect in improving relations with the Allied powers once the war was over. Compared with World War I, when Spain had derived considerable economic advantage from its position as the leading European neutral, World War II was a harsh experience, leaving economic depression and suffering in its wake and the very future of the regime gravely in doubt.[92]

Even more ironic, despite Franco's uncertain prospects after Allied victory, is the likelihood that his future would have been more bleak had Hitler actually won. The Generalissimo's persistent tacking, delays, and dissimulation had eventually so infuriated Hitler that, according to Albert Speer, he swore to get even with Franco by using his domestic enemies to overthrow him.[93]

At the same time, it must be recognized that the war years were crucial for the internal consolidation of Franco's government. The immediate post–Civil War period, coinciding with the tensions of World War II, was the time of greatest dissidence within the Nationalist elites. These years revealed grave deficiencies in the new bureaucratic and administrative structure, along with a sharp divergence of criteria among the principal political families of the regime. Franco encountered greater discontent and political resistance among the military during World War II than at any subsequent period in the history of the regime. His successive governmental reorganizations between 1939 and 1945 were therefore crucial in solidifying his own leadership over the military in particular and the entire regime in general. In the process, his self-confidence and belief in a providential mission steadily increased. The experience thus gained, together with the accompanying solidification of his regime, enabled him to face with confidence and determination the external opposition and isolation that followed the end of World War II.

92. A broader perspective on Spain and World War II is provided by the papers presented at the first symposium in the series "España y la Segunda Guerra Mundial," at the Centro Ortega y Gasset in Madrid, October 13–15, 1983; and by the lucid summary analyses of the "Resumen" by Florentino Portero in *Cuenta y Razón* 14 (Nov.–Dec. 1983), 127–33.

93. Albert Speer, *Spandau: The Secret Diaries* (New York, 1976), 183–84.

15

*Ostracism and
Realignment,
1945–1950*

During most of World War II Franco had maintained closer relations with Germany and Italy than with the Allies, not only because he favored the Axis and thought they would win but also because he recognized that an Axis defeat could have grave consequences for the future of his own regime.[1] The reassurances provided by the United States and Britain at the initiation of Torch had been encouraging, but Franco had been much too late in moving toward genuine neutrality and in developing closer cooperation with the Allies. In Brazil, the Vargas regime was overthrown in 1945 by domestic forces, and the fact that its troops had fought on the Allied side in Europe did not save it. Within the peninsula the Portuguese Estado Novo, maintaining the traditional Portuguese alliance with Britain, had been more discreet and more genuinely neutral than the Spanish government. Moreover, the origins of the Portuguese regime were remote and obscure and were not associated with Italy or Nazi Germany, while Salazar had largely (though not entirely) eschewed fascistic style and discouraged overt political identification with the central European regimes. Thus the Portuguese government escaped the ostracism of its Spanish counterpart and was later admitted to the North Atlantic Treaty Organization in 1949. Even so, the Lisbon regime carried out a formalistic lib-

---

1. In its "whitebook," *The Spanish Government and the Axis* (Washington, D.C., 1946), the United States Department of State included a quotation from a German diplomatic report of December 1943 in which Franco had agreed with the German ambassador that he could never survive the defeat of the Axis. Franco, of course, often told his listeners what they wanted to hear.

eralization of its corporative parliamentary system in 1945, giving it a greater appearance of electoral democracy.[2]

The Franco regime was judged not only in light of wartime policy but as much or more in terms of its origins during the Civil War, which had depended on German and Italian assistance. As a military dictator, Franco also reflected a much more clear-cut "fascist image" than Professor Salazar. His government was commonly described as the last fascist regime in Europe, and for the first year or more after the war was showered with rhetorical abuse and roundly denounced on almost every hand. Any distinction between Francoism and Hitlerism was generally ignored.

To this the regime responded with an air of outraged dignity, insisting on its own independence and originality and stressing the salient role of Communists in promoting the most virulent forms of hostility against it. Yet it did little good to denounce the hypocrisy involved in demonizing Franco while blithely accepting the expansion of totalitarianism throughout most of eastern Europe, for in 1945 few cared to listen. Antipathy was so intense in France that Spanish workers who had been employed in German factories were subjected to severe physical assault while being repatriated across France. Denied entrance to the United Nations, the regime was ostracized politically and militarily, while Spain's suffering economy was cut off from the international credits and opportunities necessary for more rapid regrowth. Though none of the western powers was willing to take up arms against the Madrid government, the domestic opposition was encouraged to carry out that task itself.

Revival of the Opposition

The first efforts to rally the leftist opposition in 1939–40 had been comparatively weak and easily repressed.[3] The more moderate Republican parties in exile were relatively inactive for several years but regained enthusiasm with the turn in the tide of World War II. While a broad new coalition of all the left and liberal Republican forces (minus the Communists) was organized abroad,[4] the Spanish Communist Party formed its

2. On the changes in Portugal in 1945, see Richard Robinson, *Contemporary Portugal* (London, 1979), 67–70; and Tom Gallagher, *Portugal: A Twentieth-Century Interpretation* (Manchester, 1983), 129–131.

3. For general accounts of the leftist resistance to the regime, see Víctor Alba, *Historia de la resistencia antifranquista (1939–1955)* (Barcelona, 1978, 1981). In addition, on the first phases, Cipriano Damiano González, *La resistencia libertaria (1939–1970)* (Barcelona, 1978), 3–95; and Eliseo Bayo, *Los atentados contra Franco* (Barcelona, 1976).

4. Hartmut Heine, *La oposición política al franquismo de 1939 a 1952* (Barcelona, 1983), is the best general treatment of the opposition during the 1940s. See also Víctor Alba, *Historia de la IIa República española 1936–1976* (Barcelona, 1976); Sergio Vilar, *Historia del antifranquismo 1939–1975* (Barcelona, 1984); and José Ma. del Valle, *Las instituciones de la República española en exilio* (Paris, 1976).

own armed political front in France[5] and the anarchists organized a separate coalition for direct action.[6] Both made ready for organized guerrilla activity to "liberate" Spain, and each could draw on sizable cadres of emigré veterans in France who had fought with the Free French either in regular units or in the Maquis.[7]

The first small Communist units began to filter across the border in June 1944, alerting the Spanish authorities, who moved police and troop reinforcements to the northeastern border. Larger units crossed the Pyrenees into Navarre and into eastern Guipuzcoa in October, but gained little support from the predominantly conservative rural population and were easily turned back. Spanish military commanders in some instances refused to recognize the Communist volunteers as regular soldiers and did not always take prisoners. The major effort was made by Communist units possibly totalling 4,000 (estimates vary) through the Pyrenean Vall d'Aran into Lérida, a largely rural Catalan province. Once more the "liberators" won scant popular support in a partially right-wing rural district, managing also to identify themselves with the atrocities of the Civil War by murdering several village priests. They were soon repelled by military and police forces. Most fled back into France, as had their counterparts in earlier attempts, but some made their way into the interior where they raised further recruits.[8]

The anarchists formed guerrilla bands of their own, associated with the otherwise shadowy Agrupación de Fuerzas Armadas de la Republica Española (AFARE) that was organized in connection with the Republican government in exile. These operated in mountain districts, and sometimes in the plains or urban areas, for about the next six years, their activities finally petering out toward the beginning of 1952. On February 25, 1945, an urban guerrilla squad attacked a Falangist district headquarters

5. On the Spanish Communist Party in the 1940s, see David W. Pike, *Jours de gloire, jours de honte* (Paris, 1984); and Joan Estruch Tobella, *EL PCE en la clandestinidad, 1939–1956* (Madrid, 1982).

6. Enrique Marco Nadal, *Todos contra Franco* (Madrid, 1982), is an account of the anarchist-led Alianza Nacional de Fuerzas Democrátics by the secretary-general of the underground CNT in 1946–47. On the resistance in Catalonia, see Carme Molinero and Pere Ysas, *L'oposició antifeixista a Catalunya 1939–1950* (Barcelona, 1981); Daniel Díaz Esculies, *El Front Nacional de Catalunya (1939–1947)* (Barcelona, 1983); and Jaume Fabre, Josep Huerta, and Antoni Ribas, *Vint anys de resistencia catalana (1939–1959)* (Barcelona, 1978).

7. Javier Rubio, *La emigración española a Francia* (Barcelona, 1974); Guy Hermet, *Les espagnols en France* (Paris, 1967); David W. Pike, *Vae victis: Los españoles republicanos refugiados en Francia, 1939–1944* (Paris, 1969); Louis Stein, *Beyond Death and Exile: The Spanish Republicans in France, 1939–1955* (Cambridge, Mass., 1979); Antonio Vilanova, *Los olvidados: Los exilados españoles en la Segunda Guerra Mundial* (Paris, 1969); and Miguel Angel, *Los guerrilleros españoles in Francia* (Havana, 1971).

8. Daniel Arasa, *Años 40: Los maquis y el PCE* (Barcelona, 1984); and Alberto E. Fernández, *La España de los maquis* (Milan, 1967).

in the Cuatro Caminos district of Madrid, the first overt action in the capital since Communists had claimed credit for setting off a bomb in the offices of the vicesecretariat of popular education two years earlier. Those perpetrators who could be apprehended were said to have been shot almost on the spot.

Though the Ministry of Justice announced to the British and American embassies in April 1945 that penalties for crimes committed during the Civil War were being canceled and that the Tribunal of Political Responsibilities was being dissolved that same month,[9] the renewal of opposition activity was accompanied by new repression. As indicated in chapter 11, security had been tightened in the middle of World War II when new laws for the court-martial of political rebels had been promulgated on March 29, 1941, and March 2, 1943. By their terms, any kind of organized political activity would be considered military rebellion, for the decree's fine print brought almost any act of defiance under *sumarísimo* proceedings. This was moderated somewhat and made more precise by a new Spanish penal code promulgated on December 23, 1944, but military courts continued to hold jurisdiction over opposition activity.

Though some Spanish jailers were said by those in prison to be showing greater consideration for leftist prisoners in anticipation of drastic political change, the regime's sense of danger at the same time produced a sharp increase in the number of executions during the late summer and autumn of 1944. Rumor had it that 200 or more political prisoners had been shot during August and September, and the director of prisons admitted to a British diplomat that 70 had been executed during the latter month.[10] On the recommendation of the papal nuncio, a petition for clemency was signed by all the Spanish bishops and submitted to the justice minister, Aunós, but had little immediate effect. The spate of executions began to peter out only in April 1945 when it became clearer that the regime would not have to face a major military challenge.

Wavering followers who had begun to abandon their blue shirts in anticipation of a change of regime began to rally to Franco once more when the growth of leftist activity seemed to indicate that the alternative was return of the Reds. A new paramilitary formation, the Guardias de Franco, was formed of the most fanatical young Falangists in August 1944. Franco also used indoctrinated Falangists to solidify the Army officer corps behind him, elevating a number of reservist officers from the SEU and the university Militia to regular commissions during 1944–45. Radical Falangists contributed directly to the renewed climate of violence by attacking known leftists on their own, occasionally with fatal results.

The guerrilla campaign had the compensating effect for Franco that it

9. *FF,* 4:8.
10. According to British diplomatic reports cited in Heine, *La oposición*, 293.

once more helped to close ranks in much of the military hierarchy. He reshuffled his military command on March 3, 1945, naming as chief of his personal military staff (Casa Militar) the ever faithful José Moscardó (in 1936 in charge of the defense of the Alcazar), who as captain general of Barcelona had recently repelled the Vall d'Aran incursion. The new captain general of Madrid was Muñoz Grandes, who had renewed his personal loyalty to Franco, enjoyed high prestige among his fellow generals, and now had no option but to support the regime to the bitter end. Carlist commanders were more trustworthy than main-line monarchists, and thus Solchaga was named captain general of Barcelona and Varela replaced Orgaz (who had earlier taken to conspiracy) as high commissioner of Spanish Morocco. The elderly Saliquet, a hardliner, took over the Supreme Council of Military Justice.

The monarchist opposition launched its own campaign on March 19, 1945, when Don Juan, after sending a copy to Franco, issued his "Lausanne Manifesto" from his Swiss residence. This defined the system that the heir to the Spanish throne would henceforth advocate: constitutional monarchy. The monarchy would stand as the moderate, nonleftist but potentially democratic alternative to both the dictatorship and a radical new republic. The manifesto declared that the Franco regime, "inspired from the beginning by the totalitarian systems of the Axis powers," had failed and could not hope to survive. As heir presumptive, the Conde de Barcelona (the formal title of Don Juan) offered as an alternative "the traditional monarchy," promising that its priorities would be "immediate approval, by popular vote, of a political constitution; recognition of all the rights inherent in the human personality, guaranteeing the corresponding political liberties; establishment of a legislative assembly elected by the nation; recognition of regional diversity; a broad political amnesty; a more just distribution of wealth and the elimination of unjust social distinctions. . . ."[11] Totally suppressed by the Spanish censorship, this document outlined a drastic political change whose implementation would be delayed a full thirty years and would be carried out not by the author but by his son.

In view of the international situation at the close of the war, Don Juan was convinced of the compelling logic of his position, but he could not count on an organized and unified monarchist opposition within Spain.[12] During its six years of complete power the regime had created a firm network of mutual interest—the opposition called it complicity—with all the elite elements of Spanish society and even with a considerable portion of

11. The text may be found in Fernando González-Doria, *¿Franquismo sin Franco . . . ?* (Madrid, 1974), 24–26, and in López Rodó, *Larga marcha,* 48–50.
12. Cf. the remarks of Garriga on Don Juan's lack of genuine contact with the situation inside Spain in *La España de Franco,* 2:321–43.

the middle classes, who had managed largely to sustain their interests and their way of life under the new system. Though the Pretender ordered a number of prominent monarchists in the Spanish diplomatic service to resign their ambassadorial posts under the regime, the only one to obey was the Duque de Alba, Franco's ambassador in London, and even he was induced by the Caudillo remain at his post for another six months.[13]

Immediately after the manifesto, Franco convened the longest meeting of the Army's Consejo Superior in the history of the regime, from March 20 to 22. Though there is no available record of the proceedings, it may be assumed that Franco repeated once more what he had already told the top members of the military hierarchy: that a properly installed and structured monarchy would be the logical succession to the regime, which he would in due course prepare, but that such a monarchy must not reject the principles for which they had fought, and that continuity could be maintained at this perilous moment only through his continued firm leadership, which was already planning new institutional reforms. He was apparently assured of the full support of the military, who respected his shrewd leadership of the armed forces, the firmness and equilibrium of his command, and his prudent diplomacy. They had little interest in abandoning their commander-in-chief for a liberal monarchist experiment during mounting international hostility and a powerful leftist offensive. Noted civilian monarchists responded in similar fashion. Antonio Goicoechea, number-two leader of the monarchist opposition under the Republic but governor of the Bank of Spain under Franco, spoke out publicly against Don Juan. Thus reassured, the Caudillo presided over the annual victory parade on April 1, and used the date to announce nationalization of the telephone system through an arrangement with ITT.

Franco still sought rapprochement with Don Juan through private channels. He even suggested that Don Juan take official residence in Spain, and though this was refused, announced to the National Council on July 17, 1945, that a law would be prepared to transform the Spanish state into a monarchy once more. Carrero Blanco had already pointed out that although Don Juan himself might never make an appropriate successor, it was important to try to cultivate good relations with the royal family, for his seven-year-old son Juan Carlos might be trained and educated as a more appropriate heir.[14] Though no understanding could be reached for the moment, reassurance was provided by the Conde de Bar-

13. The only other notable to renounce his position was the king's cousin, the air force general Alfonso de Orleans, who resigned as head of the Seville air district. Since he was an officer on active duty, Franco had him imprisoned for a period of time in Sanlúcar de Barrameda. See Fernández, *Tensiones militares*, 111–14.

14. Cf. Carrero Blanco's memorandum following the Manifesto in López Rodó, *Larga marcha*, 54–55.

celona's announcement in September that he would "incite no one to rebellion."[15]

The Reforms of 1945

Franco realized that he faced the most fundamental turning point in the life of the regime, which had to be altered in some ways to survive in the postwar world of social democratic western Europe. There is no indication that he ever thought of abandoning power. If he did, the fate of Mussolini and the vigor of the purges in France and the Low Countries only served to dissuade him. The caudillaje, once undertaken, was a life-and-death enterprise. As he told a leading general, "I shall not make the same mistake as Primo de Rivera. There will be no resignation: from here only to the cemetery."[16]

By the spring of 1945 Franco had a fairly clear design for his future course. Fundamental new laws would have to be introduced to give the regime more objective juridical content and provide some basic civil guarantees. A major effort would be made to attract new Catholic political personnel and intensify the Catholic image of the regime in order to win the support of the Vatican and reduce the hostility of the democracies. The Falange would be deemphasized but not abolished, for it was still useful, and no rival political organizations would be tolerated, though to some extent censorship might be eased. A municipal government reform law would be promulgated, and ultimately a new statute to legitimize the regime as a monarchy under Franco's regency would be submitted to popular plebiscite.[17]

The new formula was to create a sort of Spanish version of the old German ideal of the *Rechtsstaat*, the authoritarian state of administration based on law. This concept, which had impressed right-wing Spanish legal theorists of the preceding generation, had nothing necessarily to do with a constitutional, representative system. Aunós, the justice minister, had begun a sketch for a new legal superstructure as early as 1943, and this was encouraged by Lequerica, who urged Franco to make haste in a memorandum of June 30, 1945.[18] The project of a set of civil guarantees

15. At that same time (September 1945), the main Carlist leader Don Javier de Borbón Parma, himself a French aristocrat persecuted and imprisoned by the German occupation during the war, tried to distance Carlists from the regime by declaring that they would not fight for Franco in a second civil war. It is not clear, however, that rank-and-file Carlists would have agreed. The regime's response was to reinflate once more the pretensions of Don Javier's Carlist rival, Carlos de Habsburgo-Lorena.

16. Quoted in Kindelán, *La verdad*, 187.

17. He explained most of this in a prolix interview with Alberto Martín Artajo (soon to become foreign minister) on May 1, 1945. Javier Tusell, *Franco y los católicos: La política interior española entre 1945 y 1957* (Madrid, 1984), 50–51.

18. *FF*, 4:43–44.

had at first been assigned to Arrese but ultimately transferred to the Instituto de Estudios Políticos, where Arrese had appointed as director Fernando María Castiella, a young theorist and politican of the prewar right and later a neo-Falangist and co-author of the now embarrassing *Reivindicaciones de España*. Castiella was flexible and relatively imaginative. Assisted by several of the Instituto's intellectuals he had elaborated a new *fuero* or bill of rights for Spanish citizens that was strongly opposed by Arrese and some of the core Falangists but largely accepted by Franco.[19]

The Fuero de los Españoles, its title employing the neotraditionalist language (reminiscent of medieval fueros or specific local rights) so dear to the regime, was promulgated on July 17, 1945. It was based in part on the Constitution of 1876 but pretended to synthesize the historic rights guaranteed by traditional Spanish law, and guaranteed many of the civil liberties common to the western world, such as freedom of residence and correspondence and the right not to be detained more than seventy-two hours without a hearing before a judge. Castiella was apparently responsible for adding article 12, "Every Spaniard may express his ideas freely provided that they do not attack the fundamental principles of the State," and article 16, "Spaniards may gather together and associate freely for lawful purposes in accordance with the stipulations of the law." This worried Arrese, but the freedom pledged by these sections was curtailed in article 33, which stated that "the exercise of the rights guaranteed in this Bill of Rights may not attack the spiritual, national, and social unity of the country," while article 25 permitted them to be "temporarily suspended by the government" in time of emergency.[20]

Promulgation of the Fuero was accompanied by a major cabinet change on the following day (July 18). Its primary features were the relative downgrading of the Falange and the installation of a leading Catholic layman and political moderate, Alberto Martín Artajo, as foreign minister. The latter was until the time of his appointment president of the junta nacional of Catholic Action, and would stand as ministerial centerpiece of a major maneuver to accentuate the Catholic identity of the regime and present a new appearance to the world. (The cabinet changes were preceded by a new Law of Primary Education, which officially subordinated all elementary education to Catholic norms.) The faithful Arrese would have to go, even though his achievement had been to domesticate the Falange and modify its fascism,[21] and for the time being its secretary generalship was left vacant. However, the Falangist Girón, whose pliant dema-

19. Tusell, *Franco y los católicos*, 50–51.
20. *Fundamental Laws of the State* (Madrid, 1967).
21. Arreste retained his post in the Cortes and also his position in the good graces of the Caudillo. Two years later he produced a new book, *Capitalismo, communismo, cristianismo* (Madrid, 1947), which declared that "fascism is not a complete formula" because of its materialism and lack of religiosity, and pointed toward Catholic syndicalism as the proper solution.

gogy was quite useful, remained as minister of labor (a post that he would hold for a total of sixteen years, until 1957, making him Franco's most durable minister after Carrero Blanco). The Carlist Esteban Bilbao was replaced as minister of justice by Fernández Cuesta, and Primo de Rivera, the outgoing agriculture minister, was replaced by a Falangist of Arrese's group, Carlos Rein Segura. Blas Pérez remained as minister of the interior, and Ibáñez Martín, a very right-wing Catholic thoroughly identified with Franco, stayed on as education minister. Franco's childhood friend Juan Antonio Suanzes, head of the state INI, had already replaced the too-independent Carceller as minister of commerce and industry in the preceding partial reorganization of 1944. Asensio, who had seemed too much an "Axis general," was followed as minister of the army by General Fidel Dávila, a tiny, colorless man but reasonably competent and intelligent and always loyal to Franco. Though some of the ministers had a semimonarchist background and two of them were considered "political Catholics," this was essentially a cabinet of Franco loyalists. With every justification, Franco was confident that none of them would cause him any trouble.

The nominal exception might have been Artajo, who had discussed the wisdom of collaborating with the regime with leading Catholics from the primate on down.[22] Most though not all of them urged him to enter the government to encourage major institutional reform. He is alleged to have told associates in Catholic Action that they could expect a basic transformation within four months, and on August 28 to have remarked to the new American ambassador Norman Armour that Franco must now realize that it would soon be necessary for him to resign.[23] Franco, of course, conceded almost nothing, and Martín Artajo's goals were less than drastic, envisioning the rapid evolution of Franco's system into a corporative, Catholic, and still semiauthoritarian monarchy—perhaps not so very different from the reforms being instituted by Salazar in Portugal.[24]

On September 3 Franco received a letter from Serrano Súñer emphasizing that the regime must be reorganized on a broad national-unity basis to include representatives of "all non-Red Spaniards," that the Falange must be dissolved and a plebiscite conducted to legitimize the monarchy. Contrary to his usual habit of ignoring criticism, Franco soon afterward received his brother-in-law for a long and frank discussion, their first in three years, and revealed more than a little uncertainty about how to proceed.[25]

During cabinet meetings in September and October Franco seemed to

22. This is treated in detail in Tusell, *Franco y los católicos*, 52–79.
23. According to Serrano Súñer, *Memorias*, 394–403.
24. See Tusell, *Franco y los católicos*, 84–93.
25. For the text of the letter and Serrano's version of the meeting, see García Lahiguera, *Serrano Súñer*, 260–67.

Alberto Martín Artajo, Minister of Foreign Affairs, 1945–57

support Martín Artajo's point of view against the resistance of Girón and Rein Segura. A series of limited reforms were discussed, such as an amnesty for Civil War crimes, electoral reforms of the Cortes, a relaxation of censorship, and a referendum law. At times Franco sounded as though he really believed in a system of checks and balances, observing, for example, that Nazi Germany suffered catastrophe through "the decision of one man" and that the same danger existed in monarchies which could "lose their way if the king only looked into the mirror."[26]

Yet the changes that emerged in following months were piecemeal, minimal, and in some respects merely cosmetic. The most influential voice counseling Franco to change things as little as possible was that of Carrero Blanco. In one memorandum, Carrero stressed that the regime must above all rely on "order, unity, and staying the course [aguantar],"[27] and so it did. On October 12 new proposed legislation was sent to the Cortes that would slightly liberalize the terms of meetings and associations and individual civil guarantees, in accordance with the Fuero de los Españoles. New municipal elections were announced for the following March, with members of city councils to be chosen through indirect procedures (one-third by heads of families, one-third by the syndicates, and the remaining third by those already selected through the first two channels), though the government would continue to appoint all mayors directly. On October 20, an amnesty was announced for prisoners serving sentences for Civil War crimes, and two days later a new Law of Referendum was announced which provided that issues of transcendent national concern would be submitted to popular referendum at the discretion of the government.

The new law of associations being discussed in the Cortes did prove momentarily troublesome. Arrese and others objected that it would require associations to be authorized by the Dirección General de Seguridad (the police), but, "should the latter not approve it, the proponent could appeal to the court system, which was empowered to authorize it as it saw fit. With that, the proposal abandoned the political system established by the Alzamiento to return to the juridical state of liberalism, since to entrust political life to the decision of a judge was to implant once more a neutral state."[28] Franco seemed less alarmed, confident of his ability to channel or otherwise control any proposed reform. "Don't worry, Arrese," the latter reports him as saying, "because it would be no trouble for me to govern even with the [liberal monarchist] Constitution of 1876."[29] The proposal soon died in the Cortes.

26. According to the notes of cabinet meetings taken by Martín Artajo, in Tusell, *Franco y los católicos*, 103. Minutes were never kept of cabinet meetings, and at the beginning of 1947 Franco forbade any minister to take detailed notes of the discussions.
27. Quoted in López Rodó, *Larga marcha*, 57–58.
28. José Luis de Arrese, *Una etapa constituyente* (Barcelona, 1982), 69–70.
29. Ibid., 70.

The Falange was not to be eliminated but only downgraded. One week after the change in cabinet the vicesecretariat of popular education, which controlled the censorship, was removed from the FET and placed under the Ministry of Education, now identified as a Catholic fief. The raised-arm Fascist or Roman salute, declared the regime's *saludo nacional* in April 1937, was officially abolished over the objection of the remaining Falangist ministers on September 11, 1945. The FET bureaucracy was left under the administration of its vicesecretary, Rodrigo Vivar Téllez, a former judge whose honesty was respected. Vivar Téllez was no fascist, and could not see why the pretense of a Movement organization need be kept up.

Franco, however, was clear in his own mind regarding its value. In an earlier conversation with Martín Artajo, he had observed that the Falange was important in maintaining the spirit and ideals of the Movement of 1936 and in educating political opinion. As a mass organization it had the potential to incorporate all kinds of people, and it organized the popular support for the regime that Franco insisted he saw on his travels. It also provided the content and administrative cadres for the regime's social policy and served as a "bulwark against subversion," for after 1945 Falangists like Muñoz Grandes had no alternative but to back the regime. Finally, the Caudillo observed somewhat cynically, it functioned as a kind of lightning rod and "was blamed for the errors of the government," relieving pressure on the latter.[30] Franco declared that it was merely a sort of administrative "instrument of national unification"[31] rather than a party. Further fleeting clandestine activities by a handful of activists who resented their new subordination could largely be ignored.[32]

Falangist leaders had alternative ploys to advance. The vicesecretary of syndical organization, José María de Olazábal, suggested in a report to Franco of August 29, 1945, that one way to meet the objections of the democracies would be to liberalize the syndical system, converting it into a corporation under public law composed of free associations, partly on the basis of the preceding syndical elections. There would be no obligatory membership, but such syndicalism might take the place of political parties. This was too liberal for Franco, who, after carefully annotating the report, dismissed it altogether.[33]

A totally different maneuver was initiated by the camisa vieja and Guardias de Franco leader Luis González Vicén, who began negotiations that summer with the new clandestine secretary general of the CNT, José

30. Tusell, *Franco y los católicos*, 58.

31. Quoted in my *Falange*, 58.

32. In 1944 a number of die-hards had organized a sub rosa group called the Circulo Nosotros (Circle of Ourselves), pledged never to surrender the original goals of the Falange. It disbanded soon after the European war ended, and its members terminated most of their activities within the Movement as well. Jato, *La rebelión*, 337–38.

33. *FF*, 4:57–58.

Leiva, in Madrid. His goal was to rescue the Falange by gaining the support of opposition anarchosyndicalists for a broader, stronger and more popular national syndicalism. Franco eventually rejected the CNT's demands,[34] and the negotiations foundered the following year. Suppression of the CNT leadership was renewed.

The construction of a "cosmetic constitutionalism," as it has been called, was for the moment completed by publication of a new Cortes electoral law on March 12, 1946. It changed very little, maintaining the principle of indirect and controlled corporative elections, but provided for representation from municipal councils and increased syndical participation. None of these reforms amounted to any fundamental institutional change in the regime, but they did begin the elaboration of a facade of new laws and guarantees which its spokesmen could refer to in terms of political representation and civil rights, however stark the contrast with reality.

Thus the new line in 1945–46 was to present the regime as a limited system of government bound by law, which was partly true with respect to routine aspects but fundamentally misleading with respect to political structure. Even before the death of Hitler, an essayist in *Arriba* had declared on April 12, 1945, "Spain has a natural style of democracy capable of broad development without denaturalizing itself. An original style. One more of the twenty types of democracy registered by history and designed by political planners down to our own perilous times." On May 14, 1946, Franco would insist, "The first error [of our critics] consists in wanting to present our regime as a system of dictatorship, thus pretending to assign to its leadership extraordinary and despotic powers, when . . . judicial power is exercised by career judges and magistrates. . . . Never, in the life of a nation, has the system of justice acted with greater independence.[35] Ten months later he informed a visiting correspondent, "I am not master of what I wish to do; I need the assistance and agreement of my government,"[36] once more defining the regime as an "organic popular democracy," repeating the new catch phrase coined in 1944 that would be employed with many variations throughout the next three decades.

The Nadir of Ostracism

Throughout 1945–46 the regime mounted a press and publications campaign to try to convince foreign opinion that the Spanish government

34. According to a report presented to Franco in May 1946, the CNT leadership offered a policy of cooperation, proposing to withdraw from the Giral Republican goverment-in-exile and accept three Falangists on their national committee, but in return insisted on freedom to proselytize. Ibid., 116–22. Cf. Ellwood, *Prietas*, 210–12.

35. Quoted in Amando de Miguel, *La herencia del franquismo* (Madrid, 1976), 29.

36. *Arriba*, March 6, 1947.

was essentially a system of organic Catholic institutions and had never really been committed to or believed in the victory of the Axis. Franco had no intention of providing sanctuary for any of the major members of the Hitlerian order. Though an untold number of French collaborators and lesser Nazis had fled into Spain in the last days of the war,[37] the most conspicuous of these, Pierre Laval, was repatriated to France at the close of July 1945. When the Allies demanded on September 3 that Spanish forces evacuate the Tangier district, they soon did. During the autumn, the Spanish president of the international Catholic student organization Pax Romana, Joaquín Ruiz Giménez, toured Britain and the United States, speaking with Catholic leaders and lobbying on behalf of the regime.

None of this had much effect. The captured archives of the Third Reich yielded considerable evidence of the regime's association with Germany,[38] and many wild rumors went far beyond fact. One French intelligence report had it that 100,000 Nazis and collaborators were being sheltered in Spain,[39] while Soviet spokesmen at the United Nations charged that 200,000 Nazis had escaped to Spain, adding that atomic bombs were being manufactured at Ocaña, 70 kilometers from Madrid, and that plans were afoot to invade France in the spring of 1946. As new elections ratified the power of the left in western Europe, antipathy to the Spanish regime only increased, and on November 20 the United States ambassador abandoned Madrid, leaving the embassy in the hands of the chargé d'affaires.

Before the ambassador's departure, Franco or the former foreign minister Lequerica (attributions vary) is supposed to have told him that the Spanish government "could not be expected to throw itself out the window." In a speech at the Infantry Academy on October 26, Franco declared that he would "defend the regime to the last."[40] By that time, however, the British and American governments had made it clear that no matter how intense the diplomatic and economic pressure, there would be no direct military intervention in Spain.

Within Spain the international campaign against the regime was energetically depicted as inherently anti-Spanish, a foreign left-liberal conspiracy to tar the entire country with a new Black Legend. The role of

37. There were no genuine Nazi bigwigs in Spain, but the Axis refugee colony included the SS commando leader Otto Skorzeny, the Belgian fascist Léon Degrelle, French collaborators, a group of Romanian Legionnaires (some of whom, however, had passed through Buchenwald as prisoners), and a few Croatian Ustasi.

38. The United States Department of State published a small book, *The Spanish Government and the Axis*, early in 1946. Madrid's reply may be found in Lleonart and Castiella, *España y ONU*, 67–80.

39. This report, dated Feb. 27, 1946, is cited in Pike, "Franco," 396.

40. *New York Times*, Oct. 29, 1945, in Trythall, *Caudillo*, 204.

Soviet and Communist forces, such as the Soviet-dominated World Federation of Trade Unions, was played up to the fullest extent, while with respect to the western powers Franco himself publicly referred to the machinations of a world "Masonic superstate" that lay behind Spain's ills.[41]

To rally support, he revived his series of motor tours to various parts of the country. These were often exhausting trips that lasted from dawn to dusk for one or more days, but they brought him personally to far-flung provinces and regions where he was seen and heard by large crowds, even if the crowds sometimes had to be manufactured by the Movement.

There is little doubt that much of moderate Spanish opinion rallied to the regime during its period of ostracism. The largest disaffected strata were as usual industrial workers and the poorest or the landless peasants. Nearly all Catholic opinion, which in 1945 accounted for more of Spanish society than it had a decade earlier, supported the regime. This included most of the northern peasantry and much of the urban middle class. To what extent the non-Catholic middle class actively supported the opposition is less certain. The regime in general continued to count on the same social strata, groups, and regions on which its military victory had earlier been based. The Civil War was too recent and memories too bitter for much erosion to have occurred. During January 1946 demonstrations were held in cities all over the country in support of Franco, variously orchestrated by the Movement.

Economic conditions remained harsh, though in general not quite as grim as during the early 1940s. The weather, which had been rather good in 1944, deteriorated considerably in 1945–46, bringing severe drought. Though major efforts were being made to generate new hydroelectric resources, intermittent power shortages were routine. There was little demand abroad for Spanish minerals once the war was over, and rationing was still very much the norm, though modified by an enormous black market.

The French government temporarily closed its Pyrenean border in June 1945 and closed it indefinitely on March 1, 1946. This action was taken immediately following the Franco regime's execution of Cristino García, one of the Communist guerrilla chiefs it had apprehended, who happened also to be a French resistance veteran. In Madrid, the Foreign Ministry commented on the symbolism of the French closing a frontier across which so many thousands had fled from France to safety during the war, then published a long list of French misdeeds which included permitting attacks on Spanish consulates, border posts, and even Spanish nationals in France. On March 4 a tripartite note issued by Britain, France, and the United States condemned the regime once more and called for

41. *Textos de doctrina política: Palabras y escritos de 1945 a 1950* (Madrid, 1951), 335.

the formation of a new provisional government in Madrid. The effect of that pronouncement was, however, slightly mitigated by the fact that on the following day Churchill delivered his famous Iron Curtain speech in Fulton, Missouri. To Madrid, this indicated that, as they had hoped for and expected, the western powers were beginning to take note of other and graver concerns more consistent with the regime's own alignment.

Moreover, it had become clear particularly in the case of the United States, the power about which Franco was most concerned, that moral and political condemnation of the regime was not being allowed to stand in the way of major economic and transportation interests. Though Washington had announced that suffering Spain would be at the bottom of its general list for scarce postwar exports, it had included Madrid in the development of the transportation and communications network led by the United States. A Spanish representation had been invited to the earlier International Civil Aviation Conference at Chicago, even though that had meant that the Soviet delegation would not attend, and Spain was later allotted new Hercules transport aircraft earmarked "for friendly nations."[42] Moreover, the State Department had already informed the Republican government-in-exile that Washington would not recognize it, for having represented only one of the two parties in civil conflict it lacked full legitimacy.

Franco presented the international boycott to Spanish opinion as a matter of independent national survival, declaring to the Cortes in May 1946, "We would have to renounce our independence and sovereignty or surrender to anarchy if we wanted to quiet these campaigns."[43] As it was, he said, Spain bore the higher mission of sustaining anti-Communist resistance for all Europe. Franco declared at Burgos on October 1 (Fiesta Nacional del Caudillo) that "the targets of Communism" lay especially in the Mediterranean area and were aimed "in the case of Spain at the redoubt or bulwark of spirituality in the world. Once again Spain has a role in the world."[44]

There was no relaxation of pressure during 1946. The report of a special subcommittee of the United Nations Security Council declared that "the Franco regime is a fascist regime" and found it a "potential," though not an "actual," "menace" to peace, despite the extreme weakness of the Spanish armed forces and the complete absence of any encouragement of terrorists or subversive activity beyond its borders. Finally, on December 12, the General Assembly voted 34 to 6, with 13 abstentions, to advocate complete withdrawal of international diplomatic recognition from the Spanish

42. Cf. Trythall, *Caudillo*, 207.
43. *Textos de doctrina política: Palabras y escritos de 1945 a 1950* (Madrid, 1951), 66.
44. Lleonart and Castiella, *España y ONU*, 69.

Public demonstration supporting the regime in the Plaza de Oriente, December 1946

regime if a representative government were not soon established in Madrid.[45] This brought the withdrawal of the British ambassador, the last remaining diplomatic representative in the Spanish capital, even though no major western state went so far as to break relations completely. In anticipation of the vote, a monster rally of several hundred thousand was convened on December 9 in Madrid's Plaza de Oriente, opposite the royal palace (which Franco used on such occasions), to demonstrate support for the regime. It was perhaps the largest single gathering in Spanish history up to that point, only surpassed thirty-six years later on the occasion of the papal visit.

45. Ibid., 386–89; Huff, "The Spanish Question," 239–50.

Hispanidad: The Latin American Connection

Though Mexico and several other Latin American states were intensely hostile to the regime, Spanish diplomacy was nonetheless able to find its strongest support during the ostracism from a number of sympathetic Latin American governments. Reestablishment of close relations with the greater Hispanic world had always been a major ambition of twentieth-century Spanish nationalism. From the very beginning this was central to the regime's foreign policy, which adopted the terminology and concepts of Ramiro de Maeztu's *Defensa de la Hispanidad* (1934), as it did so many of the ideas of the *Acción Española* group. During the Civil War it gained many sympathizers among the Latin American right,[46] and subsequently on November 2, 1940, inaugurated an official Consejo de la Hispanidad (Council of Hispanity). The seventy-four official members drawn from among government officials, military and Falangist leaders, Church prelates, and right-wing intellectuals were appointed in January 1941, and three months later five different committees were organized under the Council to coordinate various aspects of Spanish relations with Latin America.

Ever since the first organization of radical Spanish nationalism emerged in 1931, it had been made clear that there was no ambition to reconquer or colonize Latin America,[47] but to restore close relations and achieve a position of hegemony for Spain. With the outbreak of World War II and Spain's tilt toward the Axis, great alarm developed in the United States in particular over the activities of Falange Exterior (the Falangist equivalent of the NSDAP Auslandsorganisation)[48] and possible Spanish imperialist designs or activities as a Nazi front.[49] In fact, the activities of Falange Ex-

46. The key work in this regard is *The Spanish Civil War 1936–1939: American Hemispheric Perspectives* (Lincoln, Nebr., 1982), ed. M. Falcoff and F. B. Pike.
47. Cf. the statements of Redondo and Primo de Rivera in chapter 4. Fermín Yzurdiaga, the FET's first director of press and propaganda in 1937, insisted that the party would reject Hispanidad if based on "physical force." *Unidad* (San Sebastián), Nov. 20, 1937.
48. José Antonio Primo de Rivera founded the first foreign section of the Falange on his last trip to Italy in August 1935. Branches of the Falange Exterior spread in Latin America during the Civil War, mainly from local initiative, and were strongest in Argentina. The first regular provisions for membership abroad under the FET were made in Political Secretariat Circular no. 27, Nov. 11, 1937, in *BMFET*, no. 12, Jan. 15, 1938. Jefaturas provinciales were established in Italy, Argentina, Cuba, Chile, Brazil, and Uruguay. Other sections were later created in Germany, Portugal, England, and Central America. Their functions were simply to serve as foreign auxiliaries to the Nationalist war effort, and to this end they disseminated hundreds of thousands of copies of pamphlets and journalistic publications. Their activity was described in the official booklet *F.E.T. y de las J.O.N.S. en el Exterior* (Madrid, 1939).
49. The most hysterical was Allan Chase, *Falange: The Axis Secret Army in the Americas* (New York, 1942); but as late as 1944 the correspondent Ray Josephs made the wild charge that "at least half the Falange budget is for work in Latin America," in his *Argentine Diary* (New York, 1944), 297. More judicious were articles by H. R. Southworth, "The Spanish Phalanx and Latin America," *Foreign Affairs* (Oct. 1939), 148–55; and Thomas J. Hamilton, "Spain Dreams of Empire," *Foreign Affairs* (Apr. 1944), 458–68.

terior had been greatly reduced as soon as the Civil War ended, but formal pronouncements that Spain harbored no designs of political domination in the western hemisphere[50] were not accepted at face value in Washington. The understanding with Germany during World War II did provide Spain with a powerful transmitter that for the first time in 1942 made it possible to broadcast directly to Latin America, yet the propaganda and information facilities opened to Germany during 1942–43 proved relatively insignificant.

With the end of the war, the government tried more than ever to propagate Hispanidad as a doctrine of cultural and religious unity. On the Día de la Raza (Columbus Day) in 1946, Franco declared that there were two different kinds of empires: "The empire that takes and . . . the empire that gives. . . . If at one point in history Spain stood first by virtue of her power, and demonstrated in her crusade the strength of her faith, her courage, and her virtues, with the coming of better times she places before these [martial values] her spiritual, social, and cultural works."[51] The goal was to gain diplomatic support that would help to overcome ostracism, and in this Franco was not disappointed.

The new Argentine government of Juan Perón provided the Spanish regime with crucial backing during the decisive years 1946–48. Leader of a new Argentine "social nationalism" that sought independence from the existing international framework, Perón regarded the Spanish system as a kind of distant brother with similar international goals and problems. He soon defied the United Nations ban and named a new ambassador to Madrid, demonstrating that at least one prosperous exporting country was willing to come to Spain's assistance. At their high point in 1948, imports from Argentina provided at least 25 percent of all goods brought into Spain and for two years guaranteed vital foodstuffs for a hungry population. Though Argentine assistance declined to a much lower level of loans and credits in 1949 as the Perón regime encountered mounting economic problems of its own, for two years its role was almost indispensable.[52]

Latin American support began to pay further dividends as a group of Latin American representatives worked in the United Nations to end the policy of ostracism.[53] Meanwhile, the Consejo de la Hispanidad had been reorganized in 1946 as the more modest and cooperative-sounding Instituto de Cultura Hispánica, and with the subsequent partial rehabilita-

50. As in Federico de Urrutia, *La Falange Exterior* (San Sebastián, n.d.); and the FET booklet, *El imperio de España* (1947).

51. *Textos de doctrina política*, 377.

52. Some discussion of Spanish-Argentine relations between 1947 and 1950 will be found in the memoir of the Spanish ambassador, José Ma. de Areilza, *Memorias exteriores 1947–1964* (Barcelona, 1984), 17–78. For an overview of postwar economic relations with Latin America, see Vicente Torrente and Gabriel Manueco, *Las relaciones económicas de España con Hispanoamérica* (Madrid, 1953), 423–526.

53. Huff, "The Spanish Question," 370–431.

tion of the regime, the doctrines of Hispanidad were modified to include cooperation with the United States in both hemispheres.[54]

The Apex of National Catholicism

Though the regime's strong Catholic identity was exploited more than ever to distinguish Francoism from fascism, the Generalissimo had been somewhat disappointed by the development of relations with the Vatican since the Civil War. Franco had hoped for an official concordat soon after the fighting ended; his government officially abolished divorce in September 1939 and resumed the state ecclesiastical subsidy (canceled by the Republic) two years later. The Vatican, however, was leery of a formal relationship with the Spanish regime after its experiences with Germany and Italy, so that the first general agreement that had been worked out in 1941 fell well short of a concordat. It did grant the Spanish state the

54. The moderate quality of Spain's postwar Latin American policy is reflected in Franco's collected speeches *Hacia la comunidad hispánica de naciones: Discursos desde 1945 a 1955* (Madrid, 1956).

The principal study of the Hispanidad doctrine and its policy implementations is William B. Bristol, "Hispanidad in South America, 1936–1948," (Ph.D. diss., University of Pennsylvania, 1947, 1951). See also Bristol's article "Hispanidad in South America," *Foreign Affairs*, Jan. 1943, 312–19; and Bailey W. Diffie, "The Ideology of Hispanidad," *The Hispanic American Historical Review*, Aug. 1943, pp. 458–71.

Among the principal theoretical statements of Hispanidad were José de los Rios, *La nueva misión de los españoles en los pueblos hispanoamericanos* (Ciudad Trujillo, 1941); Manuel Coronado Aguilar, *Influencia de España en Centro-América* (Guatemala, 1943); Rodolfo Barón Castro, *Españolismo y antiespañolismo en la América Hispana* (Madrid, 1945); Manuel García Morente, *Idea de la Hispanidad* (Madrid, 1947), a standard manual; Rafael Gil Serrano, *Nueva visión de la Hispanidad* (Madrid, 1947); Carlos Berraz Montyn, *Hispanidad y Argentinidad* (Santa Fe, 1948); and Bernardo Monsegu, C.P., *El Occidente y la Hispanidad* (Madrid, 1949).

A work by a Mexican diplomat, José Robredo Galguera, *La Hispanidad a través de los siglos* (Mexico City, 1954), provides a good description of the varying definitions and formulations of the idea of Hispanidad and of its revised tone by the 1950s. He observed that "'Hispanidad' successively was (a) 'that group of spiritual and material entities that . . . can bear the adjective 'hispanic'; (b) 'the totality of spiritual and material qualities which *are common* to all men and to all Hispanic nations, distinguished from the qualities that are peculiar to those very men and to each one of those nations'; (c) 'a new race sui generis in the world, not based on the material identity of blood and flesh, but in a *spiritual identity* of souls, ideals, and common aspirations, and in a particular manner of defining life and living it, adjusted to the Catholic religion in its Hispanic totality, to Hispanic languages, . . . to Hispanic arts, culture, and civilization, with a broad *universal* base which is the absolute *equality of all* men by their origin and by their capacity to obtain the same final glorious destiny in eternal life after temporal death'; (d) 'a geographical and territorial expression which takes in all the lands in every clime occupied and inhabited by the Hispanic nations'; (e) 'as a goal, in the near future, a regional grouping within the Charter of the United Nations, which can be a moderating element for peace that strives to realize on an international level its ideals of equality for all men in the concert of nations'; (f) and secondly, in the remote future, an organized community of Hispanic nations absolutely free and autonomous internally, but united under a single direction or council in which all participate with equal rights. . . ." (Pp. 5–6.)

right to make presentations for episcopal appointments,[55] but withheld broader authority over Church appointments. The Vatican was nonetheless pleased with the changes in Spanish policy during the final phase of World War II[56] and did not discourage Spanish prelates and Catholics in general from reaffirming their support for Franco during the crucial period of ostracism.

The decade of the 1940s brought marked revival of most aspects of religious life. Church attendance increased greatly, church buildings were reconstructed on a large scale, and virtually every single index of religious practice rose. By 1942 a new series of "popular missions" of mass evangelization were in full swing, continuing for more than a decade. In large industrial cities such as Barcelona sometimes nearly a quarter of a million people lined the streets during mission campaigns. Seminary facilities were expanded throughout Spain, though the number of new seminarians did not increase markedly until about 1945, after the new religious acculturation had had time to nurture young vocations.

One of the most remarkable features of post–Civil War Spain was the reintroduction of religious rites to most formal aspects of life.

> Religion was a natural part of social life: Christmas, with its nativity scene and processions of the Wise Men; Lenten lectures and open or closed spiritual exercises; novenas; the processions of Holy Week; Eucharistic processions and the viaticum to the sick; rosaries at dawn; the processions of the Sacred Heart of Jesus; pilgrimages to the Virgin; festivals of patron saints; the religious activities of charitable guilds and confraternities and spiritual brotherhoods. . . . The entire year was accompanied by some form of public religious manifestation.[57]

This resacralization of Spanish life affected all public affairs and institutions and was strongest in those regions and among those Spaniards who had never been fully secularized in the first place: the Catholic north, with its predominantly religious rural society, and significant portions of the middle and upper classes. It was much weaker and had much less effect among the former bastions of the revolutionary cause: the poverty-stricken rural south and the urban workers. Yet even in those areas there was some change during the 1940s, as a minority of the formerly indifferent returned to church attendance and certain forms of piety, whether under duress, conviction, or a new sense of social conformity. For a few years during the 1940s the Catholic Spain of tradition seemed once more to have been restored.

In some respects Spanish life during the 1940s was lived at extremes.

55. The Spanish state had the right to present, for episcopal appointments, one name chosen from a list of three that the papacy selected from a longer list of six agreed to by the state and the nuncio.

56. Marquina Barrio, *La diplomacia vaticana*, 311–30.

57. Rafael Gómez Pérez, *Política y religión en el régimen de Franco* (Barcelona, 1976), 156.

Franco and the Papal Nuncio, Msgr. Antoniutti

Prostitution flourished amid the penury of the postwar years, yet formal Spanish society was the most prudish in Europe.[58] The black market was a necessity for many in private life, but public expression achieved extremes of piety that would have appeared strange even before the Republic.[59]

The primate Cardinal Gomá in fact found the results of the religious revival disillusioning, confiding to the British ambassador Sir Samuel Hoare (who was Catholic) that Franco's triumph had not produced the true spiritual renewal that Gomá had anticipated. What it had produced was the "autocratic state," the danger of which Gomá had overconfidently rejected in 1937. Catholic student associations were absorbed into the Falange's SEU, Catholic social groups repressed if they competed with state syndicates, priests forbidden to use the vernacular in Catalonia and the Basque provinces (despite Gomá's intercession), and a pastoral of the primate himself suppressed as too indulgent of the opposition and obliquely critical of the government.[60] Even the pope had been censored, as in the suppression of Pius XI's anti-Nazi encyclical, *Mit brennender Sorge*, and the excision of part of his radio message of April 15, 1939, felicitating the Nationalists on their victory but also urging kindness and good will to the defeated. Gomá died in August 1940 a politically disillusioned prelate.

Gomá was exceptional among the Spanish church leaders of his day, who were in general strongly identified with the regime despite its excesses. The only notable exception was the arch reactionary Pablo Segura, cardinal archbishop of Seville, who made little secret of his detestation of the Falange and of Franco himself. He curtly refused requests for the celebration of *misas de campaña* (open field masses) at Falangist rallies, observing that this was a political spectacle which profaned holy services in a sacrilegious manner. His cathedral in Seville was said to be the only major church building in Spain that did not bear the names of fallen Falangists on its walls. During the course of a public sermon in 1940 he had the audacity to inform his listeners that the term *caudillo* had signified in classical literature the leader of a band of thieves and that Loyola's *Spiritual Exercises* classified such a figure as a demon. This provoked such wrath in El Pardo that Franco's ministers could barely restrain him from ordering the second exile of Segura, who had earlier been evicted from Spain by the Republic.[61] Franco resigned himself to the fact that

58. Cf. L. Alonso Tejada, *La represión sexual en la España de Franco* (Barcelona, 1977).

59. There are two general descriptive social histories of these years: Fernando Vizcaino Casas, *La España de la posguerra* (Barcelona, 1976); and Rafael Abella, *Por el Imperio hacia Dios: Crónica de una posguerra (1939–1955)* (Barcelona, 1978), which emphasize the bizarre and picaresque.

60. Anastasio Granados, *El Cardenal Gomá* (Madrid, 1969), 229–48.

61. Ramón Garriga, *El Cardenal Segura y el Nacional-Catolicismo* (Barcelona, 1977), 274–75.

Cardinal Segura was a cross to be borne; the Vatican finally removed him years later.

By the last years of World War II, opinion within the Church hierarchy grew more divided. The clearest opposition to the regime was expressed by Fidel García Martínez, bishop of Calahorra, who issued strongly and categorically anti-Nazi pastorals in 1942 and 1944. A few other bishops began to issue what were termed "social pastorals" that condemned the abuses and injustices of the prevailing economic structure, particularly in the countryside. These culminated in the first collective social pastoral by the bishops of eastern Andalusia in October 1945, which recommended separate worker and management associations to replace the state vertical syndical system.

Much more typical, however, were the many prelates who strongly identified themselves with and defended the regime, though only one— Eíjo y Garay, the "blue bishop" of Madrid—ever went so far as to identify himself with the Falange. Within the government, the Ministries of Justice and Education had from the start been reserved for ultra-Catholics so that religious norms would be brought to bear on the legal and educational systems. The decree establishing the state's new council for scientific research, the CSIC, in November 1939 defined its goal as "the necessary reestablishment of the basic Christian unity of the sciences, destroyed in the eighteenth century. . . ." and the new law of university organization in 1943 recognized as "supreme guide Christian dogma and morality and the authority of sacred canons with respect to teaching."[62] The subsequent Law of Primary Education went even further to bring every aspect of elementary education in line with Church doctrine.[63] Within the Syndical Organization an ecclesiastical advisor of syndicates was appointed in 1944, and similar religious advisory agencies were established under a number of other ministries and state institutions, becoming a standard feature of the next quarter-century.[64]

Enrique Pla y Deniel, Gomá's successor as primate, cooperated fully with the government's enterprise of establishing the primarily Catholic and nonfascist identity of the regime after World War II.[65] He wrote in *Ecclesia*, the central Catholic publication, on March 21, 1945: "It must be

62. Quoted in Víctor Manuel Arbeloa, *Aquella España católica* (Salamanca, 1975), 275.
63. For this period, see Gregorio Cámara Villar, *Nacional-catolicismo y escuela: La socialización política del franquismo (1936–1951)* (Jaén, 1984).
64. The principle study of church-state relations and Catholic politics under the regime is Guy Hermet, *Les catholiques dans l'Espagne franquiste*, 2 vols. (Paris, 1980–81). Among the best treatments, in addition to that by Gómez Pérez cited earlier, are Santiago Petschen, *La Iglesia en la España de Franco* (Madrid, 1977); and J. J. Ruiz Rico, *El papel político de la Iglesia católica en la España de Franco* (Madrid, 1977). Other studies include Alfonso Alvarez Bolado, *El experimento del Nacional Catolicismo* (Madrid, 1976); José Chao Rego, *La Iglesia en el franquismo* (Madrid, 1976); and Francisco Rodríguez de Coro, *Colonización política del catolicismo (1941–1945)* (San Sebastian, 1979).
65. Cf. volume 2 of Pla's *Escritos pastorales* (Madrid, 1949).

Franco and his wife, Doña Carmen, with the Primate Cardinal Enrique Pla y Deniel at the Royal Palace in Madrid, 1958

said with perfect clarity: The World War has nothing to do with the Spanish Civil War." His pastoral "Al terminar la guerra" ("On the Ending of the War"), issued on August 28, 1945, defended the regime from charges of being either statist or totalitarian. It reemphasized the classic doctrine of the right of rebellion against tyrannical regimes such as that of the Popular Front and insisted that "the episcopacy and the clergy did not exceed the limits set by the Roman pontiff. Not a single priest performed military service in the Civil War, and the ecclesiastical hierarchy blessed one of the belligerent groups only after the character of the Civil War of the first moments was transformed into a Crusade."[66] In February 1946 he defended the Nationalist cause as a genuine crusade before the College of Cardinals in Rome.

At the same time, the Church leadership expected major reform in the direction of moderation and the institutionalization of traditional legal norms. Pla's pastoral of May 8, 1945, synthesized the position of the hierarchy by endorsing the regime and at the same time urging it to acquire "solid institutional bases in conformity with our historical traditions and compatible with present realities." During the next two years Pla hailed

66. Quoted in Arbeloa, *Aquella España*, 248.

the regime's new institutional formulations and urged Catholics to participate in the system.

There were definite frustrations involved, for Franco never accepted
the ideas of his new foreign minister Martín Artajo for a modified and
semirepresentative corporative structure for the regime. The changes of
1945–47 promised more than they delivered. When direction of the censorship and of the press were removed from the Movement and early in
1946 placed in the hands of two noted conservative Catholic laymen
within the Ministry of Education, the new directors found it impossible
to reform the censorship as they had hoped. Prior censorship continued
much as before. Though Catholic publications were given greater liberty
after 1945, they were not entirely free of restrictions either. Moreover,
the new Hermandades Obreras de Acción Católica (HOAC; Worker Brotherhoods of Catholic Action), founded in 1946 to foster Catholic social concerns among workers and strongly supported by the primate himself,
were harassed by the Syndical Organization and sharply censored.[67]

Nevertheless, the balance was satisfactory from the viewpoint of the
Church. The institutional changes of 1945–47 in one sense went further
than the hierarchy might have preferred, building the Church hierarchy
into the senior advisory state leadership for the first time since the early
nineteenth century. Prelates sat on both the Council of State and the new
Regency Council, introduced in 1947, others had been appointed by
Franco to the Cortes, and two priests were among the corporatively elected
deputies in its first session. Franco told the Cortes on May 14, 1946, "The
perfect state is for us the Catholic state. It does not suffice for us that
a people be Christian in order to fulfill the moral precepts of this order: laws are necessary to maintain its principles and correct abuses."[68]
By that time the broadest assortment of religious regulations seen in any
twentieth-century western state had been established in Spain, finally
completed with a new round of dispositions in 1950–53 preceding the
signing of the eventual concordat with the Vatican.[69]

What in the late 1960s would begin to be derisively called the Spanish
system of National Catholicism[70] offered many advantages to the Church.
These included a dominant voice in primary education, a series of financial subsidies and tax exemptions, the renovation and expansion of semi-
naries, manifold opportunities for publicity and proselytizing, juridical
enforcement of Church norms, enforcement of Catholic standards in fam-

67. Both these problems are discussed in Tusell, *Franco y los católicos*, 188–220.
68. *Iglesia, Estado y Movimiento Nacional*, 75–76.
69. A four-page list of such measures has been compiled by Ruiz Rico, *El papel*, 134–37.
70. The term was coined by opposition writers to mimic the regime's earlier slogan of
nacionalsindicalismo. According to some, it was first used by the essayist José Luis L.
Aranguren.

ily law and mores, and special juridical procedure and protection for clergy accused of violating civil law.

It can be argued that the advantages to the regime were even greater, however. Guy Hermet has suggested that the relationship served it in a variety of ways,[71] the most important being to help solidify its legitimacy and expand its base of support. In addition, close association with the Church provided means through which various organizations and lay groups might participate to some extent in public affairs. It offered a sounding board for interests otherwise ill-represented (even if this was no more than a chance to blow off steam), provided new cadres from which top political personnel might be selected, and contributed to elaborating the subsequent programs and objectives of the regime.[72]

Legitimization as Monarchy

While accentuation of the regime's Catholic identity was one major strategy to achieve legitimacy during the years of ostracism, a second was to make intensified use of monarchism. The fact that Franco had spent his first nine years largely in political temporizing, refusing to introduce the institutional features of a fully formed system, had been due in considerable nature to the dynamics of the European political context. Had Hitler and Mussolini won the war, a perpetual dictatorship of at least semi-fascism would no doubt have been fully feasible. Yet Franco had been sufficiently astute to realize from the beginning that the most viable outcome for his regime would probably be an authoritarian monarchy, combining traditional legitimacy with specific new features. Thus, even after Don Juan's Lausanne Manifesto, Franco had assured the National Council of the Movement on July 17, 1945, that "to assure my succession . . . of the systems universally accepted for the government of peoples only one is viable for us: the traditional Spanish system, in accordance with the principles of our doctrines,"[73] indicating that the Cortes would shortly prepare legislation to this end.

Two months later Carrero Blanco prepared a thirteen-page memorandum for the Caudillo, defining the two cornerstones of Spanish policy. On the international level the regime need only sit tight, for Britain and the

71. Hermet, "Les fonctions politiques des organisations religieuses dans les régimes à pluralisme limité," *Revue Française de Science Politique* 23:3 (June 1973), 439–72.

72. In an unpublished paper, "The Last Theocratic Regime in Western Europe: The Role of Traditional Catholicism in Legitimizing Franco's Regime" (Rome, 1976), Amando de Miguel has termed such a symbiosis *fascismo fráiluno* (friar fascism). This is perhaps not inaccurate if it is kept in mind that it refers to the symbiosis of neotraditionalist Catholicism and an essentially right-wing, not primarily fascist, system.

73. Quoted in López Rodó, *Larga marcha*, 55–56.

United States would never run the risk of direct intervention to hand the government of Spain over to the divided, leftist Republican government-in-exile (which in fact was never recognized by any of the major powers). Internally, the solution for the future would be the monarchy, but only on Franco's terms. The monarchist politicians lacked support to impose their will; Don Juan must be weaned away from them and brought to an understanding with the regime.[74]

While hoping to gain the support of the legitimate Pretender, Franco had been careful never in public or private to endorse directly the principle of dynastic legitimacy. He claimed to regard this as especially dubious in the case of the Spanish Bourbons, in view of their family history. Referring to a promiscuous nineteenth-century queen, Franco once observed that the father of the king could not be "the last person to go to bed with Doña Isabel." Monarchical succession was a complex issue involving both ability and principles and should not be decided by biology alone. One of his typically blunt and cynical comments was to the effect that "whatever comes out of the queen's womb should be tested for ability."[75]

The Generalissimo maintained contact with Don Juan through personal intermediaries during the autumn and winter of 1945–46 and decided not to oppose the Pretender's plan to move his residence to Portugal. Franco apparently believed the move might facilitate an interview which he could use to his own advantage, and therefore he indicated approval to the Portuguese government. On February 2, 1946, Don Juan took up residence in Estoril, a stylish suburb of Lisbon, establishing a base as close to Spain as possible. Once there, he showed no interest in visiting Franco on the latter's terms, while the Salazar regime granted him full autonomy and did not permit Franco's brother Nicolás, the long-term Spanish ambassador, to supervise his activities. Moreover, his arrival in the peninsula immediately sparked rumors of a new agreement with Franco that produced a letter of support signed by no less than 458 members of the Spanish elite, including two former Franco ministers (Galarza and Gamero del Castillo).[76]

This infuriated Franco, who had Nicolás announce to the Pretender on February 15 that, given the extreme differences in their positions, relations were now broken. Soon afterward General Kindelán, whom Franco held most responsible for collecting signatures to the letter, was ordered to undergo a period of internal exile in the Canary Islands.[77]

74. Ibid., 57–60.
75. According to Martín Artajo in *Franco y los catolicos*, 58.
76. The text is in Tusell, *La oposición democrática al franquismo* (Barcelona, 1977), 114. See also Heine, *La oposición*, 352.
77. Cf. Fernández, *Tensiones militares*, 71–72. After spending seven months in the Canaries, Kindelán passed to the reserve list three years later (1949), unremitting in his opposition to Franco.

At this point Don Juan's chief political advisor was Gil Robles, the Catholic leader who had supported Franco during the Civil War but subsequently turned against him for maintaining a permanent dictatorship. Gil Robles hoped to appeal to both the left and right wings of the opposition, first attempting to consolidate the support of a number of major Carlist figures who had recently rallied to the Pretender. The resulting "Bases institucionales de la Monarquía española," issued at Estoril late in February, contradicted the Lausanne Manifesto, reserving considerable power for the king and postulating a largely corporative form of parliament, only one-third of which would be chosen by direct election.[78] The Bases did, however, promise a national plebiscite on the restoration of the monarchy as well as some decentralization of government.

Gil Robles then tried to gain the support of the non-Communist left for the holding of such a plebiscite as the first step in creating a practical alternative to Franco. Since the new Bases seemed to indicate that Don Juan was far from committed to a democratic, directly elected parliamentary system, the Republican government-in-exile rejected this proposal, though negotiations continued for some time with the Alianza Nacional de Fuerzas Democráticas, representing all the clandestine left-liberal opposition inside Spain except the Communists. Two years of complex dickering and maneuvering between the monarchist right and the non-Communist left followed. There were sporadic efforts to mediate by the most active and persistent of the military conspirators, the indefatigable Aranda, until Franco interrupted Aranda's inveterate plotting by sending him off to two months of internal exile in the Balearics at the beginning of 1947.[79]

As the months passed, Carrero Blanco urged Franco to make use of the wave of popular support for the government being created in 1946–47 (some of it genuine) to proceed with setting up a workable monarchist succession strictly on his own terms.[80] Such a move would seize the initiative from the monarchist politicians and ratify Franco's existing powers, yet legitimize them by converting the state system into a monarchy. Moreover, announcement of the Truman Doctrine on March 12, 1947, inaugurating the first official phase of western resistance to Communist expansion, began to open prospects of a polarized international situation which a relegitimized Spanish regime might exploit to end the prevailing ostracism.

78. José Ma. Gil Robles, *La monarquía por la que yo luché: Páginas de un diario (1941–1954)* (Madrid, 1976), 166–68; Tusell, *Oposición democrática*, 116–20.

79. See Heine, *La oposición*, 354–80, and Tusell, *Oposición democrática*, 152–61. Gil Robles created a sort of umbrella organization called the Confederación Española de Fuerzas Monárquicas, including representatives of the old CEDA, the Carlists, and Renovación Española. In 1947 Aranda tried to counter the rightist bias of this relatively short-lived confederation with an abortive Comunidad de Organizaciones Monárquicas de España designed to attract moderates and liberals.

80. López Rodó, *Larga marcha*, 73.

The new Succession Law was ready by March 27. Its first article stipulated, "Spain, as a political unit, is a Catholic, social, and representative state which, in keeping with her tradition, declares herself constituted into a kingdom." The second specified, "The Head of State is the caudillo of Spain and of the Crusade, Generalissimo of the Armed Forces, Don Francisco Franco Bahamonde." The Spanish state was thereby declared to be a monarchy which Franco would govern until his death or "incapacity." He would have the right to name his royal successor for approval by the Cortes. The future king must be male, Spanish, Catholic, and at least thirty years of age, and must swear to uphold the Fundamental Laws of the Regime and of the Movement. There was no mention of any legitimate dynastic right of succession in the royal family until after Franco had designated a royal successor, whereas the law reserved to him the power to cancel the right of succession of any member of the royal family in the event of "notorious departure from the fundamental principles of the state."[81]

Two new institutions, a Regency Council and a Council of the Realm, were also created. The Regency Council would be composed of three members: the president of the Cortes, the most senior general of the armed forces, and "the highest-ranking prelate serving as Councillor of the Realm for the longest period."[82] Its function would be to serve as interim regency during the transition to Franco's successor and, in the event that he were to die without having named one, convene the members of the Council of the Realm and the cabinet jointly to select one.[83]

The Council of the Realm was designed as a special deputy to the executive, creating a sort of diarchic structure for an authoritarian monarchy. It stemmed from Napoleonic precedents, and twenty years earlier had been proposed by Gabriel Maura as part of the abortive Primo de Rivera constitutional reforms. The Council of the Realm would "have precedence over the consultative bodies of the nation" and "assist the Head of State on highly important matters and resolutions falling within his exclusive competence."[84] The president of the Cortes would preside over it, joined by "the prelate of the highest rank and seniority among those who are procuradores of the Cortes,"[85] the most senior general, the head of the Alto Estado Mayor, two members each elected by the National Council of the Movement, the syndicates and local government officials, and one member selected by university rectors and the professional

81. *Fundamental Laws of the State*, 119.
82. Ibid., 112.
83. In the event that they could not identify an appropriate candidate of "royal blood," they were empowered to name a regent for whatever term they saw fit, subject to the approval of the Cortes.
84. Ibid., 113.
85. Ibid., 113.

colleges. The Council of the Realm would have responsibility to declare war and reexamine all laws voted by the Cortes.

This legislation was designed to formally legitimize the Civil War *caudillaje*, recognizing Franco as the supreme organ of the state who could not be relieved of his powers without the action of two-thirds of the government ministers and two-thirds of the Council of the Realm, followed by a two-thirds vote of the Cortes. Since all the members of these bodies had been appointed either directly or indirectly by Franco, this was an altogether implausible prospect unless he were to fall into a prolonged coma.

A direct corollary was the recognition of Franco's personal power as the sovereign constitutional organ of the state, holding the right to develop new institutions without temporal limitation on its use. In lieu of a unified written code or constitution, article 10 recognized as "Fundamental Laws of the Nation" the Fuero de los Españoles, the Fuero del Trabajo (the Labor Statute of 1938), the Constitutive Law of the Cortes, "the present Law of Succession," the Law of the National Referendum recently instituted, "and any other which may be promulgated in the future in this category."

Carrero Blanco delivered the text of this new legislation to the Pretender in Estoril on March 31, only hours before Franco announced it to the nation. This aroused rage and consternation within the royal circle, for it went even further than the project of an authoritarian reform and *instauración* of the sort proposed by *Acción Española* under the Republic, making the succession elective and dependent on the pleasure of a military dictator.[86] On April 7 Don Juan launched a public manifesto which began, "Spaniards: General Franco has publicly announced his intention to present to the so-called parliament a Law of Succession to the Head of State, by which Spain is constituted as a kingdom and there is projected a system completely opposed to the laws that have historically regulated the succession to the Throne."[87] The manifesto took a strong stand on the principle of hereditary succession, emphasizing that the new system adopted a principle of election based neither on the royal dynasty nor on a truly elected parliament. The Carlist leader Don Javier de Borbón-Parma also protested in a personal letter to Franco. Both these messages were of course completely suppressed within Spain. Through the media of the Movement the government immediately launched a campaign against Don Juan as an enemy of the regime and of Spain. Falangist bureaucrats who continued to staff the Movement were usually eager to co-

86. On the visit to Estoril and its aftermath, see Tusell, *Oposición democrática*, 161–70. The monarchist version is given in Gil Robles, *La monarquía*, 206–7; and that of Carrero in López Rodó, *Larga marcha*, 76–88.
87. The text may be found in Fernández-Doria, *Franquismo*, 38–40.

Eva Perón with Franco and his wife at the Royal Palace in Madrid, June 1947

operate, for in most cases they opposed the monarchy as their number-one enemy on the right.[88]

Franco, now defined as a sort of regent for life, spent the second half of May in Barcelona, his longest visit to any city in five years, as local factotums of the Movement organized the usual crowds. The gala reception given the following month to Evita Perón, who was in Spain from June 8 to 25, was an even more splendid occasion of international resonance.

The Law of Succession was rubber-stamped by the Cortes on June 7, with a national referendum scheduled for the following month. This did not involve any particular danger, in the government's view, for a sounding requested of the Movement's Delegación Nacional de Provincias reported that of the fifty provinces of Spain only two, the main Basque provinces of Vizcaya and Guipuzcoa, were clearly "enemies" of the regime, with six others "doubtful."[89] The indications were that the referendum would

88. Even the small dissident Falangist groups that had carried out a few feeble and marginal activities in 1945–46 directed some of their spleen toward the monarchy, distributing pamphlets entitled "Ni Rey ni Roque."

89. These included the Carlist province of Navarre, the third Basque province of Alava, one Catalan province (Lérida), Teruel, and two populous leftist provinces in Andalusia, Seville and Malaga. Tusell, *Franco y los católicos*, 163–64.

carry by at least 63 percent, and this could be expanded by an all-out propaganda campaign, supported by a pastoral letter from the primate. On June 25 the *Boletín Oficial del Estado* announced that ration cards would be requested for voter identification and would be stamped at the polling place, and other means of persuasion were also reported. Yet by that point the failure of both international diplomatic pressure and the internal insurgency was becoming apparent. Whether or not most Spaniards supported the regime in a positive sense, relatively few saw any real alternative to it. The turnout on July 6 was by all reports massive, and the government subsequently claimed that of 17,178,812 qualified adult voters, a total of 15,219,565 cast ballots. Of these, 14,145,163 were reported as voting yes, 722,656 no, and 336,592 were null or mutilated.[90] Whatever the real figures, this was a major step for the regime, creating at least a certain theoretical or polemical legitimacy as well as a mechanism for the succession to Franco, and it had been done without making any concessions.

One of Franco's first measures in the use of his newly minted "regential" prerogatives was to announce in October 1947 arrangements for creating new titles of nobility in accordance with the powers just ratified. Three of the first recipients of dukedoms in 1948 were the heirs of Primo de Rivera, Mola and Calvo Sotelo, while the status of count was awarded to those of the Carlist Pradera and the Falangist Redondo. Altogether, Franco created thirty-six new titles over the years, most of them by 1961. They were given mainly in recognition of loyal service during the early period of the regime. Two-thirds of the surviving members of the original Junta de Defensa Nacional that had elevated Franco in 1936 were ennobled and were among the twenty-two public figures of the founding decade to be so rewarded. Seventeen of the titles, or nearly half, went to the military, but only three to Falangists.[91]

Waning of the Opposition Offensive

The opposition's offensive immediately after World War II was threefold: The organization of armed maquis or guerrilla detachments to attack police outposts in the countryside and rob banks in the cities, the revival of

90. See the discussion in Max Gallo, *Histoire de l'Espagne franquiste* (Paris, 1969), 1:214. According to the figures in Sueiro and Díaz Nosty (1985), *Historia*, 2:106–7, by far the highest percentages of abstention occurred in Asturias (32.48), Madrid (30.08), and Barcelona (29.50). Vizcaya was only in seventh place with 21.59 percent abstention or no vote, and Guipuzcoa far down the line with 15.13. The fullest turnouts on behalf of the regime were registered in Valladolid and Avila.

91. Cf. the analysis by Pi-Sunyer, *El personal*, 130–33. Franco found the bureaucrats and nouveaux riches who were prominent in the later years of the regime less worthy of recognition.

Table 15.1. Summary of the Guerrilla Offensive in Spain 1943–49 (based on
official government statistics)

Armed robberies	5,963
Insurgents arrested or captured	3,400
Accomplices arrested	19,444
Civilians killed by guerrilleros	953
Insurgents or leftist "bandits" killed	2,173
Civil Guards killed	257
Army troops killed	27
Policemen killed	23

Source: Francisco Aguado Sánchez, *El maquis en
España* (Madrid, 1975).

strike activity in industrial areas, and the renewal of organized activity by
clandestine political groups. All three kinds of activity peaked during the
years 1946–47. The Communists had taken the lead in guerrilla warfare,
but the anarchosyndicalist CNT did not begin to achieve maximal operational strength until 1947, launching their first major drive in Catalonia
during the summer of that year. After 1949 the activities of both groups
rapidly waned. The Communists abandoned the guerrilla struggle in
1952, and the anarchist actions continued weakly and sporadically into
1963. Official government statistics for the main period of counterinsurgency from 1943 to 1949 are given in table 15.1.[92]

The regime's success in counterinsurgency was due to several factors.
Though the paramilitary Civil Guard did most of the police work and
fighting, sizable military forces were also committed. Large-scale Army
deployment gave the counterinsurgency the heavy preponderance of manpower necessary for success, making it possible to control the countryside
without disruption of civilian life. Moreover, many of the mountain and
forest regions of the north which were most propitious for guerrilla operations were inhabited by conservative, Catholic farmers not disposed to
shelter or support the insurgents. Though some sanctuary was available to
insurgents in southwestern France, its extent was eventually reduced by
French authorities.

Director of the Civil Guard from 1943 to 1955 was Lt. Gen. Camilo
Alonso Vega, a key figure in the regime's security policy. He had been in

92. Different statistics may be found in the appendix to Eduardo Pons Prades, *Guerrillas
españolas 1936–1960* (Barcelona, 1977); and in Enrique Líster, "Lessons of the Spanish
Guerrilla War (1939–1951)," *World Marxist Review*, Feb. 1965, pp. 53–58. See also Andrés
Sorel, *La guerrilla española del siglo XX* (Paris, 1970), which provides a brief description
of the period 1944–49 from the viewpoint of the guerrilleros; and Rafael Gómez Parra,
La guerrilla antifranquista 1945–1949 (Madrid, 1983), which deals primarily with the
Communists.

considerable measure responsible for persuading Franco not to dissolve the Civil Guard after the Civil War, when Franco, disturbed by the support of some of the Civil Guard for the Republic, had considered establishing a single unified armed police corps. Alonso Vega carried out a thorough remilitarization of his corps, choosing all its top commanders from among regular Army officers, and he enforced unbending discipline and ideological purity among its members. His policies were both successful and enduring, with effects more paradoxical than he could have anticipated; save for one major exception the Civil Guard would survive the Franco regime itself and serve the subsequent democratic system with little loss of morale, even when it had to bear the brunt of post–Franco terrorism.

The strike activity of 1946–47 was centered in the Basque provinces and Catalonia, reaching a climax in a major industrial walkout in Vizcaya that began on May 1, 1947. The state syndical system in the province broke down, and within three days at least 60,000 workers had left their jobs. Stringent measures were taken by the police and employers to break the strike. There were reports of as many as 7,000 workers temporarily arrested and another 14,000 fired from their jobs,[93] though these figures may be too high. Such tough measures achieved their goal. Unsupported by effective political activity elsewhere or any dent in the regime's internal unity or mechanism of repression, worker dissidence began to subside after 1947.

Though armed repression was left to the Civil Guard and armed police, juridical prosecution of political dissidence remained the province of military courts. All pertinent legislation in this area was recapitulated by a new Ley de Represión del Bandidaje y Terrorismo (Law for the Repression of Banditry and Terrorism) announced on April 17, 1947.

Some thousands of leftist prisoners were still under detention and there were still occasional executions, though normally only of those convicted of *delitos de sangre* (crimes of blood, usually killings). An occasional leftist militant died under police beatings. Monarchist activists were treated much more gently as a kind of semilegal opposition, though even major generals were sometimes arrested, and one of the most determined civilian leaders, the young Luisa María Narváez, Duquesa de Valencia, served various sentences that added up to twenty-two months in prison.[94]

93. L. Ferri, J. Muixi, and E. Sanjuan, *Las huelgas contra Franco (1939–1956)* (Barcelona, 1978), 94–130; and Alberto Elordi, "Euskadi: la huelga del primero de mayo de 1947," *Historia 16* 8:82 (Feb. 1983), 19–25. On Catalonia, see Cipriano Damiano González, *La resistencia libertaria (1939–1970)* Barcelona, 1978).

94. In Madrid, young monarchists formed an activist group called Avanzadilla Monárquica to engage in such modest activities as distributing literature in the street. The group was closed down by the police in 1948, but one of its militants, a youth named Carlos Méndez

Franco's success in the 1947 referendum that made the state a monarchy accelerated the division of the opposition political groups. In July, the Socialist party abandoned the Republican government-in-exile to attempt an understanding with the monarchists. Most other emigré parties began to follow their example, condemning the Republican government to the merest shadow of an existence in exile. Yet the ensuing Socialist-monarchist entente was ineffective and soon broke down. Gil Robles, the chief monarchist advisor, more or less admitted that under the circumstances which they faced, new maneuvers of that sort were virtually hopeless.[95] The regime felt sufficiently secure to hold the first public trials of oppositionists—fourteen students—in Madrid that summer.

The armed opposition was still capable of action, and on several occasions in 1948–49 there were gunbattles even in the streets of Barcelona with anarchist urban guerrillas, but the insurgency grew steadily weaker and more isolated.[96] A decree of April 7, 1948, finally ended the general terms of martial law that had been in effect since the Civil War, though all political offenses of any magnitude would continue to be tried by court-martial. In November, the government felt secure enough to implement a reform announced three years earlier, holding the first indirect corporative municipal elections. Such a controlled process involved no political risks, though in a note to Franco the foreign minister lamented the clumsiness of the first official announcement, which as he put it "unnecessarily reveals the limited character of the voting."[97]

Rapprochement with Don Juan

Though Franco acted as if he was prepared to turn his back on the direct line of the Bourbon dynasty and seek an eventual successor elsewhere, a rapprochement on his own terms with the Conde de Barcelona was by far the most desirable goal and would further strengthen the regime. The consolidation of his own position as head of state through the Law of Succession greatly increased Franco's leverage. The heir to the throne had few alternatives, for the possibilities of independent monarchist initiative had dwindled to nil. One last effort to rally the monarchists at the home of

---

González, was kept in prison almost incommunicado for months, despite a heart condition, dying in detention on November 7, 1948, the very date of the arrival of the young Prince Juan Carlos in Spain. Méndez was the only direct fatality registered by the monarchist resistance.

95. Gil Robles, *La monarquía*, 227–43.

96. For a brief general treatment of the internal opposition groups in the late 1940s, see Valentina Fernández Vargas, *La resistencia interior en la Espana de Franco* (Madrid, 1981), 109–50.

97. Quoted in Tusell, *Franco y los católicos*, 180.

a Madrid aristocrat in March 1948 featured a speech by Kindelán, but its only consequence was another brief detention for the general.[98]

Franco had intermittently sought a meeting with Don Juan for more than two years, and one was finally arranged on the Caudillo's yacht *Azor* off San Sebastián on August 25, 1948. The resulting three-hour conversation was not fully congenial, for Franco tended to treat the heir to the throne as a political ignoramus uninformed on conditions inside Spain. Nonetheless, Don Juan felt that he had no choice but to agree to a political truce. Franco explained that his own work was not yet completed and that a quick restoration would be desirable only in the event of a war with the Soviet Union (in which case Franco would have to assume active command of the military) or of national economic bankruptcy, a contingency that seemed equally unlikely. Franco promised to put an end to the propaganda against the royal family, and Don Juan himself suggested that it would soon be appropriate for his oldest son and heir, the cherubic, blond, brown-eyed Prince Juan Carlos, to continue his personal education inside Spain. Franco readily agreed to this, for it opened the possibility of training a younger eventual Bourbon heir within the framework of the regime itself.[99]

The ten-year-old prince arrived in Spain on November 7, 1948, to begin a difficult role.[100] Franco did not entirely make good on his pledge to eliminate antimonarchist propaganda, for he did not supervise the Movement very closely and he did not insist that its bureaucrats eliminate all expression of antimonarchist sentiment. Juan Carlos would encounter a great deal of intermittent hostility from some members of the regime during the next decade. It was during these adolescent years away from his family and in an uncertain environment that he developed the somewhat melancholy expression that later became familiar.

On September 19, 1949, after Juan Carlos had been in Spain ten months, his father wrote a strong letter to Franco threatening to withdraw his son, since the regime was doing little to favor the monarchy. Franco, as usual, did not reply for a full month, and when he did Gil Robles described the letter as follows:

It is a very extensive note whose two principal characteristics are overweening pride and poor syntax. The chief ideas of this absurd fabrication, doubtless edited by Franco himself, are the following: 1— that in the interview on the

98. Part of the text of Kindelán's speech is given in his *La verdad*, 351–55.
99. The principal account that we have of this famous meeting is the version of Don Juan as recorded in Gil Robles's diary, *La monarquía*, 267–73. See also Créac'h, *Le Coeur* 234–35; and González-Doria, *Franquismo*, 43–44.
100. For his early childhood before his arrival in Spain, see the heavily illustrated portrait by Juan Antonio Pérez Mateos, *Juan Carlos: La infancia desconocida de un Rey* (Barcelona, 1980).

Azor he made no promises; 2— that he ought to be thanked for having initiated the possibility of a monarchist regime with the Law of Succession, since it would have been easier to install a different system; 3— that the education of the Prince in Spain is a benefit for him and for the dynasty that has not been adequately appreciated; 4— that he fails to see that the presence of the Prince creates any equivocal situation, though this was clearly made manifest by Franco in his speech before the Cortes in May where he violently attacked the monarchy; 5— that in no way should one think about replacing the present regime; 6— that the King's attitude comes from a little clique of monarchist busybodies and the negative activity of bad counsellors; 7— that the King should consider how difficult monarchist restorations are today. All this is in a confused and exaggerated tone in which he calls himself Caudillo while addressing the King only as Highness and making repeated references to what is good for the dynasty.[101]

In this unequal contest Franco held almost all the cards. Nothing had come of Gil Robles's attempts to bring together the Socialists and the monarchist opposition, for this ploy had merely divided the left while stimulating conservative monarchists to renew their support for Franco. The most persistent conspirator of the decade, Aranda, still pursued his confabulations among the military, and as late as July 1949 tried to persuade the incumbent captains general of Barcelona and Madrid, Solchaga and Varela, to precipitate a coup that would restore the monarchy.[102] This was finally too much for Franco, who treated high-ranking generals with great tact and even indulgence, but on this occasion he promulgated special ad hominem legislation to place Aranda on the permanent retirement list, putting an end to the political vocation of the Army's most persistent gadfly of the post–Civil War decade.[103] This, along with the retirement of Kindelán, also ended the last gestures of monarchist conspiracy among the military. Early in 1950 a monarchist note was handed to the American chargé in Madrid urging support for the monarchy as an alternative to Franco and bearing several hundred names. The Generalissimo felt secure enough after obtaining a copy to have the entire list published in the monarchist *ABC* as a list of traitors to the nation.[104] For his part, Don Juan directed his followers to maintain their independent activity and tried to sustain military contacts, but had no other option save to continue the same terms of his unequal relationship with Franco.

101. Gil Robles, *La monarquía*, 308–10.
102. Heine, *La oposición*, 401–3.
103. This legislation, which became known colloquially as the "ley Aranda" (Aranda law), was promulgated on July 13, 1949, providing for the permanent retirement, at the discretion of the command, of senior officers at the rank of colonel and above who had been passed over for promotion by at least 10 percent of the holders of their rank. Aranda was given one last chance to repent, and then placed in premature retirement along with a score or so of other promonarchist officers. In 1977, just before the general's death, King Juan Carlos restored Aranda's full seniority.
104. *FF*, 4:383–87.

The End of Ostracism

Political developments abroad during 1947–48 prepared the way for an end to the formal boycott of the regime. The establishment of Communist dictatorships in the Soviet-occupied countries of Poland, Hungary, Romania, and Bulgaria in 1946–47 inevitably provoked a hostile response among the western powers, and the United States' support of the anti-Communist forces in the Greek civil war—the only analogy to the Spanish conflict in post–World War II Europe—helped to demarcate a new political boundary. In October 1947 the Soviet Union partially renounced one of its official fictions by establishing a new international Communist Information Agency (Cominform) in place of the old Comintern which it had (only formally) dissolved during the war, finding it no longer useful to disguise its promotion of Communist movements abroad. In the following month, as tensions increased in Italy and France, Communist deputies were expelled from the Italian government, as they would later be from that of France. In March 1948, the previously representative government of Czechoslovakia, the only surviving democratic country in east-central Europe, was converted into a Communist regime through à bloodless coup d'etat. The Cold War had begun.

The regime sustained its own informational counteroffensive throughout this period,[105] emphasizing that Franco had been the first and most vocal to warn of the dangers of Communist expansion in Europe. In numerous government statements and in several official interviews of Franco with foreign journalists, the regime advertised its availability for a western anti-Communist alliance, a project in which the Spanish leadership, as it was pointed out, had more experience than any other.

At the United Nations General Assembly session of November 17, 1947, a Soviet-inspired initiative which would have authorized the Security Council to take some sort of unspecified action against the Spanish regime failed to carry by the necessary two-thirds. Among those voting against it were the United States, Canada, Australia, and a large number of Latin American countries.[106] This made it clear that the international policy of ostracism was weakening, and on February 10, 1948, France opened the Pyrenean frontier for the first time in nearly two years.

105. Some of its major expressions were Tomás Elorrieta y Artazu, *La Carta de las Naciones Unidas y la postdata soviética: El llamado caso de España ante la ONU* (Madrid, 1947); Oficina de Información Diplomática, *Spain and the United Nations Organization* (Madrid, 1949); and Gonzalo Rodríguez Castillo, *Notes for Posterity. Communist World Offensive against Spain: A Report on the "Spanish Case" in the United Nations Organization (January–April, 1946)* (Madrid, 1949). Somewhat useful to the Spanish case from the American side were two historical accounts, Herbert Feis's *The Spanish Story: Franco and the Nations at War* (New York, 1948); and C. J. H. Hayes, *The United States and Spain: An Interpretation* (New York, 1951).

106. For a detailed account of this maneuver and its background, see Huff, "The Spanish Question," 342–69.

In accordance with the Truman doctrine of assisting Greece and Turkey against Communist pressure, the United States had begun to look for strategic support in the Mediterranean. In February 1948 Admiral Forrest Sherman, chief of United States Naval Operations, made an ostensibly private visit to Madrid, where his son-in-law was naval attaché, in conjunction with a Mediterranean trip. There he also met with Carrero Blanco, ever eloquent in arguing the geostrategic importance of Spain. In the following month, Representative Alvin O'Konski of Wisconsin succeeded in adding an amendment to new legislation establishing an American Marshall Plan for Europe that would have included Spain, but the Truman administration cut it out of the final bill.[107]

The Spanish government undertook new initiatives that spring, negotiating commercial agreements with Britain and France in May. The slippery and astute Lequerica, dropped from the Foreign Ministry three years earlier, was given a specially created position, director of embassies, enabling him to take up ad hoc residence in Washington, where he helped to supervise a remarkably successful Spanish lobbying campaign over the next two years. Chief representative for the subsequently notorious "Spanish lobby" was the Washington lawyer Charles Patrick Clark (who at one point was being paid a retainer of $100,000 per year), though others like the firm of Cummings, Stanley, Truitt and Cross were also used.[108] One of the first benefits was negotiation of a $25 million loan to the Spanish government from the Chase National Bank in February 1949.

Thus Franco's annual end-of-the-year address for 1948 on New Year's Eve could declare that the time of trial was over and that the postwar crisis, both political and economic, had come to an end. Later, in October 1949, he made his second and last journey outside Spain, the only true state visit during the long history of the regime, when he traveled to Portugal. After being made Doctor Honoris Causa by the University of Coimbra, he responded to a carefully controlled press conference—also the only one of his career. In a final address before the Portuguese authorities, he indulged in one of the customarily megalomaniac hyperboles of regime propaganda, intoning that the political principles "which only five years ago sounded like heresy beyond our frontiers now fill the ambit of the universe."[109]

Though President Truman remained personally hostile to Franco,[110]

107. Angel Viñas, "El Plan Marshall rechazó a Franco," *Historia 16* 6:64 (Aug. 1981), 27–42 (repr. in Viñas's *Guerra, dinero, dictadura*, 265–87).

108. The key study is R. W. Gilmore, "The American Foreign Policy-Making Process and the Development of a Post–World War II Spanish Policy, 1945–1953: A Case Study" (Ph. D. diss., University of Pittsburgh, 1967), 162–85.

109. Fernández, *Franco*, 150.

110. A Baptist and Freemason, Truman was particularly incensed at the regime's discrimination against Protestants. He is reported to have said, "I never had any use for Franco. That's all that needs to be said. . . . He wouldn't let a Baptist be buried in daylight. That's the

general American opinion was changing rapidly in 1948–49. A poll taken in Massachusetts during May and June 1948 reported that 30 percent of the opinion sampled was hostile to the Spanish regime, and a national survey in November showed 25 percent opposed to admitting Spain to the United Nations, while only 18 percent favored it. A Gallup poll at the end of 1949 reported that of the 56 percent of the sample interviewed who were able to identify Franco, 26 percent favored admission and only 18 percent were opposed.[111] Such disparate samples could not in themselves produce reliable conclusions, but the obvious inference was borne out by other evidence as well. In 1945 a rally against the Spanish regime was able to assemble 16,000 in Madison Square Garden, but a similar rally in January 1950 drew a mere 1,000.

The leaders in altering American policy toward Spain during 1949–50 were a small group of senators and congressmen headed by Pat McCarran of Nevada,[112] reinforced by members of the military. Political and geostrategic convictions seem to have been the dominant factors; there was, for example, no correlation between home-district Catholic voting blocs and congressional support.[113] McCarran liked to emphasize that the Spanish regime was "the world's most violently anti-Communist government."[114] As chairman of the Senate Appropriations Committee he sponsored three attempts to authorize a loan to Spain through the United States Export-Import Bank. The third effort, in August 1950, was finally successful. Though the Truman administration at first refused to ratify the measure, the United Nations vote of November 4, 1950, which cancelled the terms of the 1946 ban on the Spanish regime, brought a reversal of government policy. On November 16 a loan of $62.5 million was approved, and at the close of December an American ambassador, the first in four and a half years, was named to Madrid. Spain would never be included in the Marshall Plan and under the Franco regime would never be invited to join the newly formed North Atlantic Treaty Organization, while entry into the United Nations would be delayed five more years. Nonetheless, by the close of 1950 the most severe aspects of the international ostracism had come to an end.

truth. He had to be buried at night in plowed ground." Quoted in L. W. Koenig, "Foreign Aid to Spain and Yugoslavia," in *The Uses of Power*, ed. A. F. Westin (New York, 1962), 102.

111. Gilmore, "Foreign Policy-Making Process," 203–4.

112. Robert N. Slawson, "Formulation of United States Policy towards Spain since 1948, with Emphasis on Congressional Activity" (Master's thesis, University of Wisconsin, 1951), is a contemporary study of congressional policy during this period.

113. Gilmore, "Foreign Policy-Making Process," 231. Theodore Lowi, "Bases in Spain," in *American Civil-Military Decisions*, ed. H. Stein (Tuscaloosa, 1963), 667–702, pinpoints several small groups that pressed for a new policy toward the Spanish regime in the American Congress.

114. As in his article "Why Shouldn't the Spanish Fight for Us?" *Saturday Evening Post*, Apr. 28, 1951, p. 137, quoted in Gilmore, "Foreign Policy-Making Process," 176.

16

Social and Economic
Policy
in the 1940s

The policy of economic autarchy and import substitution adopted in 1939 remained in effect, with varying degrees of modification, for the next two decades. As discussed earlier, autarchy suited Franco's own predilections as well as the international conditions during World War II, and the policy of ostracism made its continuation almost inevitable after 1945. A few economic administrators such as the commerce minister Carceller had urged a more liberal and internationalist approach during the last phase of World War II, but such an option would not emerge fully until the 1950s, and even then the regime would be slow to take advantage of it.

There is no doubt that the program of autarchy was generally inefficient.[1] Policy was relatively arbitrary and frequently improvised, and it varied considerably from one sector to another with little attempt at coordination. It intended to discourage the international market and exports in general while emphasizing import substitution industries. State controls determined nominal prices and wages in most categories, and state policy reinforced the existing structure of small enterprises by providing credit no matter how inefficient the firm. Thus the economies of scale required for optimal functioning usually could not be achieved, and when new plants were established in nonindustrialized areas—laudable from the viewpoint of overcoming regional imbalance—that also increased their cost. More rapid and efficient development required intensive capital investment as well as new technology, both in short supply, while state

1. For general economic policy during 1945–50, see Ros Hombravella et al., 1:172–270. A critique of the paternalism and limited rationality of development under autarchy will be found in Carlos Moya, *El poder económico en España (1939–1970)* (Madrid, 1975), 93–119, 143–71. Miguel Capella, *La autarquía económica en España* (Madrid, 1945), presents an idealized official description of the autarchy policy at this time.

Table 16.1. Foreign Commerce of Spain, 1940–50

| | Adjusted Index | | |
	Imports	Exports	Balance in Millions of Gold Pesetas
1931	90	116	−211
1935	100	100	−290
1940	55	49	−226
1941	45	46	−29
1942	46	43	25
1943	48	56	−30
1944	41	73	130
1945	47	68	18
1946	52	56	−110
1947	63	59	−276
1948	69	72	−326
1949	69	76	−225
1950	64	98	−5

Source: Instituto Nacional de Estadística, in Viñas et al., *Política comercial exterior en España* (Madrid, 1979), 1:489.

priorities and international ostracism combined to discourage any search for foreign capital.

Autarchy was most rigorous in foreign commerce and exchange.[2] As indicated in table 16.1, Spain regained her approximate pre–Civil War level of exports only in 1950, while financial stringency and a persistently negative balance kept vital imports below the norm of 1936.

By this time Franco had abandoned his extravagant notions about Spain's national resources. He almost reversed the argument in an address to Asturian miners in May 1946, attributing Spain's lower standard of living to her lack of colonies. "Nobody in the universe works for Spain," the Caudillo declared. "Spaniards earn their bread by the sweat of their brow."[3] Such an explanation was well suited to the pompous rhetoric of the period, for it arrogated to Spain a position of moral superiority, relatively poor but honorable and nonexploitative compared with the major powers.

State policy emphasized coal and steel production and hydroelectric expansion, areas that had registered major gains by the close of the 1940s. The National Institute of Industry (INI) played a significant role, espe-

2. It has been suggested that the personalistic system of control reached its height in the "modelo Navascués," as developed by Emilio Navascués y Ruiz de Velasco in the Secretaría de Economía Exterior y Comercio from February 1947 to March 1948. Angel Viñas, "La administración de la política económica exterior de España, 1936–1979," *Cuadernos Económicos de ICE*, no. 13 (1980), 157–247. For a detailed treatment of external commercial policy in the late 1940s, see Viñas et al., *Política comercial*, 1:453–616.

3. Quoted in Trythall, *Caudillo*, 217.

cially in coal, fuels, and electric power. From 1942 to 1948 it developed major new enterprises including the national airline Iberia (1943) and ENASA (1946), which fostered Pegaso, the country's principal producer of trucks and buses, while participating in the restructuring and expansion of scores of others.[4] The railroad and telephone systems were also nationalized, and rails and highways, which had generally deteriorated, began to receive more attention beginning in 1946.

General industrial production surpassed the 1935 level by 2 percent in 1946. Textiles languished, even in 1948 reaching only 60 percent of the pre–Civil War figure. The chemical industry did not regain its 1935 level until 1950, but as early as 1940 coal output exceeded the prewar total by about 30 percent and by 1945 was more than 60 percent higher. The most spectacular growth was in electrical production, which by 1948 was nearly double that of a decade earlier even though drought still left intermittent shortages. By 1948 overall investment began to accelerate, and from that time industrial expansion was more general.[5] The first all-Spanish transport plane was produced in 1949.

Agriculture, the largest division of the economy, remained with textiles the most depressed, total production continuing well below averages for pre–Civil War years. A Ley de Intensificación de Cultivos was promulgated in 1940 to try to force landowners to bring more soil under cultivation, but state compulsion—not very rigorously enforced in Spain—had no more success than in the Soviet Union. In 1939, only 77 percent of the wheat-growing area cultivated before the war was under production, and this increased very slowly, finally reaching 90 percent ten years later.[6] The 1941 wheat harvest was only 2.4 million tons, whereas nearly 4 million tons were needed. Weather conditions were intermittently very poor for much of the decade, the drought of 1944–45 resulting in the lowest cereal harvest of the century, worse even than the calamitous year 1904 (previously the poorest). Thus wheat production in 1945 was only 53 percent of the pre–Civil War average, and by 1946 food production had risen to only 79 percent of the 1929 level, falling back temporarily to 64 percent in 1948.

The effects of prolonged drought were compounded by poor management and lack of investment and technical improvement, for which state

4. On the growth of the INI during the 1940s, see Schwartz and González, *Una historia,* 39–68.

5. Three contemporary descriptions of the Spanish economy in this period are Higinio París Eguilaz, *La expansión de la economía española* (Madrid, 1944); Manuel Fuentes Irurozqui, *Síntesis de la economía española* (Madrid, 1946); and J. M. Ruiz Morales, *La economía del Bloque Hispanoportugués* (Madrid, 1946). Félix Gordón Ordás, *Al borde del desastre: Economía y finanzas de España (1939–1951)* (Mexico City, 1952), is an extremely critical account by an emigré politician.

6. Henri Marti, "Agriculture and Politics in Spain, 1936–1960" (Ph.D. diss., University of Michigan, 1979), 206.

Table 16.2. Agricultural Investments, 1942–1950

Year	Agricultural Investments as Percentage of Total Private and Public Investments	Budget of the Ministry of Agriculture as Percentage of Total Budget
1942	4.74	0.84
1943	2.70	0.83
1944	3.69	0.84
1945	3.98	0.89
1946	3.41	0.89
1947	4.29	0.78
1948	3.67	0.86
1949	4.08	0.85
1950	4.53	0.95

Source: Henry Marti, "Agriculture and Politics in Spain, 1936–1960" (Ph.D. diss., University of Michigan, 1979), 157–58.

policy and regulations were at least partly responsible. Miguel Primo de Rivera, minister of agriculture from 1941 to 1945, had no qualifications whatever for the position, though his successor and fellow Falangist, Carlos Rein Segura, did hold a degree in agricultural engineering. The Spanish state simply paid little attention to the agricultural base of its economy in allocating production resources (see table 16.2). Throughout the decade of rationing and severe hardship it was thus necessary for a still primarily agricultural country to use much of its limited foreign exchange to import basic foodstuffs. (Spain was not alone in this; it has been a common experience for underdeveloped twentieth-century economies.)

Not surprisingly, foodstuffs were the most important commodities on the widespread black market of the 1940s. The National Wheat Service was unable to fully control grain supplies, so that about one-third of all grain produced in the country during the forties ended up on the black market.[7] Since this was sold at much higher than government prices, it provided about 60 percent of the income of domestic grain producers. A law of September 30, 1940, provided for stiff fines and prison terms for buyers and sellers in the black market, and as mentioned earlier, the death penalty was soon afterward instituted for particularly serious crimes. During the first year of the new sanctions approximately 5,000 traffickers were sentenced to prison and more than 100 million pesetas in fines were levied,[8] but this had very little effect, because of the extreme shortages and the maladministration and growing corruption of the sys-

7. Servicio National del Trigo, *Cosechas, comercio y consumo de trigo* (Madrid, 1963), in Marti, "Agriculture," 189.
8. *BOE*, Oct. 21, 1941.

tem. Moreover, new regulations in 1941 and 1943 no longer required grain growers to deliver all their wheat to the National Wheat Service, thus in effect legalizing part of the market activity. Critics pointed out that the grain growers of the north had largely supported the Nationalist cause in the war, whereas the most severe hunger and food shortages were suffered by urban workers and poor southern peasants, who had been on the other side.

Despite the reduction in the area of land cultivated, the agricultural labor population continued to grow, in part because of restrictions and unemployment in urban industry and in part because of natural demographic increase. The rural labor force increased altogether from 4.1 million in 1932 to 4.8 million in 1940 and to 5.3 million in 1950[9] before it eventually began to decline. While annulling almost completely the radical land redistribution and collectivization program of the Republican zone, the government recognized the need to pursue an agrarian reform policy, substituting its own program of technical reforms aimed at increasing income and production. This was inspired by the "hydraulic policy" that had been preached in Franco's early years by Costa and the Regenerationists and partially initiated by Primo de Rivera and the Republic. In addition, a modest program to expand land ownership among poor peasants was envisaged, but more along the lines of the limited "internal colonization" program of 1907 than that of the Republic. Thus the Servicio Nacional de Reforma Económico-Social de la Tierra, created under Franco's first cabinet in 1938, was superseded in October 1939 by the Instituto Nacional de Colonización. The latter, however, lacked funding in the penurious aftermath of the Civil War, and a law of December 1939 designed to encourage private capital to help place peasants on untilled land produced little result. New legislation of July 1942 did ease the condition of tenant farmers somewhat, and a law of April 1946 on local resettlement ("colonizaciones de interés local") managed to place land in the hands of a small number of landless peasants. A further advance was reflected by a third law of April 1949 which tied a limited amount of land redistribution to participation in new irrigation programs being developed.[10] In all, these efforts settled only a few landless peasants on new land, for the program was simply not important to the regime's agrarian policy.

By the end of the 1940s some areas began to register real improvement in expanding irrigation and providing other technical facilities to augment production. Investment in agriculture, which averaged less than 4 percent of all Spanish investment during the forties, suddenly doubled to

9. *Anuario Estadístico 1950.*

10. There is a brief summary by Ramón Tamames, "La política agraria hasta 1953," in Diario 16, *Historia del franquismo*, 327–29.

9.33 percent in 1952, and then increased further during the remainder of the fifties.[11] Approximately half of total investment came from public funds. Thus after midcentury significant changes finally began to affect Spanish agriculture, beginning the transformation that would take place during the last twenty-five years of the regime.

A major limitation on the regime's ability to prosecute more rapid autarchic development was its weak fiscal policy. Direct taxes had always been light in modern Spain, though excises weighed heavily on those of modest means. Within the system there was great resistance to changing this, for any policy of more progressive taxation smacked of socialism or collectivism, which Franco was determined to avoid. The government had absolutely no interest in redistributing income through taxation, and thus in 1948 only 14.76 percent of the measured national income of Spain was collected in state revenue, compared with approximately 21 percent in France and Italy and 33 in Britain.[12]

In this situation the big winners under the stringent Spanish economic conditions of the 1940s were the banks, particularly the big banks. The five largest banks (Central, Español de Crédito, and Hispano-Americano in Madrid, and Bilbao and Vizcaya in Bilbao) expanded at what was probably an unprecedented rate, increasing their annual profits by about 700 percent. According to estimate, they dominated about 65 percent of the mobilized financial resources of Spain in 1950,[13] an ironic commentary on the rejection of the original Falangist program of controlling the banks through nationalization of credit.

For Spain as a whole, the 1940s were a decade of prolonged hardship. Actual conditions varied somewhat from region to region, for the more advanced areas normally did better, and energetic civil governors sometimes managed to expand the food supplies for individual provinces. To some extent the black market created a new middle class and was actually necessary for survival; the civil governor of Valencia pointed out in 1947 that the daily food consumption guaranteed by rationing in his province amounted to only 953 calories.[14] Rationing, of course, was common to most of Europe throughout that decade, but the Spanish system could not guarantee the same minimum as those of the more advanced countries.

11. Marti, "Agriculture," 253.
12. According to a speech by the subsecretary of finance in the Cortes on Dec. 22, 1948, cited by Gordón Ordás, *Al borde*, 43.
13. According to a study by Fermín de la Sierra, *La concentración económica en las industrias básicas españolas* (Madrid, 1953). The Falangist intent behind this investigation, published by the Instituto de Estudios Políticos, is fairly obvious. La Sierra also concluded that 9 of 338 mining enterprises mined 55 percent of the coal output, that 10 of 42 steel manufacturers produced most of Spain's steel, and that 14 of 511 electrical power concerns generated 71 percent of the country's electricity.
14. *FF*, 4:89.

Table 16.3. Per Capita GNP in 1950
(in 1974 dollars)

Venezuela	992	Japan	662
Uruguay	978	Chile	596
Italy	935	Mexico	562
Argentina	907	Greece	556
Spain	710		

Source: David Morawetz, *Twenty-five Years of
Economic Development, 1950–1975* (Baltimore,
1977), 77–80.

Table 16.4. Recorded Unemployment in Spain, 1940–1947

1940	477,808	1943	225,493	1946	178,165
1941	450,014	1944	169,525	1947	138,771
1942	294,530	1945	147,946		

Source: "Boletín de Estadística," in Félix Gordón Ordás, *Al borde del desastre* (Mexico City,
1952), 169.

Nonetheless the overall rhythm of Spanish economic suffering was about
the same as that for Europe as a whole. Sustained development began in
1948–49, just as it did for most of Europe.

By the end of the decade Spain stood near, though not at, the bottom of
economic development in southern Europe, well behind the most prosperous countries of South America (a comparison that would change
rather dramatically in later decades) (see table 16.3). Pre–Civil War per
capita income was not regained until 1951. Compared with that of 1935,
adjusted per capita income stood at 79 in 1940, rose to 87 in 1942, held at
that approximate level during 1943–44, then sank to 71 in 1945 before
beginning to rise again.

Unemployment decreased rapidly during the first half of the decade, as
indicated in table 16.4. It should be kept in mind, however, that such figures usually ignored the massive underemployment in agriculture. Moreover, the situation was less satisfactory than it might have appeared, because of the proportionately smaller size of a labor force that employed
comparatively few women. The remaining unemployment and the much
larger agrarian underemployment could not be diminished during these
years by emigration or work abroad. Small-scale emigration could only be
resumed after 1945 and it was mainly to Venezuela, 135,487 Spaniards emi-
grating during 1945–50.[15]

15. Forty-nine percent of this came from Galicia, the region of emigration par excellence.
Vicente Borregón Ribes, *La emigración española a América* (Vigo, 1952), 117, 154.

Table 16.5. General Cost of Living
(1922–26 = 100)

1936	100	1943	335	1946	425
1940	250	1944	335	1947	560
1941	300	1945	333	1948	580
1942	330				

Source: *El Trabajo Nacional* (Barcelona), March 1949, in Gordón
Ordás, *Al borde del desastre*, 161–62.

The 1940s brought the worst inflation in Spanish history. This had
largely been avoided in the Nationalist zone during the Civil War but had
gotten completely out of control in Republican territory and in the postwar dislocation began to afflict the entire country in 1939–40. After
prices had generally increased about 150 percent over the prewar level by
the close of 1940, they were partially stabilized during 1942–45. But in
1946 they rose nearly a third, and almost as much in 1947 before tapering
in 1948, when they stood at nearly six times the level of 1936. Moreover,
the price increase was steepest in foodstuffs, which accounted for a higher
proportion of expenditures among the lower classes. Nominal wages increased much less than prices, though some of the difference was made
up by second jobs, black market activities, and the beginning of the social
security system. It was not until 1952 that the general standard of living
finally climbed above that of 1936.

The most impressive achievements of the 1940s took place in medical
care and sanitation of the most fundamental kind. There was no possibility
that a country at Spain's level of development in those years could provide
sophisticated, high-quality medical service for all, but quite a bit was accomplished in such basic areas as childbirth and infant care. Infant mortality, for example, declined from 109 per thousand live births in 1935 to
88 ten years later, and had been reduced by half—to 55—by 1955. The ma-
ternal death rate similarly declined from 2,196 for every 100,000 births in
1935 to 1,183 after a decade, and to less than half—465—by 1955.[16]

The welfare system of the regime evolved in piecemeal fashion. The
first provision for family subsidies to unusually large or needy families was
announced on July 18, 1938, and by 1942 about 10 percent of the population was receiving supplementary income from it.[17] A new state insurance
program began with the Seguro de Vejez (Old Age Insurance) on Septem-

16. Some of the achievements of the early years of the regime have been reevaluated by
Amando de Miguel in his "La autarquía, en esta tierra de secano," in Diario 16, *Historia del
franquismo*, 322–29.
17. The *Anuario Estadístico 1946* listed figures of 579,700 workers and 1,657,800 children on subsidy.

ber 1, 1939, though this was not extended to agricultural workers until February 1943, followed by the Seguro Obligatorio de Enfermedad (Compulsory Sickness Insurance) on December 14, 1942. Though the regime reversed nearly all the property transfers carried out by the Republic and the revolution, its social policy was not simply reactionary, for it preserved or adapted much of the social legislation that preceded it, and in some respects extended it.[18] One innovation was the new Ministry of Housing, eventually raised to cabinet rank in 1957, which financed construction of new housing for low income groups on a national scale for the first time in Spanish history. Though the construction of only about 13,000 units per year was subsidized during 1940 to 1944, the number increased to 20,000 in 1946, 30,000 in 1947, and more than 42,000 in 1950.[19] All this fell far short of the need, but it was the beginning of the *franquista* welfare state, a system that never convinced its original "class enemies"—industrial workers and landless peasants—but one whose provision of welfare accelerated significantly during following decades.

In his rare speeches to workers, such as the one at the inauguration of the new SEAT automobile factory at Barcelona in June 1949, Franco liked to assure them by saying, "We reject capitalism as much as Marxism."[20] What was meant by rejection of capitalism, however, was the rejection of liberal economics in favor of state regulation and the arbitration of the state's Syndical Organization. The national syndical structure was completed during the 1940s, though many workers, particularly in small towns and in the countryside, were still not included within it.[21] One of the four new vicesecretariats created under the FET in November 1941, that of Obras Sociales (Social Works), included the Organización Sindical del Movimiento, the Delegación Nacional de Excombatientes y Cautivos (veterans' organization) and the welfare agency Auxilio Social. The first vicesecretary of social works was Fermín Sanz Orrio, a Navarrese Falangist of quite different stripe from Salvador Merino. Under Sanz Orrio the Syndical Organization abandoned any ambition to direct the economy, limiting itself to the technical and social function assigned by the state. A grand total of sixteen national syndicates had been officially formed in the major branches of the economy by 1945,[22] though the ones dealing with

18. Cf. Fernando Suárez, "Las líneas generales de la política social," in Instituto de Estudios Políticos, *El nuevo Estado español: Veinticinco años del Movimiento Nacional* (Madrid, 1961), 624.

19. La Cierva, *Franquismo*, 1:325.

20. *Pensamiento político*, 1:90.

21. On the basis of the syndicates' own record, Chueca estimates that by July 1949 only 48.41 percent of Spanish workers were enrolled. *El fascismo en los comienzos del régimen*, 385–86.

22. On the development of the syndical system in this period, see Aparicio, *El sindicalismo*, 179–203.

agriculture were still not fully organized, and a National Workers Congress was then held in Madrid in 1946[23] as part of the regime's new show of representative rights.

Sanz Orrio attempted to give a minimal consistency to syndical doctrine, which generally followed a theory of Catholic state corporatism whose goal was to harmonize class conflict and carry out Catholic social principles. He was concerned that the syndicates play a real role, and under autarchy they held power to regulate certain conditions of production and to allocate imports and raw materials. For this reason, and because they were concerned about working conditions and made frequent demands for statistics on business operations, they were unpopular with business and management from the start.

Sanz Orrio sought to assuage this, and was not reluctant to stress the hierarchical nature of the system and the prerogatives of entrepreneurs within it. In 1943 he declared that the function of entrepreneurs and their profit was so legitimate and of such importance that the syndicates should when necessary undertake to protect industrial enterprises from undue state control or interference.[24] He further declared:

> It is also said that uniting workers and owners in one total syndicate is equivalent to ending the authority of the entrepreneur. In reality it is quite the contrary, since in the national syndicalist system the entrepreneur is . . . the fundamental pivot of the entire system, for to his role of business manager . . . are added those of syndical representative of a group of producers and delegate of the authority of the state and the Movement in that sector . . . , exercising on his subordinates authority directly protected by the strength of the state and the Movement.[25]

This was a remarkably frank declaration of the way in which the system really worked, though Sanz Orrio added the usual guarantees about the role of the syndicates in seeing to it that such authority was not abused.

Sanz Orrio would thus never support any degree of syndical radicalism, whether aiming at economic collectivism or simply at syndical dominance within the system. At the same time he was concerned about a somewhat greater influence and initiative for the Syndical Organization in order to give it a more coordinated policy, but he never found the exact role which he sought.[26] In concept and function his administration essentially paralleled that of Arrese and Girón in domesticating post–Falangist institutions and fitting them into the new system.

23. Congreso Nacional de Trabajadors, *Conclusiones* (Madrid, 1946).
24. Fermín Sanz Orrio, *Los sindicatos españoles: Una creación para el mundo* (Madrid, 1948), 206, 228–29.
25. Ibid., 105.
26. In a speech of 1945, for example, he tried to affirm a role for the syndicates in the supervision of monopolies to ensure distributive justice. Ibid., 227. Cf. his *Teoría y soluciones del sindicalismo nacional* (Madrid, 1948).

José Antonio Girón de Velasco, Minister of Labor, 1943

Workers' benefits and general social welfare were divided between the Syndical Organization and the Ministry of Labor, which further limited the former's influence. Whereas syndical organization was not completed for many years, general welfare benefits such as medical services were steadily developed by the labor ministry for the broader population and were not limited to syndicate members. Thus it was Girón, the labor minister, and not Sanz Orrio who directed the major share of the regime's social policy, an arrangement apparently preferred by Franco himself. The Generalissimo was confident of Girón's loyalty, however demagogic his public utterances, but maintained strict limits on the power of the Syndical Organization. This delimitation—compared, for example, with the greater power of unions in Peronist Argentina or some other systems—actually discouraged deeper social penetration by the Spanish regime, which in certain respects would never complete the full institutionalization of its own syndical structure.

A series of Delegaciones Regionales de Trabajo (Regional Labor Delegations) were created apart from syndicates under Girón's Ministry of Labor in 1941, but the chief powers of labor inspection were ultimately vested in the Delegaciones Provinciales de Sindicatos, whose basic organization dated from 1940. By the close of 1942 new labor regulations for all the main branches of industry had been worked out and promulgated. Organization began on a separate series of labor tribunals to adjudicate labor disputes, the Magistraturas de Trabajo, with their structure and functions fully defined by a law of October 17, 1944, after which the organization of the tribunals was completed.

The only representative elements were the bottom level *enlaces sindicales*, delegates of the smallest local subgroups or shops of workers, though without the authority of shop stewards in a free trade-union system. The first grass-roots elections by workers of a nominal total of 210,000 enlaces took place on October 22, 1944.[27] Though this process was by no means entirely free and many workers either did not take part or cast blank or derisory ballots, neither were the elections a complete fraud, for from that point on the enlaces sindicales did play a very limited role as worker representatives at the lowest level of the system. Three years later in August 1947 the formation of new advisory *jurados de empresa* (factory juries or councils) was announced.[28] Greater freedom was permitted for the elections of enlaces in 1950, and this was used by the left to elect more crypto-oppositionists.

In general, the syndicates were able to dominate the workers but not to generate much in the way of real support. The influence of the syndical system was particularly weak in such areas as Barcelona, Vizcaya, and Asturias, where organized labor had previously been strongest. The civil governor of Barcelona from 1945 to 1947 would write a year later with surprising frankness: "That the working masses do not always find themselves represented in their syndicates is evident. Workers often do not recognize the moral authority of their own delegates, saying that they are the servants of boss so-and-so. Others say that political influence determines that the leaders be persons who do not hold office to benefit the workers but to benefit other sectors or their own pocketbook."[29] Some of

27. The nominal functions of the enlaces were presented in the official *Representación y enlaces sindicales* (Madrid, 1963); and in Eduardo Martín and Jesús Salvador, *Los enlaces sindicales* (Barcelona, 1976). Their number was later reduced to 163,000 for an expanded labor force.

28. The jurados did not actually begin to function until 1953. Though the head of each individual firm automatically became the head of a jurado, election of worker members was relatively free and to some extent representative. Experience in the jurados may have contributed to the first independent *comisiones obreras* (worker commissions) that began to appear in Asturias and elsewhere as early as 1954–55.

29. Bartolomé Barba Hernández, *Dos años al frente del Gobierno Civil de Barcelona* (Madrid, 1948), 58, in Chueca, *El fascismo*, 102.

the most imaginative syndical leaders hoped to coopt part of the opposition and were particularly interested in the clandestine CNT, which still had significant labor support in Barcelona and a few other regions, but efforts to negotiate some sort of pact with members of the CNT leadership during 1946–47 were unsuccessful.[30] Thus Franco's cousin Salgado Araujo would write privately eight years later, "What is sad is the gulf between the mass of workers and the Syndical Organization, since the big shots are not popular leaders in contact with the workers, but superiors who exploit their positions. . . ."[31] Whatever strength the Syndical Organization possessed was derived from its status as a state bureaucratic organization, not from direct worker support.

30. Manuel Ludevid, *Cuarenta años de sindicato vertical* (Barcelona, 1977), 32–35; Ferri, Muixi, and Sanjuan, 131–35; and Damiano González, *La resistencia libertaria*, 286ff. In 1948 there apparently existed a temporary working agreement between the moderates of the CNT in Barcelona and Falange Joven, a dissident neo-Falangist group, but their cooperation soon ended, along with the very existence of the latter.

31. Salgaudo-Araujo, *Conversaciones privadas*, 142.

17

Complacent Dictator

By the close of 1950 Franco enjoyed the satisfaction of having achieved the security of his regime primarily on his own terms. Certain changes had been made in deference to international opinion. The Catholic identity of the regime had been reemphasized, and the content, though not the baroque excess, of official rhetoric had been altered, and nothing more was heard of the *reivindicaciones de España*. With the hardening of the Cold War, Franco seemed to be gaining respectability. The pope was a hardline anti-Communist who had declared members of the party excommunicate, and in September 1950 the French government forced the Spanish Communist Party out of France because of its subversive international role, requiring it to shift headquarters to Prague. Franco was now being actively courted by the American military, transforming the West's oldest and most successful anti-Communist from "fascist beast" into "sentinel of the Occident," the title of his next semiofficial biography.[1]

From all this derived a mounting sense of complacency and self-satisfaction, reinforced by the shameless rhetoric of the official organs whose tone had altered much less than their content.[2] On the Day of the Caudillo, October 1, 1949, *Arriba* hailed him as

> beyond all simple, spare, narrative description. It would be a mistake merely to place him at the level of Alexander the Great, Julius Caesar, Gonzalo de Córdoba, or Ambrosio de Spinola. Francisco Franco, the greatest sword of them all, belongs to the vanguard of providential destiny. He is the man of God, the one who always appears at the critical moment and defeats his enemies proclaiming

1. Luis de Galinsoga (with Francisco Franco Salgado Araujo), *Centinela de Occidente* (Barcelona, 1956).
2. Hence the chapter's heading, which has been borrowed from the title of the British ambassador Sir Samuel Hoare's memoir of his wartime mission to Spain (New York, 1947).

himself champion of the forces of heaven and earth. If we heed Niccolò Mac-chiavelli, he holds the titles of Caudillo, Monarch, Prince, and Lord of the Armies. Caudillo by his own military achievement; Monarch by his well proven nobility; Prince by his keen political talent and Lord of the Armies by his courage, skill and knowledge of tactics, strategy and other complex problems of war.

. . . On this day, let us devote a moment to meditation in honor of the figure of Francisco Franco. Let us renew our promise of loyalty to his person and in the name of Christ pardon those who do not understand him. On this day we see ourselves petty, dwarfish, and ridiculous by comparison.

Two months later, on December 4, he was

the man of invincible sword who belongs to the ranks of the advance guard of providential destiny. He is the man of God, as always. . . . Who can dispute his laurels of the richest, most just and honest victory? To Franco is owed the mobilization of the Vatican, of Washington, and of the entire world, even before Germany. . . . And as if that should not suffice, the Caudillo, the Monarch, the Prince, the commander of armies is beneath it all a simple and affable man, loving home and hearth, profoundly human.

Or, as the Falangist organ put it simply on October 21, 1950, "Franco is the Caudillo and star of the entire world." Perpetually bathed in this sea of absurdly extravagant rhetoric by his own press,[3] he would maintain absolute indifference, at least externally, to the harsh criticism and denunciation which still sometimes came from abroad.

Franco once indicated that he did not find the government of Spain a particularly heavy burden, and given the way in which he ran it that was doubtless the case. In an interview with an American history professor he declared that his role had been analogous to that of the sheriff in the typical American western, a cinematic genre that he enjoyed. Franco went on to observe with considerable mirth that the Spanish, rather than being rebellious and difficult as they were often portrayed, were generally patient and long-suffering. "The proof of that," he said breaking into a sudden loud cackle, "is that they have put up with [soportado] my regime for so long!"[4]

His most demanding trials came during the first eleven years when Franco was still in his prime, with abundant stamina and emotional resilience. The final quarter-century of the regime, as he gradually aged and lost his acuteness, was for him a period of routine administration conducted according to a personal schedule that was more regular than those of more famous dictators and was attuned to his own rhythm of life.

Cabinet ministers and principal subordinates were almost always given great latitude in running their departments, always of course within the general guidelines of the regime. Thus Lequerica would opine that being

---

3. For an anthology, see Fernández, *Franco*, 311–24.

4. Though sometimes of dubious authenticity, one of the best collections of personal anecdotes is Rogelio Baón, *La cara humana de un Caudillo* (Madrid, 1975).

a cabinet minister "is the only serious thing you can be in Spain. To be a minister of Franco is to be a little king [reyezuelo] who does whatever he wants without having His Excellency put a halt to his personalistic policy."[5]

This was not necessarily because of any intrinsic confidence in his collaborators. Franco's suspiciousness was notorious, though its extent has been exaggerated by his detractors. As he once remarked to Salgado-Araujo, "I must tell you that I don't really trust anyone."[6] Yet this did not lead to the morbid paranoia that possessed some other dictators, for Franco was a shrewd judge of character and was adept at assessing when and to what extent he could rely on his appointees. Moreover, like other dictators, he rarely tolerated anyone around him who might create policies or political followings of their own. As Salgado-Araujo put it, "Surely His Excellency does not want to have ministers with independent personalities who could create difficulties."[7] Franco was also forever sensitive to the balance needed between the various forces supporting the regime. Ministerial latitude gave further expression to that and in many cases was as important as direct recognition and reward.

The relative autonomy given ministers was accompanied by an almost total blind eye to malfeasance in office and corruption. From 1940 on it was commonly complained that Franco simply refused to listen to any charges of personal corruption, to the frustration of such close associates as Martínez Fuset and Muñoz Grandes. He followed his standard tack of changing the conversation, which he normally did whenever it strayed to a serious theme that he found troublesome. Occasionally, as Muñoz Grandes complained, he would reply to a critic who denounced the malfeasance within a given minister's domain, "I'll let him [the minister in question] know you have informed me of this."[8] Franco seems to have regarded corruption as a necessary lubrication for the system that had the advantage of compromising many with the regime and binding them to it.

Franco was almost always polite and correct in manner but rarely cordial. When the mood struck him, he could still be talkative in private, but the occasional vivacity of his younger years had largely disappeared except on certain convivial family occasions or hunting excursions. One of his favorite maxims was "One is a slave of what he says but master of what he keeps to himself,"[9] and his demeanor of hauteur and severity was accentuated with the passage of time. His flashes of humor became less and less frequent, though they never disappeared altogether. Words of praise were few, even

5. Quoted by Salgado-Araujo, *Conversaciones privadas*, 50.
6. Ibid., 55.
7. Ibid., 50.
8. Ibid., 178.
9. *Franco visto por sus ministros*, 128.

to those whom he trusted and appreciated the most. Some of his key ministers would complain that they were never quite sure where they stood with him, though that may have been by design. José Antonio Girón lamented that Franco was "very cold, . . . with that coldness which at times freezes the soul." [10] Lack of affect had been typical of Franco's manner on serious occasions, and it eventually froze into a routine. This also had the advantage of permitting him to discuss the most stressful and troublesome matters without altering the expression on his face or the tone of his quiet, high-pitched voice. The most arresting aspect of his facial expression had always been the keen, penetrating glance of his large brown eyes, a quality that disappeared only in the final months of his life.

His emotional tone during public ceremonies could, however, vary considerably. At appearances and meetings in commemoration of the Civil War or on other occasions when he was strongly applauded by hard-core followers, the Caudillo would reveal considerable sentiment and often grow misty-eyed. Routine public appearances were quite a different matter in which he rarely emerged from his mask. By the 1950s public ceremonies had mostly lost the animation of earlier years and were often very cold, formal, stiff and rather tense. Those meeting Franco for the first time were often taken aback by the manner of his handshake, for he held his hand fixedly by the side of his waist, almost as if it were attached to his belt, instead of extending it in the normal manner. This required much taller men to lean over and partially bow in his direction in order to grasp it.

Cabinet meetings became legendary for their marathon length and spartan style. During the 1940s Franco often dominated conversation, speaking at great length, launching into harangues, or wandering from subject to subject. As he grew older he became increasingly reticent and eventually went to the opposite extreme, speaking relatively little. In later decades cabinet meetings were held every Friday during the greater part of the year, though after 1956 they sometimes met biweekly.

Manuel Fraga Iribarne, a major figure of the 1960s, wrote:

Cabinet meetings with Franco were long and in general interesting. They began at ten in the morning, though some ministers might ask to see him earlier, if they had new and important business. . . . Meetings in the summer were held in the dining room of El Pazo de Meirás. When the morning was over [around 2 P.M. in the Spanish schedule], everyone left for lunch and returned at five in the afternoon. We then worked until we had finished, in the small hours. During my period, our longest meeting lasted until four in the morning, but in earlier times people recalled the record of the longest cabinet meeting, which ended at 8 A.M.

Franco not only did not restrict or cut off discussion, as did DeGaulle, or prevent debates, like Salazar (who only accepted reports from his ministers),

10. Quoted by Salgado Araujo, *Conversaciones privadas*, 159.

but sought confrontation among his ministers and administrators in order to clarify matters. . . ."[11]

On busy occasions, lunch might be taken on the premises and restricted to one hour. The lengthy sessions were often a trial for the ministers, since Franco did not believe in rest breaks and did not permit smoking in his presence. Even water was sometimes absent from the table. His own bladder control was legendary, and he is not known to have left a cabinet meeting to step out to the toilet until December 6, 1968,[12] after his seventy-sixth birthday. Ministers had to catch his eye to be excused or to step out for a smoke. Only in his last years did cabinet meetings grow shorter, sometimes being limited to a single morning session.

Franco's interest in and knowledge of government was quite uneven. In later years

> his attention at cabinet meetings varied considerably. Problems of ordinary administration did not interest him at all and in general he took little part in the discussions, which could sometimes be quite lively. Nonetheless, some matters visibly awakened his interest and he followed them with attention. Among these were foreign policy, relations with the Church, public order, and problems having to do with the communications media and with labor.[13]

When disagreement arose at cabinet meetings

> he rarely took positions pro or con. When he thought the matter had been sufficiently discussed, and there were not fundamental objections, he terminated the discussion and the proposal was accepted with appropriate modifications. On the other hand, when no agreement emerged, instead of imposing a solution he directed the ministers involved to study the matter further and seek a common solution to present at the next meeting.[14]

One of Franco's more attractive qualities was his optimism. He rarely communicted a sense of worry to subordinates, and this self-confidence had always been a major factor in his leadership. He expressed great pride in the fact that he had improved the mores of the Spanish people and that the nominal crime index was lower in the 1950s than in the 1930s. He believed, to some extent correctly, that he had instilled a greater respect for authority and for religion in the country, and he confided, with satisfaction, "According to what I am told, blasphemy is not heard anywhere"[15]—a pious exaggeration if ever there was one.

Though adoption of the slogan "organic democracy" was in large part a concession to the democratic climate of postwar western Europe, Franco

11. Manuel Fraga Iribarne, *Memoria breve de una vida pública* (Barcelona, 1980), 41.
12. According to Laureano López Rodó, in *Franco visto por sus ministros*, 167.
13. José Ma. López de Letona, ibid., 209.
14. Carlos Rein Segura, ibid., 74.
15. Quoted in Salgado-Araujo, *Conversaciones privadas*, 285.

was quite serious about not considering himself a dictator (as for that matter was Hitler). He claimed to derive great satisfaction from the fact that he did not personally interfere in the regular judicial system,[16] and insisted at least for the record that there should always be free discussion in the Cortes. He was undoubtedly sincere in his conviction that the regime was working for the true progress and economic development of the country, and in private was quite critical—as was common among the military—of the financial elite. Franco was convinced that Spain rested on the shoulders of the *macizo de la raza,* the ordinary middle classes, and the fact that monarchist opposition was centered in the upper classes only encouraged this conviction. He believed that in modern Spain major accomplishments came from those in the lower middle and even lower classes who had risen to the top,[17] and he looked toward a society that contained fewer rich and fewer poor. When on a later occasion (1961) he happened to be driven through a benighted slum of Seville, something not on his usual itinerary, he expressed genuine shock,[18] but typically thought that the matter would be corrected by orders given to local authorities.

There is no evidence that Franco's central ideas and values—rightist, nationalist, authoritarian, and Catholic—were ever altered substantially at any point in his life. His basic mentality was probably revealed in the script which he wrote personally for the film *Raza*[19] that appeared in February 1942 under the direction of the well-known filmmaker José Luis Saenz de Heredia, a relative of the Primo de Rivera family. Franco had a lifelong interest in movies, having himself acted in an amateur film of the late 1920s. He endeavored to stimulate the Spanish cinematic industry during the early years of the regime, and was particularly interested in communicating his fundamental values to the Spanish public through the medium of an historical melodrama. Under the pseudonym Jaime de Andrade (the most aristocratic of the Franco family names) and very possibly with the help of a ghost writer, his script featured an idealized model family with the fictional name of the Churrucas, using the name of a naval hero of 1898. This apparently represented the kind of paradigmatic *ferrolana* officer's family that he would have liked for his own. Instead of a standard middle-class town house like that of the Francos, the Churrucas seemed to inhabit a virtual castle as though they were a major aristocratic clan. The strong Catholic mother figure was clearly modeled on Franco's own, but the father was altogether different from the agnostic though pro-

16. Ibid., 207.
17. Ibid., 185.
18. Ibid., 317.
19. Meaning literally "race," though with strong patriotic-cultural (rather than merely bioethnic) connotations in Spanish.

fessionally competent Don Nicolás, no doubt representing the ideal military and patriotic father Franco would have wished. He was a sterling example of patriotic, military, and familial virtues who finally died a martyr to the Patria, going down with his ship in heroic battle. This was entirely different from the landlocked career of bureaucratic tedium laced with irregular personal conduct that had filled the long life of the elder Franco.

Franco continued to write sporadically at least through the 1940s. Perhaps because they were not fully satisfied with the journalists at their disposal, both Franco and Carrero Blanco wrote articles on Masonry and other liberal intrigues, published in the regime's newspapers under the pseudonyms Hakin or J. Boor, or Hispanicus in the case of Franco and Ginés de Buitrago for Carrero Blanco. Unafflicted with anti-Semitism, Franco found his true bête noire in Masonry. To the end of his days he was certain that a "world masonic superstate" orchestrated hostility against Spain. His articles maintained that an international Masonic conspiracy was responsible for the chief ills of the West in the twentieth century. It had supposedly gained control of the League of Nations, been momentarily held in check by Hitler and Mussolini, and then come to dominate the United Nations after 1945. "The entire secret of the campaigns directed against Spain lies in these two words: Masonry and Communism."[20]

The outcome of the Civil War, followed by the success of his policy during the 1940s, firmly convinced Franco that his role was providential. The cynical military in Morocco used to refer to his *baraka*—"Franco's luck"—but after 1936, if not before, the Caudillo saw it as divine guidance. He often attended mass at his private chapel in El Pardo and during some of the major crises of the regime was said to spend part of the night there. Yet despite the extreme formal religious emphasis of the regime, Franco did not want his own devotions publicized, feeling that Spanish opinion in general might not approve the image of a leader too dominated by religion in the affairs of state.[21] His religiosity was distinctly of the traditional Spanish type—formalistic, given to liturgy and ritual but not informed by personal meditation, religious study, or practical personal application of doctrine. Franco also believed devoutly in the efficacy of relics, his personal favorite being the remains of a petrified arm of Santa Teresa de Avila which he had obtained during the Civil War and kept on a bedstand for the remainder of his life.

20. A number of the Hakin Boor articles were later collected in the volume *Masonería*, published by the Editora Nacional in 1952 and sometimes referred to as Franco's "third book," after *Diario de una Bandera* and the script for *Raza*. There has been speculation that he may have occasionally employed as ghost writer Joaquín Arrarás, one of the regime's leading publicists, and others from the *Mundo* group headed by Vicente Gállego. Cf. La Cierva, *Franquismo*, 1:384.

21. His public statements on religion were later collected under the title *Francisco Franco: Pensamiento católico* (Madrid, 1958).

Anonymous personal threats arrived regularly in the mail down to the final days of his life. Franco rarely saw these personally, and there is no indication that they bothered him very much. His anarchist opposition showed the main interest in organizing assassination attempts, which were most frequent between 1945 and 1950. Particularly elaborate preparations were set in motion on the occasion of his visit to Barcelona in 1947 and to San Sebastián in September 1948. Though Spanish security sometimes seemed a trifle lax compared with rigorously totalitarian regimes, it was tight enough to foil each of the forty or more assassination plans developed by anarchists down to 1964, when the attempts petered out. Not a single one ever reached the point of direct action.[22]

Franco's personal tours to various parts of Spain continued at a diminishing rate through the 1960s, and the crowds rarely failed to present themselves, whether spontaneously or not. On these and other occasions he continued to deliver his regular ceremonial speeches, in addition to two or three major addresses each year. Speechwriters who could turn out elegant speeches seem to have been in very short supply at El Pardo, and Franco wrote most of his material himself. Much of his terminology was rather simple, but it was adequate to get across his main concepts. Grandiosity was not his forte, and he seems to have been the one who established in Spanish rhetoric the custom of saying "Many thanks" at the end of a speech. Before his time the style normally was to end with the peremptory and slightly arrogant "He dicho" ("I have spoken") or "He terminado" ("I have finished").

Yet his travels did not really keep him well informed, for he talked with only a limited set of people, most of whom told him what he wanted to hear. Even within the military he restricted his personal contacts more and more, and his only personal associates were family relatives and a very small circle of family friends.

After 1945 he was seen less and less often in uniform, and by the 1950s he dressed normally in well-tailored business suits, much more deftly cut than the rather crude uniforms of Civil War days. Despite his fondness for simple, hearty food such as the Asturian *fabada*, he was on a low-calorie diet by the 1950s that left him slimmer than he had been in the two preceding decades.

Franco's austere personal habits never varied. Smoking never attracted him, and he never drank more than a glass (or on special occasions, a maximum of two glasses) of wine with meals. He was normally up at 7 A.M., and in his later years breakfasted on fruit juice, tea, and dry toast. Prayers or morning mass usually followed, and Franco was ordinarily in

22. See Eliseo Bayo, *Los atentados contra Franco* (Barcelona, 1976). Of one hundred or more anarchist militants involved in such plans between 1945 and 1950, the great majority were either killed in clashes with the police or imprisoned.

his office and ready for business by nine. Tuesday morning was reserved for personal audiences with the military, and Wednesday for civilians. Foreign diplomats were received on Thursday morning, and the rest of Thursday was dedicated to a meeting with Carrero Blanco. Cabinet meetings, as indicated, took place on Fridays. Until his last years Franco devoted four full afternoons a week, from Monday to Thursday, to personal consultation with his ministers. Each minister usually talked with him for about an hour each week, and this enabled him to maintain close touch, while allowing them broad latitude in supervising their departments. Mealtime was never a major event in the life at El Pardo, since for many years the head chef was a former Civil Guard NCO of unquestioned loyalty whose gastronomic talents were limited. Franco's idea of an after-dinner drink was either a glass of manzanilla (sherry) or a cup of decaffeinated coffee. Evenings were normally quiet and domestic, sometimes with private movie screenings. In his later years, Franco became addicted to television and was especially fond of soccer matches and boxing.

Franco's reading habits were modest. Books held little attraction, and he often ignored the Spanish press since his censorship rendered it predictable and rarely interesting. He did sometimes look at the *New York Times*, considering it a "bulwark of international Masonry"[23] on which he needed to be informed and with which he could practice his limited English. (Failure to learn English well[24] and to be able to speak it seems to have been a source of continuing frustration.)

Franco had perforce to forego the private *tertulias* (social conversation parties) that he had enjoyed as a younger officer, but during the first twenty years or so of the regime he and Doña Carmen attended a certain number of Madrid's top social and entertainment functions, including operas, bullfights, and soccer matches. Daytime social and charity events were the province of Doña Carmen, who developed her own set of activities as first lady, though her individual social circle remained limited.

Franco sometimes worked long hours, but there was little danger of overwork, given the absence of stress and tension that he normally showed, and even more, the length of the vacations that he permitted himself. Though he played golf and a little tennis and enjoyed morning horseback riding, his great diversion, almost a mania, was private hunting expeditions. Franco had a small hunting domain at El Pardo and at the summer palace of Aranjuez, but was also engaged in major hunting parties arranged for him on the finest private estates and public lands throughout Spain. These were sometimes strenuous three- and four-day affairs in which

23. Salgado-Araujo, *Conversaciones privadas*, 255.

24. As Martín Artajo noted, Franco's pronounciation of English was very poor and phoneticized in Spanish style. Thus he pronounced MacArthur "Macartu" and Eisenhower "Aissenhovair." Tusell, *Franco y los catolicos*, 113.

Franco during a pause in one of his hunting excursions. At his side, Fuertes de Villavicencio, head of his domestic staff; behind, from left to right, Manuel Fraga Iribarne (Minister of Information), José Solís Ruiz (Minister of the Movement and of Syndicates), and the Marqués de Villaverde (Franco's son-in-law).

Franco did considerable hiking and climbing and fired off enormous numbers of cartridges either in the open range or in specially prepared shooting zones. Franco had the opportunity to excel in shooting in a way that he could not in other public sporting activities, and in time he became quite a good shot.[25] His absorption in hunting led to a steady stream of invitations from the wealthy and those seeking influence, and he was often attended by what were called *cazadores aduladores* (flatterer-hunters), who were seeking jobs or influence in suits and petitions, and by *cazadores comerciantes* (business-hunters) interested in government backing for business deals. Salgado Araujo, head of Franco's Casa Militar during much of the 1950s when the hunting mania was at its height, was quite critical

25. Rein Segura, agriculture minister from 1945 to 1951, recalls that when Franco first took up hunting regularly in the mid-1940s, his shooting ranged from "average to rather bad." *Franco visto por sus ministros*, 78.

of all this, noting that during November 1955 seventeen days were spent on hunting leaving at most thirteen for state business. All this gave "the impression of frivolity," as he put it succinctly.[26]

Franco suffered from no chronic health complaints whatever until well advanced in years. During his first three decades in power he suffered from only three illnesses which required him to stay in bed for a day or more: two cases of flu and one brief bout of food poisoning. Even in his sixties he displayed impressive stamina during long days in the open. Franco's personal physician, a blunt, devoted Falangist camisa vieja from Old Castile named Vicente Gil, nonetheless believed that he extended himself too greatly on these excursions, observing in November 1954: "Franco expends too much energy on these hunting parties which do not provide him with any rest since he sleeps little on them. Yesterday . . . he fired 6,000 cartridges and that is terrible for a 62-year-old man. Any day he could have a stroke."[27] His summer fishing trips in Asturias would similarly find him standing in hip-boots for hours in the icy water of mountain trout streams. There is no question that Franco derived great satisfaction from these carefully contrived slaughters, boasting in October 1959 that he had set a personal record by shooting nearly 5,000 quail on the last outing.[28] As late as 1966 the press carried stories of his fishing prowess at sea, where he was reported to have bagged 36 small whales with a harpoon gun.

For thirty-seven years summers were spent at the Galician estate of Pazo de Meirás presented to him before the end of the Civil War,[29] though considerable time was also passed on Franco's yacht *Azor*, mainly off the cooler coasts of northern Spain. Franco's primary summer sport was fishing,[30] though he also played golf and cards and sometimes practiced his painting, hanging the walls of the Pazo's spacious dining room with his still lifes of hunting and fishing trophies.

The family circle was Franco's ultimate refuge but remained constricted. His closest and most harmonious relations, after those with his wife and daughter, were maintained with his brother Nicolás, ambassador in Lisbon for many years, and with his only sister Pilar. He had virtually nothing to do with the widow and daughter of his dead brother Ramón. After the dismissal of Serrano Súñer, relations were also strained with Doña Carmen's youngest (formerly closest) sister and her husband. There was a possibility of reconciliation in 1952, when Serrano published several articles

26. Salgado-Araujo, *Conversaciones privadas*, 72. See Luis Alonso Tejada, "Las cacerías de Franco," *Historia 16* 4:37 (May 1979), 19–30.

27. Salgado-Araujo, *Conversaciones privadas*, 37. Gil eventually published his own memoir of his long service as Franco's physician, *Cuarenta años junto a Franco* (Barcelona, 1981).

28. Salgado-Araujo, *Conversaciones privadas*, 270.

29. There is a sketch of his summer activities in Fernández, *Franco*, 277–83.

30. Described by Vicente Gil, *Cuarenta años*, 63–76.

in *ABC* that were well received and when he was given good press coverage of a trip to Paris. There was talk of making him ambassador to France, but nothing came of this, and gossip ascribed it to the apprehension of Doña Carmen herself that Serrano might upset the existing balance within the government (and perhaps within the family).

Nor had the Caudillo anything directly to do with his elderly father, who had died in February 1942 at the age of eighty-seven, still living in Madrid with Augustina, his devoted, lower-class mistress, and their illegitimate daughter. The family house in El Ferrol had remained the property of Don Nicolás, who began to vacation there once more in 1935 after his wife's death. The Civil War surprised him there with his second famiy in 1936, and thus they passed the entire war in the Nationalist zone, which did not prevent the old freethinker from making scandalously negative remarks about his second son in public.[31] In 1939 Don Nicolás returned to Madrid, where he was able to live adequately on his vice-admiral's pension. Franco provided him with a private car and chauffeur, but there is no indication that he visited him regularly or even at all, as did his brother and sister and their children.

The attitude of Don Nicolás toward Franco never improved. Even after the Civil War he called his son Paco "inept" and insisted that the idea of him as a "great leader," as repeated daily in the controlled press, "was something to laugh about." Don Nicolás was pro-Jewish and detested Hitler, whom he thought would either destroy or enslave Europe. He found his son's anti-Mason mania absurd. "What does he know about Masonry? It is an association of illustrious and honorable men, needless to say greatly superior to him in learning and in openness of spirit."[32] Upon his father's death Franco quickly took possession of the corpse, but accorded it only the normal funeral honors of a vice-admiral of the Spanish Navy and barred the distraught Augustina from the ceremony.[33] There is no indication that he ever acknowledged his half-sister.

Even from the grave, his father had the last word, for the Caudillo must have been taken aback—though perhaps not totally surprised—to receive in April 1950 a brief letter from a young veteran of the Nationalist Army informing him that the author's father-in-law, Eugenio Franco Puey, was the natural son of Don Nicolás, born of a Spanish officer's wife in Cavite in the Philippines in 1889. According to the letter, Franco Puey

31. In *La Señora de El Pardo*, 170–72, Garriga recounts several undocumented anecdotes about the old man's bizarre behavior in expressing his antipathy toward his son during the Civil War.
32. According to Pilar Jaraiz Franco, *Historia*, 59–60.
33. Ibid., 29–30. Garriga has it that the cadaver was seized by a Civil Guard detachment, which carried it off from the shrieking and hysterical Augustina as a crowd of neighbors looked on.

had been legally recognized by his natural father, who had extended to
him the paternal blessing at the time of his marriage in 1918.[34] There is no
indication that Franco deigned to make contact with this alleged half-
brother, employed as a topographer in Madrid.

Until 1950 Franco's official household was comparatively restrained and
austere, not given to opulence or elaborate self-indulgence. This was considerably altered by the marriage of his twenty-one-year-old daughter
Carmencita on April 10, 1950 to Cristóbal Martínez Bordiu, the Marqués
de Villaverde. Martínez Bordiu was a young playboy aristocrat descended
in part from the famous Aragonese clan of Luna which had provided one
pope and the protagonist of one of Verdi's best-known operas. The wedding was a bit of a surprise, in that most of Madrid society had supposed
that Carmencita's leading suitor was a naval officer son of Juan Antonio
Suanzes, one of Franco's leading administrators and an old boyhood friend
who was one of the extremely few who ever addressed the Caudillo
as Paco. Carmencita, taller than might have been expected of Franco's
daughter, was a healthy and handsome, though not remarkably pretty,
young woman with lustrous dark hair and eyes and heavy brows (thinned
in later years to enhance her attractiveness). Her bridgegroom was an affable, athletic, moderately handsome young man, popular in high society
and trained as a physician and heart surgeon. Their wedding was a gala
ceremony attended by 800. Many of the vast array of presents were distributed among charities. The primate, Cardinal Pla y Deniel, officiated
at the ceremony, uttering undoubtedly the most blasphemous comparison
of his ecclesiastical career when he intoned to the young couple: "You
have a most exemplary model in the family of Nazareth and a more recent
one in the exemplary Christian home of the chief of state."[35]

The family circle thus widened to include the aristocratic parents and
brothers of the new son-in-law, creating a broader network that for the
first time began to be known as "the clan of El Pardo." Yet Franco himself
permitted little intimacy, requiring Carmencita's father-in-law to address
him always as Your Excellency. The "clan" soon became involved in extensive business and financial activities facilitated by their privileged position, activities led especially by the bridgegroom's uncle, José María
Sanchiz Sancho, known as Tío Pepe, the financial wizard of the group.
One of his operations was the creation of an extensive agricultural estate
at Valdefuentes, 21 kilometers southwest of Madrid, which became a
major food producer and was converted into a joint stock company owned
by Franco personally. Thus the Caudillo, who had in earlier years kept
himself free of such arrangements, began to be involved in the privileged

34. The letter is quoted in full in Fernández, *Franco*, 310.
35. Quoted in La Cierva, *Franquismo*, 2:89.

financial maneuvers that were already making the fortunes of his brother and sister.[36]

Carmencita was almost as prolific as her aunt Doña Pilar, the mother of ten.[37] Eventually there were seven Martínez Bordiu children, two boys and five girls, all handsome and with one exception healthy children, and one of the principal joys of the old dictator's later years. The entire family normally lived together in El Pardo, and Franco would often be visited by some of the grandchildren around nine in the morning before beginning the day's activities, a diversion that he much appreciated. Since there was no male heir in Franco's direct line, it was arranged in December 1954, after the birth of the first grandson, that the Cortes would officially legalize the reversal of his family name so that the infant would be named Francisco Franco Martínez Bordiu (rather than Francisco Martínez Bordiu Franco) and thus be in a position to perpetuate his family name.

The son-in-law was much more of a disappointment. Superficial and lacking in any capacity for seriousness and concentration, he was self-indulgent in the extreme and often behaved badly. Here Franco had little alternative but to close his eyes. For a brief time Villaverde was made "medical inspector of embassies" abroad, enabling the young couple to travel extensively at state expense and also to play a minor diplomatic role in representing the regime abroad. Though most of his time was devoted to society life and amusements and to a lesser extent business deals, Villaverde later made some effort to develop his professional expertise and became sporadically active as a heart surgeon, performing the first transplant operation in Spain (the subject of which promptly died). As the Caudillo aged, Villaverde attempted to develop some competence in the new treatment to prolong life, though again without notable success. He was eventually made head of the heart section of a major Madrid hospital and also of a specialized national medical institute, though his competence was seriously questioned. Muñoz Grandes spoke for many when he observed to Salgado-Araujo that the Francos had "not been fortunate in the marriage of their only daughter." In later years Doña Carmen would sometimes refer to Villaverde when speaking to her daughter as "that man whom you married," and Carmencita herself would eventually refer to him as *un desequilibrado mental* (mentally unbalanced).[38]

36. It should also be pointed out that at a later date, Franco made no attempt to take advantage of rezoning opportunities in the expansion of greater Madrid that would have greatly increased the value of this property, according to Vicente Mortes, minister of housing from 1969 to 1973, in *Franco visto por sus ministros*, 270.

37. Widowed at a comparatively early age, Doña Pilar managed to raise her ten children quite successfully with the profits from a series of real estate investments made available to her. Cf. Jaime Sánchez-Blanco, *La importancia de llamarse Franco: El negocio inmobiliario de doña Pilar* (Madrid, 1978).

38. As recorded in the gossip sheet published by one temporary son-in-law, Joaquín Giménez Arnau, *Yo, Jimmy (Mi vida entre los Franco)* (Barcelona, 1980). The Marqués de

The expansion of the family circle tended to alter the style and role of Doña Carmen. Whereas before she had presided with at least a certain modesty over a small and not particularly ostentatious household, after 1950 she was free to play a grander personal role as first lady. Her tendency toward pride, hauteur, and imperiousness was accentuated as she grew accustomed to more direct personal deference, and in social conversation she was said to be more intolerant of any hint of criticism than the Generalissimo himself. Her collection of jewels, furnishings, and art works expanded greatly, becoming legendary and the subject of much gossip, generally exaggerated.[39] Yet she had very few intimates, her principal companion during the 1950s being the Marquesa de Huétor de Santillán, wife of the head of Franco's Casa Civil.

Doña Carmen also played a more active role in public affairs and tended to be more controlling in the arrangement of Franco's personal schedule as he grew older. She accompanied him on most hunting trips and became increasingly vocal about political matters, especially in her resentment of aristocratic monarchism. It vexed her greatly and she apparently urged that the monarchy and its supporters be more closely restricted and receive as little official recognition as possible. Her control of Franco's social life tended to increase his isolation, for she attempted to screen him from any who might raise unpleasant questions, and she instructed guests not to discuss potentially disagreeable topics. Despite Franco's famed steadiness of nerve and serenity of mind, troublesome problems were perfectly capable of worrying him and disturbing his sleep. Similarly, though Franco had never given the slightest indication that he had a roving eye, Doña Carmen kept pretty and younger women away from his social receptions, simply to be on the safe side.

Thus Franco entered the final quarter-century of his life with a fixed routine that varied little until his death. His vacations were long, and he was shielded from conflict as much as possible, in some respects more and more out of touch with his country and the world as it changed. Personal

---

Villaverde is a favorite target of denunciation in all the other memoirs of members of the family (Salgado-Araujo, Pilar Franco, Pilar Jaraiz) and in that of the personal physician Vicente Gil.

Cristóbal Martínez-Bordiu, the younger of Franco's grandsons, who identified very much with his grandfather and briefly followed in his footsteps by earning an army officer's commission, has written a more sensible and discreet memoir of the first years after Franco's death, *Cara y cruz* (Barcelona, 1983).

39. On Doña Carmen's role and the family circle, see Garriga, *La Señora*, 222–27; Fernández, *El general Franco*, 271–73; and Salgado-Araujo, *Mis conversaciones*, 196. Gossip had it that Doña Carmen commandeered gifts from Spain's leading jewelers to the extent that they formed a kind of mutual assistance society to equalize the costs of such confiscations. Garriga's investigation found no evidence of such directly high-handed practices on her part, though she did use her position to exchange other gifts for original items of jewelry of her preference, free of charge.

isolation increased as he grew older. As his health declined in his final years he saw fewer and fewer people, so that toward the end he was very solitary. Yet after the 1940s his personal authority was never again seriously questioned within Spain. Even the opposition eventually came to think of the possibility of an alternative only after his death. He had built his regime slowly and indecisively, but the foundations laid were firm enough to endure. The regime rode a tide of ever-increasing national prosperity until death finally claimed him in his eighty-third year.

18

The Regime at
Mid-Passage
1950–1959

By 1950 the regime had taken mature form. Despite the tenseness of its relations with hard-core monarchists, the system that Franco had developed was much more like the blueprint laid down by Calvo Sotelo and the *Acción Española* theorists for "instauration" of an authoritarian monarchy than it was the fascist formulas of the Falange. All seven main points of *Acción Española* theory had been met: the legislation of 1947 had converted the system into an authoritarian monarchist state; a controlled corporative parliamentary system had been in place since 1943; economic policy was based on state *dirigiste* neocapitalism; labor relations were administered through state corporative syndicalism; since 1945 the Movimiento had been deemphasized (though far from eliminated); the system relied on the ultimate political support of the military, who had initiated it; and religious, cultural, and educational policy had developed an elaborate structure of "national Catholicism" that provided more effective support than did any remaining fervor for the Falangist program.

Serious pressure for further liberalization had come to an end, and though Franco was still persona non grata to social democratic western Europe, the domestic opposition had begun to despair of his overthrow. It had been unable to maintain any consensus of its own, and so well-informed an opponent of the regime as the celebrated British Hispanist Gerald Brenan, after describing the harsh terms of Spanish life in recent years, wrote that "Spain for some time needs to live under an authoritarian regime."[1] Greater security certainly did not induce the Generalissimo to consider further changes. According to his former army minister Varela,

1. Gerald Brenan, *The Face of Spain* (London, 1950), xvi.

413

Franco remarked privately late in 1949 on the subject of his recent visit to Portugal and Salazar's advice to him: "Salazar said that because Spain was entering a constituent period, I should concede some greater liberty to the country. I shall give Spain no further liberty during the next ten years. After that period, I will relax my hand somewhat."[2] Although there is no indication of any specific plan or timetable, that was about the way things worked out, and there were no significant changes until later in the new decade. The semiautarchist policy of state-regulated development continued with certain modifications almost until the end of the 1950s, and only when it reached a dead end in 1959 did it become necessary to liberalize economic policy and adopt a new course that would bring political and cultural reforms in its wake.

The regime continued to promote its bombastic rhetoric of triumphalism, claiming victory on every hand, with Franco the true leader of all western civilization and Spain the focus of world strategy because of its priority in opposing Communism and championing true spiritual values. It insisted on moral superiority over all the divided, multiparty regimes of western Europe, some of which struggled with sizable Communist opposition parties or were themselves led by Socialists. To each of the visiting American correspondents, whose numbers were increasing at this point, Franco liked to emphasize what he termed the moral decay of other European countries. If improvement in domestic economic conditions remained somewhat slow and 1950 was another bad year for Spanish agriculture, that could be used as the starting point for yet another grandiloquent homily on the difference between Spanish values and those corroding the rest of western Europe.

Correspondingly, west European governments remained more hostile to the regime than did Washington. Their resumption of intercourse did not bring with it full political or military acceptance as distinct from the technical proprieties of normal diplomatic, commercial, and financial relations. Franco's first nominee as new ambassador to the Court of St. James's, Castiella, was rejected because of his "fascist" background and publications hostile to England. Ironically, the subsequent candidate accepted by London was Miguel Primo de Rivera, whose fascistic credentials were presumably superior to those of Castiella. The continuing hostility of west European governments was only meagerly balanced by the friendship of many Latin American countries[3] and of the Arab states of the Middle East, the latter having supported the regime in the United Nations and used Spain as a source of arms purchases.

Of all governments in the western world, the most intransigent was

---

2. Quoted in Gil Robles, *La monarquía*, 318–19.
3. Though relations later declined rather drastically with the Peronist government of Argentina, earlier Franco's strongest supporter in Latin America.

that of Mexico, whose quasileftist state party remained strongly opposed to the Spanish regime, which it identified with the old European right and imperialism. When a Spanish diplomat was dispatched to Mexico at the beginning of 1950 to explore possible restoration of diplomatic relations, he was promptly murdered by a gunman reported by Mexican police to have been an agent of the Spanish Communist Party.[4] Normal relations were not restored until after the death of Franco.

Within Spain, living standards were finally improving more rapidly, and this, together with the obvious failure of the opposition, helps to explain the quiescent atmosphere of the 1950s, though one major disturbance did take place in March 1951. In Barcelona, discontent with continuation of rationing and low wages first found expression in a boycott of public transport to protest a new fare increase, and then quickly mushroomed into a mass industrial strike. When several hundred thousand workers walked off the job, this became the largest single industrial action in the regime's history, and was seconded a few weeks later by smaller strikes in Vizcaya and Guipúzcoa. The reaction of the police, taken by surprise, seemed weak at first, while the captain-general of Barcelona, Juan Bautista Sánchez, who was known for monarchist sympathies and congenial relations with Barcelona society, denied a request for intervention by Army troops. After several days, more forceful methods were applied and the workers began to return to their jobs,[5] but they also gained economic concessions. General Felipe Acedo Colunga, a dedicated hardliner, was then named civil governor of Barcelona province and ruled firmly for the next ten years.

On July 10 the Conde de Barcelona addressed a letter to Franco declaring that with such outbursts the regime could not expect to continue as it had for the past twelve years. He also pointed to widespread corruption and what he defined as the need for major economic improvement and foreign assistance, proposing that he and the Generalissimo work together for a new political solution of conciliation.[6] This of course implied significant liberalization and a more concrete plan for restoration, but Franco was not impressed.[7] He intended simply to shut the lid more firmly, which in fact had been done even before the royal letter arrived.

One of the strengths of Franco's personal style was that, as La Cierva

4. *FF*, 4:400.
5. On the boycott and strike in Barcelona, see F. Fanes, *La vaga de tramvies del 1951* (Barcelona, 1981); Damiano González, *La resistencia*, 167–94; and Ferri et al., *Las huelgas*, 148–74; and on the strikes in Vizcaya, Ferri et al., 175–89. A running account of events during the decade is provided by J. Lee Schneidman, *Spain and Franco 1949–59* (New York, 1973).
6. López Rodó, *Larga marcha*, 550–54.
7. Franco later replied archly that the allegation of major corruption was pure calumny, while the success of the regime's economic policy was amply demonstrated by the recent increase in industrial production to the highest levels in Spanish history. Sáinz Rodríguez, *Una monarquía*, 374–78.

has observed, he never publicly overreacted, whether to a rash of strikes, a monarchist manifesto, a minor street demonstration, or a rare shouted insult by an old guard Falangist. His tendency was to trivialize and isolate each act of defiance rather than to generalize or inflate it, thus making them all seem to be petty irritants. In this way he was able to avoid adding to any momentum they might have generated.

The first general cabinet change in six years was announced on July 19, prompted by a concern to strengthen domestic administration and liberalize economic policy slightly. It featured continuity much more than change, although it also provided some opportunity for Catholic evolutionists. The principal carryovers were the invaluable Martín Artajo as foreign minister,[8] the almost equally invaluable Blas Pérez in Interior, the eminently useful and loyal Girón in Labor, and the air force minister Eduardo González Gallarza. Carrero Blanco's subsecretaryship of the president was upgraded to cabinet rank, and he was also made secretary of the Council of Ministers. The prominent Catholic layman Joaquín Ruiz Giménez, who had assisted the regime in 1945, was named minister of education in a gesture toward moderate reformist Catholic opinion, but the powers of his ministry were also slightly reduced. A regular secretary general for the Falange-Movimiento had been appointed in November 1948, when Fernández Cuesta was given that post in addition to his regular portfolio as minister of justice. In the more relaxed atmosphere of 1951 Franco upgraded the secretary generalship to cabinet rank, thus retaining Fernández Cuesta in his cabinet while replacing him in Justice with the Carlist Antonio Iturmendi. The vicesecretariat of popular culture, in charge of censorship, was removed from Education, where it had been for the past six years, to be placed under the newly created Ministry of Information and Tourism, entrusted to the ultraright-wing Arias Salgado. Suanzes's Ministry of Commerce and Industry was cut in half, Commerce going to

8. Franco had correctly taken the measure of Martín Artajo, who played his role effectively without creating waves and apparently had a low opinion of his fellow Spaniards. A decade later, in a scholarly discourse after he had left government, Martín Artajo opined: "Spaniards commonly are deficient in the type of virtues that form the basis of social cooperation. . . . They are too intransigent in their judgments and opinions and consider the confession of error or recognition that an opponent may be right as weakness if not outright dishonor. . . . The Spaniard is also subjective, emphatic, and hyperbolic and therefore closed to dialogue and mutual discussion. He is obstinate and violent in defending his opinions. . . . He shows no interest in harmonizing his interests or opinions with those of others. . . . Spaniards are, moreover, undisciplined and ordinarily rebellious to authority and resentful of obedience. . . . When a Spaniard obeys, he does so not so much out of love and respect for the law as from fear of punishment. . . . Spaniards, finally, share no sense of common interests; they avoid participation in the common government, the *res Pública,* since it provides no personal advantage. Thus those outside government judge maliciously those occupying public positions, thinking they do so to enrich themselves. . . . The poverty of the Spanish in those virtues that are the foundation of public life, and especially of justice, makes national coexistence difficult." Alberto Martín Artajo, *La conciencia social de los españoles* (Madrid, 1961), 54; quoted in de Miguel, *Herencia del franquismo,* 167–68.

Manuel Arburúa, former subsecretary and something of a technocrat, who might be expected to reform and slightly liberalize the existing highly restrictive structure. Col. Joaquín Planell, a veteran Army engineer and INI administrator, became minister of industry. Salvador Moreno, Franco's first postwar naval minister, returned to that post, while Muñoz Grandes, probably the most prominent and prestigious figure in the military hierarchy, took over the Army Ministry, on ceremonial occasions still wearing Hitler's Iron Cross.

In general, this could be seen as another of Franco's skillful balancing acts. Major Catholic appointees were still prominent, but the Movement received greater cabinet recognition. The great majority of the members of the new cabinet were veteran hardcore Francoists who had been in one way or another associated either with the Movement or the earlier Primo de Rivera dictatorship.

Strategic Rehabilitation:
The Pact with the United States

Once a regular relationship had been established with the United States, it developed rapidly in the climate of the Korean War. The official exchange of ambassadors took place early in 1951, the oily Lequerica taking over the embassy in Washington, where interest in bringing Spain within the United States's defense network was mounting. This was stimulated by top-ranking American army and navy commanders (though not as much by their air force counterparts), seconded by conservative interests in Congress and public affairs.[9] Admiral Forrest Sherman arrived in Madrid in July to initiate exploratory talks concerning a strategic agreement. Franco's interest was manifest, including his suggestion of some form of Spanish participation among the United Nations forces in the war then raging in Korea. He could well say in his New Year's Eve message at the close of the year that "those clouded, insane years which surrendered whole clusters of peoples in Europe and Asia to Communism and which repaid Spain's neutrality in the coin of hostility have passed," though this was not true of some of the west European democracies, who refused to hear of Spain joining the new NATO organization as long as the Franco regime lasted.

Nonetheless the integration of Spain into international organizations continued. Spain entered the World Health Organization in 1951, UNESCO in 1952, and the International Labor Organization in 1953, while Franco once more offered a Spanish contingent for Korea. During a Middle Eastern swing in the spring of 1952 Martín Artajo suggested the

---

9. The forces shaping United States policy toward Spain in 1951–53 are treated in Gilmore, "Foreign Policy-Making," 269–341.

alternative of a southern tier defense alignment consisting of Spain, Italy, Greece, and several Arab states to defend the Mediterranean basin in conjunction with NATO. This ploy failed to prosper, but negotiations with the United States did, leading eventually to three executive agreements that made up the Pact of Madrid signed on September 26, 1953. These provided for mutual defense and military aid to Spain, the construction and use of three airbases and one naval base in Spain for a ten-year period, and economic assistance. The form of an executive pact was adopted because unlike full treaties this would not require ratification by the United States Senate, where residual opposition from liberals would have been an obstacle. In addition to direct military and economic assistance, Spain received significant credit and the opportunity to buy large amounts of American raw materials and surplus foodstuffs at reduced prices, and the volume of American capital investment in Spain notably increased. Official American figures place the value of all forms of American economic aid (including credits) over the next ten years at 1,688 million dollars, to which was added 521 million in military assistance.[10] The figure might have been higher had not Spanish authorities slowed negotiations during 1952–53 in order to concentrate on the new Concordat with the Vatican. Once the Korean War ended, the value of the Spanish connection declined somewhat. Nonetheless, though the amount of aid was considerably less than other west European countries had received through the Marshall Plan, its impact was considerable.

This agreement incorporated Spain geographically in the military network of the Strategic Air Command and established a significant American military presence for the next two decades. There is no doubt that such association with the greatest power in the world strengthened the Spanish regime both at home and abroad and increased its stability. Martín Artajo presented it as an admission by the United States that Franco's position had been right all along, while strict rules of conduct for American military personnel in Spain were written into the pact. Yet there was considerable opposition to the new arrangement in Spain, even though it could not be expressed openly. Critics charged that the relationship was asymmetrical and would inevitably involve Spain or at least Spanish territory in any major international conflict of the United States while falling

---

10. According to the U.S. Dept. of Commerce, *Foreign Grants and Credits by the United States,* Fiscal Year Reports 1957–1963, in R. R. Rubottom and J. C. Murphy, *Spain and the United States since World War II* (New York, 1984), 46. The principal Spanish study is Angel Viñas, *Los pactos secretos de Franco con Estados Unidos* (Barcelona, 1981). See also Arthur Whitaker, *Spain and Defense of the West* (New York, 1961.), 44–84; Eduardo Chamorro and Ignacio Fontes, *Las bases norteamericanas en España* (Barcelona, 1976), 65, 110; and Stanley B. Weeks, "United States Defense Policy Toward Spain, 1950–1976" (Ph.D. diss., American University, 1977). The Soviet version is presented by D. D. Prygov, *Trevozhnoe partnerstvo* (Moscow, 1972), 37–75.

altogether short of being a true mutual defense pact for Spain. When United States Air Force Secretary Talbott indicated that atomic bombs would be kept in Spain, this touched off protest even within the regime. Though the fact was denied, it was widely suspected that the pact contained additional secret clauses permitting such procedures. An additional secret agreement did exist, stipulating that the United States could determine unilaterally when it would use the bases to counter "evident Communist aggression," though the bases were officially under joint Spanish and American sovereignty.[11] Nevertheless, it could not be denied that the general arrangement provided a de facto strategic guarantee that had never before existed. The three major air bases were completed several years later and formed a major link in the SAC network throughout the 1960s.

Franco was immensely gratified by the American pact, giving him a recognition he had never before possessed. Coming on the heels of the new concordat with the Vatican, it marked the apogee of the regime's rehabilitation and made the annual Día del Caudillo on October 1, 1953, the most festive ever.

This was followed two years later, in December 1955, by Spain's admission to the United Nations as part of a package deal. By 1956 relations had even thawed with the new leadership of the Soviet Union, which repatriated about 4,000 Spanish nationals, mostly former child evacuees of the Civil War and relatives of Republican emigrés but also including a hundred or so captive veterans of the Blue Division who had survived thirteen or more years in Soviet prison camps.

The Spanish government then moved to the offensive as an injured victim of imperialism. An annual Gibraltar Day had already been designated for the Frente de Juventudes, and in 1956 the Spanish delegation formally presented to the United Nations Madrid's claim for the devolution of Gibraltar, a suit that would be pressed with increasing though fruitless vigor for nearly two decades.

Franco began to have second thoughts about the regime's new international relations only after the successful Soviet launching of Sputnik in 1957. This was widely taken as evidence of major Soviet breakthroughs in missile delivery systems, and Franco had a healthy, even exaggerated, respect for the achievements of the Soviet system of dictatorial order. Fear that the nearby American airbase at Torrejón might involve Madrid itself in a Soviet nuclear exchange became vocal, and during 1958–59 there were high-level discussions with American authorities seeking withdrawal of American nuclear forces from Torrejón, but the United States refused to budge. As a minor ally, Franco had to rest content with the political and

11. See Viñas, *Los pactos*, 195–250; and Rubottom and Murphy, *Spain*, 32, 73.

economic advantages gained and continue to accept the strategic risk, which turned out to be considerably less than feared.

The 1953 Concordat with the Vatican

While negotiating with the United States, the regime redoubled efforts to complete its recognition by the Church through an official new concordat that would replace the old document of 1851 cast aside by the Republic. Such an arrangement was more eagerly sought by Madrid than by Rome, where the pope commented to visitors that the Spanish regime remained an arbitrary dictatorship, sometimes abusive of law and civil rights, and Spanish Catholics played a major role in convincing the Vatican of its desirability. Negotiations were begun by Ruiz Giménez, Franco's ambassador to the Vatican from 1948 to 1951, and carried to fruition by his successor, Fernando María de Castiella, the rising star of the Spanish diplomatic corps.[12] The concordat was finally signed in August 1953. It provided the fullest possible recognition by the Church, reaffirmed the confessionality of the Spanish state, and confirmed the existing right of presentation of bishops by the head of state. At the same time, it expanded the independence of the Church within the Spanish system, guaranteeing the juridical personality of the Church and the full authority of canonical marriage, and completed the restoration of the legal privileges of the clergy that had been partially abolished in the mid-nineteenth century. The Church would be exempt from all censorship in publications dealing with religious affairs, and Catholic Action groups would be allowed "freely to carry out their apostolate," which had not always been the case.[13] Virtually coinciding with the pact with the United States, the Concordat of 1953 marked another major step in the international recognition of the regime, even though most of its provisions merely ratified the existing status quo between church and state. The neo-Catholic tactic adopted in 1945 had produced its harvest, while most of the liberalizing changes that Martín Artajo had once proposed to introduce had never taken place.

Two months later Franco described Spain as "one of the great spiritual reserves of the world"[14] and other notable public gestures followed: reconsecration of Spain to the Sacred Heart by Franco in 1954; the supervision of foodstuffs under the American pact by Caritas, the principal

---

12. There is a good account of the negotiations in Tusell, *Franco y los católicos*, 229–82.
13. *Texto del Concordato entre la Santa Sede y España de 27 de agosto de 1953 y textos anejos* (Madrid, 1961). See also Isidoro Martín, *El Concordato español de 1953* (Madrid, 1954); Eduardo F. Regatillo, *El Concordato español de 1953* (Santander, 1961); and for further aspects of the legal relationship between church and state, *El fenómeno religioso en España: Aspectos jurídico-políticos* (Madrid, 1972).
14. In a Cortes address of October 26, 1953, in *Discursos y mensajes del Jefe del Estado 1951–1954* (Madrid, 1955), 401.

Catholic charity association; and the suppression of legalized prostitution in 1956, abolishing the licensing of brothels begun fifteen years earlier. (This may have been prompted by requirements of entry into the United Nations and certain of its affiliate organizations late in the preceding year).

The obverse of state religious policy was the sharp restriction imposed on Spain's nearly 30,000 Protestants. The 1945 Fuero de los Españoles guaranteed them freedom of private worship, but all public activity and announcements were prohibited.[15] Moreover, Protestants were subjected to a variety of legal harassments, and there were occasional acts of arson and vandalism against their meeting places. Even so, some Catholic prelates still found Protestant infection a major source of danger and railed against it in public pronouncements. The most violent was Cardinal Segura, the rigidly undeviating foe of Franco in Seville, who inveighed against the new association with the liberal United States in a notorious diatribe known as the "dollars of heresy" sermon. Inspired by his example, Catholic Action youths had burned a Protestant meeting place in Seville on March 3, 1952.[16]

During the 1940s and 1950s Catholic schools not only regained but improved upon their earlier position within Spanish education. At their high point in 1961, 49 percent of all secondary students attended Catholic schools. Catholic publications also greatly expanded in number and volume. By 1956, 34 of the 109 daily newspapers being published in Spain could be defined as Catholic organs, and more than 800 other periodical publications were being brought out either by the clergy or Catholic lay associations. Subsequently, a new agreement with the state in 1962 freed official Catholic publications from prior censorship altogether, while certain Church officials continued to participate in concrete aspects of the general state censorship.

Growth in the number of religious vocations continued through the mid-1950s, as an all-time record number of new priests for the modern era (more than 1,000 a year) were ordained between 1954 and 1956. Yet certain signs of change began to appear by the late 1950s. A new mood of secularization began to emerge with economic expansion and the partial opening of Spain to foreign cultural and social influence. For the first time since the Civil War, certain indicators of popular devotion started to decline before the close of the decade. Though few observers might have credited it in 1953, the great secularization of the succeeding generation was already establishing its roots.

15. E. Guerrero and J. M. Alonso, *Libertad religiosa en España* (Madrid, 1962), tries to argue the reasonableness of state regulations concerning Protestants.

16. Advanced in years and infirm in health, Segura was finally removed by the Vatican late in 1954.

Relations with the Royal Family

The restabilization of the regime carried out by the early 1950s had dimmed hope for any immediate restoration of the monarchy. Franco in fact was correct when he declared that Spanish public opinion was not at all promonarchist. Much of the population consensually accepted the regime, whether for positive or negative reasons, and had little direct interest in the monarchy as an alternative. The leftist opposition that stood outside this enforced consensus was now totally bereft of means of action, but it also showed little interest in the monarchy as a rector of Spain's political future.

The uneasy compromise made by Don Juan with Franco in 1948 did give the royal family a certain privileged status in Spain, however, and during the 1950s the monarchists came to occupy the position of a sort of controlled and loyal opposition, concerned more to correct than to contradict the regime. The Madrid daily *ABC*, always the leading monarchist organ, was even allowed on one occasion in 1952 to attack *Arriba*, the central Falangist newspaper, which sometimes featured antimonarchist propaganda. The next significant point of conflict came in 1954 when the sixteen-year-old Prince Juan Carlos completed his secondary studies.[17] On July 16 Don Juan wrote to Franco that the appropriate time had come for the prince to pursue university study abroad in a high-caliber Catholic institution such as Louvain. This proposal apparently came from Gil Robles, who was eager to remove Juan Carlos from Franco's clutches. The very next day, as it developed, Franco prepared a letter for Don Juan stressing that the time had come for Juan Carlos to gain more advanced training in Spanish institutions and that the appropriate course for a prince in line for the throne and the rank of commander-in-chief would be to matriculate at the Academia General Militar in Zaragoza, the institution first developed and commanded by Franco and then revived by his regime. Before he could dispatch this, Franco received the letter from Don Juan, to which he immediately and harshly replied in the negative. Rather than breaking with Franco, Don Juan gave in, provoking the resignation of Gil Robles as political advisor.[18]

The next municipal elections in Madrid on November 24 attracted much more attention than usual, for they were touted as to some extent "free" elections in which for the first time one-third of the municipal councillors would be chosen individually by the direct, "inorganic" vote of heads of families and married women rather than exclusively by controlled corporate blocs. The only opposition permitted to enter alternate

17. On the early years of Juan Carlos, see Juan Antonio Pérez Mateos, *El rey que vino del exilio* (Barcelona, 1981).
18. Gil Robles, *La monarquía*, 411–18; López Rodó, *Larga marcha*, 116–17, 555–58.

candidates for the four seats involved were the monarchists, whose nominees encountered harassment at every step from official institutions and young activists of the Frente de Juventudes and Guardias de Franco. Since this came to be regarded as a sort of mini plebiscite, the government pulled out all the stops, mounting a heavy press campaign and rigorously manipulating the vote on election day, after which it announced that the official slate in Madrid had won 220,000 votes, compared with 50,000 for the monarchist independents.[19] The blatant coercion nonetheless fully revealed the regime's fear of independent opinion, even in favor of conservative monarchists, and amounted to a public relations defeat.[20]

The first meeting between Don Juan and Franco on Spanish soil then took place on December 29 at a private estate of the Conde de Ruiseñada near Navalmoral de la Mata west of Madrid. (Ruiseñada was a Catalan aristocrat who held the post of majordomo (jefe de la casa civil) to the queen mother and served as chief personal contact between Franco and the Pretender for the balance of the decade.) Don Juan apparently pressed for a series of reforms in the regime, to which Franco paid no attention whatsoever. Finding no alternative, he told Franco that he accepted the latter's plan for his son's education,[21] though he also observed that he had recently received communications from four lieutenant generals who had never before approached him.[22] Don Juan subsequently declared in *ABC* on June 24, 1955, "The monarchy has always felt solidarity with the ideals of the National Movement." That fall Juan Carlos entered the military academy in Zaragoza.

The Military in the 1950s

The armed forces had rallied strongly behind the regime throughout the years of ostracism. Franco's leadership was psychologically well adjusted to Spanish officers, who remained generally impressed with his steady discipline and imperturbability, as well as his strong and impenitent stand on behalf of his regime and refusal to bend to foreign pressure. The military entered the 1950s with relatively high morale, though this declined somewhat in the middle of the decade. Their primacy was underscored by the fact that when Franco left the country to visit Portugal in 1949 he had devolved the functions of acting prime minister on Fidel Dávila, the minister of the army.

19. Cf. Créac'h, *Le Coeur*, 338–39; López Rodó, *Larga marcha*, 117; and the article by Joaquín Bardavío in Diario 16, *Historia del franquismo*, 413.
20. Suárez Fernández is of this opinion. *FF*, 4:159.
21. López Rodó, *Larga marcha*, 117–18. Franco's version may be found in Salgado-Araujo, *Conversaciones privadas*, 63–65.
22. Créac'h, *Le Coeur*, 341–45.

General Agustín Muñoz Grandes as commander of the Blue Division in Russia, 1942

Dávila was replaced in the 1951 cabinet by Agustín Muñoz Grandes, a most singular figure in the military hierarchy and certainly one of the most prestigious. He had survived his fascist or Nazi reputation of World War II [23] and his status among his peers was based on two factors: his command of the only Spanish force in major international conflict during the twentieth century, and an extreme personal austerity and incorruptibility, which contrasted with the illicit perquisites and financial dealings common to a number of other top generals. Franco was convinced of Muñoz Grandes's reliability despite the contretemps of 1942, for Muñoz Grandes had long since burnt his bridges with the opposition, leaving his own future closely bound with that of the regime. Six years in the Ministry of the Army in fact tarnished his prestige somewhat, for Muñoz Grandes was sometimes harsh and arbitrary. He seemed to take delight in wearing his German Iron Cross on an official visit to Washington, and for some years his principal bête noire was the Falangist labor minister Girón, whom he considered a demagogue and one of the chief sources of corruption in the government, though they were reconciled in 1954. [24]

The officer corps remained a bloated 25,000, and the retirement age was the highest in Europe, making it superannuated as well. Though most older officers were on the preliminary reserve list, they still drew full pay. Franco was well aware of the waste and redundancy involved [25] and yet could never bring himself to impose a major reform, doubtless for fear of the political consequences. On July 18, 1952, provision was made for senior officers to take full-time jobs in civil service, [26] and in August the maximum age for officers and NCOs in active troop commands was reduced by two years. A second measure put into effect in July 1953 provided for the retirement with full pay and allowances of approximately 2,000 senior officers at the ranks of captain, major, and lieutenant colonel. The Army was at that point reduced from 24 to 18 divisions, and to little more than 250,000 men, which would remain its approximate troop strength for the next thirty years.

As early as January 25, 1952, the Ministry of the Army announced that Spanish small arms and artillery were being converted to accommodate United States weaponry and ammunition. [27] American military assistance

23. Salgado-Araujo, who detested him, observed at the close of 1955: "Muñoz Grandes is neither of the left nor right, neither Socialist, Communist, nor Falangist. By temperament, education and manner of being I think he is more of a leftist than anything else, but above all he is only interested in what can contribute to his personal advancement more than anything else." *Conversaciones privadas*, 156.

24. Ibid., 42. Girón, in turn, had denounced Muñoz Grandes to Franco for conspiring against the regime a decade earlier.

25. Ibid., 222 *et passim*.

26. *Diario Oficial del Ministerio de la Guerra*, July 18, 1952.

27. Ibid., January 26, 1952.

between 1954 and 1958, the period of most intense allocation, amounted to about 350 million dollars, of which some 40 percent went to the Air Force and 30 percent each to the Army and Navy. The Spanish Air Force got its first jet fighters, and the acquisition of squadrons of heavy tanks made it possible to create an armored division, something that the Spanish Army had never possessed. Nearly 5,000 young officers and NCOs received advanced training in the United States during this period.[28] Interservice rivalry was kept to a minimum, partly because the Navy and Air Force were assigned specific and delimited roles and were so much smaller than the Army.

Since 1944, the primary concern of the armed forces had been domestic insurgency and subversion rather than repelling an external threat. Some of the annual maneuvers as well as the regular unit displacements and assignment of commands were directed toward this contingency, even though after 1950 such dangers were increasingly remote. The main external challenge from the early 1950s down to the very end of the regime and even beyond did not come from Europe or the Soviet Union but from the increasing difficulty of sustaining Spain's colonial position in northwest Africa.

The prime military problem for the last two decades of Franco's life was Morocco. This was ironic, because the Generalissimo had made his reputation there and had retained a special emotional relationship with Africa, site of perhaps the happiest days of his life, ever afterward refracted in his memory through a youthful romantic glow. During the postwar ostracism, the regime had emphasized a special opening to the Arab world and placed great emphasis on maintaining its position to Morocco. It was argued that Spain's historical experience created a special relation to and understanding of Arab culture, and Spain in fact followed a somewhat more lenient policy toward native activities in its Protectorate than did France in the main part of Morocco. Yet in the final analysis native unrest sometimes had to be forcibly put down, and when all is said and done the only joint policy followed by both France and Spain during the period of ostracism was, in varying degrees, mutual repression of Moroccan nationalism.

Relations with the Arab world grew closer in the late 1940s and early 1950s, aided by Spain's nonrecognition of Israel and a mounting antipathy toward the Jewish state after it had outspokenly voted for retention of the UN boycott against Spain in 1949. Hussein of Transjordan became the first foreign head of state to visit Spain since long before the Civil War. A

28. It should not be thought that this resulted in an ecstatic wave of pro-Americanism among the Spanish military, however. There was a certain amount of resentment over the American military presence in Spain; memories of the ostracism still rankled, and the fact that the Spanish were always on the receiving end created psychological problems.

Middle Eastern tour by Martín Artajo produced a variety of economic and cultural agreements, and Arab states were generally prepared to take a benevolent attitude toward Spain's role in Morocco. Since Moroccan nationalism was primarily directed against the French, Franco's high commissioner after 1951, Lt. Gen. Rafael García Valiño, was able to follow a relatively lenient policy in the Protectorate. It was Moroccan pressure that won the reincorporation of Spain into the administration of the international zone of Tangier in 1952.[29]

After the French government deposed the sultan in Rabat, the administration of the Spanish Protectorate continued to recognize him as the legitimate Moroccan leader, and García Valiño provided sanctuary for Moroccan nationalists in the Spanish Protectorate, which became a staging area for minor raids into the French zone. This bilevel Spanish policy was designed to discomfit the French and gain favor among the Moroccans, not to promote independence. Franco's personal attitude seems to have been dominated by memories of how faithfully Moroccan troops had served under his command during the 1920s and later during the Civil War,[30] and he expressed the personal opinion that Moroccan independence lay in the distant future. García Valiño was nevertheless unable to prevent a wave of nationalist strikes, demonstrations, and minor terrorist acts that broke out in the Protectorate late in 1955 and continued into the following year.

At that point Paris reversed its policy and prepared to withdraw, allowing a Moroccan nationalist cabinet to be formed in Rabat by the end of 1955. Three nationalists had earlier been given senior administrative positions in the Spanish zone and on January 13, 1956, the Spanish Council of Ministers agreed that independence would soon have to be negotiated with Morocco (with Franco privately blaming García Valiño for going too far in backing subversive activities against the French).[31] After France officially granted independence to its major zone in March 1956, the Spanish government—facing disorders in its own minor Protectorate—had no choice but to follow suit within one month. It was a bitter outcome for Franco, and it also meant the loss of the Guardia Mora, the mounted, gaudily dressed personal guard of specially selected Moroccans who had provided the brightest note in his personal entourage. García Valiño, a tiny general who was widely respected as one of the few genuine luminaries in the military hierarchy, felt almost as though he had been betrayed. Franco had encouraged him to take a strong line in the face of

29. On the evolution of Spanish policy, see Shannon Fleming, "North Africa and the Middle East," in *Spain in the Twentieth-Century World*, ed. J. W. Cortada (Westport, Conn., 1980), 130–40.

30. Salgado-Araujo, *Conversaciones privadas*, 227.

31. Ibid., 157–58, 168, 189.

unrest within the Spanish Protectorate in 1955, then left him without instructions in a rapidly changing situation.[32] Spanish policy had revealed no "special understanding" or "relationship" with Morocco but only confusion and contradiction before collapsing completely.

Sudden loss of the Protectorate was a bitter blow to the pride of senior officers, so many of whom had built their careers there. Military pay was again falling farther behind the spiraling rate of inflation, and restiveness began to appear among the military just as the first significant signs of dissent in five' years emerged among the political opposition. General Antonio Barroso, who had recently replaced Salgado-Araujo as head of Franco's Casa Militar, expressed the opinion that the officer corps was no longer as united as it had been several years earlier, for there was a feeling that the government was not responsive to problems and that ministers stayed in power too long.[33] Not long before the withdrawal from Morocco two cadets had been expelled from the Zaragoza military academy for defacing a portrait of Franco,[34] and early in 1956 a number of small Juntas de Acción Patriótica were formed in garrisons at Madrid, Barcelona, Seville, Valladolid, and Valencia.[35] Though this might have been viewed as symptomatic of an alarming recrudescence of the military syndicalism and conspiracy that had plagued Spain in 1917–23, Franco responded in his usual calm manner, trivializing the phenomenon and virtually refusing to acknowledge it.

The limits of dissidence in the military were illustrated in the case of Juan Bautista Sánchez, the heavy-set, bespectacled, popular, and promonarchist captain general of Barcelona. Beginning in 1950 he met regularly with Don Juan's representative, the Conde de Ruiseñada, and eventually developed the notion of trying to lead a bloodless pronunciamiento that might pressure Franco into restoring the monarchy. Sánchez's political maneuvers were no secret, however, and Franco seems in part to have managed him through his close personal relationship with the army minister, Muñoz Grandes, an old comrade-in-arms from earlier years in Morocco.[36] During late autumn maneuvers of 1956 a lieutenant colonel who commanded two battalions of the Legion was said to have peremptorily told the captain general that his troops took orders only from the Caudillo.[37] When another transport strike occurred in Barcelona in January 1957, Sánchez's studied inactivity recalled his refusal to participate in labor repression six years earlier. Still uncertain as to whether to try to take the

32. According to Serrano Súñer, *Memorias*, 238–39.
33. He is quoted by Salgado-Araujo, *Conversaciones privadas*, 179.
34. According to La Cierva, *Franquismo*, 2:146.
35. A critique of the regime supposedly written by a Junta leader appeared in *Iberica* 4:10 (Oct. 1956).
36. Cf. Sainz Rodríguez, *Una monarquía*, 163–66.
37. According to La Cierva, *Franquismo*, 2:155.

lead in a bold political move, the captain general, who was known to suffer from a heart condition, suddenly died some days later during new field maneuvers, apparently of angina pectoris. Rumors abounded, but there is no evidence of foul play,[38] and Franco was relieved to be rid of his chief military dissident.

Loss of the Moroccan Protectorate did not put an end to Spanish possessions in northwest Africa. There remained the two Spanish-inhabited presidio cities of Ceuta and Melilla on the northern coast of Morocco, across the straits from Andalusia, the enclave of Sidi Ifni far down Morocco's Atlantic coast, and the broader expanses of Cabo Juby and the Spanish Sahara south of Morocco,[39] as well as the equatorial districts of Spanish Guinea well beyond. The new Moroccan state coveted all the Spanish territories along its border, and the easiest target was the enclave of Ifni, surrounded on three sides by the land mass of Morocco. On November 23, 1957, Moroccan forces in the guise of irregulars, using formerly Spanish equipment provided their regular army, attacked Spanish positions in Ifni. A few small posts were overrun, but the invaders were stopped within three days. The Spanish garrison of 2,500 troops was expanded to 8,000 by December 9 after suffering 62 fatalities in the brief combat. The French also cooperated in the Spanish buildup, for Paris wanted to defend Mauritania to the south from further Moroccan expansion. Within a month the Moroccans "unofficially" struck again, this time attacking near El Aaiun, the capital of the Spanish Sahara. They were stopped once more, this time at the price of 241 Spanish dead. Spanish air strikes helped to turn back the assailants, and again France cooperated in the Spanish buildup. By February 1958 tranquillity was restored,[40] and the military had once more rallied firmly behind the regime in a time of crisis. The activity of the clandestine juntas quickly petered out.

Though these assaults did not for the moment pose a serious threat to Spain's remaining territories in northwest Africa, they were a violent indication of the strength of irredentism in Moroccan policy and raised serious questions for the future. The district of Cabo Juby, bordering Morocco's southern frontier, was ceded early in 1958, but the Spanish government intended no further concessions. Carrero Blanco was even more emphatic than Franco that both Ifni and the Sahara must be retained as a necessary strategic shield for the Canary Islands farther to the west. To strengthen their relationship with Spain, both territories were raised to the status of Spanish provinces on January 31, 1958, following

38. The fullest discussion is in Fernández, *Tensiones militares*, 141–48.

39. On the historical evolution of these territorial demarcations down to 1960, see José Ma. Cordero Torres, *Fronteras hispánicas* (Madrid, 1960), 387–458.

40. See Ramiro Santamaría, *Ifni y Sahara: La guerra ignorada* (Madrid, 1984); and La Cierva, *Franquismo*, 2:168–72.

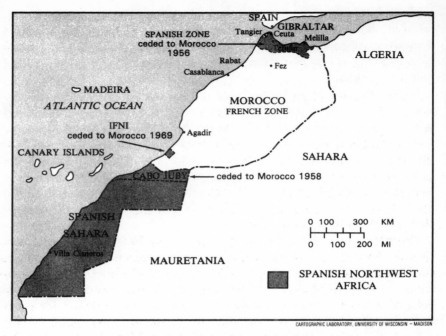

Spanish possessions in Northwest Africa

the policy earlier adopted by Portugal for its own African possessions. Plans were announced for the emigration of 30,000 Spaniards to the largely barren and uninhabited Spanish Sahara, though little ever came of that. For the time being, the two Spanish-inhabited cities of Ceuta and Melilla were safe, but nothing had been done to extract a recognition of Spain's sovereignty from the new Moroccan state at the time of independence, and the two cities were likely to become a major bone of contention in the future.

Through its policy of standing fast, the regime still upheld the military conception of Spanish honor, yet the place of the armed forces and the police in its financial priorities was steadily falling. The share of the armed forces in the state budget declined from 30 percent in 1953 to 27 percent in 1955, and then to 25 percent in 1957, whence it sank further to only 24 percent by 1959. The armed police, similarly, had become less numerous and costly by the late 1950s than under the Republic. Their total of 84,591 (with the Civil Guard) in 1958 was lower in proportion to the population than the number for 1935, and their share of the total budget had dropped from 6.3 percent in 1935 to 5.3 percent in 1958.

Falangism in the Fifties

A prime demand by the democracies during the period of ostracism had been the elimination of the Falange from Spanish life. Franco responded by further deemphasizing the FET and altering part of the terminology and nomenclature of the regime, but the Falange as National Movement remained very much a part of the bureaucracy of the system, and its own increasingly languid institutional life continued uninterrupted. Approximately 900,000 names were still carried on the membership rolls—though the active membership was far fewer—and Franco continued to regard it as indispensable to the bureaucracy and infrastructure of the regime. His remark in Granada on October 13, 1952, "The Falange is necessary to the life of Spain"[41] was repeated from time to time in different phraseology but always with the same sentiment.

The Movement was indispensable to Franco for several fundamental reasons. First, it provided a necessary cadre of leaders and manpower to staff portions of the regime. Secondly, it provided a modern social doctrine, was responsible for administering the syndical system, and had developed much of Spain's social welfare program. It also staffed the press and propaganda system and was responsible for the youth program. Finally, the Movement was the most loyal of Spanish institutions save for the military, because it had no other basis for its existence after 1945. It could even serve as a scapegoat[42] whose nominal downgrading would be evidence of reform and liberalization.

The FET's basic organizational budget had been cut drastically in 1946, when it was reduced by more than 75 percent. As indicated in table 18.1, Franco at first had not been willing to spend much money on the party, alloting it only a half of one percent of the state budget in the first two years after the Civil War. Once Arrese had taken over, this had been more than tripled for the four years 1942–45. After that, the party would never claim as much as a half of one percent of the state budget again and sometimes only a quarter of one percent. The secondary role of the party was indicated by the fact that by 1950, if not before, Franco had almost ceased to appear in Falangist uniform (save for the annual party rally), though certain Falangist ministers occasionally did so.

41. *Discursos y mensajes del Jefe del Estado 1951–1954* (Madrid, 1955), 234.
42. And Franco himself was not above mocking Falangist ideology in private, as on the occasion in 1954 when he playfully inquired of the young administrative specialist López Rodó whether he understood the concept of the "vertical syndicate" (central to Falangist doctrine), adding sardonically that he himself had never been able to figure it out. *Franco visto por sus ministros*, 165.

Table 18.1. FET/Movimiento Budget

Year	Total Pesetas	Constant Pesetas	Percentage of State Budget
1940	32,307,071	32,307,071	0.54
1941	36,802,271	31,134,721	0.54
1942	141,490,427	108,806,138	1.80
1943	179,561,041	123,717,557	1.90
1944	181,371,827	116,259,341	1.73
1945	204,374,581	117,924,133	1.92
1946	43,479,922	20,913,842	0.38
1947	41,414,779	16,980,039	0.29
1948	41,214,102	15,785,001	0.27
1949	44,476,899	15,922,730	0.28
1950	50,000,000	15,150,000	0.28
1952	61,242,125	14,330,657	0.27
1954	71,684,705	15,555,581	0.28
1956	81,770,396	15,699,916	0.23
1958	102,174,652	15,326,198	0.21
1960	154,799,850	22,291,178	0.28
1962	317,000,000	42,161,000	0.29
1964	404,800,000	50,195,200	0.33
1966	544,900,000	59,939,000	0.32
1968	603,300,000	64,553,100	0.25
1970	1,349,500,000	137,649,000	0.44
1972	1,693,265,000	152,393,850	0.40
1974	2,467,700,000	172,739,000	0.42

Source: Presupuestos Generales del Estado, compiled in Ricardo Chueca, *El fascismo en los comienzos del régimen de Franco* (Madrid, 1983), 203.

Table 18.2. Uniforms Worn by Franco and His Cabinet in the First Six Months of 1940, 1945, and 1950

	1940		1945		1950	
Type of Uniform	Franco	Cabinet	Franco	Cabinet	Franco	Cabinet
Falangist blue	44%	44%	35%	25%	—	2%
Falangist white (summer)	3	9	3	7.5	—	8
Military	50	12	40	25	87%	6
Civilian	3	35	5	55	4	71
Other (diplomat, admiral, etc.)	—	—	19	2	9	12
N	(32)	(75)	(37)	(132)	(46)	(49)

Source: Photographs in *ABC* of Madrid in Juan J. Linz, "From Falange to Movimiento-Organización," in *Authoritarian Politics in Modern Society*, ed. S. Huntington and C. Moore (New York, 1970), 151.

By 1948 he had found it useful to appoint a secretary general once more, as the reliable Fernández Cuesta returned to direct the party bureaucracy. The Movement still harbored a number of dissident elements, and Fernández Cuesta fired several officials in March 1949 in an effort to improve discipline. When the second national congress of provincial directors of the party met on July 10 of that year, there was considerable criticism of policy as it related to price controls, rationing, censorship even of the Movement, and the holding of double offices under the regime. At the beginning of 1950 a small reformist Falangist journal, *Sí*, was suspended for supporting a recent bank employees' strike, but there was no evidence that Fernández Cuesta's administrative vigor had increased since his first tour of duty. His leadership proved anodyne in the extreme.[43] Unable to give direction to the more active elements or provide a true focus for the Movement, he soon lost a good deal of whatever respect he had retained among the membership.

The security that the regime had achieved did permit a modest new cycle of Falangist political and cultural activity beginning about 1952, encouraged by Franco to counterbalance monarchism. When the able new satirical journal *La Codorniz* (*The Quail*, founded in the early 1940s in tongue-in-cheek imitation of *Le Canard Enchainé*)[44] published a satire in early 1952 of the Movement's central journal *Arriba* (*Upward*) under the title *Abajo* ("Downward"), the regime allowed its offices to be sacked by Falangist toughs. The one and only general national congress of the FET was held in Madrid late in October 1953 on the twentieth anniversary of the party's founding. Only a month earlier Franco had declared that "the Falange is superior to all contingencies, . . . flanking and supporting the constituent force of our Army."[45] Wearing a now unaccustomed black Falangist uniform, Franco addressed a crowd officially described as numbering 150,000 (though other observers suggested half that) to denounce "traitors advocating a third force," by which he meant independent monarchists. Other speakers once more differentiated the party from central European fascism, but statements from various spokesmen also revealed continuing latent dissension within the organization between radicals and bureaucratic moderates, the former urging drastic statist economic measures.[46] The Congress provided an opportunity to blow off steam, for nothing more came of it. A large national rally could not mitigate the clear

43. Cf. his bland collected speeches for the years 1950–53: *El Movimiento político español* (Madrid, 1952) and *Afirmación falangista* (Madrid, 1953).

44. Alvaro de Laiglesia, *La Codorniz sin jaula* (Barcelona, 1981), is a memoir by its founder and director.

45. Quoted in Rafael Gómez Pérez, *Política y religión en el régimen de Franco* (Barcelona, 1976), 71.

46. Créac'h, *Le Coeur* 319–20; La Cierva, *Franquismo*, 2:115–16; *FF*, 5:142–44.

fact that the Movement, as a tame bureaucratic organization with scant initiative, failed to serve as a very effective vehicle of political mobilization and was becoming increasingly ineffective in the indoctrination of Spanish youth.[47]

Cultural Differentiation and Conflict

From its inception, the Nationalist regime intended to foster a unified, broadly diffused neotraditionalist culture that would reanimate Spain's spiritual life and inculcate in the younger generation a strong sense of nationalism, religion, and tradition.[48] The two somewhat contradictory poles of this enterprise were the Church and the Falange. The Catholic revival of the 1940s did succeed temporarily in restoring wider participation in neotraditional religiosity, yet the fascistic culture of the Falange was partially antagonistic to this process as well as much less successful in its own right.

The only aspect of Falangist culture that merits attention was the work of the literary activists of the early 1940s, sometimes called a bit confusingly the liberal Falangists, represented by such writers as Dionisio Ridruejo, Antonio Tovar, and Pedro Laín Entralgo. Their main channels were several well-known journals such as *Escorial* and *Vértice*, and, on a more scholarly level the *Revista de Estudios Políticos*, first edited by García Valdecasas. They sought to promote a more dynamic and modern culture, largely secular in inspiration, that would maintain and develop much of the heritage of the Generation of 98 and of Ortega. Their chief protector had been Serrano Súñer, intellectually the most accomplished of the regime's leaders; with his ouster the more creative and critical in the Falange lost backing and opportunity for expression. Arrese's leadership of the FET incorporated part of this group under the subsequent leadership of José María Alfaro, while progressively diluting their fascism and promoting a more narrowly nationalistic and religious culture.[49]

47. The waning of the regime's youth movement in the 1950s is described in the memoir by José Luis Alcocer, *Radiografía de un fraude: Notas para una historia del Frente de Juventudes* (Barcelona, 1978).

48. There is no general study of Franquist culture as a whole as distinct from general surveys of cultural and intellectual life in Spain throughout the long history of the regime, such as Equipo "Reseña," *La cultura española durante el franquismo* (Bilbao, 1977); and Elías Díaz, *Pensamiento español (1939–1973)* (Madrid, 1974). Concerning the regime's own style and expression in art, see Antonio Bonet Correa, *Arte del franquismo* (Madrid, 1981).

49. On the critical Falangists of the 1940s, see José Carlos Mainer, *Falange y literatura* (Barcelona, 1971); the articles by Manuel Contreras and José Antonio Portero in *Las fuentes ideológicas de un régimen (España 1939–1945)*, ed. M. Ramírez Jiménez (Zaragoza, 1978), 29–80; Thomas Mermall, *The Rhetoric of Humanism: Spanish Culture after Ortega y Gasset* (New York, 1976), 17–52; and Díaz, *Pensamiento*, 27–36.

Mention might also be made of the ex-Socialist professor of law Francisco Javier Conde, who served as director of the Instituto de Estudios Políticos from 1948 to 1956. As a neo-

Only a politically mobilized regime could have seriously attempted to inculcate a Falangist culture on a broad scale, and such was not the structure of Franco's system. Its official culture was not that of fascism or Falangism but of conservative Catholicism, propagated through the Church and private media more than through official agencies.

For the common population, especially in the cities, the Spain of the first two post–Civil War decades evolved its own popular culture and entertainments as a means of distraction. Encouraged by the regime, these included comics, dime novels, radio programs, and above all large doses of cheap cinema, mostly of a sentimental variety and always within strict cultural limits. The regime encouraged athletic activities but lacked the means to do so on a large scale. By the 1950s, however, professional soccer had become very popular, and had gained the same enthusiastic mass following as sports in other western countries.

The most critical cultural commentary in Franco Spain, aside from occasional moralistic diatribes by Falangist journalists or churchmen, came from apolitical novelists. Several of the *tremendista* novels of the first years after the Civil War, such as Carmen Laforet's *Nada* (1940) and Camilo José Cela's *La familia de Pascual Duarte* (1942) and *La Colmena* (1954), commented on the hollowness or hypocrisy of social values and the injustice of some social relationships. The apolitical climate and relative cultural anomie of the 1950s was best captured in the stark and unaffected depiction of Madrid Youth in *El Jarama* (1956), by Rafael Sánchez Ferlosio, the non-Falangist son of the Falangist writer Sánchez Mazas.

Catholic conservatives came to the fore in the official cultural activities after 1945. Their main independent bases were Catholic Action, the National Association of Catholic Propagandists, and the Editorial Católica, Spain's largest and most influential Catholic publisher. Appointment of the Catholic lay leader and university professor Joaquín Ruiz Giménez to the Ministry of Education in 1951 placed educational policy in the hands of one of the most idealistic and open-minded of the major Catholic figures. Though fully loyal to Franco, Ruiz Giménez tried to initiate a new *apertura* (opening) in educational policy to expand facilities, reform and modernize procedures, and incorporate sectors of Spanish culture that had been ostracized by the regime. Formally, he was a member of the Movement and would wear a blue shirt on certain public occasions. Part of Ruiz Giménez's initial policy was to appoint some of the more able and culturally liberal Falangists to key posts in his ministry and the university sys-

Falangist after the Civil War, he had developed the most sophisticated theoretical interpretation of Franco's *caudillaje* done in Spain, and as director of the IEP devoted considerable attention to contacts with western Europe and the United States and to the social dimensions of politics. His principal writings are collected in his *Escritos y fragmentos políticos*, 2 vols. (Madrid, 1974–75).

Joaquín Ruiz Giménez, Minister of Education, 1951–56

tem, in the hope of projecting a new synthesis of the best ideals of the Movement and a kind of open-minded Catholic progressivism. Laín Entralgo was made rector of the University of Madrid, Tovar took up the rectorship of Salamanca, and one of the most adroit young Falangist academics, Torcuato Fernández Miranda, became rector of the University of Oviedo.

Though altogether lacking the financial resources to fill the many gaps in Spain's weak educational system, Ruiz Giménez held the initiative from 1951 to 1953, initiating reforms on both the university and secondary level. A new law of secondary education in 1953 partially revised the curriculum and also provided for limited inspection of Catholic schools. New university regulations established more impersonal and automatic procedures for the membership of qualifying boards (tribunales de oposiciones) for the nomination of professorial chairholders, eliminating some of the favoritism dominant since the Civil War. A major effort was made to reincorporate highly qualified university faculty who had been ostracized, providing positions for such eminent professors as the exiled Arturo Duperier, Spain's only internationally respected physicist.[50] Ruiz Giménez also encouraged liberalization of curriculum, choice of study matter, and cultural expression, which drew increasingly sharp attacks from Falangists and the extreme right.[51]

Catholic pressure during this same period had also attempted to push a new press censorship law through Arias Salgado's Ministry of Information and Tourism, since 1951 in charge of state censorship. The Junta Nacional de Prensa Católica initiated a new draft project that would have abolished prior censorship and would have been more liberal than the later reform carried out in 1966. It was much too free for the rigid Arias, a Catholic Falangist of the Arrese group, who quashed the project at the beginning of 1952. He was opposed to any overt change, and, remarkably loquacious for a censor, propounded at length in public speeches and articles what he liked to call "the Spanish doctrine of information," which required prior censorship in most instances for the well-being of the nation.[52] Nonetheless, despite the minister of information's reputation for rigidity, cultural and commercial contacts with western Europe and North America were expanding during these years, and greater diversity of opinion could be seen in Spanish publications, as the censorship made minor but broadening adjustments to accommodate the widening horizon of Spanish life.[53]

A distinctive new Catholic influence had emerged by the 1950s in the secular institute Opus Dei (Work of God). Originating as a diocesan organization, it was the most unusual Catholic group in post–Civil War Spain and perhaps in the Catholic Church as a whole. Developing from a small nucleus founded by the Aragonese priest José María Escrivá de Balaguer in 1928, it was recognized in 1947 as the first secular institute in the Church. By the time that Pope John Paul II granted it the status of the Church's first "personal prelature" in 1982, Opus Dei had expanded to a worldwide membership of approximately 72,000.

The mission of Opus Dei is the sanctification of the secular world. As

50. A very few opposition scholars of distinction such as the outstanding Catalan historian Jaime Vicens Vives, who gained a chair at Zaragoza in 1947, had been reincorporated under the second ministry of Ibáñez Martín, Ruiz Giménez's predecessor.

51. The best study of this entire phase is in Tusell, *Franco y los católicos*, 308–36.

52. Gabriel Arias Salgado, *Política española de la información* (Madrid, 1958). Censorship under the regime is treated by Manuel L. Abellán, *Censura y creación literaria en España (1939–1976)* (Barcelona, 1980); and Ramón Gubern, *La censura (1936–1975)* (Barcelona, 1981). On the period of Arias Salgado, see also Javier Terrón Montero, *La prensa en España durante el régimen de Franco* (Madrid, 1981), 83–135; and Juan A. Giner, "Journalists, Mass Media, and Public Opinion in Spain, 1938–1982," in *The Press and Rebirth of Iberian Democracy*, ed. K. Maxwell (Westport, Conn., 1983), 33–54.

53. This is reflected in the limited renascence of painting and the cinema in Spanish cultural life of the 1950s, which in these two areas was not as restricted as has often been supposed. For a survey of Spanish film, see "Le cinéma de l'Espagne franquiste (1939–75)," ed. M. Ohms and P. Roura, in *Les Cahiers de la Cinémathèque* 38–39 (Winter 1984).

conceived by its founder and leaders, the labor of disseminating spiritual values could be most effectively prosecuted through the key professions of late industrial society such as university teaching, business, finance, and the higher levels of management. Since a disproportionate number of the institute's members had careers in these areas, Opus Dei eventually developed a reputation for elitism, while the reserve displayed by leaders and members about their own association and interrelationships created a certain air of secrecy.

During the first years after the Civil War members of Opus Dei were in general less closely connected with the regime than were those of Catholic Action. Its work seemed more progressive and modern than that of most other Spanish Catholic organizations of the 1940s, and thus it was supported and encouraged by several wealthy Catholic progressives, particularly in Catalonia. Falangists on the other hand attacked and opposed the institute and its members almost from the start.

Opus Dei came to the public's attention as scores of its members gained university professorships during the 1940s and 1950s. By the fifties some alleged that as many as 20 percent of the teaching positions in Spanish higher education were held by institute members, though that is probably an exaggeration.[54] In 1952 Opus Dei opened what soon became the first completely developed Catholic university in the country, the University of Navarre at Pamplona. The organization's members came to prominence in business and financial affairs, and some developed an interest in politics, although others discouraged such activity.[55]

Though differences of opinion on public affairs developed among members of Opus Dei, the most conspicuous and vocal group formed around the journal Arbor (a publication of the National Research Council; CSIC), led by the extravagant and unstable essayist Rafael Calvo Serer and the more prudent Florentino Pérez Embid. The Arbor circle strongly supported an authoritarian Catholic monarchist succession to the regime,[56] combatting Falangism, liberalism, and narrowly bureaucratic loyalism to the system. Calvo Serer was thus critical of the regime for failing to give proper right-wing monarchist substance to the state and also a vociferous critic of Ruiz Giménez and other aperturistas for being too weak and lib-

54. Though it provides no statistics on the number of professors who were members of Opus Dei, see Antonio Fontán, Los católicos en la universidad española (Madrid, 1961).

55. Jesús Ynfante [pseud.], La prodigiosa aventura del Opus Dei (Paris, 1970), and Daniel Artigues [pseud.], El Opus Dei en España, 1928–1962 (Paris, 1971), are two detailed, hostile accounts. Jean-Jacques Thierry, L'Opus Dei: Mythe et réalité (Paris, 1973), is much more favorable.

56. Cf. Calvo Serer's Teoría de la Restauración (Madrid, 1952), an attempt to bring Franco and Don Juan closer together; and his España sin problema (Madrid, 1949), a rightist Catholic response to the book España como problema, 2 vols. (Madrid, 1949), by the reformist Falangist Pedro Laín Entralgo (Cf. Díaz, 69–79). A collection of articles by Florentino Pérez Embid was published in his Ambiciones españolas (Madrid, 1953).

eral and opening the door to radical tendencies. In September 1953 he published an article in a minor French journal of the extreme right that expressed both these viewpoints, labeling the years 1945–51 within the regime as years of nonmonarchist "rightist nihilism." This resulted in his firing as editor of the state-subsidized *Arbor.*

By 1954 rightist critics within the regime had effectively curtailed the freedom of action of Ruiz Giménez as minister of education, and the two brief years of limited *apertura* in educational and cultural matters were at an end. Nonetheless, by the mid-1950s the Spanish cultural panorama was broadening under the impact of expansion of the university system and the growth of the economy, stimulated by new international and cultural relations. For the first time in the history of the regime university students, despite their nominal compulsory organization in the Falangist SEU, began to develop dissident ideas, whether from a critical Falangist, monarchist, independent catholic, liberal, or leftist perspective.[57] By the mid-1950s the enforced consensus of Spanish cultural life was beginning to show its initial cracks.

The Crisis of February 1956

In 1953 direct opposition among university students led to the first attempt to contest SEU elections when a new circle called Juventud Universitaria (University Youth) tried indirectly to resurrect the essence of the old Republican Federación Universitaria Española. Though this was not successful, a turning point of sorts was reached on January 27, 1954, when the SEU mobilized a student crowd, as it did from time to time, to protest British control of Gibraltar. The demonstration took place in front of the British embassy on the occasion of a visit of Queen Elizabeth to the colony, but for reasons that are not clear, the armed police charged the student crowd near the end of the protest, breaking it up violently. This led to a direct clash between the students and the police, followed by a spontaneous new counterdemonstration in the central Puerta del Sol demanding the ouster of the national police chief.[58] The authorities' apparent betrayal of an organized patriotic protest helped to destroy much of the SEU's remaining legitimacy. This was the last student mob ever mobilized by a government agency, and from that time opposition in the country's largest university became more overt.

A few days later, on February 2, 1954, new workplace elections for

57. On the new attitudes of the university generation of the 1950s, see Juan F. Marsal et al., *Pensar bajo el franquismo* (Barcelona, 1959).
58. Pablo Lizcano, *La generación, del 56: La universidad contra Franco* (Barcelona, 1981), 95–97; Créac'h, *Le coeur,* 331–32. Cf. Vicente Girbau, "The Foreign Policy of Franco Spain," *Iberica* 7 (Sept.–Nov. 1959), 9–11.

enlaces sindicales resulted in the selection of a number of oppositional crypto-leftists,[59] indicating that labor activities were not as thoroughly controlled as in the past, even though the syndical system was not formally challenged. Near the close of that year a minor attack came from a totally unexpected source, when Bishop Pildain of Las Palmas (Canary Islands) attacked the syndical system in a pastoral letter, charging that its state-dominated structure violated papal teachings on social organization. This caused little excitement in Spain, where the news was censored, but sparked considerable comment abroad. During the next few weeks Spanish diplomats in several other Catholic countries labored to reduce the negative impression created.[60]

The hollow ring of the regime's rhetoric was even noted by Franco's cousin Salgado Araujo several months later in his diary:

> When I hear these pompous speeches I am often reminded of Hamlet when he said "Words, words, words." There is too much talk about the Movement, the syndicates and so on, when the truth is that the whole business as it is presently set up is supported only by Franco and the Army. . . . All the rest, the Movement, the syndicates, the Falange and all the other political operations have not taken root in the country nineteen years after the Alzamiento. It is sad to have to say that, but it is the pure truth.[61]

The sense of frustration and artificiality was at that point even keener among many Falangists, relegated to a limited and secondary role and forced now to accept, at least in theory, monarchist principles which they had always combatted. Moreover, Franco's own instructions that the Movement must become more monarchist seemed only half-hearted, for the Movement press (split off from the vicesecretariat of popular culture since 1945) continued intermittent attacks on the institution of monarchy and indirectly on the royal family.

Falangist resentment was expressed in two new efforts to form dissident, semiclandestine groups between 1952 and 1954, both soon repressed by the police.[62] The crisis of Falangism was most acute among the youth, and in January 1955 two of the principal Falangist youth publications came out with strong articles against the monarchy. A minority of ardent young Falangists were growing more radical; at the annual cere-

---

59. Créac'h, *Le Coeur,* 332.
60. Tusell, *Franco y los católicos,* 363–66.
61. The entry is for October 28, 1955, in *Conversaciones privadas,* 142.
62. The clandestine neo-Falangist Juntas de Acción Nacional Sindicalista, formed in 1952, was quickly broken up by police. During these years dissident Falangism sometimes looked for leadership to the rehabilitated Manuel Hedilla, last jefe nacional before Franco, who had been in prison from 1937 till 1941 and was later a private businessman without an official role in the Movement. In 1954 another minor dissident initiative, the Juntas de Ofensiva Nacional Sindicalista (reviving the name of the original JONS), was organized only to have its leaders soon arrested, though for several years the slogan "Hedilla-JONS" appeared on walls in Madrid.

mony on February 9 (The Day of the Fallen Student, marking the anniversary of one of the first Falangists killed by political assassins in 1934), one young militant openly shouted insults at Fernández Cuesta, the tepid and inept secretary general.[63] When he was expelled from the university, Falangist comrades organized a brief protest strike against the party leadership, for which in turn the head of the SEU was dismissed.[64] Insubordinate gestures continued through the year on a minor scale. On one occasion, at a camp of the Falanges Juveniles de Franco in July, some of the assembled Falangist youth displayed public rudeness to Prince Juan Carlos,[65] making his normally awkward role even more difficult.

Franco as usual ignored the situation. His only change in the party during the balance of 1955 was to appoint personally another 50 members of the FET National Council, naming a new member from each province. The intention was not so much to change the composition of the National Council (which had not met since 1943) as to give the FET bureaucratic leadership 150 of the 510 votes in the national Cortes instead of the old ratio of 100 out of 460.

At the November anniversary ceremony for the death of José Antonio, one young Falangist shouted "No queremos reyes idiotas" ("We don't want idiot kings"), mouthing a common phrase of Falangist resentment in defiance of official policy. Some days later a *centuria* (company) of young Falangists marching in the outskirts of Madrid chanted a song ridiculing the Caudillo himself. For these and other outbursts the head of the Frente of Juventudes was fired later that month, as was Luis González Vicén, the camisa vieja chief of the youthful Guardias de Franco.[66] In December the still nominally Falangist rector of the University of Madrid, Laín Entralgo, completed a report based on a sample of questionnaires which concluded that university youth were basically disaffected and that the university system was in need of drastic reform. Published as a pamphlet,[67] this report dealt much more with problems of moral and religious rebelliousness than with politics, and though it apparently reached his desk, made scant impression on Franco.

By 1956, at least four different small dissident student groups could be

63. Lizcano, *La generación*, 101–3. The weak, defensive posture of Fernández Cuesta is apparent in some of his collected speeches of 1953 to 1955, *Continuidad falangista al servicio de España* (Madrid, 1955).

64. Créac'h, *Le Coeur*, 352.

65. This incident is described by José Luis Alcocer, "Covaleda, 1955: La Falange desaira a Juan Carlos," *Nueva Historia* 2:15 (April 1978), 95–100.

66. A prime demand of Falangist dissidents was, as usual, a return to the pristine radicalism of the Movement, invoking the example of Ledesma's JONS and the pre–Franco leadership of Manuel Hedilla. To quash this, Tomás Romojaro, the vicesecretary general, revealed that Hedilla was receiving a monthly subsidy from the government. *FF*, 5:243.

67. *Reflexiones sobre la situación espiritual de la juventud universitaria* (Madrid, 1955).

identified at the University of Madrid, in addition to the core Falangist minority of the SEU. At the extreme left was the clandestine Communist group, seeking to encourage militant opposition. There was also a very small Socialist group, formed in part around Rafael Sánchez Ferlosio, son of the Falangist writer Sánchez Mazas. Another small set followed the now ex-Falangist writer Ridruejo[68] and sought a drastic reform, though not necessarily the overthrow, of the system, while a dissident SEU group simply wanted to reform the existing SEU.[69]

Free student elections were a prime goal, and on February 1, 1956, an oppositionist student manifesto was distributed calling for an elected national assembly of students. Official SEU candidates were then defeated for the first time in elections for the minor office of sports delegates within the Faculty of Law, principal hotbed of dissent. A centuria of the Guardias de Franco physically attacked anti-SEU students there, and a number of violent incidents ensued. The climax to these skirmishes came on February 9, when a group of student protesters ran into a column of Falangist demonstrators returning from the annual Fallen Student ceremony on a main street near the university. By the time the melee had been broken up by police, one of the Falangists lay severely wounded by a bullet in the back of the neck, probably fired either by the police or by one of his own comrades.[70] In the resulting crackdown, about fifty dissident students and their associates were arrested. Falangist leaders demanded more action, and the party press immediately launched a heated campaign about the danger to the Movement and the regime. As reports spread of a list prepared by SEU and Guardia de Franco activists for a "night of the long knives," the captain general of Madrid, Rodrigo, made it clear that the Army would brook no violence, and even placed headquarters of Falangist activists under military surveillance to keep them in line.

It is doubtless true that, as La Cierva has suggested,[71] Franco was well enough informed to realize that the February incidents involved mere handfuls of politicized youth who could be easily repressed. At first he failed to react, spending the tenth on a hunting trip, to the disgust of his cousin Salgado Araujo.[72] Not until one day later did the government de-

68. Ridruejo apparently had not yet incurred the complete displeasure of Franco, who was said to have intervened personally in 1954 to ensure that Ridruejo was awarded a literary prize of which he might have been deprived. Ridruejo's letter of gratitude is given in *FF*, 5:164–66.

69. See the analysis in La Cierva, *Franquismo*, 2:137–40.

70. The fullest collection of materials on these incidents and their background will be found in *Jaraneros y alborotadores: Documentos sobre los sucesos estudiantiles de febrero de 1956 en la Universidad Complutense de Madrid* (Madrid, 1982), ed. Roberto Mesa. See also Lizcano, *La generación*, 123–53; and Ridruejo, *Casi unas memorias*, 335–55.

71. La Cierva, *Franquismo*, 2:138–42.

72. *Conversaciones privadas*, 164. Salgado Araujo wrote on February 11, "Unfortunately frivolity and irresponsibility continue at the top, and as if nothing were happening they are going off on another hunt and not returning for five days." He further observed that four

cree for the first time the suspension of articles 14 and 18 of the Fuero de los Españoles, followed by temporary closure of the University of Madrid. Moreover, the Generalissimo could not ignore the internal decomposition and mutual conflicts of the veteran political families of the regime, some of whom were nearing exhaustion. The loyal Girón warned that there was considerable anti-Franco sentiment within the Movement.[73] It was obvious that Fernández Cuesta had been unable to maintain order among Madrid Falangist Youth, while would-be reformers within the Movement were a dangerous unknown quantity. The chief innovation of the current government, Ruiz Giménez's attempt to open up and reform education, had drawn intense opposition and eventually the hostility of Franco himself. Extreme right-wing Catholics in the cabinet such as Arias Salgado or the Carlist Iturmendi could offer little new political support of their own. One alternative might be to bring in more technical experts, something favored by Carrero Blanco, but in the winter of 1956 Franco was not willing to consider any major change.

Thus after one week, on February 16, Franco carried out a very limited cabinet realignment to replace the two ministers whose authority had been most directly challenged. The Caudillo's most trusted Falangist, Arrese, was brought back after eleven years in the wilderness to replace Fernández Cuesta as secretary general of the Movement, and the portfolio of Ruiz Giménez in Education was given to Jesús Rubio García-Mina, a university professor and former subsecretary of education. Ruiz Giménez's reformists within the ministry and the university system were replaced mostly by more orthodox personnel, though two key appointees remained: Torcuato Fernández Miranda became director general of universities and the young Manuel Fraga Iribarne took over the Instituto de Estudios Políticos.

This reorganization was carried out against a background of mounting economic distress brought on by persistently high inflation. The government granted a 20 percent across-the-board wage increase for Spanish labor on March 3, followed by another 7.5 percent in the autumn. To satisfy the military, who had been losing proportionately even more to price rises, an even greater increase—especially for junior officers—was given in the summer. Such measures did not head off major strikes in the Basque provinces in April, the first large-scale labor stoppages there in five years.[74]

---

ministers and García Valiño, the high commissioner of Spanish Morocco, were to accompany Franco, along with a coterie of big landowners and businessmen and "aristocrats who [otherwise] never compromise with the regime, black-market importers, etc. etc." In fact, Franco apparently remained in Madrid at least three more days to complete the political resolution of the crisis.

73. Ibid., 159.
74. Ferri et al., *Las huelgas*, 226–47.

Altogether, the crisis had been more significant than Franco's measured response indicated, for it was the regime's first major internal crisis in fourteen years, and the threatened Falangist "night of the long knives" had at least temporarily evoked widespread fear in Madrid. Moreover, the whole course of events had demonstrated that after fifteen years the regime was losing control of youth in the major universities, where previously it had had either limited support or at least uncontested domination. During the remaining two decades of Franco's government, opposition in the larger universities would mount steadily. In addition, those of the "critical Falangist" and "progressive Catholic" intelligentsia ousted with Ruiz Giménez would never return to the fold but would henceforth remain outside the regime. The events of 1956 marked the first glimmerings of a new, internal opposition, one that stemmed not from the Republic or the emigrés of the 1940s but from the new generation who had begun to grow up under the regime during the 1950s.

The Abortive Falangist Fundamental Laws of 1956

There is no indication that Franco had any major changes in mind after the February crisis other than tighter administration. The new secretary-general of the Movement, however, realized that the malaise of the Falange would be difficult to resolve merely through bureaucratic manipulation. He had opposed the entire monarchist direction of the Fundamental Laws in 1945–47[75] and believed that he might now be facing the last chance to guarantee a major role for the Movement in the permanent structure of the regime. Abortive projects for the institutional redefinition of the system were not unprecedented; drafts had been prepared during the 1940s by Serrano Súñer and by at least two other theorists that had come completely to naught. Arrese was nonetheless surprised and delighted to receive approval when he proposed to Franco that he assemble a new Falangist commission and prepare the text of possible new fundamental laws to redefine the role of the Movement.[76]

Even though on one occasion Franco had privately given his opinion that the Movement was fundamentally little more than a "propaganda claque,"[77] he still sought to stabilize its place in the system, for he be-

75. Ellwood, *Prietas*, 158–59, refers to a critique of the 1947 Law of Succession that he prepared for his fellow Cortes members.
76. Arrese's memoir, *Una etapa constituyente* (Barcelona, 1982), gives his account of the entire process that followed.
77. According to a memorandum of Antonio Garrigues to Martín Artajo, Jan. 8, 1957, Franco had once told Garrigues: "You must understand that for me the Movement is like a claque. Have you not observed that when there is a big crowd it is necessary to have a few start the applause so that the others will follow? Well, that is more or less how I understand the purpose of the Movement." Tusell, *Franco y los católicos*, 402–3.

José Luis de Arrese, Minister Secretary General of the Movement, 1941–45, 1956–57

lieved that it continued to fulfil certain indispensable functions. While insisting that Falangists adjust to the fact of an eventual monarchist succession, he also insisted on April 29 that "the Falange can live without the
monarchy, but what could not survive would be any form of monarchy
without the Falange."[78] What was required of Falangists was, as usual,

78. *Pensamiento político*, 1:251.

adjustment to the twists and turns of the regime. Addressing 25,000 Falangists in Seville on May 1, he declared that "in politics you cannot remain stationary; it is necessary to renew oneself, for the failure to renew oneself means the beginning of death. Therefore we cannot remain statically anchored in the past, in old routines or formulas." He invoked the old Falangist rhetoric "We are making a revolution," but added, "We shall revise whatever is necessary."[79]

A meeting of the Junta Política on May 17 approved a commission under Arrese to prepare draft projects of new fundamental laws to redefine the Movement, its principles, and its role in the system. This was seen by party leaders as the last opportunity to renew and strengthen the Falangist nature of the regime. The commission was made up of such leading party bureaucrats and notables as Fernández Cuesta, Sánchez Mazas, and Javier Conde, in addition to two other cabinet ministers, Carrero Blanco and the minister of justice, Iturmendi. There was considerable disparity of opinion at first among commission members. The most radical proposal was made by the national councillor Luis González Vicén (one of Girón's associates from Valladolid), who presented a draft in June that would not only have given the National Council a dominant institutional position but would also have reorganized the Cortes on a partially direct elective basis. Offices within the Movement would have been made directly elective on the local level and indirectly elective on higher levels. Such extensive loosening of control was obviously impossible, and after a stormy argument González Vicén resigned.[80]

By autumn three draft projects had been prepared dealing with the principles of the National Movement, a new organic law of the National Movement itself, and a proposed law of government organization (*ordenación*). The first seemed to provoke little controversy, for it carried out a drastic defascistization of the original Twenty-six Points of the Movement. Its four articles dropped all references to empire or any other radical goal, stressing instead the principles of Catholicism, the family, state syndicalism, integrity of the individual, national unity, and international cooperation. The National Movement itself was defined as "an intermediate organization between society and the state and a means of integration of public opinion."

The proposed Organic Law of the Movement was much more drastic, for its terms would have made the Movement absolutely autonomous to the point of independence after the death of Franco, with great power concentrated in the hands of its secretary general and National Council. The chief of state after Franco would hold no direct position of leadership in the Movement, though members of the National Council would be

79. *Discursos y mensajes del Jefe del Estado 1955–1959* (Madrid, 1960), 183–89.
80. For a fuller discussion of Vicén's proposals, see my *Falange*, 251–57.

partly appointed by him and partly elected by the Movement. Future secretaries general would be elected by the National Council and then named (in effect, ratified) by the chief of state, and would be responsible only to the council. The council would hold the power of a court of constitutional review and could declare invalid any legislation under consideration by the Cortes. It would also be empowered to transmit its recommendations on policy, legislation and administration to the government.

The proposed Law of Government Organization was intended to give the Movement a dominant role in the functioning of the government. It provided for the chief of state to appoint a separate president of government (prime minister) after consulting with the president of the Cortes and the secretary general of the Movement. The latter would automatically become vice-president of government at the time of Franco's death, should the latter office then be vacant. The president and his cabinet would serve for a term of five years, removable at the order of the chief of state or three adverse votes by the National Council. The secretary general was endowed with a perpetual legislative veto as a member of cabinet, for his abstention or negative vote on any issue would trigger a vote of confidence in the government by the National Council. The Cortes, by contrast, was only empowered to censure individual ministers, and its vote could be negated by an expression of confidence by the National Council. The latter would thus become an executive senate with veto power over a future prime minister and all subsequent legislation. Moreover, none of these documents ever referred to either the monarchy or the king.

In this fashion Arrese and the old-guard Falangists hoped to perpetuate a new political monopoly for the party after Franco's death. The new ambition that Arrese injected into the party resulted in a flurry of new adherents; approximately 35,000 new members joined the Movement in 1956, its last significant increase. Arrese hoped that neo-Falangist doctrine, totally rejected by social democratic western Europe, might still exert influence in the Middle East,[81] where the Spanish regime enjoyed friendly relations with Arab nationalism.

Most members of the regime hoped for a formula that could maintain basic features of the system after Franco's death, but none save core Falangists would support a proposal to give such permanent power to the secretary general and National Council of the Movement. Monarchists objected particularly to the exclusion of any mention of the Crown, and the more reform-minded also objected to the power granted a future chief of state.[82] While Carrero Blanco at first recommended revision of the pro-

81. Arrese, *Una etapa constituyente*, passim.
82. Franco later slyly observed to Salgado-Araujo that the draft legislation had to be rejected because it would have given the next chief of state enough power to place a future king in an awkward position.

posals, all the other major cabinet members, even including the Falangist minister of education, opposed them in varying degrees. Iturmendi, the justice minister, had already presented to Franco a completely different project for a non-Falangist set of new laws to complete the construction of an authoritarian Spanish Rechtsstaat or Estado de Derecho, based on detailed proposals from a new advisor, a thirty-six-year-old professor of administrative law at the University of Santiago de Compostela named Laureano López Rodó.[83] Though not a word appeared in the press, copies of Arrese's draft projects circulated widely among the regime's elite, and opposition mounted from all sides. Some of the top military commanders expressed objections, and the monarchist minister of public works, the seventy-year-old Conde de Vallellano, distributed two documents during October denouncing what he termed introduction of a "totalitarian state" and an "oriental-style politburo," emphasizing that "to declare dogmatically in a legal document that the political ideas of the Falange represent in a permanent manner the political will of the Spanish people is objectively absurd."[84]

The coup de grace was delivered by the three cardinals of the Spanish Church, who called on Franco on December 12 to present a document that declared the proposals "in disagreement with pontifical doctrine." It went on to say, "The projects of the Organic Law of the National Movement and the Law of Government Organization have no roots in Spanish tradition, but in the totalitarian regimes of certain countries after the First World War, whose doctrines or practices drew serious condemnation from the Roman pontiffs." The cardinals stated that they did not request "the liberalism of inorganic democracy," that is, a direct parliamentary system, but they did urge the Generalissimo "to promote true organic representation" rather than "a dictatorship by a single party."[85]

Arrese at first refused to give in. To underscore the absence of any Falangist domination or even broad influence under the regime to date, he prepared data for a report to the National Council on December 29, 1956. It concluded that in the current Spanish political structure, camisas viejas of the party had only the following representation in government:

2 of	16 cabinet ministers
1 of	17 subsecretaries
8 of	102 director generals

83. López Rodó proposed a new law on the principles of the Movement, a Fuero de la Corona that would define future power of the monarchy, a basic national administrative reform law, a new justice bill (Fuero de la Justicia), and a more moderate organic law on the National Council. (*Larga marcha*, 129). Most aspects of these proposals were subsequently adopted to a greater or lesser degree in the legislation of the decade that followed.

84. Créac'h, *Le Coeur*, 386. Detailed accounts of the reactions of regime notables will be found in López Rodó, *Larga marcha*, 124–35; and in *FF*, 5:306–16.

85. Quoted in Tusell, *Franco y los católicos*, 421–22.

18 of	50 provincial governors and jefes provinciales
8 of	50 mayors of provincial capitols
6 of	50 presidents of provincial assemblies
65 of	151 national councillors
137 of	575 Cortes deputies
776 of	9,155 mayors
2,226 of	55,960 members of provincial councils

"That is to say," Arrese commented, "that the original Falange occupies approximately 5 percent of the posts of leadership in Spain."[86]

Since Franco had instructed him to revise each of the proposals over the Christmas vacation, Arrese tried to interest the Caudillo in watered-down versions of the two principal projects. In the final version, the National Council would merely form part of a new Court of Constitutional Guarantees, sharing power equally with the Council of the Realm. To assuage the cardinals' wrath, a faint proposal for greater representation was advanced in the form of new *Hermandades* (brotherhoods) that could be organized within the Movement to correspond to the various groups that had originally composed it during the Civil War. As it turned out, Franco found none of this acceptable.

Ever since the preceding summer there had been talk of a general government change, and Arrese had been working toward an expansion of Falangist influence in the cabinet. By that time, however, Franco was more concerned about the continued inflation and heavy balance of payments deficit, which was becoming a severe problem. The regime needed better economic leadership, while any reaccentuation of Falangism had become futile and anachronistic and was clearly unacceptable to the major institutions and currents of opinion in the country. A more detailed and complete new elaboration of fundamental laws might be desirable, but that would have to be postponed until they could be prepared under different terms and more acceptable patronage than that of the Movement. The present climate of Spain and of international opinion instead required efficient technical administration, something that the Movement itself was unprepared to provide. In February 1957 Franco decided to shelve the Falangist proposals sine die and carry out a broad new cabinet renovation.[87]

86. Arrese, *Treinta años de política*, 1146–65.
87. Franco's dismissal of cabinet personnel was often abrupt, impersonal, and lacking in any cordiality. Outgoing ministers usually received notification from a motorized messenger who brought them a brief note of thanks from the Caudillo. Martín Artajo, dismissed in this fashion after eleven and a half years as foreign minister, replied directly:

My General:
The manner in which my eleven and a half years as minister of foreign affairs at the orders of Your Excellency come to an end grieves me. It was natural that I be dismissed when Your Excellency decided this would serve the good of the country, but I am hurt

The New Government of 1957:
Toward Technocracy and Bureaucratic Authoritarianism

There is no evidence of any specific grand design in the new ministerial appointments of 1957. Franco had decided months earlier that he would have to replace a number of key ministers but typically procrastinated over the alternatives. A memo of Carrero Blanco on January 26 emphasized the need to reinforce Franco's personal authority after the events of the past year (strikes, student disorders, the loss of Morocco and the frustrated institutional reform). Rather than stemming from the preponderance of any particular sector, new policy changes and institutional laws should be developed by the joint efforts of a cabinet that could work together as a team in conjunction with the head of state.[88] Franco's new choices thus revealed a radical downgrading of Falangists and renewed emphasis on technical expertise, yet he had always used experts freely (usually civil or military engineers or elite state lawyers). Privately he described the new cabinet as simply a renewed effort to give balanced representation to the diverse forces behind the regime, adjusted to the realities of the late 1950s.[89]

The key new appointees were mostly professionals with university or technical backgrounds, though here almost for the first time Franco encountered one or two refusals. Carrero Blanco exerted rather more influence than before, anxious to shortcircuit the Falange and bring in experts capable of reorganizing state administration and carrying out a more efficient economic policy, although Arrese may also have played a role in bringing one or two of the new people to Franco's attention.

The three key technicians in economic affairs and state administration were all members of Opus Dei and had the direct backing of the subsecretary of the presidency. The first to enter the senior level of government was Laureano López Rodó, whose administrative proposals had so impressed Carrero that he had been appointed to the newly created post of general technical secretary for the subsecretary of the presidency before

---

that having conferred with Your Excellency on the eve of the cabinet meeting in which the crisis was announced, I was not informed of your intentions, even if sworn to secrecy on a gentleman's word of honor.

The truth must be said, my General. More than an explanation and much more than any reward, I expected some word of affection, which seems to me the only conclusion worthy of a collaboration so lengthy, long, and assiduous. I have heard many ex-ministers complain of the same thing; I preferred to confide my lament to Your Excellency and to no one else.

But in any event, now as always, Your Excellency may rely on my loyalty and affection. (Quoted in Tusell, *Franco y los católicos*, 430.)

88. *FF*, 5:320–21.

89. According to Salgado-Araujo, *Conversaciones privadas*, 206–8.

Carrero Blanco addressing the Cortes, July 15, 1957

the end of 1956.[90] Though he did not receive cabinet rank in the new government, López Rodó was also named head of the Government Secretariat and of the Office of Economic Coordination and Programming, another new technical position created especially for him.[91]

Two other members of Opus Dei took over the main economic portfolios. Alberto Ullastres, a forty-three-year-old university professor, replaced Arburúa in Commerce, while Finance was occupied by Mariano Navarro Rubio, a lawyer and economist of similar age who had broad experience in the syndical system as well as having been the last subsecretary of public works. Franco held the outgoing Arburúa in some esteem, appreciating his craft and virtuosity, but the corruption and distortions in

90. López Rodó has a few discreet words about his rise in *Larga marcha* and in his *Política y desarrollo* (Madrid, 1970). He had first been brought to Carrero's attention by the priest (who also happened to be professor of canon law at Santiago and a member of Opus Dei) who had helped resolve an earlier marital problem of the admiral. Fernández, *El almirante Carrero*, 141; Garriga, *Los validos*, 274.

91. He later presented his ideas on public administration and economic development in his Royal Academy lecture, *La administración pública y las transformaciones socioeconómicas* (Madrid, 1963).

Spain's commercial administration were so severe that he had become the most criticized minister in government, and Franco reluctantly concluded that some sort of reform was needed. These three new appointees would be responsible for conceiving and executing the major changes in Spanish economic policy during the next two years (treated in the following chapter), though it is more than doubtful that Franco had any alterations of such magnitude in mind when he assembled the new government.

Franco saw to it that Falangists retained four posts. After fifteen years he replaced the veteran Girón, to date the regime's only minister of labor, whom he esteemed as "very good" and extremely loyal but also "too impetuous"[92] and politically compromised by his long tenure in power. The veteran syndical director Sanz Orrio[93] took Girón's place, while José Solís Ruiz, a suave and accommodating syndical boss who had labored to catch Franco's eye, replaced Arrese as secretary general of the Movement. Rubio, who had been in office but a year, remained in Education and, as a salve, a new Ministry of Housing was created for Arrese. Thus Falangist representation in government was not numerically diminished, but this did not disguise the fact that the withdrawal of the reform projects and the main thrust of the cabinet realignment represented a fundamental defeat for the Movement and the start of its final deemphasis. Arrese held his new post for only three years before resigning and retiring altogether from public life.

Changes occurred in both Foreign Affairs and Interior. Martín Artajo had held the former post almost as long as Girón had been in office but was now replaced by Fernando María Castiella, a professor of international law and an accomplished diplomat and, like Artajo, a member of the elite National Association of Catholic Propagandists. Originally famous for his coauthorship of the wartime *Reivindicaciones,* Castiella was also a veteran of the Blue Division and the second cabinet member to hold the German Iron Cross, but he was also more knowledgeable and experienced than most of his predecessors in this post.[94]

The outgoing minister of the interior, Blas Peréz González, equaled Girón in seniority and was one of Franco's all-time favorites because of his honesty, efficiency, calm judgment, and incorruptibility. Carrero Blanco had been intriguing to eliminate him for several years, perhaps because of his high standing with the Caudillo. The disorders in Madrid early in 1956, followed by other outbursts at the University of Barcelona in Janu-

92. Salgado-Araujo, *Conversaciones privadas,* 182.

93. Sanz Orrio's speeches and articles in his new post were published as *Pensamiento y acción social 1956–1960* (Madrid, 1960).

94. The coauthor of *Reivindicaciones de España,* José Ma. de Areilza, had replaced Lequerica as ambassador in Washington the year before when the latter became Spain's first ambassador to the United Nations.

ary 1957, finally provided Carrero with a talking point, especially after these mushroomed into a major student strike that was also supported by demonstrations in Madrid. Franco apparently felt that Pérez was finally losing his effectiveness but still hoped to retain his services for a newly created Ministry of Health. Pérez, however, was eager to turn to private practice to build his personal fortune,[95] something that he had scrupulously eschewed in government, so Franco replaced him with General Camilo Alonso Vega, the eminently successful reorganizer of the Guardia Civil. Lacking in sophistication or broad intelligence, Alonso Vega was both tough and energetic. Though Franco had earlier thought him "too harsh and inflexible" for the Interior Ministry, he soon demonstrated that he could run an effective police force.[96] The two other civilian ministers connected with repression, the Carlist Iturmendi in Justice and Arias Salgado in Information, retained their positions.

Franco changed his military ministers more frequently than any others, probably in order to avoid having any general consolidate too much personal power or influence. Yet seven of the seventeen ministers in the new government were military men: Carrero Blanco, Alonso Vega, Colonel Joaquín Planell as a holdover in Industry and General Jorge Vigón in Public Works, as well as the three Armed Forces ministers. The military thus continued as the foundation of the regime in a manner totally incommensurate with any political faction, and the appearance of such a large number of military also reflected Franco's concern to tighten up the government after the uncertainties of the past year. Muñoz Grandes was replaced as army minister by Antonio Barroso, the head of Franco's personal military staff, but in turn was promoted to captain general and became the only top commander other than Franco to hold that rank. Salgado-Araujo put this down to a certain "fear" that Franco had of Muñoz Grandes and his influence in the Army (an influence that was, in Salgado-Araujo's opinion, overestimated).[97] Concern for Muñoz Grandes's sensibility was no doubt a factor, but Franco also seems to have had genuine esteem for the crude and crusty former commander of the Blue Division, indicating that in an emergency Muñoz Grandes would be best suited to take over his own powers and if necessary even be appointed regent.[98] Franco felt that of all the top generals he would be the most faithful to the institutions and values of the regime, in part because his past made him thoroughly unacceptable to reformers and liberals. Thus his own authoritarian tendencies,

95. See Garriga, *Los validos*, 205–13.
96. The quotation is from Salgado-Araujo, *Conversaciones privadas*, 201, which also claims that Alonso Vega had so loyal an outgoing minister as Girón tailed for nearly two years, until Franco himself directed him to stop (253).
97. Ibid., 204.
98. Ibid., 236, 266.

combined with a fervent antimonarchism, made Muñoz Grandes a necessary counterbalance to the monarchists both inside and outside the regime. He was subsequently named head of the Central General Staff and,
with several of the Falangist ministers, formed a part of a fluctuating alignment of "Regentialists" who preferred that the Caudillo be succeeded by
another Franco-style regent rather than a more liberal Bourbon king.

The leading Regentialist in the new government was José Solís Ruiz,
the first minister to hold the posts of national delegate of syndicates and
secretary general of the Movement simultaneously. Solís was a veteran
syndical bureaucrat. He had helped organize the first elections of enlaces
sindicales in 1944 and was active in giving the syndical system a more representative appearance at the close of World War II, having been in charge
of the First National Congress of Workers in 1946. After appointments as
civil governor of two different provinces in succession, he became national
delegate of syndicates in 1951 before being given direction of the Movement as well in 1957. Solís was cordial in manner, the father of thirteen
children, and fluent of speech. He cultivated a popular style that attempted
the common touch and was eager to kiss babies on public occasions, becoming known in the following decade as "the smile of the regime."[99]

Solís Ruiz would spend the next twelve years announcing successive reforms of the syndical system,[100] none of which changed its essential structure but some of which did loosen its mode of functioning and allow
slightly more representation. This came from his perception that the
Movement as an organized party was little more than moribund, whereas
a more active syndical system could provide a stronger political base during a period of economic development. Thus the next elections for enlaces sindicales in the autumn of 1957 were freer than ever before, resulting in the election of more leftist oppositionists than ever before, though
Franco did not seem to be fully aware of what was taking place.

On the other hand, he took some satisfaction from two major European
events of the following year which he saw as a kind of vindication of the
need for strong government. Visiting a new industrial complex at Cartagena in October, he hailed the first Soviet space vehicle *Sputnik* as
"something that could not have been achieved in the old Russia" (in his
customary ignorance overlooking the fact that under the old semiliberal
regime Russia had in fact made several early aeronautical breakthroughs)
because "great accomplishments require political unity and discipline."[101]

99. The career of Solís Ruiz is described in the Equipo Mundo's *Los noventa ministros de
Franco* (Barcelona, 1970), 299–310.

100. The first syndical changes under Solís down to 1962 are summarized by Walther Bernecker, "Die Arbeiterbewegung under dem Franquismus," in *Die geheime Dynamik autoritärer Diktaturen* (Munich, 1982), 108–12.

101. La Cierva, *Franquismo*, 2:168.

Such unaccustomed praise from the senior anti-Communist of Europe was intended as a vindication of authoritarianism, regardless of political hue. The second development, even more applauded by Franco, was the collapse of the parliamentary Fourth Republic in France and its replacement by a presidential Republic under Charles de Gaulle, who also affirmed, though in quite different terms than Franco, that the party system did not work.

The new government made its own limited contribution toward further institutional definition by finally enacting a new version of the Principles of the Movement, promulgated on May 29, 1958. These completely replaced the old Twenty-Six Points and, similar in part to the earlier draft by Arrese, were fully sanitized of any overtly fascistic expression. They affirmed patriotism, unity, peace, Catholicism, the individual personality, the family, representation through local institutions and syndicates, and international harmony. Reflecting Carlist rather than Falangist concepts and terminology, the Movement was termed a "communion" instead of a party, and the regime itself defined as a "traditional, Catholic, social, and representative monarchy." [102] In one of his more notorious personal interviews a few days later, Franco told the French journalist Serge Groussard that he had never been influenced by anyone, not even Mussolini, and that he had "never" contemplated entering the war on Germany's side. "I also am" a democrat, affirmed the Caudillo, referring to his own nominal concept of organic democracy. [103]

The traditional leftist opposition, broken by the events of the late 1940s, would never fully recover during Franco's lifetime. Neither the passage of the dissident ex-Falangist Dionisio Ridruejo into outright opposition [104] nor a major new strike wave in Asturias and Barcelona during March 1958 [105] had much impact, though these were the most extensive strikes since 1951. The government responded by suspending nominal civil rights and declaring an *estado de excepción* (constitutional state of exception) for four months. Similarly, radicalization of clandestine student politics at the leading universities was growing apace but would not become a problem until the following decade. Major initiatives by the Spanish Communist Party failed completely. Its declaration of a Jornada de Reconciliación Nacional (Day of National Reconciliation) for May 5,

---

102. *Fundamental Laws of the State*, 19–25.
103. *Le Figaro*, June 12, 1958.
104. In an interview with the Cuban journal *Bohemia*, Ridruejo declared, "At the end of so many years we who were the conquerors now feel ourselves defeated; we want to be so considered." He had undergone a period of internal exile and was briefly placed under arrest again. Ridruejo helped to found a new clandestine social democratic group, significant more as an example than for effective action.
105. For a summary of opposition activities in the late 1950s, see Fernández Vargas, *La resistencia*, 193–208.

1958, which was to have been accompanied by local strikes and transport boycotts in many parts of Spain, attracted little support, while the following Huelga Nacional Pacífica (Peaceful General Strike), scheduled for June 18, had little support beyond the small groups of workers directly influenced by the Party.[106]

New measures were nonetheless taken to tighten police controls. A law of March 22, 1957, specified that in the case of collective illegal activities such as strikes, when it was not possible to identify directly those primarily responsible, persons in positions of responsibility or with seniority among those involved could legally be charged instead. On January 24, 1958, a new military court with special jurisdiction for "extremist activities" in all of Spain was established under the direction of Col. Enrique Eymar Fernández, who acquired a sinister reputation during the next decade. Franco felt it necessary to be fully prepared, indicating privately on June 9 that he had "direct information from the Masonic lodges" of "a campaign of great proportions against the regime."[107] There followed a new redaction of the Law of Public Order (July 30, 1960), which provided that those arrested for strikes, demonstrations, and attacks on public utilities or supplies would be prosecuted before a special court of civil judges, and there was a new Law against Military Rebellion, Banditry, and Terrorism (September 26, 1960).[108]

In fact, the number of those involved in opposition activities was quite limited, and according to the statistics of the Supreme General Staff, the annual total of those condemned by the special military tribunals was declining steadily. From 1,266 in 1954 it dropped to 902 in 1955 and again the following year, then to 723 in 1956 and to 717 in 1958, falling further to 529 in 1959.[109] The ordinary crime rate in Spain was very low during these years, so that by 1959 the prison population stood at 14,890,[110] compared with 34,526 under the Republic in 1935, when there were five million fewer inhabitants.

The only opposition that concerned Franco was that presented by monarchist legitimists. The continuing pretensions of Carlist candidates were a nuisance to be swept aside,[111] for Franco always considered his

106. A broader sketch of labor activities from an opposition viewpoint is given in José Antonio Biescas and Manuel Tuñón de Lara, *España bajo la dictadura franquista (1939–1975)* (Madrid, 1980), 320–26.

107. Salgado-Araujo, *Conversaciones privadas*, 239.

108. *FF*, 6:121–22; Biescas and Tuñón de Lara, *España*, 311–12. The new Law Against Banditry and Terrorism revived provisions of the 1943 decree that included under military rebellion any participation in politically motivated strikes, spreading "false or tendentious information" or committing any act judged detrimental to the prestige of the country, government, armed forces, or police.

109. According to Ballbé, *Orden público*, 417.

110. *FF*, 6:93.

111. In 1952 Prince Javier of Borbón-Parma, nephew through the female line of the last direct-male-line Carlist pretender, had publicly declared himself rightful king of Spain. On

most logical and appropriate successor to be either Don Juan or Prince Juan Carlos, and he was still willing, theoretically, to accept Don Juan provided that he would fully and publicly accept all the principles of the regime—something to which the Pretender never agreed.

Though the new government contained an important Regentialist faction, it marked a significant departure not only in terms of what soon became a drastic new economic policy but also because for the first time a discreet promonarchist bloc was forming. This consisted primarily of Carrero Blanco and several of the economic ministers who were members of Opus Dei. They were at one and the same time loyal to Franco[112] and reasonably determined to promote a legitimate monarchist succession at the appropriate time. López Rodó, who soon became the key member of the group after Carrero, assiduously cultivated the Conde de Ruiseñada, Don Juan's principal representative in Spain, and tried to develop as much influence as he could with the modest, affable, somewhat retiring young Juan Carlos. One result was an article by Ruiseñada in *ABC* on June 11, 1957, which avowed that the monarchy, while rejecting "totalitarianism" and the domination of any "minority," always remained within "the line of the 18th of July [1936] without deviations of any kind."

Don Juan broadened his base further near the end of 1957, a decade after he had first gained to support of a significant number of Carlists. To reaffirm this, more than sixty Carlist leaders and representatives met in Madrid on December 1, after which forty-four of them traveled to Estoril to ask Don Juan to accept the principles espoused by Don Alfonso Carlos (last Carlist pretender in the direct male line). Don Juan signed a document accepting five basic principles of Carlism—which, except for the recognition of regionalism, were generally similar to the new Principles of the Movement promulgated the preceding year—in return for their recognition and support.[113] This seemed to complete his swing to the right that had slowly been developing since 1947. At this stage both he and Franco were doing what they could to avoid direct conflict, and a rather long period of amicable if not cordial relations ensued between Estoril

---

May 5, 1957, his eldest son, named Hugo, showed up at the annual Carlist rally at Montejurra in Navarre to present himself as "Carlos-Hugo" and direct heir to the throne. He was quickly sent back to France by Spanish authorities, Franco deeming the Borbón-Parma branch not Spaniards but Frenchmen, which indeed technically they were.

112. Carrero was alleged to have encouraged collection of signatures for an extraordinary collective letter to Franco in December 1957 which urged that, in view of the fact that he had been miraculously favored by Divine Providence and had rendered greater services to Catholicism than any ruler in Spain's history, a national commission of illustrious personages be authorized to negotiate with the Vatican his appointment to the College of Cardinals. Franco had the sense not to encourage this preposterous maneuver, and it is not clear that Carrero ever supported it either. Cf. Fernández, *Franco*, 175–76, and *El almirante Carrero*, 145–46.

113. López Rodó, *Larga marcha*, 149–50.

and El Pardo. This was not particularly disturbed by a semipublic meeting of dissident monarchists opposed to the regime, held at the Hotel Menfis in downtown Madrid on January 29, 1959, which led to temporary arrests and the imposition of large fines on the chief organizers and participants. What Don Juan would not do, however, was make the full public endorsement of the regime and its principles that Franco wanted, and even more, recognize that the monarchy would be its direct successor and continuation. However much he might accept certain common principles, he continued to hold to his position that the monarchy remained distinct and was the alternative to rather than continuation of the present system.

The decade closed in 1959 with two major events in the life of Franco, the opening of the Valle de los Caídos (Valley of the Fallen) on April 1 and the visit of Eisenhower to Madrid in December. Construction of the grandiose tomb and national monument 40 kilometers northwest of Madrid had begun in 1940 and was long delayed (by "Masonic influences," Franco feared), sometimes employing the labor of political prisoners.[114] Franco participated personally in its design, selecting the site for his own interment below the high altar in the sanctuary. He also intended it, secondarily, to shelter the remains of a small number of Republican veterans as well as Nationalists, observing that many Republican troops were not bad fellows but simply deceived or drafted.[115] The opening of this great monument, a sort of twentieth-century rival to Philip II's El Escorial, was ultimately timed to coincide with the twentieth anniversary of final victory in the Civil War and bore eloquent witness to the presence of death and history in Franco's own consciousness.

Some months later he was described by Arnold Toynbee in the *New York Times Sunday Magazine* (Nov. 2, 1959) as

> perhaps the arch-example, in our time, of a powerful personality that has triumphed by finesse. Like Hitler, Franco has flown in the face of the spirit of the age; but while Hitler came to grief, Franco has so far gotten by. He managed to drive the Falangists and the Carlists in double harness, and he persuaded the Italians and the Germans to give him military help without making any reciprocal military commitments to them. Here is a personality who has got the better of potent impersonal forces by the technique of Chinese boxing.

The brief visit of Eisenhower to the Spanish capital, in which Franco and the American president toured the center of the city standing together in the same open car to the applause of hundreds of thousands, was the international apotheosis of Franco's career. For a short time he abandoned the frigid coldness of his official style and recaptured some of the

---

114. Cf. Daniel Sueiro, *La verdadera historia del Valle de los Caidos* (Madrid, 1976).
115. Salgado-Araujo, *Conversaciones privadas*, 215. Yet this sentiment never moved him to provide military pensions for disabled Republican veterans.

President Eisenhower parts from Franco with a Spanish *abrazo*, December 1959

animation of his younger years, aspects of which were caught in several striking photographs.[116] At no other point would he command greater acceptance or recognition.

116. Benjamin Welles has related the background to one of these scenes: "Franco helped break the ice by telling a story that seemed to him appropriate, about a young French major who was having a bullet removed from his brain when a messenger from Napoleon brought the news that he had been appointed to general. The hero jumped off the operating table and on to his horse. When the surgeon protested, the young man shouted as he galloped away: 'I'm a general now; I don't need brains any more!'" *Spain: The Gentle Anarchy* (New York, 1965), 250–51. The transcript of the principal conversation between Franco and Eisenhower is presented in *FF*, 6:140–52.

PART IV

---

*Developmentalism
and Decay
1959–1975*

19

The Desarrollo

The last twenty-five years of the Franco regime, from 1950 to 1975, were the time of the greatest sustained economic development and general improvement in living standards in all Spanish history. In one sense this was not so remarkable, because it coincided with the greatest period of sustained prosperity and development in all world history as well. Nonetheless, the proportionate rise in living standards and general productivity and well-being was greater than in other right-authoritarian regimes such as that of Portugal or those in the Middle East, Africa, and Latin America, and it was also greater than in the totalitarian socialist regimes in eastern Europe, Asia, or Cuba. Only Japan made greater proportionate progress than Spain during this period.

If Franco were to be resurrected and questioned about this, he would doubtless reply that such had been his plan all along. Certainly from the very beginning Franco and other spokesmen emphasized their determination to develop Spain's economy and achieve a higher level of well-being, yet the policies and institutions under which the *desarrollo* was consummated were quite different from those on which the regime had originally embarked in the 1940s. Moreover, the reestablishment of Spanish influence in the world that was to accompany this never really occurred, while the remarkable cultural and religious counterrevolution carried out in Spain during the late 1930s and 1940s was totally undermined by the social, cultural, and economic changes wrought by development, as, in the long run, were the basic institutions and values of the regime itself.

The Last Phase of Autarchy

The regime's economic policies during the 1940s continued to be based on a modified semi-autarchy and import substitution. Rapprochement with the United States brought closer association with the international economy, but it only partially altered official policy, which was based on the firmly fixed world view of Franco and his closest associates. The outer world, even in the West, was seen as fundamentally hostile to the regime and to Spanish culture,[1] so that it would always be incumbent on the country's domestic economy to become as strong and as independent as possible. Though he considered economics of prime importance, Franco did not believe that economics required autonomy or needed to respond to market forces. Like most twentieth-century dictators, he continued to believe in the primacy of politics and that state power was capable of bending economics to its will.

The goal of force-drafting the economy with annual investment rates of 15 percent or more per year was largely achieved during the 1950s. Investment had begun to rise in 1948. It provided increasing support for electrical development and certain key industries by 1950, the commercial structure by 1951, the banking system by 1952, and public works by 1953. This policy continued to offer major tax advantages and even guaranteed profits to favored firms, requiring the consumption of domestically produced goods as much as possible irrespective of price. Imports continued to be restricted, foreign exchange controlled, foreign trade regulated by the state, and direct intervention practiced through incentives and licensing for both exports and imports, together with the major investments of the Instituto Nacional de Industria (INI). Whereas the INI pushed fuels, fertilizers, and electric power during the 1940s, in the fifties it emphasized metallurgy and automobiles through large new enterprises such as ENSIDESA (Asturias) and SEAT (Barcelona). It was empowered to borrow large amounts of money from the Bank of Spain at only three-quarters of one percent interest, and savings institutions were required to place half their investment funds in INI stock.[2]

This import-substitution industrialization registered major gains during the 1950s. Its real growth of GNP at an average annual rate of 7.9 percent

1. To the ends of their days, Franco and Carrero Blanco believed that the implacable enmity toward the regime of the Communist world was paralleled by that of "international Masonry" in the West. Even after economic policy had changed, Carrero Blanco would hector the foreign minister on the conspiracies of the "three Internationals": Communism in the East, Socialism in western Europe, and Masonry in liberal countries generally. Cf. Viñas, *Guerra, dinero, dictadura*, 230–35.

2. On the INI in this period, see Schwartz and González, *Una historia*, 68–85. The nationalist doctrines underpinning autarchist policy were presented fairly clearly in a collection of articles from *Arriba* in 1953–54 reprinted in *Notas sobre política económica española* (Madrid, 1954).

Table 19.1. Spanish Industrial Production, 1942–59

Year	Instituto Nacional de Estadística	Consejo Nacional de Economía
1942	100	100
1943	107	88
1944	108	101
1945	102	97
1946	120	112
1947	122	111
1948	125	112
1949	119	113
1950	136	123
1951	153	128
1952	175	147
1953	184	153
1954	191	169
1955	214	186
1956	236	198
1957	249	216
1958	272	254
1959	282	298

Source: Joseph Harrison, *An Economic History of Modern Spain* (New York, 1978), 163.

from 1951 to 1958 was at one of the highest rates in the world. In seven years industrial production doubled, and since agriculture failed to make equivalent gains, its share of total national production dropped from 40 percent in 1951 to 25 percent in 1957.

Nevertheless this was growth from a shallow and uneven base. For years the system suffered from major bottlenecks, especially in the poorly developed road and transport system. Electrical output expanded rapidly, but demand grew even faster. Consumption remained low because of limited productivity and low wages (and the absence of special demand from a military-industrial complex). Moreover, the quality of many goods produced under state protection for a captive home market was inferior.

Insulation from international trade limited the market and the scale of production as well as the import of necessary goods and technology. Already by the mid-1950s a significant proportion of plants and tools were thoroughly antiquated, while an increasingly sophisticated industry would demand more complex and expensive capital goods from abroad which could not yet be produced at home.

The economic ministers of the 1951 government had realized that the maze of artificial controls and the partial separation from the world economy were creating restrictions that needed to be overcome. Manuel Arburúa, minister of commerce from 1951 to 1957, who was considered by many to epitomize the corruption inherent in the system of arbitrary state regulation, was in fact a limited reformer. He encouraged more foreign trade, reducing the number of variable exchange rates from 34 to 6, and managed to close the autonomous accounts of some agencies while reducing others, all in the effort to achieve greater coherence. The rationing of basic necessities ended early in 1952, and tourism began to expand. Imports increased rapidly, doubling during the 1950s, in part simply because of the accelerating purchase of food and other items of consumption to fuel a rising standard of living. Yet little was done to promote exports, which had registered a 15 percent increase between 1947 and 1948 and then another 10 percent in 1950 but largely stagnated in the decade that followed. The basic system of controls and restrictions remained, along with all the malpractices and distortions to which it gave rise.[3]

American aid provided an important stimulus between 1953 and 1956, but further difficulties emerged. Continuing high inflation was due above all to the constant public deficits from 1954 on that were created in considerable measure by large state investments in the autarchist industrial program. Comparatively minor in 1954 and 1955, the deficit became severe by 1956. The demagogic across-the-board wage increases engineered by Girón were designed to boost consumption and thus encourage domestic production, but above all they accelerated inflation. The government printed more and more money but was tardy in stimulating agriculture, whose low output required growing purchases of food from abroad. Increased imports did raise the standard of living, but since little attention was given to diversifying and expanding the export base, the trade deficit became so severe that it threatened future expansion.[4] Though the number of acknowleged unemployed declined from 175,000 in 1950 to 95,000 by 1959, underemployment was endemic. New capital investment and technology were indispensable, but they could only come from abroad, and could only be paid for after a reorientation of policy that would encourage accelerated production of goods and services for the international market.[5]

3. The policy failures of the last phase of autarchy are discussed in Ros Hombravella et al., *Capitalismo*, 2:19–51; and in Viñas et al., *Política comercial*, 1:726–40.
4. The best treatment of foreign trade problems of the mid-1950s will be found in Viñas et al., *Política comercial*, 2:868–988.
5. Several contemporary surveys of uneven value dealing with the Spanish economy and its problems in this period include Heinrich Klaus, *Strukturwandlungen und Nachkriegsprobleme der Wirtschaft Spaniens* (Kiel, 1954); Antonio Robert, *Perspectivas de la economía española* (Madrid, 1954); Jacques Milleron, *Etude sur l'économie espagnole* (Rabat, 1955); Fermín Labadíe Otermín's brief *Notas al futuro económico español* (Madrid, 1958); and two relatively uncritical surveys by Higinio París Eguilaz, *Factores del desarrollo económico español* (Madrid, 1957) and *Expansión, recesión y reactivación económica, 1951–1961* (Madrid, 1962).

The Stabilization Plan of 1959

The economic ministers of the new government of 1957 were determined to confront these problems but had no coherent theoretical model or integrated general policy. When inflation or deficits climbed, the tendency within the regime had always been to blame poor administration or lack of government control rather than a fundamentally mistaken policy. Indeed, the first reforms introduced were those of López Rodó to rationalize the central state administration, probably a necessary concomitant of any effective policy change.[6] The resulting Ley de Régimen Jurídico de Administración del Estado of July 1957, followed by the Ley de Procedimiento Administrativo (Law of Administrative Procedure), sought to coordinate the structure more efficiently and gave more direct authority to the presidency of the government (i.e., the prime minister, Franco), while institutionalizing the office of subsecretary of the presidency, Carrero's post, which was also given the powers of the presidency in certain circumstances. This did not involve a drastic reform or reorganization as much as a recodification and realignment of the earlier policies and procedures drafted by the public administration specialists in the Instituto de Estudios Políticos during the 1940s. The new legislation was intended to draw public administration together more efficiently and permit some streamlining of procedures.

A series of piecemeal economic reforms were undertaken during 1957–58, designed to help balance the budget and to introduce sounder monetary and exchange policies. In a major breakthrough, Ullastres unified the multiple foreign exchange rates but did not undertake a major devaluation or find the means to remove the numerous restrictions on commerce and investment. Navarro Rubio, the finance minister, tried to stem inflation by raising the rediscount rate of the Bank of Spain and limiting the amounts discounted.

Franco and Carrero Blanco were not anticipating any major change of economic policy but rather some adjustment and tightening of the existing system. Near the end of 1957 Carrero Blanco circulated a new proposal

6. As Angel Viñas has put it in a somewhat different context: "The Spanish administration has never represented an organizational translation of the Weberian model of a rationalizing bureaucracy, and certainly did not under the Franco regime. . . . On the contrary, the weight of personal relations, the preference for grand lines of thinly structured policy, the interpenetration of collegial structures by means of the interaction between various administrative corps, the appearance and development of parallel channels of authority to reconcile contradictory approaches and the institution of promotions not by merit but based on other variables often given greater weight have all created a particular kind of organizational style that would inevitably be very sensitive to changes in orientation created by the lack of coordination between different departments." "La administración de la política económica exterior de España, 1936–1979," *Cuadernos Económicos de ICE*, no. 13 (1980), 196–97.

through the offices of the top economic administrators for "a coordinated plan to increase national production." Rather than reform, this recommended an intensification of autarchy, insisting that a massive, almost Stalinesque mobilization of national resources would be the surest path to economic strength. It meant continued avoidance of the international market or the need to export, and the solution of the balance of payments problem by drastic reduction of imports. "We categorically reject, as unjust and egotistical, the easy argument of some that Spain is a poor country. . . ." The goal should be "not to have to import more than vital elements of production."[7] This was of course not so much an economic proposal as a doctrinal projection, and there is no indication that it had any effect on the top economic administrators.

It flew directly in the face of the powerful new trend toward economic cooperation in western Europe, and such was its intention. Treaties to establish the European Economic Community (the Common Market) had just been ratified by six west European governments. The EEC officially came into existence at the beginning of 1958 and was a dynamic success from the start. The achievements of west European economic integration were already apparent to most Spanish administrators, and the development of the Common Market almost immediately exerted strong influence on many of them, who were soon convinced that the road to Spain's future prosperity could not lie apart from the rapid economic growth of the western economy as a whole. The position of Franco and Carrero Blanco became the minority view even among the top economic administrators of the regime.

Somewhat slowly, Navarro Rubio, Ullastres, and López Rodó began to sketch the partial outline of a new program of economic liberalization and stabilization, while the inflation-fueled strike wave beginning in the spring of 1958 added further pressure. Navarro Rubio distributed a questionnaire to the directors of the state's leading economic agencies to elicit their response to a possible liberalization of the autarchic system in the interest of international economic cooperation. Most were supportive, led by the administrators of the Syndical Organization, who now encouraged economic integration with Europe (with the hope that stronger sustained economic development might give them more influence in the Movement and the regime).[8] Administrators of the Bank of Spain were

7. Quoted in Viñas, *Guerra, dinero, dictadura,* 228–29.
8. When the First Syndical Congress met in Madrid from February 27 to March 6, 1961, it took a reasonably enlightened stand on partial economic liberalization. The Congress repudiated an inflationary economic policy and endorsed major foreign investment in Spain, thus reversing a long-standing principle. Its main recommendations, characteristic of the Syndical Organization during the decade that followed, urged a strong national minimum wage (*salario mínimo interprofesional*), achievement of greater equality between regions, rationalization of the tax system with more progressive taxation, the need for an antitrust

more cautious, stressing monetary policy and the control of inflation, while Suanzes and the INI directors were the most intransigent, demanding retention of a nationalist/interventionist policy.[9]

The next change was the Ley de Convenios Colectivos (Law of Collective Bargaining) that appeared in April. It introduced the novel principle of local collective bargaining between employers and labor under the framework of the Syndical Organization, if this were found preferable to the industry-wide norms that the Ministry of Labor had supervised heretofore. Though the ministry retained the power to dictate agreements when collective bargaining broke down, the law provided much greater individual and local initiative, allowing more active and efficient firms and syndical units to determine their own norms and to that extent giving the Syndical Organization a more direct role than before. Collective bargaining nonetheless got off to a slow start, because of the deflationary, recessionist conditions of 1959–60. Only one local collective bargaining agreement was signed in 1958, followed by 179 in 1959, the number rising to 412 by 1962.[10]

As first steps in a new direction, in 1958 the regime entered the Organization for European Economic Cooperation (OEEC), the Export-Import Bank, and the International Monetary Fund. The new Spanish budget provided special incentives to export and for the first time timidly widened the door to foreign investment.[11] Late in the year the principal west European countries made their currencies freely convertible, increasing pressure on Spain to do likewise. The pathology of Spain's situation was underscored in December 1958 when police caught two Swiss banking agents in a massive *evasión de pesetas* (illegal smuggling of Spanish currency abroad). The agents were also caught with a list of 1,363 wealthy or prominent figures—including of course various officials high in the regime—whose secret Swiss bank accounts they serviced.[12]

A crisis was reached in mid-1959 after four years of severe balance of payments deficits and inflation. In May the OEEC issued a report on Spain, pointing the way to major reform. By July the Instituto Español de Moneda Extranjera (Spain's foreign currency exchange) was very close to having to declare suspension of payments, while the stock market had gone into decline after the restrictive measures of the preceding year.

policy, promotion of the agrarian reform, and state encouragement of small business. See Juan Velarde Fuertes, *Sobre la decadencia económica de España* (Madrid, 1967), 141–434.

9. González, *Política económica,* 172–80.

10. Biescas and Tuñón de Lara, *España,* 325.

11. Cf. Organización Sindical Española, *Oportunidades del capital extranjero en España* (Madrid, 1959).

12. Some of those involved seem to have been given de facto immunity while the rest were merely required to repatriate their funds without penalty. The fullest account is in Garriga, *La Señora,* 265–67.

With the government facing bankruptcy, the economic ministers concluded that a fundamental change of direction could no longer be delayed.

Franco did not at first agree. In several recent speeches, he had used the term "crisis of growth" to explain the present difficulties. He was willing to grant the need for a measure of reform and retrenchment, but resisted abandonment of the regime's framework of statist autarchy. During the Civil War he had maintained a fixed, high rate of exchange for the peseta against much advice, and the policy had proven a success through the end of the conflict. Moreover, he fundamentally distrusted liberal economics as much as any other aspect of liberalism. His rejection of a freer form of capitalism was reflected in a memorandum that he prepared about the economic situation at that time:

> The interest of the nation, the common good and the will of the Spanish people require above all a transformation of the capitalist system, acceleration of economic progress, a more just distribution of wealth, social justice, transformation and modernization of credit, and the modernization of many basic elements of production. The fact that the state nationalizes certain industries and services is criticized as socialism when this is accepted in many countries who are considered liberal but adopt this from socialism as good and proper.[13]

Thus when Navarro Rubio presented to Franco the outline of a new plan of stabilization and liberalization, Franco "did not at first have the slightest confidence in it,"[14] discerning merely the abandonment of much of the regime's program in favor of unregulated interests. Moreover, he had always viewed greater economic liberalism as inherently tied to political and cultural liberalism, and reliance on foreign investment and international commerce as inevitably opening the door to subversive foreign political and religious influences. To reject the proposal might require another change of government after two and a half years, however, and Franco had a favorable opinion of the new economic ministers, particularly of Navarro Rubio, who had been wounded three times as a Civil War volunteer and subsequently became a member of the Military Juridical Corps. The finance minister therefore pressed upon him an overwhelming weight of technical arguments and data[15] and at the same time astutely appealed to his sense of patriotism and national pride, insisting that no other alternative could save the government from bankruptcy. Franco was never a fanatic, and after several days allowed himself to be convinced by this combination of technical reasoning and call to patriotic responsibility, opening a new phase in the evolution of the regime.

On July 22, 1959, after Ullastres had arranged a $544-million loan in

13. Quoted in *FF*, 6:107–8.
14. According to Navarro Rubio in *Franco visto*, 89.
15. There is a broader account of the economic background of the policy-making process in Charles W. Anderson, *The Political Economy of Modern Spain* (Madison, 1970), 3–128.

Washington, a new decree law was issued for a "plan de estabilización interna y externa de la economía." Its goal was retrenchment, deflation, and above all a liberalization that would open the economy to the international market. The peseta was devalued from 42 to 60 to the dollar, and by the end of the year, eighteen government control agencies had been abolished and a wide variety of items freed from regulation in both domestic production and foreign trade. Restrictions were placed on credit, and the Bank of Spain's rediscount rate was again raised, this time from 5 to 6.25 percent. Import licensing was abolished for 180 commodities deemed essential imports, representing about 50 percent of all imported goods, while controls were retained on less important items to protect foreign exchange. Internal investment was largely freed from government restriction, more careful guidelines were set for state investment, and new regulations encouraged foreign investment for up to 50 percent of the capital investment in any individual enterprise. The previous limit had been 25 percent, and even that had been hedged with serious restrictions and limited to certain kinds of firms. The new regulations, which greatly simplified and expedited procedures, applied to all firms and allowed foreign investors to repatriate freely annual dividends of up to 6 percent. This was obviously not a program of full free-market economics, for many restraints remained, but it did create a significant opening to market forces. Much though not all of the "Falangist" system of semiautarchist economic nationalism had been demolished at one stroke.[16]

The Stabilization Plan gave a jolt to the man in the street, temporarily increasing unemployment and bringing a slight drop in real income for about a year, but its main goals were soon achieved. The danger of suspension of payments was averted, and within five months, by the close of 1959, Spain's foreign exchange account showed a $100-million surplus. New foreign investment rose from $12 million under the old restrictions in 1958 to $82.6 million in 1960, while between 1958 and 1960 the annual number of tourists doubled from three to six million and thenceforth continued to rise rapidly.[17]

The turnaround was hailed as a major success for the new economics ministers, who gained the sobriquet "technocrats." In addition to introducing a new policy, they inaugurated a different style, free of the ideological bombast and rhetoric of the autarchist spokesmen, for the Opus Dei ministers addressed problems in direct and practical language that

16. González, *Política económica*, 199–226, provides a good description of the Stabilization Plan. See also Ros Hombravella et al., *Capitalismo*, 2:228–50; the chapter by Juan Sardá in *El Banco de España: Una historia económica* (Madrid, 1970), 467–79; and, on the commercial liberalization, Viñas et al., *Política comercial*, 2:989–1167, which emphasizes the role of Ullastres.

17. The immediate effects of the Stabilization Plan are treated in González, *Política económica*, 227–77.

reflected their policy priorities.[18] After his initial doubts, Franco gave the new orientation his full endorsement.[19]

Further reforms followed. A new tariff in 1960 systematized the changes in levels of protection. Two years later the Bank of Spain was nationalized and new antimonopoly regulations imposed on industry and commerce to encourage competition. A modest tax reform was then carried out in 1964 that simplified the tax system and made it slightly more progressive.

The economics ministers admired the indicative planning of French administrators during the past decade that presented broad outlines and goals but did not attempt to regulate particular details or enterprises, and they prepared to introduce somewhat analogous development planning into Spain. A major study of the country's economy by the World Bank in 1962 pinpointed most of the problems and helped show the way.[20] The first Spanish Plan de Desarrollo was subsequently announced in 1963 and introduced in 1964. The final version was toned down to be more palatable to Carrero Blanco and even then was strongly attacked by INI directors. It particularly emphasized metallurgy, machine tools, shipbuilding, irrigation, the chemical industry, road building, the mechanization of agriculture, and the development of fishing.[21] The powers of the state were still used to reward favored sectors through credits, tax breaks, export subsidies, and the combination of any of these in *acciones concertadas* which might be carried out with favored firms or entire industries,[22] but

18. The unadorned and direct style of Ullastres, as in the collected speeches of 1958–62 in his *Política comercial española* (Madrid, 1963), may be contrasted with the ideological extravagances of Suanzes even in recent years, as in the Instituto Nacional de Industria's *El Estado ante el desarrollo económico* (Madrid, 1960).

19. In a speech of October 2, 1961, Franco quoted his own words of 1942, "No people on earth can live normally from its own economy alone," which had indeed sought to encourage foreign trade but not at all the sort of liberalization that began in 1959. *Discursos y mensajes del Jefe del Estado 1960–1963* (Madrid, 1964), 332.

20. Economic Survey Mission to Spain, *The Economic Development of Spain* (Baltimore, 1963). Cf. *El desarrollo económico de España: Juicio crítico del Informe del Banco Mundial* (Madrid, 1963), ed. E. Fuentes Quintana.

21. Laureano López Rodó, *Plan de Desarrollo Económico y Social para el período 1964–1967* (Madrid, 1964; Eng. tr., Baltimore, 1965). The new Comisaría del Plan de Desarrollo Económico also published a briefer *Resumen del Plan de Desarrollo Económico y Social 1964–1967* (Madrid, 1964). *Líneas del crecimiento económico español* is another government description.

All the new economic legislation of the late 1950s and early 1960s was collected in the Secretaría General Técnica de la Presidencia's *Legislación económica*, 4 vols. (Madrid 1965), and studied in Herbert J. Becher, *Wirtschaft, Recht und Steuern in Spanien* (Berne, 1965), and F. Javier Paniagua, *La ordenación del capitalismo avanzado en España, 1957–1963* (Barcelona, 1977).

22. For a broad critique of the economic policies and emphases of the 1960s, see Carlos Moya, *El poder económico en España (1939–1970)* (Madrid, 1975), 181–243. The reactions of Spanish businessmen to the new policies of the 1960s are given in Juan Linz and Amando de Miguel, *Los empresarios ante el poder público* (Madrid, 1966).

the emphasis was on new investment, expansion of exports, and greater integration with the international economy. This did not involve precise overall planning, and indeed, the primary effects of the plan were the result of general policy priorities and psychological benefit rather than of any detailed blueprint.

The liberalization initiated the greatest cycle of industrialization and prosperity that Spain had ever known. Proportionately the most successful years were 1961 to 1964, the years before the plan was in effect, for they registered a real growth in GNP of 8.7 percent a year, on a higher base than in the fifties. During those years inflation was held to an average rate of less than 5 percent annually.[23] Moreover, most aspects of national economic policy had been brought into the open and were henceforth subject to varying degrees of criticism, creating something of a national economic debate during the last fifteen years of the regime, in sharp contrast to the official dictates and closed-door dealing of its first two decades.

Foreign investment and export growth were vital to this program. The former came by means of massive and growing tourist expenditures and by major direct investment in industrial enterprises. Spain's tourist industry blossomed into one of the most efficient in the world, drawing 21 million annual visitors by the close of the decade and still increasing.[24] At one point it accounted for at least 9 percent of the gross national product, centered on Madrid and on the eastern and southern coasts. Dour, neotraditionalist Spain was rapidly transformed into a "good-time" vacationland, with cultural consequences to which the native population could not be immune. Spanish expertise even made it possible to mount small technical assistance programs to a few Latin American countries attempting to develop their own tourist industries.[25] Export growth itself always remained far from sufficient to balance the trade deficit, resulting from increasingly large imports of food and capital goods, but as table 19.2 indicates, receipts from tourism were responsible for covering most of the remaining gap during the next fifteen years.

Second only to the receipts from tourism was the total of direct foreign investment, which from 1960 to 1974 came to more than $7,600,000,000. Of this, nearly five billion was invested in properties, over two billion in

23. The best contemporary study of the Spanish economy during this phase was probably Ramón Tamames, *Estructura económica de España* (Madrid, 1964), later revised and expanded, and his briefer *Introducción a la economía española* (Madrid, 1968).

24. Juan Fuster Lareu, "El turismo," *La Espana de los anos 70*, ed. M. Fraga Iribarne et al. (Madrid, 1973), 2:805–33.

25. On technical assistance to the Spanish economy and limited Spanish technical aid, primarily to Latin American and Arab countries, see the OECD's *Technical Assistance and the Economic Development of Spain* (Paris, 1968).

Table 19.2. Tourism and the Balance of Payments, 1959–75

Year	Tourists (thousands)	Foreign currency receipts from tourism ($ millions)	Balance of trade deficits ($ millions)
1959	4,194	128.6	253
1960	6,113	297.0	57
1961	7,445	384.6	279
1962	8,668	512.6	634
1963	10,931	679.3	1,004
1964	14,102	918.6	1,056
1965	14,250	1,156.9	1,737
1966	17,251	1,292.5	1,964
1967	17,858	1,209.8	1,745
1968	19,183	1,212.7	1,548
1969	21,682	1,310.7	2,333
1970	24,105	1,680.8	2,360
1971	26,758	2,054.4	2,025
1972	32,506	2,486.3	2,911
1973	34,559	3,091.2	4,405
1974	30,343	3,187.9	8,340
1975	30,122	3,404.3	8,516

Source: Joseph Harrison, *An Economic History of Modern Spain* (New York, 1978), 156.

direct commercial and industrial investment, and the remainder in stock market purchases.[26] More than a billion dollars in additional funding was made available from foreign sources through various loan and credit devices. Of the direct investment, more than 40 percent came from the United States, nearly 17 percent from Switzerland (of whatever origin), slightly more than 10 percent each from Germany and Britain, more than 5 percent from France, and almost 5 percent from the two Low Countries combined. Foreign investment was heaviest in automobile manufacturing (where more than 50 percent of industrial capital was of foreign origin by 1970) and in electronics and the chemical industry (where foreign capital amounted to 42 and 37 percent of the totals, respectively, by the end of 1973). Altogether, before the close of the regime, 12.4 percent of all the capital invested in the 500 largest industrial enterprises was of foreign origin.[27] Some industries such as textiles, the oldest in Spain, received very little foreign investment. That investment was disproportionately concentrated in the new industries of the central area around Madrid, which received nearly 36 percent of the total, and in Catalonia, which got 26

26. Eric Baklanoff, *La transformación económica de España y Portugal* (Madrid, 1980), 74–75.
27. Ibid., 79.

percent. The established industrial zone of the Basque provinces, specializing in metallurgy, received only 10 percent, and much of that went to the newly industrializing province of Alava.[28]

Of the ministers involved in the new economic policy, López Rodó received the widest public recognition. He did not gain full cabinet rank until 1965 but was placed in charge of the Commissariat of the Plan of Development in 1962. At this point the leading ministers of economics, by then known colloquially as the Opus ministers, gained greater unity when Joaquín Planell, the elderly Army engineers general who had held the Ministry of Industry for a decade and was still wedded to semi-autarchist thinking, was replaced by the elegant thirty-nine-year-old Gregorio López Bravo, former naval engineers officer and industrial administrator and also a member of Opus Dei.

The strongest opposition came from certain sectors of the Movement and within the state economic structure from Suanzes and the INI. Suanzes himself resigned before the close of 1963, and although one of the oldest friends of the Caudillo, broke off relations with him.[29] The new policies tended to limit investment in the INI, yet its holdings continued to grow. By the time of Franco's death they were responsible for or involved in 15 percent of all exports, 76 percent of all shipbuilding, 64 percent of heavy trucks built, 50 percent of the coal mined, 67 percent of the aluminum, 58 percent of the iron, and 45 percent of the steel, 46 percent of the automobiles produced, 37 percent of the petroleum refined, and 23 percent of the electrical energy produced.[30] Yet the INI was not a truly powerful autonomous institution, for it lacked independence and was poorly coordinated. It increasingly came to serve as a state safety net for inefficient and failing private enterprises, and in later years was required to take over and compensate for the losses of leading shipbuilding and coal-mining companies. The direction and central administration of the INI was not in itself inefficient, but it maintained a total of 4,000 executive positions throughout Spain, half of which were political sinecures. The lack of rationalization and coordination among its enterprises as well as the stagnation in some of them became clearer with each passing year. After 1970 an entire generation of reorganization and reform was initiated, as more and more of the older enterprises operated at a loss.[31]

28. Juan Muñoz, Santiago Roldán, and Angel Serrano, *La internacionalización del capital en España 1959–1977* (Madrid, 1978), esp. 68, 115, 130, 132.

29. For the INI in the 1960s, see Schwartz and González, *Una historia*, 89–134; and Moya, *El poder*, 208–17.

30. Schwartz and González, *Una historia*, 3; and also "The 30th Anniversary of the Founding of the I.N.I.," *Spain Today*, no. 19 (Jan. 1972), 55–60.

31. Schwartz and Gonzalez, *Una historia*, 147–216; and Robert Graham, *Spain: A Nation Comes of Age* (New York, 1984), 82–83.

Table 19.3. Net Spanish Emigration, 1961–75

1961	107,557	1966	−1,085	1971	70,348
1962	96,661	1967	−25,000	1972	40,369
1963	82,311	1968	18,000	1973	−9,073
1964	80,128	1969	68,869	1974	−84,473
1965	60,600	1970	65,674	1975	−45,485

Source: Banco de Bilbao, *Informe Económico 1976*, in Eric Baklanoff, *La transformación económica de España y Portugal* (Madrid, 1980), 123.

The new policies were generally supported by the Syndical Organization but were at first unpopular with the workers, since wages were nearly frozen between 1957 and 1961. The temporary decline in real income during the initial main phase of stabilization in 1960 stimulated what soon became a wave of Spanish surplus labor migration to the labor-short industries and service jobs of France, Germany, Belgium, and Switzerland, as western Europe absorbed nearly a million Spanish workers during the next decade.[32] This supplemented the great expansion of employment in Spain that followed, eventually making possible almost complete elimination of urban unemployment and much of rural underemployment, while the remittances of foreign workers provided further sources of international exchange.

In general, the productivity of Spanish industrial labor was so low that in 1960 the temporary freeze made sense. It stood at less than half that of Italy and only a small fraction of that of West Germany. Subsequently both productivity and real income increased steadily, real wages rising between 1961 and 1964 at rates varying from 8 to 11 percent a year, making up what they had lost and more.

Results from the First Plan of Development of 1963 were nonetheless never quite according to plan, despite impressive growth figures. A high rate of internal investment was sustained for several years, with nearly 23 percent of the GNP invested in 1965 thanks to the easy terms of credit for productive enterprises. Yet industry itself was financing only 27 percent of its own investment directly through reinvested savings and profits. In 1965 the inflation rate shot up to 14 percent, leading to new deflationary restrictions not foreseen in the plan. The second half of the decade was a time of "stop-and-go" in Spanish industrial policy, with minicrises in 1966–67 and to a lesser degree in 1970–71. The main neoliberal phase could be said to have ended in 1966. Spain still had two and a half times the level of tariff protection of the average non-Communist industrialized

32. On worker emigration during the 1960s, see Francisco Sánchez López, *Emigración española a Europa* (Madrid, 1969), which presents thorough statistics.

Table 19.4. Yearly Rates of Increase of the Gross
Industrial Product, 1959–71

Year	Rate %	Year	Rate %
1959	0.2	1966	9.3
1960	2.7	1967	4.5
1961	13.6	1968	6.0
1962	11.3	1969	11.4
1963	12.2	1970	7.1
1964	13.3	1971	3.9
1965	9.4		

Source: Sima Lieberman, *The Contemporary Spanish
Economy* (London, 1982), 213.

Table 19.5. Average Increase in Real Income per Capita

1906–30	0.95%	1940–60	2.8 %
1931–36	0.00%	1961–70	6.45%

Source: Manuel J. González, *La política económica del franquismo, 1940–1970* (Madrid, 1979), 300.

country (and nearly twice that of Japan). A new decree of 1967 limited the
installation, expansion, or transfer of industrial enterprises once more.
Further policy reform was needed at that point, but as Franco's health and
energy declined, leadership became less assertive and no one could or
would take responsibility for changes. Following a major increase in the
minimum wage in 1966, a deflationary program the following year further
devalued the peseta by 17 percent, cut the national budget, and temporarily froze prices and wages. Temporary restrictions were reimposed in
1969, though followed by further liberalization of terms of foreign investment and reform of monetary policy in 1970–71. The average growth rate
from 1966 to 1971 was only 5.6 percent a year, distinctly less than for the
earlier part of the decade though still impressive in terms of sustained
growth.[33]

33. González, *Política económica*, 324–30; Jacint Ros Hombravella, *Política económica
española (1959–1973)* (Barcelona, 1979), a lucid essay; and also Luis Gámir, *Política económica de España* (Madrid, 1972). Michel Drain, *L'économie de l'Espagne* (Paris, 1968), is a
brief general survey from the period of the First Plan; and Gonzalo Barroso Gippini, *España
1970: Estudio de su desarrollo comparativamente con otras economías* (Madrid, 1971),
presents a comparative analysis. Manuel Román treats some of the salient problems of these
years in *The Limits of Economic Growth in Spain* (New York, 1971).
The Ediciones del Movimiento presented official accounts in *Marcha del desarrollo
económico-social de España* (Madrid, 1967) and *Balance del Primer Plan de Desarrollo*
(Madrid, 1968). Projections for the Second Plan were published by López Rodó's Comisaría
in multivolume format as *II Plan de Desarrollo Económico y Social* (Madrid, 1967).

Expansion temporarily accelerated once more early in the seventies, so that Spain's average annual growth rate for the fifteen years 1960 to 1975 was 7.2 percent—certainly the highest figure in Europe and second in the entire world only to Japan. Industrial productivity per worker was still less than 40 percent that of Germany and less than 45 percent that of France in 1970, but in 1969 Spain achieved the rank of twelfth largest industrial power in the world, and later climbed to eleventh. In 1971 it was momentarily the world's fourth largest shipbuilder.[34]

The regime's leaders recognized that severe regional economic imbalance was a fundamental feature of Spanish underdevelopment which must be overcome. Under the development plan, special "poles of development" were targeted for six underdeveloped areas: Vigo in the northwest, Burgos, Valladolid, and Zaragoza in the north, and Huelva and Seville in the south.[35] This strategy was not generally successful, for massive investments would have been required to overcome the lack of infrastructure and sociocultural prerequisites in the more backward agrarian provinces. As it was, part of the state investment was poorly or improperly employed. Huelva received vastly disproportionate funding and developed a huge chemicals complex but remained an industrial island in a backward agrarian province. The only other two "poles" to approximate their goals were Vigo and Valladolid, though Zaragoza profited considerably from increased private investment.[36]

Greater Barcelona and the northern part of the Basque provinces remained the chief industrial centers and were joined for the first time by Madrid. Several other key northern provincial capitals, such as Pamplona and Alava, were also transformed by industrialization. Spain became a country of larger and larger cities; by 1970 40 percent—and by the time

34. The broadest general study of recent Spanish economic development in English is Sima Lieberman, *The Contemporary Spanish Economy: A Historical Perspective* (London, 1982). See also Baklanoff and Alison Wright, *The Spanish Economy 1959–1976* (New York, 1977).

35. Comisaría del Plan de Desarrollo Económico y Social, *Polos de promoción y de desarrollo industrial* (Madrid, 1966).

36. From the mid-sixties a large literature dealing with regional problems and economic imbalances developed: José Ma. Codón, *Regionalismo y desarrollo económico* (San Sebastian, 1964), represented an early attempt to put this in international comparative perspective; while Friedrich Buttler, *Growth Pole Theory and Economic Development* (Lexington, Mass., 1975), presented a foreign critique of the Spanish case. The Instituto de Desarrollo Económico offered its own two-volume *Evaluación económica de los Polos de Desarrollo* (Madrid, 1973); and Sebastián Martín-Retortillo, *Descentralización administrativa y organización política*, 3 vols. (Madrid, 1973), presented a lengthy politico-administrative analysis. Some of the major regional economic studies are the official *Acción de planes provinciales en Galicia* (Madrid, 1971); Xavier Costa Clavell, *Perfil conflictivo de Galicia* (Barcelona, 1976); Jesús A. Expósito Fernández, *Asturias frente a su reconversión industrial* (Madrid, 1968); Francis Fourneau, *El impacto del Polo de Desarrollo en la provincia de Huelva (1964–1974)* (Seville, 1978); Ernest Lluch, *La vía valenciana* (Valencia, 1976);and Carlos Carrasco-Muñoz de Vera, *La alternativa de Castilla y León* (Madrid, 1978).

of Franco's death in 1975 50 percent—of its population lived in cities of 100,000 or more. In some respects development merely accentuated centralization, as Madrid burgeoned into one of the largest megalopolises of Europe. On the other hand, the two chief Basque provinces of Vizcaya and Guipúzcoa, which led all Spain in per capita income at the close of the sixties,[37] received proportionately less infrastructural support. Due to a complex variety of problems, their relative well-being declined decidedly during the decade that followed, fueling resentment and exacerbating regional nationalism.

Rapid development reduced somewhat the concentration of banking sources that had developed in the 1940s, so that by 1967 the five largest banks controlled only 56 percent of the country's private banking resources and the eleven largest about 75 percent, amounting to decreases of 12 and 8 percent respectively over the preceding decade. The financial power of Spanish banks was not greatly diminished, however, and the state in some respects did little to regulate them, allowing them to maintain the highest bank margins in western Europe. Though 30 percent of all deposits were nominally required to be invested in state-approved projects, Spanish industry became heavily dependent on private banks, which controlled 40 percent of all industry by the time of Franco's death. The Caudillo himself voiced private doubts as to the wisdom of state financial policy, both before and during the development programs, which in some respects encouraged the power of the banks and the concentration of resources among them, with some 57 percent of all banking resources concentrated in Madrid.[38] The proposed merger of two of the largest Madrid banks in 1965 was apparently vetoed by Franco.[39]

Agriculture

Agriculture, which in the early years of the regime had received limited investment and comparatively little attention, continued to lag. This situation, common to countries pressing industrialization, meant that food production would remain the Achilles heel of the economy, doing

37. The major compilations of data for Vizcaya and the Basque provinces during these years were the Bilbao Chamber of Commerce's *Análisis de la economía vizcaina y su proyección, 1968–1971* 5 vols. (Bilbao, 1968–69); and *Aspectos de la estructura económica de Alava, Guipúzcoa, Navarra, y Vizcaya,* 2 vols. (San Sebastian, 1973).

38. Juan Muñoz, *El poder de la banca en España* (Algorta, 1970), 101–12. Ramon Trías Fargas, *El sistema financiero español* (Barcelona, 1970), provides a sound account of the financial system of the 1960s; while his *Las fuentes de financiación de la empresa en España* (Madrid, 1972), treats the role of the banks in industrial development. A. González Temprano et al., *La Banca y el Estado en la España contemporánea (1939–1979)* (Madrid, 1981), emphasizes financial concentration and association with the state. See also Graham, *Spain,* 90–105.

39. Salgado Araujo, *Conversaciones privadas,* 428, 458–59.

Table 19.6. Distribution of Agrarian Property by Category of Owner, 1960

Size of Property, in hectares	Number of Owners	% of All Owners	Property in Hectares	% of All Property	Parcels per Owner	Average Total Property per Owner
Minifundia						
Less than 1	3,128,953	52.23	1,808,747	4.23	15.56	.57
Small properties						
1 to 5	1,805,012	30.13	2,707,518	6.33	2.35	1.50
5 to 10	552,655	9.23	3,592,257	8.40	1.07	6.50
Total	2,357,667	39.36	6,299,775	14.73		
Medium properties						
10 to 50	401,922	6.71	8,038,440	18.79	.93	20.
50 to 100	49,812	.84	3,735,900	8.74	1.34	75.
Total	451,734	7.55	11,774,340	27.53		
Large properties						
Over 100	51,283	.86	22,881,100	53.51	.80	446.
Grand total	5,989,637	100.	42,763,962	100.		

Source: G. García Badell, "La distribución de la propiedad agraria de España en las di-
ferentes categorías de fincas," *Revista de Estudios Agro-Sociales*, no. 30 (Jan.–Mar., 1960),
cited in Xavier Flores, *Estructura socioeconómica de la agricultura española*, (Barcelona,
1969), 103.

little more than keeping pace with growth in population, which increased
from 25 million in 1936 to 35 million by 1975. The existence of hundreds
of thousands of landless peasant families in the latifundist districts of the
south and west had long been recognized as one of the country's predominant social ills, and its alleviation had been one of the major goals of the
original Falange. Though the regime canceled virtually all wartime property transfers, it did set up an Instituto Nacional de Colonización to enable landless families to obtain plots of their own. With its limited authority and scant funding, its accomplishments were modest, though
some 90,000 landless families had been settled on new land by 1968.[40]
Meanwhile, a certain number of the existing smallholders were abandoning the land altogether, and the net result was that during the first quarter-
century of the regime the basic structure of land ownership remained unaltered.[41] The distribution of agrarian property as of 1960 is shown in
table 19.6.

40. Jose López de Sebastián, *Política agraria en España 1920–1970* (Madrid, 1970),
302–5.
41. Cf. Juan Martínez Alier, *La estabilidad del latifundismo* (Paris, 1968).

Table 19.7. Indices of Rural Wages and
Wholesale Prices, 1950–72
(1935 = 100)

Year	Index of Rural Wages	Wholesale Price Index
1950	424	651
1955	540	631
1960	1,125	916
1965	2,170	1,173
1970	3,787	1,289
1972	5,030	1,465

Source: Lieberman, *The Contemporary Spanish Economy*, 80.

Minifundia—tiny, often widely separated uneconomical cultivation plots—were as much a problem as latifundia, and the state sponsored a Servicio Nacional de Concentración Parcelaria (founded in December 1952) to concentrate small plots into economically viable units. It was empowered to reorganize whenever either 60 percent of the landowners or those owning 60 percent of the land in a district requested concentration. Ultimately about 4 million hectares, or about 10 percent of the farmland of Spain, was so reconcentrated, but even in the last years of the regime millions of uneconomic minifundia remained.[42] Thus one study in 1965 found that 48 percent of all landowners, the true minifundists, had a cash income even lower than that of rural day laborers.[43]

Many agrarian producers increased their incomes significantly in the black market of the forties, and the elimination of rationing in 1952, which destroyed the black market, temporarily depressed their condition. The only benefits for the lower strata of agrarian society provided by the regime's own regulations during the early years were security of tenure for renters at relatively fixed rates and a kind of minimum wage for laborers. In general, the income of laborers and some minifundists declined during the 1940s, like that of urban workers and much of the middle classes, but the wages of farm laborers began to rise rapidly after 1950 and spurted upward during the later years of that decade.

The government enacted legislation for the eviction of landlords who did not properly use their land or tend to larger estates, and it provided for the collectivization of large units under carefully delimited conditions,

42. As late as 1972, such northern provinces as Burgos, La Coruña, and Zamora still contained more than a million plots of less than one hectare, even though the number of such plots had been reduced by approximately half. Ramón Tamames, *Introducción a la economía española* (Madrid, 1973), 84.

43. Jose Ma. Naredo, *La evolución de la agricultura en España* (Barcelona, 1977), 87–88.

but such powers were rarely invoked. Much more successful were the large-scale efforts to promote the reforestation of large tracts of barren hillsides which by the 1960s had considerably increased the amount of tree cover in the peninsula. Irrigation facilities were also greatly expanded, sometimes in connection with hydroelectric projects. One major rural regional project, the Plan Badajoz, was implemented in Extremadura during the 1950s. It attempted to combine new irrigation facilities, electrification, resettlement of landless families, reforestation, and the development of secondary agrarian industries,[44] but it was not a complete program of regional development and met only limited success. In fact, the irrigation programs undertaken by the regime during its first two decades tended primarily to benefit larger landowners, and though they did expand production, at first had limited effect on the structural and social problems of the countryside.

Agrarian policy became more active during the 1950s, and the following decade of the sixties was in some respects even more decisive for agriculture than for industry. Grain production was stimulated by a new pricing policy in the fifties, and after 1958 the state introduced an increasing array of incentives, loans, and credits to stimulate productivity and modernization. New opportunities for higher wages in domestic industry or abroad in western Europe provoked a mass exodus of underemployed agrarian laborers and minifundists. The shrinking labor supply, together with the general prosperity, further stimulated the dramatic increase in rural wages. Bountiful credits and loans helped to dramatically expand mechanization and the use of fertilizers, the number of tractors spurting from one for every 228 hectares in 1962 to one for every 45 hectares by 1970 and the number of motor cultivators increasing with equal or greater rapidity. Beginning about 1962 there was a dramatic decrease in small farms, for under these conditions the individual cultivation of tiny plots inherited from the Antiguo Régimen no longer made any sense. Within the next ten years, about half a million minifarms simply disappeared and the average size of holdings increased from 14.9 to 17.9 hectares. Only farms in the category of 50 to 100 hectares increased in number. Major agrarian problems remained, but the profound socioeconomic dilemma of the early twentieth century had largely disappeared in the face of more modern, large-scale commercial agriculture, accompanied by the emigration of a large part of the formerly depressed population.[45]

44. *Plan general de ordenación económico-social de la provincia de Badajoz*, 2 vols. (Madrid, 1948); Manuel Martín Lobo, *Un luchador extremeño: La conquista del Guadiana (El Plan de Badajoz)* (Badajoz, 1962); López de Sebastián, *Política agraria*, 318–36.
45. Xavier Flores, *Estructura socioeconómica de la agricultura española* (Barcelona, 1969); Arturo López Muñoz and J. L. García Delgado, *Crecimiento y crisis del capitalismo español* (Madrid, 1968), 115–52; José Luis Leal et al., *La agricultura en el desarrollo capitalista español (1940–1970)* (Madrid, 1975); and J. L. García Delgado and S. Roldán López,

Agriculture's percentage of the total Spanish GNP shrank from 24 in 1960 to only 13 in 1970, representing proportionately less than in Italy, Greece, or Portugal. The active agrarian population diminished from 4.9 million in 1960 to 3.7 million in 1970, and by 1970 represented only 22 percent of Spain's active population. Even in some of the prosperous agrarian areas of the northeast, the agrarian population declined because of the inherent unattractiveness of a rural lifestyle in an urban, hedonistic, consumer-oriented society. Prosperous family farms transferred in one form or another from generation to generation over centuries disappeared in the Basque provinces and Catalonia not because they were economically unprofitable but simply because agriculture was disagreeable.[46] At the same time, one of the traditionally most backward agrarian provinces, Almería, made a dramatic turnaround in the 1960s and 1970s, adjusting to new financial and marketing opportunities and specializing in exportable produce, with a dramatic effort on provincial income. Continuing problems of agrarian and regional underdevelopment, however, persisted in the primarily rural districts of the south and west.[47]

Social and Cultural Transformation

The real Spanish revolution was not the defeated struggle of 1936–39 but the social and cultural transformation wrought by the industrialization of the 1960s and 1970s. Rapid urbanization sucked population from the small rural towns and farming districts that at least in the north had provided much of the backbone of the traditional society and culture. By the time of Franco's death, 40 percent of the labor force was employed in services (reflecting the massive growth of tourism), 38 percent in industry, and only 22 percent in agriculture, the primary sector. This pace of development reoriented social psychology, which became attuned to the com-

"Contribución al análisis de la crisis de la agricultura tradicional en España: Los cambios decisivos de la última década," in *La España de los años 70*, ed. M. Fraga et al., 2:253–322. A striking portrait of the effect of the regime's agrarian policies of the 1960s and 1970s on an Aragonese village may be found in Susan Friend Harding, *Remaking Ibieca: Rural Life in Aragon under Franco* (Chapel Hill, 1984). There are a number of anthropological studies in Spanish and English on the changes in rural life during this period. One of the best is Carmelo Lisón Tolosana, *Belmonte de los Caballeros* (Oxford, 1966).

46. See especially Davydd J. Greenwood, *Unrewarding Wealth: The Commercialization and Collapse of Agriculture in a Spanish Basque Town* (Cambridge, 1976); and also E. C. Hansen, *Rural Catalonia under the Franco Regime* (New York, 1977).

47. On the changing social structure and economic problems of the rural population, see Jesús M. de Miguel, *Notas sobre la estructura social del campo español* (Madrid, 1970); Víctor M. Pérez Díaz, *Pueblos y clases sociales en el campo español* (Madrid, 1974); and Juan Maestre Alfonso, *Modernización y cambio en la España rural* (Madrid, 1975). The continuing problems of eastern Andalucía were examined in Manuel Siguán, *El medio rural en Andalucía oriental* (Madrid, 1972); and the *Estudio socio-económico de Andalucía* (Madrid, 1970), 195–224.

Table 19.8. Wages and Salaries as a Percentage of National Income in Spain, 1958–74

Year	Eguilaz & Anderson	FOESSA	Alvargonzález	Lázaro Araujo & Muñoz Cidad	Carr & Fusi
1958	56				
1960			49.5	53.0	53.0
1961		49.0	49.1		
1962	67.5		51.7		
1963			53.4		53.9
1964		55.1	55.0		
1967			56.5		
1970				58.8	56.9
1974					61.8

Year	Banco de España	Fuentes Quintana	In France	In Italy
1960	53.0		58.3	51.5
1961	52.4			
1962	52.2			
1963	53.5		62.4	56.6
1964	54.5			
1967	57.7			
1970	57.2			
1973	59.8	55.6	62.9	59.8
1974	61.0		69.3	67.9

Source: H. París Eguilaz, *Desarrollo económico español, 1906–1964* (Madrid, 1965), in and corroborated by C. W. Anderson, *The Political Economy of Modern Spain* (Madison, 1970), 50; Fundacion FOESSA, *Informe sociológico sobre la situación social de España* (Madrid, 1966), 82; Rafael Alvargonzález, *Estrategias de actuación para la sociedad española* (Madrid, 1967); L. Lázaro Araujo and C. Muñoz Cidad, "La distribución de lo producido," *La España de los años 70* (Madrid, 1973), 2:916; R. Carr and J. P. Fusi, *Spain: Dictatorship to Democracy* (London, 1979), 77; Banco de España, *Informe Anual*, 1970, 1974; and E. Fuentes Quintana, "Economía y política en la transición democrática española," *Pensamiento Iberoamericano*, no. 1 (1982), 148.

mon consumerist and hedonist culture of the western world in the second half of the twentieth century.

Massive development not only expanded the general national income but also began to redistribute it as the population became better educated, more urban, and industrially employed. At the beginning of the new economic program, income was more unevenly distributed in Spain than in northwestern Europe, though considerably better distributed than in Latin America.[48] Depending on the measurements employed, esti-

48. One study published in 1963 found a pre-tax index of economic inequality of 0.421 for Spain, compared with 0.366 for England, 0.399 for Sweden, and 0.540 for Mexico. Bruce M. Russet et al., *Handbook of Basic Political and Social Data for Cross-National Comparison* (New Haven, 1963).

Table 19.9. Comparisons of Spanish Living Standards

	1960 ($1=60 ptas)	1970 ($1=70 ptas)
Income levels ($ per capita)	290	818
Illiteracy level (per 100)	11.2	5.7
Book titles published	12,038	19,900
Consumer durables (per 1,000 people)		
Telephones	59	135
Automobiles	9	70
Television sets	5	70
Refrigerators	1	25
Washing machines	3	15
Dwelling units	257	270 (1969)
Consumption of industrial products		
Steel (kg./person/year)	65	260
Cement (kg./person/year)	173	493
Electricity (kw. hours/person/year)	612	1,515
Gasoline (liters/person/year)	32	102

Source: Ramón Tamames, "La España de 1985," *Actualidad Económica,* July 14, 1973, p. 16, adapted by Wm. T. Salisbury and Jonathan Story, "The Economic Positions of Spain and Portugal in 1980: The Official View," p. 4 (1975).

Table 19.10. Increase in Consumer Goods, 1960–75 (in percentages of families owning)

Goods owned	April 1960	July 1975
Refrigerator	4	87
Washing machine	19	55
Television set	1	89
Phonograph	3	41
Automobile	4	48

Source: Compilation of various national surveys by Juan J. Linz.

mates of the increase in the share of national income gained by salaries and wages differ considerably, as indicated in table 8, but the more modest projections indicate that the share rose by nearly 20 percent during the last fifteen years of the regime, and by 1975 was not behind that of other western countries at approximately the same levels of development. The subsequent increase between 1975 and 1978 was even more dramatic.

The accompanying rise in living standards was of course the most dramatic in Spanish history. Varying measurements of the changes in living conditions and the increase in consumption are given in tables 19.9,

Table 19.11. Changes in Spanish Living Conditions, 1950–75

Indicator	1950	1975
Average daily caloric consumption	2116	2968
Grams of protein daily	64.6	92.1
Number of persons per room in homes	1.08	0.90
Average age of housing units	53.3	33.8
Vacancies	2.4	12.4
Domestic conveniences (on a scale of 95)	35.3	75.8
% of population protected by social security	29.4	78.7
Inhabitants per physician	650	106.2
Life expectancy	62.1	73.3
Mortality	10.8	8.2
Automobiles per 1,000 inhabitants	3.17	135.51
Suicides per 100,000 inhabitants	6.69	4.95
Violent deaths per 100,000 inhabitants	27.78	43.73

Source: Jose García-Durán de Lara and Pedro Puig Bastard, *La calidad de la vida en España* (Madrid, 1980), 149–80.

19.10, and 19.11.[49] At the same time, the average work week declined from 49 hours in 1964 to 44 hours in 1975.[50]

The regime always made much of its social welfare goals. Despite the hunger of the 1940s, health conditions improved as measured by certain key indicators, and general conditions improved more rapidly during the following decade. Infant mortality per thousand live births, for example, descended steadily from 123.75 in 1930 to 113.76 in 1940, to 69.84 in 1950, to 43.66 in 1960, and to 28.12 in 1970.[51] The latter figure, though still high compared with northern Europe, approached that of a developed country. During the 1970s Spanish infant mortality dropped well below that of the Soviet Union.

In the 1940s the Ministry of Labor initiated a modest social security system. Regular contributions were paid by both workers and employers. At first the system was restricted basically to industrial labor and the service sector. In a comparatively youthful population, retirees were relatively few, and payments caused little strain, despite a low level of contributions. Social security was greatly expanded in 1964 to include the agricultural population.[52] This added nearly two million names to the rolls at the same modest rate of contribution, insufficient to fund the system in

49. For further indicators on the rate of change in the mid-1960s in comparison with other countries, see Gonzalo Barroso Gippini, *España 1970: Nivel de vida europeo* (Madrid, 1967).

50. José García-Durán de Lara and Pedro Puig Bastard, *La calidad de la vida en España* (Madrid, 1980), 42.

51. Ibid., 269.

52. A comprehensive inventory is provided in *Seguridad Social, Sanidad, y Asistencia Social* (Madrid, 1967).

the long run. Small shopkeepers and others who were self-employed were included in 1971 on much the same terms, but by that point retirements were increasing and the Spanish system began to run a deficit for the first time. Reforms of 1972 increased contributions somewhat, but those workers who had not yet been covered were then included in the system. Deficits became severe by 1974, and there were many complaints of fraudulent claims and too-lenient terms for disability. (Eventually some provinces would contain more nominally disabled workers than regular retirees.) As in other systems, the tendency was to pay much the same benefits to everyone, regardless of amount or number of years of contribution. These would soon become standard problems in other western industrial countries. The Spanish system was more poorly designed than some, but a welfare state had been created, accompanied by very rigid job security enforced by the syndical system.

The growth in educational facilities was proportionately even greater in some respects than that of industry. By 1970 the Spanish state for the first time was spending more on education than on the armed forces. The last full year of Franco's life, 1974, marked the first year in history in which elementary school was available to almost every Spanish child (with the exception of those in a few isolated mountain villages). The quality was uneven and often left a good deal to be desired, but the schools were there and available to nearly all. By that time, with the opening of a second chain of universities, the number of Spanish universities had nearly doubled to twenty-two. The volume of university students increased rapidly during the 1960s, then skyrocketed between 1970 and 1974 with a breathtaking 500 percent increase. This was a reflection, despite the radical nature of student politics, of the new embourgeoisement of Spanish life and of the great transformation of status, income, and aspirations. Such an increase also swamped many of the universities, and made any approximation of adequate training a virtual impossibility, especially in the huge Complutense of Madrid. The book publishing industry followed suit. The number of titles published worldwide approximately doubled between 1955 and 1975, and those published in Spain nearly quadrupled from 4,812 to 17,727, facilitated by the easing of censorship after 1966.

Massive shifts in employment, along with the dramatic improvements in consumption and education, led to decisive changes in social structure and in social self-definition. In 1950 no more than a third of the Spanish population could have been considered middle and lower-middle class, and then only if many of the peasant smallholders were included.[53] The

53. In *Las clases medias españolas* (Granada, 1959), the first contemporary measurement by a sociologist, Francisco Murillo calculated that the middle classes amounted to 27 percent of Spain's population in 1950. Another sociologist calculated that as of 1957 they amounted to 38.8 percent. See José Cazorla Pérez, *Factores de la estructura socio-económica de Andalucía oriental* (Granada, 1965) and *Problemas de estratificación social en España* (Madrid, 1973).

systematic FOESSA study published in 1970, however, revealed that by that point slightly more than 6 percent of the population classified themselves as upper or upper-middle-class, 49 percent middle- or lower-middle-class, and about 45 percent lower-class. Forty percent of Spanish skilled workers, for example, defined themselves as lower-middle-class by 1970, and some social scientists calculated that the broader middle classes made up as much as 54 percent of society.[54] The 1975 FOESSA study classified heads of households by occupational group and social strata as being 5 percent upper- and upper-middle-class, 35 percent middle-class, 20.3 percent lower-middle-class, 33.6 percent working-class, and 6.1 percent still "poor." Though others disagreed with so large a measurement,[55] there was little doubt that within just a few years, those considering themselves in some general sense part of the middle classes had increased by half, while the self-defined lower class had declined by at least a third.

The Limits of Development

During the last fifteen years of the regime Spain thus became an industrial, and by world standards relatively affluent, land for the first time. Modernization, a national problem since at least the seventeenth century, was finally being achieved at an accelerated pace. By the end of 1973 annual per capita income passed the coveted threshold of $2,000 (which López Rodó had earlier declared would be sufficient to prepare Spain for democracy). In real dollars, this figure was equivalent to that of Japan only four years earlier. At that point Spain ranked ahead of Ireland ($2,034) and far ahead of Greece ($1,589) and Portugal ($1,158),[56] not to speak of Latin American or Third World comparisons.

54. Ignacio Fernández de Castro and Antonio Goytre, *Clases sociales en España en el umbral de los años 70* (Madrid, 1974), 306–7; and José Félix Tezanos, *Estructura de clases en la España actual* (Madrid, 1975).

55. Luis García San Miguel has contrasted the following estimates by social scientists for approximately the year 1970 (in *Las clases sociales en la España actual* [Madrid, 1980], 213–24):

	Upper classes or strata	Middle classes or strata	Working classes or strata
Ramón Tamames	2.5	28	69.5
Amando de Miguel	6–7	40–45	49–52
José Félix Tezanos	4.8	54.9	39.1

More recently, Amando de Miguel has suggested the following pattern of transformation (in *Diario 16, Historia del franquismo*, 412):

	1860 (%)	1950 (%)	1970 (%)
Urban upper and middle classes	24	26	41
Self-employed farmers	29	17	14
Industrial workers	13	24	35
Farm laborers	34	33	11

56. Richard Gunther, *Public Policy in a No-Party State* (Berkeley, 1980), 58.

Economic policy was nonetheless subject to an unprecedented barrage of criticism from the mid-1960s on. The new economic leadership itself brought the discussion of government policies out into the open, while the censorship reform that took place in 1966 made it possible in most cases to criticize strictly social and economic problems without penalty, as long as the politics and legitimacy of the government were not called into question. Critics held that Spain had largely failed to overcome major structural defects, that the development was dependent on foreign capital and the international boom of the sixties. Much of this was really a veiled form of political opposition, criticizing state policy, the influence of the big banks, failure to overcome the imbalance between the regions, the inadequacy of housing and municipal services in the expanded industrial zones, the inability to provide employment for the entire labor force without large-scale emigration, and the limited share of labor in the national income.[57]

Some of these criticisms obviously referred to major failings, while others simply lamented the normal facts of economic development. Major investment transfers from abroad are a standard feature of modern capitalist development, beginning most notably with the development of the United States itself. The large national banks did exert major influence but no more than in Belgium, and probably only slightly more than in France and West Germany. The three successive economic plans all expressed an intention to redistribute income; if the process was slow, it corresponded to the standard rhythm of such changes proportionate to the overall level of economic development. The Third Plan in 1973 made more of an effort than the earlier ones to invest in the backward provinces, yet little was accomplished there. As in nearly all countries, capital flowed to the major regions where it could obtain the best return, nor for that matter have the two different socialist models of the Soviet Union and Yugoslavia been very successful in altering the economic rank of the diverse regions of their own lands.

Other problems, however, stemmed directly from economic policy, for certain limitations were never overcome and new ones became accentuated. The system was never fully opened to the market, for a broad variety of price and exchange controls remained for specified activities, as well as a continuing fairly high degree of industrial regulation, trade protection, and artificial agricultural supports. The corruption that had been a major byproduct of autarchy may have diminished, but it nevertheless continued to be widespread. In most industries, the optimal scale of enterprise was not fully attained, making it difficult to achieve complete ra-

57. On the remaining pockets of poverty in Spain, see Demetrio Casado, *Introducción a la sociología de la pobreza* (Madrid, 1971) and *La pobreza en la estructura social de España* (Madrid, 1976).

tionalization, cost efficiency, and the most sophisticated application of technology. Despite the general transformation of agriculture, food production was increasingly specialized and was generally inadequate for Spanish needs, requiring perpetual large-scale imports. Though inflation was reduced in the 1960s, it was never eliminated and in later years was greatly stimulated by easy credit and other official policies. The Syndical Organization both restricted and overprotected workers, official regulations making it difficult to fire redundant employees for sloth, minor misdemeanors, inefficiency, or sheer redundancy, and this promoted featherbedding and discouraged more rapid advances in productivity. Nevertheless, the rapid growth in industrial employment (contrasted with the enormous shrinkage of the agricultural population) was never sufficient to provide full employment without major emigration of workers. When emigration began to decline, starting in 1973–74, the result was increasing unemployment. The notable efforts to expand further the scale and coverage of state welfare in the last years of the regime increased industrial costs and fueled inflation. Industrial investment remained dependent on cheap credit provided by state policy and the banking system, and to a lesser degree on foreign capital—factors that would be much more difficult to sustain after 1973. Several key industries, such as Basque metallurgy, began to age, failing to renovate their capital investment and technology. The INI had become a bloated white elephant by the end of the regime, for the attempted restructuring of the early 1970s turned out to be inadequate to convert many of the subsidized industries into going concerns. Though this was often the case with nationalized or state-supported industries around the world, such knowledge provided scant comfort.

Despite the statist economic pretensions of the regime during its first two decades, by its close the Spanish government's domination of economic resources was proportionately the least of any country in Europe. The limited reforms of 1957 and 1964 did not greatly alter the fact that the fiscal system remained highly regressive and ridden with loopholes. Even when social security and other welfare categories were added, the state budget in 1973 amounted to only about 21 percent of GNP. Regular taxes were equivalent to only 13.5 percent of GNP, compared with 15.6 percent in Japan and 22.5 percent in France, to contrast Spain with the two most lightly taxed of the major industrial countries. Approximately 44 percent of all Spanish taxes were indirect, a figure exceeded only marginally by France at 45 percent.[58]

Limited state income was a major factor in the failure to develop some aspects of public services. This was especially true in roads and transportation, and in the limitations of municipal services and of low-cost housing

58. Gunther, *Public Policy*, 59, 61.

to accommodate the massive shift of population to the cities. Such short-comings revealed a major gap in the development strategy, leaving Spanish urban centers relatively poorly cared for by general west European standards in the 1970s.

The Spanish economy was protected from the immediate effects of the international oil crisis of 1973 by government policy, which kept petroleum prices well below the European average. Spain then depended on petroleum for 69 percent of its energy, and scarcely 2 percent of that was produced domestically. The overriding goal was to sustain the general growth rate, which for 1974 was 5.4, slightly below target yet still a worthy achievement.[59] Yet the oil price rise greatly burdened the foreign exchange account and was a prime factor in increasing the inflation rate to 18 percent in 1974, beginning the steep new Spanish inflation that would reach even higher rates during the remainder of the decade.

By the time of Franco's death, the Spanish economy was faced with a major international recession, a sharp decline in foreign investment, and a drastic falloff in the growth rate. Some of the major industries such as metallurgy and shipbuilding proved unable to compete in the new environment, and the unemployment rate soared.[60]

Despite the broad transformation of Spanish social structure, severe economic inequalities remained between advanced and lagging regions and between the rich and the poor. Though much of the population was becoming more or less middle class, in 1970 the wealthiest 1.23 percent had a larger share of the total national income (22.39 percent) than did the lower 52.2 percent of the population (who had only 21.62 percent of the national income).[61] By the time of Franco's death, "the richest ten percent were nearly twice as rich as their opposite numbers in the United Kingdom."[62]

Yet these limitations did not obviate the achievements of the development itself. Most of the problems of the post-Franco era were recognizable as the common problems of west European industrial countries (even though more severe in the case of Spain) and were no longer those of the largely agrarian economy of the early twentieth century. The fact

59. The Third Development Plan spanned the last four years of the regime, 1972–75. It was presented in the *Tercer Plan de Desarrollo 1972–1975* (Madrid, 1971), and officially presented by López Rodó to the Cortes on March 14, 1972, in a speech subsequently published as *Nuevo horizonte del desarrollo* (Madrid, 1972). López Rodó replied to interpellation on January 22, 1973, when he presented his *Informe sobre el III Plan de Desarrollo Económico y Social* (Madrid, 1973). The *Memoria sobre la ejecución del III Plan de Desarrollo Año 1975* (Madrid, 1976) is an official report.

60. The first phase is treated in the Agrupación de Periodistas de Información Económica's *La economía española en crisis: Informe 1947–1975* (Madrid, 1975).

61. Antonio de Pablo Masa, "Estratificación y clases sociales en la España de hoy," in FOESSA, *Informe . . . 1975*, 758.

62. Carr and Fusi, *Spain*, 77.

remains that Spain during the third quarter of the century did better than any country in its development range, and acquired the resources that enabled the new regime of 1976–77 to cope with recession, survive the loss of most new foreign investments and most worker remittances, take back large numbers of emigrant workers, and still make adjustments that would enable it to compete and carry forward.

The Consequences of Development

During the 1960s diversion of political attention toward the rewards of economic expansion became a standard practice of the regime, accentuating a trend that had already begun in the previous decade. Given the enduring stability of the system, combined with further partial reforms and the new economic opportunities (compounded by the weakness, antiquated ideas, and division of the opposition), this tactic was at least temporarily successful.

What the regime leaders had not counted on was the profound social and cultural changes that accompanied development. Full employment and steady, unprecedented increases in income for nearly all social sectors created the first experience in mass consumerism in the life of Spain. The possibility of a new society oriented toward materialism and hedonism, never before remotely within reach of the bulk of the population, quickly became a reality. Rural and small-town society—in the north the sociogeographic backbone of the Movement during the Civil War—was progressively uprooted. Despite continuation of a steadily attenuated state censorship, foreign cultural influences entered Spain on a scale previously unimaginable. Mass tourism, combined with the movement of hundreds of thousands of Spaniards abroad and then home again, exposed much of society to styles and examples widely at variance with traditional culture but often most seductively attractive. This was accompanied by mounting bombardment from the contemporary media and mass advertising. The transformation of the cultural environment was absolutely without parallel.

The first victim of this transformation was not the regime but its primary cultural support, the traditional religion. A highly urban, sophisticated, materialist, nominally educated, and hedonistic Spain, increasingly attuned to the secular and consumerist life of western Europe, simply ceased to be Catholic in the traditional manner. Though the majority of Spaniards did not reject their religious identity, they no longer identified with the traditional values and practices of the religion per se. The Church in Spain was one of the branches of Catholicism most profoundly affected by the cultural and religious crisis stemming from Vatican II, which concluded in 1965, and the subsequent generational revolt of the clergy.

During the course of the 1960s, the regime found that it was less and less able to count on the Church, and by the end of that decade many of the clergy had become the primary public spokesmen for the opposition.

Though Franco was never seriously challenged as long as he lived, the surviving government administrators would find that by the time of his death, the kind of society and culture on which the regime had primarily been based had largely ceased to exist, and that would make it impossible for the regime to reproduce itself. Ultimately the economic and cultural achievements that took place under the regime, whether or not they were intended to develop as they did, deprived the regime of its reason for being.

20

Continuity and Reform
during the 1960s

The plateau achieved by the regime during the 1950s extended through its third decade, well into the 1960s. It had developed a system of essentially bureaucratic, politically almost unmobilized authoritarian government, and the success of the new economic policy along with the impotence of the opposition seemed to indicate that it had little to fear until the demise or incapacity of Franco. An elaborate ceremony in Burgos, site of the original investiture, celebrated the twenty-fifth anniversary of Franco's elevation to power on October 1, 1961. In an address to the National Council on the following day, Franco reaffirmed the doctrinal basis of his state in traditional principles:

> The great weakness of modern states lies in their lack of doctrinal content, in having renounced a firm concept of man, life, and history. The major error of liberalism is its negation of any permanent category of truth—its absolute and radical relativism—an error that, in a different form, was apparent in those other European currents [of Fascism and Nazism] that made "action" their only demand and the supreme norm of their conduct. . . . When the juridical order does not proceed from a system of principles, ideas, and values recognized as superior and prior to the state, it ends in an omnipotent juridical voluntarism, whether its primary organ be the so-called majority, purely numerical and inorganically expressed, or the supreme organs of power.

Only "organic democracy," in the terminology used by the regime since 1945, was based on firm institutions and principles, and its propagandists claimed for it the status of the only "true democracy."[2]

Yet as Franco neared the end of his seventh decade, intimations of mortality were increasing. His entourage was thrown into momentary con-

1. *Discursos y mensajes del Jefe del Estado 1960–1963* (Madrid, 1964), 320–21.
2. Quoted in Fernández, *Franco*, 9.

494

sternation when a faulty exhaust in the official limousine left both Franco and Doña Carmen sick and nauseous after returning from one of his customary provincial tours in January 1960. During the following year physicians first diagnosed symptoms of Parkinson's disease in Franco, an apparent sequela of infection from the great influenza epidemic of 1918–19. On December 24, 1961, he had the only notable hunting accident of his career, when a defective cartridge exploded in the barrel of his hunting rifle, shattering part of it and fracturing several bones in Franco's left hand and index finger. The injury was severe enough to make it difficult to hide it from the public. Though not life-threatening, it was painful and complicated, requiring an operation more than an hour long and months of recuperation. At first the hand failed to heal properly, making extensive rehabilitative therapy necessary,[3] and the recovery was never absolute, though Franco regained general use of the hand.

Though no public acknowledgement was made of the presence of Parkinson's disease until 1974, the fact became widely known at least a decade earlier. By the mid-1960s the symptoms were becoming evident in his personal appearance, marked by increasing rigidity and somewhat vacillating walk, facial inexpressiveness, weak and monotonous speech, and tremor in the hands. Though the effects of this condition could be controlled to some extent by medication, it tended to reduce his alertness and energy, both of which generally declined from the mid-1960s on.

In his later years, Franco's personal appearance became more gentle and even rather kindly. He normally appeared in conservative business suits and projected the image of a fragile, sometimes gentle grandfather—an appearance accentuated by his quiet, courteous manner. In the final phase of his life, this air of mild-mannered, benevolent patriarch presented an ironic contrast to the military style and fascistoid bombast of the early years of the regime.

The aging and decline of the Caudillo underscored the uncertainty of the political succession, for which the heirs of the royal family remained primary candidates. Franco never failed to speak of the royal family with relative respect, even in private. He declared Don Juan to be "an agreeable person," though always influenced by the last councillor to speak with him, and observed, "Don Juan is very pleasant and the fact that he is so weak and liberal is a great source of frustration for me."[4] Franco added that he did not want to have the Conde de Barcelona officially excluded from the succession, since there was always the possibility that he might change his position, but by 1960 Franco became increasingly confident

---

3. Ramón Soriano, *La mano izquierda de Franco* (Barcelona, 1981), is a moderately interesting memoir by the specialist in surgical therapy who attended Franco. It is notable mainly for its collection of the Caudillo's personal remarks about sundry subjects great and small.

4. Salgado-Araujo, *Conversaciones privadas*, 27–78, 308.

that the Conde would cede his rights to his son, Prince Juan Carlos. The Generalissimo continued to completely exclude Carlist candidates from consideration on the grounds that their direct line had ended and that the Carlists had no appropriate candidate who was Spanish and known to the Spanish public. He always emphasized his agreement with most Carlist doctrines but concluded that the regime had integrated them directly already.

On March 29, 1960, Franco had his third meeting with Don Juan at the Ruiseñada estate west of Madrid. The encounter was amicable but somewhat frustrating for both, since there could never be a true meeting of minds between Caudillo and Pretender. It was agreed that Juan Carlos, now twenty-two, would continue his studies in Spain, but considerable tension remained concerning his training and role. The press releases issued by the two principals after each returned home differed widely in political content. That of Don Juan treated the two essentially as equals and paid no lip service whatever to the regime as such. From that time on, Franco began to lose any lingering hope of a full accommodation with Don Juan and turned his attention more and more to his son.

The prince had lived under Franco's aegis for more than a decade and in addition to his university studies had received training in all three branches of the armed forces. His tutors were changed in 1960. Martínez Campos was replaced as principal counsellor by General Castañón, and the scholar-priest Federico Suárez Verdaguer (a *numerario* of Opus Dei) became religious counsellor and confessor. One of the shrewdest of the new generation of regime bureaucrats and politicians, the Asturian law professor Torcuato Fernández Miranda, was placed in charge of coordinating his further studies and administrative visits to learn more of the functioning of various branches of the government. Miranda was a veteran theorist of "organic democracy" as it had evolved under the regime[5] and the author of several political textbooks. He was a staunch formal defender of orthodoxy, later writing that "the 'Succession' must be continuity. . . . The King . . . must be the incarnation of the historico-national legitimacy which the Spanish state created by the eighteenth of July incarnates."[6] In fact, the rhetorically sinuous Miranda, with his sharp wizard's face, was one of the wiliest figures in the regime, fully cognizant of its manifold shifts of emphasis. He was alert to the opportunity that Juan Carlos represented and tried not only to indoctrinate him but also to provide a broader political education within the framework of the regime's evolution. The relationship thus begun between the two in the early 1960s would become decisive for the future of Spain after Franco's death. Meanwhile, in recognition of Juan Carlos's status and growing maturity,

5. Cf. his principal work of this period, *El hombre y la sociedad* (Madrid, 1960).
6. *Arriba,* Nov. 29, 1966.

the reconstructed Palacio de la Zarzuela was given to him in November 1961 as his official princely residence.

During this period, Juan Carlos met and won the hand of Princess Sofía, daughter of Queen Frederica of Greece. The bright and winsome young royal couple were married with appropriate circumstance in Athens in May 1962. Juan Carlos, whose path would continue to be difficult, was fortunate in his bride and and future queen. She was intelligent and discreet, adjusted well to the Spanish ambiance, and managed to impress Franco himself favorably. Princess Sofía was a steadying influence and a reliable source of support for Juan Carlos in the "long march toward the monarchy" that still lay ahead. Three children were born to them during the next years, first two daughters and then the desired son and heir, Prince Felipe, a handsome blonde boy of precocious presence and unusual athletic skill.[7]

Franco was generally quite pleased with Juan Carlos and seemed convinced that his ploy was working. Snide comments in Madrid society that the Prince's smiling good nature and shy manner bespoke naiveté and limited intelligence failed to impress him for he knew better. When asked his reaction to one of the personal visits of Juan Carlos, he replied: "Magnificent, and of course the rumor circulated by his enemies that he is not bright is unfounded. Not at all, since he is a lad who talks very well and thinks for himself and not just what he may hear from his friends or followers. I do not believe that he is dominated by his father in political affairs."[8] Even so, the Caudillo showed no inclination to recognize Juan Carlos or anyone else as his successor.

Slow Recrudescence of the Opposition

Having reached a low point in the 1950s, the domestic opposition became more active by 1960 and slowly but steadily expanded during the following decade. For the first time in some years, the number of arrests began to rise, though the change was not dramatic, and the tendency was for prosecution to become increasingly lenient. Alonso Vega, the minister of the interior, lacked the intelligence and dexterity of his predecessor, Blas Pérez, but he was a disciplinarian who ran a tight ship. His standing with Franco was high, a situation that was reinforced by the relative popularity of his wife Ramona within the family circle. He also tried to expand the network of police information and informers, though this was limited by Franco, who doubted the need to spend large amounts of money on such

7. Fernando González-Doria, *Juan Carlos y Sofía* (Madrid, 1962), was the principal contemporary account. Pilar R. Ferrer, *La familia real española* (Madrid, 1976), is a large, ornate illustrated volume that describes aspects of the life of the Spanish royal family, mainly in the 1960s and early 70s.

8. Salgado-Araujo, *Conversaciones privadas*, 369.

Lt. General Camilo Alonso Vega (Minister of the Interior) and Carrero Blanco during a cabinet meeting at Franco's summer home, August 18, 1967

activities. Franco considered the eight or more secret service and information agencies already attached to various state institutions adequate, though much duplication was involved and most were superficial.[9]

A series of incidents occurred in Catalonia and the Basque country during 1960 that reflected a regrowth of regionalist sentiment, while a new clandestine group that called itself DRIL (Directorio Revolucionario Ibérico de Liberación) set off a number of explosions in Madrid. This may have been only a dying gasp of the old anarchist resistance, but the

9. The Dirección General de Seguridad maintained a regular Servicio de Investigación, while information was also collected by its Brigada de Investigación Social. Other *servicios de investigación* were maintained by the presidency of the government, by the Guardia Civil, and languidly by the Confederación de Ex-combatientes. Separate ones also existed in each of the three armed forces, where they were normally known as the "segunda Bis" and, in the case of the Army, organized at the level of the ministry, captaincies general, and each regimental office. A central Servicio de Información del Ejército (SIE) was also maintained by the Alto Estado Mayor. Cf. Jesus Ynfante [pseud.], *El Ejército de Franco y de Juan Carlos* (Paris, 1976), 24–31.

expanding industrial labor force showed increasing signs of militance. A major strike wave began in Asturias during April 1962 and in the following month expanded, spreading through the Basque provinces and the Barcelona region.[10] A new style of labor opposition was taking form in the clandestine *comisiones obreras* (worker commissions) being organized by Communists and dissident Catholic social activists, sometimes jointly. The first fully developed commission was formed in an Asturian mine in 1958, and by 1962 such groups were beginning to appear in other parts of the industrial north.[11] The commissions were not intended to be organized trade unions but ad hoc factory committees to serve as representatives chosen directly by informal groups of workers themselves. In coming years they would coexist with and in some cases overlap with the official Syndical Organization, in which Communist activists energetically participated at the lowest level.

Though a "state of exception" was declared in three industrial provinces in May, 1962, the government's response was the softest ever taken toward strikers to that date. Leaders of the Syndical Organization were hearing more frequent demands for "authentic unions" and had themselves proposed several reforms that were blocked in part by Fernández Cuesta and the old guard in the Movement. In an unprecedented step, Solís Ruiz, head of the Syndical Organization, went to the industrial centers to talk to leaders of some of the strikers. A number of workers were either arrested or fired but not as many as in previous strikes, and the special powers of repression reenacted by decree two years earlier were for the most part not used. A new law of July 1962 provided for worker representatives in the councils of industrial plants and for management representatives on workers' syndical committees,[12] while a big jump in the minimum wage was enacted the following month. At the same time, the next northern strike wave during the following year was repressed somewhat more rigorously.

A new opposition front began to emerge from what would have seemed one of the least likely groups, the clergy. The massive generational shift within the Spanish clergy during the preceding two decades that produced an influx of new young priests reconstituted the priesthood with younger clergymen who were particularly susceptible to the new currents of liberalization coming from abroad and from the international Roman

10. See the summary in Biescas and Tuñón de Lara, *España*, 339–44.

11. The historical development of comisiones obreras and other opposition labor groups in the later years of the regime is narrated in F. Almendros Morcillo et al., *El sindicalismo de clase en España (1939–1977)* (Barcelona, 1978).

12. Nominal changes in the Syndical Organization through 1965 are included in Carlos Iglesias Selgas, *Los sindicatos en España* (Madrid, 1965). Fred Witner, *Labor Policy and Practices in Spain* (New York, 1965), presents an analysis of the way labor relations really functioned during the early 1960s.

Catholic Church. This was particularly the case among the younger clergy in the Basque provinces and Catalonia, strongly identified with their regions, and with lay activists of Catholic Action determined to carry out initiatives among industrial workers that were often more politico-economic than spiritual in intent.

The beginning of clerical oppositionism may be formally dated from the letter of May 30, 1960, signed by 339 Basque priests to protest the absence of freedom and self-determination among the Basque clergy and in the Basque provinces generally. Even the conservative Cardinal Primate Pla y Deniel, though disapproving of the latter initiative, dispatched a very strong letter to Solís Ruiz on November 15, 1960, protesting the repression of the Hermandades Obreras de Acción Católica (HOAC; Worker Brotherhoods of Catholic Action) and demanding full freedom for their activities.[13] When Pope John XXIII issued a strong encyclical urging more progressive social policies (*Mater et magistra*) Franco did his best to finesse the situation by responding, when asked about it: "We welcomed it joyfully because we had been leading up to it for twenty years."[14] By the time of the 1962 labor disturbances, the Catholic organ *Ecclesia* publicly defended the right to strike, while in September, 102 intellectuals, writers, and artists signed a protest against the force used to repress industrial stoppages.

Nonetheless, the only notable gesture of organized political opposition during the first half of the decade was what the regime's propagandists called the *contubernio de Munich* (cohabitation or mesalliance of Munich), in which a sizable number of moderates representing both internal and external opposition groups met in the Bavarian capital from June 5 to 8, 1962. This represented an effort by diverse opposition elements to demonstrate that the Civil War was indeed over and that both moderate left and moderate right could meet together, with 80 of the 118 signatories of the final document, led by Gil Robles and Ridruejo, coming from within Spain. The meeting occurred four months after Spain's first petition to enter the European Common Market, which was likely to be rejected for political reasons, and it was thus designed to dramatize the fact that only different leadership and a democratic system could bring Spain into the new international community. The participants by no means agreed among themselves, for the veteran Salvador de Madariaga and other emigrés sought some sort of international pressure against the regime, a tactic not supported by representatives of the internal opposition. They all signed an agreement on the internal changes needed in Spain before it could ex-

13. The Church saw to it that this letter was widely circulated, portions of it appearing in the *New York Times*, Jan. 1, 1961. On the development of Catholic worker opposition, see Juan Domínguez, *Organizaciones obreras cristianas en la oposición al franquismo (1951–1975)* (Bilbao, 1985).

14. Angelo del Boca, *L'Altra Spagna* (Milan, 1961), 146, in Trythall, *Caudillo*, 233.

pect to make a successful application to enter the Common Market. This action was not necessary to freeze the eventual response to the Spanish petition, but it obviously did not help, and subversion of Spain's international relations thus became the technical basis for the action taken against members of the internal opposition on their return. On June 8, article 14 of the Fuero de los Españoles (concerning freedom of residence) was suspended for two years and returning participants were temporarily confined in the Canaries. Given the currently cooperative relations between the royal family and regime, Don Juan disavowed the liberal monarchists who had participated.[15] The whole affair gained greater notoriety than it otherwise would have through the shrill denunciations of the participants that were broadsided for several days throughout the regime's press. It drew considerable notice abroad, so that *Time* magazine began an article of June 22 on Spain with the injunction "The end of the Franco era is near."

The next few years were in fact quiet ones, the most notable event of 1963 being the execution on April 20 of the clandestine Communist leader Julián Grimau for alleged crimes involving torture and murder committed as a Republican police officer during the Civil War. ("Ordinary" Civil War political crimes were covered by amnesty, but not "major" offenses or *delitos de sangre*.) A Communist central committeeman, Grimau had been apprehended after he reentered Spain, and his execution became an international cause célèbre, even the Queen of England joining those who attempted to intercede. Despite the adverse publicity abroad, Franco was implacable in such cases.

This affair nonetheless helped to produce one change, coming as it did on the heels of an investigation by the International Commission of Jurists. The results of the investigation were published late in 1962 as *The Rule of Law in Spain*, and severely criticized limitations on civil rights, particularly the continued authority of military courts as distinct from standard civil courts.[16] The Council of Ministers first discussed the desirability of terminating military jurisdiction in December 1962. One year later, on December 2, 1963, a new law established a Tribunal of Public Order, composed of civil judges, to deal with most categories of nominal political subversion or political crime. Its work replaced most of what had previously been done by courts-martial and the Special Tribunal for Re-

15. The best account is in Tusell, *La oposición democrática,* 388–420. The principal groups participating in the Munich meeting were the liberal monarchists of a group called Unión Española, Gil Robles's Democracia Social Cristiana, Dionisio Ridruejo's minuscule Acción Democrática, the Basque nationalists (PNV), the Socialist Party, surviving Left Republicans, the most liberal wing of Acción Católica, and the small left-wing Catholic Frente de Liberación Popular. As a result of the assembly Gil Robles, who had been included once more in Don Juan's Consejo Privado, was dropped again.

16. The government's reply appeared as *España, Estado de Derecho (Réplica a un Informe de la Comisión Internacional de Juristas)* (Madrid, 1964).

Table 20.1. Crimes Most Frequently
Prosecuted before the Tribunal
of Public Order, 1964–76

Category	No. of Cases
Illegal propaganda	2,269
Illicit association	1,193
Public disorder	1,004
Illegal possession of arms	843
Illegal demonstration	691
Defaming the chief of state	478
Terrorism	235
Illegal meeting	93
Clandestine publication	87
Personal	45

Source: Compilation by Miguel Cid in Diario 16,
Historia de la transición, 126.

Table 20.2. Sentences of the Tribunal of Public Order,
1964–76

Year	Acquittals	Convictions	Total
1964	30	98	128
1965	39	74	113
1966	37	108	145
1967	42	114	156
1968	53	168	221
1969	108	247	355
1970	80	236	316
1971	78	254	332
1972	77	248	325
1973	119	387	506
1974	126	441	567
1975	164	363	527
1976	31	170	201
	984	2,908	3,892

Source: Compilation by Miguel Cid in Diario 16, *Historia de la
transición,* 126.

pression of Masonry and Communism that had operated since 1940.
Though military courts still held jurisdiction over certain categories,[17] the
years 1964–68 were the only period in the history of the regime partially

17. Even during the heyday of the new civil tribunal, the following numbers of civilians
were convicted by military courts, according to the statistics of the Alto Estado Mayor: 312
in 1963, 372 in 1964, 329 in 1965, 322 in 1966, 232 in 1967, and 254 in 1968. Ballbé, *Orden
público,* 427.

free of political prosecution by military courts. (Later, in 1968, jurisdiction over violent political crimes was returned to *tribunales de guerra.*)

The Reforms of the 1960s

At the height of the industrial strikes in May 1962 Franco addressed a large outdoor rally of former Alféreces provisionales, and aware of their criticism of the regime's new leniency, preempted it with a hard-line speech pledging to maintain undiminished the principles and institutions for which they had fought. He had come to support the new economic orientation, however, and had no interest in attempting to reimpose a harsh line as in earlier times. When after the Munich affair he decided on a partial renovation of the cabinet, the direction chosen was that of a further *apertura* or opening, though always along carefully controlled lines that would hold the monarchists at bay.

Foremost among the changes in the partially new government of July 10, 1962, was the appointment for the first time of a vice-president of government and lieutenant to Franco himself in the person of the veteran Muñoz Grandes, who retained his post as head of the Alto Estado Mayor. Most of the key ministers remained, the economic leadership being reinforced when the young former naval engineer Gregorio López Bravo, another member of Opus Dei, replaced Planell, the elderly army officer and old autarchist, as minister of industry. It gained further support by the appointment of two other newcomers who were considered *afectos* (friends or associates) of the Opus Dei ministers: Manuel Lora Tamayo, a member of Catholic Action, as minister of education, and Jesús Romeo Gorría as minister of labor (the latter a Falangist camisa vieja but one who had made his career as an elite jurist of the Council of State). The best-known Falangist in the preceding government, Arrese, had resigned as minister of housing in 1960 after failing to gain a desired budget increase.[18] The army and navy ministers were once more replaced, but the most notable change was the dropping of Arias Salgado in Information and Tourism and Sanz Orrio in Labor after both had spent twenty years in high government posts.

Arias Salgado was in poor health, and had been the target of criticism even from within the regime for the continuing rigidity of the censorship and the heavy-handedness of much of the regime's press. On November 1960 a petition was signed by many leading Spanish writers and intellectuals—including even a veteran cultural luminary of the regime like Pemán—asking for more careful regulation of the censorship, along with juridical guarantees and public identification of responsible censors. For

18. Arrese's public stand was given in his *Política de vivienda* (Madrid, 1960).

Franco presiding over a meeting of his cabinet ministers at the Palacio de Pedralbes in Barcelona, 1963. On his right, Carrero Blanco; on his left, Muñoz Grandes.

several years Church hierarchs had also been demanding greater freedom and flexibility in information, and this had involved the ultra-Catholic minister of information in an embarrassing polemic with the bishop of Málaga, Herrera Oria. And finally, the minister had handled the Munich affair clumsily, conducting a hyperbolic and counterproductive propaganda campaign against the participants, further alienating opinion abroad and even implicating Don Juan, who had supported the regime throughout. Arias had thus won the enmity at one and the same time of European liberals, the monarchists, and the Church hierarchy, and Franco somewhat reluctantly let him go.[19]

The new minister of information and tourism was the forty-year-old Manuel Fraga Iribarne, holder of the most impressive credentials of any younger official of the regime and a product of what its publicists liked to call the "bureaucracy of competence." An outstanding student and youthful winner of a chair of political science, Fraga had already occupied a wide variety of university and government administrative positions and had had limited experience abroad with UNESCO. He had been identi-

19. A year earlier, in July 1961, Franco had observed: "Arias Salgado is not energetic and because of his softheartedness does not ask very much of his subordinates, but he is very loyal and I am quite fond of him." Salgado-Araujo, *Conversaciones privadas*, 339.

fied with the reformists of the Movement but had carefully dissociated himself from the antiregime positions of such figures as Laín, Tovar, and Ruiz Giménez. Extraordinarily energetic and concerned to bring the regime abreast of new currents in society and culture, Fraga soon became known at home and abroad as a reformer who would encourage further transformation of the system.

The new cabinet, which with minor changes would last for seven years, harbored two different somewhat fluid and overlapping sets of rivalries. One was between the technocrat-monarchists, supported and to some degree led by Carrero Blanco, and the so-called Regentialists (or at least lukewarm monarchists), to some extent led by Muñoz Grandes and including Solís Ruiz and the new navy minister, Pedro Nieto Antúnez, a former naval aide of the Caudillo. Fraga, though basically a supporter of the monarchist succession, tended to be allied with the Regentialists. The second rivalry was between reformists and those who wished to avoid major internal political change while concentrating on economic development. The reformists were led by Castiella, the foreign minister, Fraga, and Solís (though the three did not necessarily agree among themselves as to the character and content of reform) and were "frequently aided by Romeo Gorría and occasionally by López Bravo."[20] They also drew some support from Muñoz Grandes and Nieto Antúnez, while Iturmendi (Justice) and Navarro Rubio (Finance) fluctuated. For the most part on the other side were Carrero Blanco, Alonso Vega, Vigón (Public Works), and to a lesser degree Martín Alonso (Army), who were more concerned with the succession than with internal reform. That was also the position of López Rodó, though he did not oppose all the goals of the reformists.

The role of Muñoz Grandes was a limited one, basically that of watchdog and guarantee of Franco, and a check on the more ardent monarchists. Had Franco suddenly died at any point in the following five years, Muñoz Grandes would at least temporarily have been his successor, with some opportunity to try to undo the working of the Law of Succession, should he have chosen. From Franco's point of view, he played his role the more effectively because of his very lack of a broader constituency. Fraga Iribarne admired the crusty old general and urged him to become more active:

> I always had great respect for his deep humanity, disinterestedness, and feeling for the people. He suffered from ill health, which greatly limited his action, and he put up little struggle to make his vice-presidency more effective. He did not install himself in Castellana 3 [the address of the presidency and vice-presidency, the Spanish equivalent of 10 Downing Street] but continued in his military headquarters at the Alto Estado Mayor, receiving political visits beside a model of a machine gun. I tried to get him to take on a Secretario General

20. Manuel Fraga Iribarne, *Memoria breve de una vida pública*, 41.

506   IV. Developmentalism and Decay, 1959–1975

Técnico and gave him a long list of names, beginning with Federico Silva Muñoz [an abogado del Estado and professor of political economy who was a leading figure of the ACNP and became minister of public works in 1965]. He completely refused, and the strings of power became concentrated in the hands of Carrero Blanco.[21]

Carrero was aligned with the technocrats, who did not seek immediate reform as much as a kind of technocratic depoliticizing of the system. Spain's political future would be assured not by reformist or quasi-Falangist ploys but through the full institutionalizing of the monarchy. They sought to guarantee the succession by having Juan Carlos recognized as heir while Franco still lived, meanwhile striving more and more to dismantle the Movement. The result would be a progressive, modern, and rationalized authoritarian structure guided by technocracy and crowned with monarchy. López Rodó, the economic commissar of the plan and key figure among the technocrats, has been described with little exaggeration as seeking a '"symbiosis between Catholic values, an authoritarian political system, and the American way of life."[22]

The reformists were somewhat more skeptical about the institution of monarchy, and sought to introduce direct political reform in the existing system that would enable it to gain strength, evolve with the times, and survive into the future. They stressed that economic development must be accompanied by new political development, not mere political demobilization. This would involve reform of the Syndical Organization to achieve greater representation, flexibility, and responsiveness, and a reorganization of the Movement to allow it to incorporate new political tendencies involving broader participation of the people. All this was to be accompanied by further social reforms to raise living standards and balance the disequilibria created by rapid industrial expansion.

These complex rivalries in the new government had little to do with the classic political "families" of the regime in earlier years. The original sectors of old-guard Falangists, Carlists, doctrinaire monarchists, semiauthoritarian traditionalist Catholics, and right-wing generals had mostly fallen by the political wayside. The various institutions of the regime were still full of survivors from all these groups, but they were rarely any longer at the top, for their ideologies no longer represented options for an increasingly industrialized country in the social democratic western Europe of the 1960s.

The new government of 1962 quickly introduced a certain change in public style. The new ministers emphasized personal contact with highly diverse groups and segments of society. Unlike their predecessors, they were increasingly on the move, traveling through Spain and even abroad,

21. Ibid., 43.
22. Raymond Carr, *Spain 1808–1975* (Oxford, 1982), 756.

speaking at length to the press, and participating in a constant round of lunches, dinners, and other public forums large and small.

The initial champion of reform had been the affable and oily glad-handing Solís Ruiz, "the smile of the regime." After replacing Arrese in 1957 he had dropped Arrese's talk of institutionalizing the existing Move-ment in favor of broadening it to include "the full incorporation of the ac-tivities of the people."[23] Within the Movement itself he had organized a new National Delegation of Associations to try to generate new organs of association or limited representation within the existing system and to at-tract new members to the Movement. Such ploys might lend at least mod-est substance to the regime's prating of "organic democracy" and give the impression that the Spanish system was approximating those of contem-porary western states.

The disturbances of 1962 encouraged Solís to proceed with limited re-forms in the Syndical Organization. An amendment to the penal code in September 1962 freed labor actions "for nonpolitical ends" from prosecu-tion, though at no time would the regime ever legalize strikes as such. According to the Syndical Organization, the following number of labor ac-tions took place without prosecution during the next five years:[24]

1963	777
1964	484
1965	232
1966	179
1967	567

In preparation for the next local syndical elections in 1963, workers were in some cases allowed to hold meetings entirely on their own in syndical offices, and in the following year for the first time separate commissions representing workers and employers were formed within the syndicates to negotiate wages and working conditions.[25] Yet so many oppositionists were elected that in a later series of crackdowns and combouts, between 1963 and 1966, about 1,800 low-level syndical officeholders would be fired from their factory jobs.[26] Similarly, all strike actions deemed political were still repressed in varying degrees by the authorities.[27]

23. Jose Solís Ruiz, *Nueva convivencia política* (Madrid, 1960), 13–39.

24. Report of the General Secretariat of the Syndical Organization at the Fourth Syndical Congress in Tarragona in 1968, cited in George Hills, *Spain* (New York, 1970), 347.

25. Iglesias Selgas, *Los sindicatos*, 49–50, 125–30. The new image sought for the Syn-dical Organization was reflected in the official *Eficacia sindical y sindicalismo* (Madrid, 1967). The formal version of agrarian syndicalism in this phase was given by Francisco López Santamaría, *Sindicalismo agrario español* (Madrid, 1960).

26. According to a paper by José Ma. Maravall, "The Evolution of Industrial Conflict in Spain, 1939–1975," at the Conference on Contemporary International Labor Problems, University of Wisconsin–Madison, Dec. 1–2, 1977.

27. On the labor disputes of the 1960s in general, see Maravall, *Dictatorship and Politi-*

The pace of reform remained slow and was not accelerated by two bombs which exploded in Madrid police and syndical headquarters on July 29, 1963, causing many injuries. Some of the sympathetic interest in Fraga Iribarne as a younger, more liberal minister of information disappeared during the course of 1963, particularly after his hostile rejection of a letter signed on September 30 by many leading writers and intellectuals asking for an investigation of the alleged torture of miners during recent strikes. Fraga did, however, permit the founding of a new critical journal by Catholic progressives called *Cuadernos para el Diálogo (Notebooks for Dialog)*, which came to play a crucial role in the development of opinion during the decade that followed.

On April 1, 1964, there began a major propaganda campaign in honor of the "twenty-five years of peace," marking the quarter-century since the end of the Civil War.[28] A major celebration was held in the Valle de los Caídos, while Franco dispensed another general pardon for certain minor categories of those under sentence for political crimes. The new color documentary film *Franco, ese hombre*, directed by José Luis Sáenz de Heredia, turned out to be the most effective celluloid celebration of the Caudillo and something of a hit in Spanish movie houses when it came out in the winter of 1964–65. With the economy growing rapidly, the regime seemed stronger than ever and ready to continue for many years.

Nevertheless, the relatively hostile attitude of the Common Market caused discomfort, providing further incentive for the regime to make renewed efforts to give its authoritarian "organic democracy" greater credibility in western Europe. It had always been standard for Franco to drop remarks about the evolution and "perfection" of the system, and by 1964 *dialogue* had become a fashionable word in the government's public relations. For the first time in the short history of Spanish television, several ministers appeared before controlled question-and-answer programs. Fraga's administration of the censorship was somewhat more moderate and in certain respects distinctly more rational than that of his predecessor.

The question of further institutional reform and redefinition had been in the air for years, since the Arrese project of 1956. With the further increase in Carrero Blanco's influence following the cabinet change of 1957, Carrero and the technocrats had proposed that a new Fundamental

---

cal Dissent: Workers and Students in Franco's Spain (New York, 1978); Jacques Georgel, *Le franquisme* (Paris, 1970), 136–71; and, for a chronicle of dissidence in the middle and late sixties, Angel Ruiz Ayúcar, *Crónica agitada de ocho años tranquilos* (Madrid, 1974), and F. Jáuregui and P. Vega, *Crónica del antifranquismo* (Barcelona, 1984), vol. 2, which covers 1963 to 1970.

28. In addition to a series of laudatory works on the regime's achievements bearing the title of the anniversary, a series of new idealized handbooks on political structure were published during the following year, including *Evolución política* (1965), *Permanencia y renovación del sistema político* (1965), *La administración y el público en España* (1965), and, for the local level, the *Manual de representantes familiares en la administración local* (1964).

Law on the Monarchy follow the redefinition of the Principles of the Movement, which would further define the powers and structure of the monarchist succession. Franco had apparently vetoed that in 1958, though he continued to agree to the possibility of a new Organic Law of the State that might recodify certain aspects of government structure. In May 1958 López Rodó and several colleagues prepared the first draft of a new Organic Law, while also beginning work on a sketch of a new Organic Law of the Movement to replace the abortive Arrese legislation. In March 1959 Carrero Blanco presented revised drafts to Franco, who reacted negatively and froze both projects.[29] The new government of 1962, with its relative reformist orientation, soon showed interest in developing new proposals. During 1963 both Solís Ruiz and Fraga presented separate sketches of new plans, that of the latter being more complete and complex, consisting of a 105-article "Borrador para un Anteproyecto de Constitución del Estado español."[30] The Generalissimo, however, remained skeptical about any major institutional redefinition, even though he did not reject it in theory.

During 1964 Solís Ruiz made increasing use of the phrase "political development,"[31] and that summer the Movement's National Delegation of Associations moved ahead with a vague project concerning the *hermandades* ("brotherhoods" of political orientation) first proposed in the Arrese projects of 1956, and began to sketch drafts for the introduction of some sort of "political associations" within the Movement. Such associations were not to be political parties but simply expressions of several diverse elements in the Movement. They would remain under the control of its National Council and make the Movement more pluralistic and representative while expanding its role within the system. Solís thus obtained approval from the National Council to prepare means by which "the Movement [would] promote the associative process within its institutional framework . . . pluralizing . . . if possible the means for a constant fulfillment of the Fundamental Principles."[32]

Four different groups in the cabinet concurrently prepared their own reformist proposals. While Solís and Fraga worked on separate plans, the foreign minister Castiella had his own pet reform and in September 1964 presented to the cabinet a proposed draft for a new law of religious toleration which he deemed highly advantageous to the regime's foreign relations. Meanwhile, López Rodó and his allies further revised their original sketch for a general new Organic Law which Carrero Blanco handed to Franco on November 25, 1964.[33]

---

29. *FF*, 7:70–71, 95–96.
30. López Rodó, *Larga marcha*, 208.
31. Cf. Jesús Fueyo Alvarez, *Desarrollo político y orden constitucional* (Madrid, 1964).
32. José Solís Ruiz, *España: Su Monarquía y el futuro* (Madrid, 1975), 300.
33. López Rodó, *Larga marcha*, 224.

The Caudillo remained skeptical, fearing innovations that might restrict the government's authority or open a dangerous Pandora's box of political novelties. Even though the draft of the proposed new law of associations within the Movement carefully avoided any appearance of introducing real political parties, to Franco it smacked of that danger and he ordered it withdrawn. Franco still attracted large crowds, however artfully assembled, and loud applause on his visits to provincial centers. As Fraga put it: "Franco continues to enjoy popular appeal and loud ovations on every hand. This is his main argument whenever we talk to him of changes. And, in fact, popular applause that summer [of 1964] made him grow colder toward the notion of accepting certain reforms."[34] Nonetheless he began to yield in principle on two points, and his annual end-of-the-year address mentioned the preparation of a new Organic Law of the State and the prospect of greater religious toleration.

The tug-of-war within the government continued during 1965. On January 15 Franco's closest associate in the cabinet, Alonso Vega, told him that Spanish opinion was worried about the future and that the top priority should be to complete the institutionalization and succession of the regime, with a younger president of government appointed in place of the aging Caudillo.[35] The only notable new opposition activity appeared in the major universities, where there was a steady rise in tension that began with a large demonstration at the University of Madrid demanding more freedom and final abolition of the SEU. Incremental liberalization continued slowly, producing the first interpellation of a minister by the Cortes in the history of the regime on April 27.[36]

Within the cabinet, however, the reformist ministers encountered steady resistance from Franco. The most heated debate took place on April 2, with Fraga Iribarne speaking vehemently on the need for new legislation. López Rodó has written that this session included "moments of great tension. At one point Franco said, 'Do you think that I don't realize that, do you think that I am a circus clown?' The debate lasted an hour and a half, but most of the time Franco simply listened smiling to the opinions of the ministers."[37]

The Generalissimo carried out another partial cabinet reorganization on July 7. Six ministers were replaced, and López Rodó, who already attended meetings, gained official cabinet rank as minister without portfolio in charge of the Commissariat of the Plan of Development (he had held that for three years). More than Castiella, Fraga, or Solís, López Rodó

34. Fraga, *Memoria breve*, 115.
35. López Rodó, *Larga marcha*, 225.
36. The target was the relatively incompetent minister of agriculture, Cirilo Cánovas García, eight years in office. As a professional agrarian engineer, he actually had better technical credentials than most of his predecessors.
37. López Rodó, *Larga marcha*, 229–30. Fraga published part of his rationale for reform in his *Horizonte español* (Madrid, 1965).

had already become the key member of the government,[38] hailed as the inspiration of the current economic boom. He was forty-five years old and an avid tennis player, and cut a trim figure of exclusively gray tones—hair, suits, socks, and neckties. López Rodó was much execrated by the opposition and old-guard Falangists as the evil genius of the materialistic new style of technocratic-bureaucratic authoritarianism that now seemed destined to continue far into the future.

This time the military ministers remained, but Navarro Rubio and Ullastres were replaced in Finance and Commerce by two new professionals, Juan José Espinosa San Martín and Faustino García Moncó. Federico Silva Muñoz, later lauded as *el ministro eficacia* ("Mr. Efficiency"), followed Vigón in Public Works and Adolfo Díaz Ambrona Moreno took over the controversial post of Agriculture. Antonio Ma. Oriol replaced Iturmendi as the *carlista de turno* in Justice, while the latter became president of the Cortes. This reshuffling balanced right-wing Catholics from the ACNP like Silva and a Carlist such as Oriol against those associated with Opus Dei, and the remaining quasi-Falangists like Fraga and Solís against regime monarchists. Though none knew it at the time, this would be the last of the classic cabinet balancing acts of Franco.

During the following month Fraga Iribarne scored the first triumph of the new cabinet, gaining approval of his new press law over the objections of Carrero Blanco and Alonso Vega. He has recorded Franco as conceding reluctantly: "I do not believe in this [new] liberty, but it is a step required for many important reasons. And furthermore I think that if those weak governments at the beginning of the century could govern with a free press, amid that anarchy, we will also be able to get along."[39] After further polishing, the final version was approved by the government in October and subsequently sent on to the Cortes, which eventually ratified it on March 15, 1966. Two weeks later prior censorship formally ended. The argument behind this reform was that contemporary Spain had become much more literate, cultured, and politically united than its predecessor a generation earlier, and that Serrano's old legislation was no longer appropriate. Censorship would henceforth be "voluntary," and no official guidelines would be imposed (though many informal ones would be laid down). Publishing enterprises would also be free to name their own directors rather than having to gain ministerial approval as before. A variety of sanctions, such as stiff fines, suspension, confiscation, or even arrest, could still be imposed on those publishing material damaging to the state, religion, or general mores, and any editor in doubt was invited to submit preliminary material for consultation.[40]

38. Some of his speeches and writings of these years are collected in his *Política y desarrollo* (Madrid, 1970).

39. Fraga, *Memoria breve*, 145.

40. For further discussion of the press law and its effects, see Ebba Lorenzen, *Presse*

This certainly did not establish freedom of the press, but it considerably eased the restrictions and boundaries on what might be published and opened the way for general liberalization and expansion. Newspaper circulation increased from less than 500,000 in 1945 to 2,500,000 in 1967, and the 420 publishing firms of 1940 had grown to 915 by 1971. In 1970 Spain published 19,717 titles, the fifth highest total in world, amounting to more than 170 million books.[41]

Fraga's notoriety rivaled that of López Rodó. In constant motion and generating new publicity on every hand, he was associated with new glamour projects in the massive expansion of the tourist industry, while the passage of the press law made him appear the focus of reformism. Fraga also tried to foster the first relatively scholarly study inside Spain of the Civil War by appointing a special study section within his ministry headed by Ricardo de la Cierva, who began to produce a stream of major new publications, less partisan than anything yet published under the regime. Publishers and writers sometimes privately criticized Fraga when they felt the force of those censorship sanctions that remained, but they soon adjusted to the new terms and used their partial freedom to expand greatly the discussion of certain kinds of issues. Franco himself regarded Fraga with some uncertainty, apprehensive that his reformism might go too far, while Carrero Blanco saw him as a distinct danger and determined to cut him down.[42]

Routine political infighting continued, as was Franco's wish. The primary duel was that between his two principal surrogates, Carrero Blanco as minister subsecretary of the presidency and Muñoz Grandes as vice-president of the government. It was an unequal contest, given Muñoz Grandes's severely declining health and incapacity for effective intrigue. On January 20, 1966, during one of his regular daily sessions with Franco, Carrero tried to convince the Caudillo that Muñoz Grandes must be relieved of his post as head of the Alto Estado Mayor as soon as he reached the mandatory age to pass to reserve status, coming very soon.[43] His pri-

unter Franco (Munich, 1978), 261–304; Javier Terrón Montero, La prensa en España durante el régimen de Franco (Madrid, 1981), 135–288; Gonzalo Dueñas, La Ley de Prensa de Manuel Fraga (Paris, 1969); and Manuel Fernández Areal, La libertad de prensa en España (1938–1971) (Madrid, 1971), 67–234. The effect of the new regulations on radio and television is discussed in García Jiménez, Radiotelevisión y política cultural, 485–97.

41. Fernando Cendán Pazos, Edición y comercio del libro español (1900–1972) (Madrid, 1972).

42. Two flattering portraits of Fraga as minister may be found in Manuel Milián Mestre, Fraga Iribarne: Retrato en tres tiempos (Barcelona, 1975), 103–251; and Octavio Cabezas, Manuel Fraga: Semblanza de un hombre de Estado (Madrid, 1976), 101–242.

43. Muñoz Grandes in return protested privately the promotion of Carrero Blanco to the rank of full admiral that same month. Though separated from naval service since 1941, the minister subsecretary was nonetheless promoted all the way up the hierarchy of ranks. Cf. Fernández, Tensiones militares, 149–52, and El almirante Carrero, 173–74. By contrast, Solís Ruiz had asked to be temporarily suspended from his rank of lieutenant colonel in the

mary concern was that an avowed antimonarchist might be in a position to try to thwart the instauration of the monarchy after Franco's death. The Caudillo replied dryly that Muñoz Grandes "is sick and will not last" and that there was nothing to worry about. He did agree to stipulate that in the proposed new Organic Law of the State the most senior general on the active list (not the reserve) would be the ex officio military member of the Council of the Realm, which would ratify the succession.[44]

Debate over these and other terms was conducted against a background of slowly rising opposition from university students, progressivist priests, and industrial workers.[45] In November 1965 the new justice minister Oriol was able to declare on television that Spain had the second lowest prison population in the world. This was technically correct because of the remarkably low civil crime rate (well below that of most democracies or Communist regimes), but as political penalties were lessened, dissidence increased. On March 9, 1966, there occurred the *capuchinada* in Barcelona, in which a Democratic Syndicate of Students was organized by university rebels in a Capuchin convent. Two months later, 130 priests marched in the streets to protest the use of torture by the political police. An effort was made to counter unrest by organizing a series of visits by Franco to Catalonia in June. This was one of the last of his grand triumphal tours, for his energy declined as he neared seventy-five, but the customary crowds were assembled and by official standards the visit came off well.

The major political event of 1966 was the presentation of the new Organic Law of the State, so long in gestation. The law incorporated features discussed in the cabinet as early as 1958 and was designed not to be a new Fundamental Law in the sense of introducing major institutional features but rather to serve as a codification, clarification, and partial reform of existing practices. It was intended to complete the process of institutionalization and round out the "open constitution" of the regime, giving full and mature definition to "organic democracy." It reflected primarily the position of Carrero Blanco and López Rodó (and of Franco himself), whose notion of reform was administrative and economic rather than directly political, and it was a frustration to Fraga and Solís, who sought to introduce a certain amount of institutional political change.

The Organic Law reconciled various inconsistencies among the six Fundamental Laws (the Fuero de Trabajo, the Law on the Cortes, the Fuero de los Españoles, the Law on the Referendum, the Law of Succes-

---

Military Juridical Corps when he became a cabinet member, resuming his rank and rising to general only after leaving the government.

44. López Rodó, *Larga marcha*, 238.

45. José Ma. Maravall, *El desarrollo económico y la clase obrera* (Barcelona, 1970), studies aspects of the strikes of 1966–67.

sion, and the Fundamental Principles of the National Movement) and eliminated or altered certain lingering vestiges of fascist terminology. It separated the functions of the president of government (prime minister) from those of the chief of state, and modified secondary details of the Law of Succession while accentuating somewhat the institution of monarchy. Membership of the Council of the Realm was increased to sixteen and the council's advisory functions increased. Membership of the National Council was expanded to 108 (40 appointed by the Caudillo, 50 elected by the provincial sections of the Movement, 12 elected by the Cortes, and 6 appointed by its president), with the presidency to be held by the president of government. The appeal of *contrafuero* (approx. "unconstitutionality") was established, which specified that either the National Council or the standing committee of the Cortes might lodge an appeal against any new legislation or government measure held to contradict the Fundamental Principles. A decision would be rendered by a special committee reporting to the Council of the Realm, which would thus become a decisive institution. Some changes were also introduced in the organization of the Cortes, expanding its membership to 565, of whom 307 would be chosen through indirect corporate representation and 108 chosen directly for the first time by the vote of "family representatives."[46]

Amendments to the Fuero de Trabajo, the basic labor law, did away with the old fascistic designations of national syndicalism and the unitary "vertical syndicate" (which Franco claimed never to have understood). Somewhat greater flexibility was introduced, together with division of local syndicates into management and labor components. The Syndical Organization was declared to be autonomous and to provide a channel for the "free participation" of all, though no structural or procedural reforms were introduced to make that possible.[47]

Rather than being the real opening sought by some reformists, the Organic Law represented the final readjustment of the system during the phase of Franco's life when he was rapidly losing physical and political energy. No basic changes were introduced, thus maintaining the structure and mechanisms on which the regime had long rested. An answer to the key question of the succession had not been significantly advanced beyond the formula of 1947, so that the specific choice of a successor or the option of a neo-franquist "regency" remained (even though Franco did nothing personally to encourage the latter alternative). At the same time, typically, there were a few modest indications of change, involving a slight liberalization in the selection of Cortes representatives and some words about the need to encourage "the contrast of opinions."[48]

46. *Fundamental Laws of the Spanish State*, 57–107.
47. Ibid., 41–56.
48. As specified in article 21 of the Organic Law, dealing with the National Council.

When presenting the Organic Law and its attendant legislative amendments to be rubber-stamped by the Cortes on November 22, Franco labeled it a "broad democratization of the political process," adding that "political parties are not a permanent necessity for the functioning of democracy." He declared, "We do not close the door to subsequent modifications and complements, but these will have to be made along the established course . . . to avoid dangerous improvisations," closing with the warning that "the Spanish must remember that every people is beset with its familiar demons: those of Spain are an anarchic spirit, negative criticism, lack of mutual cooperation, extremism and mutual enmity."[49]

This was accompanied by another partial amnesty for political crimes and was followed by a massive propaganda campaign for the national referendum on the Organic Law to be held on December 14. Franco appeared on television the night before to urge full participation and support. The government afterward announced that 80 percent of the eligible voters participated; of these 95.9 percent were declared to have voted yes and only 1.8 percent no. Whatever the exact figures, the operation resulted in a temporary propaganda success for the regime.

The Organic Law was followed with two supplementary pieces of legislation by the middle of the following year: a new Law on Religious Freedom and an electoral Law on Family Representation. The former provided specific guarantees for the expansion of religious liberty in Spain, even though certain restrictions would remain. The second defined procedures for electing the 108 "family representatives" to the Cortes, to be chosen by direct vote of heads of families and married women. They would hold less than 20 percent of the seats in the Cortes, and their candidacy was hedged about with stringent nomination requirements.[50]

All this amounted to much less than the "new constitution" promised in the subtitle of a booklet released by the Ministry of Information for the referendum campaign, but the Organic Law and lesser related measures completed the legal structure of the state and would be described, together with the Fundamental Laws, as comprising the "Spanish constitution."[51] Critics suggested that the regime had lost perhaps its last major

49. *Discursos y mensajes del Jefe del Estado (1964–1967)* (Madrid, 1968), 317–19.

50. To be eligible to stand for election, a prospective "family representative" had to be either (a) a former procurador (deputy); (b) nominated by five current procuradores; (c) nominated by a certain proportion of local representatives in his municipal council or provincial Diputación; or (d) nominated by a number of heads of families or married women in his district equivalent to one-half of one percent of eligible voters.

51. Rodrigo Fernández-Carvajal, *La constitución española* (Madrid, 1969), the same title used for the government's subsequent publication of the Fundamental Laws, *La constitución española: Leyes Fundamentales del Estado* (Madrid, 1971). There were detailed expositions in José Zafra Valverde, *Régimen político de España* (Pamplona, 1973); Jorge de Esteban et al., *Desarrollo político y constitución española* (Barcelona, 1973); and Fernando Garrido Falla's compendium, *Leyes políticas de España* (Madrid, 1969). The most lucid analyses

opportunity to secure genuine popular support for a serious liberalization of the system. That is most doubtful, since Franco made it abundantly clear that he had no intention of ever permitting basic alterations that might weaken what he termed in 1967 "a modern state with authority."[52] He fully realized that it was one thing to liberalize policy and quite another to liberalize the basic structure of an authoritarian system, which would then rapidly erode altogether.

The coup of the Greek colonels, which took place in April 1967 while the final reform measures were being discussed, merely served to reenforce Franco's long-standing political prejudices and relieve his sense of isolation in Europe. Within two days he reaffirmed the regime's unyielding opposition to the return of political parties and for the last time in his life felt a slight swing of historical change in his direction.

The system of the late 1960s was beyond all doubt more open, moderate, and responsive than that of ten or twenty years earlier. Though the Cortes never became a parliament and never gained the right to initiate legislation, its members became slightly less timid and occasionally criticized aspects of legislation proposed by the government or even carried through a few minor changes.[53] Membership remained oligarchic in the extreme, about half the procuradores always being higher state functionaries who held other positions as well.[54] Turnover was about 40 percent

were published abroad especially by José Amodia, *Franco's Political Legacy* (London, 1977); and E. Ramón Arango, *The Spanish Political System* (Boulder, 1978). Earlier foreign studies included Walther Wefers, *Grundlagen und Ideen des spanischen Staates der Gegenwart* (Bonn, 1967); Giuseppe Loi Puddu, *España: Desarrollo histórico-político-constitucional* (Milan, 1967); and Jean Testas, *Les institutions espagnoles* (Paris, 1975).

52. In a speech to the Cortes of November 17, 1967. *Pensamiento político*, 2:370.

53. Franco even alleged that the government failed to advance certain kinds of legislation to the Cortes "due to the lack of receptive atmosphere there." *Conversaciones privadas*, 390.

The official version of improvements in the representative process was given in Jesús Vasallo, *Participación de los españoles en la política* (Madrid, 1970). On the changes in the Cortes, see Carlos Iglesias Selgas, *Las Cortes españolas* (Madrid, 1973); and Bernardo Díaz-Nosty, *Las Cortes de Franco* (Barcelona, 1972), 25–75; and, on its technical functioning, M. M. Fraile Clivellés, *Comentario al Reglamento de las Cortes* (Madrid, 1973). Other aspects are treated in Antonio Cillán Apalategui, *El léxico político de Franco en las Cortes españolas* (Zaragoza, 1970); Antonio Remiro Brotons, *Las Cortes y la política exterior española (1942–1976)* (Valladolid, 1977); and Angel Garrorena Morales, *Autoritarismo y control parlamentario en las Cortes de Franco* (Murcia, 1977). The best brief analysis of the evolution of the Cortes is Juan J. Linz, "Legislatures in Organic Statist-Authoritarian Regimes—The Case of Spain," in *Legislatures in Development*, ed. J. Smith and L. D. Musolf (Durham, N.C., 1979), 88–124.

54. Even after the 1967 reform, 47 percent of the members of the tenth and final Cortes chosen in 1971 were state functionaries, and that figure was very near the average for the entire history of the Cortes since 1943, according to the findings of Rafael Bañón Martínez, *Poder de la burocracia y Cortes franquistas (1943–1971)* (Madrid, 1978), 175.

from one legislature to the next,[55] the most extensive changes coming in 1946 (when National Catholicism came to the fore), 1958 (when the new economic leadership and Solís's takeover of the Syndical Organization brought in new cadres), and 1967, with the slight liberalization of representation. Some of the new family representatives made brief gestures of independence in the next legislature. Unable to get an adequate hearing in the regular chamber, they temporarily formed a rump *Cortes viajeras* or *transhumantes* ("travelling Cortes") until their informal meetings were prohibited by the minister of the interior in September 1968.[56]

The state administrative system also remained relatively elitist. Those who played the leading roles in it came from proportionately higher social background than was the case in most other western countries, with the partial exception of France.[57] Technical competence on certain levels increased significantly during the 1960s, but personal influence and clientelism remained powerful factors, though in a diminishing degree, to the end of the regime.

Franco's only significant new decision of 1967 was announced on July 22, when he relieved Muñoz Grandes of his functions as vice-president of government. This was commonly ascribed to the influence of Carrero Blanco, though it may have been due as much to Muñoz Grandes's extreme ill health, which had led him to request dismissal two years ear-

---

55. Jesús M. de Miguel and Juan J. Linz, "Las Cortes españolas 1943–1970: Un análisis de cohortes," *Sistema* 8 (Jan. 1975), 85–110.

56. Díaz-Nosty, *Cortes de Franco*, 77–104; and Josep Meliá, *El largo camino de la apertura* (Barcelona, 1975), 131–44. The most notorious member of the "Cortes transhumantes" was the Barcelona furniture manufacturer Eduardo Tarragona, who resigned in frustration in 1969. See Franco Estadella, *El senor Tarragona: semblanza política* (Barcelona, 1971), and the *Libro negro del procurador familiar Tarragona* (Barcelona, 1971).

57. One study developed the following categorization of high-ranking bureaucrats according to social origin (Juan J. Linz and Amando de Miguel, "La elite funcionarial española ante la reforma administrativa," in *Sociología de la administración pública española* [Madrid, 1968], arranged by Richard Gunther, *Public Policy in a No-Party State* [Berkeley, 1980], 14):

Occupational Status of Father	United States	England	France (general)	France (grandes écoles)	Spain
Upper and upper-middle-class	37%	32%	43%	65%	69%
Middle-class	43	50	49	33	27
Working-class	21	15	3	2	4

Miguel Beltrán, *La elite burocrática española* (Madrid, 1977), 99, comes to roughly similar conclusions, defining as upper-class in origin 65 percent of the bureaucratic elite in Spain, compared with 55.5 percent in France and 25 percent in Italy.

lier.[58] The Caudillo was by then seventy-five, and the influence of those around him grew as his own initiative declined. For the first time in the history of the regime, Doña Carmen and the family camarilla attempted to exert direct influence on government affairs, but their role could scarcely be compared with that of Carrero Blanco. His quarter-century of devoted service had made him a true *valido,* with preeminent status over all other advisors and cabinet members. This was formally recognized on September 21, 1967, when Franco raised him to the position of vice-president while allowing him to retain his existing post of minister subsecretary of the presidency.

With reformism at an end, the late 1960s were a time of mounting opposition and disorder within the universities and the industrial north. The opposition shadow syndicates, the Comisiones Obreras, were strong enough in several districts to make little effort at concealment, while the two largest and most politicized universities, Madrid and Barcelona, were in a state of constant uproar that would continue with only momentary remission until Franco's death. Various faculties were periodically shut down altogether, and henceforth it would be unusual to complete a full academic year without partial closure. Despite intermittent crackdowns, the police were carefully restrained in the degree of repression they were allowed to exercise in the universities. This provoked strong criticism from the ultraright, while leftists took it as a sign of the weakness and senility of the regime, unable to apply the police pressure of earlier years. Franco observed on March 23, 1968, "Many leftists say that we are in the time of the fall of Primo de Rivera's government or of Berenguer. They are completely wrong and confuse the serenity of the government with weakness."[59] With his constant awareness of the parallel experience of Primo de Rivera, Franco may not have wished to repeat the policy that united the universities in a solid phalanx against Primo's regime. At any rate, he was on record as having directed the police to go easy, though the minister of education, Lora Tamayo, soon resigned because of conflict with the minister of the interior, Alonso Vega, who directed the repression.[60] It remains a moot point whether the relative restraint of Franco's policy was due in part to the benumbing effects of Parkinson's disease and the medication taken to control it. He had always responded to threats and challenges without excitement, but in the past had calmly adopted rigorous measures. Here, however, the moderation of repression was fully conso-

58. The formal argument was that under the new Organic Law, holding the office of vice-president was incompatible with his ex officio membership in the Council of the Realm as head of the Alto Estado Mayor. That problem could obviously have been resolved simply by replacing him as head of the latter.

59. Salgado-Araujo, *Conversaciones privadas,* 525.

60. Lora Tamayo has given a brief account of his problems in *Franco visto,* 132–33.

nant with the evolution of the regime's policy over the past decade and more. The new education minister of April 1968, José Luis Villar Palasí, initiated a broad expansion and upgrading of educational facilities, which though fully laudable in itself could only compound the immediate political problems.

It was not the laxness of the police that produced the rebelliousness of university youth, but the broad changes in society and culture during the previous decade. The secularization that had suddenly become so marked had its ideological counterpart, for, even though the regime's own ideologists followed Daniel Bell in announcing the "twilight of ideologies"[61] and urged Spaniards to concentrate on economic advancement, students and the younger intelligentsia, now in much closer contact with western Europe than a decade earlier, discovered a new materialistic ideology in the neo-Marxist ideas which they imported en masse from France and Italy. The new Spanish-style *marxismo cañí* ("gypsy Marxism") amounted to no more than a transcription of foreign ideas with scant elaboration or originality, but it provided a mental framework congenial to the new intelligentsia growing up in a suddenly materialistic and semiaffluent society still subject to political repression. Spain, which had never had a real Marxist intelligentsia during the revolutionary generation of the 1930s, began to acquire a second-hand one in the late 1960s.

For the new vice-president, this scandalous state of affairs was due to the disastrously libertine character of the Press Law of 1966 and Fraga's indulgent direction of the Ministry of Information. In a memo to Franco of July 10, 1968, he detailed:

> The situation of the press and the other organs of information must be corrected from the inside out. This is producing positive moral, religious and political deterioration. The windows of all the bookstores and the stands of the Book Fair are crowded with Marxist works and the most licentious erotic novels. Moreover, the growth of immorality in public entertainment has been tremendous in recent times. The damage being done to public morality is grave and we must put a stop to it. . . . I greatly fear that the present Minister of Information is incapable of correcting this state of things.[62]

Criticism from within the government by Carrero and López Rodó of what was seen as Fraga's dangerous tendency toward reformism led the minister of information to introduce new legislation transmitted to the Cortes restricting information about material designated as official secrets. This took so stringent a form that the bill in turn had to be modified by carefully controlled amendments so as not to undo some of the accom-

61. Most notably Gonzalo Fernández de la Mora, *El crepúsculo de las ideologías* (Madrid, 1965).
62. Quoted in Fernández, *Franco*, 216.

plishments of the earlier press reform.[63] Franco was also suspicious of Fraga, but unlike the ultras he had less illusion that it would be possible to go back to an earlier order of things.

The government responded much more sharply to mounting labor unrest and nationalist agitation, especially the latter, in the Basque provinces. The new Basque extremist organization, Euskadi ta Azkatasuna (ETA; Basque Land and Liberty), turned to violence in August 1968 with the retaliatory assassination of the head of the political police (Brigada social) in Guipúzcoa. This provoked a severe crackdown which soon brought the arrest of many ETA members and temporarily restricted its activities greatly. A new decree once more broadened the jurisdiction of military courts over political offenses (which had been reduced five years earlier). Continued disorder in the universities and unrest in the Basque provinces led to declaration of a legal State of Exception for two months between January 24 and March 22, 1969.[64] It was followed a few days later, however, on April 1, thirtieth anniversary of the end of the Civil War, by a final and conclusive amnesty for those few still under legal sanction or liable to prosecution for their activities during the Civil War, though this measure still did not bring military pensions for disabled Republican veterans nor rehabilitation of teachers and civil servants fired in 1939.

The Movement in Suspension

The defeat of the Arrese proposals of 1956 was a major setback for Falangists from which the official Movement never quite recovered, though there was a continuing effort to give it a new function that would assure its future within the structure of the regime. On ceremonial occasions the Caudillo reiterated to Movement members that he was with them and that the organization was still essential to the regime, insisting that "the Movement is a system and there is a place for everyone in it."[65] Later in 1967 he would avow that "If the Movement did not exist, our most urgent task would be to invent it."[66] Franco was fully aware that camisas viejas had criticized him for many years from the firm conviction that he had never desired a strong party (which of course was correct), but he privately insisted that he had always wished to strengthen the Movement. Franco laid the blame for its weakness on the intransigence of the camisas

63. Cf. the discussion in Gregorio Morán, *Adolfo Suárez: Historia de una ambición* (Barcelona, 1979), 176–77.

64. *Anuario político español 1969*, ed. M. Martínez Cuadrado (Madrid, 1970), 221–42. On the internal opposition during the middle and late sixties, see Fernández Vargas, *La resistencia*, 231–315; and on the growth of ETA, see Robert P. Clark, *The Basque Insurgents: ETA, 1952–1980* (Madison, 1984), 3–56.

65. *Discursos y mensajes del Jefe del Estado 1960–1963* (Madrid, 1964), 324.

66. Fernández, *Franco*, 214.

viejas who wished to maintain the original doctrines and the predominance of the early leaders, failing to adjust their postulates in order to attract a broad and diverse new membership.[67]

For many years the Movement admitted no decline in numbers. The 1963 report of the National Delegation for Provinces declared a membership of 931,802 militants,[68] roughly the same as for every year since 1942, but there was strong suspicion that the names of inactive members were never removed from the lists. The Sección Femenina had reported only 207,021 members for 1959, scarcely more than a third of the total of two decades earlier, but still only a little less than the number of women affiliated with Catholic Action[69] (though the latter's statistics were more reliable). The reality was quite different, however, for active members in the Movement were relatively few, and in many local districts individual sections had become moribund. A special report of May 19, 1958, that apparently reached Franco analyzed the the organization of the Movement in fourteen northern provinces (including some such as Valladolid in which it had once been very strong) and found the infrastructure uniformly weak.[70]

The secretary of the Movement during this phase, Solís Ruiz, represented the logical evolution of the Arrese style of leadership imposed by Franco. There were nonetheless differences, for Arrese had been an authentic camisa vieja and party veteran, however docile, who represented a large number of his original comrades. Solís was not a party veteran but a military juridical officer and an administrator of the syndical bureaucracy who had scarcely any contact with the original fascist movement whatever. Jovial, garrulous, and histrionic, he realized that the old-style party was dead and could not be revived. His vicesecretary general was Alfredo Jiménez Millas, a true camisa vieja in the Arrese tradition and proud of it. Friction increased between the two, as Jiménez Millas tried to revive residues of the semifascist past and complained of the rhetorical and disordered administrative style of Solís, who perpetually traveled and talked but showed no interest in reconstituting the party structure. After a series of personal snubs, Jiménez Millas resigned early in 1961.

He was replaced by a protege of Solís, the former number-three man in the Movement (national delegate of provinces), Fernando Herrero Tejedor. The new vicesecretary general was a total contrast to the old, a suave and subtle politician who happened to be both a high official of the Movement and a member of Opus Dei. Thus even more than Solís he represented the perfect blend of qualities for the bland reformist era of the sixties. Herrero Tejedor showed a pronounced ability to gear his activities

67. Salgado-Araujo, *Conversaciones privadas*, 344.
68. Joaquín Bardavío, *La estructura del poder en España* (Madrid, 1969), 117–18.
69. Linz, "From Falange to Movimiento-Organizacion," 167.
70. *FF*, 6:49.

to catch Franco's eye, and took over the staging of the Asamblea Internacional de Excombatientes at the Valle de los Caídos in October 1963. This
was the first international assembly ever held in Spain in support of the
regime, bringing in exfascist veterans from all over western Europe. Herrero was no fascist himself, but he correctly judged that this tribute from
the military past would be greatly appreciated by the Caudillo and managed to seize much of the limelight for himself.[71]

More symptomatic of the direction of the Movement had been the appointment of three Opus Dei members as provincial governors and provincial chiefs of the Movement: Hermenegildo Altozano Moraleda in
Seville, Santiago Galindo Herrero in Tenerife, and Juan Alfaro in Huelva.
At that point in the regime new provincial governors were named through
mutual agreement between the secretary of the Movement and the minister of the interior, Alonso Vega. López Rodó, meanwhile, had managed to
win appointment of an Opus Dei member as director general of local administration, facilitating the appointment of three governors who were
not only indifferent to the Movement's Falangist past (that might have
been said of most) but overtly anti-Falangist in their political attitudes.
The most outspoken was Altozano in Seville, who gained a reputation for
having been the first nominal provincial chief of the Movement to refuse
ever to wear the Falangist blue shirt under any circumstances and to suppress the other classic emblems. His independence was so extreme that
even the supple Herrero found it impossible to deal with him.[72]

The most severely eroded of all the Movement institutions was the
SEU, its university student syndicate. The national chief of the SEU appointed in 1957 following the crisis of the preceding year was a moderate,
Jesús Aparicio Bernal, of Catholic reformist leanings. He attempted to
follow a somewhat liberal policy while placating and restraining the diverse currents of neo-Falangists, pragmatic careerists, and Opus Dei-
associated or Catholic-based reformists within the organization. In 1961
Altozano Moraleda promoted an attempt to "democratize" the student
syndicate by the leadership in Seville that was quickly repressed by the
national directors, and in 1962 both Bernal and Altozano were replaced
when there was a change in government. The new national chief, Rodolfo
Martín Villa, attempted a more rigorous policy, while trying to focus activities on pragmatic objectives such as apolitical student cooperatives
under the SEU, but by 1964 found the situation unmanageable. His successor lasted only two months, by which time the SEU had reached a
state of collapse. Appointment of the radical young neo-Falangist José Miguel Ortí Bordás as new chief of the syndicate proved ineffective in reviv-

71. See the commentary in Morán, *Adolfo Suárez*, 138–43.
72. Ibid., 110–18.

ing an organizational cadaver.[73] The SEU was officially dissolved on April 5, 1965. The elite youth group of the Movement, the Guardias de Franco, was also in decline, but as an expression of the hard core it managed to maintain its organizational structure more effectively.[74]

Though Spanish youth were now lost to the Movement, senior figures in the old guard jealously preserved their remaining posts and continued to express hostility to the new technocratic leadership of the 1960s. Their chief remaining leader was José Antonio Girón, though he no longer held a major position, and hence their criticism had to be voiced primarily by the top Falangist journalists. Chief among these was Emilio Romero, director of the newspaper *Pueblo* and possessor of the most agile and trenchant journalistic pen in Spain,[75] and Rodrigo Royo, who edited *Arriba*. An editorial by the latter on January 30, 1962, invoked once more the original Falangist leadership of José Antonio, Ledesma, and Redondo, denouncing by contrast the "planning projects of the triumvirate" in charge of economic affairs. Royo was fired immediately but later gained a measure of revenge through his novel *El Establishment* (1974), an unflattering portrayal of the new government leadership. For camisas viejas, the "Opus ministers" represented a "new right" who were selling the Nationalist birthright for a mess of foreign investment pottage, and at one Movement meeting in Madrid in June 1964 they accused the technocratic government of killing the spirit of the Eighteenth of July. In April 1966 Franco complained of these criticisms, lamenting that "the only newspapers who do not say what their owners want are those of the Movement."[76] Verbal assaults on Opus Dei, however veiled, became so persistent that on October 28 Msr. Escrivá de Balaguer, founder and director of the institute, wrote directly to Solís to protest "the campaign against Opus Dei carried on so unjustly by the press of the Falange, which is under your order."[77] So little satisfaction was gained that the matter was carried to the pages of the French daily *Le Monde*. It was typical of Franco that he did not try to bring the Movement press fully to heel, for its hostility to the technocrats maintained pressure against them as well as something of the political counterbalance that he always sought within the system.

73. See ibid., 147–64; Alcocer, *Radiografía*, 153–66; Lizcano, *La generación*, 227–34.

74. The membership of 225,000 reported for all the youth organizations of the Movement's Frente de Juventudes in 1963 was a modest figure for a country of more than 30 million, and even that was probably subject to the customary statistical misrepresentation. *Informe, Sesión del Pleno del IX Consejo Nacional* (Madrid, 1963).

75. Romero's main writings of the 1960s, collected in book form, were his *Cartas a un Príncipe* (Madrid, 1964); *Cartas al pueblo soberano* (Madrid, 1965); and *Los "Gallos" de Emilio Romero* (Madrid, 1968).

76. According to the new minister of finance, Juan José Espinosa San Martín, in *Franco visto*, 154.

77. Quoted in *España perspectiva 1974* (Madrid, 1974), 70–71.

A small minority went even further and was still capable of occasional public outbursts. On November 20, 1960, at the annual commemoration of the death of José Antonio—now held at his new burial site in the Valle de los Caídos—a young militant shouted "Franco, you're a traitor!," bringing his immediate arrest and five years in prison.[78] A new current of "dissident Falangism" had emerged at the end of the 1950s in the Guardias de Franco that sought to recover the original doctrines of José Antonio, Ledesma, and Hedilla. This led to the formation in Madrid during 1959 of the first of the semidissident "Círculos Doctrinales José Antonio" under the leadership of Luis González Vicén, sometime leader of the Guardias and still a member of the National Council of the Movement. He lost the latter post in 1964, however, and in 1965 was succeeded as head of the Círculos Doctrinales by Diego Márquez Horquillo, under whose leadership they expanded to seventy local sections the following year, in some cases including separate youth, labor, or student groups. This was the largest neo-Falangist organization, but the weaker the official Movement became, the more tiny dissident neo-Falangist groups began to proliferate, half a dozen others being founded before the close of the sixties,[79] each more insignificant than the last.

By the mid-1960s only two possibilities remained to the leaders of the Movement: one was to enhance the role of the Syndical Organization, as Solís Ruiz attempted to do, and the other was to try to revive the Movement by acquiring for it some sort of new representative function. Latin American models were vaguely invoked, for an expanded state syndicalism suggested a parallel to Peronism, whereas a more open and representative hegemonic party that encouraged semipluralism within unity raised the specter of the Mexican PRI. In fact, neither alternative was feasible. The Fourth Syndical Congress held at Tarragona in May 1968 was to have reflected the development of a more powerful and influential Syndical Organization, but by that time it had become painfully clear that the system could never achieve authenticity or even the control that it had once had. Not only did it not determine the workers' opinions, but it was becoming

78. Sueiro, *Verdadera historia*, 273–86; Alcocer, *Radiografía*, 74–76.

79. In 1963 the veteran camisa vieja Narciso Perales led organization of a tiny Frente Nacional de Trabajadores. Intense conflict later developed between this group and its student arm, the Frente de Estudiantes Sindicalistas, leading to a realignment in 1965 in which Perales and several associates broke with the latter to form a new Frente Sindicalista Revolucionario. One year later Manuel Hedilla, the last national leader of the independent Falange before Franco, was induced to step outside his new life as a Madrid businessman to become president of the new FSR's central committee. Though the authorities quickly declared it an illegal organization, the police did not bother to arrest its leaders. In 1968 Hedilla broke with Perales to form his own Frente Nacional de Alianza Libre, whose activities largely came to an end with Hedilla's death two years later. Meanwhile several other dissident neo-Falangist splinter groups attempted to function more or less simultaneously. See Ellwood, *Prietas*, 226–40.

increasingly unable to control their collective action. The development of collective bargaining and the broadening of representation within the syndicates at the level of enlaces sindicales and factory committees (jurados de empresa) created opportunities that industrial workers were not slow to seize, but the results overflowed the syndical structure. From 1967 on, strike actions were no longer sporadic but were comparatively regular and had little or nothing to do with the official syndicates. The Syndical Organization lacked the strength and the authenticity to develop into a Spanish Peronism, an outcome that had really been decided when Salvador Merino was cut down in 1941. It did constitute a center of antagonism to Carrero Blanco and the economic ministers, but its criticism had little effect on policy[80] and the attempts to broaden its base ended in failure.[81]

There remained the intermittent debate that had gone on since 1957 over whether the old form of the Movement as "organization" should give way to a new form of the Movement as a broader "communion" of Spanish society that would guarantee its future not as a single party but as a broader multicurrent channel for participation and representation. This was essentially the meaning of "political development" as used in the Movement during the mid-1960s. During his term as vicesecretary general Herrero Tejedor prepared the draft of a proposal to redefine the function of the Movement by authorizing the formation of associations of heads of families and married women within its ranks. This gained initial approval, but was withdrawn at the beginning of 1965 after meeting a firestorm of disapproval in the Cortes from the Church hierarchy, reformist Catholics, and Carlist spokesmen.[82] Another broader constitutional project drawn up by Herrero and other Movement leaders was directly vetoed by Franco, and thus they had little influence on the eventual Organic Law that was approved in 1966, which made no mention of the National Movement. It referred only to the latter's National Council, and its authors evidently intended to reduce the Movement to the functions of the National Council alone.

One of the last determined Falangist leaders in the history of the regime was Alejando Rodríguez Valcárcel, who replaced Herrero as vice-

80. The Syndical Organization's Dionisio Martín Sanz was possibly the Cortes's most outspoken critic of López Rodó and the Development Plans, which he scored for lacking a national ideology, relying too much on foreign capital and the emigration of labor and abandoning agriculture. Martín Sanz, *En las Cortes españolas: Crítica del Segundo Plan de Desarrollo* (Madrid, 1969), and *La planificación española la Olimpiada de las ideologías: Crítica del Tercer Plan de Desarrollo* (Madrid, 1972).

81. The last effort to negotiate with elements of the clandestine CNT in Catalonia was apparently made in 1965, while ongoing efforts were made to negotiate with opposition elements at the lower level of the Syndical Organization itself. Cf. *FF*, 8:223–25.

82. *FF*, 7:181–82.

secretary general from 1966 to 1969. He insisted that "the Movement must be the chief actor in the progress and growth of Spain."[83] To recover some of the ground lost in the Organic Law, the Movement leadership prepared a separate new "Organic Law of the Movement and of Its National Council" that was officially approved on June 28, 1967. This measure ratified once more the position of minister secretary of the movement, and again defined the functioning of its provincial and local councils, safeguarding its organizational structure. When López Rodó protested to Franco that this was in contradiction to the general Organic Law so recently approved, Franco dismissed the matter on the grounds that the new Organic Law of the Movement was mere ordinary legislation that could be changed at any time, while the Organic Law of the State was a "Fundamental Law" that would take precedence and could only be modified by national referendum.[84] In fact this indicated that Franco, who was never worried about legal contradictions when they served his purpose, was not necessarily ready to dispense with the Movement as a political organization. Nonetheless, none of this did anything to strengthen its operations or add membership, so that by 1968 even the docile Fernández Cuesta would lament that the lack of concreteness and new goals left the Movement "in a gaseous state."[85]

The only remaining option was to broaden membership and participation through the ploy of "associationism," a concept toyed with for a decade. Some lip service had been paid to this in the Organic Law of the State, which declared that one of the goals of the National Council was to "stimulate authentic and effective participation of national entities" and "the legitimate contrast of opinion." Therefore a new Organic Statute of the Movement was planned in the last months of 1968 to redefine its functions, terming it "the communion of the Spanish people in the Principles of the Movement," to imply broader participation than that of a single-party membership. Rodríguez Valcárcel's proposal to grant the Movement a massive budgetary increase for political and organizational work and control over propaganda and ordinary state jobs was quickly vetoed, perhaps by Franco himself, and attention focused on article 15, which raised the possibility of "associations" that might be legitimized "within the Movement" for the "legitimate contrast of ideas."

83. Alejandro Rodríguez Valcárcel, *Una etapa política* (Madrid, 1969), 67.

84. López Rodó, *Larga marcha*, 263.

85. Quoted in José Ma. Martínez Val, *¿Por qué no fue posible la Falange?* (Barcelona, 1975), 11. All this was, as usual, obscured by the barrage of propaganda published by the Ediciones del Movimiento and allied organs: *Nueva etapa política* (Madrid, 1966); *Ley Orgánica, Movimiento y democracia* (Madrid, 1967); *Tiempo nuevo y Movimiento Nacional* (Madrid, 1967); *Nuevo horizonte del Movimiento* (Madrid, 1968). The Servicio Informativo Español began its *Crónica de un año de España* for 1968–69 by declaring, "The movement toward institutionalization and reform of the National Movement has been one of the fundamental concerns of the period from July 1968 to July 1969."

A small group in the old guard, led by Fernández Cuesta, opposed any sort of "associations" as opening the door to the return of political parties, but the statute was approved by the National Council in December 1968 in terms that recognized the possibility of "constituting associations for the development of family participation in public life and promoting and defending the interests of the family," presumably an acceptably conservative goal. In addition, it was stipulated that associations of the Movement might be formed for other goals, such as defending professional interests not represented by the Syndical Organization, promoting national culture, and studying and implementing the doctrines of the Movement itself, as well as any other that might be specifically approved by the National Council.[86] Yet none of these options would be forthcoming until the latter prepared and approved a new law specifically defining the terms of association and until this was officially ratified by Franco.

Ultras asked aloud "What is the difference between a political association and a political party?" but the new "Anteproyecto de Bases del Régimen Jurídico Asociativo del Movimiento" prepared during the spring of 1969 seemed to bring that danger well under control. The new statute on associations that was approved unanimously by the National Council on July 3 defined them as "associations of opinion" whose organizers would have to collect 25,000 signatures in order to register them legally. The National Council would have complete control over their legal authorization, and there was no specification of the goals or functions of such associations should any ever be authorized. Once more a measure toward aperturismo and greater participation was made so limited in practice as to frustrate any serious reform. Moreover, the statute was never approved by Franco, who had serious doubts about going even that far.[87]

With each passing year membership in the Movement simultaneously aged and shrank. A check of membership records indicated that in Lérida province in 1965 85 percent of the affiliates were more than forty-five years of age, while in 1974 the average age among Madrid members was at least fifty-five. Though a few new members were gained every year (27,806, for example, in 1969), they did not compensate for those who dropped out or died, and came mostly from the semirural Catholic and conservative provinces of the north.[88]

---

86. On the effort to develop associationism in 1968, see Juan Ferrando Badía, *El régimen de Franco* (Madrid, 1984), 165–72.

87. J. A. González Casanova, "Asociaciones políticas y Monarquía moderada," *España perspectiva 1974* (Madrid, 1974), 101–22.

88. Zamora, for example, provided 6,210 of the new members in 1969. A total of 2,485 more were registered in Orense, while Lérida, which at that point had a zealous provincial governor and Movement chief, acquired 1,819. The lowest enrollments were in Gerona and Guipuzcoa, with only 25 new members each. Formerly Carlist Navarre, changing rapidly under the impact of accelerating industrialization, ranked third from the bottom with only 47. A total of 28,513 entered Movement youth groups that year, scarcely more than one

On November 23, 1969, a middle-aged camisa vieja, Francisco Herranz, shot himself in front of the large church in Madrid's Plaza Santa Barbara to protest the ultimate marginalization of the Falange. It was to no avail. A subsequent law of April 3, 1970, ratified the definitive abolition of the official name, Falange Española Tradicionalista y de las JONS, in favor of National Movement; the earlier decree of 1945 had been inadequately worded and had failed to achieve complete derogation of the nomenclature established by the original decree of April 1937. Henceforth the name Falange would belong to various dissident neofascist groups organized semiclandestinely in opposition to the regime. The official movement would endure seven more years, until its formal dissolution in 1977.

Foreign Policy in the 1960s

The last twenty years of the regime were relatively static in foreign relations. Castiella, foreign minister from 1957 to 1969, acted with more vigor and ambition than some of his predecessors, though he achieved no triumphs equal to those of Martín Artajo. Castiella hoped to develop a more genuinely Spanish policy that would avoid excessive dependence on the United States, but he had only a limited success.[89] All the while, Spain grew ever closer to western Europe in economics and culture, even though the regime would never become politically acceptable to most of the west European democracies.

Franco always opposed the notion of a united Europe and publicly attacked "Europeanism" as late as 1961. Yet that same year Britain, Denmark, and Norway all applied to join the European Economic Community, and even Greece made an agreement of association. When the EEC came up with a common agricultural policy that would hamper Spanish exports at the beginning of the following year, Franco saw the handwriting on the wall and authorized Spain's application to join the Common Market as well. The EEC members persistently dragged their feet, largely for political reasons, and Franco was in no hurry to enter, realizing that it would require massive structural readjustments in Spain. He correctly pointed out that much more than mere political antagonism was involved.[90] Ullas-

---

percent of their national age group, while the Feminine Section gained only 2,913 new members. Martínez Val, *¿Por qué?* 158–69.

89. For a brief discussion of Castiella's policy, see Armero, *Política exterior,* 171–200.

90. "Although there is no alternative to entry, since we belong to Europe, I do not know if it is really in our interest or may be prejudicial, given that our farm products are sold in the other countries, especially Germany. Nonetheless, our industry—particularly the small enterprises, which are the most numerous—might suffer from such competition," Franco complained in 1961; "I need an able economist to provide guidance on these problems, but I can't find the right one," indicating a continuing lack of confidence in López Rodó and the latter's associates. "Moreover," he added, "with the embargo against our regime, they create many obstacles, complaining that we are not democratic, that we are authoritarian, and so

tres was eventually dispatched as Spanish ambassador to the EEC in 1965, but not until April 1967 did the Common Market leadership deign slowly to begin negotiations.[91]

Franco had much more interest in an association with NATO and after Spain's admission to the United Nations began to hope that such a rapprochement would become possible. The smaller social democracies of northwestern Europe were firmly opposed to Spain's entry, however, and no such alignment would be possible as long as the regime remained in power. Failing that, Spanish diplomacy toyed with the possibility of some sort of parallel southwest European defense group that would include the four Latin countries and overlap with NATO, but they gained no support for such an alternative. During 1959 there arose the possibility of limited military cooperation with West Germany, which needed broader space for troop and particularly air force training maneuvers. Yet the German government feared the appearance of encouraging neofascism and made limited arrangements with Portugal instead.

Though Franco was pleased with the American relationship for the political reinforcement and military security that it provided, he considered Americans "infantile" and observed that he would have preferred the British to lead the western alliance. He criticized the Kennedy administration for its irresolution and clumsy handling of the Bay of Pigs fiasco, and harbored the notion that Washington had erred in not "unleashing" Chiang Kai-shek against the Chinese Communists.[92] Yet his reply to Lyndon Johnson (in response to a message explaining the new American initiative in Vietnam in 1965) urged caution, shrewdly observing that it would be difficult to win such a contest completely in military terms and that the political and military problems involved were probably too complex for a simple solution.[93] The Spanish leadership hoped for more favorable terms when the initial ten-year pact with the United States expired in 1963, for Communist Yugoslavia had begun to receive aid at the same time without providing any direct quid pro quo, and over a period of twenty years would obtain more aid from the United States than would Spain.

Castiella's display of greater independence was thus calculated to exact a higher price.[94] NATO overflights across Spain to Portugal were re-

---

on. Then they pull other complaints out of their sleeves. The main point is to delay our entry as long as possible. There are countries like Italy or France that have no interest in our inclusion in the Common Market. . . ." Quoted by Soriano, *La mano izquierda*, 82–83. Similar remarks are quoted by Salgado-Araujo, *Conversaciones privadas*, 333, 334.

91. For a detailed acount of this frustrated relationship, see William T. Salisbury, "Spain and the Common Market, 1957–1967" (Ph.D. diss., Johns Hopkins, 1972).

92. As quoted by Soriano, *La mano*, 70–72.

93. Franco to Johnson, Aug. 18, 1965, in *FF*, 7:203–6.

94. Yet there were severe limits to any gestures critical of the United States. When the

stricted, and an effort was made to establish a special relationship with France. Madrid generally enjoyed more favorable contact with De Gaulle's Fifth Republic than with its predecessors, despite occasional incidents such as the sanctuary provided by ultra-Falangists to the French rebel general Salan for six months during 1960–61.[95] In April 1963 the French finance minister came to Madrid to conclude a new commercial treaty after several minor military agreements had been reached. Yet the execution of the Communist leader Grimau temporarily chilled relations, and the pact with the United States had to be renewed largely on American terms.[96]

In 1964 the regime hired the publicity firm of McCann-Erickson (which held the contracts for Coca-Cola and Old Gold cigarettes) to improve its image in the United States.[97] The conviction that the assistance provided and the risks run on behalf of collective security were disproportionate was reinforced by the Palomares incident of January 17, 1966, in which a B-52 crashed in the Mediterranean very near the southern coast of Spain, losing four unarmed hydrogen bombs, one of which was not recovered for several months. Though no contamination resulted, Washington subsequently agreed that American planes flying over Spain would no longer carry nuclear weapons. By the time that the second renewal of the American pact came due in 1968 Franco hoped to exact much more military assistance, but by then Spain had lost at least some of its strategic significance for the United States. An interim agreement signed in March 1969 provided for only a small fraction of the billion dollars of military aid that had been requested.[98]

The regime persisted in its efforts to maintain a special relationship with Latin American countries. In 1965, as financial circumstances improved, it made a certain amount of money available for development loans, hoping not to be totally outdone by the United States's Alliance for Progress. Spanish diplomacy was surprisingly friendly to Fidel Castro, though relations were temporarily suspended in 1960 following an incident in one of Castro's television marathons to which the Spanish ambas-

---

ultra-right-wing director of the Instituto de Cultura Hispánica, Blas Piñar, published an article in *ABC* on January 19, 1962, entitled "Hipócritas" and clearly referring to the United States, he was promptly fired.

95. According to Serrano Súñer, who was implicated in this, the principal arrangements were made by the ardent camisa vieja Narciso Perales. Saña, *Conversaciones*, 340–42.

96. The new ambassador in Washington, Antonio Garrigues, played a major role in rescuing the negotiations. See Benjamin Welles, *Spain: The Gentle Anarchy* (New York, 1965), 299–308; and, more generally, R. R. Rubottom and J. C. Murphy, *Spain and the United States Since World War II* (New York, 1984), 77–84; and Ronald F. Hadian, "United States Foreign Policy towards Spain, 1953–1970" (Ph.D. diss., Univ. of Calif. at Santa Barbara, 1976), 53–62.

97. As reported in the London *Sunday Express*, May 27, 1964.

98. Rubottom and Murphy, 84–90; and Hadian, 81–110.

sador responded in person at the Havana television studio. Franco naturally supported the United States during the Cuban missile crisis, but commercial relations with Cuba were resumed in 1963. Favorable commentary on the Cuban regime was occasionally allowed to be published in Spain, and Iberia, the national airlines, maintained a direct flight to Havana.[99] Spanish diplomacy also cultivated cordial relations with Third World countries at the United Nations, successfully angling for their support on the Gibraltar issue.

Nominally the worst relations, though hardly the most problematic, were as usual those with the Soviet Union. Here the most dramatic incident was Nikita Khrushchev's tirade against the Spanish regime at the United Nations on October 1, 1960, to which Lequerica vigorously responded. This virtually coincided with Spain's official cancellation of a European Cup match between the Spanish and Soviet teams which was to have been held in Spain, bringing an international fine against the Spanish soccer federation. Franco privately explained that he feared incidents, pro or con, and determined to refuse the Soviet government the propaganda advantage of flying its flag and having its anthem played in Spain.[100]

The most troublesome relations continued to be with Morocco, an area which was increasingly dominated by Carrero Blanco. Several Spanish technicians were kidnapped in the Sahara in 1961, but Madrid took a tough line and such incidents soon ended. The final contingent of troops left the territory of the old Protectorate on August 31, 1961, but pressure then increased against the remaining possessions of Ifni, the Spanish Sahara, and the cities of Ceuta and Melilla. On July 30, 1962, Morocco declared the extension of its territorial waters to a distance of twelve miles off the coast in order to hinder Spanish fishing operations. Madrid refused to recognize such an unusual unilateral definition and declared that it would protect the rights of its fishermen, a problem that continued to fester for more than twenty years. The small district of Ifni, Spain's last remaining enclave in the main part of Morocco, was peacefully relinquished in 1969.

The Gibraltar Question

Gibraltar, a perennial rallying point for Spanish nationalists, came to the forefront in the mid-sixties. British domination of this small district near the southern tip of Spain dates from the early eighteenth century and was ratified by the Treaty of Utrecht in 1713. The terms of that treaty were subsequently broken by British permission for non-Spanish immigrants (Maltese, Jews, etc.) to enter the territory, and the boundaries were also

99. Relations with Cuba are summarized in Hadian, 69–77.
100. Salgado-Araujo, *Conversaciones privadas*, 290–91.

slightly expanded, especially during the Civil War when Britain built an emergency landing strip on agreed neutral ground that played a vital role in World War II. During Britain's dark summer of 1940, London indicated that it considered the future of "the Rock" to be negotiable, echoing a line first used during earlier difficult moments of the eighteenth century. Needless to say, nothing more was heard of such a disposition after 1945. By that time the population had come to be heterogeneous in the extreme, enjoying local self-government on a democratic basis (something obviously not available in Spain) and a higher standard of living than the Spanish norm.

Franco first took restrictive measures in 1954, following a visit to Gibraltar by Queen Elizabeth that Madrid thought provocative. No more permits were issued to allow Spanish workers to cross over to work in British territory, and tourists were no longer allowed to leave Spain directly through Gibraltar. The issue was placed before the United Nations in 1963, which subsequently urged bilateral negotiations to restore Spanish sovereignty. Further restrictions were imposed by Spain two years later that eventually had the effect of cutting Gibraltar's commerce by 40 percent. In October 1965 the regime announced a special building program for the Campo de Gibraltar, the Spanish territory around the enclave, to raise its living standards and present a more attractive alternative.

Castiella met with the British foreign minister in London to begin bilateral negotiations on May 18, 1966. Spain proposed cancellation of article 10 of the Treaty of Utrecht, thus restoring Gibraltar to Spain, and simultaneously offered to guarantee Britain the use of Gibraltar as a military base well into the future, along with special "personal status" for the population of the district to be guaranteed by the United Nations. Britain proposed instead to allow a Spanish commissioner to reside in Gibraltar, to provide Spain with its own military facilities there, and to suppress all contraband activities (another perennial Spanish complaint). Following this impasse, the Spanish government denied permission for all overflights to Gibraltar and rejected a request to submit the dispute to the International Court of Justice. The United Nations General Assembly, where Spanish diplomacy had courted Third World representatives, voted repeatedly to urge Britain to withdraw from Gibraltar, but it also requested Spain to prepare to decolonize its remaining Moroccan enclave of Ifni and the Spanish Sahara. Britain countered with a plebiscite on September 10, 1967, in which the population of Gibraltar voted with virtual unanimity to remain under British rule. Two United Nations resolutions in 1967 and 1968 nonetheless condemned the British position and on December 18, 1968 demanded termination of "the colonial situation in Gibraltar not later than October 1, 1969." During 1969 the Spanish government proceeded to isolate Gibraltar as much as possible. As the deadline neared, the frontier was closed and telephone communications, ferry service, and the fresh water supply all cut off. Despite the pressure placed on Gibraltar's economy, which had to be subsidized by Britain, no progress was made toward resolution of the dispute and no further initiatives were forthcoming after 1969. Franco rejected all suggestions inside his government for more extreme measures, recognizing that Spain was in no position to force the issue to its final conclusion and that it could be settled only by British withdrawal and not by Spanish seizure, a withdrawal that he realized would not be likely until after his own death.[101]

The Problem of Spanish Guinea

After the independence of the Moroccan Protectorate in 1956, the former Dirección de Marruecos y Colonias in the Spanish government was changed to the Dirección de Plazas y Provincias Africanas. It functioned under the thumb of the minister-secretary of the presidency, for Carrero Blanco dominated Spanish policy in Africa until his assassination. A Law of Provincialization in 1959 followed the example of Salazar's Portugal in giving the colonial population equal rights with Spanish citizens and providing for their nominal representation in the Cortes.

A turning point in the future of Iberian colonialism in sub-Saharan Africa was reached in the spring of 1961, when revolt broke out in the key Portuguese colony of Angola. Portuguese possessions were of course much larger and more significant than the remaining Spanish holdings, and the Salazar government, after tense internal controversy, determined to stand fast. It expected moral and possibly physical support from Madrid, but there Castiella emphasized the impossibility of Spain and Por-

101. See the remarks attributed to Franco by his finance minister of the late 1960s, Espinosa San Martín, in *Franco visto,* 156–58. Spain's first elected Socialist government reopened the border in 1984.

The best history of the long controversy over Gibraltar is George Hills, *Rock of Contention: A History of Gibraltar* (London, 1974). Don Lawson, *The Lion and the Rock* (New York, 1969), and Ernle Bradford, *Gibraltar: The History of a Fortress* (London, 1971), are general histories, while C. E. Carrington, *Gibraltar* (London, 1966), is a scholarly essay, and John D. Steward, *Gibraltar: The Keystone* (London, 1967), focuses on the 1950s and 1960s.

The Spanish case was presented in the Foreign Ministry's *The Spanish Red Book on Gibraltar* (Madrid, 1965), the compendium *Razones de España sobre Gibraltar* (Madrid, 1966), and Antonio Figueruelo, *Informe sobre Gibraltar* (Barcelona, 1968). General Spanish accounts include Jose Pla Cárceles, *El alma en pena de Gibraltar* (Madrid, 1953), and "Hispanus" [José Díaz de Villegas], *El Estrecho de Gibraltar* (Madrid, 1953). Gil Armangué Rius, *Gibraltar y los españoles* (Madrid, 1964), collects the opinions of leading Spaniards over a period of two hundred years, while Gumersindo Rico, *La población de Gibraltar* (Madrid, 1967), emphasizes the heterogeneity of Gibraltar's population. The ultranationalist position was well-articulated in Blas Piñar's lecture, *La España irredenta* (Madrid, 1965). Juan Velarde Fuertes, *Gibraltar y su campo: Una economía deprimida* (Madrid, 1970), describes the poverty of the surrounding Spanish territory.

Carrero Blanco and members of the Youth Organization from Guinea

tugal holding out where Britain and France had already withdrawn. The Spanish regime would do what it could to maintain the stability of the Salazar regime at home, though it is a moot point whether or not Franco would have been willing to intervene directly in Portugal had either the military conspiracy of 1961 or the Beja revolt of 1962 against Salazar gotten out of hand.[102] It prudently dissociated itself from a policy of diehard colonialism in Africa. In 1962 the Spanish government declared that the two territories of Rio Muñi and the island of Fernando Poo, which constituted Spanish Guinea, could have their independence within a reasonable time if they so desired.

In June 1963 a limited autonomy statute was promulgated for these tropical African districts, and after further prodding from the United Nations, a referendum in December arranged for a single internally autonomous administration to include both territories. Subsequently a long conference was held in Madrid during 1967–68 to work out an independent constitution. Spokesmen for the more numerous population of Rio Muñi demanded a single unified system of government, while those from the

102. As was rumored in Lisbon. Cf. Benjamin Welles, "Salazar in Trouble," *Atlantic Monthly*, July 1962.

smaller Fernando Poo feared domination and preferred separate independence or a continued autonomous relationship with Spain. In a second referendum of August, 63 percent of the combined population voted for independence, which was officially granted to the new state of Equatorial Guinea on October 12, 1968.

The limited Spanish presence that remained was deeply resented by the sinister new president, a former functionary of the Spanish administration once known as Francisco Macías. After rioting in March 1969 and an attempted coup against Macías by the foreign minister (following a trip to Madrid), United Nations assistance was invoked to evacuate the remaining Spanish citizens. Macías, who had reverted to his original name Nguema Masie Byoto, then imposed a harsh personal dictatorship—rhetorically decked in the garb of "scientific socialism"—that stood out even among the bloody new African regimes of the 1970s for its genocidal propensities. As in many other areas, there was really no case for the hasty decolonization of Spanish Guinea except for the prevailing climate of political hysteria that made it difficult for Spain to remain. The final steps were accelerated by Madrid partly in the hope of building a stronger case for the devolution of Gibraltar, but the price that its new ruler exacted of this unfortunate region was among the most devastating in all the recent disasters of African independence.[103]

103. See Castiella's *España y la Guinea Ecuatorial* (Madrid, 1968), and three works by Donato Ndongo-Bidyogo: *Historia y tragedia de Guinea Ecuatorial* (Madrid, 1977); "Una merienda de blancos," in *España en Africa*, a special issue (Extra IX) of *Historia 16* (April 1979), 105–16; and "Guinea: Diez años de independencia," *Historia 16* 3:30 (October 1978), 11–18.

Macías had been vice-president of the autonomous government under Spain and also counselor of public works. He had a reputation for incorruptibility unusual among African politicians and won the first elections of 1968 after registering a protest against the new Spanish-administered constitution. The Cuban regime devoted some attention to Spanish Guinea as early as 1962, and Macías was later protected by a Cuban guard. His self-image was messianic in the extreme; he preferred to quote Hitler almost as much as Lenin. His power base lay among the more numerous Fangs of Rio Muñi, while the regime's massive violence was primarily directed against the rival Bubis of Fernando Poo. Of this unhappy little land's original population of 350,000, it has been estimated that as many as 50,000, mostly Bubis, were killed outright (with hundreds executed by the hand of Macías himself) and another 40,000 enslaved on state-owned plantations, while up to 100,000 either fled the country or were driven out. Toward the end, Macías was said to be drinking a pint of human blood a day, according to an eyewitness report cited in the *International Herald Tribune,* Jan. 28, 1980. As one investigation concluded: "At the time of independence from Spain in 1968, Equatorial Guinea was potentially one of the wealthiest countries of the African continent. . . . It had a promising tourist industry, with fine hotels, nightclubs, and casinos. Thanks to the rich volcanic soil, the country shipped almost 40,000 metric tons a year of the world's best cocoa to Europe and America. . . . [Over the course of Macías' rule from 1968 to 1979] cocoa production dropped to 5,000 metric tons a year, and of 98,000 acres of plantation land in 1968, all but 7,400 acres have reverted to jungle. Apart from killing about a fifth of the population, the dictator also forced more than 100,000 people to go abroad." *New York Times,* Sept. 12, 1982.

The "Operación Príncipe"

During the mid-1960s the regime weathered the rise in student, labor, and regionalist unrest with little loss in stability, and few Spaniards really expected its collapse or overthrow before the death of Franco. General expectation tended to accept Franco's own conclusion that he had prepared the institutions to succeed himself, and so hostile an observer as the American historian Gabriel Jackson, long a foe of the regime, published an article on October 7, 1968, entitled "Fascism for the Future." He prognosticated that "a Franquist type of dictatorship may continue for decades in Spain and by so doing may provide a 'model' for other nations that achieve a minimum of economic prosperity in the absence of strong traditions of political liberty."[104]

Some of Franco's closest collaborators in the government, led by Carrero Blanco and López Rodó, nonetheless were uneasy about the future of Spanish institutions unless Franco took decisive action to give the system greater legitimacy and continuity by recognizing as successor a legitimate heir to the throne, more precisely, Prince Juan Carlos. Even the Caudillo's older brother Nicolás became concerned, supposedly drawing this typically sly retort from the elderly dictator: "Don't worry, Nicolás. We Francos are a long-lived family and moreover we die in order: you are the oldest."[105]

A proposal introduced by one of Franco's more extravagant sycophants in the Cortes in 1966 would have declared Franco himself rightful king of Spain, with his powers transmitted through his daughter to his oldest grandson, who would according to the petition succeed him.[106] Franco had better sense than that, but the ranks of serious pretenders to the throne expanded during the mid-sixties. Not only did the son of the principal Carlist heir change his name to Carlos Hugo and advance his own candidacy in 1963, but the elder son of Alfonso XIII, Jaime de Borbón y Battemberg, who had formally renounced his own rights to the line of succession as a deaf-mute, recanted his own renunciation in 1964 after his second wife taught him to speak a bit. Though he himself received little attention, his own elder son, Alfonso de Borbón y Dampierre, had established residence in Spain in order to learn Spanish and gain Spanish nationality.[107] Tall, dark, suave, and handsome, this prince was a generally agreeable young man who entered the Spanish diplomatic corps on matu-

104. *The New Republic*, October 7, 1968.
105. According to José Ma. Pemán, *Mis encuentros con Franco* (Barcelona, 1976), 82.
106. Fernández, *Franco*, 204.
107. Don Jaime de Borbón y Battemberg had earlier requested the assistance of Franco in gaining custody of the two sons from his first marriage when their mother was keeping them in Switzerland. There is a facsimile of his letter of January 16, 1953, in Salgado-Araujo, *Conversaciones privadas*, 371.

rity and soon attracted attention. Franco, who occasionally had second thoughts about Juan Carlos during the early 1960s,[108] said of Alfonso de Borbón y Dampierre in February 1963, "He is cultured, patriotic, and might be a solution [sic] if Juan Carlos doesn't work out."[109] At that point only Carlist candidates were categorically excluded. As the Caudillo put it, "For me the bad thing about the Traditionalists is not their doctrine, which is very good, but their determination to bring a foreign king to our country whom no one knows, who has always lived in France, and for whom the Spanish people feel nothing."[110] He himself denied the request of the Carlist Borbón-Parma branch to become Spanish citizens.

At no point did Don Juan, as direct legitimate heir to the Spanish throne, either in word or thought relinquish his own claim. During the preceding decade he had seemed to draw closer to the regime (for lack of any alternative), but by 1964 he realized that little had been accomplished to advance his candidacy. In February, Don Juan sent a personal memorandum to Franco urging him to take the step prepared for in the Law of Succession by institutionalizing the monarchy through the official recognition of himself, the legitimate heir, as Franco's successor. This Franco categorically refused,[111] and from that time relations between the two became increasingly hostile once more. During the next two years the Conde de Barcelona added prominent monarchist liberals to his personal council, in 1965 naming as his new political delegate in Spain the former regime politician and diplomat José Ma. de Areilza, who renounced his own past and invested his not inconsiderable talent in the cause of parliamentary monarchy. With the change in the censorship, Don Juan's supporters became more outspoken. On July 21, 1966, the young monarchist writer Luis Ma. Ansón published an article in *ABC* entitled "the Monarchy of Everyone," which invoked "the European monarchy, the democratic monarchy, the popular monarchy" proclaimed by the Conde de Barcelona, bringing confiscation of the edition and temporary exile to the author.

By the early 1960s Carrero Blanco and his associates had firmly set their sights on Juan Carlos as the only appropriate heir to the throne and successor to Franco. In May 1965 Juan Carlos first took the place of honor beside Franco at a major military parade, and both López Rodó and Fraga Iribarne, from somewhat different political perspectives, began publicly to promote the prince's candidacy to the extent permitted within the sys-

108. On April 4, 1963, Franco declared Juan Carlos to be "somewhat subject to his father," but added immediately, "I consider him an intelligent person and of good character." He admitted that "many think he is a bit juvenile" but that this impression would pass as he matured. Ibid., 377.

109. Ibid., 369.

110. Ibid., 311.

111. *FF*, 7:127–29.

tem. Supporters of Juan Carlos within the government worked vigorously to distance the prince from his father politically and to separate him as much as possible from his father's political supporters. Individually and in succession they belabored him (in what López Rodó called successive "Stuka dives") to beware of "opportunists" such as Areilza and others who sought to create conflict between himself and Franco. Partly as a consequence, Juan Carlos informed Franco that he would not be among those attending a major monarchist assembly in Estoril to honor his father on March 5, 1966.[112]

Juan Carlos had long been painfully aware of the narrow line that he must walk. He would later refer to it privately as many "years playing the fool in this country," [113] for he realized that he must avoid controversy to the point of appearing insipid and would only reach the throne through the monarchist succession created by Franco. Thus on a private trip to the United States in January 1967 he assured journalists that he supported the Movement and its principles, stressing that the monarchy would be restored "as continuation" of the present regime, a position that he reiterated at a working breakfast with four provincial Movement leaders in Barcelona on July 2. [114]

Franco remained generally pleased with the prince, gratified by the relative simplicity of his life style (maintained on a slender budget) and his attentive manner. He made very little attempt to personally indoctrinate Juan Carlos, and was perhaps even willing to accept the possibility that the prince might make certain changes in the regime after his own death, apparently showing little alarm over an intelligence report which indicated that Juan Carlos had met with a small group of moderate liberals and leftists on May 27 and expressed a preference for a two-party electoral system under a restored monarchy. [115] The Caudillo observed approvingly near the end of 1966: "I am certain that little by little the entire country will develop affection for Prince Juan Carlos and Doña Sofía, for their conduct is irreproachable and a model in every way. They lead lives of absolute simplicity and austerity, and always try to be in touch with the needs of the Spanish people. And they do so entirely on their own initiative without my having to prompt them, for I believe they should be free in their own style of activity." [116]

None of the alternative candidates had the slightest success. Solís Ruiz and Nieto Antúnez, as two of the leading "Regentialists," toyed briefly with the possibility of trying to promote Alfonso de Borbón y Dampierre.

112. *FF*, 7:326.
113. As quoted by a leading participant in the Fundación Ortega y Gasset Symposium on the Transition (Toledo), May 11, 1984.
114. *FF*, 7:374, 395.
115. *FF*, 7:328–29.
116. Salgado-Araujo, *Conversaciones privadas*, 488–89.

If they had to accept Juan Carlos, they hoped to do so on terms that would give a broader place to the Movement,[117] but that seemed increasingly unlikely, especially since Juan Carlos was the chief candidate of their rivals in the government. At one point in 1968 Solís even attempted to establish direct contact with the Conde de Barcelona, but that was a desperate gesture.

Nor did the main *juanistas* do any better. Areilza placed considerable emphasis on trying to rouse military pressure against Franco but failed to gain any response. The bizarre writer and would-be politician Calvo Serer, sometime noted figure of Opus Dei, moved steadily to the left and became a devout juanista, all to no avail. His article in the daily *Madrid* (controlled by a group of his friends, some of them members of Opus Dei) on May 30, 1968, addressed the current "May crisis" in France with veiled allusions to Spanish affairs. It was entitled "Retirarse a tiempo; No al general De Gaulle." Franco did not take kindly to the suggestions that old generals retire from positions as heads of state. The newspaper was temporarily closed, and eventually it was suppressed altogether.[118]

In June 1968 Juan Carlos reached thirty years of age, the age required by the Law of Succession to accede to the throne. That summer he was even being quoted in the international press as having let the diplomatic corps know that he was willing to accept power directly from Franco and bypass his father in the line of succession.[119] The Conde de Barcelona himself doubted that Franco would ever name a successor in his lifetime, and later in the fall wrote to his son telling him that he had fulfilled his responsibilities well in Spain but must hold firm to dynastic principles and the proper chain of succession.[120] On his part Juan Carlos, being briefed regularly by several cabinet members, believed that Franco would name him as his successor in a year or so.

By the autumn of 1968 Juan Carlos had begun to act with greater assurance, and his father may indeed have feared that Franco had succeeded in winning him over. In fact, Juan Carlos, behind his manner of winsome naiveté, had become a master of telling each person more or less what that person wanted to hear. Yet in an interview published in the French *Point de Vue* on November 22, 1968, he was quoted as stating categorically that he would never reign as long as his father lived. Though the authenticity of these remarks was quickly denied by a spokesman for

117. That had been the point of Emilio Romero's widely sold *Cartas a un Príncipe* (Madrid, 1964), which spoke in Aesopian terms of the need for a restored monarchy to be more popular and broadly based.
118. The final closing took place in November 1971. Calvo Serer had in the meantime gone into exile, where he came to collaborate with the Communist Party. See his *La dictadura de los franquistas, I: El affaire del "Madrid" y el futuro político* (Paris, 1973).
119. *New York Times*, July 10, 1968.
120. Quoted in full in González-Doria, *Franquismo*, 73–76.

Juan Carlos, they horrified the principal Franco-monarchists (Carrero, López Rodó, Silva Muñoz, et al.), who immediately began to work on the Prince once more to convince him of his responsibilities to the nation as they saw them.

Meanwhile, mindful of the total physical collapse of Salazar a few months before in Lisbon, they pressed Franco more vigorously than ever to proceed with recognition of a successor before absolute infirmity struck. These conversations normally involved strong doses of the most extreme flattery, assuring the Caudillo that no other historic personality would ever hold his degree of authority and legitimacy and that therefore only he and he alone could guarantee the continuation of the regime by personally investing his choice as successor with his own legitimacy at the present moment, when his prestige and authority were undiminished. Meanwhile, to avoid any further confusion, the most active Carlist pretender, Hugo de Borbón-Parma ("Carlos Hugo") was expelled from Spain at the close of the year because of active political gestures.[121]

Juan Carlos adopted a different tone in an interview with the official news agency EFE on January 7, 1969, when he declared himself ready to make "sacrifices" and "to respect the laws and institutions of my country"—with respect to Franco's Fundamental Laws—"in a very special way." These remarks were carried in all the media[122] and pleased Franco greatly. When he next met with Juan Carlos on January 15, the increasingly decrepit Caudillo gave him to understand that he intended to name him as successor before the end of the year. According to one version, Franco urged him, "Be perfectly calm, Highness. Don't let yourself be influenced by anything else. Everything is prepared." Juan Carlos is said to have responded, "Don't worry, *mi General.* I have already learned a great deal of your *galleguismo* [slyness]," and after both laughed, Franco added, "Your Highness does it very well."[123] During the spring Carrero Blanco, López Rodó, and Alonso Vega continued to work on Franco to make the

121. Hugo de Borbón-Parma was the elder son of Don Javier, nephew of the last Carlist pretender in the direct male line. Don Javier was himself descended through the female line—the original cause for Carlist disqualification of the main branch of the dynasty in 1833—but nonetheless had declared his own rights to the throne in 1953. Hugo, a French citizen and trained as a French paratrooper, first took up residence in Spain to learn Spanish and officially changed his name to Carlos Hugo. In 1964 he married Princess Irene of the Netherlands and subsequently advanced his own candidacy to the Spanish throne. At one point he was patronized by a small group of Spanish monarchists, some of them members of Opus Dei. He originally supported Carlist traditionalism, switched to democratic socialism about 1966, then back to traditionalism, and later campaigned after the death of Franco on a platform of "self-governing socialism." Under the regime this bizarre French aristocrat was twice expelled from Spain. On "Carlos Hugo" see Javier Lavardín, *Historia del último pretendiente a la corona de España* (Paris, 1976); and Josep Carles Clemente, *Historia del carlismo contemporáneo 1935–1972* (Barcelona, 1977), 211–72, 310–50.

122. Cf. *Cambio social y modernización política: Anuario político español 1969,* ed. M. Martínez Cuadrado (Madrid, 1970), 173–74, 180–86.

123. López Rodó, *Larga marcha,* 301.

Prince Juan Carlos de Borbón signing the Law of Succession, July 1969

declaration, while Juan Carlos spent a week with his father at Estoril in
June, and whether or not the two came to a direct agreement, apparently
found that Don Juan would not go so far as to forbid him to accept the
succession.[124] Finally, the prince also consulted with his few trusted advisors, especially his highly esteemed former tutor, the Movement politician Fernández Miranda, who is said to have reassured him that further
reforms would be perfectly feasible once he had fully inherited the constitutional structure of the Franquist state.[125]

124. López Rodó has Juan Carlos telling his father on this occasion, "If you forbid me to
accept, I'll pack my bags, take Sofi and the children, and leave [Madrid]. I have not intrigued in order to have the choice fall on me. I agree that it would be better that you become king, but if the decision has been taken, what can we do?" Ibid., 331–32.
125. Joaquín Bardavío, *Los silencios del Rey* (Madrid, 1979), 49–50. It was Fernández
Miranda above all who guided the prince through the political maze of Franco's system. As

On July 21, 1969, Franco finally presented the designation of Juan Carlos to the Council of the Realm and one day later to the Cortes. A special ruling arranged by Herrero Tejedor, attorney general (fiscal) of the Supreme Court, provided that the vote of ratification would be public so as to minimize opposition. The Cortes registered its approval by a vote of 491 to 19, with 9 abstentions, as a handful of die-hard Falangists and hardcore "Regentialists" held out to the end. On the following day, July 23, Juan Carlos officially swore "loyalty to His Excellency the Chief of State and fidelity to the Principles of the Movement and the Fundamental Laws of the Kingdom." [126] It seemed then that the long struggle for the instauration of a corporative and authoritarian monarchy, begun by *Acción Española* in 1932, [127] was about to reach fruition.

Adolfo Suárez put it, "Torcuato Fernández Miranda held a great ascendancy over Juan Carlos; he could explain to him many things." Symposium on the Transition, May 13, 1984.

126. Díaz-Plaja, *La España política del siglo XX*, 4:412–17.

127. Cf. R. A. H. Robinson, "Genealogy and Function of the Monarchist Myth of the Franco Regime," *Iberian Studies* 2:1 (Spring 1973), 18–26.

21

Twilight of the Regime
1969–1973

The ceremony of July 1969 finally solved the immediate question "After Franco, who?" It did not necessarily answer the accompanying query "After Franco, what?" The general assumption was that despite the increase in dissent and a certain decline in the internal coherence and determination of the regime, Franco had managed to institutionalize a system that would sustain its main features for at least a certain period after his death. The cautious, mild, smiling, somewhat diffident young Prince was given little credit for political insight or ability, and general opinion in 1969 held that if he really expected to reign he could do so only by living up to his oath and affirming the laws and institutions of the regime in order to gain the support of the military and the leaders of other state institutions. Though there was little confidence that the system could continue for very long after Franco's death, neither was any drastic alternative within view. Informed interest therefore focused much more on further changes and reforms within the system than either its prospective overthrow or its replacement.

A new cabinet took office on October 29, 1969, three months after the recognition of Juan Carlos. It was a different sort of government from any of its predecessors and it is not clear that Franco had had any such alteration in mind at the time the Prince's oath was sworn. The change was precipitated rather suddenly by the greatest financial scandal in the history of the regime and of all Spanish government—the MATESA affair, which first became news on August 13. The acronym stood for the first multinational corporation in Spanish industry, Maquinaria Textil, S.A., which manufactured textile machinery in Pamplona with outlets and subsidiaries in the process of formation in Latin America. Its director, Juan Vilá Reyes, was an entrepreneur of unusual breadth of interest and ability who had developed a new mechanical loom for export. Even though the new development program was geared for increasing exports, financial regulations still did not readily assist sales of machinery abroad but had been designed to encourage finished consumer goods. Vilá Reyes was unable to obtain export credits without being able to present firm orders for his products; since these were slow to develop, he inflated orders through his own subsidiary firms to gain credits from the government's Banco de Crédito Industrial. Vilá later insisted that officials were adequately informed beforehand of his modus operandi, required by the rigidity of the Spanish financial structure. The credits involved were quite substantial and the irregularities eventually became more widely known. They were formally denounced on July 17, 1969, by Víctor Castro San Martín, an old-guard Falangist and director general of Spanish customs. The charges were debated by the cabinet in August. There was no doubt that Vilá had been involved in irregular procedures, but considerable uncertainty existed as to the extent of complicity in higher circles of government. The issue was quickly seized by Movement leaders to discredit the Opus Dei economics ministers, who were at a loss to quiet the affair, even though irregularities in official financial dealings had been a way of life in much of big business since the start of the regime.

The scandal was made public in mid–August and was investigated by a Cortes commission the following month. The press was given broad freedom to report the case, and indeed, the Movement organs led the charge in denouncing fraud,[1] hoping thereby to discredit the economics ministers who had gained the upper hand in the cabinet during the past decade and secured the recognition of Juan Carlos. Vilá Reyes had enjoyed good relations with government personnel who were members of Opus Dei, and it was loudly whispered that some of the funds unaccounted for had been sent abroad to finance the activities of Opus Dei in other countries. The facts in the affair were so complicated that they have still not been fully clarified after nearly two decades. The defense claimed that MATESA's basic operations were in order until widespread negative publicity provoked massive cancellation of orders, and that all losses on orders supported by government credit had been fully insured, though the government made no effort to require the insurance company to pay. A subsequent investigative report released only in 1981 concluded that the firm had total assets of more than 14,000 million pesetas and despite outstanding debts

---

1. The disposition to publicize scandals possibly connected with the economics ministries had been demonstrated a month earlier, when on June 19 *Arriba* denounced a housing disaster in Segovia that resulted in many deaths.

had retained a positive balance of approximately 1,000 million pesetas.[2] Whatever the full facts, Vilá Reyes was arrested and his corporation taken under government control.[3]

For Carrero Blanco and López Rodó the scandal was an acute embarrassment, coming on the very heels of their signal victory in wringing the recognition of Juan Carlos from Franco. The Caudillo, however, had made his choice, and had come to rely much too heavily on his vice-president and the latter's closest associates to permit the triumph of the Regentialists who had been combating them for the past seven years. As repercussions mounted, it became clear that the ministers of finance and commerce, Juan José Espinosa San Martín and Fuastino García Moncó, allegedly implicated in varying degrees, would have to go, but this would be balanced by the elimination of the principal Regentialist and Movement figures, producing a broad cabinet reorganization. To Carrero, Fraga Iribarne was a "dangerous liberal" who had opened Spain to Marxism and pornography, while the minister-secretary of the Movement, Solís, was painted as a dangerous intriguer, a veritable new Salvador Merino of the Syndical Organization who sought to establish the dominance of the labor bureaucracy within the system. To a lesser degree Castiella was also a target, blamed for the abrupt, graceless, and destructive decolonization of Guinea and for conniving with liberal currents in the Vatican.

Franco no longer had the energy or the opportunity to renew his standard balancing act in forming a new government, relying primarily on Carrero Blanco. Aware of his own declining health and energy, he even suggested to the latter that the time might have come for him to take over directly the office of president of government (prime minister), though to this Carrero demurred, insisting that as long as Franco retained any degree of physical health he ought not to step aside.[4] Such dogged loyalty

2. Miguel Ramos, "La Carta que Asustó a Carrero," *Cambio 16*, Dec. 5, 1983; and Alberto Anaut, "La Guerra entre 'Azules' y Tecnócratas," in Historia 16, *Historia del Franquismo*, 2:722–27. Vilá insists that in the long run the government never lost any funds because of MATESA.

3. The charge has been summarized as follows: "The loans had been made to facilitate the production of textile machinery for export, yet of the 20,381 machines for whose manufacture the company had negotiated loans with the government, only 13,450 had actually been produced. Of these only 10,636 had been exported, out of which only 2,321 had actually been sold. Remaining unsold in warehouses outside Spain were 8,315 machines. In addition, the money diverted from 7,381 machines that had not even been manufactured had been used by MATESA to acquire subsidiary companies in Spain and other textile companies in foreign countries, to pay personal expenses of the company directors, and to make loans to companies not affiliated with MATESA. Thus not only had money been fraudulently used but also the money legitimately used had gone into the manufacture of equipment no one seemed to want." E. Ramón Arango, *Spain's Political System: Franco's Legacy* (Boulder, Colo., 1978), 150.

4. According to López Rodó, *Larga marcha*, 445.

carried to the point of absolute sycophancy was what had gained Franco's complete trust, and the new cabinet of October 1969 represented a complete victory for Carrero Blanco. The broadest change in twelve years, it became known as the *gobierno monocolor*—"monocolor" because virtually all its key members were either members of Opus Dei or the ACNP, associates of those members, or otherwise known to be identified with their policies, even though the new cabinet was publicly presented as representing considerable diversity of viewpoint. Fraga, Solís, Castiella, and Nieto Antúnez were all dropped, as were the tainted incumbents in Finance and Commerce. Carrero Blanco, López Rodó, Silva Muñoz, Oriol, and Villar Palasí retained their positions. The joint portfolios of the Movement and the Syndical Organization previously held by Solís were divided. Torcuato Fernández Miranda was named minister–secretary general of the Movement, where he was expected to complete its final and definitive transformation into a totally servile bureaucratic front. The new minister without portfolio in charge of the Syndical Organization was Enrique García Ramal, a reliable "Falangist monarchist." López Bravo, who had become one of Franco's favorites, took over Foreign Affairs, where the United States government had earlier indicated that it would be pleased to see Castiella replaced. The new finance minister, Alberto Monreal Luque, was a professional economist fully attuned to the existing personnel and policies. The elderly Alonso Vega, of whom Franco was always fond even though he thought him unnecessarily rigid, had finally to be dropped as minister of the interior because he had reached eighty years of age. He was replaced by a military juridical officer, Tomás Garicano Goñi, already experienced in political administration after serving for thirteen years as governor of Barcelona. Fraga was replaced by Alfredo Sánchez Bella, a veteran diplomat of ultra-right-wing Catholic background, who was imposed personally by Franco (according to gossip, grateful for Sánchez Bella's private information concerning Castiella's negotiations with the Vatican).[5]

By this time it was Carrero Blanco much more than Juan Carlos who had come to represent the succession to and continuation of the regime. Franco obviously saw him as his natural successor as president of government, the surviving prime minister who would guarantee that the transition to Juan Carlos would take place under strict continuation of the laws and institutions of the regime. Carrero Blanco's success was due in large part to his strict personal fidelity to Franco and his lack of overweening ambition for himself. He was an introverted and retiring man of absolutely fixed and unremitting ideas, totally convinced that the world in general was dominated by the "three internationals," as he termed them,

5. Cf. Morán, *Adolfo Suárez*, 198–99.

of Communism, Socialism, and Masonry. The father of five children and grandfather of fifteen, he spent a very large part of his time reading and writing,[6] and continued to prepare sizable memos for the Caudillo, though not at such great length as in the past. He was largely immobilist with respect to major domestic institutions, and viewed foreign affairs in similarly intransigent and apocalyptic terms, holding that it would be preferable for all his descendants to die in an atomic war than survive as slaves of the Soviet Union. Even within the regime he had no large coterie of associates, and a foreign journalist described him as "a shy man, standing alone at social functions, somberly dressed and rarely smiling. With his dark, bushy eyebrows, he bears some resemblance to Leonid Brezhnev, the Soviet leader."[7]

Franco had allowed himself to be convinced by Carrero in the selection of the new cabinet, but despite his declining faculties retained enough political instinct to harbor some doubt whether an essentially immobilist new government that was not even representative of the regime in general would be effective. He himself lacked the physical energy or political stamina to lead a more diverse and representative group of ministers, but voiced his doubts as to the durability of the new arrangement when Fraga Iribarne called on him to take his leave from government.

Meanwhile the MATESA affair ground slowly on. In the following year the Spanish Supreme Court indicted both of the outgoing ministers who were implicated, as well as the former finance minister Navarro Rubio[8] and six others. Vilá Reyes was himself convicted of wrongdoing and sentenced to a large fine and several years incarceration. While in prison awaiting an appeal, on May 5, 1971, he directed a blunt letter to Carrero Blanco, warning that if the government did not take action to absolve him in some fashion he would make public extensive documentation that was in his possession concerning widespread smuggling of funds abroad during the years 1964–69. His letter included a "documentary appendix" listing various materials that he could present dealing with such activities by 453 leading individuals and business firms, many of whom were closely connected with the regime.[9] This well-documented threat seems to have achieved results. Carrero convinced Franco that if the whole business were not soon hushed up it would reflect even greater discredit on the government and might even do irreparable damage to the regime. Sev-

6. A posthumous edition of his *Discursos y escritos 1943–1973* (Madrid, 1974) included all the shorter writings published under his name, though not his pseudonymous newspaper articles.

7. *New York Times*, June 9, 1973. A revealing three-page interview by Emilio Romero was published in *Pueblo* on October 7, 1968.

8. Navarro Rubio later wrote his own version of *El caso de MATESA* (Madrid, 1979).

9. The text of the letter appeared in *Cambio 16*, Dec. 5, 1983.

eral months later, on October 1, 1971, the thirty-fifth anniversary of his elevation to the Jefatura del Estado, Franco granted an official state pardon to all the principals involved, feebly camouflaging it by a general pardon to more than 3,000 others still suffering the penalties of political convictions in earlier years. There had as yet been no trial save for the preliminary prosecution of Vilá Reyes and hence no verdict save in that one case, though the financial inquiries involved would extend for more than a decade further, beyond the end of the regime and well into the 1980s. Attended by major publicity under the relaxed censorship and occurring at a time of growing mobilization of political opinion, the whole scandal probably brought more discredit on the regime than any other single incident in its long history.

The Movement in Paralysis

The new minister-secretary of the Movement, Torcuato Fernández Miranda, was a master of the rhetorical doubletalk of the system[10] and in some respects reflected Franco's own thinking about the Movement, which he intended to adjust to a completely pragmatic and bureaucratic function. He could not in any particular sense have been considered a Falangist, and was the first minister-secretary to eschew the old blue shirt of the Falange altogether in favor of a white bureaucrat's collar, later abolishing the blue shirt as official dress, eliminating yet another fascist residue.

One alternative remained unsettled, however, and that was the lingering issue of political associationism, now more than a decade old. Proponents of apertura within the Movement insisted that its future lay only as a *Movimiento-Comunión*, mobilizing broader support among Spaniards of nonregime background, rather than as a *Movimiento-Organización*, the mere residues of the old semifascist single state party. The path to a broader *comunión* would lie in making the Movement the vehicle of multiple associations representing broader and reformist points of view. After initial approval of the Statute on Associations on July 3, 1969, four distinct groups had begun to take the initiative in forming associations. The first, called Acción Política, was led by moderates such as Pío Cabanillas and José García Hernández, together with well-connected newcomers such as the civil engineer Leopoldo Calvo Sotelo. A second, composed of reformist veterans of the Frente de Juventudes, proposed to form an association called Reforma Social Española, led by the Falangist reformist Manuel Cantarero del Castillo. Another handful of Movement members, led

10. His basic work of political theory on "organic democracy," *El hombre y la sociedad,* was reissued in a new 1969 edition.

by a national councillor, announced their intention to form a group called Democracia Social, while the ultrarightists of Blas Piñar and the journal *Fuerza Nueva* declared that "against their own will" they would assume the responsibility of forming an association to defend Franquist orthodoxy. As of late 1969, however, all this was beside the point, since Franco had never ratified the Statute on Associations.

Neither Franco nor Carrero Blanco approved of the idea of associations, yet they did not take the step of quashing the idea altogether, probably for lack of any other reformist alternative. A loyal servant, Fernández Miranda grasped that his assignment was to make haste slowly. He thus began with a meeting of the National Council on December 15, 1969, in which he presented a new project for the reorganization of the General Secretariat of the Movement and its relationship to the National Council. This increased the powers of the secretariat, which would in fact take over some of the functions of the National Council, and abolished the National Delegation of Associations, replacing it with the National Delegations of the Family and of Political Action and Participation. He insisted that the aim was not to eliminate the development of associations but to make better preparation for them. Fraga Iribarne, now looking toward a political career in the post–Franco era, protested that despite such verbal reassurances, the Delegation of Associations was being abolished and that the word associations never appeared once in the new proposal. He also observed that the text of the Organic Statute of the Movement passed in 1968 had still not been officially published, but emphasized that a golden opportunity lay at hand to transform the Movement behind a great national "centrist policy." Miranda's changes were finally approved, though against the unusual opposition of twelve negative votes and four abstentions.[11]

Fernández Miranda held that the "pluralism" of political parties could never be accepted but that the "pluriformism" within unity of the Movement could still provide opportunity for participation in some form of associationism.[12] As an alternative to parties, he later advanced the slogan of "an integrating national socialism," and on March 4, 1971, declared that "the only authentically effective attitude in the face of Marxism is a radical and profound national socialism that carries to its consequences the national revolution, the revolution of the Movement, and the achievement of social justice."[13] This partial rephrasing of traditional Falangist demagogy evidently referred to the benefits of industrialization, full employment, and state welfarism and was picked up by other regime pub-

11. On this session and Fraga's speech, see Ferrando Badía, *El régimen de Franco*, 174–79; and the *Anuario Político Español 1969*, 409–38.

12. In a series of newspaper interviews and Miranda's *El Movimiento y el asociacionismo* (Madrid, 1970).

13. Quoted in Amando de Miguel, *La herencia del franquismo*, 147.

licists.[14] Thus the Movement leadership continued to manipulate the standard rhetoric, augmented by occasional new terms but no new concepts.[15]

Immobilism was accentuated in April 1971 with the dismissal of Fernández Miranda's young vicesecretary general, Miguel Ortí Bordás. Once one of the hard-line young radicals of the Movement who had published a notorious article urging nationalization of the banking system, Ortí Bordás was an ambitious Movement politician who claimed to favor apertura and earned the enmity of the old guard. He was also, from Fernández Miranda's point of view, a less than reliable subordinate and was replaced by a veteran camisa vieja literally twice his age, Manuel Valdés Larrañaga, a companion of José Antonio and one of the founders of the party. The appointment of Valdés was strictly a sop to the old guard that would protect Fernández Miranda's right flank; he was given no significant authority or responsibility within the Movement administration.

Yet an aperturista minority did exist within the Movement and the Cortes, and at the beginning of 1970 a small group of reformist members of the National Council, led by the former vicesecretary general Herrero Tejedor, presented a petition to Fernández Miranda, urging that arrangements for political associations be speedily brought into effect. A month later members of the minority of directly elected Cortes deputies ("family delegates") prepared their own proposal for political associations, denying the jurisdiction of the National Council of the Movement and insisting that the right of association be legislated by parliament.[16]

The situation was then confused by a new decree-law published in the *Boletín Oficial del Estado* on April 3 concerning "the normative faculties of the organs of the Movement." This stipulated that certain decisions of the National Council could have the effect of laws or decrees and that the secretariat could issue ministerial orders, in effect placing the Movement on the level of the Cortes or the government's own council of ministers. This abrupt decree, personally dictated by Franco on the basis of his authority as head of state as originally defined in 1938–39, was not the product of any legislative or ministerial reform project but was an executive order suddenly carried out to redefine and enlarge the power of the Movement bureaucracy, protecting state authority from erosion in a time of change. Its effect was confusion and widespread criticism, since it contradicted the reforms of 1966–68, and these new powers were never exercised.

Fernández Miranda kept his word not to forget the associations project

14. Cf. Pablo Castellanos's ironic "Los nuevos socialistas," *Cuadernos para el Diálogo* (April, 1971).

15. *Nuevo horizonte del Movimiento* (Madrid, 1970); *Balances y rumbos nacionales: Plataforma 1972. Realidades y perspectivas 1973* (Madrid, 1973); and *El Movimiento Nacional, las Leyes Fundamentales y el sistema de instituciones* (Madrid, 1973).

16. Ferrando Badía, *El régimen de Franço*, 220–22.

and on May 21 presented a new draft outline for associations of political action to the permanent commission of the National Council. This stipulated that any proposed political association must consist of no less than 10,000 signed members. The members of the organizing commission of each association would be required to sign a notarized document stating that they respected the Principles of the Movement and the Fundamental Laws, and in addition would have to obtain the signed agreement of three members of the National Council who pledged themselves to supervise and guarantee the reliability of the association. It would then have to be approved by a special new organizations committee to be created by the council, by the new national delegate for political action, by the minister-secretary general, and by a full meeting of the National Council. Thus the Movement bureaucracy and the council would hold full authority over any associations, and no provisions were made either for elections or any representative or legislative authority, the terms of future elections to be taken up by subsequent legislation.[17]

There the project remained for the next three years. Franco and Carrero Blanco quickly drew back before even such a carefully controlled scheme, and the associations project was buried, further discussion by the National Council avoided. On February 15, 1971, the family representatives in the Cortes attempted to interpellate the government on this issue but gained no satisfaction. When the National Council finally met again two days later, political associations were not on its agenda. One further effort was made by reformists to air the issue in the press and other forums in the spring of 1972, but by that time Fernández Miranda had received clear orders. Echoing the terminology of Franco, he declared publicly that any action which attempted to reintroduce political parties would be a mere "dialectical trick," and in November 1972 informed the Cortes: "To say yes or no to associations is simply a Sadducean trap. . . . The question is to see whether in saying yes to political associations we also say yes or no, or whether we do not say yes or no, to political parties."[18]

A minority of younger reformists nonetheless remained active within the Movement, emerging as the Group of Thirty-Nine at the beginning of 1973. They were led by Ortí Bordás and Rodolfo Martín Villa, one of the last SEU chiefs, and continued to try to turn the Movement toward political associations and a semirepresentative system during the final phase of the regime.

The Falangist old guard, largely displaced from the direction of the

17. See ibid., 194–97, 231–32.
18. Quoted in Carr and Fusi, *Spain*, 190. On Fernández Miranda's handling of the problem of associations, see Josep Meliá, *El largo camino de la apertura* (Barcelona, 1975), 169–200.

Movement itself since 1957, persisted in their traditional rhetoric, hold-
ing that only in reviving the Falangism of the regime and restoring a
Falangist program would survival and continuity be assured. Thus José
Antonio Girón, still hoping for a political comeback, would state to the
National Council on October 29, 1972 (thirty-ninth anniversary of the
founding of the party):

> The Spanish state, at the end of thirty-six years, can only justify itself, as it faces
> the future, as the executor of the National Revolution. If the state or its execu-
> tive arm—the government—were one day to abandon this goal, not only would
> it be left without substance but it would draw upon itself the disenchantment
> and wrath of the entire people. But the fact is, further, that the Spanish state,
> which has had to carry out an effective but delayed constituent period, can now
> attempt, with much more guarantee of success than thirty-five years ago, the
> unfulfilled aims of the National Revolution.[19]

Some of the original Falangist organizations, such as the Vieja Guardia,
the Guardias de Franco, and the Frente de Juventudes, continued to
exist, declining in numbers, activities, and fervor. In the last years of
the regime, however, neo-Falangist enthusiasm was found mostly outside
the main currents of the Movement. The broadest expression of neo-
Falangism, the Círculos Doctrinales José Antonio, was still nominally associated with the official Movement and continued to expand, numbering
101 Circles by 1973 and 231 by 1976. Its leaders and those of other neo-
Falangist groups planned a large national rally to be held in Alicante on
November 20, 1970, thirty-fourth anniversary of the execution of José Antonio Primo de Rivera. Fernández Miranda saw to it that the police
refused to authorize it as a legal assembly, but 4,000 neo-Falangists nonetheless assembled in Alicante. When it was learned that the order prohib-
iting their assembly came from the minister-secretary general, the neo-
Falangist leaders meekly submitted, limiting themselves to a public mass
in memory of José Antonio in a large church. In June 1973 the Círculos
Doctrinales held their own fourth national assembly in Toledo, which
abruptly ended when a disturbance broke out during a speech by the new
vicesecretary general, Valdés. In punishment, Fernández Miranda ordered the Círculos Doctrinales closed throughout Spain for the next
three months. The "alphabet soup" of tiny neo-Falangist dissident grouplets continued, with a half dozen new ones formed during the first half
of the 1970s.[20] One of these was the Frente de Estudiantes Nacional-

19. Quoted in Enrique de Aguinaga, *Informe sobre la Falange de José Antonio* (La Coruña, 1973), 56.
20. The appearance and disappearance of these minigroups followed in dizzying succession. The Acción Sindicalista Revolucionaria and Frente Sindicalista Unificado, Juntas de
Oposición Falangistas and Frente de Estudiantes Nacional Sindicalistas were followed in
1970 by the Confederación de Obreros Nacional Sindicalistas (reviving the old Falangist
name) and the Frente Sindicalista Universitario, then by the Falange Española Nacional Sindicalista (1971), Unión Falangista (1972), Alianza Revolucionaria Sindicalista (1973), Juventudes Obreras Falangistas (1974), and the Juventudes Falangistas Universitarias (1975).

Sindicalistas, organized by Sigfrido Hillers, a radical but generally ultra-orthodox student group of limited numbers that by 1970 enjoyed the distinction of being the only publicly active nonleftist student political group at the University of Madrid.

Neo-Falangism surpassed even the revolutionary left in its divisiveness and internal schisms. This of course reflected the normal sectarian factionalism and exclusiveness of the twentieth-century radical political religions of whatever stripe, but in the Spanish case also seemed to express an unusually high degree of anarchic personalism and voluntarism, qualities most salient in the neofascist culture. This divisiveness might have been partially overcome if any one of the grouplets had generated any support.[21] None did, however, and post–Franco elections would show that all the neofascist elements combined could not muster two percent of the popular vote, though of course José Antonio's original movement had done even more poorly in 1936.

Not only had Falangism reached a state of terminal confusion, but the other original primary constituent of the Movement, Carlism, was in process of a kind of reversal of ideologies. Under the uncertain leadership of "Carlos" Hugo, the main group of neo-Carlists came out for *el socialismo autogestionario* (self-managing socialism), the leading new catchphrase of the Spanish left by the early 1970s, derived from French Socialist terminology.[22] Even before the death of Franco, the primary forces of the original Movement had become totally eroded and ceased to exist as viable political options.[23]

Membership sometimes overlapped, particularly between the nominally syndicalist and student groups. Of the first neo-Falangist organizations of the 1960s, the Frente Nacional de Alianza Libre still survived, absorbing several of the smaller grouplets in 1974 and still trying to work within the official movement. Its companion, the Frente Sindicalista Revolucionario, finally split in two in 1975, one section forming a new Partido Sindicalista Autogestionario (employing the fashionable "self-managing" socialist terminology of the period). During the final political associations phase of the regime in 1974–75, Hillers tried to form a Falange Española Independiente, while Fernández Cuesta and other members of the old guard organized a new Falange Española y de las JONS. Other grouplets followed after the death of Franco. See Ernesto Cadena, *La ofensiva neo-fascista* (Barcelona, 1978); Ellwood, 241–46; Diego Márquez, *Círculos "José Antonio"* (Bilbao, 1977); and Sigfrido Hillers de Luque, *Estilo y ética falangistas* (Madrid, 1974) and *España: Una revolución pendiente* (Madrid, 1975).

21. *Falange, hoy* (Madrid, 1973), ed. Miguel Veyrat and J. L. Navas-Migueloa, presents the attitudes of a sizable group of Falangist (mostly neo-Falangist) leaders and spokesmen during the final phase of the regime. Perhaps the most coherent statement was Manuel Cantarero del Castillo's *Falange y socialismo* (Barcelona, 1973), though by the time that the book was published Cantarero had ceased to be a neo-Falangist.

22. The neo-Carlists even claimed that such ideas had formed the core of earlier Carlist corporative doctrine. Several veteran Carlists made an effort to clarify this deep confusion and mystification by publishing a brief primer of orthodox doctrine: Francisco Elías de Tejada et al., *¿Qué es el carlismo?* (Madrid, 1971).

23. On the last phase of the Movement, see the work by Martínez Val cited earlier. Girón, one of the last two major spokesmen for a form of orthodoxy, published his *Reflexiones sobre España* (Madrid, 1975), while one of the most reflective discussions by a Falangist

Last Phase of the Syndical Organization

Since the mid-sixties Solís Ruiz had been preparing a major new reformist syndical law which was finally presented to the Cortes on October 3, 1969. Its basic intent was to endow the Syndical Organization with autonomy and to make it a much more representative institution, with lower-level leaders to be elected by the membership (even though the nomination process would be partially controlled) and the president to be named by Franco, not directly but from a list proposed by the organizations's syndical council. Earlier drafts had proposed even more drastic autonomy, such as the selection of the president at national syndical congresses, and Solís also hoped to extend the organization into new areas such as professional colleges, mutual aid associations, and chambers of commerce.[24] Such aims, and most concretely the new syndical law, were the primary source of Solís's downfall. Carrero Blanco keenly resented his ambition, saw him as a potential source of opposition to prevailing policies, and objected to the growing infiltration of left-wing oppositionists into the lower levels of the Syndical Organization.

Solís's successor, García Ramal, pursued some of the same policies with more political prudence. There was continued emphasis on making aspects of the Syndical Organization more representative, expanding benefits for workers, and codifying new reforms in a syndical law that would replace Solís's abortive project. A watered-down version was finally completed in May 1971. The old fascistic language of "vertical syndicates" had already been replaced in the Organic Law of 1966 with the simple definition "associations of employers, technicians and workers." Whereas the Syndical Organization had previously been labeled "an instrument in the service of the state," the new Syndical Law of 1971 called it "the channel for the professional and economic interests of the workers" and declared it to be autonomous.[25] Technically it would no longer be necessary to be a member of the Movement to hold office higher than that of enlace sindical.

In the wake of the new syndicates law an extensive series of reforms were carried out. Workers' rights of assembly were broadened, lower-level syndical officials received more autonomy as well as a partial guarantee of greater security in their positions, workers' rights of legal appeal were extended, and a new welfare jurisdiction (Tribunales de Amparo) was created. Social assistance was increased, a number of professional col-

---

in these years was Juan Velarde Fuertes, *El nacionalsindicalismo cuarenta años después (Análisis crítico)* (Madrid, 1972).

24. *FF*, 8:165, 174–75; and the discussion in Meliá, *El largo camino*, 237–64.

25. *Spain Today*, no. 10 (Feb. 1971), 21–36. A detailed chronicle and critique of the developing controversy over changes in the syndical law may be found in J. N. García-Nieto, A. Busquets, and S. Marimón, *La nueva Ley Sindical: análisis de una protesta* (Barcelona, 1970).

Table 21.1. Spanish Strike Statistics, 1967–76

Year	Strikes	Workers on Strike	Hours Lost on Strikes
1967	402	272,964	2,456,100
1968	236	1,114,355	2,224,100
1969	459	174,719	5,549,200
1970	817	366,146	6,950,900
1971	601	266,453	8,186,500
1972	688	304,725	7,469,400
1973	811	441,042	11,120,251
1974	1,193	625,971	18,188,895
1975	855	556,371	10,355,170
1976	1,568	3,638,952	110,016,240

Source: Data from the Organización Sindical Española in W. L. Bernecker, "Die Arbeiterbewegung unter dem Franquismus," in *Die geheime Dynamik Autoritärer Diktaturen* (Munich, 1982), 131.

leges were formed, and in general, both the range of activities and the opportunity for worker participation were increased.[26] On July 1, 1970, an elderly Caudillo even admitted, to the applause of many thousands of workers dutifully assembled in Barcelona's Ciudadela Park, that some of the poorer in the nation were still not sharing equally in the benefits of the great economic boom.[27] When the next national syndical congress was held in 1973, nearly all the delegates and officers were elected by the workers. Nonetheless, the president of the Syndical Organization continued to be named by the chief of state, and the basic chain of command remained vertical. Though workers had greater autonomy, rights of participation, and economic justice, the system was still one whose framework was organized and ultimately controlled by the state. Though major public relations efforts had been made during the past decade, even including extensive questionnaires about reforms distributed among workers, the basic right to strike or form independent unions was never even mentioned. Thus all the nominal changes, though they did introduce a semipluralism and a limited freedom of expression, had no effect whatsoever in pacifying industrial labor.

The statistics in table 21.1 indicate considerable growth in strike activity, technically illegal, from 1967 on. The strategy of the Syndical Orga-

26. García-Ramal presents his own case for improvements made during his term of office in *Franco visto por sus ministros*, 282–86. After the new law was enacted, the ministerial title, which had been minister-national delegate of syndicates, was changed to minister of syndical relations.

27. Franco declared that the average level of income had reached a satisfactory level but that the same could not be said of proportionate distribution, "since some of the population gain a great deal, while other poorer sections remain behind." *Pensamiento político*, 2: 515–16.

nization was to combine somewhat greater freedom with firm repression of those active in labor disputes. The arrest and firing of militants together with the ejection of dissident low-level representatives within the syndical structure continued at a high rate. The Communist labor organizers, Catholic dissidents, and others who cooperated in forming broader semiclandestine workers' commissions had succeeded to some extent in infiltrating parts of the Syndical Organization at the shop level. Labor militancy was greatest in some of the new industries (while it dropped off in older ones like the declining coal industry of Asturias), and for the first time strike actions were undertaken by professionals such as doctors and teachers and white-collar workers such as postoffice and bank employees. Moreover, there was more evidence of politics in the strike activity from 1967 onward, including a number of solidarity or sympathy strikes after the dismissal of radical enlaces and occasional public demonstrations to mark May Day.[28] The most lethal incident occurred in Granada when a police charge killed three demonstrating strikers on July 21, 1969.[29]

By the early 1970s there were several cases of strike actions virtually expanding into area general strikes, particularly in the Basque provinces of Vizcaya and Guipúzcoa, where collective actions were more directly politically motivated than in any other part of Spain. It is true that during the entire history of the regime no sector of the economy was ever crippled or paralyzed by strike action, and such key areas as transportation, tourism, and electricity were scarcely ever affected, the Madrid subway workers strike of 1970 being broken by military mobilization of the strikers. By 1973, however, the annual loss of more than ten million work hours on strikes had become troublesome, and during the two months January–February 1974 there were at least 4,379 firings from jobs and 66 expulsions from low-level syndical positions for helping to lead

28. Jon Amsden, *Collective Bargaining and Class Conflict in Spain* (London, 1972), treats the evolution of labor conflict through the late 1960s. The syndical strategy of both the Organization and the opposition during the last years of the regime is well summarized in Bernecker, 145–53. For a sympathetic account of one of the longest strikes of the period, see Joan Font, *La Vaga de l'Harry Walker de Barcelona de 17-12-70 al 15-11-71* (Paris, 1972). Faustino Miguélez, *La lucha de los mineros asturianos bajo el franquismo* (Barcelona, 1977), deals mainly with the Asturian strikes of 1969–73 (pp. 89–304); while CCOO, *Luchas obreras en España* (Lausanne, 1974), provides brief accounts of the main Comisión Obrera strikes during 1972–73. Contemporary discussions by "experts," such as those published in *Los conflictos colectivos de trabajo* (Madrid, 1970), sometimes bore little relation to reality.

29. Such violence by police was highly unusual in the later years of the regime and was triggered by substantial provocation, as explained by a later article entitled "Carta de Granada" in the opposition Paris-based *Cuadernos de Ruedo Ibérico*. The workers' demonstration in Granada was sparked by controversy over terms of a large new road-construction contract, and protesters who gathered in front of the fancy new provincial syndical headquarters were so many and vehement that nervous, ill-trained police had no confidence in controlling them except by gunfire. Local police commanders were summoned to Madrid and roundly berated by superiors for their inefficiency and violence.

strikes.[30] The next syndical elections nonetheless returned even more oppositionists at the grass-roots level than before, indicating that the Syndical Organization relied as much as ever on ultimate police controls to
sustain whatever authority it still had.

The Growth of Opposition

The opposition was no nearer gaining power to overthrow the regime in
the early 1970s than in the late 1940s, but it increased greatly in scope
and intensity, aided by the limited freedom of expression that had slowly
but steadily grown since 1966. Opposition continued to function at three
different levels. There was a sort of loyal opposition consisting of semi-
liberals and reformists within the system and the Movement itself, who
wished to reform rather than overthrow the regime. There continued to
exist a semilegal opposition of middle- and upper-class monarchists and
Christian democrats, whose activities were never directly legalized but
frequently tolerated, and beyond it lay the illegal opposition of radical and
revolutionary groups that was still directly (though never totally) repressed. The radical opposition in turn was made up of three primary elements: university students, industrial labor, and regionalists.[31]

On December 23, 1969, 131 of the principal leaders and intellectuals
associated with the semilegal and illegal opposition presented an open
letter bearing their signatures to Franco. It rejected the concept of restricted political associations within the Movement and demanded democratic reforms. Though the Caudillo was unimpressed and made no response, neither were there serious reprisals.

Throughout the later years of the regime, the great bulk of even the
leftist opposition was moderate and restrained, for it had little hope of
fundamental change until after the death of Franco. This was as true of the
well-organized Communist Party, largest and most active of the hard-core
opposition, as it was of the Socialists and most smaller leftist groups.
Though the regime had become halfway tolerant compared with its first
two decades, it retained all its power, and even during its very final phase
would occasionally pass out long prison sentences for no more than semiclandestine labor organization.

Violent opposition was restricted primarily to a new revolutionary form

30. According to J. M. Maravall, "The Evolution of Industrial Conflict in Spain, 1939–
1975," presented at the Conference on Contemporary International Labor Problems at the
University of Wisconsin, Madison, Dec. 1–2, 1977.

31. The best contemporary analysis of the opposition in the late 1960s and early 1970s
was Juan J. Linz, "Opposition in and under an Authoritarian Regime: The Case of Spain," in
Regimes and Oppositions, ed. R. A. Dahl (New Haven, 1973). For a chronicle of opposition
activities during the last years of the regime, see Fernando Jáuregui and Pedro Vega, *Crónica del antifranquismo*, vol. 3 (Barcelona, 1985).

of Basque nationalist resistance (ETA), and to a much lesser degree, a subsequent minor Marxist terrorist organization in Madrid (FRAP). Radicalization of some of the youth in the Basque nationalist movement is explained in considerable measure by the vertiginous social and cultural changes that took place in the Basque country during the 1960s. Secularization struck a still largely religious society with great impact, while the most intensive pattern of urbanization and industrialization in the entire peninsula engulfed a society of villages and small towns. Between 1950 and 1970 the population of the Basque provinces swelled more than 60 percent, from approximately 1,500,000 to more than 2,400,000, most of it resulting from massive inmigration of non-Basque workers. Formerly semirural areas were transformed into almost solidly industrial zones, destroying ancient patterns of landholding and traditional ways of life and producing extraordinary cultural disorientation and anxiety, the blame for which was often projected outward onto the encompassing Spanish environment. Destabilization of a tightly integrated religious and distinctive regional culture in Vizcaya and Guipúzcoa thus had quite different consequences from the migration of peasants from Andalusian or Leonese villages. Those displaced peasants simply moved away, often never to return, but hundreds of young Basques responded to the trauma of drastic change and continued centralized repression by developing a violent resistance organization of students, young workers, and young middle-class employees. The new movement, ETA, raised the most direct challenge to the regime that it was to face in its last years.[32]

The first fatality exacted by ETA gunmen occurred in 1968 when the head of the *Brigada social* (political section) of the police in Guipúzcoa was shot at the door of his home partly in retaliation for the earlier killings of two *etarras*. Several ETA leaders were captured in the resulting crackdown (which produced nearly 2,000 arrests in the Basque provinces during 1969), and military prosecutors eventually decided to place those most responsible for violence on public trial. The reason for this unusual show procedure was the calculation that public exposure of the violent methods and revolutionary aims of ETA, who by late 1970 had killed three members of the security forces, would build public support for the regime against its challengers. This calculation, opposed by some in the govern-

32. The best succinct analysis of the sources of the radicalization of Basque nationalism during the later years of the regime is Peter Waldmann, "Sozio-ökonomischer Wandel, zentralistische Unterdruckung und Protestgewalt im Baskenland," in *Die geheime Dynamik*, 199–286. For a general treatment of Basque nationalism in this period, see Robert P. Clark, *The Basques: The Franco Years and Beyond* (Reno, 1981). There is now a growing bibliography on the history and evolution of ETA, beginning with José Ma. Portell, *Los hombres de ETA* (Barcelona, 1976). The most comprehensive account is Robert P. Clark, *The Basque Insurgents: ETA, 1952–1980* (Madison, 1984). See also G. Jáuregui Bereciartu, *Ideología y estrategia política de ETA* (Madrid, 1981); and José Ma. Garmendia, *Historia de ETA* (San Sebastian, 1981).

ment, proved to be a major mistake, for the publicity generated by the resulting court-martial had the opposite effect. ETA had been considerably weakened by the repression of 1968–69, and according to some reports was threatened with internal breakdown. A plan to assassinate Franco near his summer residence in Galicia in 1970, possibly the major nonanarchist assassination plot in the history of the regime, had to be abandoned for lack of organizational infrastructure.[33] The court-martial of the leading ETA prisoners at Burgos in December, however, resulted in a flood of favorable publicity that helped to revive and expand the movement.

All the leftist groups gave the trial as much attention as they could, stressing that court-martial procedures merely exemplified the military and repressive nature of the system. On August 18, an old *gudari* (Basque Nationalist soldier of the Civil War) set himself afire and threw himself from the upper level of a *frontón* in San Sebastian in front of Franco, attending a jai-alai game there. The pope publicly requested leniency for the accused *etarras* while the leadership of the European Community urged "maximum clemency." On December 2 ETA activists kidnapped the German consul in San Sebastián, after which guarantees were suspended in Guipúzcoa for three months, and then more briefly for all of Spain.

The trial at Burgos in December 1970 thus became a cause celebre, the defendants outspoken in their denunciations of the military judiciary and occasionally making physical lunges at them. In Madrid a sizable demonstration on behalf of the unity of Spain was convened before Franco in the Plaza de Oriente. If this was not as spontaneous as the regime claimed, there nonetheless seemed to be genuine enthusiasm in the denunciation of Basque separatists by the crowd. When the proceedings were completed at Burgos on December 28, nine of the defendants were condemned to death,[34] though after a unanimous recommendation by his cabinet[35] Franco prudently commuted all the sentences to life imprisonment three days later.

The consequence of all this, nonetheless, was to refurbish the image of ETA among Basques generally and young Basques particularly and to reemphasize the general image of the repressiveness of the regime. The youth of the accused, their burning enthusiasm and dedication to the

33. C. Fernández et al., "ETA quiso matar a Franco y a Arias Navarro," *Cambio 16,* Dec. 17, 1984, pp. 86–89.

34. Kepa Salaberri, *El proceso de Euskadi en Burgos* (Paris, 1971), is the version of a Basque nationalist; while Gisele Halimi, *Le procès de Burgos* (Paris, 1971), adds that of the French and west European left. Federico de Arteaga, *ETA y el proceso de Burgos* (Madrid, 1971), is favorable to the regime. Angel Suárez–Colectivo 36, *Libro blanco sobre las cárceles franquistas 1939–1976* (Paris, 1976), 147–308, presents a denunciation of prison conditions during the regime's last years.

35. The account of two cabinet members, the foreign minister López Bravo and the interior minister Garicano Goñi, may be found in *Franco visto por sus ministros,* 124, 201–2.

Table 21.2. Repression in the Basque Provinces, 1968–75

Year	Arrested	Exiled	Imprisoned	Years Sentenced	Wounded by Police
1968	434	38	—	—	—
1969	1,953	342	862	786	—
1970	831	128	396	1,104	416
1972	616	—	328	226	216
1973	572	—	316	635	178
1974	1,116	320	315	786	105
1975	4,625	518	632	—	—

Source: Luis C.-Núñez Astrain, *La sociedad vasca actual* (San Sebastian, 1977), 121. Data not available for 1971.

Basque cause, the severity of the initial sentences, the obvious sympathy of a large portion of the Basque clergy for the accused (two priests were among the indicted), and the general outpouring of international sympathy and appeals on their behalf—all had a profound effect on Basque opinion. The government was completely unable to find any formula that might have conciliated some of the moderates in Basque society, other than minor concessions for part-time *ikastolas* (Basque language schools). Repression was simply increased, though not to the level that would have been necessary to stamp out dissidence (see table 21.2). Altogether, between 1968 and 1975, ETA would claim a total of 47 victims, while 27 of its members would die at the hands of the police. ETA activists had certain undeniable advantages in their work: the mountainous configuration of Vizcaya and Guipúzcoa provided shelter, the clergy sometimes gave them major assistance, their language was virtually impermeable to Spanish police, and the contiguous French border offered easy sanctuary. The movement gained in strength during the closing years of the regime, and by the time of Franco's death, Basque opinion was very much more inflamed than it had been a mere decade earlier.

The Ecclesiastical Revolt

A potentially even more serious source of dissidence than radical Basque nationalism was the drastic change in the policy of the Church, coupled with the active political dissent of much of the younger clergy. The liberalizing reforms and redefinitions of the Catholic Church's Council of Vatican II, which were concluded in 1965, had probably a greater impact in Spain than in any other country, if only because Spain had hitherto been more conservative than any other major Catholic country.

Formal association with the state persisted, but the Vatican clearly indicated that it wanted a complete change, and in fact many of the clergy had become the de facto leaders of the visible (as distinct from clandestine) domestic political opposition. From petitions in the early 1960s they had moved to protest marches in Barcelona in 1966 and then to occupations of buildings and to independent politicized assemblies, all of this accompanied in the larger cities by inflammatory sermons and agitation by individual priests. A few of the most radical proclaimed the need to put an end to capitalism and solemnly declared that "exploiters" could not expect to receive the sacraments in a state of grace. Christian-Marxist dialogues, either clandestine or conducted outside of Spain, became all the rage. Hundreds of clergy were involved in political activities that a quarter-century earlier would have brought immediate imprisonment, beatings, and long prison terms to laymen. Since the clergy had special juridical privileges under the Concordat, they were treated with kid gloves, however. Only the most conspicuous were arrested for civil (that is, political) offenses, and even then it was necessary to consult with the ecclesiastical superior. Eventually a special *cárcel concordataria* (lit. "Concordat jail") was set up in the Leonese city of Zamora and housed more than a score of inmates by 1969. While the hierarchy generally attempted to hold the wave of agitation in check, at least to some extent, this was less true with each passing year. When the liberal José Ma. Cirarda was appointed bishop of Bilbao on the death of the ultraconservative incumbent near the close of 1969, the insurgent Basque clergy of Vizcaya in effect had one of their own as leader. After the regime declared a temporary state of emergency at the beginning of 1969, a delegation from the hierarchy urged the minister of justice to lift it as soon as possible.

All this provoked a new kind of anticlericalism never before seen in Spain, the anticlericalism of the extreme right. Publications of old-line Falangists and other ultrarightist groups were given relative license in their verbal attacks on the "red clergy," and there were occasional physical assaults as well. In July 1971 the minister of justice publicly protested the "Marxistization" of the Church, echoing the language of a report presented by the minister of the interior six months earlier on the penetration achieved by subversive groups and ideas.

The most outspoken supporter of the regime among the Church hierarchy was Msgr. José Guerra Campos, former auxiliary bishop of Madrid (and later bishop of Cuenca), an appointive deputy in the Cortes and for several years secretary of the Episcopal Conference (the leadership structure of the Church developed after Vatican II). He had delivered possibly the most important and effective Spanish address at Vatican II (on the theme of Christianity and Marxism), but could count on no more than about 15 percent of the votes in the Episcopal Conference to support a direct proregime stand. Later, in September 1974, he issued a pastoral letter in Cuenca entitled "The Church and Francisco Franco," declaring that in the late twentieth century it was "singular" that "a son of the Church has tried to project in public life his Christian faith and the law of God proclaimed by ecclesiastical teaching," as a result of which Franco had received special recognition from popes and bishops that "can scarcely be found with respect to any other personage of recent centuries."[36] Farther yet to the right there were several efforts to form new activist lay groups. The most extreme were the strong-arm squads known as the Guerrilleros de Cristo Rey (Warriors of Christ the King), which were fully repudiated by the Church leadership.

The peak of clerical activism was reached in the early 1970s. Support for it from the highest level of the Church was demonstrated in 1972 when Pope Paul's liberal nuncio, Msgr. Luigi Dadaglio, indicated that it was appropriate to have offered church sanctuary to a group of 111 priests, students, and workers pursued by police for having demonstrated on behalf of Basque nationalism.

Abandonment of the traditional Spanish ideology by the greater part of the clergy filled Franco and Carrero Blanco, its last major historical avatars, with perplexity and a certain consternation. At a meeting late in 1972 with the liberal Cardinal Tarancón, new president of the Episcopal Conference, Carrero Blanco reiterated the devotion of the Spanish state to the Church, pledging that it was prepared to do even more juridically and financially and that all it asked in return was that the Church be its firmest support. Carrero gained no reassurance from Tarancón. At a subsequent cabinet meeting on December 7, the vice-president presented a statement detailing the financial support provided the Church by the regime, together with the amount which the regime had invested in the construction of new church buildings and the propagation of the faith, amounting, he claimed, to some 300 billion pesetas. The Church leaders may have forgotten, concluded Carrero, "but God does not forget." This statement was then leaked to the press, one official organ describing it as "Carrero's hammer-blow."[37] It was conceptually extremely difficult for the leaders of the Spanish regime in their old age to grasp that the Church no longer thought in such traditional terms, and the very last years of their lives were to this extent a time of bewilderment.

At the beginning of 1973 the foreign minister (himself a member of Opus Dei) gained an audience with the pope to present a personal letter of protest from Franco, but this elicited no change of ecclesiastical policy. Soon afterward the Spanish hierarchy released a document "La Iglesia y la Comunidad Política" ("The Church and the Political Community") that

36. Quoted in Amando de Miguel, *Franco, Franco, Franco* (Madrid, 1976), 23.
37. Tarancón's version of the meeting and his reaction to the subsequent announcement is given in J. L. Martín Descalzo, *Tarancón, el cardenal del cambio* (Barcelona, 1982), 191–92.

came out in favor of democratic pluralism.[38] During 1973 a number of leftist laymen and clergy formed a group called Cristianos por el Socialismo,
while the newest appointee as bishop of Bilbao, Antonio Añoveros (who
was even more liberal than his predecessor), conducted an official ceremony of excommunication against a number of policemen who had beaten
up an activist priest in his diocese. In November the ecclesiastics held
prisoner in the cárcel concordataria at Zamora staged a prison riot, wreck-
ing much of the furniture and other appointments, and were supported by
demonstrations of sacerdotal solidarity in various parts of the country.

The Question of a New Concordat

The question of a new concordat or institutional relationship which would
grant the Church greater autonomy became a central issue during the
final decade of the regime. Both the Vatican and the Spanish Church were
concerned to eliminate the close institutional association with the state,
particularly the government's partial control of the selection of bishops.
Most of the clergy seemed willing to renounce their juridical privileges in
favor of a new political and institutional framework that would provide
greater freedom for all Spaniards. Certain specific reforms, however, such
as the issue of the ecclesiastical subsidy, raised major practical problems,
and these restrained the Church from denouncing the Concordat directly.
From the point of view of the government, the cost of the subsidy was a
small price to pay for the residual benefits of the Concordat. Its proportionate expense had dropped from about one percent of the total state
budget in 1940 to only about one-half of one percent in 1970.

The Vatican initiated negotiations for a new concordat in 1968, but the
regime dragged its feet. Church leaders favored a series of limited agreements on specific issues rather than a mere revision of the old concordat,
but Franco and his ministers had little interest in a new relationship, the
old one having suited their purposes optimally. Yet the regime could not
completely resist personal pressure from the Pope, and a draft sketch of a
possible new concordat was released by the government at the beginning
of 1971. This proved unsatisfactory to the Church, for it resulted in only
limited liberalization.

From that point the Vatican became increasingly assertive, virtually dic-
tating the choice of new prelates by offering the regime only one name for
new vacancies, in technical violation of the Concordat, or else appointing
auxiliary bishops, a procedure that did not require the approval of the
state. Franco had little alternative but to swallow such treatment in his

38. Reprinted in *Documentos colectivos del Espiscopado español, 1870–1974* (Madrid,
1974), 520–24.

declining years, and as a result of the Vatican's strategy, by the time of his death almost as many (seventeen) episcopal sees had no full titular incumbent as in the Republican zone when Franco completed its conquest in 1939.

Even so, the regime sustained its national Catholic identity to its dying day, continuing on frequent public occasions to affirm its own peculiar theology, as if the position of the Roman Catholic Church in general had not changed since 1939 or 1953. Despite acute political tension between portions of the clergy and the government, most members of the hierarchy continued to play much the same ceremonial roles on public occasions. Even though there were few ministers who were primarily "Catholic ministers" in Franco's final government,[39] three bishops sat as Franco's personal appointees in the regime's last parliament, and an archbishop sat in the government's Council of State and Council of the Realm to the very end.

Educational Reform and Expansion

Shortly before his death, Franco complained that the trouble with most of his education ministers was that they had been professors more interested in protecting their own guild interests than in developing sound education.[40] This could not be said of José Villar Palasí, brought in to deal with the problems of the Ministry of Education in 1968, whose approach paralleled that of his fellow government technocrats who were also members of Opus Dei. He aimed for rapid development of educational facilities, accompanied by major reforms, though with the assumption that a greatly expanded and modernized educational system would continue to operate within the existing cultural and institutional modalities.

Such a drastic change could probably not be managed without the personal support of the Caudillo, and in order to gain his approval Villar Palasí emphasized the need for educational modernization in order to bring an end to the constant disorder in the major universities. This argument from national security helped carry the day with Franco, who gave

39. The best composite analysis concludes that about one-fourth the ministers of the Franco regime could be identified politically as primarily "Catholic," so long as one includes in that general designation a number of the military ministers of somewhat ambiguous identity. Ten ministers (7.7 percent of the total) came from Catholic Action or the ACNP. Fourteen of the "technocratic" ministers of the 1960s were of overtly Catholic background, members of or otherwise identified with Opus Dei, and accounted for 11.9 percent of Franco's ministers. To these may be added four Carlists, four military ministers either with CEDA connections or closely associated with other ministers who were members of Opus Dei, and five neo-Falangist ministers during the early years of the regime who were originally connected with the CEDA. Guy Hermet, *Les Catholiques dans l'Espagne franquiste* (Paris, 1980), 1:336–37.

40. Vicente Pozuelo Escudero, *Los últimos 476 días de Franco* (Barcelona, 1980), 54–56.

the ambitious new program his blessing. To convince other departments of the government and the Cortes, a special White Paper, *La educación en España: Bases para una política educativa*, appeared in April 1969, prepared mainly by Ricardo Díez Hochleitner, former director of educational planning and finance for UNESCO, who became Villar's subsecretary. This served as the basis for a broad new education law that provoked sharp and extended debate in the Cortes and a number of amendments before it was finally approved in July 1970.[41]

The new program, theoretically scheduled to extend over a decade, was the first general reform of Spanish education since the original Moyano Law of 1857 that had established the country's modern school system. It criticized Spain's existing educational structure for being technically backward, impractical, and incapable of providing equal access to all Spanish society. Its aim was not to develop a new culture distinct from the present one (as in revolutionary regimes) but to build a more highly trained and skilled society able to sustain a higher level of economic development. In the process, in the words of the ministry, it proposed to make education "the decisive instrument of social mobility" in Spain, thus achieving the social renovation that the vaunted National Syndicalist revolution, aborted in earlier years, had failed to bring about. The goal was therefore to expand all levels of education at the same time, while trying to integrate them through new content and techniques. For the first time in Spanish history, national elementary education became compulsory, since for the first time the state possessed resources to begin construction of schools adequate for the entire population. A new program of *educación básica general* was instituted for the first eight years of schooling, divided into two different cycles. Secondary education was reorganized around a three-year cycle (in the Institutos Nacionales de Enseñanza Media), plus a pre-university year for those going farther. The university system was geared to three cycles: a three-year undergraduate cycle, a two-year professional degree sequence, and the doctorate. In addition, plans were laid for expansion of vocational and adult/extension programs.[42]

As late as 1964 Spain had been spending only about 2 percent of its GNP on education (not counting private and religious schools, which were numerous), less than any other European country save Portugal. Several World Bank Loans were obtained to expedite reform and expansion, so that between 1969 and 1971 spending on education increased 66 percent in constant pesetas. By 1971 the proportion of GNP spent on education had more than doubled compared with 1964, and had in-

---

41. Gestation of the education reform is treated in Gunther, *Public Policy*, 166–72.

42. John M. McNair, *Education for a Changing Spain* (Manchester, 1984), studies the educational reform of 1970 and its consequences.

Table 21.3. Changes in Spanish Government Spending Priorities
(Spending on each function as percentage of total budget)

Function	1953	1958	1963	1968	1973	1975
Defense	30.4	20.9	19.3	14.7	13.2	13.8
Education	8.2	8.0	9.6	12.2	17.7	17.8
Social assistance	3.8	1.8	5.3	5.3	7.4	8.7
Housing	0	9.8	7.3	4.0	2.5	2.8
Economic services	15.3	27.3	30.0	26.8	24.9	21.5
Justice and police	9.1	7.9	6.8	7.1	6.6	7.5

Source: Richard Gunther, *Public Policy in a No-Party State* (Berkeley, 1980), 50.

creased much more in real terms, due to the rapid expansion of the economy. The steady rise in the percentage of the state budget devoted to education is indicated in table 21.3 and about 1970 the number of secondary students educated in state schools for the first time began to surpass the total of those in Catholic institutions.

This was proportionally the broadest educational reform and expansion being attempted anywhere in the western world. It challenged the vested interests of veteran teachers and professors and of some students who had partially completed the requirements of the old system. At the universities it roused strong protests from both radical students and reactionary professors. In more objective terms, the reform tried to do too much too fast and was often poorly administered, with Díez Hochleitner resigning under considerable fire in mid-1972. The university student population, about 150,000 in 1969, increased to nearly 400,000 by the time of Franco's death six years later. This academic population explosion produced a volatile mass of new students for whom adequate facilities were often lacking, and only reinforced the tendency among *universitarios* toward disaffection and strong political opposition. There is little doubt that the educational reform and expansion, one of the prouder achievements of the regime's later years, contributed significantly to its partial destabilization.[43]

The Military During the Final Phase

Throughout the 1950s and 1960s, whenever worried supporters pressed Franco about the question of the succession and the future, he usually responded that no one need worry, for in extremis there was always the Army, which could be relied upon to defend the institutions of the regime

43. Carrero Blanco was by no means oblivious of this and rather feared some of the consequences of the new policies, at one point calling Villar Palasí "crazy." Dr. Vicente Gil, *Cuaranta años junto a Franco* (Barcelona, 1981), 57. He sought to have him dropped from the cabinet, and in the next government replaced him with a much more conservative, less imaginative minister.

Table 21.4. Percentage of Military Ministers in the Governments of Franco

1938	41.6	1943	46.1	1956	31.2	1969	26.3
1939	42.8	1944	38.4	1962	42.1	1970	26.3
1941	46.1	1945	50.0	1965	31.6	1973	20.0
1942	46.1	1951	37.5	1967	31.6	1974	15.8

Source: Computation by Rafael Bañón Martínez, "Las Fuerzas Armadas durante la Transición Política," cuadro 11.

and guarantee continuity. This assurance was well founded to the extent that the Spanish military remained fully identified as Franco's own Army to the very end. The officer corps, with only the fewest exceptions, supported the regime and always looked to Franco as their Caudillo. Yet he had managed to develop an institutionalized system rather than a merely pretorian or military regime, and had always been successful in avoiding political intervention by the military while retaining their political loyalty. Though many senior officers had participated in government, they did so not primarily as representatives of the armed forces but as individual administrators in formal state institutions which recruited on a semipluralistic basis. Moreover, the number of military personnel in cabinet positions declined noticeably after 1951, dropping from nearly 50 percent in some of the first governments to 32 percent in 1965 and to 26 percent in 1969. In Franco's final government of 1974–75 only the armed forces ministers themselves were of military background.[44] To a certain degree Franco encouraged professionalization and the attitude that the function of the military was to serve rather than to dominate. Thus he not only trained the officer corps to serve his own regime faithfully but he also, however ironically, began its preparation to adjust to an apolitical role during the democratization of Spanish institutions after his death.

One of the most important functions that military institutions continued to play in the regime to the very end was to expedite political repression. A new decree of 1969 even authorized military mobilization of striking workers in the interest of national security and was used to break a subway strike. Yet such exploitation of military institutions had never been altogether popular among officers, and on December 1, 1970, just before the notorious Burgos trial began, Lt. Gen. García Valiño (who had voted in the Cortes against Franco's choice of successor) wrote to the captain general of the Burgos district, where the trial was to be held, protesting the use of military courts in this way.[45] On the other hand, resentment

44. Altogether, Rafael Bañón Martínez has calculated that 32.4 percent of all Franco's cabinet ministers were military officers and 76.3 percent state bureaucrats in one area or another, whether civil or military. M. Baena, R. Bañón Martínez, et al., *Burocracia y política en la realidad española* (Madrid, 1976).

45. *FF*, 8:218.

increased among ultra officers in the face of the government's subsequent vacillations and commutation of sentences, leading to semisecret meetings in a number of garrisons during the closing days of 1970 that were said to have involved hundreds of officers. A subsequent decree of November 1971 finally reduced once more the jurisdiction of military courts, so that, according to the *Anuario Estadístico Militar,* the number of civilians sentenced by such tribunals dropped from 403 in 1970 to 231 in 1971 and 222 in 1972.

Franco was fully aware that one of the main deficiencies of the modern Spanish army lay in the hypertrophy of its officer corps and the excessive share, sometimes up to 80 percent, of the budget devoted to salaries, leaving much too little for equipment and training. Yet, though he privately criticized successive ministers of the army for being slow to deal with the problem, he himself took little initiative, hesitating to create disturbances or resentment where almost none existed. Slowly but steadily the size of the Army in general, the officer corps, and the proportion of the budget devoted to the military were pared down during the last twenty years of the regime. From a total force of 320,000 (including 29,500 officers) in 1950 the Army was reduced to 240,000 (including 19,300 officers) in 1970. Lt. Gen. Antonio Barroso, army minister from 1957 to 1962, cut the number of divisions from eighteen to twelve, and more extensive reorganization was initiated in 1965. This ultimately divided Army units into two different groups, the Fuerzas de Intervención Inmediata (FII) and the Fuerzas de Defensa Operativa del Territorio (FDOT). The first was organized for external defense at the Pyrenees and the southern coast, the second primarily for antisubversive operations within Spain.[46]

Much of the manpower was provided by an annual contingent of between 100,000 and 150,000 draftees, who served for eighteen months, while volunteers enlisted for two years. One of the most necessary reforms, however, was to lower the retirement age, much higher than in most other armies, so as to remove the elderly, superannuated, usually not fully competent generals who made up the swollen senior echelon, yet this was never seriously attempted, at least partly for political reasons. A personnel reform was introduced in the Navy during the 1960s, but this was a much smaller arm and one much less capable of generating political repercussions.

46. The FII (international defense) forces consisted of three divisions (one armored, one mechanized, one motorized) and three brigades (one parachute, one air transport, one cavalry). The FDOT comprised two mountain divisions, eleven infantry brigades, and two artillery brigades. These units were maintained at about 70 percent strength, with a tank park that in 1975 contained about 800 vehicles, of which about 350 were American M-47 and M-48s, 50-ton tanks with 90-mm guns (the standard American tanks down to 1960). Another 250 were smaller American models, while 200 were French AMX-30s, relatively light tanks with 105-mm guns that were the Army's most modern combat vehicles.

Unlike the situation in many other contemporary military establishments, the Army always got the lion's share of the military budget, though its percentage declined from 72 in 1945 to 53.4 in 1970. This might have seemed surprising in view of Spain's exposed peninsular position, which would have argued development of the Navy and Air Force, but it obviously stemmed from inertia and from political considerations. The Navy consisted of but one cruiser, ten submarines, some thirty destroyers and frigates, and a variety of smaller craft. The Air Force came to comprise eleven squadrons of relatively modern jet fighter-bombers, varying in size from twelve to eighteen aircraft per squadron. Three of these, however, were equipped with obsolescent subsonic Saeta and Super Saeta jets, originally designed by Willy Messerschmitt but manufactured in Spain. Most of the rest were older American aircraft, though during the last year of the regime twenty-one late-model Mirage jets were purchased from France. The Spanish Air Force also included approximately one thousand transports and miscellaneous planes.

The aid received from the United States at any one time was comparatively modest, often consisting of obsolescent equipment that the United States Army no longer wanted. Outright gifts of material were sometimes accompanied by an agreement that further amounts were to be purchased commercially. The severe limit to American generosity, combined with the perennial backwardness and shortage of materiel in the Spanish armed forces, led to a certain amount of resentment among the military over the terms of the relationship with the United States.

Certainly a regime primarily devoted to economic development and exhibiting a largely passive foreign policy felt no need to spend much money on its armed forces. Not only did the Spanish government maintain a relatively small military establishment compared with other European coun-

Table 21.5. Military Expenditures per Soldier and
Sizes of Armies in Western and Central
Europe, 1969

Country	Dollars Spent Annually per Soldier	Troops under Arms per 10,000 Population
Great Britain	12,763	77
France	12,087	103
Sweden	11,775	108
Norway	9,285	92
Czechoslovakia	6,835	150
Hungary	3,627	98
Portugal	1,660	192
Spain	1,783	94

Source: Antonio Sánchez Gijón in *Madrid*, Nov. 3, 1969.

Table 21.6. Military and Police Expenditures as Percentages of the National Budget, 1967–75

Year	Military Expenditures	Police Expenditures
1967	16.2	5.1
1968	14.7	4.8
1969	13.5	4.5
1970	12.7	4.4
1971	12.2	4.1
1972	12.8	4.6
1973	13.2	4.8
1974	14.2	5.2
1975	13.8	5.8

Source: Richard Gunther, *Public Policy in a No-Party State* (Berkeley, 1980), 167.

tries (table 21.5), but it steadily reduced the military share of the state budget (table 21.6). By 1973 Spain was devoting only 1.5 percent of its GNP to defense, a lower proportion than that of any other west European country save Luxemburg, and after 1970 for the first time in Spanish history, Spain spent more on education than on the armed forces.

The senior military command enjoyed great recognition and prestige, but opinion polls among Spanish youth in the 1960s indicated that a low-paid military career attracted little interest and that in the new urban, industrialized Spain a military career was not generally viewed as a prestigious one. Between 1964 and 1970 the number of new cadets in Franco's old Academia General Militar at Zaragoza dropped by two-thirds. The officer corps was increasingly isolated from the new urban society and had become largely self-recruited. During the years 1964 to 1968 in the Army academy, 79.6 percent of officer candidates were sons of officers or other military personnel, and the corresponding figures for the Navy were 65.8 and for the more modernistic Air Force 56.2.[47] Moreover, salaries remained so low that 65 percent of the officers held part-time jobs to make ends meet.[48] It should be kept in mind, though, that this situation was to some extent characteristic of Spanish society in general, for most elite groups were to a significant degree self-recruited within their own cadres and *pluri-empleo* was a common middle-class phenomenon.

The attitudes and values of the gerat majority of officers remained con-

47. Julio Busquets Bragulat, *El militar de carrera en España* (Barcelona, 1971), 201–2. José Antonio Olmeda has arrived at the variant percentages of 71.7, 73.6, and 47.1 for officer candidates during the broader period of 1960–1976, while including sons of Civil Guard and police personnel. "La Burocracia Militar en España," 244.
48. Busquets, 270.

servative, Catholic, and nationalist. They were rightly considered the most reliable part of the state system, along with the two bodies who maintained public order, the 60,000-man Civil Guard and the 20,000 armed police (colloquially known as *grises*, from the color of their grey uniforms). The other state employees—approximately 350,000 in the central bureaucracy, 190,000 in local government administration, and more than 100,000 in the Syndical Organization—were much less significant, even though they were disproportionately concentrated in central rather than local government administration.[49] Beginning in 1972, the regime began to increase, slightly, expenditures on the military and the police in the face of a burgeoning political opposition that had become better organized and more overt.

If the military never wavered in support of the regime, what they thought of the current government was sometimes another story. In 1968 Carrero Blanco set up a new intelligence unit, which in March 1972 became the Servicio Central de Documentación de la Presidencia del Cobierno (SECED), under his own branch of government. It was to gather systematic information about political attitudes and activities, including possible subversion, in key sectors of Spanish society and institutions, including the military.[50]

Army "ultras" resented the influence of the civilian technocrats in the regime, who had introduced reforms and were dedicated to an uncertain monarchist succession, neither of which were pleasing to some of the old hard-liners. In January 1971 Fernando Rodrigo Cifuentes, captain general of Granada, was relieved of command for making a speech in which he denounced the nefarious power of the "White Masonry" (a common allusion to Opus Dei), but he received a telegram of congratulations from the thirtieth annual assembly of the alféreces provisionales of the Civil War.[51]

49. A 1977 study found that the approximately one million central state employees (including the military) amounted to 81 percent of the grand total of 1,247,000 government employees. Within the EEC countries, local government employees were proportionately more than twice as numerous as in Spain, averaging 41 percent of the total compared with 19 percent. This reflected the neglect of Spanish local government in modern times and the political priorities of the regime, though in general the Spanish bureaucracy was small, only 9.3 percent of the active population, compared with an average of 16 percent in the heavily bureaucratized social democratic states of the European Community. J. Junquera González, "La Burocracia en la 'Europa de los nueve'," in *Papeles de Economía Española* 2 (1980), 175, quoted in D. Nohlen and C. Huneeus, "Elitenwettbewerb in der Spätphase des Franco-Regimes," in *Sozialer Wandel und Herrschaft im Spanien Francos* (Paderborn, 1984), ed. P. Waldmann et al., 351–52.

50. This special intelligence unit was originally created under the Ministry of Education to assist in dealing with the crisis in the universities. It later worked closely with the Ministry of the Interior before being placed directly under Carrero's subsecretaryship of the presidency in 1972. José Ignacio San Martín, *Servicio especial* (Barcelona, 1983), is a memoir by its head.

51. Fernández, *Tensiones militares*, 188–93.

The chief representative of strict professionalism within the military command was Lt. Gen. Manuel Díez Alegría, who had a reputation for professional competence and who succeeded Muñoz Grandes as head of the Alto Estado Mayor. His book *Ejército y sociedad* (1972) presented an irreproachable philosophy of civil-military relations, emphasizing the professional role and apoliticism of the officer corps. Díez Alegría, whose brother was a notorious representative of the radicals among the dissenting Jesuits within the Spanish clergy, was considered a dangerous liberal by the ultra factions, yet his goal of apolitical professionalism for the military was not far from the thinking of many of his fellow officers. Only a handful of senior generals such as Díez Alegría, Castañón, Vega, and Gutiérrez Mellado (and perhaps a majority of the Air Force generals) were directly sympathetic to aperturismo and reform within the regime. The vast majority of generals and officers, however, felt little desire for the officer corps to have to take responsibility for government again, and hence their reluctance to contravene its normal processes, whether under an aged Caudillo or a young king.[52]

Foreign Relations

The relationship with the United States remained the cornerstone of Spain's foreign policy, and it had even been rumored that American pressure was a factor in the *cese* of Castiella as foreign minister, since he had been trying, however unsuccessfully, to take a hard line in negotiations for renewal of the bilateral pact. In fact, it is doubtful that American pressure had much to do with it. Castiella had become an object of some suspicion because of his liberalizing position on religious relations and the Vatican, while the appointment of López Bravo as his successor was thoroughly in line with the monocolor tone of the new cabinet. López Bravo had been director general of external commerce and head of the Spanish Institute of Currency Exchange (Moneda Extranjera) before serving as minister of industry. Though he did not continue Castiella's tougher line toward the United States, he did institute a new Spanish *Ostpolitik*, travelling to Moscow at the beginning of 1970 to discuss opening relations with the Soviet Union. Soon afterward an agreement was signed to buy Mirage jet fighters from France, and in June a limited agreement was signed with Paris concerning future joint military maneuvers and a modest program of arms manufactures.

52. H. C. Felipe Mansilla, "Politik und Militär in Spanien," in Waldmann et al., *Die geheime Dynamik*, 1–60, presents an accurate summary of the evolution of the military during the course of the regime, together with the pertinent bibliography. On the military during the last days of the regime and afterward, see Jesús Ynfante [pseud.], *El Ejército de Franco y de Juan Carlos* (Paris, 1976); and Carlos Fernández, *Los militares durante la transición* (Madrid, 1982).

Franco valued the American connection highly for reasons of prestige, political reinforcement, and international strategy, and consequently López Bravo dropped his predecessor's insistence on large amounts of military aid in favor of increased "scientific, educational, social and economic aid,"[53] in accordance with the priorities of the new government. This quickly led to the signing of the new five-year Agreement of Friendship and Cooperation with the United States in Washington on August 6, 1970. Like its predecessors, this pact failed to provide any direct security guarantee for Spain, but the secret clause agreed to in 1953 was finally canceled, and for the first time the bases used by American forces were designated simply "Spanish military installations." The new pact specified that "in case of foreign threat or attack against the security of the West, the time and method of use by the United States . . . will be the object of urgent consultation between the two governments."[54] American assistance from 1970 to 1975 came to approximately 300 million dollars, much of it in nonmilitary aid.[55]

President Richard Nixon followed the new pact with a very brief visit to Madrid during his west European swing in October 1970. This was reciprocated by a trip of Juan Carlos and Sofía to Washington at the end of January 1971, which proved quite successful. The intelligent, discreet, English-speaking royal couple impressed American officialdom favorably and set policy-makers to thinking of the importance of a transition to reformist monarchy in Madrid before the irremediable decay of the regime dangerously destabilized the country.

In the following month Nixon sent General Vernon A. Walters, deputy chief of the CIA, to Madrid for a talk with Franco. Walters found the Generalissimo looking "old and weak. His left hand trembled at times so violently that he would cover it with his other hand. At times he appeared far away and at others he came right to the point." He quickly volunteered "that what he felt the President was most interested in was what would happen in Spain after his own demise," stressing that the transition would be "orderly" and that "there was no alternative to the Prince." He acknowledged that "Spain would move some distance along the road we favored but not all the way, as Spain was neither America nor England nor France. . . . He . . . expressed confidence in the Prince's ability to handle the situation after his death. . . . He smiled and said that many people

53. *New York Times*, April 15, 1970.

54. *FF*, 8:195.

55. For a lucid brief summary of Spanish-American relations during these years, see Benjamin Welles, "Spain and the United States," in *Spain in the 1970s*, ed. W. T. Salisbury and J. D. Theberg (New York, 1976), 136–51; and also Rubottom and Murphy, *Spain*, 91–94. Manuel Vázquez Montalbán, *La penetración americana en España* (Madrid, 1974), 13–25, presents the text of the agreement and a denunciation from the viewpoint of the leftist opposition.

doubted that these institutions would work. They were wrong; the transition would be peaceful. . . . He had faith in God and the Spanish people."[56]

Despite an official State Department denial, the Washington Post reported on July 28, 1971, that the Nixon administration was waging a low-key campaign to convince Franco that he should turn the reins of government over to Juan Carlos before his physical decline produced a crisis. During the year a number of high-ranking American officials visited Madrid to reinforce this point, while the current ambassador, Robert P. Hill, went to considerable lengths to cultivate the Prince.

López Bravo's principal achievement in foreign affairs lay in negotiations with the European Community, with whom Spain entered into associate status through a treaty in June 1970 that provided preferential terms of trade. This arrangement opened the Common Market partway to Spanish exports without disturbing too greatly the Spanish protective tariff. Though full membership in the Community lay far in the future (and would not be arranged until a decade after Franco's death), the agreement of 1970 offered Spain much of the best of both worlds, providing a new outlet for Spanish goods without subjecting the domestic economy to greatly increased competition.

Beyond this, López Bravo's effort to carry on a more active foreign policy involved more travel and publicity than substance and achievement. Though Carrero and other hardliners prevented full resumption of relations with the Soviet Union, a commercial agreement was signed, a TASS office was opened in Madrid, and an EFE (Spanish news service) office was opened in Moscow. Regular diplomatic relations were established with East Germany and China, as well as consular agreements with Hungary, Poland, Bulgaria, Romania, and Czechoslovakia. López Bravo also paid special attention to relations with other Mediterranean countries and with Latin America. He made three trips to Latin America in 1971, visiting every country in the region except Mexico.[57] This accelerated activity could not change the fact that Spain would never enjoy fully normal relations with its west European neighbors as long as the regime remained in power.

56. Vernon A. Walters, Silent Missions (New York, 1978), 555–56.

57. López Bravo summarized his general approach in a lecture before the CESEDEN (Center of National Defense Studies) on Feb. 3, 1971, published in English as Some Considerations about the Spanish Foreign Policy. A brief overview of López Bravo as foreign minister and the functioning of his ministry is provided by Angel Viñas, "La política exterior española del franquismo," Cuenta y Razón, no. 6 (Spring 1982), 61–76. López Bravo's Ostpolitik is treated by J. Lee Shneidman, "Eastern Europe and the Soviet Union," in Spain in the Twentieth-Century World, ed. J. W. Cortada (Westport, Conn., 1980), 169–73. Manuel Cantarero del Castillo, "La politica exterior," in España perspectiva 1973 (Madrid, 1973), 47–86, presents a critique of López Bravo's activity during 1972–73. Fernando de Salas López, España, la OTAN y los organismos militares internacionales (Madrid, 1974), treats the Spanish relation to western defense.

Politics During the Monocolor Government

It is doubtful that Franco really believed that he could guarantee the full perpetuation of his regime after his death, but he did intend to see that its key institutions survived and was convinced that his dispositions had fundamentally achieved that goal. In his New Year's Eve speech of 1969 he made his notorious declaration about the succession that *"todo está atado y bien atado"* ("everything is tied and well tied"). The future of the regime would ultimately rest more with Juan Carlos than with Franco, of course, and the accuracy of the Caudillo's wager on the Prince.

After being recognized officially by Franco as heir to the throne, Juan Carlos very slowly but surely began to assert himself as the fundamental factor in the country's future. Obstacles were plentiful, for he had never been popular with the die-hards of the regime and was spurned by nearly all the leftist opposition as "Franco's prince" and puppet. His height and coloring did not create a very Spanish appearance (except to the historically minded few who recalled that at the apex of Spain's power all the Spanish Habsburg kings, as well as the last two Trastámara rulers, had been blondish), and his soft-spoken, affable manner was not likely to impose itself quickly on the Spanish political culture. The country had been conditioned to expect hauteur, arrogance, and high-sounding rhetoric from its leaders, all qualities alien to this friendly, discreet, somewhat shy but nonetheless highly calculating young man. During long years of waiting and preparation, Juan Carlos had been careful to say little of substance. His reputation stemmed almost more from his well-cultivated avocations than from his political role, so that when he became prince he was "best known for being a yachtsman, judo expert, and radio ham."[58] In the early seventies Madrid was full of Juan Carlos jokes, all turning on his lack of promise as the future king.[59]

Yet once named official successor, Juan Carlos became a major focus of political attention, hundreds of aspiring young bureaucrats and politicians beating a path to his door. The new cabinet was composed of regime administrators who backed the *juancarlista* succession, and the new director general of Spanish television, Adolfo Suárez, did everything possible to cultivate the Prince and present him in the national media in the most favorable light. The political contacts of Juan Carlos burgeoned, as he endeavored to maintain effective relations with key elements of the regime while gaining more and more information about the state of public opinion and the opposition.

In some respects, Franco left him a remarkable degree of freedom. He

58. Robert Graham, *Spain: A Nation Comes of Age* (New York, 1984), 147.
59. For a more positive evaluation of the abilities and prospects of Juan Carlos at that particular point, see my "In the Twilight of the Franco Era," *Foreign Affairs* 49:2 (Jan. 1971), 343–54.

had never tried to indoctrinate him directly or in detail, and often even failed to respond with any precision to the Prince's questions about future political issues. According to Juan Carlos, on one occasion the Caudillo replied, "Why do you want me to give you advice? You certainly will not be able to govern as I have!"[60]

> In fact the Prince, analyzing his conversations with Franco on political themes, reached the conclusion that the latter left him complete liberty, not wanting to mortgage his future, and that it was very possible that Franco honestly did not seek to condition the man who would have to face a future that Franco could not determine.
>
> Or perhaps he thought that the Prince, in his silence, in his observer's stance, was thoroughly imbued with Francoist spirit and that that would lead him to maneuver effectively without ever moving his feet from the regime of the Eighteenth of July. It is very hard, not to say impossible, to know exactly what Franco thought. It is nonetheless easy to learn how he acted. And with Juan Carlos he acted without imposition, almost without pressure, but with vague indications and paternal counsel that were merely general orientations concerning given themes. But he never indoctrinated him explicitly. He never told him what he must do.[61]

In general, Franco preferred that Juan Carlos make as few political statements as possible, both to avoid complications for the current regime and to allow him a freer hand of his own in the future. There was rarely cause for concern, since the Prince was known for his discretion, yet he occasionally felt the need to reach out to broader opinion. Thus early in 1970 he told Richard Eder of the *New York Times* that in the future, Spain would need a different kind of government than at the time of the Civil War and that as king he would become the heir of all Spain. This was published on February 4, 1970, under the headline "Juan Carlos Promises a Democratic Regime," with Eder further noting that those who talked with the Prince now found him better informed and more mature and determined than he had been, though still unsure how to proceed in certain respects.

Since the regime had for a quarter-century relied on official doubletalk about the "profoundly democratic," "organically democratic" nature of the current system, Franco could not take great umbrage at verbal gestures made to American correspondents. He was nonetheless reported to be greatly annoyed by subsequent remarks made by Juan Carlos a year later on his official visit to the American capital, as reported by the *Washington Post*. The Prince therefore called on Franco immediately after his return to Madrid to gauge his reaction personally, but the Generalissimo merely observed sardonically, "There are things that you can and ought to

60. Joaquín Bardavío, *Los silencios del Rey* (Madrid, 1979), 51.
61. Ibid., 51–52. Bardavío adds, "On one occasion I had the opportunity to explain this interpretation of mine to Don Juan Carlos personally, and he completely confirmed it."

say outside Spain and things that you ought not to say inside Spain. It may not be appropriate to repeat here what is said outside. And, at times, it might be better if what is said here is not picked up outside."[62]

Even more clearly annoying were the continuing political activities of José Ma. de Areilza, chief political representative of the Conde de Barcelona. Franco counted on Juan Carlos having achieved a certain political independence from his father, and that was the case to the extent that the two were rumored not to have spoken to each other for some six months after the Prince was officially recognized as successor. Yet personal relations were soon restored, and in February 1970 Juan Carlos reported to Franco about a recent luncheon that he had had with Areilza, who sharply criticized the regime. The Generalissimo responded tersely, "Ya lo sabe, Alteza; o Príncipe o persona privada" ("You know how it is, Highness; either be Prince or a private citizen").[63] He was further put out by reports that Foreign Minister López Bravo, who had been one of his favorites, was asking the help of European Community leaders, during conversations in Brussels, in steering Spain toward a reformist democratic regime.[64]

Personal relations between Caudillo and Prince did not follow an altogether easy rhythm, for sometimes long periods would pass without a meeting, on occasion punctuated by a peremptory summons from Franco. Juan Carlos urged Franco during several conversations in 1970 to appoint a prime minister so that it would not be up to him to name the first president of government to follow Franco, but he was always answered vaguely that this would be done in good time. Franco did suggest that the Prince come to El Pardo once a week to participate in some of his conversations with cabinet ministers, but Juan Carlos politely declined, not wishing to be involved to that degree in Franco's administration.[65]

The Generalissimo himself was displeased by the apparent eagerness of certain ministers to make spontaneous gestures of their own to the Prince or to involve him in special visits or study tours. Franco preferred that Juan Carlos only participate in specially approved public activities, and tried to see to it that his appearances were largely restricted to the major ceremonies of the regime, though in practice so narrow a schedule could not be enforced. At this point Juan Carlos was relying to some extent on López Rodó and Fernández Miranda, who drew up memoranda for his somewhat irregular conversations with Franco.[66] Despite certain differences, never carried to the point of extreme tension, Juan Carlos man-

62. Bardavío, *Los silencios del Rey*, 53–54.

63. López Rodó, *Larga marcha*, 401. José Ma. de Areilza has published a memoir concerning his political activities in this period, *Crónica de libertad* (Barcelona, 1985).

64. According to Calvo Serer, *La dictadura de los franquistas*, 170.

65. López Rodó, *Larga marcha*, 404.

66. Ibid., 405.

Franco and his recognized successor, Don Juan Carlos de Borbón, Prince of Spain, at the official ceremony marking the 39th anniversary of the founding of the Falange, October 30, 1972

aged to continue to be discreet and convincing, generally maintaining the respect and even the modest affection of Franco while having the almost unwaveringly strong support of Carrero Blanco.[67]

Though the new government had pledged publicly to continue the "development" and "evolution" of the system, its apparent monocolor tone was deceptive, and the cabinet soon divided to some extent between hardliners and advocates of greater apertura, with the former gaining the upper hand. One of the first victims was the proposed new Ley de Bases del Régimen Local being prepared by the Ministry of the Interior. The law proposed that mayors be elected by local municipal councils, and would have permitted two or more provincial governments to form "Mancomunidades" for specific limited goals. It was strongly denounced by

67. Thus they forgave his remarks to foreign journalists and did not blame him for the continuing attacks from his father's political representatives. Areilza, for example, managed to publish an article in *ABC* at the end of March 1970 suggesting that Spain would never be allowed to enter the European Community without fundamental domestic reforms, by which he implied democratization. A reply was carried on April 2 from "Ginés de Buitrago" (Carrero Blanco himself), totally denying Areilza's thesis and impugning the history of parliamentary liberalism and democracy in Spain. At least in one respect Carrero was not altogether mistaken, for it took nearly a decade after Spain's democratization before it was allowed to enter the Common Market.

hardliners for weakening authority and reviving the spirit of Catalan and Basque separatism and was eventually killed altogether.[68]

On April 14, 1970, the government took a slight step to the right when Silva Muñoz ("el ministro eficacia") was replaced in Public Works by Gonzalo Fernández de la Mora, the subsecretary for foreign affairs. Fernández de la Mora was one of the most active ideologues of the unreconstructed authoritarian right, an admirer of Maurras, Donoso Cortés, and Maeztu. He held that party politics should be permanently replaced by authoritarian technocracy, arguing that the regime was fully justified by its practical achievements, all of which would be endangered by any fundamental reform. He would later term the system an Estado de Obras (State of Works) whose practical benefits far transcended any limitation of strictly political liberty.

Carrero Blanco still sought to encourage further "evolution," and in January 1971 handed Franco a detailed memorandum urging him to name a president of government in order to preserve his own strength and energy and maintain undiminished the prestige of chief of state. Carrero outlined a ten-point program for the first prime minister other than Franco himself to hold the presidency of government, but these had to do mostly with technical reforms and the reinforcement of authority. The only proposal involving political development was the suggestion for some sort of scheme of political associations.[69] Though Franco made no positive response to this, he did agree to a proposal by Carrero and López Rodó to clarify the terms of succession, publishing a decree on July 15, 1971, that conferred upon Juan Carlos the powers that properly pertained to the officially declared heir to the throne as stipulated in article 11 of the Organic Law. These included the right to take over the interim functions of chief of state whenever Franco might be physically incapacitated or out of the country. Meanwhile a special effort was made by Carrero Blanco and Fernando Liñán, the director general de política interior, to elect a number of new procuradores to the Cortes who were supporters of the succession of Juan Carlos. This objective was generally accomplished so that the final Cortes of the regime, which convened in November 1971, contained proportionately fewer old-guard Movement loyalists or die-hard members of the Bunker[70] than its predecessor.[71]

In general, the two years 1971 and 1972 were the last relatively quiet

68. Cf. the remarks of the interior minister, Garicano Goñi, in *Franco visto por sus ministros*, 201–2.

69. *FF*, 8:238–39.

70. The term invented by a Madrid journalist and popularized by Santiago Carrillo, head of the Spanish Communist Party, to designate die-hard supporters of the regime in the early 1970s.

71. Cf. López Rodó, *Larga marcha*, 408–9. On the work of the chamber chosen in 1971, see Díaz Nosty, *Las Cortes*, 141–83.

period of the regime. A protest culture continued to spread in the universities and among the intelligentsia, and the autumn of 1971 saw the first firebombings of left-leaning bookstores by ultrarightist squads (often indirectly subsidized by the government) to protest the expansion of leftist propaganda in Spain. This had little effect, for there were no new restrictions in the press laws, and with each passing year the de facto limited freedom of the press was used more widely, creating an alternative "parliament of paper" to the controlled assembly of the Cortes. In Catalonia an only partially clandestine Asamblea de Catalunya was formed, representing nearly all the leftist and liberal democratic opposition shadow parties and grouplets that had begun to spring up in that region. Nonetheless all this led only slowly to any significant mobilization. Most young people did not want to become involved, and nearly all those who did were careful to abide by the restrained rules of shadow opposition politics that had begun to evolve in those years. The consumer society and the new television culture were by that time in full development, and the great majority of Spanish youth were relatively apathetic about politics.[72] Thus there was no attempt to revert to the tight police crackdowns of earlier years, and the regime merely responded with its customary swagger and bombast. When a new head of the Civil Guard, Lt. Gen. Carlos Iniesta Cano, was sworn in at the close of 1971, the ceremony was attended with even more pomp and circumstance than usual and witnessed by no less than eleven cabinet ministers, yet it portended no alteration in the moderate police policy of the current years.

A new scandal erupted in March 1972 after revelation of the disappearance of a large part of the national olive oil reserve that had been stockpiled by the minister of commerce to assure supplies and commercial equity. Unidentified elements had apparently been allowed to sell off a portion of these stocks for their own profit; among the names bandied about in this connection was the Caudillo's brother Nicolás.[73]

Franco was by then in his eightieth year. The slow but steady decline in physical vitality left him extremely tired and nonfunctional for a significant part of every day, and he rarely had much to say in cabinet meetings, sometimes dozing off altogether. Though his mind remained completely clear when he had the energy to talk to visitors and attend meetings, his stamina had become so uncertain that diplomatic audiences were becoming a hazard and an increasing worry to his aides. At the annual victory parade in May 1972, the Caudillo had to use a portable golf seat in order to maintain the illusion of standing upright through the entire review. He was also undergoing extensive oral surgery for serious fungus infections in

72. J. R. Torregosa, *La juventud española* (Barcelona, 1972), 131–48.

73. José Rey, *El caso REACE* (Barcelona, 1974); Jesús Ynfante [pseud.], *Los negocios ejemplares* (Toulouse, 1975), 118–29; and La Cierva, *Franquismo,* 2:355–56.

the mouth, a condition aggravated by his somewhat obstructed respiration and habit of oral breathing. In May, Franco then began to suffer severe pains in one leg, inaccurately reported as a bout of phlebitis. This proved to be a side effect of the oral infection and ended after the oral surgery was completed.[74]

Hope that the current cabinet would take the lead in further *apertura* had meanwhile faded. It was sorely divided on policy and received no leadership whatever from Franco, who seemed content with immobilism. Moderate opinion therefore looked more and more to Juan Carlos as the only hope for a breakthrough, and a new political tendency, *juancarlismo*, emerged as the focus of those who sought new personal opportunities as well as peaceful reform in the future. The regime's own media encouraged this by the constant publicity given "the generation of the Prince,"[75] basically the affluent, relatively well-educated young middle- and upper-middle-class Spaniards between twenty and forty years of age who had grown up under the regime and were urged to regard Franco's heir as their symbol and public personification. Some of the more politically minded had by this time come to do so.

During 1972 prospects for a smooth and potentially reformist legitimist succession were temporarily clouded by the marriage of Franco's eldest granddaughter, María del Carmen Martínez Bordiu-Franco, to Alfonso de Borbón-Dampierre, the elder son of Don Jaime (deaf-mute elder son of Alfonso XIII), who had attempted about a decade earlier to retract his official renunciation of a place in the line of succession. Don Alfonso, a tall, dark, handsome, and suave Latin prince, had completed his education in Spain and developed a career in the Spanish diplomatic service. During the mid-1960s he had had some success in Madrid society and had met the pretty, graceful young granddaughter with dyed blonde hair when she was a teenager in an exclusive finishing school in Switzerland in 1966. The engagement was announced in December 1971 and the wedding took place on March 8, 1972.

With serious deterioration in Franco's health, Doña Carmen played a more important role than she ever had before in Franco's personal relations and to some extent even in political affairs. She immediately initi-

74. Dr. Vicente Gil, *Cuarenta años junto a Franco* (Barcelona, 1981), 42–43.

75. On a more serious level, three books that appeared in Madrid in 1972 were Juan Luis Calleja, *Don Juan Carlos, ¿por qué?*, an Editora Nacional publication explaining the theory and logic of the succession; Miguel Herrero de Miñón, *El principio monárquico*, a discussion of the legal structure and powers of the new monarchy that stressed its theoretically broad authority; and José Luis Nava, *La generación del Príncipe*, which treated some of the younger politicians and public figures who had associated themselves with the Prince. Two collections of the speeches of Juan Carlos were published, one containing remarks on common ceremonial occasions, *Palabras de Su Alteza Real el Príncipe de España Don Juan Carlos de Borbón* (Madrid, 1972), and a second concerning more important and diplomatic remarks, *Por España, con los españoles* (Madrid, 1973).

ated a campaign to have Don Alfonso recognized as "His Royal Highness" and a full prince of the royal family, with the ultimate goal, it was thought, of changing the line of succession itself and placing her eldest grand-daughter on the Spanish throne. The maneuver was supported by ele-ments of the ultraright, who thought an Alfonso married to a Franco a more secure succession than the possibly dangerously liberal Juan Carlos.

Had Franco remained in full possession of his faculties he might have quashed this illegal and undignified claim. As it was, Doña Carmen and other members of the family first tried to have the Council of the Realm and Cortes grant official recognition of the marriage, as required for princes of the royal family by the Law of Succession, and then ratify for Alfonso the full legal titles of Prince and Royal Highness. An increasingly weakened Franco lent himself feebly to these maneuvers, which were stoutly resisted by most of the members of the cabinet, with the active assistance of Juan Carlos and Don Juan from Estoril. Franco had not yet lost all sense of dignity and appropriateness and ultimately did not insist, thereby skirting the danger. A final moment of peril occurred shortly be-fore the wedding, when Don Jaime, the father of the bridegroom, took it upon himself to "confer" the Toisón de Oro (the order of the Golden Fleece) upon Franco, though he had no legal right to do so. It was feared that the aged dictator might appear at the wedding ceremony wearing this decoration, thereby further fueling ambitions concerning the alleged inheritance rights of Don Alfonso, but he retained enough of his native prudence not to do so. The minister of information, Sánchez Bella, ordered the director general of radio and television, Adolfo Suárez, to give full live coverage to the lavish wedding ceremony. Suárez, an ambi-tious *juancarlista* bureaucrat of the younger generation, refused to do so and presented his resignation. He had already caught the eye of Carrero Blanco as a promising new talent, and the vice-president intervened, sav-ing Suárez's position and arranging that the wedding be telecast exten-sively, but not fully live, without changing normal programming.[76]

Doña Carmen and the ultra groups mounted as much pressure as they could against Juan Carlos, hoping to make his life unpleasant enough to drive him out. Franco was gotten to order Carrero Blanco not to have the

76. Letter of Javier González de la Vega to the editor, *Cambio 16,* May 30, 1983. Suárez in fact generally reported directly to Carrero Blanco, whom he cultivated assiduously, rather than to his nominal supervisor, the minister of information. Morán, *Adolfo Suárez,* 214–51; Fraga Iribarne, *Memoria breve,* 282. The formal wedding publicity was presented in a so-ciety glamour book by José Ma. Bayona, *Alfonso de Borbón—María del Carmen Martínez Bordiu* (Barcelona, 1971).

These maneuvers and pretensions elicited the scorn of much Madrid opinion. Don Al-fonso had earlier enjoyed a modest degree of popularity, but now he was jeeringly referred to by some as "El Doño" (a typical Madrid witticism that may be rendered in slightly bowd-lerized form as "Her Lordship").

Prince accompany ministers any longer on official trips, but such a decision was in fact very much to Juan Carlos's liking. He and Sofía were determined to stand fast, realizing that they were gaining increasing support of their own as Franco neared his end.

As a member of the diplomatic corps, Alfonso temporarily accepted assignment as ambassador to Sweden but resigned after only a few months when the Scandinavian winter began to set in. He was offered the ambassadorship to Argentina but insisted on remaining in Madrid, where he requested the post of national delegate of sports in the Movement, according to gossip hoping that this might be upgraded to minister of sports. The government's sense of the ridiculous enabled it to resist this, thanks to a firm and cleverly reasoned stand by Fernández Miranda,[77] but even Carrero Blanco, ever a supporter of Juan Carlos, was prevailed upon to ask the Prince to approve for Don Alfonso the title Príncipe de Borbón, since Juan Carlos had been given the title Príncipe de España in 1969. Juan Carlos rejected this proposal; rather than creating a special title, he suggested instead the vacant title of Duque de Cádiz, which had belonged to Francisco de Asís before his marriage to Isabel II (1833–68). This was agreed upon,[78] together with the rank of Alteza Real (Royal Highness), and some observers conjectured that Franco himself might even have been pleased to see Juan Carlos show himself so firm and decisive. Subsequently the position of president of the Instituto de Cultura Hispánica in Madrid was created for Alfonso (a purely honorific post, since it already had a director), and in December his bride gave birth to Franco's first great-grandchild.

Whatever coordination the government enjoyed was mostly provided by Carrero Blanco, who on July 18, 1972, obtained from Franco the promulgation of two laws, one establishing the unified authority of the king over the government at the time of succession and the other providing that the vice-president would automatically assume the powers of president of government (prime minister) should the position of chief of state temporarily fall vacant at a time when no other president of government was about to be named. These regulations were designed to guarantee a smooth transition should Franco suddenly die without having named a president of government, avoiding the danger that elements of the Bunker would temporarily gain control and thwart the succession.

Meanwhile such prominent recent cabinet members as Fraga Iribarne and Silva Muñoz took advantage of the permissive press climate to come

77. According to Morán, *Adolfo Suárez*, 213–14, Fernández Miranda reported directly to Franco, informing the Caudillo that as secretary of the Movement he had rejected this request because he could never consent that he rule over "grandchildren of the Caudillo," who would thereby have been placed under his orders.

78. The intrigues involved are related by López Rodó, *Larga marcha*, 421–38.

584 IV. Developmentalism and Decay, 1959–1975

out in favor of new political representation within the regime.[79] During his Christmas speech of 1972, even Franco seemed to refer to the desirability of a new apertura, declaring, "We have to depart from any closed and exclusivist criterion. . . . The disparity of ideas and tendencies is not only legitimate but necessary."[80] For a moment, proponents of reform inside the system thought that a new signal was being given, forgetting that Franco had used some of the same generalizations as early as 1937.

Political publications and news reporting became increasingly daring and outspoken, representing a wide range of tendencies and opinions and serving as a surrogate for a political life that could have no formal existence. The weekly news magazine *Cambio 16* soon established itself as the leading national news reporter and the most widely circulating advocate of democratic change, as its title implied. The Marxist economist Ramón Tamames, who earlier had written the most widely read general study of Spain's economic structure, in 1973 published a new history of the Republic, Civil War, and Franco era as the final volume in a new multivolume paperback history of Spain directed toward the mass university audience. Intellectually undigested neo-Marxism and French *gauchisme* were all the rage, as the latest radical theories from Paris and Milan were uncritically reprinted in Spain.

The scope of ETA violence broadened, bringing a spiral of assassinations, kidnappings, and bank hold-ups. In 1973 it was flanked by a small new Marxist-Leninist terrorist organization, known by the acronym FRAP, centered in the capital.[81] On May Day, as police were breaking up a leftist demonstration in Madrid, a young policeman was attacked by FRAP militants in an alley and literally hacked to death. The government attempted selective new police crackdowns and tightened up certain aspects of the Law of Public Order, but it was no longer in a position to command the full authority or apply the ruthlessness of former times. Moreover, the Spanish judiciary was also increasingly influenced by the growing liberalization of society and institutions and tended to be more solicitous of the civil rights of citizens than in earlier years.[82]

The extreme right, now at the margin of the regime, attempted a counteroffensive of its own. Public rallies were held in Madrid, and at the funeral for the slain policeman there were incendiary demonstrations and demands for an end to government permissiveness and for a return to martial law. All proposals for political associations were stoutly rejected,

79. Manuel Fraga Iribarne, *El desarrollo político* (Madrid, 1971); Federico Silva Muñoz, "Pluralismo y participación," *ABC*, Oct. 27, 1972.
80. *Tres discursos de Franco* (Madrid, 1973).
81. See Alejandro Diz, *La sombra del FRAP: Génesis y mito de un partido* (Barcelona, 1977).
82. Cf. "Justicia Democrática," *Los jueces contra la dictadura (Justicia y política en el franquismo* (Madrid, 1978), which draws examples from the years 1971–74.

while ultra spokesmen in the Cortes denounced López Bravo's concil-
iatory policy toward eastern Europe and the suggestion of pensions for
Republican Civil War veterans. The Fuerza Nueva group of Blas Piñar
(indirectly subsidized by Carrero Blanco) came to the fore, working with
direct-action squads such as the Guerrilleros de Cristo Rey. Though the
Guerrilleros normally but not always stopped short of homicide, they
added to the climate of extremism at the margin of public life.

The growth of political violence tended to paralyze whatever initiative existed within the government for further reform. Though Carrero
Blanco seemed to support some sort of associationism in his speech before
the National Council on March 1, 1973, subsequent developments led
him to draw back. The subsecretary of the interior had resigned the preceding month in protest against continuing government division and immobilism, ventilating part of his disgust in the press.[83]

As Carr and Fusi put it,

> Something deeper than a mere ministerial malaise was afflicting the Francoist
> state: a crisis of the regime which had begun with the debates over political
> associations in 1967–69, a crisis of contradictions. Spain was officially a Catho-
> lic state, yet the Church was at odds with the regime. Strikes were illegal but
> there were hundreds of them every year. Spain was an anti-liberal state yet des-
> perately searching for some form of democratic legitimacy. . . . 'In Spain,' the
> ultra right-winger Blas Piñar said in October 1972, 'we are suffering from a cri-
> sis of identity of our own state.'[84]

Division within the cabinet became increasingly pronounced. It had become abundantly clear that Franco was unable to provide further leadership, and as early as the beginning of 1971 the minister of industry, López
de Letona, had presented to him a lengthy proposal that the Fundamental
Laws be set in motion to choose a president of government different from
the chief of state.[85] Doña Carmen took verbal initiatives of her own, complaining directly to Carrero Blanco in February 1973 that something must
be done about the "disloyalty" of such cabinet members as the interior
minister, Garicano Goñi, and López Bravo, whom she accused of siding at
home and abroad with elements of the opposition.[86]

Garicano tendered his resignation on May 7, six days after the May Day
incident, in a letter that expressed his "worry over the activity of certain
ultra elements" whose "triumph would be fatal for Spain's interests." He
insisted that "when a minister is in complete disagreement with the policy and tendencies of other cabinet colleagues which are followed by the
government on certain occasions, even though they do not dominate the

83. *La Vanguardia* (Barcelona), Feb. 7, 1973.
84. Carr and Fusi, *Spain*, 194.
85. José Ma. López de Letona, in *Franco visto*, 212–15.
86. According to an extract from "Diario de Fernández Miranda," *ABC*, Dec. 20, 1983.

latter, the situation becomes intolerable and creates problems of conscience." Garicano stated flatly that "people no longer have anything to do with the rundown, deserted headquarters of the Movement in provincial capitals and local areas; there remain only a few older people of our generation, with few exceptions those who have some sort of paid position," and concluded, "I think a genuine aperturismo is necessary."[87]

Franco finally accepted the fact that he was no longer in condition to run the government himself, and for the first time placed in operation the mechanism to appoint a new president of government. This required the Council of the Realm to present a list of three names from which the chief of state would choose. Franco apparently indicated that he wished to have Carrero Blanco on the list, to which the council added Fraga Iribarne and the old guard Falangist Fernández Cuesta. On June 8 the Caudillo officially appointed Carrero Blanco, the first time in the history of the regime that anyone other than Franco held the position of prime minister.

The new cabinet was almost exclusively Carrero's election, its common denominators being loyalty to the regime combined with reasonable technical competence and an at least moderate support of further aperturismo. Carrero's chief lieutenant was not López Rodó nor any other member of the Opus Dei group but the enigmatic, seemingly pedantic Fernández Miranda, who remained minister-secretary of the Movement and also received the post of vice-president. Carrero appreciated his political shrewdness and discretion and his willingness to combine flexibility with immobilism whenever that was required. After eleven years López Bravo disappeared from government—some said because of his rudeness to the pope during his last trip to Rome but more probably because of the enmity of Doña Carmen—and was replaced as foreign minister by López Rodó. Sánchez Bella was dropped from Information because of his ultra tendencies and support of the "Doño," to be replaced by the veteran Movement bureaucrat Fernando Liñán. Fernández de la Mora remained in Public Works, while Francisco Ruiz Jarabo, a one-time follower of Girón who had become more moderate, took over Justice. Several ministers may have received their positions primarily on the basis of technical ability, but the appearance of the ultra Julio Rodríguez in Education, with limited qualifications, was an anomaly.[88] The only name imposed by Franco was that of Carlos Arias Navarro, military prosecutor during the Málaga repression of 1937, director general of security under Alonso Vega

87. Tomás Garicano Goñi in *Franco visto*, 203; and the full text in López Rodó, *Larga marcha*, 440–42.

88. To some extent, this may simply have been an administrative error. The appointment was apparently intended at least in part to reward Rodríguez for effective management of the new Autonomous University of Madrid, though credit was due primarily to his subordinate, Luis Sánchez Agesta.

from 1957 until 1965, and more recently mayor of Madrid, to replace Garicano in Interior. Arias had a reputation as a *duro* and had long gone out of his way to favor and cultivate the Franco family, who encouraged his appointment.

Formation of the Carrero Blanco government was seen by most of the now very extensive opposition as little more than an expression of immobilism, designed to provide for the continuation of Francoism after Franco. It actually represented a degree of change and timidly proposed to consider new reforms. This was not so much a monocolor government as a practical administration of reliable but flexible moderates.[89] Like its predecessor, it no longer represented the old political families of the regime who had fallen into irremediable decay, while Franco's traditional balancing act had ceased to be feasible once the Caudillo lost the vigor to direct the cabinet himself. The hope of Juan Carlos that Franco might retire at this point was quickly dashed, yet the feebleness of his health guaranteed that the end could not be long delayed. Carrero Blanco recognized the need to generate additional apertura, and a new mixed commission representing the cabinet and the National Council of the Movement began once more to study the issue of political participation during the autumn of 1973.

Fernández Miranda thought that he saw the green light for some sort of pluriform political associations for a new if limited electoral network. In mid–November he submitted to the minister a document "on the opportunity and convenience of presenting to the Cortes the project of a General Law on the political participation of the Spanish people." The minister–secretary general of the Movement directly posed the question "of whether or not the National Movement is today capable of attracting new support." He declared that "whatever contributes to generating popular support is politically sound" and stressed that "one must run the risks that liberty brings."[90] At a government meeting on November 14, Fernández Miranda stated emphatically:

. . . some adulators of the Prince talk to him about the strength of "pure monarchy" by itself. They are preparing a trap for him by encouraging him to do away

89. For example, the new minister of planning and development, Cruz Martínez Esteruelas, had turned out a little book two years earlier, *La enemistad política* (Barcelona, 1971), in which he discreetly supported reformism and participation, though without suggesting specific changes. The only ministerial memoir produced by this short-lived government was that of the education minister, Julio Rodríguez Martínez, *Impresiones de un ministro de Carrero Blanco* (Barcelona, 1974), more an expression of piety than a memoir.

90. Quoted by López de Letona in *Franco visto*, 215–16. The proposal also insisted on its own absolute loyalty and orthodoxy, insisting that "this system of associations rejects political parties and . . . ideological and party groups. It functions within the doctrinal parameters of the National Movement. It rejects all parallel representation as contrary to Point VIII of our Principles." *FF*, 8:342.

with the Movement after a prudent interval. A monarchy without the Movement would fall apart. The Movement must be renovated with an eye toward the future. We must now organize the King's Movement, which was a Francoist Movement in its origin but which will become that of the King. I don't want to have the Movement trapped in a street with no exit. The only means of winning support for the Movement in 1974 is from a posture of freedom. There must be free associations within the Movement open to all Spaniards.[91]

Carrero's government subsequently began to discuss the proposal at several cabinet meetings devoted exclusively to this issue. Another was scheduled for the same theme on December 20, when the government abruptly came to an end.

The Assassination of Carrero Blanco

The assassination of Carrero Blanco on a sidestreet near the center of Madrid at 9:25 A.M. on the morning of December 20, 1973, was in form perhaps the most spectacular of the century. It was directed not merely against the existing government but against the future of the regime, so as, in the words of the assassins, "to break the rhythm of evolution of the Spanish state, forcing it into an abrupt leap to the right."[92] Personal security for Carrero Blanco was lax, as tended to be the custom in Spain except in the case of Franco himself. Carrero was very much a creature of habit, attending Mass daily in the same church in mid–Madrid near the American embassy. The ETA team that executed the assassination rented a tiny basement apartment on the one-way street along which his official car—a Spanish-built Dodge Dart—drove each morning after Mass en route to the nearby office of the presidency of the government at Castellana, 3. They devoted ten days to digging a tunnel with a jackhammer that burrowed under the center of the street directly beneath which his car passed. Such an operation naturally created considerable noise and debris, but the *etarra* squad passed themselves off as sculptors creating large new art works with mechanical techniques. The manager of the apartment building was himself a part-time police employee but found nothing amiss in their peculiar activities, all of which was a further demonstration of the lessened police control during the later years of the regime. Electrical wiring enabled them to set off an enormous blast precisely underneath Carrero's vehicle as it drove slowly down the street on the morning of the twentieth, creating a huge hole in the pavement and lifting the president's car high into the air, finally depositing it right side up on top of the fourth-floor roof of the church and Jesuit monastery

---

91. Quoted by López Rodó, *Larga marcha*, 456–57.
92. Julen Agirre [Genoveva Forest], *Operation Ogro* (New York, 1975).

across the street, driver, police escort, and passenger still in one piece but all quite dead.[93]

This created the most serious governmental crisis in the history of the regime. The date of December 20 had been chosen by the assassins because the trial of the main group of leaders of the primarily Communist Workers' Commissions was to begin that day, and as many as a hundred illegal demonstrations were scheduled to erupt in towns all over Spain. As news of the magnicide spread, it was accompanied by a general sense of foreboding. All but three of the demonstrations were abruptly canceled, and the leadership of the clandestine Communist Party, largest and most active of the opposition groups, quickly moved to dissociate itself from the assassination. In Madrid some shops closed early and street traffic fell off as many citizens remained in their homes. The only confusion resulted from an intemperate order by the new head of the Civil Guard, Lt. Gen. Iniesta Cano, directing provincial commanders to open fire, if necessary, to control any disorder. The acting president of government, Fernández Miranda, moved quickly to cancel the order and was supported by the interior minister Arias Navarro and the navy minister Pita da Veiga (who according to regulations took over the functions of the minister of the army in the absence of the latter).[94] Military units were placed on alert, but there were no disorders whatever, though the assassins escaped into Portugal and from there back to France.[95]

Burial ceremonies on December 22 were not well organized. Franco, who had accepted news of the assassination with his usual outward icy calm, was ill with a cold and was represented by Juan Carlos. No more than 20,000 mourners were present, though groups of ultras shouted "Ejército al poder" ("The Army to power") and greeted the reformist president of the Episcopal Conference, Cardinal Tarancón, with cries of

93. The assassins' own account is presented in the previously cited book by Forest, herself an activist of the Madrid section of the Communist Party and a major accomplice. On the collaboration of Madrid Communists, who provided the principal collateral support for the Basque assassination team, see Lidia Falcón, *Viernes trece en la calle del Correo* (Barcelona, 1981). Some further information may be gleaned from Manuel Campo Vidal, *Información y servicios secretos en el atentado al Presidente Carrero Blanco* (Barcelona, 1983), 1–44. "Argala," the ETA leader who actually triggered the explosion that killed Carrero, was himself blown up exactly five years and one day later by a bomb device in his car in France, evidently set by foreign agents of the Spanish security forces. Cf. *Cambio 16*, May 20, 1985, pp. 26–36.

94. Iniesta Cano has given his version of this rather famous incident in his *Memorias y recuerdos* (Barcelona, 1984), 218–22. He claims that Fernández Miranda had nothing to do with rescinding the order, though this seems doubtful.

95. Detailed accounts of the events of that day are given by Rafael Borrás Betríu, *El día en que mataron a Carrero Blanco* (Barcelona, 1974); and Ismael Fuente et al., *Golpe mortal* (Madrid, 1983). It may be noted that among the rumors widely circulated in the aftermath of the assassination was the notion that it had been planned or at least supported by the CIA, an idea still held by a few to this day.

"Tarancón al Paredón" ("Tarancón to the firing squad"). The formal memorial service took place one day later, and on that occasion an aged Franco sank for a moment into the arms of the cardinal archbishop, sobbing uncontrollably over the loss of his closest and most trusted collaborator.[96]

96. Martín Descalzo, *El cardenal*, 200. Carrero Blanco's most positive qualities were his austerity and incorruptibility, combined with his habit of hard work and his rigid devotion to duty. After more than two decades as Franco's right hand, he left an estate amounting to no more than his admiral's pension, a less than luxurious though good apartment still not fully paid for, a savings account of less than 500,000 pesetas (about $8,000), and a fully paid-for tomb in the cemetery, according to Fernández, *El almirante Carrero*, 258.

22

The Death of Franco

The assassination interrupted the continuity planned by Franco, as was its intention. A new prime minister would have to be found, yet there was no one who could take the place of Carrero Blanco in the Generalissimo's thinking, which relied more on selection and continuity of personnel than on the role of institutions, even of the institutions designed by Franco himself. The functions of president of government for the moment automatically devolved on the vice-president, the owlish and enigmatic Fernández Miranda, whose sorcerer's visage reflected the complex role that he played in the regime's affairs. During the immediate crisis he acted with calm and prudence, reassuring the official institutions and the public at large. He had been loyal to both Franco and Carrero Blanco, but he was fully aware that an immobilist dictatorship had little future. Carrero Blanco had appreciated his intelligence, discretion, and political ability, but the future lay with Juan Carlos and the succession. This formed Fernández Miranda's political horizon by the close of 1973, though he would maintain formal loyalty to Franco as long as the Generalissimo lived.

The choice of Carrero Blanco's successor would be, as it turned out, Franco's last major decision. He had never had close relations with Fernández Miranda and was somewhat opposed to the acting president because of the latter's independence and aperturista tendencies.[1] Moreover, all of the regime's old guard were unanimous in their opposition to such a nomination, while more moderate elements found him cold, abstract, antipathetic, and lacking in popular appeal or capacity for new leadership

1. Vicente Gil, Franco's physician, said to him of Miranda, "In all positions he has placed young people who are either socialists or of doubtful background. Just look at the kind of example he has set with all the Delegates of the Frente de Juventudes and the Guardia de Franco." Gil, *Cuarenta años*, 140.

as distinct from manipulative and administrative ability. Franco's first preference was apparently Admiral Pedro Nieto Antúnez, a leading Regentialist as navy minister in the 1960s but more flexible and moderate than the extreme ultras. He was also a fellow-Galician and something of a personal friend. Nieto Antúnez, however, was seventy-five years old, and unlike such austere military figures as Carrero Blanco and Muñoz Grandes, was heavily involved in business ventures and could scarcely present an image of self-abnegation. Moreover, he was opposed by certain groups in the military.

Throughout the final week of 1973 Franco was ill with the flu, and despite his normal optimism, depressed by illness and the assassination. Gossip held that at this moment Doña Carmen and other members of his personal circle (such as his physician, his aide, naval captain Antonio Ucelay, and General Gavilán, deputy head of his personal military staff) intervened in possibly the only major camarilla intrigue of the regime to pressure Franco into accepting their own candidate, the interior minister Carlos Arias Navarro. This may overstate the case. Gil, his physician, has claimed that the Caudillo was anguished and uncertain. Doubts had indeed been building in his mind ever since Carrero had become vice-president in 1967, and he was no longer able to assess the political future very clearly. He finally decided on Arias Navarro on the morning of December 28.[2]

This was a questionable choice, for Arias's primary experience had been in local government and police work, and his ministry had failed to maintain adequate security to prevent the recent magnicide. His most positive achievement had been a relatively successful administration as mayor of Madrid in the preceding decade, when traffic routes were reconstructed. Yet Arias Navarro had always carefully cultivated the Franco family, and his wife was on good terms with Doña Carmen and Franco's sister Pilar. His loyalty to the Caudillo was unquestionable, and unlike Nieto he was still of active age. Franco thus instructed the Council of the Realm to include Arias among the three names in the *terna* to be presented him that afternoon, and the council members added those of two other veterans of the Movement, Solís Ruiz and José García Hernández, the latter a somewhat obscure abogado del Estado who had made a career in the Ministry of the Interior.

The Arias Navarro government that was announced on January 3, 1974, would be the last to serve under Franco and represented an extensive

2. The longest narrative of the events surrounding formation of the new government is by Carrero's press director, Joaquín Bardavío, in *La crisis: Historia de quince días* (Madrid, 1974). See also Gil, *Cuarenta años*, 139–60; José Oneto, *Arias entre dos crisis 1973–1975* (Madrid, 1975), 37–39; Diario 16, *Historia de la transición* (Madrid, 1984), 19–23; and Fraga Iribarne, *Memoria breve*, 321.

turnover of personnel, only about one-third of Carrero Blanco's ministers retaining their portfolios. Arias was advised especially by Antonio Carro Martínez, a former law professor and his recent general technical secretary in Interior, and by Pío Cabanillas, a notary who held the post of secretary of the Council of the Realm and had been a subsecretary under Fraga Iribarne. The new cabinet was largely composed of remnants of the bureaucratic inner core of the regime, with Arias relying especially on top personnel from his own Ministry of the Interior, the largest of Spain's ministries. Franco named only the three military ministers and the new foreign minister, Pedro Cortina Mauri (senior member of Spain's diplomatic corps and a lieutenant of Castiella's), while recommending that the able Antonio Barrera de Irimo be retained in Finance. Not one but three vice-presidents were named, including the new minister of the interior, García Hernández, the labor minister, Licinio de la Fuente, and Barrera. Carro became minister subsecretary of the presidency and Cabanillas entered the cabinet as minister of information.

This was the first all-civilian cabinet (with the exception of the heads of the military ministries themselves) in the history of the regime, and it also included a few relatively nonpolitical technical appointees. Gone were the members of Opus Dei and their associates (though Franco apparently would have preferred to retain López Rodó), putting a sudden end to years of hysteria about the supposed Opus domination. Whereas Carrero Blanco had at least gone through the motions of consulting with Juan Carlos in preparing his government, Arias Navarro ignored the Prince of Spain altogether, and with the exception of Barrera, included no one with a very overt monarchist identity. Thus the new government had little appearance of aperturismo and seemed designed to guard the deathwatch of Franco.

Yet such an appearance was deceiving, for its members were also in large measure bureaucratic pragmatists and included only one genuine doctrinaire, the Falangist Utrera Molina as minister secretary of the Movement. Arias Navarro's chief advisors, Carro Martínez and Cabanillas, managed to convince the new president that the pace of aperturismo had to be accelerated. To some extent they also managed to include in this inner core of consensus his other main stalwart, the first vice-president and interior minister García Hernández, though the latter held reservations. This produced agreement that a system of political associations must finally be introduced and that the government must move toward recognition of more distinct cultural and regional pluralism. Cabanillas, as image-maker for the president, tried to set the tone.[3]

3. Cf. Joaquín Bardavío in *Historia de la transición*, 83–84; and, for a slightly different view, Oneto, *Arias*, 37–51.

IV. *Developmentalism and Decay, 1959–1975*

Arias Navarro's first major public address on February 12, 1974, promising significant reforms, nonetheless came as a surprise. The speech itself was apparently written by Gabriel Cisneros, a young journalist who as a national councillor of the Movement represented the younger generation of aperturistas within the regime and served Arias as subdirector general of the presidency of the government. The address began by vowing the most complete loyalty to the regime and affirming that the historical legitimacy of the succession of Juan Carlos lay in the "Eighteenth of July." Arias then declared, "Due to exceptional historical circumstances, the national consensus backing Franco was expressed in terms of support [*adhesión*]. In the future, the national consensus in support of the regime must be expressed in the form of participation." He specifically promised (1) to withdraw the current new proposal for a law on local government and to replace it with another by May 31 that would permit the election of mayors and of presidents of provincial assemblies; (2) to send to the Cortes before June 30 a new law regulating *incompatibilidades* (conflicts of interest) for those holding parliamentary seats; (3) "immediate acceleration" of a new syndical law that would permit more "autonomous" activity; and, most important of all (4) to prepare a new statute regulating the right of association in order, in the torturous language of the regime, "to promote the orderly concurrence of criteria"—that is, the expression of political viewpoints—though without setting any timetable.[4]

Soon after becoming president, Arias had been convinced that at least minor reforms and some appearance of movement would be necessary to sustain a government. He hoped to guarantee the continuity of the regime by limited changes that might conciliate moderate opposition and even more, win back the critical and reformist sectors within the regime itself, thus making possible reconstruction of its internal basis. His proposals implied much more representative local government, would supposedly strike against syndicate leaders and other officials doing double duty in the Cortes and elsewhere, might give the syndicates some degree of autonomy, and offered the hope of finally providing some direct political representation through associations. Though his proposals made no impression on most of the organized opposition, Arias's policy was well received by moderate critics of the system and also by the aperturistas and reformists within the regime, and it succeeded in generating some hope and expectation during the next eight months.[5]

4. The full text may be found in *El año Arias: Diario político español 1974*, ed. Jesús de las Heras and Juan Villarín (Madrid, 1975), 104–32.

5. For several years, moderate reformers had been pointing out in guarded language the possibilities for significant change that existed within the institutions and structure of the regime itself. This was in part the burden of the works by Herrero de Miñón and Jorge de Esteban cited earlier, as well as of two articles published by Luis García San Miguel in January 1973 and January 1974, reprinted in his *Teoría de la transición* (Madrid, 1981), 21–79.

Of Arias's ministers, Cabanillas had by far the most immediate impact. He launched a major campaign to present Arias as the chief avatar of enlightened reformism, a modern conservative who understood the requirements of the times and would carry out a conservative but genuine *apertura*. This brought the new president considerable publicity abroad, and some observers thought that he almost came to believe his own propaganda. Most important, Cabanillas virtually eliminated what remained of general censorship in Spain, except with regard to direct criticism of Franco and the government. With Ricardo de la Cierva as director general of popular culture, the office in charge of publication guidelines,[6] the Ministry of Information largely ceased to prosecute or otherwise restrict publishers, who took greater and greater latitude. Censorship was increasingly left to whatever sense of prudent restraint still existed or to the initiative of state prosecutors within the regular criminal justice system. The latter was not staffed to deal with the minutiae of Spain's large and highly diverse publishing industry, though individual publishers were still occasionally fined or prosecuted. Thus 1974 became the year of the great *destape*—the "uncovering"—as the eruption of nudity in common publications far exceeded even the increase in political discussion.

The winter of 1973–74 closed with two new causes célèbres. The first was provoked by the new bishop of Bilbao, Antonio Añoveros, originally a Navarrese Carlist chaplain in the Civil War but now aligned with ecclesiastical progressivism and the spirit of Vatican II. Influenced by his Basque Nationalist vicar general, on February 24, 1974, he delivered a sermon on the application of religious norms to society that at one point called for Basque cultural freedom and a change in government policy concerning regional rights. This was stated in vague, general, and almost Aesopian language but was read in more than 90 percent of the churches of Añoveros's diocese. It brought from the government an immediate order of house arrest, and Arias and García Hernández (an arch-representative of the new phenomenon of right-wing anticlericalism) even sent a plane to Bilbao to fly him out of the country into exile. Meanwhile the permanent commission of the Episcopal Conference met concurrently in Madrid, some of its members urging preparation of articles of excommunication against key government leaders. Cabanillas worked energetically to calm Arias and García Hernández, while Franco himself, who despite his feebleness continued to meet with the cabinet almost every week, intervened to veto any drastic action. This was fully in keeping with the priorities of the Generalissimo, who claimed to have counseled Perón at the time of the Argentine church-state crisis in 1955 to "have patience; re-

6. La Cierva had been appointed to that office in October 1973, and his declarations during this period are collected in his *La cuarta apertura* (Madrid, 1976), 39–111. La Cierva personally made possible the publication of my book *El nacionalismo vasco* in 1974.

member that the Church is eternal and our regimes are transitory."[7] The sensible Tarancón then arranged for Añoveros to go on a long vacation, defusing the crisis.[8]

This was followed on March 2 by the execution of Salvador Puig Antich, a young Catalan anarchist of good family, who had been convicted of killing a policeman while resisting arrest, and by the execution of a common criminal of Polish origin for having murdered a Civil Guard. An international campaign had been organized for commutation of the death sentence, but Franco proved implacable on this occasion, only the second and third executions in Spain in eight years. The death of Puig Antich excited great feeling and public disturbances in Catalonia, where it was interpreted as a symbolic punishment of Catalan regional aspirations.[9]

The uproar over the Añoveros affair and the execution of Puig Antich severely tarnished the new image of the Arias administration as a reformist government. Months passed with little progress toward the promised legislation except for a preliminary sketch of a new local government bill. The government's main activity consisted of a long series of personnel changes in the senior administration. During its first three months a total of 158 *altos cargos* (high officials) appointed during the lengthy hegemony of Carrero Blanco and the technocrats were replaced. The police stepped up their activity, arresting 325 political dissidents, mainly young Basques and members of the new revolutionary Marxist-Leninist groups. At length Arias himself, together with several other ministers, traveled to Catalonia, always one of the major focuses of discontent, to promise that there would be movement toward new associations, but he coupled this with strong emphasis on regime orthodoxy and maintaining the full continuity of institutions, leaving an impression of doubt and confusion. Cisneros, his aide and speechwriter, admitted privately to journalists that the government had suffered as much erosion in three months as might normally have occurred in three years.[10]

The Portuguese revolution suddenly erupted on April 24, dramatically though almost bloodlessly overthrowing the longest-lived authoritarian regime in the western world. Downfall of the Portuguese regime was provoked by protracted colonial war in Africa, a conflict from which Franco had carefully dissociated his own regime. Nonetheless the Portuguese Estado Novo had always protected the Spanish regime's western flank; its overthrow could not but encourage all those forces seeking fundamental change in Spain. The main difference between the political situation in

7. According to Soriano, *La mano*, 73.

8. Tarancón's version is given in Martín Descalzo, *El cardenal*, 203–17. Carlos Santamaría Ansa, *La Iglesia hace política* (Madrid, 1974), briefly presents the new political posture of the Church.

9. Oneto, *Arias*, 63–67.

10. Cf. ibid., 79–105.

the two countries was that the Spanish military had not been undermined by protracted colonial conflict and remained loyal to Franco. The revolution prompted increasing conservatism in Spanish military policy, nevertheless, particularly with regard to new appointments and promotions, and several of the state intelligence agencies increased their monitoring of opinion and activities within the officer corps of the Spanish armed forces.

Though Spanish policy toward Portugal generally followed the moderate tack taken by the United States, the subsequent course of events there, in which a semisocialist revolution was promoted by some of the officer corps, was bewildering to Franco. He is supposed to have remarked, "What can be expected of an Army that is led by its supply corps [Intendencia]?" referring to the fact that the Portuguese Armed Forces Movement was based on officers in home garrisons and supply and training cadres. Even worse was the flood of favorable comment in the Spanish press over the revolution in Portugal, which Franco complained amounted to "a press campaign in reverse."[11]

Later, at the height of the abortive "Tancos revolt" in March 1975 which helped to provoke the most radical phase of the revolution, the defeated Portuguese General Spínola asked for Spanish intervention under the mutual defense terms of the old Iberian Pact. Franco prudently refused, declaring that the Portuguese government earlier had effectively voided the Pact. Nor were conservatives granted asylum in the Spanish embassy, for if it had been attacked by radical mobs, Spain would have had no choice, according to Franco, but to send in paratroopers, virtually involving the two countries in war.[12]

The success of the Portuguese revolution confirmed the worst fears of Spanish ultras. It further slowed the pace of aperturismo in Madrid and stimulated a new campaign by the Bunker directed especially against Cabanillas and the relaxation of censorship. This was led by José Antonio Girón, who on April 28 with the connivance of Antonio Izquierdo, the ultra editor of *Arriba*, published an apocalyptic diatribe against the consequences of reformism. Franco had at first considered Girón for president after the assassination of Carrero and still thought highly of the old Falangist, who accused Cabanillas of permitting public ridicule of Franco himself and prepared special portfolios of examples of the new Marxist publications and increasingly widespread sexual pornography for the perusal of the Caudillo. The cabinet itself was divided. The new minister-secretary of the Movement, José Utrera Molina, led the ultras, while outside the government Girón and the old guard proclaimed that they could

11. López Rodó, *Larga marcha*, 469.
12. According to Franco's last personal physician, Dr. Vicente Pozuelo Escudero, *Los últimos 476 días de Franco* (Barcelona, 1981), 136–37.

598   IV. Developmentalism and Decay, 1959–1975

count on extensive support among the military, the bureaucracy, and the veterans of the Movement and thus could generate the means to impose themselves on the government if need be.[13]

Their only public success, however, was to gain the dismissal of the leader of professional reformism in the military, Lt. Gen. Manuel Díez Alegría, as head of the Alto Estado Mayor on June 20. Díez Alegría was the strongest advocate of strict apolitical professionalism in the armed forces, though personally fully loyal to Franco. Trained also as a lawyer and engineer, he devoted himself to technical reform but had a reputation as a moderate liberal and had earned the disfavor of Franco, who had not received him for several months. The nominal ground for his dismissal lay in a recent private trip to Romania to seek medical assistance for his wife, during the course of which he had with government approval accepted a dinner invitation from the Romanian Communist dictator Ceauşescu.[14]

Ricardo de la Cierva, the director general of popular culture, acknowledged privately to reporters that the current reform effort (in his terminology the third, following those of Ruiz Giménez and of the technocrats) constituted the regime's last opportunity, which, if frustrated, "will be followed by a fourth, but one that can no longer be carried out by this regime, or another born of it."[15] Some identified the chief obstacle to significant change as lying not so much in the government or in the ultras beyond it as in the Franco family, which feared to see power slipping from its grasp.[16]

On July 9 Franco was felled by an attack of thrombophlebitis, apparently due to the pinching of one foot by the tight and stiff Army-issue black leather shoes that he had worn for many decades, eventually leading to creation of an abcess beneath a callous.[17] Forced to enter a hospital (appropriately the Clínica Nacional Francisco Franco), he considered turning over the acting powers of chief of state of Juan Carlos, who did not express any eagerness to receive them. The Prince feared being compro-

13. *El reto de los halcones: Antología de la prensa apocalíptica española en la apertura (Febrero de 1974–Junio de 1975)*, ed. C. J. Cela Conde (Madrid, 1975), is an anthology of the ultra press. Jesús Vasallo, *Madrid: Kilómetro cero* (Madrid, 1975), collects articles in the regime press by an ultra journalist during 1974; while the commentary of Emilio Romero's *Prólogo para un Rey* (Barcelona, 1976), is more sophisticated. Carlos E. Rodríguez, *Continuidad o cambio: Vigencia y perspectivas del Estado del 18 de julio* (Madrid, 1975), a collection of articles from *Arriba* and other official organs, accurately observed that "a modern state is never overthrown: it surrenders itself" (p. 12).

14. Santiago Carrillo, secretary of the Communist Party, had recently made a reference to Díez Alegría as a leading force for liberalism and prudence within the military hierarchy during a public interview in Paris, which further prejudiced him in the eyes of Army ultras.

15. Quoted in Oneto, *Arias*, 92.

16. "The problem lay in the fact that the Franco family would not resign itself to inevitable change and did not allow to be done what needed to be done." Fraga Iribarne, *Memoria breve*, 342.

17. On the course of Franco's affliction in 1974, see the medical memoir by Pozuelo Escudero, *Los últimos 476 días*.

Stricken with thrombophlebitis, Franco enters the Clínica Nacional Francisco Franco on July 9, 1974.

mised by having to act temporarily as chief of state under the Franco system without full authority of his own, and told the Caudillo that he did not wish to appear to be in any hurry or trying to push Franco out. The latter is said to have replied that there was little alternative, since this might be the end for him. On July 19 he suffered a hemorrhage, and Juan Carlos did assume his duties, but by the end of the month Franco was recovering and had returned to his residence in El Pardo. Juan Carlos presided over his first cabinet meeting there early in August and later, on August 30, directed a second cabinet meeting at Franco's summer residence of Pazo de Meirás in Galicia.

The entire month was a period of intense speculation amid all manner of political conversations, including some that began to take the form of virtual conspiracy. The boldest was the position advanced by Cabanillas (and supported to some extent by Carro Martínez and Barrera de Irimo, the minister of finance, who directed economic policy). This strategy would have insisted that the logic of the situation and of Spain's succession laws must no longer be resisted and that the only responsible course was to proceed directly to the coronation of Juan Carlos and his investiture with full powers, even while Franco still lived. Arias Navarro was torn by agonizing doubts. His first vice-president, García Hernández, had begun to criticize the policy of apertura as early as April, though it was said that the most overt ultra representative, the Movement secretary Utrera Molina, might support an immediate coronation if he were rewarded with the jefatura del Movimiento, a post always held by Franco himself. While political oppositionists sought to pressure Juan Carlos's father, Don Juan, into a strong stand on behalf of a complete break with the regime that might advance his own candidacy to the throne, Franco's son-in-law, the playboy surgeon Marqués de Villaverde, sought to play the role of family leader and Franco's own political surrogate. He traveled to Málaga to consult Girón about the best means of thwarting the present course of government and encouraged Franco, now seeming to recover rapidly, to reassume his powers as soon as possible.[18]

According to some reports, the three spokesmen for apertura—Cabanillas, Carro, and Barrera—agreed during the cabinet meeting of August 30 to resign if Franco should resume full power. Arias Navarro could not bring himself to take a resolute stand one way or the other, but García Hernández, having swung to the side of the ultras, is said to have informed Franco directly of the situation, and Villaverde redoubled pressure on his father-in-law. Fully informed of developments, Franco was apparently further stimulated to resume control as soon as possible by a report (possibly distorted) concerning a telephone conversation between

18. Cf. the account by Carmelo Cabellas in *Historia de la transición*, 85–87.

the Prince and his father in mid-July soon after Franco entered the hospital. This reawakened all Franco's suspicions of Don Juan and his fear of the latter's influence on Juan Carlos. On September 1, only two days after the last cabinet meeting, Franco abruptly called Arias Navarro to declare that he was "cured" and would be resuming power right away. This took place officially on September 3, with Juan Carlos barely being informed of the fact before it hit the newspapers. To intimates, Franco justified his precipitous return by the diplomatic crisis developing with Morocco over the Spanish Sahara.[19]

In some respects this first severe illness of Franco's old age brought out the better side of his character, for he generally demonstrated patience, discipline, and relative good humor throughout the ordeal and the recuperative period that followed. He nonetheless had to undergo considerable therapy in order to regain a modicum of health, for he had become depressed in the middle of the illness and for some time had seemed to lose the will to act. It became necessary for him to learn to walk again more or less normally and to swing his arms again as he did so, and considerable practice was required to regain reasonable speech articulation. His voice, which had been fading for several years, never fully returned, but by mid-autumn Franco had made an impressive recovery, conducting a full complement of daily interviews and even resuming his hunting, although on a limited scale.

The political opposition had meanwhile become increasingly active, and 1974 was already well on its way to its record as the greatest year for strikes in Spanish history to that date (with the possible exception of 1936). Most of this was being reported in the largely uncontrolled Spanish press. The most direct repression took place in the Basque provinces, where political opposition was by far the most overt. During the years 1973–75 more than 6,300 Basques were arrested by police, although the majority were soon released.

The sensation of the late summer was a gruesome terrorist act, the bombing of a coffee shop, the Cafetería Rolando, across the street from the Dirección General de Seguridad (national police headquarters) in Madrid's Puerta del Sol. The explosion in this crowded coffee shop, much frequented by policemen and Interior Ministry employees, resulted in twelve deaths and eighty injuries. Of the victims, one of those killed was an elderly woman police clerk, while thirteen of the injured were police employees. This, the bloodiest of all terrorist acts against the regime, was carried out by a two-member ETA team with the aid of individual Communist accomplices in Madrid. Since it totally failed to achieve its goals of

19. On political developments during Franco's illness and the role of Juan Carlos, see Bardavío, *Los silencios del Rey*, 95–102; Diario 16, *Historia de la transición*, 50–59; and La Cierva, *Franquismo*, 2:412–16.

spectacularly destroying a large number of policemen, the Basque organization denied responsibility and tried to label it a terrorist provocation by the ultraright. The leaders of the Communist Party, which organizationally had no contact with terrorists, were embarrassed by the key role of individual Communists and cut off all contact with those charged as accomplices.[20]

Franco finally acted to tighten up the government when he intervened directly to order Arias to dismiss Cabanillas because of his information policy and relaxation of the censorship. After this was announced on October 29, it was followed by the resignations of Barrera de Irimo, Francisco Fernández Ordóñez (new president of the INI), Ricardo de la Cierva and Marcelino Oreja (subsecretary of information), and of other aperturistas holding state administrative positions below cabinet rank. This was a major blow not only to apertura but also to reforms in economic policy introduced by Barrera.[21]

Arias Navarro found himself trapped in mid-stream. While state policy became more rigid in some areas, he tried to salvage part of his program by moving ahead with the proposal for political associations. This was the most important of the promised reforms, and two different versions were being prepared, one along the lines of previous proposals by Utrera Molina, the minister-secretary of the Movement, the other by a young aperturista, Juan Ortega Díaz-Ambrona, appointed by Carro director of the Instituto de Estudios Administrativos.

The latter formed a committee in his institute of young reformers such as Gabriel Cisneros and Rafael Arias Salgado, son of the former information minister. Their project proposed to open the right of association broadly to all Spanish citizens, not restricting it to membership in or the control of the Movement. When the initial project was ready in August, it was edited by Carro and then passed on to Arias Navarro. The president eventually transmitted it to Franco for his approval on November 14, but Franco quickly gutted the project to bring it back under the control of the Movement once more. Ortega Díaz-Ambrona then resigned his post on

20. See Diario 16, *Historia de la transición*, 65–73, and the memoir by the indirect accomplice Lidia Falcón, *Viernes y trece en la calle del Correo* (Barcelona, 1981). One of the two principal Communist accomplices was the writer and psychiatrist Genoveva Forest, wife of the Communist dramatist Alfonso Sastre. She had also been an accomplice in the assassination of Carrero Blanco and was also "Julen Agirre," pseudonymous author of *Operation Ogro*. Nonetheless, after approximately one year the accomplices were rather inexplicably released by police.

21. Nearly a year earlier, in November 1973, Barrera de Irimo had launched a new fiscal plan to control inflation, tighten tax collection, and fill a number of loopholes, making the system slightly more progressive. See J. L. Pérez de Ayala, "La Reforma Barrera en materia fiscal y económica," *España perspectiva 1974* (Madrid, 1974), 143–69. Barrera had also encouraged further liberalization of the still very extensive network of state economic controls, protection, and subsidies.

November 26, after police arrested a number of key leaders of the democratic opposition at a private meeting.[22]

This opened the way for Utrera's project, which was developed by a select committee of the National Council composed of remaining Movement leaders such as Jesús Fueyo and Fermín Labadíe Otermín. Utrera
was proud of the fact that he was the first minister secretary who had entered the Movement as a "flecha" (member of the adolescent youth group)
and thus had passed his entire life within it, working his way from the
bottom to the top. Preparation of a controlled statute of political association formed part of his program for revitalization of the Movement, on
which he worked actively throughout 1974. This was to involve the reform of the organizational structure itself, stimulating the activity of local
members and the role of the local and provincial councils of the Movement. One major goal was to encourage the ideological rearmament of the
regime by reanimating the Instituto de Estudios Políticos under Fueyo
and creating new cultural and recreational centers for the Movement on
the local level. Another major goal was revival of the moribund youth organizations of the Movement, and to that end Utrera visited most of the
remaining youth camps during the summer of 1974 to try to whip up enthusiasm.[23] He drew at best a limited response, for most affiliates had long
since abandoned the Movement, while even some of the remaining nominal leaders were not convinced that it had any future and were looking
toward reformist alternatives. Arias Navarro had come to resent Utrera as
the leader of the ultras within the government, a subverter of the original
reform plan who sought to develop a major power base of his own. Arias
had originally sought to eliminate Utrera in the minicrisis of October
which ousted Cabanillas, but Franco would not hear of it at that time.

The opportunity for Utrera to substitute his National Council draft on
associations came after Franco's initial resistance to the text prepared by
Ortega Díaz-Ambrona's group. At that point Arias Navarro is said to have
naively asked assistance from Alejandro Rodríguez Valcárcel, former vicesecretary general of the Movement and currently president of the Cortes,
in gaining the Generalissimo's approval. Rodríguez Valcárcel was fundamentally an ultra and close to Girón politically. He in turn sought out
Jesús Fueyo, Utrera's head of the Instituto de Estudios Políticos, and they
transmitted to Franco the essence of the National Council draft, whose
main points were superimposed by the Caudillo in place of the govern-

22. Ortega Díaz-Ambrona has given his own version in the *Historia de la transición*,
117–18. For the varying attitudes of hope and rejection this elicited among the opposition,
see J. A. González Casanova, "Asociaciones políticas y Monarquía moderada," *España perspectiva 1974*, 101–22; and José Amodia, "El asociacionismo político en España: Aborto inevitable," *Iberian Studies* 3:1 (Spring 1974), 9–14.
23. Utrera Molina explains his goals in *Franco visto por sus ministros*, 322–32.

ment's draft. This cleared the way for its adoption by the National Council on December 16. The measure was promulgated by Franco by decree five days later and subsequently ratified by the Cortes in January.

This new Estatuto Jurídico del Derecho de Asociación Política still restricted associations to the ideological orbit and organizational control of the Movement, but unlike the earlier proposal by Fernández Miranda, did not technically require members of proposed associations to also be members of the Movement. It authorized formation of political associations that were in accord with the principles of the Movement, subject in each case to final approval by the National Council. Each association must achieve a minimum membership of 25,000 distributed through at least fifteen provinces. In thinly inhabited provinces with less than 500,000 legally responsible residents (*población de derecho*), a minimum of 2 percent of that population must be registered with the party in order for that province to qualify, a figure reduced to 1.5 percent for provinces with between 500,000 and a million in that category, and to 1 percent in those with more than a million. The Movement was to contribute toward the financing of each qualifying association, which would be authorized to participate in whatever electoral processes might be established by law. Three categories of fines were set up to punish associations that might subsequently infringe the terms of these regulations.[24]

Fernández Miranda declared in an interview that "the political associationism of our system is not primarily based on ideological pluralism, the basis of a party system, but finds its true source in the pluriformism inherent in our National Movement since its origin."[25] One critic wryly observed, "This gives the impression that the new decree-law primarily favors the association of those who have never permitted us to associate ourselves,"[26] and the well-known sociologist Salustiano del Campo succinctly defined it as "a typical Spanish invention." García Hernández declared the following May, "The government is trying to carry out the great operation [of transformation] of the established system, but still within the same system,"[27] while Ricardo de la Cierva wrote that the biennium since Carrero Blanco first became president was "possibly achieving the difficult goal of joining together the disadvantages of both authoritarian and democratic regimes, without the clear advantages of the one or the other."[28] The Bunker vociferously denounced the proposed freedom to associate as the beginning of a limited political party system that would totally alter the basis of the regime, while a series of opinion surveys taken

24. Ferrando Badía, *El régimen*, 246–56.
25. *ABC*, Jan. 11, 1975.
26. Juan Antonio Ortega in *Tele-Exprés*, Jan. 11, 1975.
27. Quoted in *Mundo*, May 17, 1975.
28. In La Cierva's *Crónicas de la transición* (Barcelona, 1975), 29.

between 1969 and 1975[29] made it evident that by 1975 a clear majority of Spaniards favored a democratic parliamentary system.[30]

Yet Franco himself stalled the *apertura* during his final months, fearing to see the whole system unravel. To the end of his days, the Caudillo remained convinced that the only hope of a *monarquía instaurada* lay in strict maintenance of the institutions of the regime, observing privately in December 1974 that if a plebiscite were held, the monarchy on its own would gain less than 10 percent of the vote.[31]

Thus after a full year, the Arias government could produce no evidence of fundamental change. Opposition mounted steadily, faced by a weakening and sclerotic regime, producing the closing even of a provincial university such as Valladolid and a continuation of the strike wave that included theater actors, and more covertly, some low-level administrative employees of the regime. On February 6, 1975, 500 ranking bureaucrats in the state administration petitioned the government for a genuine democratization, as a new round of political meetings began among reformers and oppositionists and speculation mounted on all sides.

The second crisis of the Arias Navarro government erupted on February 20, when its third vice-president and minister of labor, Licinio de la Fuente, resigned under fire from cabinet hardliners and national employers councils. For months he had sought to develop a new law of labor relations that would liberalize existing provisions. After this had been blocked, he concentrated on a new strike law that would legalize strikes within a single firm, provided that it had been voted by at least 60 percent of the

29. These ordinarily used small samples, but the most extensive was conducted by the Fundación FOESSA in 1969. Attitudes expressed in the latter were very cautious, but the resulting chapter was nonetheless suppressed by the censorship. It later appeared in abridged form as Amando de Miguel, "Spanish Political Attitudes, 1970," in *Politics and Society in Twentieth-Century Spain*, ed. S. G. Payne (New York, 1976), 208–31. A majority of all social sectors save university students were registered in the 1969 survey as favoring no more than a liberalization of the existing system, but this response was circumstantial and was taken before the population felt itself at liberty to express its full opinion, which moreover evolved rapidly during the early 1970s. See also Antonio López Piña and Pedro L. Aranguren, *La cultura política en la España de Franco* (Madrid, 1976), on political attitudes during the last years of the regime.

30. A small poll sponsored by *Cambio 16* reported on May 31, 1974, that 60 percent of those sampled wanted general participation in politics, while only 18 percent favored one-man rule. Of the 48 percent expressing a political preference, socialism led with 14, followed by the Movement with 12 and Christian Democracy with 11. A survey based on 1,500 interviews, published in *El Europeo* April 19, 1975, reported that 56 percent favored a multiparty system, with socialists and Christian Democrats the most popular choices.

31. According to Pozuelo Escudero, *Los últimos*, 122. The official Francoist doctrine of the *instauración* was vigorously publicized during the final year of Franco's life. In addition to the many minor treatments, the principal book-length presentations were Juan Ferrando Badía, *Teoría de la instauración monárquica en España* (Madrid, 1975), a thorough exposition published by the Instituto de Estudios Políticos; Manuel Martínez Ferrol, *La Sucesión* (Barcelona, 1975); and Carlos Iglesias Selgas, *Mañana la monarquía* (Madrid, 1975).

Franco's last cabinet at his summer home, August 22, 1975

workers involved, was exclusively economic in purpose, and took place after the existing contract had expired or in protest against the failure to fulfill existing norms. This was strongly opposed by the minister-delegate for the Syndical Organization and by the minister of the interior (for reasons of public order), leading to La Fuente's immediate resignation.

Arias became determined to use this opportunity to carry out the kind of government reorganization that he would have preferred the preceding October. While replacing La Fuente in Labor, he also insisted on relieving his two ultra ministers representing the Movement, Utrera Molina and Ruiz Jarabo (in Justice). Franco was at first completely opposed, having formed a positive opinion of the reliability and orthodoxy of Utrera. The insistence by Arias Navarro marked another first in regime annals, for he stood fast and managed to convince Franco that the president must have the authority to reorganize his own cabinet, possibly even threatening resignation.[32]

When the new government was finally announced on March 5, it had been reorganized in a more reformist direction, with the Ministries of Commerce and Industry also changing hands. The new minister-secretary of the Movement presented a striking change in the person of Fernando Herrero Tejedor, vicesecretary general under Solís Ruiz in the sixties and

32. Antonio Carro presents a version favorable to Arias in *Franco visto*, 356–59. Journalists provided extensive coverage of the events of 1974–75. In addition to works already cited, Equipo de Estudios, *Al filo de las crisis* (Madrid, 1975), chronicles the events of late 1974 and early 1975; and for the final year of the regime there are useful chronicles by Jesús de las Heras and Juan Villarín, *El último año de Franco* (Madrid, 1976); and by José Luis Granados, *1975: El año de la instauración* (Madrid, 1977).

more recently attorney general of the Supreme Court. He was the only major figure in the Movement who was also a member of Opus Dei, was (with Fernández Miranda) one of the two most trusted and influential political contacts of Juan Carlos, and was an avowed aperturista. As vice-secretary he brought in his young protégé Adolfo Suárez, the sometime favorite of Carrero Blanco, who was also close to the Prince and, together with Herrero, had been among a very small number of reformist politicians within the regime who had been asked by Juan Carlos during the preceding autumn to submit to him their personal outlines for a possible fundamental reform or transformation of the system.[33] Franco accepted his appointment because he was impressed with Herrero Tejedor's honesty, ability, and discretion and especially by the official report that he had prepared on the assassination of Carrero Blanco. Moreover, the Generalissimo knew that Herrero was not one of Arias's cronies and so would balance the new cabinet. Herrero Tejedor underlined his loyalty to the regime, declaring, "We have a political system in which there is no place for political parties" and requiring his lieutenant Suárez to wear the old Falangist blue shirt that had been passing out of fashion.

This was something of a smokescreen to obscure the fact that he had his sights firmly set on the transition to the monarchy, perhaps with the ambition to become Juan Carlos's prime minister. As minister-secretary, one of his key functions would be to preside over the Permanent Commission of the National Council, which held the power to approve the new political associations. His plan seems to have been to exploit to the maximum the possibilities of this new alternative, the centerpiece of which was to be a new centrist-reformist association called the Unión del Pueblo Español (whose acronym was UDPE, to distinguish it from the old UPE of Primo de Rivera). He even considered leading it himself. Herrero Tejedor apparently was convinced that a system of associations could provide the vehicle for a transition to a reformed system under the monarchy,[34] though it is not clear how far and how fast this would go.[35]

By late spring seven *proyectos asociativos* had been presented. These included a conservative Christian Democratic group called Unión Democrática Española; a Unión Española of monarchist militants aiming for a democratic monarchy; a nominally social democratic Reforma Social Es-

33. According to testimony at the Ortega Foundation's Symposium on the Transition (Toledo), May 13, 1984. Cf. Graham, *Spain*, 150.

34. Herrero Tejedor's alleged plans are briefly presented in Morán, *Adolfo Suárez*, 285–96; and in Campo Vidal, *Información*, 90–98. They evidently built on earlier preparation by Nieto Antúnez and others, a sketch of which Nieto presented to Franco in February 1975. *FF*, 8:381–82.

35. Fraga Iribarne drew the impression from a conversation with Herrero Tejedor on April 27 that "the definitive plan is to build a great association that is continuist more than reformist." *Memoria breve*, 355.

pañola, led by the dissident ex-Falangist Manuel Cantarero del Castillo,[36] with most of its members drawn from former affiliates of the Frente de Juventudes; an Alianza del Pueblo led by Solís Ruiz and other Movement associates; another, called Mayoría Silenciosa Unida (United Silent Majority); and even a group called Falange Española de las JONS, led by Girón and Fernández Cuesta.

Yet the whole associationist ploy seemed doomed, for the bulk of the opposition and even many moderate reformists refused to participate.[37] By September 1975 only eight associations had been formally registered, and of these only the UDPE of Suárez had gained the requisite 25,000 members. Six of the eight originated from various segments of the Movement, and at most three or four stood for serious reform.[38]

Fraga Iribarne was then the most widely publicized politician in the country, and one survey of political opinion in mid-January had found that those thought to have the best chances of leading effective political associations were Fraga, Cabanillas, and Girón, in that order.[39] Yet Fraga decided not to participate and was rumored to have rejected Herrero Tejedor's offer of the leadership of the new UDPE. He decided that the present government would be unable to complete significant reforms, for its only real achievement during the spring of 1975 was the eventual promulgation of a new decree-law on strikes, containing some of the changes originally proposed by La Fuente.[40] This had no measurable effect on opinion, and Fraga chose to join a group of associates in forming a separate study group, FEDISA, which remained aloof from the political associations.[41]

A general scramble had already begun among those currently or previously associated with the regime and its administration to define new identities for themselves. Such a stampede was developing that the monarchist writer Luis Ma. Ansón wrote an article entitled "Moral Cowardice" that appeared in *ABC* on May 20, 1975:

> In political Spain one now hears with greater frequency each day the interminable call of sheep and the loud cackle of chickens. There is also the sound of

36. Cantarero's earlier political writings were collected in his *Ideas actuales* (Madrid, 1970).
37. For example, the informal Christian Democratic coalition of intellectuals, administrators, lawyers, and businessmen called Tácito, which published a thoughtful book by the same name (Madrid, 1975), decided not to form an association.
38. Jesús Conte Barrera, *Las asociaciones políticas* (Barcelona, 1976), is a survey.
39. *La Vanguardia* (Barcelona), Jan. 21, 1975.
40. The text of the Decree-Law of May 22, 1975 is given in *La España franquista en sus documentos*, 573-86, and in Granados, *1975*, 247-55.
41. In October 1975, when Franco was virtually moribund, Fraga clarified his position in a series of newspaper articles in *ABC* which specified a sweeping series of necessary changes and held categorically that the legitimacy of a post-Franco regime could only be established through competitive elections under general suffrage. His earlier books, *Desarrollo político* (Barcelona, 1970) and *Un objectivo nacional* (Barcelona, 1975), had naturally been more abstract.

rats abandoning the ship of the regime. Each day moral cowardice takes hold of greater and greater sectors of our political class. Such a spectacle of fear and desertion gives one a vicarious sense of shame.

. . . Without sharing their ideas, I nonetheless must proclaim my admiration for those Franquists and Falangists who still defend, within the logical evolution of time, those principles for which they earlier fought bravely in war and peace. And shame rises to my face for those other Franquists and Falangists, for those men of the regime, for those chickens of the system who sometimes dissimulate what they used to be, at other times deny their own convictions, and besmirch the principles and symbols with which they formerly enriched themselves in order now to align themselves with the change and continue to fill both cheeks in the future. There are some ready to proclaim the most humiliating repentance so long as they can gain a single sentence of praise from those new leftist journals who hand out democratic credentials or impart Red blessings according to their own caprice.

Moderate opinion, which by 1975 was the largest single current of opinion in a prosperous, reasonably sophisticated Spanish society, looked beyond Franco to the monarchist transition for representative reform of Spanish institutions. On May 31, 1975, the new American president Gerald Ford made a hurried visit to Madrid during a European tour and somewhat naively encouraged Juan Carlos to accelerate the succession to a more democratic monarchy.[42] The Prince's father, Don Juan, remained totally suspicious of Franco's succession mechanism. On June 14, at a dinner given in his honor in Lisbon by a group of loyal supporters, Don Juan publicly offered once more to the people of Spain the institution of the legitimate monarchy as a bloodless solution to the problems of succession, reform, and true parliamentary democratization. This again enraged Franco, who five days later denied him the right to set foot on any part of Spanish soil.

At approximately the same time (June 12), the new aperturista minister-secretary of the Movement, Herrero Tejedor, was suddenly killed in a highway accident.[43] This was a major blow to reformist plans of the government, for though Arias suggested the young aperturista Rodolfo Martín Villa as a possible replacement,[44] Franco preferred to return to the veteran Solís Ruiz, who resumed his old post for the next six months.

This also required removal of Herrero's lieutenant Adolfo Suárez, who had been drawing increasing publicity in connection with Herrero's re-

42. On the role of the United States Embassy and American policy in the final phase of the regime and during the transition, see Samuel D. Eaton, *The Forces of Freedom in Spain, 1974–1979: A Personal Account* (Stanford, 1981).
Negotiations had already begun with the United States for the next renewal of the bases agreement, which was to terminate in 1975. Talks would drag on throughout the final year of Franco's life and only be successfully concluded in mid-1976 in the form of a regular mutual defense treaty, once Juan Carlos had had an opportunity to begin the democratization. Thus for the first time Spain gained a specific security guarantee, as well as further reduction in the American military presence and slightly more assistance.
43. See Campo Vidal, *Información*, 90–99.
44. According to Antonio Carro, *Franco visto*, 359.

formist maneuvers. It was known that Suárez had the blessing of Juan Carlos, and on July 2 the widely read magazine *Blanco y Negro* hailed him as "politician of the month," declaring that he could play a major role in the imminent transition. Herrero had tried to make him secretary of the nascent UDPE, though that was at first vetoed by other eminentoes because of Suárez's lack of earlier achievement in the Movement. Solís Ruiz nonetheless found it expedient to name him "coordinating president" of the political association that was cast in the role of a "Spanish PRI" (the PRI was the Mexican government-electoral party) on July 17.

The regime's final six months were largely devoid of further reforms. New syndical elections in 1975 got so far out of control that plans for a further syndical reform law were dropped, while the new law on "incompatibilidades de procuradores" (conflicts of interest among Cortes deputies)—one of the original reform promises of February 12, 1974—was finally so watered down as to be ineffective. García Hernández, the first vice-president, did persevere in his plans for local government reform, proposing direct universal suffrage elections for municipal councils and the recognition of some regional rights (including restoration of the old *concierto económico* for Vizcaya and Guipúzcoa), but this got bogged down during Franco's final illness. A decree of November 7 merely established a commission to study the problem, while the draft of a new local government law, published on November 19, the day before Franco's death, stopped short of full, free local elections.

The opposition, sensing the weakening of the regime and enjoying unprecedented freedom, accelerated its efforts, to which the government responded with intermittent barrages of fines, prohibitions, and arrests. A state of exception was declared for Vizcaya and Guipúzcoa in April, partially suspending civil guarantees. During the final year of the regime a total of 4,625 arrests were made in the Basque provinces, and by the moment of Franco's death 632 Basques were serving sentences in Spanish prisons[45]—though this was not in itself a remarkable level of repression given the extent and activity of the opposition in the Basque region. Unrest was to some extent stimulated by the slowdown in the economy after the oil shock of 1973, which sharply increased inflation, and by the second half of 1975 the economy was beginning to register recession for almost the first time since World War II. On the other hand, the number of strikes ceased to grow. Though 1975 had begun with a major new series of labor stoppages, the record strike wave of the preceding year was not quite equaled.

The first new effort to unify the opposition had been announced by

45. These statistics are from Núñez Astrain, *La sociedad vasca;* and from *Documentos Y* (San Sebastian, 1981), quoted in Morán, *Los españoles que dejaron de serlo,* 362. Pierre Celhay, *Consejo de Guerra en España* (Paris, 1976), is mainly an account of the situation in Vizcaya and Guipúzcoa during 1975.

the Spanish Communist Party in Paris on July 30, 1974, with the formation of a pseudodemocratic umbrella organization called the Junta Democrática. The bizarre nature of this lay in the identity of the Communists'
chief allies who, aside from two minor neo-Marxist parties, were the new
version of the (formerly Carlist) Comunión Tradicionalista (that now
preached "self-managing socialism" under "Carlos" Hugo) and the weird
monarchist publicist Rafael Calvo Serer, member of Opus Dei and former
leader of right-wing integrism who had by this point, as the saying went,
"evolved."[46] With memories of Communist domination during the Civil
War still partially alive, all other major opposition groups shunned the
Junta. In June 1975 the democratic leftist and liberal parties came together in their own non-Communist coalition, the Plataforma de Conver-
gencia Democrática. A major practical difference between the Communists' position and that of the majority opposition parties grouped under
the Plataforma lay in the former's demand for a provisional government,
possibly under Don Juan, to replace the regime after Franco's death,
whereas the latter were implicitly willing to accept some sort of negotiation with the government of Juan Carlos. The Junta Democrática even
managed to conduct a public session of its own in a congressional hearing
room in Washington on June 10, 1975, in an attempt to influence American policy to exert direct pressure on the Spanish government during the
forthcoming transition.[47]

On July 29 a minor bombshell burst with the arrest of eleven Army officers who about a year earlier had formed a small clandestine Unión Militar Democrática Española to generate military support for a democratic
system and social reform and to avert any subsequent military intervention that might prop up the surviving institutions of the regime.[48] They

46. José Martí Gómez, *Calvo Serer: el exilio y el reino* (Barcelona, 1976), largely presents
Calvo's own version of his grotesque career as extravagant publicist and frustrated political
busybody.

47. A left-liberal pressure group called the Fund for New Priorities in America sponsored
this session in the Caucus Room of the House of Representatives on June 10, 1975. Its burden was that the United States should have little further to do with the present Spanish
government but should exercise all possible suasion to bring about a fully democratic transition and to discourage the Spanish military from preventing a formal break in the regime.
Having been invited to participate, I pointed out that (a) the Junta Democrática was essentially a Communist front; (b) Juan Carlos would probably be capable of leading the reform of Spanish institutions himself without a formal *ruptura* or outside interference; (c) the
Spanish Socialist Party would potentially be able to organize a viable democratic alternative
within the transition; and (d) the Spanish military were not altogether eager to stick their
necks out politically and would, however reluctantly, probably go along with any reform carried out in an orderly and legal fashion and supported by the great majority of Spanish
people. All these points, though mostly contradicted by those assembled, proved to be entirely correct. The proceedings were later published as *Spain: Implications for United States
Foreign Policy*, ed. S. Chavkin et al. (Stamford, Conn., 1976).

48. *Unión Militar Democrática* (n.p., ca. 1976) is a small volume prepared and published
semiclandestinely by the UMD officers to set forth their position. In a separate incident,
two officers associated with the group had been arrested in February 1975.

later claimed to have the support of 242 officers, though this was subsequently reduced to 84 officers ready "to participate actively" with them.[49] Communist Party leaders meanwhile established contact with one senior general (Vega) through a non-Communist member of the Junta Democrática,[50] but the armed forces remained solidly in support of the regime, and the conservative senior hierarchy remained firmly in control until Gutiérrez Mellado was made chief of staff in June 1976, seven months after the death of Franco.

Franco's Last Moroccan Conflict

The final months of the regime were further complicated by a rapidly accelerating conflict over Spain's last remaining colonial territory, the Spanish Sahara, which constituted the westernmost part of the great desert that stretched to the Atlantic coast and bordered southern Morocco. Spain had obtained dominion over this territory early in the century but only effectively occupied it in 1934. Most of the region fell temporarily under the control of native insurgents, supported by Morocco, in 1957, though it was reoccupied by the following year with French assistance. Major phosphate deposits were discovered as early as 1950, but capital and technology for their exploitation became available only in 1973. Soon more than 1,500 Spanish workers were engaged, as the region exported two million tons of phosphates in 1974 and nearly three million in 1975. The entire population consisted of only 70,000 indigenous inhabitants, primarily bedouin. The Sahara became a nominal Spanish province in Carrero Blanco's legislation of 1959, and in 1967 the government created a provincial assembly called the Djemaa which it stocked with one hundred indigenous notables, a few of whom were also made procuradores in the Cortes in Madrid. In addition a sort of collaborationist political front, the Partido de Unión Nacional Saharaui (PUNS) was created, though its erstwhile leader later absconded to Morocco with much of the party's treasury.

King Hassan's government in Rabat had long coveted the Sahara, and flash points had periodically flared with Spain ever since Morocco's inde-

---

49. Articles on the UMD in *Diario 16* (Madrid), June 30 and July 1, 1980. Both the Socialist and Communist leaders maintained contact with UMD organizers, though both parties disavowed any formal connection, fearing it would be counterproductive vis-à-vis the military as a whole. Carrillo is said to have convinced Julio Busquets, chief ideologue of the group, to withdraw a preliminary draft manifesto that directly espoused socialism. Testimony at the Toledo Symposium, May 12–13, 1984.

Fifteen officers were eventually arrested and prosecuted. Convicted of military indiscipline, they did not regain their commissions under the succeeding democratic regime, which feared to offend military orthodoxy or condone politics among the armed forces. The two lengthiest accounts of the UMD are Francisco Caparrós, *La UMD: Militares rebeldes* (Barcelona, 1983); and José Fortes and Luis Otero, *Proceso a nueve militares demócratas: Las Fuerzas Armadas y la UMD* (Barcelona, 1983).

50. According to testimony at the Toledo Symposium.

pendence. Fishing rights were one persistent problem, since the fishermen of the Canary Islands do much of their work in waters near Morocco. This issue produced considerable disagreement in 1972–73, though it was temporarily resolved. As domestic opposition mounted in Morocco, Hassan II found expansion of the nation's borders southwards one of the easiest ways of enhancing political support, though the ambitions of Morocco from the north and Mauretania from the south were challenged within the Sahara by an indigenous liberation movement, the Frente Polisario, organized by western-educated, socialistic young *Saharauis* and backed by the leftist government of Algeria to the northeast.

Faced with what might soon be irresistible pressures, Franco on September 21, 1973, promised self-determination to the Sahara but in his customary way refused to set a date. The Arias Navarro government prepared a new Statute of the Sahara in May 1974, but this did not go directly into effect. Meanwhile a United Nations commission visited the region and was not impressed by the puppet PUNS but reported favorably on the claims of the radical nationalist Frente Polisario. In September 1974, however, Hassan managed to gain a postponement of any final United Nations verdict until the World Court had the opportunity to hear Morocco's claim. To increase the pressure on Madrid and score more points at home, Hassan at the beginning of 1975 also asserted Morocco's rights to the Spanish-inhabited enclave cities of Ceuta and Melilla on Morocco's Mediterranean coast.[51] Several frontier incidents occurred between Moroccan irregulars and Spanish patrols in the northern part of the Sahara, and on May 23, 1975, Arias announced that Spain would proceed with the devolution of self-determination to the people of the Sahara as soon as possible. Since the Moroccan government had no interest in self-determination but wished to take over the region directly, it steadily increased the pressure against Madrid during the waning months of Franco's life.[52] Given the cordial relations between Washington and Rabat, suspicion mounted in Madrid that somehow the United States was encouraging the increasingly aggressive policy of Morocco.

The Final Phase

By the summer of 1975 Spain had developed a broad new parapolitical life, with a largely free press and a whole series of semiclandestine politi-

51. Robert Rezette, *The Spanish Enclaves in Morocco* (Paris, 1976), describes their situation in the 1970s.

52. The best studies of the Saharan conflict are Francisco Villar, *El proceso de autodeterminación del Sahara* (Valencia, 1982); and Maurice Barbier, *Le conflit du Sahara accidental* (Paris, 1982). Briefer accounts include Ramón Criado, *Sahara: Pasión y muerte de un sueño imperial* (Paris, 1977); Juan Maestre Alfonso, *El Sahara en la crisis de Marruecos y España* (Madrid, 1975); Juan Segura Paloma, *El Sahara: razón de una sinrazón* (Barcelona, 1976); and Juan Bta. Vilar, *El Sahara español* (Madrid, 1977).

cal groups organizing and expanding themselves to undertake increasingly elaborate maneuvers. Yet nearly all of them remained convinced, correctly, that the regime would not undergo further fundamental change until after the death of Franco.

Sixty of the more ultra *procuradores en Cortes* petitioned the chief of state to prorogue the present Cortes, elected in November 1971 and due for renewal in a few months. This scheme was not favored by most of the cabinet but was devised by Franco himself and the ultra Cortes president, Rodríguez Valcárcel, who feared that even under the existing system a new election might produce significant changes, possibly ousting Rodríguez Valcárcel. A veteran of the Movement and practitioner of the most dreadful purple rhetoric, the latter's function as president of the Cortes would be crucial in any transition, because this post carried with it the presidency of the Council that would propose specific names for new presidents of government. Prorogation of the current Cortes was officially decreed on August 1 on the grounds that the present legislature had much uncompleted work before it. (In fact, during the six years that Valcárcel served as president, the Cortes had dealt with only 98 legislative proposals from the executive, the great majority of which had passed unanimously, while 101 Decree-Laws had been promulgated by the government.)[53]

This was the most violent year in Spain since the days of the guerrilla maquis of the forties, with eight policemen killed during the first eight months of 1975. Their funerals were occasions for semiviolent right-wing demonstrations insisting on a crackdown. Rightist groups fire-bombed leftist bookstores, sometimes beat up members of the opposition, and even engaged in one or two minor assaults on the cars of cabinet ministers.

A tough new antiterrorist law was imposed in August, restoring *sumarísimo* court-martial proceedings and mandatory death penalties for the killing of security officers. It was then applied retroactively to the cases of eleven revolutionaries from ETA and FRAP who were convicted of responsibility for the deaths of three policemen.[54] This occasioned the biggest international campaign in years against the regime by the west Euro-

53. During those six years there had been only six regular sessions of interpellation, only one of which had occurred during the Tenth Legislature then in session. Though individual procuradores did sometimes voice mild criticism, record a few individual no votes, and manage to add an occasional minor amendment to government legislation, no law prepared in the Cortes was ever accepted by the government. A total of 120 procuradores, 21.4 percent of the total, were still directly appointed by the chief of state or the government, and the rate of turnover became very high. During the four years 1971–75, 180 deputies resigned or were dismissed and were replaced by 172 new appointees, for a "coefficient of fluidity" of 32 percent. Miguel Angel Aguilar, *Las últimas Cortes del franquismo* (Madrid, 1976), 11–15.

54. Pedro J. Ramírez, *El año que murió Franco* (Barcelona, 1985), narrates the entire affair.

pean left, some of whom exhibited much greater indignation over the determination to punish these killers than they had, for example, over the Soviet invasion of Czechoslovakia. Pope Paul VI showed extraordinary interest in the fate of the condemned, twice urging commutation of the sentence. Both Don Juan and Prince Juan Carlos made the same request, as did the Generalissimo's elderly and ailing brother Nicolás, oldest living representative of the Franco family.[55] After the Burgos trial five years earlier, Franco had commuted the maximum penalty, apparently at the behest of his cabinet, but in September 1975 he and the more intransigent government figures deemed it necessary amid the rise in opposition activity to sustain the spirit of the recent antiterrorist law. Franco did commute the sentences of six of the condemned, but five were executed on September 27.[56] This touched off massive and emotional demonstrations against the regime in many European cities, on at least two occasions led by prime ministers. Spanish tourist offices, banks, and consulates were assaulted, and the venerable embassy in Lisbon was totally gutted.

To the end, Franco professed to be unmoved and untroubled, yet the tension of September took its toll. He had become increasingly agitated and for some days could scarcely sleep. Such strain was very likely a factor in the onset of his fatal illness the following month. The usual crowd assembled in the Plaza de Oriente on October 1, 1975, to hail him on the thirty-ninth anniversary of his elevation to power, the last that he would celebrate. Adolfo Suárez and other leaders of the new UDPE association were among the massed throng. The Caudillo expressed his customary disdainful satisfaction, declaring "that everything which has been going on in Europe is due to a Masonic-leftist conspiracy of the political class in collusion with Communist-terrorist subversion, which honors us as much as it degrades them," concluding that "evidently being Spanish is once again a serious thing in the world. Arriba España!"[57] Though the words repeated his standard idées fixes, gone was the icy aplomb of earlier times, for Franco's voice was unusually feeble and his expression sad and teary-eyed. For one instant he even turned to fall sobbing into the arms of

55. Nicolás had written to his brother, "Dear Paco: Don't sign that sentence. I tell you because I love you that it is not the thing to do. You are a good Christian and will regret it afterwards. We are old now; listen to my advice, for you know how much I love you." Quoted in Diario 16, *Historia de la transición*, 144.

56. Curiously, at approximately the same time Spanish courts began to release five Communists charged as accomplices in the Calle del Correo bomb slaughter of 1974, at least one or two of whom had also acted as major accomplices in the assassination of Carrero Blanco. Cf. Falcón, *Viernes y trece*, 13. Direct corroborating evidence was said to be unavailable, yet the police held confessions from two of the principals. Unexplained anomalies such as this contributed to the air of mystery surrounding both crimes, and the widespread belief, despite the lack of any other evidence, that "other forces" were involved in the Carrero assassination.

57. Diario 16, *Historia de la transición*, 144.

The last public demonstration on behalf of Franco, October 1975

Juan Carlos (who stood behind him), just as with Tarancón at the funeral of Carrero Blanco. That same day, four policemen were slain in different parts of Madrid by a new terrorist organization called GRAPO, and several more died four days later.

However weary, aged, and melancholy, Franco would not slacken as long as he could breathe. Though he realized that Juan Carlos would make changes, he yet hoped that some of the regime's most basic institutions might survive. During these last days, for example, Adolfo Suárez came to El Pardo to report on the progress of his new political association. Taking him aside, Franco asked Suárez if he thought the Movement could survive "after the death of General Franco" (speaking of himself in the third person). The young politician replied that he did not believe so. Franco then inquired if Suárez thought the future of Spain was "inevitably democratic," as Franco put it, and after receiving an affirmative reply, said no more.[58]

Franco's final public appearance took place on October 12, the Día de la

58. According to testimony at the Toledo Symposium.

Hispanidad (formerly Día de la Raza), in a ceremony at the Instituto de Cultura Hispanica, where his grandson-in-law, the Duque de Cádiz, presided. The first report of a new decline in his health two days later indicated that he was merely suffering from a cold. At that point the Caudillo's son-in-law, the Marqués de Villaverde (who had recently had his nose broken in a brawl with a Dutchman in a Marbella nightclub), stepped in to supervise operations for the family and called once more on Dr. Pozuelo, who had seen Franco through the affliction of the preceding year. On October 16 the International Court of Justice ruled in favor of independence for the Spanish Sahara, while King Hassan threatened a mass march of Moroccans to occupy the territory. On the following day Franco presided over a meeting of the Council of Ministers strapped with electrodes connected to a monitoring machine attended by physicians in an adjoining room. When he heard the latest report on Morocco, he immediately suffered a mild coronary infarction; he had had one several days earlier.

Franco felt weak and ill after awakening on October 18 and soon sat down to draft his final testament to the Spanish people, to be read after his death. Villaverde informed President Arias that the time had come for Juan Carlos to assume the functions of chief of state once more, but when notified, the Prince shrewdly replied that he would do so only if Franco signed an agreement ratifying the definitive succession and transfer of powers. He had no intention of being subjected to the almost comic indignities of the summer of 1974. Arias Navarro, fearing to try too hard, was unable to obtain such an agreement, and on October 19 it was simply announced that Franco had the *gripe* (flu).[59]

At this juncture the Moroccan government announced its readiness to launch a "Green March," the mass movement of more than a hundred thousand civilians (including not a few foreigners eager for excitement) across its southern border into the Sahara. On October 21 Solís Ruiz was dispatched to Rabat to talk with Hassan, who agreed to bilateral negotiations. That night it was announced in Madrid for the first time that Franco was suffering a coronary affliction.

His symptoms seemed to moderate on the following day, but by the twenty-third he was clearly worse. Villaverde consequently tried to convince Juan Carlos to come to El Pardo so that together with Arias and the physicians they could convince Franco formally to transmit his powers. Counseled by López Rodó not to agree,[60] the Prince refused. During the week that followed, Franco's condition declined further, with severe gastric hemorrhage and pulmonary edema added to his maladies.

59. Concerning the control of information and commentary on Franco's last illness, see Dolores Alvarez et al., *Noticia, rumor, bulo: La muerte de Franco. Ensayo sobre algunos aspectos del control de la información* (Madrid, 1976).

60. According to López Rodó's *Larga marcha*, 487–90.

The evacuation of Spanish civilians from the Sahara began on October 29,[61] though on the next day the Algerian government warned Madrid that to hand the Sahara over to Morocco would constitute an act of war. This raised international tension to the maximum, and Franco, convinced that he would soon die, ordered on the thirtieth implementation of article 11 of the Organic Law whereby Juan Carlos once more would assume interim functions. The Prince then for the first time presided over a cabinet meeting in his own residence, the Zarzuela, and on November 2 flew his own plane to the Sahara to raise the morale of Spanish troops.[62] Since the Spanish government still had not given in, the Green March was officially begun on November 6 and moved about three kilometers into the Spanish Sahara, with Spanish troops naturally unwilling to fire on a great mass of civilians. Three days later, before the marchers might suffer the misfortune of running into a Spanish minefield, Hassan gave the order to withdraw and bilateral negotiations were resumed. On November 14 it was agreed that Spain would withdraw from the Sahara by February 28, 1976. In the interim there would be coadministration by representatives of Spain, Morocco, and Mauretania in conjunction with the Djemaa, supposedly representing the will of the Saharauis. The whole procedure was simply a formula for handing over the Sahara—whose defense by Spain would have been totally counterproductive at that point—to Morocco, which would then face a very long war against its several African rivals.

Franco's stoicism and personal discipline were never needed more than during his agony. For weeks the suffering was intense, as one malady was added to another. At one point, after nearly being asphyxiated by a large lump of coagulated blood in his pharynx, he was heard to say, "Dios mío, cuánto cuesta morirse" ("My God, what a struggle it is to die").[63] When the gastric hemorrhaging became uncontrollable, he underwent an emergency operation in El Pardo on November 3. This required seven liters of transfused blood and prompted a further remark from the aged stoic, "Qué duro es esto" ("How hard this is"). Symptoms of thrombophlebitis and partial kidney failure also appeared at this time. The return of massive hemorrhaging finally required removal to a hospital on the seventh, where a second operation removed much of his stomach to extirpate eleven ulcers, requiring another transfusion of six liters of blood. From this point on the Caudillo was heavily sedated and he scarcely spoke. By

61. The annual observance of the founding of the Falange took place as usual that day in Madrid. According to López Rodó, a woman shouted at the meeting, "I demand to speak! Spain is Franco's and the heir to Franco is his grandson Cristóbal." She was ejected. Ibid., 491.

62. On the activity of Juan Carlos during the final days, see Bardavío, *Los silencios,* 113–41.

63. Dr. Pozuelo dates this as simply before Franco's removal from El Pardo on November 7. *Historia de la transición,* 164.

November 14, the sutures from the last operation had broken and further signs of grave degeneration appeared, requiring a third and final operation.

It is often overlooked that, quite aside from the natural desire of Franco's family, physicians, and closest supporters to save his life, there was a more immediate objective involved in prolonging his life for a few weeks. On November 26 the term of Rodríguez Valcárcel as president of the Cortes and of the Council of the Realm would end. If Franco were able to recover power by that date, he could ratify Valcárcel for a second term and thus guarantee that the Council of the Realm, which controlled nomination for future presidents of government, would remain under reliable Francoist control. Even if Franco should die shortly thereafter, it would be very difficult for Juan Carlos to inaugurate a different policy or appoint a more genuinely reformist prime minister without authorization from the Council of the Realm. But without Franco's recovery, a new head of the Cortes and Council of the Realm would soon be chosen, greatly facilitating the options of Juan Carlos for sweeping change.

Security forces began to carry out the first phase of "Plan Lucero" (Morning Star), the contingency plan to guarantee the security of the regime during the transition. Leaders of the leftist opposition, particularly Communists, began to be rounded up as a preventive measure, while groups of ultras issued threats to opposition leaders on a much broader scale (though later they made little effort to follow up on them).

Religious gestures of all manner were made throughout Spain. Sacred relics were dispatched from the provinces to join the petrified arm of Santa Teresa, Franco's chief personal relic since the Civil War, on his bedstand. Meanwhile, according to reports, champagne supplies were several times exhausted at the headquarters of emigré opposition parties in Paris, where the successive notices of Franco's deteriorating condition provoked several premature celebrations. For the last two weeks Franco was suspended between life and death as a sort of mechanical man, full of tubes attached to medical machines. After the third operation, his daughter Carmencita suggested that artificial procedures be discontinued and the old soldier left to die naturally and peacefully.[64] During the final ten days Franco was scarcely conscious and at the end weighed only 40 kilos (88 pounds), after having received 70 liters of blood. After life-support systems were finally withdrawn late on the nineteenth, he expired on November 20 (the anniversary of the execution of José Antonio Primo de Rivera), fourteen days short of his eighty-third birthday. The final medical report on the cause of death read like a medical dictionary: "Parkinson's

64. Cardinal Tarancón agreed, observing that "we should have pity on the elderly and allow them to die peacefully." Quoted in Garriga, *La Señora de El Pardo*, 354.

disease, cardiopathy . . . , acute recurrent digestive ulcers with repeated massive hemorrhages, bacterial peritonitis, acute kidney failure, thrombophlebitis . . . , bronchial pneumonia, endotoxic shock, and cardiac arrest."[65]

At ten that morning Arias announced Franco's death on national radio and television and read the farewell message to the Spanish people that Franco had written a few weeks earlier:

> Spaniards: When the hour comes for me to surrender my life before the Most High and appear before His implacable judgment, I pray that God may receive me graciously in His presence, for I sought always to live and die as a Catholic. In the name of Christ I glory, and my constant will has been to be a faithful son of the Church, in whose bosom I am going to die. I ask pardon of all, as with all my heart I forgive those who declared themselves my enemies, though I might not have held them to be such. I desire and believe to have had none other than those who were enemies of Spain, which I love until the final moment and which I promised to serve until my last breath, that I know to be near.
>
> I wish to thank all who have collaborated with enthusiasm, commitment, and abnegation in the great task of making Spain united, great, and free. In the love that I feel for our Fatherland, I ask you to persevere in unity and in peace and to surround the future King of Spain, Don Juan Carlos de Borbón, with the same affection and loyalty that you have offered me, and that you grant him at all times the same support and collaboration that I have had from you.
>
> Do not forget that the enemies of Spain and of Christian civilization are alert. Keep watch yourselves and subordinate every personal concern to the supreme interests of the Fatherland of the Spanish people. Do not be diverted from achieving social justice and cultural advancement for all citizens of Spain and make of that your prime goal. Maintain the unity of all the lands of Spain, exalting the rich diversity of its regions as the source of the strength of the Fatherland's unity.
>
> I should like, in my final moment, to join the names of God and of Spain and to embrace you all to cry together, for the last time, at the moment of my death:
>
> Arriba España! Viva España!

Hundreds of thousands filed past his bier in Madrid as he lay in state on November 21–22. According to a public opinion survey, 80 percent of Spaniards polled qualified his death as a loss, but 90 percent declared their positive opinion of the succession of Juan Carlos[66] (in one sense validating Franco's own judgment), who took the oath as king of Spain on the twenty-second. On the following day the last great avatar of the traditional Spanish national-Catholic ideology was laid to rest in the grand but

---

65. The final illness has been described by "Yale," *Los últimos cien días* (Madrid, 1975); Germán Lopezarias, *Franco, la última batalla* (Madrid, 1975); and José Oneto, *Cien días en la muerte de Franco* (Madrid, 1976). There is a brief memoir by Dr. Manuel Hidalgo Huerta, *Cómo y por qué operé a Franco* (Madrid, 1976).

66. Granados, *1975*, 541–59.

austere mausoleum that he had constructed at the Valle de los Caídos,[67] and with him was buried a millenary tradition dating in some respects from the eighth century.

67. "Soon the abbey of the Valle de los Caidos began to receive numerous letters, from foreign countries as well as Spain, proclaiming the one buried there to be a saint (or to be holy) and asking for objects that had come in contact with his tomb, to keep in the form of relics." Sueiro, *Verdadera historia*, 272. Though some visitors during the next few years would deposit petitions on Franco's tomb as though it were a holy shrine, it never became the major religious center that the family might have wanted. As the years passed, its attraction was primarily for tourists, domestic and foreign.

23

The Franco Regime
in Perspective

The definition and classification of the regime obviously presented an increasingly complex problem the longer that Franco's system endured. This was due in part to its very length, spanning the fascist and post–fascist social democratic eras, and even more to the successive metamorphoses of the regime's priorities and policies. Nietzsche once observed that "whatever has a history cannot be defined," and certainly the Franco system had a longer history and underwent more historical change than have most non-Marxist dictatorships. Beyond that, the calculated ambiguity and procrastination of Franco's personal style and modus operandi installed a certain polyvalent character in the regime from the beginning. Hence one of its earliest theorists wrote soon after Franco's death:

> It turns out to be difficult to understand Francoism because its very development relied on ambiguity and changes of direction. The political forms that Franco established did not undergo direct continuous development, but underwent pauses and superpositions. . . . I have sometimes thought that preoccupation of his against the force of chance led him to play with two decks when he spread his cards on the table, to have available the greatest number of combinations. . . .[1]

Any typology is rendered complex and confusing by the two metamorphoses of the Spanish regime, whose history may be divided into three periods: (1) the semifascist, potentially imperialist phase of 1936 to 1945; (2) the decade of National Catholic corporatism from 1945 to 1957 that witnessed the further irremediable subordination of the fascist component; and (3) the developmentalist phase of so-called technocracy and a

1. Juan Beneyto, *La identidad del franquismo* (Madrid, 1979), 10–11.

sort of bureaucratic authoritarianism from 1957/59 to the end.[2] This in turn has raised the question, frequently answered in the negative, as to whether Franco had any consistent doctrine or ideology other than the conservation of personal power at all costs. He himself never produced a significant work of theory, reserving his doctrinal statements for public speeches, while the Fundamental Principles of 1958 differ fundamentally from and in some ways directly reject key aspects of the Twenty-six Points of 1937.

Certainly Franco never defined in theory a clear-cut formal ideology comparable to any of the major political theologies of the twentieth century, but he always possessed a fundamental set of beliefs whose basic priorities and values changed comparatively little. His political attitudes stemmed to some extent from his Catholic and military background but only took full form during the decade 1926 to 1936, the time in which most of his political and economic reading was concentrated. He believed in nationalism, central unity, the Catholic religion, strong authoritarian government without political parties, and a program of modern economic development determined as much as possible by political and nationalistic priorities, with social reform a secondary byproduct of economic growth. Franco's nationalism was grounded in Spanish tradition, aspects of which he revered. He was fundamentally monarchist in political principles, though he was also tempted by some of the more radical ambitions of fascism before 1943, temptations to which he never fully succumbed.

Like most major political actors, Franco basically used the ideas of others. The eclecticism of the authoritarian coalition which he established during the Civil War was not merely a matter of opportunism, for to a degree he shared some of the key ideas of each of the major political families of the regime while rejecting the full ensemble of ideas of any one of them. From the monarchists he accepted the principle of monarchical legitimacy but totally redefined it to suit himself. He shared the nationalism and to some extent the imperialism of the Falangists, together with their insistence on authoritarian rule and the form if not all the substance of their social and economic policies. He praised Carlist traditionalism, Catholicism, and defense of traditional monarchy while rejecting Carlist dynastic politics. He believed in the military sense of patriotism and national security, together with the elitist function of commanders and officers, but rejected any notion of a corporate military function that would give the armed forces institutional independence. In many ways, the right radical program defined by Calvo Sotelo between 1933 and 1936

2. In his *España 1939–1945: Régimen político e ideología* (Madrid, 1978), Manuel Ramírez Jiménez labels the periods those of the "totalitarian regime," the "empirico-conservative dictatorship," and "tecno-pragmatic Francoism."

most nearly anticipated the guidelines of the regime, though there is no indication that Franco consciously followed this particular blueprint systematically, and he rejected the dynastic legitimacy supported by some of Calvo Sotelo's principal associates.

It has been frequently observed that Franco's thinking was defined as much by what it opposed as by what it espoused. He was firmly convinced that a fully developed parliamentary party system could not work in Spain, and he was equally opposed to Marxism, cultural liberalism ("Masonry"), laicism, materialism, and internationalism. He apparently never ceased to have certain misgivings about the opening up of economic policy after 1959,[3] however gratifying its immediate technical achievements.

The Primo de Rivera dictatorship made a major impression on his thinking, and in most respects Franco always regarded himself as continuing the same policies while avoiding the basic "Primo de Rivera mistake" of failing to institutionalize an authoritarian nationalist regime. The Civil War trauma provided a unique opportunity for Franco and from his own point of view created a fundamental legitimacy of its own, for as he made clear in his correspondence with the Conde de Barcelona during 1944–45, he believed in a quintessential "right of conquest" not altogether different from that of a sixteenth-century conquistador. At the same time, he was sophisticated enough to realize that this was too crude for public consumption and could easily be used against him, so that public pronouncements dwelt on unity and common support in the achievement of victory.

The nearest historical analogy to the Francoist form of *caudillaje* would be elective but absolute monarchy, a role to which he believed himself called by the decision of the Junta de Defensa Nacional. The earliest modern prototype was Napoleon Bonaparte, and Franco certainly showed himself to be influenced either directly or indirectly by certain Bonapartist formulas, specifically the use of the referendum and the concept of the dyarchic monarchist state which employed a royal council to guarantee legitimacy, continuity, and proper authority. Though somewhat far-fetched, the earliest Spanish analogy might lie with Enrique de Trastámara, winner of the great Castilian civil war of the 1360s. Enrique had no legitimate claim to the throne but presented himself as true champion of law, religion, and tradition in opposition to the supposed heterodoxy and arbitrary despotism of Pedro the Cruel. Foreign assistance was also fundamental to Enrique's victory, which proclaimed the triumph of true religion and proper respect for tradition.

Despite the prevalence of military dictatorship and "caudillos" in Latin America, there is no evidence that Franco was ever influenced by Latin American models. He himself viewed his regime, correctly, within the

3. Cf. his remarks to the Catalan syndicates in Barcelona, July 1, 1970. *FF*, 8:210.

comparative context of European nationalist and authoritarian systems. Except for the temporary exception of Peronism between 1945 and 1949, the official Spanish media reflected a degree of ambiguity about most Latin American dictatorships. The regime's censorship discouraged any use of the term *caudillo* for Latin American rulers to avoid cheapening the concept.

Franco believed in imperialism, having won his spurs in a colonial war. He hoped to restore Spain's prestige in the world and develop a new empire in Africa, a little like the way in which Portugal had replaced Brazil with Angola and Mozambique. When circumstances made that impossible, the adjustment was made, though grudgingly.

One of the most novel aspects of the regime within the European context was its archaizing effort to revive cultural traditionalism. The concept of the neotraditionalist community, basic to Franco's social and cultural thought, seems to have been taken largely from Carlism. Creation of community was fundamental to many modern European nationalist movements, but no other emphasized neotraditionalism to the same extent. The attempt to revive traditionalism and religious fundamentalism was carried to a degree unprecedented by any other European regime, and was almost more akin to Islamic revivalism than to Italian Fascism.

Yet Franco was a conscious and determined economic modernizer, however limited his grasp of economics. He always held that effective social and economic policy was vital for any contemporary state, absorbing doctrine from both conservative and Catholic corporatism, from economic nationalism, and from fascistic national syndicalism. He was not as totally oblivious of the potential contradiction between economic modernization and cultural traditionalism as it may have seemed, but hoped to contain the problem, as have Communist regimes, by partially sealing off the outside world. When Spain's economic limitations made this impossible, the cultural erosion of the regime greatly accelerated.

Franco always emphasized his willingness to reconsider individual policies as distinct from fundamental principles, but it is not clear that an absolute distinction was always maintained. Critics maintained that the only abiding "fundamental principle" was the maintenance of Franco's personal power. Though that may be something of an exaggeration, in the ultimate sense it was true enough. One thing that Franco would never concede or truly compromise was his personal prerogative, influenced above all by the examples of Primo de Rivera in 1930 and Mussolini in 1945. He realized that though individual policies may be relaxed or even changed, a personal dictatorship cannot be disbanded halfway, for that would ultimately leave the dictator no choice but to flee abroad, an enterprise which he judged hazardous in the extreme.

Whereas opponents usually labeled the regime as "fascist" or "totalitarian" during its early years, these appellations had become less persuasive by the 1950s. In 1956 an unsympathetic critic such as Herbert Matthews defined it as perhaps not fascist but certainly "fascistoid."[4] During the 1960s even that attenuation seemed inadequate, and other phrases of description such as "authoritarian regime," "corporatism," "authoritarian-conservative"[5] and "a unitary limited pluralism"[6] were employed.

Juan J. Linz, the most persuasive taxonomist of totalitarianism and authoritarianism,[7] presented in 1964 his classic definition of the Spanish system as a semipluralist rightist "authoritarian regime," specifying:

> Authoritarian regimes are political systems with limited, not responsible, pluralism: without elaborate and guiding ideology (but with distinctive mentalities); without intensive or extensive political mobilization (except at some points in their development); and in which a leader (or occasionally a small group) exercises power within formally ill-defined limits but actually quite predictable ones.
>
> . . . Personal leadership is a frequent characteristic but not a necessary one, since a junta arrangement can exist and the leader's personality might not be the decisive factor. Furthermore, the leader does not need to have charismatic qualities, at least not for large segments of the population nor at all stages of development of the system. In fact he may combine elements of charismatic, legal and traditional authority in varying degrees, often at different points in time—though the charismatic element often tends to be more important than the legal authority, at least for some sectors of the population.[8]

That the Spanish regime was obviously authoritarian, not totalitarian, is first of all simply an inescapable fact, for it did not attempt to control the entire economy and all social, cultural, and religious institutions. Totalitarianism in terms of total control of institutions is a construct that accurately describes only the most extreme Stalinist type of socialist dictatorships (and possibly the final phase of Nazi Germany).[9] It fell into disfavor during the 1970s because of genuine or merely supposed alterations in Communist systems but remains an accurate and useful classificatory device for the fully Stalinist-type polity.[10]

4. Herbert L. Matthews, *The Yoke and the Arrows* (New York, 1957).

5. Jean Blondel, *Comparing Political Systems* (New York, 1972).

6. Pi Sunyer, *El personal político*, 149.

7. Juan J. Linz, "Totalitarian and Authoritarian Regimes," in *Handbook of Political Science*, ed. F. Greenstein and N. Polsby (Reading, Mass., 1975), 3:175–411.

8. Juan J. Linz, "An Authoritarian Regime: Spain," in *Cleavages, Ideologies and Party Strategies*, ed. E. Allardt and Y. Littunen (Helsinki, 1964), 291–341.

9. This is the de facto conclusion of Hannah Arendt, *The Origins of Totalitarianism* (New York, 1966), in her analysis of Fascist Italy, Nazi Germany, and the Soviet Union. She judges that the Hitler regime did not approach full totalitarianism until its radical death throes during 1944–45.

10. For recent discussions of authoritarianism as distinct from totalitarianism and vice versa, see Amos Perlmutter, *Modern Authoritarianism: A Comparative Institutional Analysis* (New Haven, 1982); and Jeane J. Kirkpatrick, *Dictatorships and Double Standards* (New York, 1982). Perlmutter would apply totalitarianism only to the most rigorous phase of the Soviet Union down to 1953. More recently, however, the term has been regaining currency

Clear analysis is sometimes confused by the fact that the term is never used by Communist regimes, having been invented by early opponents of the Mussolini regime in Italy. By 1925 it had been officially adopted as a positive slogan and goal by the Duce himself and was also employed by Franco and other officials during the first years of the Spanish regime, just as the slogan was picked up in several other right-authoritarian systems. The word was apparently invented by the Italian liberal and militant anti-Fascist Giovanni Amendola in May 1923 to refer to the prospect of a total concentration of political power in the hands of the Mussolini government, while Mussolini later inflated its meaning ambiguously. Antonio Gramsci, Italian communism's leading thinker during that decade, confused the issue further by references to "progressive" totalitarianism of the left (because Marxist revolutionary) and the "false" totalitarianism of the right, though this had the merit of correctly implying that genuine totalitarianism—insofar as it was an accurate empirical or structural description and not a mere epithet—pertained to total revolutionary state socialism.[11]

José Antonio Primo de Rivera was aware of at least some of the problems involved and abandoned use of the term "totalitarian state,"[12] while Franco qualified his own vague usage during the Civil War by referring with even greater ambiguity and in fact downright confusion to its supposed invention by the builders of the united Spanish monarchy in the fifteenth century. In the first years of the Spanish regime the term tended to refer to the concentration of all political power and the fostering of a single and consistent doctrine of national unity.[13] That structural totalitarianism could only describe something like the Soviet state but not the nascent Franco regime was grasped by the Jesuit theorist Azpiazu— more systematic than some of his fellow countrymen—in the midst of the Civil War.

Yet if the regime never was nor was intended to be structurally totalitarian, it at first absorbed a good deal of fascistic doctrine through the incorporation of the Falange and the latter's program. From 1937 to 1945 the Franco regime was doctrinally at least a semifascist state, the categorical fascism of the FET as state party being mitigated above all by the

in light of the absence of fundamental structural and policy reforms in the Soviet Union. Cf. William E. Odom, "A Dissenting View on the Group Approach to Soviet Politics," *World Politics* 28:4 (July 1976), 542–89; and Walter Laqueur, "Is There Now, or Has There Ever Been, Such a Thing as Totalitarianism?" *Commentary*, Oct. 1985, pp. 29–36. The fullest recent treatment is Pierre Hasner and Jacques Rupnik, *Totalitarismes* (Paris, 1984).

11. Origins of the term are clarified by Meir Michaelis, "Anmerkungen zum italienischen Totalitarismusbegriff," in *Quellen und Forschungen aus italienischen Archiven und Bibliotheken* (Rome, 1982), 270–302.

12. Cf. his *Obras completas*, 571; and the work by Arrese cited earlier.

13. This is the argument—in my judgment, a correct one—made by Vicente Marrero, *La guerra española y el trust de cerebros* (Madrid, 1967), 293–95.

confessional nature of the regime—creating the strange hybrid known to some as clerical fascism and to Amando de Miguel as *fascismo frailuno* (friar-fascism)—and also by the explicit syncretism avowed by Franco from the outset.

The early regime was an extreme form of dictatorship, in juridical structure (or lack of it) nominally the most arbitrary in Europe until after the end of World War II. Politically and institutionally, however, the place of the FET was even weaker than that of the Partito Nazionale Fascista in Italy, where from the first the party was subordinate to the state rather than vice versa. The military hierarchy, on the other hand, had a special relationship to the state, even though not directly institutionalized, that found no counterpart in either Germany or Italy.

The most direct parallel might be encountered in a military/rightist regime such as that of Antonescu in Romania from 1940 to 1944, which maintained an alliance with a fascist-type movement for six months before subduing it. Even in eastern Europe, however, the right authoritarian systems differed substantially from the Spanish regime, for the efforts of Pilsudski and the colonels in Poland or of King Alexander in Yugoslavia were carried out to some degree within the context of preexisting political institutions and did not produce as radical a break as in Spain.

Horthy's Hungary was the first twentieth-century European state to restore a monarchy (1920–44) and install a military leader as regent for life, but the Hungarian system involved the direct restoration of a regime and a constitution that had ceased to exist less than two years earlier, and did not at all require the radical break and the incisive new dictatorship that was the case of Spain. Moreover, Horthy's Hungary occupied a kind of border position between genuine authoritarian regimes and true parliamentary systems, permitting multiple political parties, partially authentic elections, and free trade unions.

The similarities between Mussolini's system and the early Franco regime during its first eight years are rather greater than is sometimes thought. Both employed subordinated state fascist parties that were merged with and subsequently incorporated nonfascist elements. Both permitted limited pluralism in national society and institutions under executive dictatorship. In neither case was the institutionalization of the regime developed primarily by revolutionary fascist ideologues but rather by monarchist or semimonarchist figures of the radical right in conjunction with fascist moderates. Though Franco enjoyed much more complete executive authority than did Mussolini, he eventually converted the form of his regime into that of monarchy, which already existed in Italy. In both cases the challenge of militant fascist national syndicalism was soon faced and thoroughly subordinated (in the *sbloccamento* of Rossoni's national syndicates in 1928, and the suppression of Salvador Merino's attempt at a more integral and autonomous radical national syndicalism in 1940).

The sequences of development of the two regimes were also somewhat parallel, finally diverging radically at the level of foreign policy. In both cases, an early coalition phase without official institutional structure (Italy, 1922–25; Spain, 1936–37) was followed by a phase of institutionalization (Italy, 1925–29; Spain, 1937–40) that was in turn succeeded by a period of equilibrium which was longer in Italy than in Spain. All this is of course a fairly common pattern for new systems, but should not lead one to overlook some fundamental differences in policies and ambitions. Mussolini made a somewhat greater effort at ideological development, and always harbored certain socially revolutionary goals that required more continuing effort at political mobilization. Foreign policy and international context marked the ultimate points of divergence, for the eventual structure of the Spanish regime was to a large extent dependent on world affairs. Whereas Mussolini tried to play an independent role from 1933 on, Franco accepted the need to wait on events. Had Hitler won the war, there seems little doubt that Franquism would have become less conservative and rightist and more radical and overtly fascist in form. Acceptance of the term *fascist* was fairly common though never official during the first year of the Civil War, and all the trappings of "Franco! Franco! Franco!" in the early period were simply imitations of Italian Fascism (or occasionally National Socialism), including various agencies and institutions of the party and regime such as the Vicesecretaría de Cultura Popular (derived from the Italian MinCulPop) or the Auxilio de Invierno (from Winterhilfe).

The defascistization of the Franco regime began as early as 1942 and proceeded in several stages. The first was that of the 1940s, more precisely from 1942 to 1947, when the FET was deemphasized, the system of monarchy established, and gestures made toward representation and civil rights through the introduction of a corporate and controlled Cortes and the Fuero de los Españoles. The second phase was that of 1956–58, when any form of Falangist restoration or major new institutionalization was ruled out, the regime moved from nationalist autarchy in economic policy to an internationalist semiliberalism, technocratic bureaucracy became the order of the day, and the fascistic program of the FET was thrown out in favor of the bland Principles of the Movement. The final phase began with the reforms of the 1967–68 which redefined the Movement as a vague national "communion," after which it was deprived of most of the remaining vestiges of its continuity and ultimately faced with total political reorganization if it intended to survive. The Movement was finally officially dissolved by King Juan Carlos in April 1977, and the memory of its long, attenuated life was reflected only in the pullulation of a variety of competing, minuscule neofascist grouplets, both singly and collectively as weak in support as the individual organizations were large in number.[14] All combined, they were scarcely able to gain one percent of the popular vote in democratic elections after the death of Franco, a collective show-ing not only much weaker than the neo-fascist MSI in Italy but even weaker than the feeble support for the neo-Nazi organizations in Germany. Moreover, a number of the neofascist groups in post-Franco Spain have identified more with Nazism than with the native Falangist tradition in their symbolism and rhetoric, diminishing even further their nationalist legitimacy and appeal.

Comparison with the Portuguese regime of Salazar and Caetano reveals other similarities and differences. Despite its lack of socioeconomic development, Portugal has persistently shown more political prococity than some other parts of southern Europe. It had the first royalist semi-dictatorship in southwestern Europe in the authoritarian government of João Franco in 1907–8, followed by the extraparliamentary government of General Pimenta de Castro in 1915, and the short-lived insurrectionist, plebiscitary effort at an authoritarian presidentialist regime under Sidonio Pais and his República Nova in 1917–18. It also had a Partido Nacionalista in the very first years of the century, before such an organization had ap-peared in Italy, much less Spain.

The forty-eight-year dictatorship that governed from 1926 to 1974 was originated, like those of Spain and various countries of eastern Europe and Latin America, by military revolt, yet it was unable to institutionalize itself or even to govern effectively as a strictly military regime. There is considerable analogy between the Portuguese military dictatorship of 1926–28 and the Primo de Rivera regime of 1923–30, the difference being that the Portuguese dictatorship found and rather grudgingly ac-cepted a leader capable of developing and institutionalizing it. A partially civilian phase began with Antonio de Oliveira Salazar's entrance as eco-nomics minister in 1928; he soon became the dominant figure and by 1933 had built the first "corporative republic" in Europe.[15] Salazar derived his inspiration mainly from right-wing Catholic corporative doctrine. The

14. Spanish neofascism has been nothing if not eclectic as well, featuring several attempts at neo-Nazi as well as various neo-Falangist groups, and by 1983 even a tiny Legión de Miguel Arcángel, reviving the nomenclature of the Romanian Iron Guard, with whose mystical reli-gious nationalism Falangists had always felt considerable affinity. Cf. Horia Sima, *Dos movi-mientos nacionales: José Antonio Primo de Rivera y Corneliu Zelea Codreanu* (Madrid, 1960).

15. The best general treatments of the Portuguese regime will be found in Richard A. H. Robinson, *Contemporary Portugal: A History* (London, 1979), 32–166; Tom Gallagher, *Por-tugal: A Twentieth-Century Interpretation* (Manchester, 1983), 38–164; and the miscellany *O fascismo em Portugal* (Lisbon, 1982).

role of the Catholic and radical rights in the Portuguese Estado Novo[16] was somewhat analogous to that of their counterparts in Spain, but Salazar never developed a fully confessional state.

More than in the case of Spain, there is considerable analogy between the Portuguese regime and those of interwar eastern Europe—corporative or semicorporative, institutionalized (in most cases), systematically authoritarian but most of the time not viciously repressive, and without any significant fascist component. Moreover, like some authoritarian systems in Latin America, Salazar maintained the form of a constitutional republic, with regular elections for the presidency (he was de facto permanent prime minister) and largely fictitious parliamentary elections. This constitutional facade, so different from that of the Franco regime between 1937 and 1945, enabled Salazar to escape the degree of opprobrium suffered by Franco in 1945 and to become a member of NATO four years later. (The absence of such bloody and well-publicized historical origins as the Spanish Civil War or any ties with Germany and Italy were also important factors.) Salazar's state political organization, the National Union, was a semiartificial front organization more nearly resembling Primo de Rivera's formalistic Unión Patriótica than a generically fascist state party like the Falange.

A real fascist movement did develop briefly in Portugal, the blue-shirted National Syndicalists of Rolão Preto, who claimed to be expanding into a mass movement in 1934–35. Salazar exiled Preto in 1934, denouncing the National Syndicalists' fascistic "exaltation of youth, the cult of force through direct action, the principle of the superiority of state political power in social life, and the propensity for organizing masses behind a single leader."[17] In 1935 the National Syndicalists attempted a revolutionary coup against the regime in vague conjunction with anarchosyndicalists but were easily crushed.[18]

The Portuguese regime was nevertheless influenced by Italy, at least after 1936, and Salazar was not as opposed to the Rome-Berlin Axis as he preferred to have it appear after 1943. The Estado Novo participated in the general tendency toward fascism in the Iberian peninsula and in southern and eastern Europe generally during the years of the Spanish Civil War. During 1936–39 the regime became more overtly authoritarian, expanded the National Union and set up a new political militia, the

16. On the radical and Catholic rightists in Portugal, see Carlos Ferrão, *O Integralismo e a República* (Lisbon, 1964); Manuel Braga da Cruz, *A origem da democracia-cristã em Portugal e o salazarismo* (Lisbon, 1979); and his article "O Integralismo lusitano e o Estado Novo," in *O fascismo*, 105–39.

17. Jacques Ploncard d'Assac, *Salazar* (Paris, 1967), 107.

18. See João Medina, *Salazar e os fascistas* (Lisbon, 1979); and Antonio Costa Pinto's thesis, "O Nacional Sindicalismo" (Universidade Nova de Lisboa, 1987).

National Legion, to supplement the police, and organized a national youth movement. Both the latter organizations employed the fascist salute. The move toward fascism was arrested by the outbreak of the war, however, and went into reverse at about the same time that the first phase of defascistization began in Spain. Yet the Portuguese regime had been influenced by the fascist vertigo of the late 1930s, so that in the proper circumstances it too would probably have become a fellow traveler of fascism and become more fascist.

What the Italian, Spanish, and Portuguese regimes all had in common were (1) political authoritarianism; (2) generally corporative economic systems; (3) a bureaucratized, nonautonomous, essentially nonrevolutionary state political organization; (4) semipluralist autonomy for influential segments of society; and (5) imperialist foreign policies, at least in the years 1937–45.[19] At the same time, a kind of continuum could be readily established, with Italy at one extreme, Portugal at the other, and Spain in the middle. The Italian regime was always under a more continuing tension with the most intrinsic and revolutionary aspects of Fascism, a more dynamic pattern of independent development, and a more active and ambitious foreign policy.

Though the Spanish regime increasingly gave up efforts at systematic political mobilization after 1945, the Salazar system scarcely ever tried any broad pattern of mobilization. Similarly, it failed to develop a cultural offensive equivalent to the new culture and religious expansion of the first years of the new Spanish state. Even its corporatism was never completely developed,[20] though it further elaborated its facade of constitutionalism in 1945, staying formalistically far ahead of the nominal reforms and changes in the Spanish regime.[21] The Portuguese regime was weak in terms of economic development policy, however, and this in turn was not unrelated to the absence of fascistic ambitions of national growth and new grandeur. Portuguese society consequently changed proportionately less than did that of Spain under Franco. Yet a third area in which the two regimes followed opposite policies was colonialism. Spanish ambitions to retain territories in northwest Africa grew progressively more modest from 1945 on, and by 1956 the Madrid regime had, *faute de mieux*, joined the ranks of the west European decolonizers. Salazar, on the other hand, was deter-

19. For further development of this comparative analysis, see Manuel de Lucena, *A evolução do sistema corporativo portugûes* (Lisbon, 1976), 1:23–51.
20. Cf. Lucena and Howard J. Wiarda, *Corporatism and Development: The Portuguese Experience* (Amherst, Mass., 1977).
21. The best succinct definition of the changing political structure and character of the Estado Novo is Braga da Cruz's article "Notas para uma caracterização política do salazarismo," in *A formação de Portugal contemporâneo: 1900–1980* (Lisbon, 1982), 773–94. (This volume is a reprint of issues no. 72–74 of the journal *Análise Social*.)

mined to cede nothing. He may have been encouraged in this by the fact that the Portuguese African territories, the main base of the colonies, presented the least resistance of any of the African regions during the 1950s. Yet his policy did not change after an armed independence movement broke out in Angola,[22] nor was he willing to concede anything to India in the hopeless enterprise of maintaining Portuguese Goa, soon snatched away by force.

Salazar was an intellectual and a man of greater cultural depth than Franco, but he was also less attuned to various problems and exigencies of the twentieth century. Franco once observed after a meeting with Salazar that he felt as though he had been talking to "the mayor of Barcelona."[23] Franco was obviously more resourceful and more political in that he was capable of adjusting to and dealing with a greater variety and complexity of problems, whether or not his solutions endured.

Nonetheless Salazar's regime did survive him by six years and probably would have had a considerably longer life had it not been for the colonial conflict. The Estado Novo continued for six years not because it was any more securely institutionalized than Franco's regime, but because Portuguese society was less sophisticated and demanding and because Portugal remained a smaller, simpler, less developed country that presented many fewer challenges to government than did Spain.[24]

Another major difference lay in the relationship with the armed forces. Franco's Army was his own creation, built during the fiery ordeal of total civil war, and despite individual resentments, sealed in loyalty to its own Caudillo. Professor Salazar was an outsider to the Portuguese military, and serious friction was intermittent throughout the long history of the Estado Novo. Military leaders emerged at various points as the nominal leaders of the opposition, both the tolerated and the illegal opposition, and a military conspiracy eventually overthrew the regime altogether.[25]

During the 1960s, as Latin American countries tended to fall back under military rule once more, new efforts were made to understand the phenomenon of authoritarian government in Hispanic countries, resulting in the development of such concepts as "bureaucratic authoritarian-

22. For a balanced account of Portuguese colonialism, see Malyn Newitt, *Portugal in Africa: The Last Hundred Years* (London, 1981).

23. Saña, *Conversaciones*, 375.

24. On the *caetanato*, the six-year continuist but also semireformist regime of the professor who succeeded Salazar from 1968 to 1974, see Lucena, *A evolução*, vol. 2; Robinson, *Contemporary Portugal*, 167–93; and Gallagher, *Portugal*, 165–90.

25. For partial overviews of the relationship between the military and the Estado Novo, see Douglas Wheeler, "The Military and the Portuguese Dictatorship, 1926–1974," in *Contemporary Portugal*, ed. L. Graham and H. Makler (Austin, 1979), 191–220; Lawrence S. Graham, "The Military in Politics," ibid., 221–56; João B. Serra and Luis Salgado de Matos, "Intervenções militares na vida política," *A formação de Portugal contemporáneo*, 1165–96; and Douglas Porch, *The Portuguese Armed Forces and the Revolution* (Stanford, 1977).

ism"[26] and the "corporatist tradition"[27] which were also sometimes applied to Spain. It was suggested, with at least a degree of accuracy, that the Spanish regime was to be understood not as part of a greater phenomenon labeled fascism but as an aspect of distinctively Luso-Hispanic political culture and tradition. Franco had always had more than a few admirers in Latin America,[28] but the only dictator who showed any distinct ambition to try to imitate him was the short-lived Onganía in Argentina during the late 1960s. As I have argued elsewhere,[29] the Latin Americanist concept of bureaucratic authoritarianism can to a considerable extent be applied to the Portuguese case, and during its later nonmobilizational phases the Franco regime certainly showed some of the same characteristics. But in general, the intensity and mobilization of Spanish politics in the 1930s far exceeded anything seen in Latin America until about 1970, and consequently resulted in a regime that was more radical and more mobilized and institutionalized than any of the rightist dictatorships in Latin America. During the reformist final decade of the Spanish regime, Movement leaders occasionally looked to the Mexican PRI and to the limited political groups permitted to function under the military government of Brazil as potential models for the metamorphosis of the Movement and a new system of limited political associations. Yet the modernization of Spanish society already exceeded that of Brazil or Mexico, and continuing development only accelerated the participatory expectations of much of the Spanish public, making it more than doubtful that any such scheme could have long endured.

For most of his long career Franco was well aware of his status as primary resident ogre of western Europe. It is instructive in this regard to compare attitudes toward Franco with attitudes toward Tito after 1945. Tito, like Franco, had come to power in a civil war in which, propaganda to the contrary, he devoted more energy to fighting Yugoslavs than to fighting Germans and Italians. The bloodbath in Yugoslavia in 1945 was proportionately much greater than that in Spain during 1939 and the new dictatorship much more rigorous and repressive, in fact a direct, self-proclaimed attempt to copy the Stalinist totalitarianism of the Soviet Union. International circumstances prompted moderation and change in

26. The concept was first developed by Guillermo A. O'Donnell, *Modernization and Bureaucratic Authoritarianism in Latin America* (Berkeley, 1973), criticized and refined by *The New Authoritarianism in Latin America*, ed. David Collier (Princeton, 1979). See also Alfred Stepan, *The State and Society: Peru in Comparative Perspective* (Princeton, 1978).
27. *Politics and Social Change in Latin America: The Distinct Tradition*, ed. Howard J. Wiarda (Amherst, Mass., 1974); *The New Corporatism: Social-Political Structures in the Iberian World*, ed. F. Pike and T. Stritch (Notre Dame, 1974); and *Authoritarianism and Corporatism in Latin America*, ed. James M. Malloy (Pittsburgh, 1977).
28. See *The Spanish Civil War*, ed. Falcoff and Pike, cited earlier.
29. "Salazarism: 'Fascism' or 'Bureaucratic Authoritarianism'?" in *Estudos de historia portuguesa: Homenagem a A. H. de Oliveira Marques* (Lisbon, 1983).

Yugoslavia as in Spain, and eventually Tito's regime emerged as a non-totalitarian, semipluralist dictatorship and major Marxist heresy. It stood in contrast to most Communist states as did Franco's to the fascist regimes of the World War II era. Yet to the very end of Tito's life the Yugoslav regime remained more thoroughly controlled and repressive than was the case in Spain (despite its authoritarian quasifederalism and a degree of worker self-management in factories), and it failed to register the economic, social, and cultural progress of Spain. After Tito's death there followed no democratization, but a more collegial form of dictatorship. Yet Tito was often hailed even in the western press as a great reformer and innovator, a kind of beacon of progressive achievement, and due to specific international circumstances, gained more and earlier foreign assistance from the West.

Franco maintained a personal dictatorship for nearly four decades, and firmly guaranteed that there would be no genuine parliamentary representation for Spaniards until after his death. During its early years the regime was repressive in the extreme, executed approximately 30,000 people, most of them for "political" crimes, and maintained the discriminatory division of Spanish society into victors and vanquished for many, many years. Regional rights, languages, and cultures were suppressed as much as possible. Even in the later, less repressive phases of the system all the civil rights common to other western countries did not exist. Political authoritarianism was paralleled by extreme favoritism, monopolies, and often a high degree of corruption, geared to the peculiar mechanisms of the regime. All this directly repudiated the cumulative achievements of Spanish constitutionalism from 1875 to February 1936. In toto it is a weighty responsibility, one which Franco claimed to accept as answerable only to God.

Measurements differ not simply according to commentators but also according to the kind of question asked. Judgments of Franco and the regime became progressively less negative as the modernization of Spain proceeded apace and its quality of life improved. One of the most widely read biographies of a twentieth-century European dictator, Alan Bullock's *Hitler: A Study in Tyranny,* closes with a view of Germany in ruins and concludes by quoting the Latin aphorism, "If you seek his monument, look around." Applying such a method to Franco, the observer finds a country raised to the highest level of prosperity in its history, converted into the ninth industrial power of the world (before it slipped later into tenth, then eleventh, place), with the "organic solidarity" of the great majority of its population increased and its society surprisingly well prepared for harmonious coexistence and a remarkable new enterprise in decentralized democracy. By such standards, Franco might be seen not only as one of the most dominant personalities in all Spanish history but also as the definitive modernizer of Spain and leader of the most successful of all the twentieth century's would-be "development dictatorships."

Thus a decade after his death, an article in a leading upper-middle-brow American publication would declare: "What he actually accomplished was the proto-modernization of Spain. . . . Franco left Spain with institutions of technocratic economic management and a modern managerial class which have enabled what was once a poverty-stricken agricultural country at the time of its civil war to acquire productive resources and a standard of living approximating those of its southern European neighbors. Can this be what its civil war was about?"[30]

Franco's legion of critics decry the superficiality of any such conclusion, insisting that the great achievements of Spanish society under his rule came either in spite of his regime or at least were not directly promoted by it. In some respects such qualifications are undeniably correct, though they are often applied too categorically. One of the better approaches is that of Walther L. Bernecker, who has divided some of the major developments during the regime into three categories: those planned and engineered by the regime, those not directly designed but simply taken advantage of once they began to develop, and those that were unforeseen and potentially counterproductive to the regime.[31]

Even Franco's enemies have sometimes tended to give him a measure of credit for his World War II diplomacy. Ironically, as has been seen in chapter 13, he may have deserved less praise in this regard than has been offered by some of his opponents. Only in 1942 did Spanish diplomacy fully acquire the characteristics often imputed to it. Though Franco did keep Spain out of the war—a fact for which all Spaniards could ultimately be grateful—he fell far short of designing and implementing an optimal policy of neutrality.

Similarly, though economic modernization was always a primary goal of the regime, evaluation of its role in this regard is also complex. It is frequently observed that the major phase of growth came after the alteration in economic policy in 1959, which partially renounced the statism and autarchy (sometimes called "fascist economics") of the first two decades. This is absolutely correct, but overlooks the significant growth already achieved during the decade 1948–58. It is true that the international liberal market economics fueling European expansion in the 1950s and 1960s was not the sort of economic development planned and preferred by Franco, and to that extent the liberalization policy falls into Ber-

30. William Pfaff, "Splendid Little Wars," *The New Yorker*, March 24, 1986.

31. Walther L. Bernecker, "Modernisierung und Wandel eines autoritären Regimes: Spanien während des Franquismus," in *"Modernisierung" versus "Sozialismus": Formen und Strategien sozialen Wandels im 20. Jahrhundert*, ed. K.-H. Ruffmann and H. Altrichter (Nürnberg, 1983), 113–66. An extended debate has been carried on by Ricardo de la Cierva and Sergio Vilar, *Pro y contra Franco* (Barcelona, 1985).

necker's second category, that of adjustment to developments not within the parameters of the regime's preferred policies. Yet not all authoritarian regimes, whether of left or right, have been willing to make such adjustments, and in that regard the creative pragmatism of the regime must be recognized.

It is idle to insist, as do many of Franco's critics on the left, that a utopian progressive democracy would have produced better government for Spain. That goes without saying, but substitutes a strictly theoretical value judgment for an empirical comparison. Historical analysis and utopian desires are two different things. No such democratic utopia was at hand in Spain in 1936, which in fact had produced quite the opposite. Electoral democracy had resulted in absolute polarization between left and right, eliminating virtually all centrist liberal influence and thus creating a latent authoritarian situation before Franco appeared on the scene. His regime must thus be judged not by utopian invocations which have no contact with reality but in terms of historical alternatives that actually existed. These were few and in no case idyllic. Had the Nationalists lost the Civil War, it is difficult to conclude that the result would have been political democracy. The revolutionary wartime People's Republic was not a liberal democracy, but was driven by powerful revolutionary forces determined to proscribe the other side altogether. Its mass political executions were as extensive as those by Franco's supporters. The effect of the Civil War, irrespective of the victor, was to temporarily banish democracy from Spain. Franco's solution was very far from optimal—indeed at first one of the worst feasible responses (the best having been Miguel Maura's proposal for a centrist constitutional "national Republican dictatorship"). Nonetheless, the strength of the subsequent dictatorship was not derived from its rigorous repression alone, however important that was, but also from the knowledge in much of Spanish society that the alternative had not been very different.[32] An evolutionary authoritarianism was in a certain sense about as much as the Spanish could expect from the impasse into which they had maneuvered themselves.

The regime did eventually develop certain semirepresentative, though never democratic, institutions of its own, but these innovations were also

32. Julián Marías has written quite accurately: "The Spanish were deprived of many liberties, which I always found intolerable, but not all of these were missed. Moreover, they enjoyed others, particularly those affecting private life, which they feared to lose. Such deprivation came from the outcome of the Civil War, but the majority were persuaded that if that outcome had been the reverse, the sphere of liberty would not have been greater because both belligerents had promised the destruction of the other, and they had both carried it out during the war itself. Thus it was not easy to mobilize Spaniards toward an *inversion* of the result of the war, and since that basically was what the most politicized fragments of the country were proposing, the majority remained relatively indifferent. It can be said that a large number of Spaniards *waited without haste* for the end of the regime. . . ." *España inteligible* (Madrid, 1985), 379.

at least in part adjustments to the triumph of liberal democracy in western Europe, not the result of any primary blueprint of the regime. Franco's own convictions were basically monarchist, though only equivocally so between 1936 and 1943 and never to the detriment of his own authority. Planned restoration of the monarchy was the best possible succession mechanism for the regime, nonetheless, and as it turned out, Juan Carlos the best possible choice for successor. Yet both these choices were the product of creative adjustments rather than primary aims, though it must be pointed out that the espousal of restoration during the Civil War itself would probably have weakened the Nationalist cause at its most crucial point.

One of the planned goals of the regime was achieved: a greater spirit of cooperation and social solidarity was created through the introduction of national corporatism, broad economic growth and eventual redistribution of income, and proscription of partisan politics. All this was consciously programmed by the regime from the start, and its accomplishment was reflected in the conclusion of a prominent American anthropologist in 1975, "It is clear that the organic solidarity of Spain as a whole has increased."[33] The regime's relation to the enormous improvement in the educational level of Spanish society is more equivocal. Since nearly all Spaniards were educated either in state or state-subsidized schools, it might seem that this too was a conscious part of the regime's modernization program, but educational development as a top priority was adopted only in the last phase, and then because it seemed an ineluctable counterpart to economic modernization and political stability. Even after the General Education Law of 1970 educational expenditures still did not compare favorably with many other industrial countries, and thus educational modernization would fall into the second category.

Paradoxically, another feature of institutional modernization achieved by Franco was the relative depoliticizing of the military, even though the regime began as a military government and even though Franco was also explicit in his reliance on the military to avoid any destabilization. He always maintained a special relationship with the military hierarchy while holding them at a certain distance, manipulating them, switching and rotating top posts, and generally avoiding any concentration of power among them. The fact that military men held so many cabinet positions and other top administrative posts, especially during the first half of the regime, tended to obscure the fact that Franco sought to avoid any military interference in government and eliminated any possibility of an independent corporate or institutional role for the military outside their own sphere of the armed forces. Officers who held positions in government

33. Stanley H. Brandes, *Migration, Kinship, and Community* (New York, 1975), 76.

bureaus or institutions or who sat in the Cortes did so as individual administrators or representatives of military background who participated in coordinated and integrated state institutions, not as independent corporative representatives of the armed forces. The relative demilitarization of the political process was accompanied by steadily increasing demilitarization of the state budget, due not so much to Franco's respect for education (uncertain at best) as to his disinclination to spend money on a professional and technological modernization of the armed forces which might have altered their internal balance.

From its own point of view, the regime's great domestic failure lay in its inability to sustain its neotraditionalist cultural and religious policies. This failure was the almost inevitable counterpart of social and economic transformation on a massive scale, compounded by the momentous changes within the Roman Catholic Church as a whole in the 1960s. Franco was not unaware of the contradictions that might result, and hence his great initial reluctance to alter economic policy and lower national barriers in 1959. Continuation of the regime itself was made impossible not so much by the mere death of Franco—for the passing of Salazar had scarcely brought the Portuguese dictatorship to an end—as by the disappearance of the system of Spanish society and culture on which it had originally been based in 1939. Francoist society and culture had largely been eroded away even before the Caudillo physically expired. Moreover, the absence of any clear regime ideology after 1958 made it impossible for any consensus in support of a Francoist orthodoxy to develop among the regime's political and administrative elites in its later phase.

In some ways the aftermath of the regime was more extraordinary than the long history of the regime itself, for the democratization brought about by King Juan Carlos and his collaborators between 1976 and 1978 was unique in the annals of regime transitions before then. After his resignation as director general of popular culture in October 1974, Ricardo de la Cierva was asked at a press conference in Barcelona for an historical example of an institutionalized authoritarian regime that had transformed itself into a democracy without formal rupture or overthrow, as the more advanced aperturistas proposed to do in Spain. He replied that he was studying that very question at the moment,[34] but the answer was of course that no such example existed.[35] Never before had the formal institutional mechanisms of an authoritarian system been used peacefully but systematically to transform the whole system from the inside out.

34. M. Vázquez Montalbán, "Adios, De la Cierva, Adios," *Triunfo*, Nov. 1974.
35. The democratization of Turkey after 1945 might be adduced as an earlier example, but the Kemalist regime in Turkey had always been a sort of Third World "guided democracy"—one of the first of its kind—rather than an institutionalized new authoritarian regime of the European fascist era.

It will not do to suggest, as have a few, that Franco can be given credit for the tolerant and democratic Spain of the 1980s. A dictatorship is not a school for democracy, and Franco was not responsible for the democratization of Spain. While permitting limited liberalization, he fought any basic alteration to the last, only accepting the prospect to some degree in the very last weeks of his life for lack of personal energy or political alternatives to do otherwise. Despite this, some of his fundamental policies and achievements ironically became indispensable prerequisites for successful and stable democratization without rupture or violence. One of the most important of these preconditions was inherently negative, though quite significant, for the depolarization and depoliticization of Spanish society pursued by the regime after 1945 did leave behind it a situation in which a new start could be made, free of the extremism of the Civil War generation. Other indirect contributions included first of all the basic institutional structure of an "open" and evolving, semipluralistic authoritarian constitution and the framework of evolving liberalization, which created peaceful mechanisms for further change and accustomed many Spaniards to peaceful, gradual, and legalitarian evolution. Restoration of the monarchy was decisive, for only the monarchy held the legitimacy and authority to lead a peaceful process of legal democratization. Only Juan Carlos, of all monarchist candidates, possessed the requisite combination of unusual qualities to undertake the process successfully, and Franco had not only selected him but had always left him a certain amount of freedom and distance with which to develop his own political personality, even though the outcome for which Franco hoped was quite different. Social and economic modernization, finally carried out under the regime, were indispensable, for the middle-class Spain that replaced the old internally antagonistic society of the 1930s provided the necessary base for democracy. Corporative solidarity, despite the numerous frauds committed by the regime in its name, also seems to have made a contribution, but only after authoritarian corporatism was transformed into a kind of consensual corporatism by Adolfo Suárez and his successors.[36] The peculiar structure of demilitarization built by Franco was also of some assistance, though it had to be managed by the leaders of the transition with extreme care.

Franco's own policies and values represented an end and not a begin-

36. One professor, lamenting the moderation and tepidity of post–Franco society, has written: "These three phases of the same extreme dictatorship will probably be seen as a continuum of capitalist development in our land, during which Francoism *permitted* the passage from a Third World condition to post–modernity and in which Franco transfused his own frozen blood into the contemporary sang-froid of the Spanish, who are no longer susceptible to fanatization either by Tejero or ETA and who will never again be disposed to die for any ideal but only to live modestly, indeed as well as possible." J. A. González Casanova, "El franquismo a diez años vista," *Historia 16* 10:115 (Nov. 1985), 35–40.

ning. He managed to liquidate some of the problems of the past, though others were merely suppressed. He could not build the new Spain of the future, either in the form that he had planned or, much less, in that assumed by Spain after his death. His importance to Spanish history lies not in his mere endurance in power for so long, but rather in the enormous changes that took place in Spain during his rule, some of them directly encouraged or even engineered by his regime and others ultimately flying in the face of all that it stood for. Franco shaped the climax to one period and one trend of Spain's past, but his era became the decisive transition to a very different one in which the new leaders of Spain have shown impressive ability to learn some of the lessons of history, even though not specifically the ones which their didactic Generalissimo endeavored to teach them.

Selected Bibliography

Index

Selected Bibliography

Biographies of Franco and General Works
on the Regime to 1986

The first brief biography of Franco, entitled simply *Franco* (San Sebastián, 1937), came from the pen of Joaquín Arrarás and was accompanied by two shorter accounts from foreign authors, Dr. Rudolf Timmermans, *General Franco* (Zurich, 1937), and Georges Rotvand, *Franco en la nouvelle Espagne* (Paris, 1937), as well as Víctor Ruiz Albéniz, *Héroes de España: Francisco Franco* (Avila, 1937). There followed José Millán Astray's eulogy, *Franco el Caudillo* (Salamanca, 1939), and Johann Froembgen, *Franco: Ein Leben für Spanien* (Leipzig, 1939), while four years later came Angel Pérez Rodrigo, *Franco, una vida al servicio de la Patria* (Madrid, 1943), and Fernando de Valdesoto, *Francisco Franco* (Madrid, 1943).

A hiatus of more than a decade ensued, finally broken in 1955 by the first serious foreign publication, S. F. A. Coles's *Franco of Spain* (London, 1955). The most ambitious official biography to that date, Luis de Galinsoga's *Centinela de Occidente* (written in collaboration with Salgado-Araujo), appeared in Barcelona one year later, offering a newer Cold War image. Several further eulogies that appeared in the next few years had little more to offer: Fernando Rubio, *Francisco Franco* (Madrid, 1958), Francisco Salva Miquel and Juan Vicente, *Francisco Franco* (*Historia de un español*) (Barcelona, 1959), and J. M. Sánchez Silva and J. L. Sáenz de Heredia, *Franco, ese hombre* (Madrid, 1964).

The first completely critical treatments finally appeared in 1964 in the attempted psychological interpretation by Luis Ramírez [pseud.], *Francisco Franco, historia de un mesianismo* (Paris), and Salvador de Madariaga's brief satire, *Sanco Panco* (Mexico City). Three major, relatively favorable accounts by foreign writers appeared next: Claude Martin, *Franco, soldat et chef d'Etat* (Paris, 1965), Brian Crozier, *Franco: A Biographical History* (London, 1967), and George Hills, *Franco: The Man and His Nation* (London, 1967). There were also more minor treatments abroad: Sven Andersen, *Francisco Franco* (Stockholm, 1968), Alan Lloyd, *Franco* (Garden City, N.Y., 1969), and Anton Stefanescu, *Francisco Franco* (Paris, 1969). This series of works climaxed in 1970 with J. W. D. Trythall, *El Caudillo* (New York). Though not as detailed as the biographies by Crozier and Hills, Trythall's book was the most accurate and best balanced and remains in certain respects the best biography ever written, though its data base has been superseded in recent years.

645

The last of the official biographies and by far the best and most informative was Ricardo de la Cierva, *Francisco Franco: Un siglo de España*, 2 vols. (Madrid, 1972–73). A thoroughly revised and better balanced edition appeared in Barcelona in 1986. Several minor biographies appeared in Germany, France, and Spain during the mid-1970s, without new information or insights. There were two more specialized treatments in French: Philippe Noury, *Francisco Franco: La conquête du pouvoir, 1892–1937* (Paris, 1975), which dealt primarily with the rise to power, and Edouard de Blaye, *Franco, ou la Monarchie sans Roi* (Paris, 1974), which concentrated more on the final decade. Of a number of brief attempts at biographies in Spain during the 1980s, two stand out. Carlos Fernández, *El general Franco* (Barcelona, 1983), though abbreviated and thematic, was the first since that of La Cierva to present new material, while Juan Pablo Fusi, *Franco: Autoritarismo y poder personal* (Madrid, 1985), finally superseded Trythall as a brief account and ranks as the most lucid and profound treatment by a Spanish author.

The first descriptive surveys of the new Spanish regime were prepared by friendly German and Italian journalists at the close of the Civil War, particularly Otto Schempp, *Das autoritäre Spanien* (Leipzig, 1939), and Arrigo Solmi, *Lo stato nuovo nella Spagna di Franco* (Milan, 1940). Emmett J. Hughes, *Report from Spain* (New York, 1947), was the first important critical account, while Sheila M. O'Callaghan, *Cinderella of Europe* (New York, 1949), was more favorable to the regime. The only new assessment in the 1950s was Herbert M. Matthews, *The Yoke and the Arrows* (New York, 1956). Arthur P. Whitaker, *Spain and Defense of the West: Ally and Liability* (New York, 1961), offered the first strictly scholarly account, written primarily from the viewpoint of international relations. Benjamin Welles, *Spain: The Gentle Anarchy* (New York, 1965), was a journalist's treatment that especially stressed the politics of the 1950s and early 1960s, and Ludovico Garruccio, *Spagna senza miti* (Milan, 1968), presented the first major new assessment in Italian. Soviet accounts concentrated much more on the activities of the opposition than on discussion and analysis of the regime. The first Soviet work was G. N. Kolomiets, *Ispaniya segodnya* (Moscow, 1961), followed by N. Grenadov, *Ispaniya: 30 let spustya* (Moscow, 1966), and I. N. Ksenofonton, *Ispaniya: novy etap borby* (Moscow, 1969).

The first attempt at a full history of the regime was Max Gallo, *Histoire de l'Espagne franquiste*, 2 vols. (Paris, 1969). There followed George Hills's survey *Spain* (London, 1970), Klaus von Beyme, *Vom Faschischmus zur Entwicklungsdiktatur* (Munich, 1971), the first new German study, and Jacques Georgel, *Le franquisme: Histoire et bilan (1939–1969)* (Paris, 1970), the best political analysis to that date. The first critical study of the period to appear in Spain was Ramón Tamames, *La República; La era de Franco* (Historia de España Alfaguara VII) (Madrid, 1973), a Marxist structuralist account. Guy Hermet, *L'Espagne de Franco* (Paris, 1974), gave a brief overview.

Ricardo de la Cierva published the first complete history of the regime from 1939 to Franco's death in his two-volume *Historia del franquismo* (Barcelona, 1975–78), though Amando de Miguel's *Sociología del franquismo* (Barcelona, 1975) possessed greater analytical depth. Javier García Fernández, *El régimen de Franco*

(Madrid, 1976), offered a brief political analysis, and Juan Alarcón Benito, *Resumen político de la paz de Franco: 1 abril 1939–20 noviembre 1975* (Madrid, 1977), a chronological survey. Manuel Vázquez Montalbán, *Diccionario del franquismo* (Barcelona, 1977), identified the major names and terms connected with the regime. Two concise political analyses of the regime's structure appeared after Franco's death: José Amodia, *Franco's Political Legacy* (London, 1977), and E. Ramón Arango, *The Spanish Political System: Franco's Legacy* (Boulder, Col., 1978). Clear and penetrating surveys of the regime may be found in Raymond Carr and J. P. Fusi Aizpurúa, *Spain: Dictatorship to Democracy* (London, 1979), Shlomo Ben-Amí, *La revolución desde arriba: España, 1936–1979* (Barcelona, 1980), and in Walther L. Bernecker's brief *Spanien seit dem Bürgerkrieg* (Munich, 1984).

The lengthiest apology for any twentieth-century regime is presented in the detailed and well-informed eight volumes of Luis Suárez Fernández, *Francisco Franco y su tiempo* (Madrid, 1984), while Manuel Tuñón de Lara and J. A. Biescas, in *España bajo la dictadura franquista (1939–1975)* (Madrid, 1980), display equal bias in the opposite direction. Daniel Sueiro and Bernardo Díaz Nosty, *Historia del franquismo*, 2 vols. (Barcelona, 1985), offer a derisory thematic treatment that does not attempt systematic history.

Other Repeatedly Cited Works

Abella, Rafael. *La vida cotidiana durante la guerra civil: la España nacional.* Barcelona, 1973.

Abendroth, Hans-Henning. *Hitler in der spanischen Arena.* Paderborn, 1973.

Alcocer, José Luis. *Radiografía de un fraude: Notas para una historia del Frente de Juventudes.* Barcelona, 1978.

Anderson, Charles W. *The Political Economy of Modern Spain.* Madison, 1970.

Anuario Estadístico de España, 1940–1975.

Aparicio, Miguel A. *El sindicalismo vertical y la formación del Estado franquista.* Barcelona, 1980.

Arbeloa, Víctor Manuel. *Aquella España católica.* Salamanca: 1975.

Armero, José Mario. *La política exterior de Franco.* Barcelona, 1978.

Arrarás, Joaquín, ed. *Historia de la Cruzada española.* 8 vols. Madrid, 1940.

Arrese, José Luis de. *Una etapa constituyente.* Barcelona, 1972.

Arrese, José Luis de. *Treinta años de política.* Madrid, 1966.

Aznar, Manuel. *Historia militar de la guerra de España.* 3 vols. Madrid, 1958.

Baklanoff, Eric. *La transformación económica de España y Portugal.* Madrid, 1980.

Ballbé, Manuel. *Orden público y militarismo en la España constitucional.* Madrid, 1983.

Bañón Martínez, Rafael. *Poder de la burocracia y Cortes franquistas, 1943–1971.* Madrid, 1978.

Bardavío, Joaquín. *La crisis: historia de quince días.* Madrid, 1974.

Bardavío, Joaquín. *La estructura del poder en España.* Madrid, 1969.

Bardavío, Joaquín. *Los silencios del Rey.* Madrid, 1979.

Bayo, Eliseo. *Los atentados contra Franco.* Barcelona, 1976.

Beaulac, Willard L. *Franco: Silent Ally in World War II*. Carbondale and Edwardsville, 1986.

Beltrán Güell, Felipe. *Preparación y desarrollo del Movimiento Nacional*. Valladolid, 1938.

Ben-Ami, Shlomo. *Fascism from Above: The Dictatorship of Primo de Rivera in Spain, 1923–1930*. Oxford, 1983.

Beneyto, Juan. *La identidad del franquismo*. Madrid, 1979.

Biescas, José Antonio, and Manuel Tuñón de Lara. *España bajo la dictadura franquista (1939–1975)*. Barcelona, 1980.

Blinkhorn, Martin. *Carlism and Crisis in Spain 1931–1939*. Cambridge, 1975.

Boletín Oficial del Estado. (BOE)

Boletín Oficial de la Junta de Defense Nacional. (BOJDN)

Boletín del Movimiento de Falange Española Tradicionalista. (BMFET)

Bonmatí de Codecido, Francisco. *El Príncipe don Juan de España*. Valladolid, 1978.

Bravo Morata, Federico. *Franco y los muertos providenciales*. Madrid, 1979.

Burdick, Charles B. *Germany's Military Strategy and Spain in World War II*. Syracuse, 1968.

Busquets Bragulat, Julio. *El militar de carrera en España* Rev. ed. Barcelona, 1971.

Cabanellas, Guillermo. *Cuatro generales*. 2 vols. Barcelona, 1977.

Cabanellas, Guillermo. *La guerra de los mil días*. 2 vols. Buenos Aires, 1973.

Calvo Serer, Rafael. *Franco frente al Rey*. Paris, 1972.

Campo Vidal, Manuel. *Información y servicios secretos en el atentado al Presidente Carrero Blanco*. Barcelona, 1983.

Cantarero del Castillo, Manuel. *Falange y socialismo*. Barcelona, 1973.

Carr, Raymond. *Spain, 1808–1975*. 2d ed. Oxford, 1982.

Carr, Raymond, ed. *The Republic and the Civil War in Spain*. London, 1971.

Casas de la Vega, Rafael. *Las milicias nacionales*. 2 vols. Madrid, 1977.

Chao Rego, José. *La Iglesia en el franquismo*. Madrid, 1976.

Chueca, Ricardo. *El fascismo en los comienzos del régimen de Franco*. Madrid, 1983.

Cierva, Ricardo de la. *Los documentos de la primavera trágica*. Madrid, 1967.

Ciano's Diary, 1937–1938. London, 1952.

Ciano's Diplomatic Papers. Edited by Malcolm Muggeridge. London, 1948.

Clark, Clyde L. *The Evolution of the Franco Regime*. 3 vols. Washington, D.C., 1950.

Clark, Robert P. *The Basque Insurgents: ETA, 1952–1980*. Madison, 1984.

Cordero Torres, José Ma. *Fronteras hispánicas*. Madrid, 1944.

Cortada, James W., ed. *Spain in the Twentieth-Century World*. Westport, Conn., 1980.

Coverdale, John F. *Italian Intervention in the Spanish Civil War*. Princeton, 1975.

Créac'h, Jean. *Le Coeur et l'épée*. Paris, 1959.

Damiano González, Cipriano. *La resistencia libertaria (1939–1970)*. Barcelona, 1978.

Detwiler, Donald S. *Hitler, Franco und Gibraltar: Die Frage des spanischen Eintritts in den Zweiten Weltkrieg*. Wiesbaden, 1962.

Diario 16. *Historia de la transición*. Madrid, 1984.

Días, Elías. *Pensamiento español (1939–1973)*. Madrid, 1974.

Díaz Nosty, Bernardo. *Las Cortes de Franco*. Barcelona, 1972.

Díaz Plaja, Fernando, ed. *La España franquista en sus documentos*. Esplugues de Llobregat, 1976.

Díaz Plaja, Fernando, ed. *La españa política del siglo XX*. Vol. 4. Barcelona, 1972.

Díaz Plaja, Fernando, ed. *La historia de España en sus documentos. El siglo XX*. Madrid, 1963.

Documenti Diplomatici Italiani. Settima Serie, 1922–1935. Rome, 1955.

Documents on German Foreign Policy, 1918–1945. Series D. Washington, D.C., 1950.

Doussinague, José Ma. *España tenía razón (1939–1945)*. Madrid, 1950.

Ellwood, Sheelagh. *Prietas las filas: Historia de Falange Española, 1933–1983*. Barcelona, 1984.

Equipo Mundo. *Los noventa ministros de Franco*. Barcelona, 1970.

Escobar, José Ignacio. *Así empezó*. Madrid, 1974.

España perspectiva 1974. Madrid, 1974.

Falcón, Lidia. *Viernes y trece en la calle del Correo*. Barcelona, 1981.

Fernández, Carlos. *El almirante Carrero Blanco*. Barcelona, 1985.

Fernández, Carlos. *El alzamiento de 1936 en Galicia*. La Coruña, 1982.

Fernández, Carlos. *Tensiones militares bajo el franquismo*. Barcelona, 1985.

Fernández Cuesta, Raimundo. *Discursos*. n.p., 1939.

Fernández Cuesta, Raimundo. *Intemperie, victoria y servicio: Discursos y escritos*. Madrid, 1951.

Fernández Vargas, Valentina. *La resistencia interior en la España de Franco*. Madrid, 1981.

Ferrando Badía, Juan. *El régimen de Franco*. Madrid, 1984.

Ferri, L., J. Muixi, and E. Sanjuan. *Las huelgas contra Franco (1939–1956)*. Barcelona, 1978.

Flores, Xavier. *Estructura socioeconómica de la agricultura española*. Barcelona, 1969.

Fraga Iribarne, Manuel. *Memoria breve de una vida pública*. Barcelona, 1980.

Fraga Iribarne, Manuel, J. Velarde Fuertes, and S. del Campo, eds. *La España de los años 70*. 4 vols. Madrid, 1974.

Franco, Pilar. *Nosotros, los Franco*. Barcelona, 1980.

Franco Bahamonde, Francisco. *Discursos y mensajes del Jefe del Estado, 1951–1954*. Madrid, 1955.

Franco Bahamonde, Francisco. *Discursos y mensajes del Jefe del Estado, 1955–1959*. Madrid, 1960.

Franco Bahamonde, Francisco. *Discursos y mensajes del Jefe del Estado, 1960–1963*. Madrid, 1964.

Franco Bahamonde, Francisco. *Discursos y mensajes del Jefe del Estado, 1964–1967*. Madrid, 1968.

Franco Bahamonde, Francisco. *Discursos y mensajes de Su Excelencia el Jefe del Estado a las Cortes españolas, 1943–1961*. Madrid, 1961.

Franco Bahamonde, Francisco. *Textos de doctrina política: Palabras y escritos de 1945 a 1950*. Madrid, 1951.

Franco Salgado Araujo, Francisco. *Mis conversaciones privadas con Franco.* Barcelona, 1979.

Franco Salgado Araujo, Francisco. *Mi vida junto a Franco.* Barcelona, 1977.

Franco visto por sus ministros. Angel Bayod, ed. Barcelona, 1981.

Fundación FOESSA. *Informe sociológico sobre la situación social de España.* Madrid, 1966.

Fundación FOESSA. *Informe sociológico sobre la situación social de España 1970.* Madrid, 1970.

Fundamental Laws of the State. Madrid, 1967.

Gallagher, Tom. *Portugal: A Twentieth-Century Interpretation.* Manchester, 1983.

Gallego Méndez, María Teresa. *Mujer, Falange y franquismo.* Madrid, 1983.

Gárate, José Ma. *Alféreces provisionales.* Madrid, 1976.

García Durán, José, and Pedro Puig Bastard. *La calidad de la vida en España.* Madrid, 1980.

García Jiménez, Jesús. *Radiotelevisión y política cultural en el franquismo.* Madrid, 1980.

García Lahiguera, Fernando. *Ramón Serrano Súñer: Un documento para la historia.* Barcelona, 1983.

García Venero, Maximiano. *Falange en la guerra de España.* Paris, 1967.

García Venero, Maximiano. *El general Fanjul.* Madrid, 1967.

Garriga, Ramón. *La España de Franco.* 2 vols. Madrid, 1976.

Garriga, Ramón. *El general Juan Yagüe.* Barcelona, 1985.

Garriga, Ramón. *Nicolás Franco, el hermano brujo.* Barcelona, 1980.

Garriga, Ramón. *Ramón Franco, el hermano maldito.* Barcelona, 1978.

Garriga, Ramón. *Las relaciones secretas entre Franco y Hitler.* Buenos Aires, 1965.

Garriga, Ramón. *La Señora de El Pardo.* Barcelona, 1979.

Garriga, Ramón. *Los validos de Franco.* Barcelona, 1981.

Gil, Dr. Vicente. *Cuarenta años junto a Franco.* Barcelona, 1981.

Gil Robles, José Ma. *La monarquía por la que yo luché: Páginas de un diario (1941–1954).* Madrid, 1976.

Gil Robles, José Ma. *No fué posible la paz.* Barcelona, 1968.

Gomá y Tomás, Cardenal Isidro. *Pastorales de la guerra de España.* Madrid, 1955.

Gómez Pérez, Rafael. *Política y religión en el régimen de Franco.* Barcelona, 1976.

González, Manuel Jesús. *La política económica del franquismo (1940–1970).* Madrid, 1979.

González Doria, Fernando. *¿Franquismo sin Franco . . . ?* Madrid, 1974.

Gordón Ordás, Félix. *Al borde del desastre: Economía y finanzas de España (1939–1951).* Mexico City, 1952.

Graham, Robert. *Spain: A Nation Comes of Age.* New York, 1984.

Granados, Anastasio. *El Cardenal Gomá, Primado de España.* Madrid, 1969.

Granados, José Luis. *1975: El año de la instauración.* Madrid, 1977.

Gunther, Richard. *Public Policy in a No-Party State.* Berkeley and Los Angeles, 1980.

Harper, Glenn T. *German Economic Policy in Spain during the Spanish Civil War.* The Hague, 1967.

Hayes, Carlton J. H. *Wartime Mission in Spain.* New York, 1946.

Heine, Hartmut. *La oposición política al franquismo de 1939 a 1952.* Barcelona, 1983.

Hermet, Guy. *Les Catholiques dans l'Espagne franquiste.* 2 vols. Paris, 1980.

Hoare, Sir Samuel. *Complacent Dictator.* New York, 1947.

Iglesia, Estado y Movimiento Nacional. Madrid, 1963.

Iglesias Selgas, Carlos. *Los sindicatos en España.* Madrid, 1966.

Iribarren, José Ma. *Con el general Mola.* Zaragoza, 1937.

Jackson, Gabriel. *The Spanish Republic and Civil War, 1931–1939.* Princeton, 1965.

Jaraiz Franco, Pilar. *Historia de una disidencia.* Barcelona, 1981.

Jato, David. *La rebelión de los estudiantes.* Madrid, 1967.

Jáuregui, Fernando, and Pedro Vega. *Crónica del antifranquismo.* 3 vols. Barcelona, 1982–85.

Javier Conde, Francisco. *Escritos y fragmentos políticos.* 2 vols. Madrid, 1974–75.

Jerez Mir, Miguel. *Elites políticas y centros de extracción en España, 1938–1957.* Madrid, 1982.

Jiménez Campos, Javier. *El fascismo en la crisis de la segunda República española.* Madrid, 1979.

Kindelán, Alfredo. *Mis cuadernos de guerra.* Madrid, 1945.

Kindelán, Alfredo. *La verdad de mis relaciones con Franco.* Barcelona, 1981.

Kleinfeld, Gerald R., and Lewis A. Tambs. *Hitler's Spanish Legion: The Blue Division in Russia.* Carbondale and Edwardsville, 1979.

Ledesma Ramos, Ramiro. *¿Fascismo en España?* Madrid, 1935.

Lieberman, Sima. *The Contemporary Spanish Economy: A Historical Perspective.* London, 1982.

Linz, Juan J. "From Falange to Movimiento-Organización," in *Authoritarian Politics in Modern Society,* ed. S. Huntington and C. Moore. New York, 1970.

Linz, Juan J., and Alfred Stepan, eds. *The Breakdown of Democratic Regimes: Europe.* Baltimore, 1978.

Lizcano, Pablo. *La generación del 56: La universidad contra Franco.* Barcelona, 1981.

Lleonart, A. J., and F. J. Castiella, eds. *España y ONU (1945–1946).* Madrid, 1978.

Lojendio, Luis Ma. de. *Operaciones militares de la guerra de España, 1936–1939.* Barcelona, 1940.

López de Sebastián, José. *Política agraria en España, 1920–1970.* Madrid, 1970.

López Rodó, Laureano. *La larga marcha hacia la Monarquía.* Barcelona, 1978.

López Rodó, Laureano. *Política y desarrollo.* Madrid, 1970.

Marquina Barrio, Antonio. *La diplomacia vaticana y la España de Franco (1936–1945).* Madrid, 1983.

Martín Descalzo, J. L. *Tarancón, el cardenal del cambio.* Barcelona, 1982.

Martínez Bande, José M. *La guerra en el norte (hasta el 31 de marzo de 1937).* Madrid, 1969.

Martínez Bande, José M. *La lucha en torno a Madrid*. Madrid, 1968.

Martínez Bande, José M. *Vizcaya*. Madrid, 1971.

Martínez Cuadrado, Miguel, ed. *Cambio social y modernización política: Anuario político español 1969*. Madrid, 1970.

Martínez de Campos, Carlos. *Dos batallas de la Guerrra de Liberación*. Madrid, n.d.

Martínez Val, José Ma. *¿Por qué no fue posible la Falange?* Barcelona, 1975.

Meliá, Josep. *El largo camino de la apertura*. Barcelona, 1975.

Merkes, Manfred. *Die deutsche Politik im spanischen Bürgerkrieg, 1936–1939*. Rev. and exp. ed. Bonn, 1969.

Mesa, Roberto, ed. *Jaraneros y alborotadores: Documentos sobre los sucesos estudiantiles de febrero de 1956 a la Universidad Complutense de Madrid*. Madrid, 1982.

Miguel, Amando de. *Herencia del franquismo*. Madrid, 1976.

Morales Lezcano, Víctor. *Historia de la no-beligerancia española durante la Segunda Guerra Mundial (VI, 1940–X, 1943)*. Las Palmas, 1980.

Morán, Gregorio. *Adolfo Suárez: Historia de una ambición*. Barcelona, 1979.

Morán, Gregorio. *Los españoles que dejaron de serlo*. Barcelona, 1982.

Moya, Carlos. *El poder económico en España (1939–1970)*. Madrid, 1975.

Muñoz, Juan. *El poder de la banca en España*. Algorta, 1970.

Núñez Astrain, Luis C.-. *La sociedad vasca actual*. San Sebastián, 1977.

Olaya Morales, F. *La conspiración contra la República*. Barcelona, 1979.

Olmedo Delgado, Antonio, and José Cuesta Monereo. *El general Queipo de Llano*. Barcelona, 1957.

Oneto, José. *Arias entre dos crisis, 1973–1975*. Madrid, 1975.

Pabón, Jesús. *La otra legitimidad*. Madrid, 1945.

Payne, Stanley G. *Falange: A History of Spanish Fascism*. Stanford, 1961.

Payne, Stanley G. *Politics and the Military in Modern Spain*. Stanford, 1967.

Payne, Stanley G. *The Spanish Revolution*. New York, 1970.

Pérez Mateos, Juan Antonio. *El rey que vino del exilio*. Barcelona, 1981.

Pike, David W. *Vae Victis: Los españoles republicanos refugiados en Francia, 1939–1944*. Paris, 1969.

Pozuelo Escudero, Vicente. *Los últimos 476 días de Franco*. Barcelona, 1980.

Preston, Paul, ed. *Revolution and War in Spain, 1931–1939*. Barcelona, 1984.

Primo de Rivera, José Antonio. *Obras completas*. Madrid, 1952.

Proctor, Raymond L. *Agonía de un neutral*. Madrid, 1972.

Proctor, Raymond L. *Hitler's Luftwaffe in the Spanish Civil War*. Westport. Conn., 1983.

Raguer, Hilari. *La espada y la cruz*. Barcelona, 1977.

Ridruejo, Dionisio. *Casi unas memorias*. Barcelona, 1976.

Ridruejo, Dionisio. *Escrito en España*. Buenos Aires, 1964.

Robinson, R. A. H. *Contemporary Portugal*. London, 1979.

Rodríguez Aisa, Ma. Luisa. *El Cardenal Gomá y la guerra de España*. Madrid, 1981.

Romero Cuesta, Armando. *Objectivo: matar a Franco*. Madrid, 1976.

Ros Hombravella, J., et al. *Capitalismo español: De la autarquía a la estabilización (1939–1959)*. 2 vols. Madrid, 1973.

Rubio, Javier. *La emigración española a Francia*. Barcelona, 1974.

Rubottom, R. Richard, and J. Carter Murphy. *Spain and the United States since World War II*. New York, 1984.

Ruhl, Klaus-Jörg. *Spanien im Zweiten Weltkrieg*. Hamburg, 1975.

Ruiz Ayúcar, Angel. *Crónica agitada de ocho años tranquilos*. Madrid, 1974.

Ruiz Rico, Juan José. *El papel político de la Iglesia católica en la España de Franco*. Madrid, 1977.

Ruiz Vilaplana, Antonio. *Doy fe: Un año de actuación en la España de Franco*. Paris, 1938.

Sainz Rodríguez, Pedro. *Un reinado en la sombra*. Barcelona, 1981.

Sainz Rodríguez, Pedro. *Testimonio y recuerdos*. Barcelona, 1978.

Salas Larrazábal, Jesús. *Intervención extranjera en la guerra de España*. Madrid, 1974.

Salas Larrazábal, Ramón. *Cómo ganó Navarra la Gran Cruz Laureada de San Fernando*. Madrid, 1980.

Salas Larrazábal, Ramón. *Los fusilados en Navarra en la guerra de 1936*. Madrid, 1983.

Salas Larrazábal, Ramón. *Historia del Ejército Popular de la República*. 4 vols. Madrid, 1973.

Salas Larrazábal, Ramón. *Pérdidas de la guerra*. Barcelona, 1977.

Saña, Heleno. *El franquismo sin mitos: Conversaciones con Serrano Súñer*. Barcelona, 1982.

Sanz Orrio, Fermín. *Los sindicatos españoles: Una creación para el mundo*. Madrid, 1948.

Schwartz, Pedro, and Manuel J. González. *Una historia del Instituto Nacional de Industria*. Madrid, 1978.

Serrano Súñer, Ramón. *Entre el silencio y la propaganda, la historia como fue: Memorias*. Barcelona, 1977.

Serrano Súñer, Ramón. *Entre Hendaya y Gibraltar*. Mexico City, 1947.

Smyth, Denis. *Diplomacy and Strategy of Survival: British Policy and Franco's Spain, 1940–41*. Cambridge, 1986.

Solé i Sabaté, Josep M. *La repressió franquista a Catalunya 1938–1953*. Barcelona, 1985.

Soriano, Ramón. *La mano izquierda de Franco*. Barcelona, 1981.

Southworth, Herbert R. *Antifalange*. Paris, 1967.

Southworth, Herbert R. *Le mythe de la croisade de Franco*. Paris, 1964.

Sueiro, Daniel. *La verdadera historia del Valle de los Caídos*. Madrid, 1976.

Sueiro, Daniel, and Bernardo Díaz Nosty. *Historia del franquismo*. Madrid, 1977.

Suero Roca, Teresa. *Los generales de Franco*. Barcelona, 1975.

Terrón Montero, Javier. *La prensa en España durante el régimen de Franco*. Madrid, 1981.

Thomas, Hugh. *The Spanish Civil War*. 2d ed. rev. and exp. New York, 1977.

Tusell, Javier. *Franco y los católicos: La política interior española entre 1945 y 1957*. Madrid, 1984.

Tusell, Javier. *La oposición democrática al franquismo, 1939–1962*. Barcelona, 1977.

Tusell, Javier, and G. G. Queipo de Llano. *Franco y Mussolini*. Barcelona, 1985.

United States Department of State. *The Spanish Government and the Axis.* Washington, D.C., 1945.

Vigón, Jorge. *Mola (El conspirador).* Barcelona, 1957.

Vilanova, Antonio. *Los olvidados: Los exiliados españoles en la Segunda Guerra Mundial.* Paris, 1969.

Viñas, Angel. *La Alemania nazi y el 18 de julio.* Rev. ed. Madrid, 1979.

Viñas, Angel. *Guerra, dinero, dictadura.* Madrid, 1984.

Viñas, Angel. *El oro de Moscú.* Rev. ed. Barcelona, 1979.

Viñas, Angel. *Los pactos secretos de Franco con Estados Unidos.* Barcelona, 1981.

Viñas, Angel, et al. *Política comercial exterior de España (1931–1975).* 2 vols. Madrid, 1979.

Viver Pi Sunyer, C. *El personal político de Franco (1936–1945).* Barcelona, 1978.

Waldmann, Peter, ed. *Die geheime Dynamik authoritärer Diktaturen.* Munich, 1982.

Whitaker, John T. *We Cannot Escape History.* New York, 1943.

Ynfante, Jesús (pseud.). *El Ejército de Franco y de Juan Carlos.* Paris, 1976.

Index

Fraga Iribarne on, 549; Franco on, 549, 602, 603–4; Herrero Tejedor on, 550, 607; in Movement (Falangism), 509, 510, 525, 526–27, 548–49, 550–51, 603–4; as pluriform, 509, 549, 587, 604

Asturias, 43, 49, 395; Nationalists in, 138–39, 142; strikes in, 455, 499

Auditoria de Guerra del Ejército de Ocupación, 214

Aunós, Eduardo, 24, 26, 29, 184, 227, 349

Autarchy, 248–53, 267, 468; demolished, 471; Franco on, 470; as inefficient, 384–85; last phase of, 464–66; ostracism affects, 384, 385; semi-, 414; syndicalism in, 393

Authoritarianism, 5, 10–11, 15, 25, 49–50; bureaucratic, 633–34; Catholic church on, 202; in Falangism, 165; in Latin America, 633–34; in monarchy, 49–50, 369, 413; of Nationalist regime, 322, 369, 413, 623, 626, 639; of Miguel Primo de Rivera, 19–33

Automobile industry, 474

Avanzadilla Monárquica, 377–78n94

Axis, Rome-Berlin, 127, 161, 356; Falangism on, 340; Franco on, 253–54, 258, 269, 313, 314, 339, 340, 343; Serrano Súñer on, 285. *See also* Germany; Italy

Azaña Díaz, Manuel, 36–38, 45, 65, 82, 98–99; army reforms by, 77, 81; government of, 88, 102, 103 (*see also* Republic, Second)

Aznar, Agustín, 170, 174, 188

Azores, 284, 333

Azpiazu, José, 204–5, 627

Bahamonde, Pilar (mother of Franco), 68

Balboa, Benjamin, 103n30

Baleares, 325

Bank of Spain, 467, 468, 471, 472

Banks, 57, 58, 389, 479, 489

Barcelona, 8, 17, 18, 21, 35, 101, 220, 337, 395, 396, 478; strikes in, 415, 455, 499; student unrest in, 452–53, 513, 518; tragic week in, 5, 12

Barcelona, Conde de. *See* Juan de Borbón, Don

Barea, Arturo, 71–72n11

Barrera de Irimo, Antonio, 593, 600, 602

Barrón, Antonio, 135

Barroso, Antonio, 428, 453, 568

Bases institucionales de la Monarquía española, 371

Basque Land and Liberty. *See* ETA

Basque provinces, 8, 35; agriculture in, 483; Carlism in, 304, 306; civil war in, 141, 142, 202; clergy in, 200, 214, 500, 560, 562; as industrial, 475, 478, 479; language in, 231, 560; nationalism in, 13, 42–43, 198, 200, 214, 498, 500, 520, 557–58, 562, 595; repression in , 559–60, 601, 610; strikes in, 377, 443, 499, 556; unions in, 27; violence in, 520, 557–58. *See also* Guipuzcoa; Vizcaya

Batallones Disciplinarios de Soldados Trabajadores, 224–25

Bautista Sánchez, Juan, 135, 415, 428–29

Bayle, Constantino, 205

Beaulac, Willard, 268n6

Begoña affair, 306–9

Beigbeder y Atienza, Juan, 235, 255, 256, 257, 267, 271, 295

Belchite, battle of, 143

Bell, Daniel, 519

Beneyto Pérez, Juan, 241, 622

Benjumea Burín, Joaquín, 262

Berlin. *See* Germany

Bernal, Jesús Aparicio, 522

Bernecker, Walther L., 636

Besteiro, Julian, 223n40

Bilbao, 8, 47, 55, 101, 142, 181, 306–9

Bilbao, Esteban, 235, 260, 317, 324, 351

Black market, 252, 253, 294, 365, 387–88, 389, 481

Bloque Ibérico, 299

Bloque Nacional, 49–50, 51

Bloque Obrero-Campesino (BOC-POUM), 39–40, 42

Blue Division, 282, 283, 298, 300, 301, 302, 316, 333–34, 419

Bolivia, 192

Bombings, 139–40, 220, 508, 580, 601–2, 614

Borbón. *See* Juan de Borbón, Don; Juan Carlos, King of Spain

Brazil, 343

Brenan, Gerald, 413

Britain: and Azores, 284, 333; bribery by, 275; on Canary Islands, 284; civil war in, 209; credit from, 247; and Gibraltar, 274,

286; and Poland, 255, 256; recognizes Nationalist regime, 154; relations with Spain of, 122–23, 154, 155–56, 254, 261–62, 266–71, 278, 301, 314–15, 319, 333–34, 335–36, 338, 341, 343, 344, 356; on Spain in World War II, 266–78, 284, 318–19; and Spanish civil war, 105, 108, 112, 123, 127, 128, 129–30, 134, 135, 139, 146, 153–54, 155, 156–57, 159–60; in Spanish domestic policy, 191–92, 299–301, 314–15; in Spanish mining, 155, 156, 254; Spanish press on, 299, 332, 335, 336; Spanish workers in, 283–84, 344; submarines supplied, 269, 276, 284, 298. *See also* Hitler, Adolf

Gibraltar, 278; British in, 274, 283, 439, 531–32; Spain claims, 267, 269, 283, 419, 531–32; strategic position of, 269–70, 276; U.N. on, 532

Gil, Vicente, 70n7, 407, 592

Gil Robles, José María, 41, 42, 44, 50, 51, 79, 98, 118, 163, 173, 378, 422; and CEDA, 80, 90; as minister of war, 80–81; as opposition, 371, 500; on succession, 379–80

Giménez Arnau, José Antonio, 182

Giménez Caballero, Ernesto, 52–53, 65

Giral, José, 122

Girón de Velasco, José Antonio, 174, 288, 289, 303, 350–51, 353, 393, 394, 400, 416, 425, 608; in cabinet, 287, 452; and Falange, 443, 523, 552; as opposition, 261, 443; on reform, 597

Goebbels, Paul Joseph, 264

Goering, Hermann Wilhelm, 254

Goicoechea, Antonio, 348

Gomá y Tomás, Isidro, Cardinal, 198, 199–200, 201–2, 207, 214, 365

Gómez Jordana, Francisco, 180, 234, 235, 274, 309, 311, 316–18, 329, 332, 333, 334, 336, 340

González Bueno, Pedro, 181, 183, 185, 186, 221

González de Canales, Patricio, 261

González Gallarza, Eduardo, 416

González Vélez, Fernando, 174, 175, 188

González Vicén, Luis, 354–55, 441, 446, 524

Grain production, 482

Gramsci, Antonio, 627

Granada, 218, 556

Gran Cruz Laureada de San Fernando, 133

GRAPO, 616

Great Britain. *See* Britain

Greece, 14, 227, 516

Grimau, Julián, 501, 530

Grises, 571. *See also* Police

Gross national product, 390, 473, 476, 478, 483, 490

Groussard, Serge, 455

Guadalajara, 131, 146

Guadalhorce, Conde de, 31

Guardia Moro, 427

Guardias de Franco, 346, 423, 441, 442, 523, 524

Guernica, 139–41, 220, 246

Guerra Campos, José, 561–62

Guerrillas, 345–46, 378

Guerrilleros de Cristo Rey, 562, 585

Guipúzcoa, 479, 520, 558, 610; strikes in, 415, 556. *See also* Basque provinces

Guitarte, José Miguel, 239

Gutiérrez Mellado, Manuel, 612

Hassan, Muley, 197n1

Hassan II, 612–13, 617, 618

Hayes, Carlton J. H., 268n6, 313, 332, 334

Haz, 239

Hedilla Larrey, Manuel, 164, 165, 170, 171, 172–73, 175, 204, 213, 440n62, 524n79

Hermandades Obreras de Acción Catolica (HOAC), 368, 500

Hermet, Guy, 369

Herraiz, Ismael, 335–36

Herranz, Francisco, 528

Herrera, Angel, 24, 25

Herrera Oria, Francisco, 215n21, 504

Herrero Tejedor, Fernando, 521–22, 525, 542, 550, 560, 606–7, 609

Hidalgo, Diego, 78–79

Hill, Robert P., 574

Hillers, Sigfrido, 553

Himmler, Heinrich, 272

Hispanidad, 360–62

Hitler, Adolf: and Franco, 128, 154–55, 272–73, 277–78, 340, 342; on Gibraltar, 276; influence of, 47, 55; military strategy of, 266, 332; and Mussolini, 127, 257; and Soviets, 161, 255; on Spain, 127, 315, 316; on Spain in World War II, 269, 273, 275, 276, 277, 319, 340, 341;

Navy, 103–4, 107*n2*, 120, 121, 244–45, 291, 568, 569

Nazi-Soviet Pact, 255

Negrín, Juan, 103, 151

Neutrality, 7, 156, 253–57, 267–68, 318, 333, 335, 337, 339; not genuine, 341; of Portugal, 269, 298, 299, 343; of press, 337; in World War I, 65–66, 341–42; in World War II, 266, 274–75, 343, 636

Nieto Antúnez, Pedro, 505, 538, 546, 592

Nin, Andrés, 39–40

Nixon, Richard, 573, 574

Nonbelligerence, 267–68, 298, 313, 314, 333

Obra Nacional Corporativa, 185–86

Oil crisis of 1973, 491, 610

O'Konski, Alvin, 382

Olaechea, Bishop, 198, 213

Olazábal, José María de, 354

Olive oil scandal, 580

Operation Felix, 276

Operation Puma, 280

Opposition, 375–78, 489; from abroad, 355–59; in army, 245–46, 295, 297, 328–31, 342, 428–29, 568, 611–12; clergy as, 499–500, 513, 561; communists as, 557; in Falangism, 260–62, 443, 524, 557; labor as, 440, 499, 507, 513, 518, 520, 556, 557; leftist, 344–49, 455, 554, 580, 584; monarchist, 294–95, 347–48, 377, 378, 422–23, 456–58, 557; Munich cohabitation as, 500–501, 504; non-communist, 371; regional, 520, 557, 601 (*see also* ETA); repression against (*see* Repression); student/university, 378, 439–44, 452–53, 455, 510, 513, 518–19, 520, 556, 557, 580; in 1960s, 497–503, 518–19, 520; in 1970s, 557–60, 601, 610–11

Opus Dei, 437–38; in cabinet, 450, 451, 471–72, 475, 503, 511, 523, 546, 593; and Falange, 522, 544; v. monarchists, 457

Oreja, Marcelino, 602

Organic Law of the State, 448, 449, 509, 513–15, 525, 554; Franco on, 510, 513, 515, 526

Organization for European Economic Co-operation, 469

Orgaz, Luis, 92–93, 109, 112, 134–35, 287, 295, 331, 347

Oriol, Antonio María, 511, 513, 546

Orlov, Alexander, 137, 138

Ortega Díaz-Ambrona, Juan, 602–3

Ortega y Gasset, José, 19, 24, 434

Ortí Bordás, José Miguel, 522, 550, 551

Ostracism, 343, 344, 355–59, 361, 381–83, 384, 385, 426

Pacelli, Cardinal, Eugenio, 202

Pact of Madrid, 418

Palomares incident, 530

Pamplona, 108, 478

El Pardo, 232, 405

Pardo Bazán, Emilia, 68, 232

París Eguilaz, Higinio, 249*n43*

Parkinson's disease, 495, 518

Parliamentarianism, 10, 12, 23

Partido de Unión Nacional Saharaui, 612, 613

Partido Nacionalista Español, 32, 169

Partido Republicano Nacional, 94

Parties, political, 12, 510, 515, 516 (*see also* Associationism); state (*see* Falangism; Unión Patriótica)

Paul VI, Pope, 615

Pazo de Meirás, 232, 407

Pegaso, 386

Peiró, Joan, 223*n40*

Pemán, José María, 28, 32, 503

Peña Boeuf, Alfonso, 181, 235

Penal code, 346, 507

People's Army. *See* Republicans/Popular Front, People's Army of

Perales, Narciso, 524*n79*

Pereda Julián, 224

Pérez de Cabo, José, 294

Pérez Embid, Florentine, 438

Pérez González, Blas, 309, 310, 311, 351, 416, 452–53

Pérez Pujol, Eduardo, 23

Permartín, José, 205

Perón, Eva, 374

Perón, Juan, 361

Peronism, 524

Phosphates, 612

Piasecki, Boleslaw, 59, 192

Picasso, Pablo, 139

Pildain, Bishop, 440

Piñar, Blas, 549, 585

Pius IX, Pope, 365

Pius XI, Pope, 201

Plan Badajoz, 482

382, 530, 572; and Germany, 122–23,
154, 155–56, 254, 261–62, 266–71, 278,
301, 314–15, 319, 333–34, 335–36, 338,
341, 343, 344, 356; on Gibralter, 267,
269, 283, 419, 531–32; and international
trade, 465–66, 470–71; and Italy, 23,
112, 131, 154, 169, 253–54, 256–57, 267,
278, 340, 343, 344; and Japan, 333, 338–
39; and Latin America, 339, 360–62,
414–15, 530–31, 574; living standards in,
415, 463; modernization in, 488, 635–36,
638; and NATO, 417, 418, 529–30; natural resources of, 247, 385; neutrality
of, 7, 9, 65–66, 156, 161–62, 253–57,
267–68, 318, 333, 335, 337, 339, 341,
636; nonbelligerance of 267–68, 298,
313, 314, 333; Old Regime in, 4; polarization in, 8–9, 35, 36–45, 87–88; and Portugal, 254, 257, 269, 630–33; revolutionary confederation of, 102–3; social/
cultural life in, 365, 435, 483–88; solidarity of, 638, 640; in Tangier, 268, 274–
75n28, 356, 427; totalitarianism in,
204–5; and United Nations, 339, 344,
358–59, 361, 381, 383, 419, 531, 532,
534, 535, 581, 613; and United States,
247, 279, 313–14, 332, 333, 337, 338,
339, 341, 356, 357–58, 382–83, 397,
417–20, 426, 464, 466, 470–71, 474,
528, 529, 530, 531, 569, 572, 573–74,
609, 611, 613; and USSR, 126, 127–28,
131, 136–38, 146, 149, 153, 154, 156–57,
158–59, 160, 339, 381, 419, 531, 572,
574; and Vatican, 418, 419, 420–21; welfare in, 391–92, 394, 486–87; in World
War II, 161–62, 266–78, 279–80, 284,
285, 298, 305–6, 313, 318–19, 335,
339–42

Spanish Guinea, 269, 429–30, 533–35
Spanish ideology, 7–8, 25, 32, 47, 48, 193,
199, 206, 320, 562
Spanish Phalanx, *See* Falangism
Spanish Sahara, 268, 429–30, 531, 532,
612–13, 617
Special Tribunal for Repression of Masonry
and Communism, 501–2
Speer, Albert, 342
Speer, Geoffrey, 139
Stabilization plan of 1959, 468, 470–72,
476
Stalin, Joseph, 146, 161
State of exception, 40, 455, 499, 520, 610

Strategic Air Command, 418, 419
Strikes, 376, 468, 507, 525, 601, 610; in Asturias, 455, 499; in Barcelona, 415, 455,
499; in Basque provinces, 377, 415, 443,
499, 556; in Catalonia, 377; clergy on,
500; communists on, 456; law on, 456,
605–6; miners' 43, 508; repressed, 556;
student, 453; Syndical organization on,
499, 555–57; white collar, 556
Students. *See* Universities
Suanzes, Juan Antonio, 181, 251, 351, 416,
469, 475
Suárez, Adolfo, 575, 582, 607, 609–10,
615, 616, 640
Suárez Verdaguer, Federico, 496
Subirán, Sofía, 70–71n9
Succession, 371, 412, 510, 600; clouded,
581–82, 583; Falange on, 441, 446–47;
Franco on, 175, 298, 326, 369, 370, ,372,
378, 456–57, 495–96, 509, 513, 542,
573–74, 575 579, 618, 638; Don Juan on,
373, 537, 609; Juan Carlos in, 379–80,
506, 536, 537, 538, 539–42, 579, 640;
law on, 372, 373, 374–75, 378–79, 505,
513–14, 537; monarchists on, 373,
378–79, 537; pretenders to, 189, 327,
456, 536–37, 540, 553, 581, 582, 611
Sweden, 341
Syndicalism, 49, 55, 181, 183, 184, 554; in
army, 428; Arrese on, 57–58; in autarchy
393; of Carlists, 185–86; in Cortes, 324;
of Falange, 50, 56, 57–58, 165, 185, 246,
262–65 (*see also* Syndical Organization);
and fascism, 53; Italian, 26, 628–29; labor in, 392, 393, 394, 395–96, 413; Portuguese, 47, 631; reform in, 454, 610
Syndical Law of 1971, 554
Syndical Organization, 181, 184–85,
262–65, 366, 368, 392–93, 394, 396,
490, 506; as autonomous, 514, 554, 555;
and collective bargaining, 469; on economic reforms, 468, 476, 525n80; last
phase of, 554–57; leftist opposition in,
554; reform in, 499, 507, 524–25,
554–55; separated from labor ministry,
262; on strikes, 499, 555–57; workers'
commissions in, 556

Tamames, Ramón, 584
Tangier, 268, 274–75n28, 356, 427
Tarancón, Cardinal Vicente Enrique y, 562,
589–90